REFE

The European Political Dictionary

THE EUROPEAN POLITICAL DICTIONARY

Ernest E. Rossi
Barbara P. McCrea
Western Michigan University

Santa Barbara, California

©1985 by Ernest E. Rossi and Barbara P. McCrea

All rights reserved. No part of this publication may be reproduced, stored in a retrieval system, or transmitted in any form or by any means, electronic, mechanical, photocopying, recording, or otherwise, except for the inclusion of brief quotations in a review, without prior permission in writing from the publishers.

This book is printed on acid-free paper to meet library standards.

Library of Congress Cataloging in Publication Data
Rossi, Ernest E.
   The European political dictionary.

   (Clio dictionaries in political science: 7)
   Includes index.
   1. Europe—Politics and government—1945— —Dictionaries.
I. McCrea, Barbara P. II. Title. III. Series.
JN12.R65   1985   320.94'003'21   84-24389
ISBN 0-87436-046-3
ISBN 0-87436-367-5 (paper)

10 9 8 7 6 5 4 3 2 1

ABC-CLIO, Inc.
Riviera Campus
2040 Alameda Padre Serra, Box 4397
Santa Barbara, California 93140-4397

Clio Press Ltd.
55 St. Thomas Street
Oxford, OX1 1JG, England

Manufactured in the United States of America

*To Jean
and
To George*

Clio Dictionaries in Political Science

1 *The Latin American Political Dictionary*
Ernest E. Rossi and Jack C. Plano

#2 *The International Relations Dictionary,* third edition
Jack C. Plano and Roy Olton

#3 *The Dictionary of Political Analysis,* second edition
Jack C. Plano, Robert E. Riggs, and Helenan S. Robin

#4 *The Soviet and East European Political Dictionary*
Barbara P. McCrea, Jack C. Plano, and George Klein

#5 *The Middle East Political Dictionary*
Lawrence Ziring

#6 *The African Political Dictionary*
Claude S. Phillips

#7 *The European Political Dictionary*
Ernest E. Rossi and Barbara P. McCrea

#8 *The Constitutional Law Dictionary* Volume 1: *Individual Rights*
Ralph C. Chandler, Richard A. Enslen, and Peter G. Renstrom

#9 *The Presidential-Congressional Political Dictionary*
Jeffrey M. Elliot and Sheikh R. Ali

10 *The Asian Political Dictionary*
Lawrence Ziring and C. I. Eugene Kim

Forthcoming

#11 *The International Law Dictionary*
Robert L. Bledsoe and Boleslaw A. Boczek

#12 *The State and Local Government Political Dictionary*
     Jeffrey M. Elliot and Sheikh R. Ali

#13 *The Constitutional Law Dictionary* Volume 2: *Governmental Powers*
     Ralph C. Chandler, Richard A. Enslen, and Peter G. Renstrom

#14 *The Dictionary of Arms Control, Disarmament, and Military Security*
     Jeffrey M. Elliot and Robert Reginald

#15 *The Dictionary of Public Policy*
     Earl R. Kruschke and Byron M. Jackson

SERIES STATEMENT

Language precision is the primary tool of every scientific discipline. That aphorism serves as the guideline for this series of political dictionaries. Although each book in the series relates to a specific topical or regional area in the discipline of political science, entries in the dictionaries also emphasize history, geography, economics, sociology, philosophy, and religion.

This dictionary series incorporates special features designed to help the reader overcome any language barriers that may impede a full understanding of the subject matter. For example, the concepts included in each volume are selected to complement the subject matter found in existing texts and other books. All but one volume utilize a subject matter chapter arrangement that is most useful for classroom and study purposes.

Entries in all volumes include an up-to-date definition plus a paragraph of *Significance* in which the authors discuss and analyze the term's historical and current relevance. Most entries are also cross-referenced, providing the reader an opportunity to seek additional information related to the subject of inquiry. A comprehensive index allows the reader to locate major entries and other concepts, events, and institutions discussed within these entries.

The political and social sciences suffer more than most disciplines from semantic confusion. This is attributable, *inter alia*, to the popularization of the language, and to the focus on many diverse foreign political and social systems. This dictionary series is dedicated to overcoming some of this confusion through careful writing of thorough, accurate definitions for the central concepts, institutions, and events that comprise the basic knowledge of each of the subject fields. New titles in the series will be issued periodically, including some in related social science disciplines.

—Jack C. Plano
Series Editor

CONTENTS

A Note On How To Use This Book, **xii**
Preface, **xiii**
Guide To Countries, **xvii**

1. The United Kingdom, **1**
2. France, **79**
3. The Federal Republic of Germany, **157**
4. Western European Regionalism, **243**
5. The Soviet Union, **273**

Appendix A: Maps, **369**
Appendix B: Tables, **373**
Index, **377**

A NOTE ON HOW TO USE THIS BOOK

The European Political Dictionary is organized so that entries and supplementary definitions and data can be located in several ways. First, entries are grouped alphabetically within chapters dealing with the United Kingdom, France, the Federal Republic of Germany (West Germany), Western European regionalism, and the Soviet Union. For example, readers who want to find an entry on the French Socialist party can turn to the chapter dealing with France. Similarly, entries dealing with the European Community will be found in the chapter dealing with Western European regionalism. Second, readers can consult the comprehensive general index when doubtful about where a term might be found. Page numbers for entries appear in the index in boldface type; subsidiary concepts and persons that are discussed within entries are identified by page numbers in regular type. Third, the Guide to Countries deals with all references to nations located in Europe. References to other countries are located in the general index. Fourth, certain geographic, political, economic, and social data on the nations of the European Community and the USSR are found in Appendixes A and B.

Readers who wish to explore topics of related interest may use the extensive cross-references found at the end of the first (definition) paragraph of each entry. Cross-references include page numbers for easy access to related entries.

The format of this book offers the reader a variety of useful applications. Each entry has two paragraphs. The first paragraph begins with a concise definition phrase and supplies additional information. The second paragraph, labeled *Significance,* puts the topic into historical or political focus, and offers interpretations, analyses, and conclusions. The design of the book and its reader-aids offer the reader a variety of useful applications. These include its use as: (1) a *dictionary* and *quick reference guide* to European topics and political personalities; (2) a *study guide* for students who want to review the field; (3) a *supplement* to textbooks and monographs for use in college courses in political science and cognate fields, such as history and economics; and (4) a *social science aid* for use in government, education, business, and journalism.

PREFACE

The traditional importance of Europe in world affairs has not diminished despite the relative decline that followed World War II. Although other regions of the world command the attention of daily newswriters and newscasters, Europe still stands supreme as the most significant locus of East-West confrontation. The postwar American commitment to defend Western Europe, casting its power again in the European balance, has not diminished despite the passage of 40 years and recurring cycles of tension and detente. Western European powers, though weakened, have reestablished themselves as regional powers with global economic interests. Their unprecedented move to economic, military, and political integration has created a bewildering number of organizations, many of which have similar names. And the European superpower, the Soviet Union, has assumed a global role equivalent to that of European imperial powers of the past.

This book was written to describe and evaluate these developments within a comprehensive structure that highlights the institutions, processes, and events of the four major powers of Europe—the United Kingdom, France, the Federal Republic of Germany, and the Soviet Union. The Soviet Union is examined in detail because of its intrinsic importance to the Western states and to serve the needs of students in courses devoted to the major European powers. A separate chapter devoted to Western European regionalism attempts to clarify the perplexing institutions of the region.

This book is intended mainly for college students, the general public, and others who seek a handy and quick reference to check certain facts. The format is simple and useful. The volume is organized into five chapters dealing with the four powers and with Western European regionalism. Each entry has two paragraphs, the first descriptive and the second, labeled *Significance*, intended to be analytical. We have tried to keep interpretations to the *Significance* paragraph, present a balanced view, and report opinions of knowledgeable observers.

This dictionary is easy to use, either as a topical study guide or as a quick reference. Through the users' aids, the Index, appendixes, Guide to Countries, and cross-references, a reader can locate information quickly and follow related themes easily. There are about 325 main entries in this dictionary; in addition, more than a thousand other concepts, institutions, and individuals are defined or identified. The Index lists over 200 abbreviations and acronyms.

We have selected entries with a view to keeping the book a convenient size, and yet detailed enough to cover comprehensive themes for those seeking a college course supplement or study guide. We have followed a few principles of selection so that comparisons can be made across nations. For each of the four powers, we included the major structures of the executive, legislative, judicial, and administrative branches of government; national political parties and interest groups; the political culture; summaries of the most recent national elections; and names and dates of principal officers of government since World War II. The selection of historical terms, necessarily limited, was based on our judgment of the relevance and importance to the present time, and of those terms one is most likely to encounter in academic study. For quick reference, Table 1 in Appendix B lists the names of the heads of state and the cabinet composition of the ten states of the European Community, and Portugal and Spain. Students can pursue comparative themes by consulting the Index and the Guide to Countries.

We believe that the entries dealing with theory will be particularly useful to students. We have identified, briefly described, and commented on some of the more important empirical theories, approaches, models, and typologies that attempt to classify and explain the European political scene. These entries are often alphabetized under the key word in the most appropriate country section, for example, Catch-All Party Thesis in West Germany. But we have also gathered a number of theories under general rubrics, such as Socioeconomic Theory (France) and Explanatory Theory (USSR).

Regarding the use of foreign words, we have retained those terms most often untranslated in English-language books, or to explain the origins of common abbreviations and acronyms, such as the Nazi SS or *Samizdat*. When a word or proper name has come into common English usage, we have dropped italicization and treated it as an English word; for example, Bundestag. For ease of reading, foreign words are italicized only in the entry title and first use within entries. We have usually indicated plural spellings of foreign words, but we have also used English plurals for Russian words in contexts where this is common practice; for example, *oblast*s.

As there is no entirely satisfactory answer to the problem of transliterating Russian words into English, we have used a modified Library of Congress system. When a name or a word has become familiar to American readers in a simplified form (Trotsky, not Trotskii; Czar, not Tsar), that usage has been followed. Because pre-Communist Russia used the Julian Calendar, which differs from the Gregorian Calendar by 13 days, the Julian dates are retained for all events that occurred before

February 1918, when the Bolsheviks adopted the Gregorian Calendar, the calendar now commonly used throughout the world. For example, the Bolshevik Revolution occurred in October by the Julian system and is frequently known as the October Revolution, even though its Gregorian date places it in November.

We are indebted to the many fine scholars, writers, and informed persons whose works we have consulted in preparing this book. To retain the rigid format and concise style we have seldom cited names unless a particular contribution is directly associated with the name, as in a theory or interpretation. We are also indebted to our students, who have often challenged us to be concise and precise, to identify actors and institutions, and to analyze the significance of current political events. The organization and format of this dictionary series is based in large part on these fundamental objectives.

We also thank our friend, colleague, and editor, Jack C. Plano, a noted lexicographer, who first developed the unique two-paragraph format for political dictionaries 25 years ago. His careful editing has saved us from stylistic errors and verbosity. We especially thank Jean Enzler Rossi, who quickly and cheerfully typed the manuscript through several revisions.

—Ernest E. Rossi
—Barbara P. McCrea
Western Michigan University

GUIDE TO COUNTRIES

This Guide contains references to European countries only. For other countries, see the Subject Index, p. 377.

Albania
Cominform, communist party as member of, 282
refuses Soviet dominance, 282
Warsaw Treaty Organization (WTO), withdraws from, 366

Austria
in Austro-Prussian War, 190
European Free Trade Association (EFTA), as member of, 259
in German Confederation, 189–190
union with Germany, 157–158

Belgium
Benelux, as member of, 243–244
Commission of European Communities, representation on, 244
European Communities, as member of, 253, 254, 257
European Parliament, representation in, 261
NATO, as member of, 267
and NATO missiles issue, 251–252
Western European Union (WEU), as member of, 272

Bulgaria
COMECON, as member of, 285
Cominform, communist party as member of, 282
Warsaw Treaty Organization (WTO), as member of, 366

Czechoslovakia
as arms supplier to Third World, 366
COMECON, as member of, 285

Cominform, communist party as member of, 282
and Italian Communists support of 1968 reform, 291
and Munich Agreement, 205–206
resists Soviet missile emplacement, 367
revolt of 1953, 305
Soviet invasion of (1968), 276
and the treaty with West Germany (1973), 217
Warsaw Treaty Organization (WTO), as member of, 366

Denmark
Commission of European Communities, representation on, 244
European Communities, as member of, 253, 254, 255
European Free Trade Association (EFTA), as former member of, 259
European Parliament, representation in, 261
NATO, as member of, 267
Nordic Council, as member of, 266

Finland
European Free Trade Association (EFTA), as associate member of, 259
independence of, 363
Nordic Council, as member of, 266
and trade links with COMECON, 285

France
administrative law in, 90
and Algerian war, 80–81
antisemitism in, 79

and armed forces not under NATO, 268
army of, 80, 81
army, political activities of, 80–81, 124–125
Bonapartism in, 82–83
bureaucracy in, 110–111, 117–118
business associations in, 83–84
cabinet instability in, 108
Catholic political party in, 131–132
centrist parties in, 84–85, 134–135, 138
and colonial relations, 80–81, 113
Commission of European Communities, representation on, 244
communist party in, 111–112
conservative parties in, 126–127, 135–136
constitution (1946), 107–108
constitution (1958), 98–99
constitutional interpretation in, 87–89
constitutions, list of, 89
declaration of rights, 90–91
dependencies of, 113–114
elections of 1981, 92–93
electoral alliances of, 92, 96
electoral systems in, 93–96
empire of, 104–105
Euratom, as member of, 253
European Coal and Steel Community (ECSC), as member of, 253
and European Defense Community (EDC), 272
European Economic Community (EEC), as member of, 257
and European Parliament elections, 263
European Parliament, representation in, 261
farmers' associations in, 97–98
Fascism in, 79
foreign policies in, 96–97, 115–116, 124–125
Gaullism and, 114–117
Gaullist parties in, 135–136
German occupation of, 138–139, 154–155
and the Indochina war, 118–119
interest groups in, 83–84, 97–98
judicial system in, 119–120
leftist radicalism in, 119
legal system of, 85–86, 90
legislative process in, 87–89
legislature of, 95–96, 99–100, 103–104
local government in, 122–123, 123–124, 133
May 1958 events, interpretations of, 125
monarchical systems of, 82, 83, 120–121
nationalization of industry in, 127–128
NATO, cooperation with, 268
NATO, as member of, 267

nuclear weapons, arguments pro and con in, 106
nuclear weapons strategies in, 96–97, 128–129, 152–153

Paris Commune in, 86
political culture of, 129–130
political party system in, 100–101, 108–109
presidency of, 94–95, 101–102
prime minister office in, 102–103
Prussia, war against, 93–94
public administration in, 117–118, 122–124, 133
referenda in, 136–137
and resistance in World War II, 138–139
revolutions in, 82, 83, 86, 120, 139–140
rightist movements in, 79, 81
and scandals in Third Republic, 150–152
and settlers in Algeria, 80, 81
social classes in, pre-1789, 82
socialism in, 127–128, 130–131, 142–144
socialist parties in, 121, 142–144
socioeconomic theories on, 144–148
suffrage in, 96
trade unions in, 153–154
Western European Union (WEU), as member of, 272

Germany, East. *See also* German Democratic Republic in Subject Index
as arms supplier to the Third World, 367
Berlin Wall and, 161–162
COMECON, as member of, 285
constitution of, 191
and the East Berlin uprising (1953), 305
and espionage in West Germany, 198
international organizations, as member of, 191
and Oder-Neisse line, 216
political parties in, 191
population of, 191
resists Soviet missile emplacement, 367
as Soviet zone of Germany, 222, 242
and treaty with West Germany, 159–160
Warsaw Treaty Organization (WTO), as member of, 366

Germany, West. *See also* Germany; Prussia; German Empire; German Democratic Republic (GDR); Weimar Republic in Subject Index
agriculture in, 180

antinuclear forces in, 195–196
Berlin airlift and, 160–161
Berlin wall and, 161–162
boundary with East Germany, 216
bureaucracy in, 240–241
business associations in, 166–167
chancellor's powers in, 181
Christian Democracy in, 168–169, 170–171
the church in, 171–172
civil service in, 240–241
Commission of European Communities, representation on, 244
communists in, 189
compared to Weimar Republic, 162–163
constitution (1949), 158–159
courts in, 201–202
democracy in, 162–163
democracy, support for, 218
economic conditions in, 174–175
economic policy of, 228–229
elections of 1983, 176–177
electoral systems in, 177–179
environmentalist party in, 195–196
espionage affairs in, 198–199
Euratom, as member of, 253
European Coal and Steel Community (ECSC), as member of, 253
European Economic Community (EEC), as member of, 257
and European Parliament elections, 263
European Parliament, representation in, 261
farmers' associations in, 180
federalism in, 183–184
and foreign policy to East, 159–160, 199, 217–218
foreign workers in, 197–198
Free Democratic party in, 186–187
functional representation in, 188
interest groups in, 166–167, 180, 230–231
judicial review in, 174, 182–183
legal system in, 201–202
legislative process in, 164, 165
lessons of Weimar applied in, 235, 236
local government system in, 204–205
media, role of, 171, 229–230
nationalists in, 206–207
NATO, as member of, 267
and NATO missiles issue, 251–252
Nazism effects on, 207–210
nonconfidence procedure in, 174–175
occupation period effects on, 160–161, 214–215
parliament of, 163–164, 165–166
political culture, 218–219
political party system in, 167–168,
194–195, 220–221, 231–232
population of, 192
Potsdam conference, effects on, 222
president's powers in, 185
proportional representation in, 177
refugees and escapees in, 225–226
and relations with East Germany, 192
rule of law in, 223
Saar, relationship to, 226
Social Democratic chancellors, list of, 228–229
socialism in, 194, 227–228
states, governmental system, 202–203
states, list of, 186
states, political party system in, 203–204
states' rights in, 183–184
terrorism in, 224–225
trade unions in, 172–173, 230–231
and treaties with Eastern Europe, 159–160, 217–218, 239
and union with Austria, 157–158
urban problems in, 205
war crimes trials by, 213
West Berlin governmental system in, 238–239
West Berlin, relationship to, 222, 238–239
Western European Union (WEU), as member of, 272
and worker participation in management, 172–173, 230–231
Yalta conference effects on, 241–242

Greece
Commission of European Communities, representation on, 244
and European Communities, 253, 254, 257
European Parliament, representation in, 261
NATO, as member of, 267

Hungary
COMECON, as member of, 285
Cominform, communist party as member of, 282
rebellion of 1956, 305
Warsaw Treaty Organization (WTO), as member of, 366

Iceland
European Free Trade Association (EFTA), as member of, 259
NATO, as member of, 267
Nordic Council, as member of, 266

Ireland, Republic of. *See also* Northern

Ireland; Ulster in Subject Index
Commission of European Communities, representation on, 244
and Commonwealth, 11
dominion status of, 59, 71
and Easter Rising, 32, 59
as Eire, 59
Euratom, as member of, 253
European Coal and Steel Community (ECSC), as member of, 253
European Economic Community (EEC), as member of, 257
European Parliament, representation in, 261
and government of Ireland Act of 1920, 42
as Irish Free State, 42, 59, 71
and Irish Republican Army (IRA), 32, 42
legislature of, 59
Northern Ireland, relationship to, 44, 71
parties in, 59
population of, 73
and relations with Britain, 60
religion and politics in, 59–60
republic status in, 59, 71
Ulster, relationship to, 71
United States, relations with, 2–3

Italy
Cominform, communist party as member of, 282
Commission of European Communities, representation on, 244
Communist party supports Czech reforms, 291
Euratom, as member of, 253
Eurocommunism in, 251, 282, 291
European Coal and Steel Community (ECSC), as member of, 253
European Economic Community (EEC), as member of, 257
European Parliament, 261, 263
NATO, as member of, 267
and NATO missiles issue, 251–252
Western European Union (WEU), as member of, 272

Luxembourg
Benelux, as member of, 243–244
Commission of European Communities, representation on, 244
European Communities, as member of, 253, 254, 257
European Parliament, representation in, 261
NATO, as member of, 267
Western European Union (WEU), as member of, 272

Netherlands
Benelux, as member of, 243–244
Commission of European Communities, representation on, 244
European Communities, as member of, 253, 254, 257
European Parliament, representation in, 261
NATO, as member of, 267
and NATO missiles issue, 251–252
Western European Union (WEU), as member of, 272

Norway
European Free Trade Association (EFTA), as member of, 259
NATO, as member of, 267
Nordic Council, as member of, 266

Poland
annexes German territory, 214, 216
COMECON, as member of, 285
divided by Nazi-Soviet pact, 206
expells Germans, 216
Gomulka, Wladyslaw, as leader of, 305
independence from Russia, 363
invasion of by the USSR, 363
and Oder-Neisse line, 216
and Pale of Settlement, 348
rebellion of 1956, 305
Warsaw Treaty Organization (WTO), as member of, 366

Portugal
European Community membership expected, 255
European Free Trade Association (EFTA), as member of, 259
NATO, as member of, 267

Romania
COMECON, as member of, 285
and Moldavia (Bessarabia), 363
rejects COMECON role, 286
rejects Soviet dominance, 282
and Warsaw Treaty Organization (WTO), 366

Spain
Civil War in, 282
Eurocommunism in, 250–251
European Community membership expected, 255

Sweden
European Free Trade Association (EFTA), as member of, 259
Nordic Council, as member of, 266

Switzerland
European Free Trade Association (EFTA), as member of, 259

Union of Soviet Socialist Republics.
See also Russia, czarist in Subject Index
administration of, 308, 318, 325, 335–336, 346
agriculture in, 280–281, 320, 327, 356–357
and anti-Soviet agitation and propaganda, 299–300
appeal to developing countries, 283–284, 334
boundaries of, 362–363
budget of, 277–278
bureaucratization in, 312–313
censorship in, 349–350, 355
Central Committee, 288–289
citizen participation in, 279, 329, 334
civil rights in, 279–280, 306–307
Civil War in, 365
climate of, 362
COMECON, 285–286
Communist Party of the Soviet Union (CPSU), 286–298
Congress of, 290–291
Council of Ministers, 284–285, 343
crimes in, 299–302
defense budget of, 283, 303
Defense Council, 303
de-Stalinization in, 305–306
and dissent, 305–307, 326, 353–355
Eastern Europe, relations with, 276–277, 282, 285, 305, 327, 365
economic planning in, 283, 310, 314–315, 319–321, 340
education in, 308, 328, 338–339, 349
elections in, 303–304
and expansion of Russian Empire, 362
explanatory theories in, 311–317
federalism in, 318
foreign policy of, 276–278, 281–282, 285, 327, 339–340, 365
General Secretary, 291–292
geography of, 362–363
government institutions in, 277, 284, 303, 330, 335–336, 343–345, 360–361
head of government, 343
head of state, 343–344
Helsinki Accord and, 280, 307
ideology of, 330–334
interest groups in, 321, 336, 344, 365
judicial system in, 324, 345, 349
KGB in, 295, 306, 326, 349, 359
and leadership selection, 292–293
legislative process in, 284–285, 329–330
and legitimation of party dominance, 289, 293, 341–342, 356
local government (*raion*), 346–347
mass organizations in, 279, 303, 307, 328, 334–335
military, 293–294, 326, 348, 349
ministers, role of, 323, 335–336
and missiles in Europe, 252, 265–266
nationalism in, 341–343, 348–349, 364–365
new economic policy (NEP), 336–337
and *nomenklatura*, 297, 310, 337
oblast', 289, 337–338
occupation of Germany and, 214–215
party schools in, 338–339
peasants in, 288, 336, 351–352
planning in, 311, 319–321, 323, 340–341
policy process in, 294–295, 316, 321, 359
Politburo, 294–295
political culture of, 311–312, 338–339, 341–343
political parties in, early, 273–275
population of, 362–363
at Potsdam Conference, 221
Primary party organization (CPSU) in, 295–296
private farm plots in, 328
Procuracy, 345–346
raion, 346–347
religion in, 300, 307, 342, 348, 350
revolutions in, 274–276
second economy in, 329, 350–351
Secretariat, 297–298
secret police in, 305, 322, 326–327
and socialist law, 353
Soviet bloc, 276–277, 285–286
soviets (councils) in, 355–356
State committees, 326, 359
Supreme Court, 359–360
Supreme Soviet, 343–344
territorial-administrative divisions in, 289, 318–319, 337–338, 346
territorial size, 362
terrorism in, 280, 296, 305–306, 322, 326
trade unions in, 334
union-republics in, 318–319, 364–365

Warsaw Treaty Organization (WTO)
and, 365–366
women in, 288, 328
at Yalta Conference, 241–242

United Kingdom. *See also* England; Scotland; Wales; Northern Ireland in Subject Index
administration of government in, 70–71
administrative complaints in, 46
agricultural policy in, 27, 245–246
antinuclear groups in, 7–8
budget of, 70–71
and budget of European Community, 262
business associations in, 5–6
cabinet, 6–7
churches in, 22–23
civil service, 9–10, 70–71
class system in, 21–22
colonies of, 4–5, 16, 73
Commission of European Communities, representation on, 244
Common Agricultural Policy and, 27, 245–246
Commonwealth, 11–12
Conservative party in, 12–13, 49–50
constitution, 3–4, 8–9, 57–58
decline of, 14–15
decolonization of, 16
deference in, 62–63
dependencies of, 73
devolution acts in, 17–18, 61–62
economic conditions in, 14–15
economic policies of, 66–67
elections of 1983, 19–20
electoral system in, 20–21
elites in, 33–34
empire of, 4–5, 16
Euratom, as member of, 253
European Coal and Steel Community (ECSC), as member of, 253
European Economic Community (EEC), as member of, 257
European Free Trade Association (EFTA), as former member of, 259
European Parliament elections (1984), 263
European Parliament, representation in, 261
and European referendum, 23–24
and Falklands' War, 25–26
farmers' associations in, 26–27
foreign policy of, 2–3, 18–19, 65–66
guild mentality in, 70
House of Commons, 28–29, 53–54
House of Lords, 30–31
hunger strikers in, 32
interest groups in, 5–6, 7–8, 24–25,
26–27, 67–70
and Ireland, 59, 71
judicial system in, 34–35
labor policy, 67, 70
Labour party in, 35–37, 49–50
legal system in, 10–11
liberalism in, 36–37
Liberal party in, 1–2, 36–37
local government, 37–38
London government, 28
members of parliament, 40
monarchy, 41–42
NATO, as member of, 261
and NATO missiles issue, 251–252
nonconformists in, 23
Northern Ireland and, 32–33, 42–46, 70–73
opposed to European Economic Community (EEC), 246
parliamentary opposition in, 46–47
Parliament in, 15–16, 40, 47–48
political culture of, 51–52
political party system in, 39–40, 48–50, 52–53
political violence in, 32–33
population of, 73
at Potsdam Conference, 221
prime minister office in, 53–54
public administration in, 9–10, 46, 56–57, 70–71
public corporations in, 56–57
reform acts, 57–58
representation acts, 58
royal houses of, 31–32
scandals in, 55–56
Scotland and, 17–18, 60–62
Social Democratic party in, 63–64
socialism in, 24–25, 35–36
spies in, 55–56, 64–65
and Suez crisis, 65–66
trade unions in, 67–70
and Ulster, 71
and Ulster parties, 45–46, 71–73
Wales and, 17–18, 50–51, 74
welfarism in, 66–67, 75–76
Welsh party in, 50–51
Western European Union (WEU), as member of, 272
at Yalta Conference, 241–242

Yugoslavia
COMECON, trade links with, 285
Cominform, communist party as member of, 282
Cominform, expulsion from, 282
refuses KGB control of secret police, 327
repudiates bilateral treaties with USSR, 366

The European Political Dictionary

1. The United Kingdom

Alliance   An electoral coalition between the Liberal party and the Social Democratic party (SDP). The Liberal-SDP Alliance was formed in 1982 and contested the parliamentary elections of June 1983. The parties agreed to a joint manifesto and not to compete against the other in elections. The 1983 manifesto criticized the Labour party's policies on the economy and defense, and the European policies of both the Labour and Conservative parties. The Alliance called for no further nationalizations or denationalizations, continued membership in the European Community, continued membership in NATO, nuclear arms limitation talks, retention of the nuclear deterrent, but cancellation of Trident missile purchases. It also advocated programs to reduce unemployment by creating jobs through government-financed programs; modernization of private industry through government assistance; and improvements in social security benefits. In the 1983 election, the Alliance won 25.4 percent of the popular vote, but it won only 23 seats in Parliament, 186 fewer than Labour. The disparity between popular votes and seats, caused by the fact that three large groups competed in the single-member district electoral system, led the Alliance to call for a system of proportional representation. In 1984 the two parties of the Alliance continued to cooperate in local government elections and elections to the European Parliament. *See also* ELECTIONS OF 1983:BRITAIN, p. 19; LIBERAL PARTY, p. 36; POLITICAL PARTY SYSTEM: BRITAIN, p. 52; SOCIAL DEMOCRATIC PARTY (SDP), p. 63.

Significance   The Alliance of the Liberal and Social Democratic parties presents a major challenge to the Labour party as the second party in Britain. Although the 1983 election yielded few seats, the Alliance may be in a position to benefit from the continuing breakdown of the

British two-party system. Thus far, the Conservative party has been the sole beneficiary. Some observers believe that the nation is going through a period of "partisan dealignment," in which traditional voter ties to parties are breaking down; others believe the 1970s have ushered in a transition period in which the Labour party will fall to third place because of the decreasing size of its social base. By maintaining an electoral coalition the parties of the Alliance may benefit from these developments as voters search for an alternative to the party in power.

Atlanticism   A fundamental postwar British foreign security policy that stresses the importance of the North Atlantic Treaty Organization and the United States commitment to defend Western Europe. The British foreign policy of Atlanticism is based on the assumptions that (1) the security of Britain requires the maintenance of a balance of power on the continent of Europe; (2) the postwar threat to the balance is the expansive foreign policy of the Soviet Union; (3) neither Britain nor any other Western European power singly or in concert can defend the area from a USSR conventional or nuclear attack; (4) the military forces of the United States must be relied on to defend Europe; and (5) within the context of the Atlantic alliance, Britain has a "special relationship" with the United States that sets it apart from other Western powers. British governments applied the principle of Atlanticism in different ways, but the key features that survived over a 35-year period include (1) promoting the collective defense of Western Europe by keeping conventional British forces on the continent (British Army of the Rhine, BAOR); (2) strongly supporting NATO and the American military presence in Europe; (3) developing a nuclear deterrent force that is supplied with American nuclear weapons; (4) retrenching from global military responsibilities and concentrating defense resources in Europe; and (5) promoting detente and arms control measures, but not at the expense of sacrificing the Atlantic alliance or the nuclear deterrent. *See also* EAST OF SUEZ, p. 18; NORTH ATLANTIC TREATY ORGANIZATION (NATO), p. 267; SUEZ CRISIS OF 1956, p. 65.

Significance   At the end of World War II, Atlanticism became one of the two fundamental parts of postwar British foreign policy, the other being the attempt to maintain its position as a global power with overseas commitments and interests. Although the second policy was subjected to great revision as Britain's weaknesses became increasingly apparent, every British government—Labour and Conservative—has pursued an Atlanticist policy. Despite the economic need to reduce military commitments to NATO and occasional disagreements with European allies, British governments have consistently stationed forces in Europe and cooperated fully in NATO operations. The special relationship with the United States places extra burdens on the British prime minister, particularly when the two governments disagree on American policies toward other parts of the world. The foreign policy of the United States is a matter of frequent debate in Britain, and the opposition often criticizes the government for American foreign policy actions. British governments attempt to dissuade the United States from undertaking policies or actions that would limit American commitments to Europe or involve it in a conflict that might engage Europe. Some aspects of the policy of Atlanticism, particularly those involving nuclear defense of Europe by American nuclear weapons and nuclear submarine bases in Britain, are very controversial and have been politically disruptive. But it seems likely that so long as nuclear weapons are believed to be the key deterrent to war in Europe, British governments will continue to be strong supporters of American forces in Europe and of NATO's nuclear strategy.

British Constitution The fundamental rules and practices that empower and delimit the authority of British governmental institutions and processes. The British constitution is not found in one document, but developed over time from organic acts of Parliament, judicial decisions, and constitutional conventions or practices. It is therefore said to be "unwritten" or uncodified. Important acts of Parliament that are sources of the constitution relate to: the composition of the political community (such as the Act of Union with Scotland of 1706), the powers of governmental institutions (e.g., Parliament Act of 1949 concerning the powers of the House of Lords), and acts pertaining to the rights of citizens (e.g., Reform Act of 1832 on suffrage). Some documents of great importance are known as great charters or historic acts because they represent a settlement of a major constitutional crisis; examples of this are the Magna Charta (1215), the Petition of Right (1628), and the Bill of Rights (1689). A second source is the common law legal system and the judicial decisions that established and interpret it. Although British courts may not declare an act of Parliament unconstitutional, the constitutional system has been affected by their interpretation of the law. Constitutional conventions are those binding practices and usages on matters of fundamental importance whose violation would cause a constitutional crisis. Examples of constitutional conventions include the responsibility of the cabinet to the House of Commons; the requirement that the monarch assent to laws enacted by Parliament; and the requirement that the prime minister resign or a new parliament be elected if the government loses a motion of nonconfidence. Two principles are considered to be most fundamental in the British constitutional system: the supremacy of Parliament, according to which there is no legal authority superior to Parliament; and the rule of law, which forbids arbitrary governmental actions. Other important constitutional principles include: a unitary, not a federal form of government, in which all governmental authority is located in the central government; the parliamentary or cabinet system, in which the political executive is responsible to the House of Commons; constitutional monarchy, in which the sovereign is a nonpartisan head of state; political democracy, in which the people through universal suffrage and free, competitive elections choose their representatives; a bicameral legislature, which is dominated by the lower chamber, the House of Commons; and an independent judiciary that interprets the law, but does not have the power to declare laws unconstitutional. *See also* MONARCH, p. 41; PARLIAMENT, p. 47; PARTY GOVERNMENT, p. 48.

Significance The most important source of the British constitution is the act of Parliament, which can override traditional conventions and principles of the common law. Although constitutional conventions are not codified, they are crucial to the operation of parliamentary government. When disputes arise over whether a particular practice has the force of constitutional law, the works of scholarly authorities are often cited. Ultimately the question is decided in the political arena through the operation of the most basic principle—the supremacy of Parliament. The British constitution is said to be flexible because a simple act of Parliament is all that is required to make a constitutional change. Yet, although the political system is adaptable, opinion is conservative concerning constitutional change, and formal amendment through statute is politically difficult. Generally, there is widespread agreement in Britain on the constitutional rules and pride in the institutions.

British Empire Territorial possessions and dependencies of Great Britain, which reached their peak in the late nineteenth and early twentieth centuries. The British Empire consisted of crown colonies, self-governing colonies, leaseholds and concessions, protectorates, mandates, and trusteeships, and other dependent territories having a variety of legal relationships with Britain. The Empire was established over several hundred years, beginning in the sixteenth century, and was expanded in various stages. By the nineteenth century it included territories on every continent and ocean, comprising one-fourth of the world's population. Typical forms of rule included (1) chartered companies; (2) indirect rule, whereby local indigenous rulers were supervised by British colonial officers; and (3) direct rule from the Colonial Office. In 1867, Canada, and later Australia and New Zealand, were given self-governing dominion status. After World War I, nationalist pressures for independence precipitated the beginning of the Empire's decline and the process of decolonization. In the twentieth century, the term "British Empire and Commonwealth" gave way to "Commonwealth of Nations" and later with near-complete decolonization to "Commonwealth." The Commonwealth is a loose association that includes Britain and most of the former colonies of the Empire. *See also* COMMONWEALTH, p. 11; DECOLONIZATION, p. 16; UNITED KINGDOM OF GREAT BRITAIN AND NORTHERN IRELAND, p. 73.

Significance The British Empire was one of the greatest empires in modern world history, and its influence on current global political, social, and economic institutions and processes is hard to measure. The influence of the Empire has been greatest where English people settled in relatively empty lands like North America and Australia, but it is also important in other areas of colonial domination, like Africa and South Asia. Along with the other European imperial powers—France, Spain, Portugal, Belgium, and Holland especially—Britain helped spread European people, customs, language, and ideas over the face of the earth. Many nations still retain the English system of law, parliamentary institutions, and administrative arrangements; 17 former colonies recognize the British queen as their head of state; and 46 have elected to remain within the Commonwealth. The Empire was made possible and contributed to British naval, military, commercial, and financial power. The exploitation of resources of foreign lands directly promoted Britain's economic development as a manufacturing state; it helped structure the policy of free trade and contributed to internal democratic demands for political reform. The English people were fond of saying that "the sun never sets on the British Empire." Only 13 scattered island dependencies remain of the once great Empire, and its recent passing promotes both nostalgia and bitter memories. These feelings contribute to support for overseas military operations, such as the one taken in the Falklands War of 1982.

Business Associations: Britain Associations of employers in industry, commerce, and finance. Over 800 business associations serve the needs of British employers. The largest and most influential body is the Confederation of British Industry (CBI), a peak organization of about 180 trade and employers' associations, and about 12,000 individual industrial and commercial firms. The CBI was formed in 1965 by amalgamating the Federation of British Industries, the National Union of British Manufacturers, and the British Employers' Confederation. The CBI includes small and large firms, but is dominated by larger industrial firms. The CBI has a president, director-general, national council, and a large staff of about 400 persons. Other business associations include the Association of British Chambers of Commerce, with a membership of 60,000 firms, and the Retail Consortium, a confederation of retailers' associations.

Significance The great number and variety of British business associations resembles the situation in other highly industrialized nations. By amalgamating three major industrial and manufacturing associations, the Confederation of British Industry increased its potential power to influence public affairs, but it also increased the possibility of internal conflict. Not all firms agree with its policy statements. The CBI is not affiliated with a political party, as the trade unions are to the Labour party, but it takes political positions and tries to influence the government and public opinion. CBI members are sympathetic to the Conservative party, but its leaders have not always been in agreement with the policies of Prime Minister Margaret Thatcher. The ability of British pressure groups to influence the government and the legislature is less than in the United States, where decentralization of governmental power and undisciplined political parties provide many opportunities for penetration and influence. In Britain, some business associations may be weaker than single multinational corporations that employ thousands of workers and make important decisions whether to invest and expand in Britain or abroad. The policy views of the "City," the banking and financial district of London, equivalent to the American Wall Street, are well represented in any British government, even though the City lacks a central association. The operations of the City expanded in the late 1970s after the financial failures that followed the oil crisis of 1973–74; by 1982 it had attracted 450 foreign banks, making London again the world's leading center of finance and credit. The British economy is so dependent on international trade that Labour and Conservative governments often show a continuity in foreign economic policy. Hence, the influence of commercial, industrial, and financial firms on governments is based less on a similarity of socioeconomic background or attitudes of the major actors, but more on the coincidence of interests of British companies and the nation's economic well-being.

Cabinet The inner policy-making body collectively responsible for the operations of the British government. The cabinet comprises from 20 to 25 ministers, most of whom are drawn from the House of Commons; 2 to 4 members are chosen from the House of Lords. The prime minister, who presides over the cabinet, has the power to appoint and dismiss its members. The cabinet is the inner group of the larger "government" or ministry, the political executive. The "government" comprises the cabinet, noncabinet ministers, and junior ministers (undersecretaries and parliamentary secretaries), the whole totaling about 100 persons. Cabinet ministers, who are in many cases the most influential and powerful politicians in the majority party, are given leadership posts in Parliament and head important administrative departments of government. As established by law and custom, the functions of the cabinet are to: (1) determine the policies to be submitted to Parliament; (2) control the national executive in accordance with the policy established by Parliament; and (3) coordinate and delimit the activities of the administrative departments. A constitutional convention requires that cabinet members maintain "collective responsibility." This means sharing responsibility for, and defending, cabinet decisions in public. *See also* PRIME MINISTER (PM), p. 53.

Significance The cabinet is the keystone in the British system of responsible parliamentary (or cabinet) government. It illustrates in a fundamental way the principle of fusion of powers because its members, who stand at the peak of the political executive, all have seats in the Parliament. The interpretation of the actual role of the cabinet in policy making has been subject to some dispute, however. The prime minister (PM) clearly dominates the cabinet, and lesser cabinet officials may have little influence on matters outside their respective departments. But the PM cannot ignore the advice of senior colleagues, most of whom are potential rivals and command the loyalty of some backbenchers.

Campaign for Nuclear Disarmament (CND) A citizens' pressure group in Britain that promotes antinuclear objectives by engaging in demonstrations and acts of civil disobedience. The Campaign for Nuclear Disarmament (CND) became very active in the 1980s, when various antinuclear groups joined forces under its banner. It is the latest of a series of antinuclear protest groups in Britain, a number of which have supported unilateral nuclear disarmament (UND). CND supports a nuclear freeze and UND; it opposed the deployment of American-made cruise missiles in Britain and British purchase of American-made Trident submarine missiles. Various CND groups engage in public protests like marches in cities and attempts to blockade entrances at British and American bases. Some camp outside bases in protest, and others engage in sit-down demonstrations in city streets. The CND became especially active in 1983 and 1984 over the issue of deployment of cruise missiles in Britain.

Significance The activity of various Campaign for Nuclear Disarmament groups has resulted in thousands of arrests or fines for acts of civil disobedience. Instances of massive demonstrations and arrests occurred during a sit-down demonstration in London's Trafalgar Square in 1982, and when CND groups blocked gates to military bases in 1983. The antinuclear movement received support from the opposition Labour party in 1982 and 1983, when the party conferences supported UND; this view is not supported by some Labour leaders, however. In 1983 public opinion polls showed that a majority of those polled opposed deployment of NATO cruise missiles in Britain, but a larger majority opposed unilateral nuclear disarmament. The policy of the Conservative government of Margaret Thatcher acknowledges the right of CND to engage in peaceful protest, but it takes measures against violent or disruptive acts. Despite much media attention, the CND movement failed to prevent the deployment of NATO cruise missiles in Britain. And the government continues to develop Britain's nuclear deterrent while promoting nuclear arms limitation talks.

Charters and Acts Historic documents in British constitutional development that represent the settlement of a major political issue. Some of the more noteworthy great charters and acts of Parliament in the over 700 years of British constitutional development include the following. In the Magna Charta (Great Charter) of 1215, which King John was forced to accept from rebellious barons, the king guaranteed nobles legal and judicial rights that he had arbitrarily withdrawn. Although based on the feudal rights of nobles, the Magna Charta established the principle of a constitutional monarchy, one limited by law. In the Writ of Summons of 1295, Edward I summoned a Parliament ("the Model Parliament") that for the first time was representative of three estates—lords, clergy, and commons. In the Petition of Right of 1628, initiated by Chief Justice Edward Coke, Parliament forced Charles I to agree that taxes could only be levied with the consent of Parliament and that restrictions be placed on the use of martial law and the quartering of troops in homes. The Habeas Corpus Act of 1679 made illegal the crown's practice of holding prisoners without a charge or a trial. The Bill of Rights of 1689, a landmark in British constitutional development, proclaimed the rights of Parliament, not of individual persons, as in the United States. The Bill of Rights was passed by the "Convention Parliament" after the defeat of the Catholic Stuart king, James II. It proclaimed the supremacy of Parliament, removed powers from the monarch, reaffirmed established rights, called for frequent and free elections, and provided that no Catholic could ascend the throne. The Act of Settlement of 1701 confirmed that Parliament determine the succession to the throne. In the Act of Union with Scotland of

1707, Scotland joined England and Wales in a single parliamentary union. Ireland was formally included by the Act of Union of 1801, but only Northern Ireland remained part of the United Kingdom after 1922. The Reform Acts of 1832, 1867, and 1884 enlarged the suffrage and eliminated inequalities between election districts. The Parliamentary Acts of 1911 and 1949 removed the financial powers of the House of Lords and reduced its power to delay the enactment of legislation by the House of Commons. *See also* BRITISH CONSTITUTION, p. 3; REFORM ACTS, p. 57.

Significance The great charters and acts are landmark documents in the evolution of the British constitution, and are part of a long evolutionary process of constitutional development. Some authorities believe that the Magna Charta, which limited the crown, and the Bill of Rights, which established Parliamentary supremacy, are the foundations upon which the entire constitutional system rests. These charters and acts are supplemented in the British "unwritten" constitutional system by practices and usages that establish important working principles in the operation of the system, and by the common law system that evolved over time.

Civil Service The permanent nonindustrial public employees of the central British government. The civil service is a classified, career-based, merit system that employs about 700,000 persons. This number includes employees in special branches like the Foreign Service that are controlled by departments, professional and specialist occupational groups, and the great bulk of employees who are controlled by the Treasury department, which supervises matters dealing with salaries, pensions, and administrative reorganization. Prior to 1971 most civil servants were divided into three groups: clerical, middle management, and the top administrative class. These groups are now integrated into a single classified system, but the topmost grades, of about 2,500 to 3,000 senior officers, retain the great influence they had in the past. Each administrative department has a civil service head, the permanent secretary, who ranks just below the government minister or secretary of state. The civil service carries out the routine administrative functions of government, and prepares legislative proposals and administrative regulations for approval by government ministers. The permanent secretary and top grades keep the department minister informed, prepare his speeches and answers to questions raised in Parliament, and give him advice on public policy matters. The group formerly called the "administrative class" has an upper-middle-class background, and many have gone to a "public" school (i.e., elite private preparatory school) and to

"Oxbridge" (Oxford or Cambridge universities). The central administrative apparatus of the British government is often referred to as "Whitehall," after the London district where many government ministries are located. *See also* CABINET, p. 6.

Significance In addition to handling routine administration, the civil service plays an influential role in the British political system. The service is comprised of a highly qualified and respected body of people who are tenured in permanent positions, thus providing a continuity of personnel that the political executive lacks. Government ministers rarely stay beyond two or three years in a department. Long tradition requires that civil servants practice anonymity, be impartial, and faithfully execute government policy. But the top administrative grades constitute a type of elite that holds and promotes views that are often incorporated into public policy. This aspect of their influence is important, but the general role of the bureaucracy in Britain is much less expansive than that in France. The British civil service has remained relatively small despite the enlargement of government services, and it rarely undertakes initiatives that involve long-range planning.

Common Law A system of judge-made law that is one of the sources of the British constitution. The common law is said to be "unwritten law" or "case law" because it was developed by traveling judges in the twelfth century who based their decisions on prevailing local custom. Gradually, through the process of reapplying decisions, a "common law" was created for the nation. By the fourteenth century the common law was used regularly in national courts in London as judges followed precedent and applied the principle of *stare decisis* (let the decision stand). Typical common law principles and practices include the supremacy of law, trial by jury, and settling civil controversies by the recovery of money damages after an injury. Another branch of law that developed in England was equity law, which is based on the idea of fairness or justice, rather than custom. By appealing to the king or the chancellor, a person might secure a fair or just redress of a civil grievance that was not possible in the common law courts. Typical equity writs (court orders) are the writ of mandamus, which orders a specific action to be performed; an injunction, which is a court order preventing an unfair action from occurring; and a writ of *habeas corpus,* which prevents arbitrary arrest by requiring that a prisoner be charged before a court. Both common law and equity law can be overridden by statutory law, a law enacted by a legislative body. Much British common law has been superseded by statutory law, which is organized into codes, similar to those in code law countries like France. The common law fills gaps in statutory law, and its principles are used by judges in interpreting statutory law. *See also* CODE LAW SYSTEM, p. 85; JUDICIAL SYSTEM: BRITAIN, p. 34.

Significance The common law system is used in England and Wales; the legal system in Scotland is based on the Roman code law system. The English common law system was carried to its colonies and is currently used in the United States (except Louisiana), Canada (except Quebec), Australia, New Zealand, and a number of the newer Commonwealth states. Although much British law is enacted by Parliament, the fundamental aspects of the system are grounded in common law principles. Through judicial interpretation, the system provides a degree of flexibility that is usually lacking in code law systems.

Commonwealth A voluntary intergovernmental association of 47 independent states including the United Kingdom and most former colonies of the British Empire. The Commonwealth, formerly called the British Commonwealth of Nations, was established in 1931 by the Statute of Westminster, an act of the British Parliament. The statute formally recognized the independence of the dominions (self-governing territories like Canada and Australia), declared that all member states were equal to Britain, and that all were united in allegiance to the British crown. From a nucleus of seven original members, the Commonwealth expanded greatly from the decolonization following World War II, when most former dependencies chose to remain members of the association. Major exceptions today include South Africa and Pakistan, which withdrew, and Ireland, Burma, and the former Arab dependencies, which chose not to join upon gaining full independence. The major institutions of the Commonwealth are (1) the Head of the Commonwealth, the reigning British monarch, who is primarily a figurehead who provides unity even though some member states are republics; (2) the Heads of Government or Conference of Prime Ministers, which is a biennial meeting of prime ministers whose decisions are not binding on member states; and (3) the Commonwealth Secretariat, located in London, which provides administrative and consultative services to member states and administers various programs including those of the Commonwealth Fund for Technical Cooperation. Meetings of finance ministers take place annually, and other ministerial meetings occur less frequently. *See also* BRITISH EMPIRE, p. 4.

Significance The Commonwealth functions primarily as a consultative body whose members cooperate in various fields when overlapping interests so dictate. Although Britain has been traditionally the most influential member, in recent years Third World Commonwealth states have become important. These states have promoted policies condemning racial discrimination in South Africa, the expansion of economic assistance for developing nations, the promotion of technical and economic cooperation, and speedier efforts in decolonization. Although Queen Elizabeth functions primarily in a symbolic role as Commonwealth head, she has taken a deep interest in the affairs of less-developed member states. It is unlikely that the Commonwealth will develop into a closer political or economic union, for the association contains over a billion people scattered over all continents and oceans. Not all have retained the British system of parliamentary government, and a number are in close competition and occasionally in conflict with fellow members. But since the association is voluntary and some benefits—especially economic—accrue to all members, it is likely that the Commonwealth will continue to function.

Conservative Party The oldest and most dominant major party in British politics. The Conservative party is descended from the Tory party, from which it inherited its support for the monarchy, the established church, and the Empire. This inheritance included an upper-class social base of support, paternalistic attitudes, and belief in the rightness of Conservative rule. Officially titled the Conservative and Unionist party, reflecting its nineteenth-century support for union with Ireland and later for union with Northern Ireland, the party is sometimes still called the Tory party. Under Benjamin Disraeli, originally a traditional conservative, the party developed in his second ministry a social reform approach called "Tory democracy" to complement its imperialism and traditionalism. In the nineteenth and twentieth centuries, the Conservative party's combination of community-minded conservatism and moderate social reform enabled it to survive challenges from parties advocating laissez-faire liberalism, social welfare liberalism, and doctrinaire socialism. Lacking an ideology and claiming to speak for the entire community, the party developed a multiclass base in the modern period. It draws support from the upper class, business interests, middle classes, and one-third of the working class. Its leaders, reflecting different tendencies within the party, have been drawn from the patrician, middle class, and Tory democracy traditions of the party. The party structure is hierarchical and its members of Parliament cohesive; and there is a strong tendency to follow the leadership so long as it produces victories. The party's change in leadership styles, its cohesiveness, and its policy changes have enabled it to dominate the two-party system since 1951. Conservative governments under Winston Churchill, Anthony Eden, Harold Macmillan, and Alec Douglas-Home ruled Britain from 1951 to 1964; from 1970 to 1974 under Edward Heath; and from 1979 under Margaret Thatcher. In the 1983 election Prime Minister Thatcher led the party to a smashing victory, winning a 144-seat majority over all other parliamentary groups. *See also* ELECTIONS OF 1983: BRITAIN, p. 19; PARTY ORGANIZATION, p. 49; POLITICAL PARTY SYSTEM: BRITAIN, p. 52; THATCHERISM, p. 66; WHIGS AND TORIES, p. 76.

Significance The Conservative party is one of the most successful political parties in the Western world. By adapting its program, membership, organization, and leadership to changing circumstances, the party maintained its long-run position as the dominant party in English politics. The party's willingness to adapt and change with the times is seen in its peaceful and rapid liquidation of the Empire, moving Britain into the European Common Market, promotion of social welfare, and selection of a woman as party leader. Yet the party retains its traditional biases in favor of free enterprise and private property and its opposition to disruptive trade unions. This mixture, with an added measure of military victory in the Falklands War, served it well under Prime Minister Thatcher in the 1983 elections. Yet, despite its success in winning elections, the Conservative party reflects the support of less than a majority of the people. This tempers its leadership and keeps it from moving too far from the center-right.

Crown The representation of the supreme executive authority in Britain. The crown symbolizes the unity of the state. It is the institution to which citizens give their loyalty and to which ministers are formally responsible. The "Crown in Parliament" is the expression of the ultimate source of all authority in the British constitutional system. The crown is the office held by the reigning monarch. Although it is to be distinguished from the particular queen or king on the throne, the crown's authority is exercised in that person's name. In a formal sense, the ministers and civil servants are servants of the crown, but in actuality the executive powers of the state are wielded by these officials. *See also* CABINET, p. 6; MONARCH, p. 41; PARLIAMENT, p. 47.

Significance The crown is often called an idea, a symbol, or an abstraction for the British state. The popular identification of the monarch with the crown is understandable because the abstraction is difficult to grasp, and because the concept of the state was not well developed in English history. All authority and power at one time emanated from the monarch, who was considered to be "sovereign." In a republic, sovereignty is formally located in the people, but it was retained in the crown in Britain. With the ascendancy of Parliament in the seventeenth century, the monarchy kept the symbols of office, but the real power was transferred to Parliament and its political executives.

Decline of Britain Differing interpretations about the causes and potential remedies for the general malaise that pervades Britain. For the last 20 years, a continuous debate concerning the decline of Britain has been going on among intellectuals and politicians. Aspects of the British political economy often cited as evidence of the decline include such matters as economic stagnation, recession, low productivity, high inflation, high unemployment, trade imbalances, budgetary deficits, currency devaluation, strikes, mass demonstrations, and racial and political violence. Theories that attempt to explain the reasons for Britain's decline tend to stress the following factors: (1) broad historical developments, such as the decay of the British industrial system as it competes with newer and stronger powers; (2) the political culture, which takes a conservative attitude toward change and adopts a piecemeal approach to problem solving; (3) outmoded economic institutions and mentalities such as the gentrified and nonaggressive spirit of British bankers and industrialists, the nonprofessionalism and lack of innovation of British managers, and the guild mentality of trade unions; (4) political institutions, such as the amateurism in the upper civil service and veto power of vested interests; and (5) government policies of any type, whether they promote socialist collectivization, Keynesian intervention, or free market neoliberalism. *See also* THATCHERISM, p. 66.

Significance The debate on the decline of Britain shows no sign of diminishing. The large number of books, articles, journalistic pieces, and political tracts offers conflicting explanations for Britain's ills, some of which seem plausible. There is little agreement on the cure, however, and some writers say that the decline was inevitable and cannot be reversed. Government policies engineered to solve some problems partially succeed, but they tend to exacerbate others. Thus Prime Minister Margaret Thatcher's experiment with neoliberalism and monetarism was abandoned in part because, although it eventually reduced the inflation rate, it contributed to an economic recession. Inflation dropped from 22 to 4 percent, but unemployment rose from 5 to 13 percent; output fell as interest rates rose and strikes flourished. Some analysts point out that Britain is on the verge of becoming "deindustrialized," i.e., of becoming a net importer of industrial goods. They note that North Sea oil has disguised the deterioration in the balance of trade; moreover, production is reaching a peak and will fall dramatically by the end of the decade. Other observers argue that British political institutions are firmly based on an adaptable political culture, and that although the people are more difficult to govern today, the country will survive its current economic malaise.

Decline of Parliament The thesis that the House of Commons as an independent legislative assembly no longer exercises the power to make policy as it did in the nineteenth and early twentieth centuries. The decline of Parliament is attributed to the development of strong, disciplined political parties whose leaders are able to impose discipline on rank and file members of Parliament (MPs). Since the leaders of the majority party in Commons, through the operation of the parliamentary system, become the cabinet, the decision-making power is transferred to the executive branch. Developments in the party system have been reinforced by twentieth-century social, economic, and national security developments. These factors have contributed to the demand for increased government services, expanded social welfare programs, detailed regulation of the economy, and expensive national defense programs. These demands and needs have greatly expanded the size and functions of the executive branch. Individual members of Parliament can do little, for they lack the time, information, staff, and resources to assess the many complex issues brought before them. Fiscal, budgetary, and legislative policy is formulated, proposed, and guided through Parliament by the government. MPs are members of a team who are expected to support (or oppose if in the opposition), the government's proposals. Party whips enforce the discipline demanded by party leaders. Thus Parliament becomes the arena where interparty struggles are manifested and not the locus of power as it was before strong parties emerged. *See also* PARLIAMENT, p. 47; PARTY GOVERNMENT, p. 48; POLITICAL PARTY SYSTEM: BRITAIN, p. 51.

Significance The decline-of-Parliament thesis provides an explanation for the widely observed phenomenon of the dominance of the executive branch within the British political system. The British phenomenon has also occurred in those industrialized democracies whose political party systems show a similar degree of simplicity, centralization, and discipline, such as West Germany. Where parties are undisciplined and decentralized, such as in the Fourth Republic of France or the United States, the legislature is able to maintain a large degree of independence vis-á-vis the executive branch. Supporters of Parliament point out that the rise of the cabinet has made meaningless the constitutional principle of the supremacy of Parliament, and they especially regret its occurrence in the land of the "Mother of Parliaments." Other observers argue that Parliament's proper role is to choose and sustain a set of leaders, that the system produces responsible and effective governments, and that these developments have been ratified by the people through the electoral process.

Decolonization   The liquidation of the British Empire after World War II. Decolonization proceeded rapidly after the war, as India and Pakistan were granted independence in 1947, the Palestine mandate was relinquished in 1948, and Burma became a republic and opted out of the Commonwealth in 1948. Many North African, Mediterranean, sub-Saharan African, and Asian territories became independent in the 1950s and early 1960s, and continental American and Caribbean possessions in the 1960s and 1970s. By the early 1980s only about a dozen territories remained as dependencies of Britain; of the more noteworthy, Hong Kong, Gibraltar, and the Falkland islands are under pressure respectively from China, Spain, and Argentina. *See also* BRITISH EMPIRE, p. 4; COMMONWEALTH, p. 11; UNITED KINGDOM OF GREAT BRITAIN AND NORTHERN IRELAND, p. 73.

Significance   The Empire was made possible by Britain's control of the seas, its financial resources, its military strength, and the apparent skill or good luck of British governments in responding to a variety of local circumstances. Historically, when these factors failed, independence movements were successful, as in North America. The rapid postwar decolonization, however, is traced to the rapid decline of Britain's diplomatic, military, and economic power, and its inability to resist the demands of strong nationalist movements. Britain was successful against Malayan communist guerrillas and Kenyan Mau Mau rebels in the 1950s. But, except for maintaining order among disputing indigenous groups, as in Cyprus and Aden, Britain refused to be committed to fighting colonial wars. For the most part, decolonization therefore came peacefully and after local nationalists were able to agree on a majority rule constitution. Since the American Declaration of Independence, all of Britain's colonies have achieved their independence through joint action with the exception of Rhodesia, which issued a unilateral declaration of independence (UDI), initially based on white minority rule. After years of pressure from the British government, the United Nations, and local guerrillas, a joint declaration granting independence to the new state of Zimbabwe based on the majority rule principle was proclaimed in 1980. Unlike France in Indochina and Algeria, Britain was spared the domestic political trauma from failed colonial wars. Most former colonies opted to remain within the Commonwealth and continue to maintain good relations with Britain.

Devolution The granting of legislative and executive powers to regional governments by the national government. Although devolution had been promoted for some time, it became an important national issue in the late 1960s when strong nationalist movements rose in Scotland and Wales. The Welsh nationalist party (*Plaid Cymru*) and the Scottish National party (SNP) won seats in by-elections in 1967 and 1968. The Labour government of Harold Wilson in 1968 created a royal commission to study the issue of devolution, and in 1973 the commission proposed the creation of assemblies in Scotland and Wales with legislative powers and responsible ministries. In October 1974 the SNP dramatically increased its share of the Scottish vote to 30 percent, and the smaller Plaid Cymru continued to win a few sets. Fearful of losing Labour's strong electoral base in Scotland and Wales, the Labour government proposed a devolution bill along the lines of the commission's report, but the bill met strong opposition and failed to clear the House of Commons. Two revised bills were adopted in 1978 after a dilution of the power to be granted to Wales, but Parliament provided they would become effective only after approval by a plebiscite vote. The Scotland Act of 1978 provided for an assembly with wide powers, including, with some exceptions, education, health, local government, transport, social services, and police. International, taxation, and economic powers were retained by the national government. Most national-regional jurisdictional disputes were to be resolved by the Judicial Committee of the Privy Council, or by the Parliament in Westminster. A Scottish first secretary (prime minister) would head a cabinet responsible to the assembly. The Wales Act of 1978 provided for an assembly without independent powers or a single executive; committees would supervise the administration of devolved powers. The acts required that a popular referendum be held in the two regions and that at least 40 percent of the eligible voters agree before devolution became operational. On March 1, 1979, devolution was soundly defeated in Wales: only 12 percent of the electorate supported the plan, including only 20 percent of those voting. In Scotland a bare majority of 51.6 percent of those voting favored devolution, but inasmuch as this represented only 32.8 percent of the electorate, the plan was also defeated. The acts were repealed when Conservatives returned to power in 1979. *See also* PLAID CYMRU, p. 50; SCOTTISH NATIONAL PARTY (SNP), p. 61.

Significance The devolution acts would have set up a quasi-federal form of government, at least for Scotland. The Scotland Act of 1978 would have delegated much authority to the regional government, but retained ultimate power in the national government, which could amend the act at any time. The devolution acts were made possible not only because of the rise of nationalist parties, but also by the politics of the

Labour party. Had the two assemblies been created, it is likely that the Labour party would have controlled Wales, and either Labour or the Scottish National party would have controlled Scotland. With the return of the Conservatives to power under Margaret Thatcher in 1979, strongly reaffirmed in the 1983 election, devolution to Scotland and Wales became remote. In Northern Ireland, which had a devolved parliament before sectarian violence brought direct rule from London, a return to a Northern Ireland government with substantial devolved power also seems unlikely in the near future. The devolution referendum in Scotland and Wales was the second instance of Parliament going directly to the people, the first being the European Community referendum in 1975. Critics believed this violated the spirit of the British constitution, which is based on parliamentary government. In both cases a Labour government submitted the question to the people, primarily to relieve its leadership of a political burden. The Conservative government that took power in 1979 is much less inclined, and finds it less necessary, to use referenda to solve its internal political problems.

East of Suez   A foreign policy adopted by the Labour government of Harold Wilson in 1966–67 that greatly reduced Britain's military commitments in the Far East and southern Asia. Indications of a new policy for areas east of Suez were made in 1966 when a defense review paper proposed that Britain maintain only a military presence in those areas and undertake military operations only jointly with allies. In 1967 the Wilson government announced that a complete withdrawal east of Suez would take place by the early 1970s. The policy was applied erratically, however, and the Conservative government of Edward Heath (1970–74) decided to retain bases and deploy forces in Singapore, the Indian Ocean, and the Persian Gulf. Upon Wilson's return to power in 1974, the government decided to withdraw or substantially reduce forces east of Suez and in the Mediterranean (Cyprus and Malta), and to terminate a naval base agreement with South Africa. *See also* ATLANTICISM, p. 2; SUEZ CRISIS OF 1956, p. 65.

Significance   The east-of-Suez policy was justified by the Wilson government on economic grounds. Although Wilson recognized Britain's traditions and interests in the East, he believed that, given the precipitous decline of the British economy, the nation could no longer maintain bases in the area. In 1967 Wilson was forced to devalue the pound sterling, but this brought little relief to the economy. The attempt by Prime Minister Heath to reverse the east-of-Suez policy was based on traditional British interests, but also on an inadequate appreciation of the defense capabilities of the nation's economy. Also, many Britons were not ready to concede a global role for the country and accept the reality that Britain was only a regional power. Some observers argue that Britain's insistence on maintaining the pound as an international reserve currency with a fixed exchange value and its slowness in attempting to join the European Economic Community account for much of the nation's poor economic performance. Wilson and Heath attempted to reverse these economic decisions in the late 1960s and early 1970s, but it was too little and too late to prevent the pullback from global military commitments.

Elections of 1983: Britain   British parliamentary elections in which the Conservative party led by Prime Minister Margaret Thatcher won a sweeping victory. The 1983 elections to the House of Commons were called one year before its term expired. Thatcher, who had become prime minister after the 1979 elections, sought to take advantage of her increased popularity following the British victory in the Falklands War and the disarray within the Labour party. Of the 650 seats to be filled (formerly 635) in the Commons, the Conservatives won 397 (compared to 339 in 1979); the Labour party won 209 (down from 268); the Liberal party took 17 (up from 11); and the new Social Democratic party won only 6 (a loss of 23 seats of members who had joined the party after the 1979 election). The Scottish Nationalist party and the Welsh nationalists (*Plaid Cymru*) retained 2 seats each. In the Northern Ireland constituencies, Ulster Unionists, divided into four parties, won 15 seats; the Social Democratic and Labour party (SDLP) retained its single seat; and the candidate of the Provisional *Sinn Fein,* the political wing of the Irish Republican Army, defeated the moderate Catholic socialist Gerald Fitt. Although the percentage of Conservative votes fell from 43.9 in 1979 to 42.4, the party won a 144-seat majority. Labour's percentage fell from 36.9 to 27.6; the Liberal-Social Democratic Alliance won 25.4 percent, compared to the 13.8 percent the Liberals won in 1979. The election results were, as in the past, much affected by the operation of the single-member district system. With less than a majority of the vote, the Conservatives won 61 percent of the seats; the Alliance received only 2 percent less in the popular vote than the Labour party, but won 186 fewer seats. *See also* ELECTORAL SYSTEM: HOUSE OF COMMONS, p. 20; POLITICAL PARTY SYSTEM: BRITAIN, p. 52.

Significance   The British elections of 1983 produced the greatest landslide for a single party since the Labour victory of 1945. The victory of the Conservatives is considered to be even more remarkable because Prime Minister Thatcher was doing poorly in public opinion polls before the Falklands War of April–June 1982. The election victory was considered to be a personal triumph for Thatcher, the first woman to be elected prime minister, who was also the first Conservative to be reelected to a second term in this century. Thatcher benefited from the resurgence of British patriotism, her hard-line stand against Irish nationalist hunger-strike prisoners, her opposition to high European Community budget assessments on Britain, and her defusing of the unemployment issue by stressing the substantial drop in the inflation rate. The poor Labour showing ultimately led to the election of Neil Kinnock to replace Michael Foot as leader. Although the Alliance did well in the popular vote, it was seriously damaged in its quest to replace the Labour party as the parliamentary opposition; two of the four original SDP leaders failed to be reelected (Shirley Williams and William Rodgers). Yet the Conservative victory can be attributed to the electoral system, for the party won only 42.4 percent of the popular vote. The big discrepancy between popular votes and seats won gave added impetus to those forces who argue for some form of proportional representation.

Electoral System: House of Commons A single-member district system with election by simple plurality. In the electoral system for the House of Commons, electoral districts (called constituencies) are recommended to Parliament by nonpartisan electoral boundary commissions, which take into account sociogeographic factors and local government boundaries. Redistricting occurred prior to the 1983 election, and the number of seats in the House was increased from 635 to 650. Candidates for office are nominated by ten local citizens; candidates must submit a deposit of £150 ($225), which is returned if they receive at least one-eighth of the votes cast. Suffrage is extended to persons over age 18 who are citizens of the United Kingdom (UK) and to citizens of the Commonwealth and the Republic of Ireland who are resident in the UK. Members of the House of Lords may not vote in elections to the House of Commons. The formal election campaign is brief, about three weeks from the dissolution of Parliament to election day. Campaign expenditures of constituency candidates are strictly controlled, but these campaigns are overshadowed by the national campaigns of party leaders, which are professionally run by public relations firms and attract much media attention. National leaders must run for a constituency seat, and they are usually reelected whether or not their party wins a majority because they run in safe constituencies. MPs need not live in the constituencies they represent. Those candidates are elected who have won a simple plurality of votes, i.e., received more votes than any other single candidate, whether or not it is a majority of the total votes cast. The British sometimes refer to this as the "first-past-the-post" system. When a seat falls vacant, a new MP is chosen in a by-election. These elections sometimes reveal shifts in public opinion that may threaten a government's slim majority in Commons. *See also* ELECTIONS OF 1983: BRITAIN, p. 19; PARTY GOVERNMENT, p. 48; POLITICAL PARTY SYSTEM: BRITAIN, p. 52.

Significance The simple plurality electoral system often results in a large discrepancy between the percentage of votes cast for a party and the percentage of seats it wins. Since only one MP is elected in each constituency, the votes cast for other candidates are ineffective. For the two largest parties, this tends to balance out across the country, but minor parties are seriously disadvantaged if their votes are diffused across many districts, like the Liberals. Regional parties, the Scottish, Welsh, and Ulster nationalist parties, which concentrate their votes within a few districts, are less affected by the plurality system. Thus in 1979 Conservatives received 43.9 percent of the vote and won 53.4 percent of the seats; Labour won 36.9 percent of the vote and 42.2 percent of the seats; but the Liberals received 13.8 percent of the vote and only 1.7 percent of the seats. In the 1983 election, Conservatives won 42.4 percent of the votes and 61 percent of the seats; Labour won 27.6 percent of the vote and 32.2 percent of the seats; but for the Liberal-Social Democratic Alliance 25.4 percent of the vote yielded only 3.5 percent of the seats. As the party most hurt by the plurality system, Liberals have been arguing for a system of proportional representation (PR). But until a third party or alliance can break the dominance of the two big parties it is unlikely that a PR system will be adopted by Parliament. Defenders of the plurality system point out that it produces strong majorities in Commons and stable single-party governments, which are preferred by the people over unstable coalition governments. The plurality system in itself does not necessarily result in or require strong party discipline (as, for example, in the United States). In the British case, however, the electoral system in combination with the cabinet system of government helps produce cohesive and disciplined parties because divided parties could not win or maintain a majority in Parliament.

Embourgeoisiement **Thesis** The theory that the traditional working class is being absorbed into an ever-growing middle class. According to the *embourgeoisiement* thesis, the traditional sharp division between the working class and the middle class or bourgeoisie has been blurred by the higher standard of living, increased opportunities, and growing affluence of the working class. As applied to Great Britain, the thesis argues that British social structure is greatly affected by the consequent attitudinal and political behavior changes that result from working-class affluence. Evidence adduced for the thesis cites the improvements in the working-class standard of living, the decline of class antagonisms, and that at least one-half of the British people do not think of themselves in traditional class terms. Critics of the thesis point out that although living standards of workers are higher, self-perceptions have not changed— almost as many people regarded themselves as working class in the 1970s as did after World War II. Although "working-class Tories," laborers who usually vote for the Conservative party, have usually comprised one-third of the working-class vote, the Labour party still received the bulk of it. *See also* LABOUR PARTY, p. 35; POLITICAL PARTY SYSTEM: BRITAIN, p. 52.

Significance The embourgeoisiement thesis is a social science theory that typically draws a relationship between socioeconomic status and political behavior. Although many British workers have not changed their voting preferences for the Labour party, the thesis may not be invalid. In a more complex form of the theory, attitudinal change rather than voting behavior is the key. Thus, moderate supporters of the Labour party may well have contributed to the moderation of Labour party leadership and programs in the 1960s and 1970s. When left-wing leaders captured the party organization in the late 1970s, moderate leaders organized the new Social Democratic party (SDP). Other observers argue that British social structure is being increasingly "declassed" into a large amorphous group. The loss of many Labour voters to the Liberals and Conservatives in the late 1970s and to the SDP in 1983 may well be a reflection of the "middle-classing" of the working class, or the "declassing" of British politics.

Established Church A church that is recognized in law as the organization for the official religion of the state. There is no one established church for all of the United Kingdom. In England the established church is the Church of England, also called the Anglican or Episcopalian church, particularly in other countries. About 40 percent of the people in England are baptized into the Church of England. Institutional linkages between the government of the United Kingdom and Church of England include (1) the queen as head of state is also head of the church; (2) the archbishops of York and Canterbury and 24 other senior bishops are members of the House of Lords; (3) official appointments of bishops are made by the monarch on the advice of the prime minister; and (4) the Book of Common Prayer, the service book of the church, is approved by Parliament. The Anglican church was disestablished in Ireland in 1869 and in Wales in 1914; in Scotland the established church is Presbyterian. Northern Ireland is technically a of the most important intellectuals in Britain. Influential Fabians included Beatrice and Sidney Webb, George Bernard Shaw, Graham Wallas, H. G. Wells, Harold Laski, and G. D. H. Cole. Political figures who were members included Ramsay MacDonald, Clement Atlee, and Hugh Gaitskell, all leaders of the Labour party. The society took its name from the Roman general, Quintus Fabius Maximus, who used delaying tactics against the Carthaginian general Hannibal, thus reflecting the society's piecemeal and gradualist approach. The Fabians' direct impact is difficult to measure, for many of their ideas have permeated major sectors of British political life.

Falklands' War   A 74-day conflict in 1982 between Britain and Argentina for possession of the Falkland islands, a British dependency in the South Atlantic. Called the Malvinas by Argentina, the Falklands are located 400 miles off the Argentine coast and 8,000 miles from Britain. On April 2, 1982, the islands were invaded and quickly taken by a sizable Argentine task force; South Georgia, 800 miles further east, a dependency of the Falklands, was also taken. The military government of Argentine President Leopoldo Galtieri justified the action on the basis of a long-standing claim to sovereignty over the islands and the failure of lengthy and sporadic negotiations with the British government. The invasion caused a sensation in Britain and an emotional outburst of patriotic fever in Parliament. Prime Minister Margaret Thatcher's government, calling the action aggression, responded by dispatching a hastily built naval task force to retake the islands. As the force slowly made the long trip, the United States attempted to mediate, but when this failed, it helped Britain with military intelligence and equipment. The United States and European Community members backed Britain's request for a financial, trade, and arms embargo against Argentina, and many Commonwealth nations supported the British. The military operations were marked by costly and destructive aeronaval engagements. Five thousand British troops were landed under fire and engaged in forced marches in extreme weather across difficult terrain. After a series of British night attacks that resulted in the defeat of the larger Argentine force on the main island of East Falkland, Argentine forces surrendered on June 18, 1982; the British captured 10,800 prisoners, who were later returned to Argentina. The war took 255 British lives and 712 Argentine lives. Britain lost 2 destroyers, 2 frigates, 2 other ships, and 34 aircraft; Argentina lost 1 cruiser, 1 submarine, 3 other ships, and over 100 aircraft. The cost of the war for Britain was estimated at $1.4 billion worth of ships and equipment.

Significance   The war had a major impact on British politics. Prime Minister Thatcher's standing in public opinion polls, which had reached a postwar low, shot up. This was reinforced by her surprise visit to the islands in January 1983. Despite the opposition's criticisms, her image as a resolute and confident leader was much enhanced, and this contributed to the big Conservative victory in the 1983 parliamentary elections. The Labour opposition, which initially supported the decision to retake the islands, could make no headway by criticizing the Foreign Office's failure in prewar negotiations and its poor assessment of Argentina's intentions. Although the foreign secretary, Lord Carrington, resigned, this apparent acknowledgement of fault was drowned in the ebullience following the British victory over a larger Argentine force that had seven weeks to prepare defenses. The new Social Democratic party, which had won an important by-election one week before the invasion and had been receiving much media attention, was driven off the front pages and began to fade. After the war, a number of reports were written by official commissions. The "military lessons" to be derived from the war have received much comment. Of interest are the royal navy's first battle in the missile age; the use of new weapons and military equipment; the amphibious landings 8,000 miles from Britain; and the tremendous logistic problems of the war. Lord Shackleton's report on the economic development of the islands noted the need for strong and costly measures for economic viability, and Lord Franks's commission assessed the question of responsibility. The Franks commission absolved the Thatcher government but criticized failures in the British intelligence community. After the war, the Thatcher government decided to maintain a garrison of about 3,000 troops, build a strategic airport, and develop local industry and tourism facilities. Critics say this is being done for an area that has little strategic or economic value, and that Prime Minister Thatcher tied Britain's policy too much to the wishes of 1,800 Falklanders, many of whom are employees of one British firm that owns 40 percent of the land. Although no British government could concede the islands after the Argentine invasion, critics say that the continued hard line is counterproductive to an eventual settlement. They argue that the victory perpetuates the false idea that Britain is a major global power, and the expenditure of defense funds in the Falklands undermines Britain's commitment to NATO. In Argentina, President Galtieri was removed from office and high-ranking officers in the military services were purged because of the poor showing of the Argentine navy and army in particular. In 1983, the military permitted elections to occur and returned power to civilians, but the new democratic government of Raúl Alfonsín continued to stress Argentina's right to sovereignty over the islands.

Farmers' Associations: Britain Organizations of agricultural interest groups that pressure the government for favorable treatment.

The largest farmers' association is the National Farmers' Union (NFU), which represents about 80 percent of the farmers in England and Wales. There are separate farmers' unions in Scotland and Wales. The number of farmers in Britain is small, compared to workers in industry; only 3 percent of the work force is engaged in agriculture. The 200,000 members of the NFU are primarily owner-occupiers, who benefit from the agricultural information and services the NFU provides, but especially from highly favorable agricultural policies. The NFU deals with the Ministry of Agriculture, Fisheries and Food on a regular basis concerning matters dealing with agricultural subsidies of various kinds; this includes guaranteed prices, tax benefits, grants for capital investment, and agricultural information. Every year there is a review of farm incomes, costs, and profits that is used to determine the level of government support for the coming year. Generally, the agriculture ministry supports farmers' demands within the government. Farmers typically affiliate with the Conservative party, but given their small size, their power comes from the role they play within the British economy. *See also* COMMON AGRICULTURAL POLICY (CAP), p. 245.

Significance Before Britain joined the European Community (EC) in 1973, farmers' associations were in a relatively weak position. For over a hundred years, British agriculture had received little protection, and Britain imported much of its food cheaply from older Commonwealth nations. After World War II, price supports encouraged increased production, but the greatest benefits came to farmers through the operation of the EC Common Agricultural Policy (CAP). In the CAP system of agricultural subsidies, farmers receive guaranteed prices, protection against non-Community commodities, and a market for their surpluses. The CAP greatly benefited British farmers, who modernized equipment and techniques and put more land under cultivation; this increased food production to 70 percent of Britain's needs, a remarkable rise. However, the price of food rose as well, consumers complained, the reputation of farmers fell, and urban interests, including trade unions, agitated unsuccessfully to pull Britain out of the Common Market. In the CAP system surplus food is sold on the world market, while Community prices are maintained. The CAP also takes 70 percent of the EC budget, which is apportioned among members. In 1983–84, Prime Minister Margaret Thatcher demanded a $1.3 billion rebate on Britain's share of the $21 billion EC annual budget on the grounds that Britain contributed much more to the budget than it received in grants and subsidies. In July 1984 Britain was granted some budgetary relief, but the problem of high agricultural prices and surpluses remained, and British consumers still had misgivings about membership in the Common Market.

Greater London Council (GLC)   The local government for the metropolitan area of greater London. The Greater London Council has authority for administering services similar to those of a county—strategic planning, traffic, transport, housing, police, fire, and refuse services for the seven million people in the greater London area. The City of London and 32 London boroughs are subunits of the GLC, in much the same fashion as districts are the second tier under counties. The authority of these subunits varies in accordance with their size, but the historic City of London retains a large measure of independence. *See also* LOCAL GOVERNMENT: BRITAIN, p. 37.

Significance   The Greater London Council was created by the reform act of 1963, which abolished the old London County Council, retained the London boroughs and the City of London, and reallocated authority within the new structure. Like the similar 1972 local government reforms, the GLC changes were aimed at a rationalization of powers and functions. Also, as in other local governments, local taxes and spending have risen sharply to pay for the many services provided to the people of the metropolitan area. Local rates (property taxes) cover less than 30 percent of local services, which must be financed in large part by national government grants. Disputes between the Labour-dominated Greater London Council and the Conservative government of Margaret Thatcher over GLC spending led to proposals that the GLC be abolished and its powers distributed to the London boroughs. In July 1984 the House of Lords defeated a government bill that would have abolished the GLC and other metropolitan councils in 1986. In its unusual move, Lords objected to the provision that council elections for 1985 be cancelled and councils be replaced by interim appointed bodies. The bill was withdrawn, but the possibility of abolition of the GLC and the metropolitan councils remained.

House of Commons   The popularly elected and more powerful house of Parliament. Representatives in the House of Commons (called members of Parliament, MPs), are elected from 650 single-member constituencies. MPs are elected for five-year terms, but Commons may be dissolved earlier by the queen on the advice of the prime minister, and new elections called. MPs are organized by the political parties into the majority (usually a single party), which provides the prime minister and most other government officers, and the opposition. Important officers of Commons include the speaker, a nonpartisan presiding officer whose function is to determine the sense of the body and provide for an orderly transaction of business; the leaders of the government and the opposition; and chief whips in both parties who inform and instruct rank and file party members (backbenchers) on issues before the house. The constitutional powers of Commons include lawmaking, levying taxes and appropriating funds, making constitutional changes, investing and supporting governments, opposing, criticizing, and standing ready to replace the government, debating policy questions, and checking on the administration of government. The functions of criticism and providing an alternative to the government are performed by the opposition. The question time, in which government ministers must reply to written and oral questions from MPs, provides an important opportunity to scrutinize the administration or question policy. Most bills enacted by Commons are those proposed by the government; private members' bills receive little consideration and those that are enacted concern noncontroversial matters or, in some cases, highly controversial matters, such as the issue of capital punishment. Because party discipline works at all levels, the legislative committees of Commons have little influence in changing the content of government proposals. Important votes in Commons are usually taken by a "division lobby" in which MPs file past tellers, rather than by a roll call as in the United States. *See also* DECLINE OF PARLIAMENT, p. 15; ELECTORAL SYSTEM: HOUSE OF COMMONS, p. 20; MEMBER OF PARLIAMENT (MP), p. 40; PARLIAMENT, p. 47.

Significance   The House of Commons is the arena in which the major political forces of Britain struggle rather than the locus of power within the system. Because of strong party discipline, enforced by party whips, and because legislative initiatives come from the cabinet, Commons in modern times has become largely a policy-validating rather than deliberative body. Much importance is placed on parliamentary debates, even though debates seldom result in major shifts of opinion within Commons. But debates help to educate and inform the public, identify leaders who are effective in extemporaneous speech, and satisfy the minority that their case was presented and considered. Although the fundamental constitutional principle is the supremacy of Parliament, the House of Commons is limited by the political culture and the disposition of political forces in the house. The system of strong party discipline and single-party governments helped transfer real power to the majority party leaders, who exercise the executive powers of the state. In the 1970s, however, the breakdown of strong majorities resulted in backbenchers and opposition parties being able to force amendments and withdrawals of government bills. This has been reversed by the strong majorities Prime Minister Margaret Thatcher won in 1979 and 1983. So long as the electoral system produces stable single-party majorities, it seems likely that the House of Commons will continue to play a secondary role in the British political system.

House of Lords   The upper and less powerful house of the British Parliament. The House of Lords includes hereditary peers (whose titles pass to their eldest sons), life peers (whose titles do not pass on), law lords, who have life appointments, and the Lords Spiritual (2 archbishops and 24 senior bishops of the Church of England). In 1983 there were 1,184 members of Lords, distributed as follows: 800 hereditary peers, 337 life peers (including 46 life peeresses), 26 Church of England prelates, and 21 law lords. Only about 300 peers participate regularly. Life peers were created under the Life Peerages Act of 1958, which also created life peerages for women. The Peerage Act of 1963 permitted hereditary peers to renounce their titles, thus making them eligible to be elected to the House of Commons. The legislative powers of Lords have been seriously restricted by the Parliament Acts of 1911 and 1949. The House of Lords has no power over finance bills, no right to veto legislation, and since 1949 it can only delay legislation for 13 months at most. A bill rejected by Lords can be passed again by Commons in the next session. Despite these restricted powers, Lords exercises the powers to: (1) scrutinize bills and recommend amendments to Commons; (2) expedite consideration of noncontroversial legislation; and (3) inform the public through its debates on important issues of national policy. The House of Lords is also the highest court of appeal for England and Wales, but this function is performed for the body by the law lords. Reform of the House of Lords has often been suggested, but none has succeeded; a 1969 Labour government proposal was defeated by a cross-party backbench revolt in the Commons. The most often suggested proposals would either abolish the house, confine membership to life peers, provide that only life peers may vote but permit hereditary peers to speak, and reduce the delaying period to six months or eliminate it entirely. *See also* HOUSE OF COMMONS, p. 28; PARLIAMENT, p. 47.

Significance   The House of Lords is the largest and oldest legislative body in the world. Its history can be traced back to medieval times, and its past influence was extensive. But Lords lost its legislative power in the twentieth century when it thwarted or delayed the House of Commons from enacting legislation desired by the popular majority. Since 1949 Lords ordinarily does not attempt to delay legislation, and its proposals for amendment are withdrawn if objected to by Commons. In an unusual action in July 1984, however, Lords defeated a Conservative government bill that would have cancelled the 1985 local council elections in metropolitan counties and the Greater London Council. Although the bill also proposed that these counties be abolished in 1986, Lords believed the election-cancellation provision to be undemocratic, and the government withdrew the measure despite its large majority in

Commons. The Life Peerages Act changed in part the overwhelming Conservative political composition of Lords by enabling Labour supporters to enter through appointment. The large majority of peers are still Conservative, however. About 10 to 15 peers have renounced their titles, the most noteworthy being Alec Douglas-Home (Lord Home), who thus was able to become prime minister; his rival Quentin Hogg (Lord Hailsham), who later was appointed to a life peerage and is the lord chancellor; and Anthony Wedgewood Benn, the leader of doctrinaire socialists in the Labour party. Since 1980 the Labour party has again proposed the abolition of the House of Lords, an idea that seems to have little support outside the doctrinaire socialist wing.

House of Windsor   The family name of the British royal house that provides the monarchs of the United Kingdom. The House of Windsor is headed by the reigning monarch, Queen Elizabeth II. Succession to the throne is determined by traditional rules and British law. Sons of the sovereign and their descendants have precedence over daughters, and daughters and their descendants have precedence over lateral lines. In December 1984 the order of succession to the throne was: the queen's firstborn son, the heir apparent, Charles, Prince of Wales; his first son, Prince William; his second son, Prince Henry; the queen's other children, Prince Andrew, Prince Edward, and Princess Anne; Anne's children, Peter Phillips and Zara Phillips; the queen's sister, Princess Margaret; and Margaret's children, David (the Viscount Linly) and Lady Sarah Armstrong-Jones. Since the eighteenth century British law mandates that the crown is to be conferred on Protestant descendants of Princess Sofia of Hanover; inasmuch as the sovereign is also head of the Church of England, certain ecclesiastical qualifications also obtain. Thus, in the abdication crisis of 1936, Edward VIII, Elizabeth's uncle, was pressured to abdicate the throne because of his intention to marry a divorced woman, Wallis Simpson. His brother, George VI (1936–52) succeeded; Elizabeth is George's firstborn daughter and the great-great-granddaughter of Queen Victoria (1837–1901). In 1947 Elizabeth married her third cousin, Philip Mountbatten (Prince of Greece & Denmark), the Duke of Edinburgh, later styled Prince Philip. Elizabeth II is not only queen of the United Kingdom and head of the Commonwealth, but she is also queen of 17 other independent nations, former colonies that retained the monarchy after independence, such as Canada, Australia, and New Zealand. *See also* MONARCH, p. 41.

Significance   Family members of the House of Windsor are direct descendants of the House of Hanover, upon whom Parliament settled the British crown in the eighteenth century. Edward VII (1901–10) reigned as a member of the House of Saxe-Coburg and Gotha, which was named after Prince Albert, the consort of Queen Victoria. In 1917 during the war against Germany, George V (1910–36) changed the family name to Windsor. In 1960, Queen Elizabeth decreed that the family name of Windsor would be retained for princes and princesses, but except for women who marry, her descendants shall bear the name of Mountbatten-Windsor.

Irish Republican Army (IRA)   A nationalist guerrilla organization that seeks to bring about the unification of Ireland through violent means. The Irish Republican Army (IRA) has passed through several transformations since it was first organized by Michael Collins to fight the British after the failure of the Easter Rising in Dublin of 1916. In 1922 the IRA split into a Collins group that supported the creation of the Irish Free State and the Eamon De Valera wing that opposed it. During the 1920s and 1930s, the IRA engaged in numerous bombings, shootings, and violent acts in Ireland, Northern Ireland, and England. Outlawed by the British and by the Irish government of De Valera, the IRA lost public support among many Catholics and was relatively quiet in the 1940s and part of the 1950s. It rose again in the late 1960s when Catholic civil rights demonstrations and civil disturbances broke out in Northern Ireland. In the early 1970s the IRA split again into two wings: (1) the Official IRA, which advocated political and social action to achieve a united, socialist Ireland; and (2) the Provisional IRA, based in Ulster, that advocated violence and terrorism. The Official IRA was originally larger, but as the violence in Ulster increased, the Provisional IRA ("Provos") became the major group conducting an urban guerrilla war. Actions were taken against the Northern Irish government, Ulster Unionist groups, British troops, and Catholics who cooperated with the Ulster or British governments. Their operations claimed the lives of many innocent citizens in Northern Ireland and England who were victims of random terrorist bombings. The Provisional IRA also suffered internal disagreements, but it has always been committed to using violence; it is dominated by Belfast leftist radicals. *See also* NORTHERN IRELAND, p. 42; NORTHERN IRELAND: POLITICAL GROUPS, p. 45; REPUBLIC OF IRELAND, p. 58; ULSTER, p. 71.

Significance   The Provisional wing of the Irish Republican Army is small, but it was effective in contributing to the fall of the Ulster government and the installing of British direct rule. By fighting British troops it increased latent support among Catholics in Ulster; and its political arm, the *Sinn Fein,* profited. IRA actions are often labeled as despicable and outrageous—such acts as the murder of Queen Elizabeth's cousin Lord Louis Mountbatten in 1979, the bombing of restaurants and pubs, the slaughter of moderate Catholics, and the bombing of a London department store during the 1983 Christmas season. Yet condemnations of these actions by the civilized world have had little effect. Actions sometimes attributed to the IRA are actually performed by the smaller and extremely violent Irish National Liberation Army (INLA). The INLA was very active in the 1982 election period when it assassinated a number of Protestant Unionist candidates as well as Catholics. Harsher measures by Britain, such as internment and long prison terms, and not giving special status to imprisoned hunger-strikers, seem to be counterproductive. In 1980 about 500 prisoners convicted of political violence began a hunger strike in the Maze prison outside Belfast. They demanded special status to be treated as prisoners of war instead of as common criminals. Prime Minister Margaret Thatcher refused despite many public protests in Ireland and Ulster. After ten prisoners died, beginning with Bobby Sands, the strike was ended in October 1981. Strong British actions tend to increase support among Catholics in Ulster and Ireland, and among Irish-Americans. The IRA is connected to the international terrorist network, and is able to acquire sufficient arms, finances, and intelligence to bring off spectacular operations.

Iron Law of Oligarchy The thesis that every society is ruled by a few. The Iron Law of Oligarchy was propounded by Robert Michels (1876–1936), a German sociologist who argued that society requires a dominant class, and that a small minority (oligarchy) always rules over the large majority. In large social organizations, political parties, and labor unions, even those based on socialist or working-class egalitarian ideals, the small minority rules. True democracy is not possible in large-scale units because complete equality of members and full participation in policy making does not occur when a representative system is used. Since this is evident in the most democratic-oriented and mass membership organizations extant—the socialist and working-class parties and trade unions—it must be true everywhere. Democracy is not possible because large-scale organization requires leadership, and the administration of social justice requires bureaucracy.

Significance The Iron Law of Oligarchy is a form of elitist theory that has been applied to British socialist and working-class mass membership organizations. Detailed studies of the Labour party and trade unions confirm Michels's view that rank and file members are not real participants in the decision-making processes of these organizations. Critics of the thesis point out that although Michels believed representative democracy could never be truly democratic, no other form of democracy is practical within mass organizations or populous societies. Michels himself believed that democratic ideals could not be achieved and that leaders of mass organizations would become like aristocratic oligarchs, but the people should strive to reduce the degree of oligarchic rule.

Judicial System: Britain   The organization and operation of the court system in the United Kingdom, England and Wales having a different system than Scotland and Northern Ireland. In England and Wales, the judicial system is organized into civil and criminal courts at lower and appellate levels. At the apex of the court system is the House of Lords. Magistrates' courts hear petty criminal offenses and some civil cases; appeals are taken to the Crown Court, which also hears serious criminal cases. Criminal case appeals are made to the criminal division of the Court of Appeal. Lesser civil cases originate in county courts, and more important civil cases are heard in the High Court. This court is organized into the Queen's Bench Division for common law cases, the Chancery Division for equity law cases, and the Family Division for divorce and child custody cases. Appeals from the High Court go to the Civil Division of the Court of Appeal. The House of Lords, the highest court in the land, receives appeals from the court system in England and Wales, and civil cases from Scotland. The appellate jurisdiction of the House of Lords is exercised by the Judicial Committee, which consists of the Lord Chancellor, Lords of Appeal in Ordinary (law lords), and other peers who have held high judicial positions. Appeals from British dependencies and some Commonwealth nations are heard by the Judicial Committee of the Privy Council. The lord chancellor is head of the judiciary; he advises the crown on judicial appointments, and at times acts as a judge. Magistrate courts are staffed by lay justices of the peace who are appointed by the lord chancellor. Judges are drawn from experienced lawyers who are mostly barristers (lawyers permitted to appear before courts) rather than from solicitors (lawyers who handle ordinary legal matters). Judges are appointed for a life term by the government. *See also* COMMON LAW, p. 10; HOUSE OF LORDS, p. 30; PRIVY COUNCIL, p. 54.

Significance   The complexity of the judicial system is derived in large part from the traditional conservatism of the British in retaining ancient institutions, the separate strands of law that evolved such as common law and equity law, and the differing histories of major parts of the United Kingdom. Although appointed by the government, judges have typically exercised a high degree of independence. Courts in the United

Kingdom do not have the power to declare laws of Parliament unconstitutional, but they do review executive actions for legality, and an action may be declared void if it is found to be *ultra vires*, beyond the bounds established by the law. Since the 1960s, some judges have expanded their interpretation of this judicial power in an activist fashion and have called for the adoption of a bill of rights. Britain lacks a bill of rights, in the sense of constitutionally guaranteed rights of citizens protected by the courts against infringement by the executive or Parliament. Such a concept is contrary to the fundamental constitutional principle of the supremacy of Parliament, and has little support.

Labour Party The democratic socialist party that enacted a large measure of social welfare and socialist programs in postwar Britain. First formed in 1900 as the Labour Representation Committee, which united various socialist groups to bring working-class representation in Parliament, the Labour party took its present name in 1906. The Fabian Society served as an important formative influence in its rejection of Marxist socialism and adoption of evolutionary or gradualist socialism. Clause IV, an important part of the party's constitution, calls for the collectivization of the means of production. The party grew rapidly, replacing the Liberals as the second largest group in Parliament in 1922, and it organized its first minority government in 1924 under Ramsay MacDonald. The party participated in Winston Churchill's coalition government in World War II, and in 1945 under the leadership of Clement Atlee it won an overwhelming victory. From 1945 to 1951 the Labour government nationalized important portions of British industry, adopted a comprehensive social welfare program that included the Health Service, promoted an Atlanticist foreign policy, and decolonized India and Burma. While it was out of power, Hugh Gaitskell and Harold Wilson moved the party more to the center, and it returned to power in 1964. As the economic problems of Britain mounted, Wilson's government lost much of its effectiveness from 1964 to 1970. Nevertheless, the Labour party again won power in 1974, and Wilson and James Callaghan led the country to 1979 in a period of economic stagnation, unemployment, and inflation. Callaghan's minority government was overthrown in 1979, and Labour lost the subsequent election to Margaret Thatcher's Conservatives. When the trade union and socialist wings moved the party to the left in 1981, a group of pro–Common Market members split and formed the Social Democratic party (SDP). In the 1983 elections under the leadership of Michael Foot the Labour party nearly fell to third place in the popular vote, barely outpolling the SDP-Liberal Alliance by 27.6 percent to 25.4 percent of the popular vote. Foot resigned as party leader and was replaced by Neil Kinnock.

See also ELECTIONS OF 1983: BRITAIN, p. 19; FABIAN SOCIETY, p. 24; PARTY ORGANIZATION, p. 49; TRADE UNIONS: BRITAIN, p. 69.

Significance   The Labour party is a federation of trade unions, constituency parties, socialist societies, and cooperative societies. The party has always had several factions, including a pacifist wing, a doctrinaire socialist group, a large trade union group, and a moderate and pragmatic group that is willing to compromise socialist principles to attain and keep government power. Trade unions are the largest group, supplying over 90 percent of the affiliated members and 90 percent of the party's funds. In the early 1980s the left wing led by Anthony Benn and the trade unions captured control of the party. They restructured the organization to give more power to unions and local party units, and adopted a socialist and neutralist manifesto for the 1983 election. The manifesto called for recollectivization of industries that had been returned to private enterprise by the Conservatives, an increase in personal tax allowances, a new wealth tax, more collectivization, a massive rise in public spending, increased power to unions to help government make economic assessments and distribute funds, withdrawal from the European Community, an immediate nuclear freeze, cancellation of Trident nuclear missile purchases, and adoption of a nonnuclear defense. In the context of British politics, observers called this 15,000 word document the "longest suicide note in history." Given the split of the SDP and the Labour's worst electoral performance since 1918, some observers question whether the party can recover. In the postelection 1983 annual conference, delegates led by trade unionists adopted a unilateral nuclear disarmament resolution over Kinnock's and Callaghan's objections. But the conference agreed to stay in the European Community for the term of the next Parliament, and it expelled leaders of the Militant Tendency, a Trotskyist faction. The future of the Labour party will depend on the fate of the Liberal-SDP Alliance and the new leadership's ability to move the party back to the center-left.

Liberal Party   A minor party of the political center that was one of the two major parties from the 1860s to the 1920s. The Liberal party succeeded the Whigs and drew their support from the middle and lower middle classes. In the nineteenth century, under William Gladstone, Liberals supported free trade, religious and political liberty, electoral reform, laissez-faire economic policies, and low budgets. In the early twentieth century, the party promoted Irish home rule, labor and social legislation, increased suffrage, and limitations on the financial and legislative powers of the House of Lords. This period was also marked by conflicts between the free trade and laissez-faire wings of the party against the progressive, social welfare group; the party also suffered from the personal rivalry between party leaders Herbert Asquith and David Lloyd George. After 1918 the Liberals went into decline as the newly enfranchised working class was attracted to the Labour party. The Liberal popular vote fell from 44 percent (1910) to 26 percent (1918), to 11 percent (1931). The Liberal decline is attributed to its position on Irish home rule, the enfranchisement of workers, the birth of a working-class party, and the Liberals' inability to retain their natural base of support in the middle class. Once the Liberal party fell behind Labour in popular votes, the operation of the electoral system hastened its decline in Parliament. In the period from 1945 to 1970, Liberals usually won 6 to 12 seats. In February 1974 the Liberal popular vote rose again to 19 percent, but this produced only 14 seats in the 635-seat House of Commons. Liberals joined the new Social Democratic party (SDP) in an electoral Alliance for the 1983 election, and although the Alliance received 25.4 percent of the popular vote, it won only 3.5 percent of the seats; the Liberals took 17 seats in the enlarged 650-seat house. Postwar policy positions of the Liberal party include programs favoring joining the European Community, antidiscrimination legislation, social welfare improvements, worker participation in management in private industry, a federal form of government, and proportional representation. Party leaders in the postwar period were Jo Grimond (1956–67), Jeremy Thorpe (1967–76) and David Steel (since 1976). *See also* ALLIANCE, p. 1; ELECTIONS OF 1983: BRITAIN, p. 19; ELECTORAL SYSTEM: HOUSE OF COMMONS, p. 20; POLITICAL PARTY SYSTEM: BRITAIN, p. 52; WHIGS AND TORIES, p. 76.

Significance In the postwar period to the 1970s, the Liberal party played an insubstantial role in the British party system. It often fielded over 300 candidates in parliamentary elections, but its vote was so diffused that it won few seats. The dramatic rise to 19 percent of the vote in 1974 is attributed to the nation's general dissatisfaction with the two major parties. From 1977 to 1978 Liberals lent their support to a minority Labour government in a "Lib-Lab" pact to gain credibility as a party of government. This was short-lived, and Liberals voted along with Conservatives and Scottish nationalists to bring down James Callaghan's government in 1979. The Liberal vote dropped to 13 percent in the subsequent election. The 1981 Electoral Alliance with the Social Democrats, of which Liberals are the stronger partner, gives them renewed hope that they might again become part of the second force in British politics that challenges the Conservatives for power.

Local Government: Britain The system of subnational government that was reformed in the 1970s. The new system of local government was created by Parliament for England and Wales in 1972 and for Scotland in 1973. The greater London area has a separate form of government, which was reformed in 1963. In England and Wales (outside London) the two basic units of local government are counties and districts. There are 53 new counties and 369 new districts. In addition about 10,000 parishes ("communities" in Wales) are organized below the districts, but only about 7,000 have councils. The counties are of two types, nonmetropolitan (or shire) counties and metropolitan counties, which are used in the six heavily populated areas of England. County councils have wide-ranging responsibilities in education, housing, planning, libraries, transport, fire, police, and sanitary services; districts have other functions, appropriate to their size. The allocation of duties is different between metropolitan counties and districts. A 1973 reform for Scotland created nine regions, which are divided into 53 districts. The authority exercised by local governments is delegated by Parliament and supervised by relevant agencies. Local revenues are derived from national government grants, about 60 percent of the total; local taxes on real estate (called "rates"), about 26 percent; and fees for services. Local councils are elected by voters, usually every four years, from single-member wards or electoral districts; proportional representation is used in Northern Ireland. Since reorganization, most local elections are contested by candidates affiliated with national parties; and although voter turnout is below 40 percent, voting results are interpreted as an assessment of the policies of the national government. *See also* GREATER LONDON COUNCIL (GLC) p. 28.

Significance The local government reforms of the 1970s replaced a complex system of county councils, county boroughs, noncounty boroughs, and urban and rural districts. Parish councils were relatively untouched by the changes. The new system attempted to introduce uniformity and a more appropriate division of authority, and to promote a professional managerial approach. In the British unitary form of government, all local government authority is delegated from Parliament in the central government. The English tradition is midway between the direct supervision of local authorities by a national officer, as in France, and the decentralized system of local self-government, as in the United States. Local governments are given much authority in Britain, but they are supervised so that they do not exceed their statutory authority. Local authorities must carry out functions that have been delegated to them. Local government structure reforms, however, have not solved a major local problem: that of financing public services. Recent sharp increases in local rates have led to proposals for increased central government intervention in local government affairs. As metropolitan county expenditures rose, increasing pressure for central government grants, the government of Margaret Thatcher proposed a bill that would have abolished these counties and the equivalent Greater London Council in 1986. The bill would have cancelled council elections scheduled for 1985 and replaced councils with appointed interim bodies. In a very unusual move, the House of Lords in July 1984 defeated the bill on the grounds that cancelling elections was undemocratic. Conflict between Labour-dominated metropolitan councils and the Conservative government over local expenditures continued unresolved, however.

Mandate Doctrine   The idea that a government constructed after winning an election has been given a popular mandate. The doctrine of the mandate has two forms. The first, supported by all parties, holds that the government has a mandate to rule. Some observers comment that in this general or weak form the doctrine has little meaning because it simply restates the obvious. Since the coming of universal suffrage and the ascendancy of the House of Commons over the House of Lords, majority parties have the right and the power to govern. A stronger form of the doctrine, held by supporters of the Labour and Liberal parties, holds that a victorious party has been given a mandate to enact the entire program of policies it set forth in its election manifesto (platform). Moreover, members of Parliament elected from that party are bound to support their leaders in pursuing the enactment of the program; they should not act as independent delegates who are free to vote according to their consciences or in accordance with the particular interests of their constituencies. *See also* MEMBER OF PARLIAMENT (MP), p. 40; POLITICAL PARTY SYSTEM: BRITAIN, p. 52.

Significance   The central issue concerning the interpretation of the doctrine of the mandate is whether the voters have selected a team of leaders or whether they have selected a set of policies as well. Although it may appear more restrictive, the Conservative view would give more leeway to the government to pursue policies not provided for in the manifesto. The Labour party's view seems more expansive because its manifesto is more in line with the socialist tradition of proposing major reforms of governmental, economic, and social structures. But the Labour view would restrict government policies to those specified in the winning party's manifesto. The constitutional issue of the electoral mandate is further clouded by the roles the parties assume as either government or opposition. In the former role, parties wish to be freer, and in the latter, they often criticize the government party for going beyond its manifesto. Although some observers raise the doctrine of the mandate to a constitutional convention, it seems unlikely that this is the case. Manifestoes are often vague, and voter choice is seldom based wholly on the party's program. The conflicting interpretations of the meaning of the doctrine and its unsettled status are likely to prevent the doctrine from attaining the status of a constitutional principle.

Member of Parliament (MP) A person elected to a constituency seat in the House of Commons. Although each member of Parliament (MP) represents a single constituency (district), the roles and influence of MPs vary. The prime minister, and almost all of the 100 members of the government are MPs, except for a few peers who are members of the House of Lords. The speaker, who like all other MPs is elected from a constituency, is a nonpartisan presiding officer who usually runs for reelection unopposed. The chamber of the House of Commons is furnished with two banks of benches facing each other across a middle aisle. The "front bench" to the right of the speaker is occupied by the prime minister and cabinet ministers, and the left front bench by the leader of the opposition and the shadow cabinet. "Backbenchers" therefore are rank and file MPs who sit on benches behind their leaders. "Private members" are MPs not holding a position in the government, whether they be in the majority or opposition group. A "private member's bill" is a legislative proposal submitted by an MP not in the government; although the MP may be a member of the majority, the bill is not part of the government's program of legislation. The duties of MPs vary with their other positions; generally, rank and file MPs are expected to (1) handle grievances and represent the interests of their constituents before government agencies; (2) vote for the party's positions in Commons; and (3) support party leaders, attend party meetings, and assist the parliamentary party generally. *See also* HOUSE OF COMMONS, p. 28; PARLIAMENT, p. 47.

Significance Although a member of Parliament has a seat in one of the most prestigious and constitutionally powerful legislative assemblies in the world, the duties of a typical MP are often routine and his votes perfunctory. Inasmuch as decision-making power has passed to the government, the backbencher is primarily a supporter rather than a main actor. Independent backbenchers may have some influence in party meetings, but consistent opposition to the leaders is not tolerated by the leaders or the MP's constituency party. MPs are paid a salary and since the 1960s have been given small offices, but apart from the 100 MPs who hold government posts, their influence and perquisites of office are quite unlike those of the members of the American Congress.

Monarch   The king or queen who is the formal head of state of the United Kingdom. The person of the monarch, since 1952 Queen Elizabeth II, is distinguished from the office of the crown, which symbolizes the executive power of the state. Formally, the British monarch has extensive powers (called royal prerogatives), including: the right to summon, prorogue (dismiss without dissolution), and dissolve Parliament; open each session of Parliament with a speech from the throne; assent to legislation; call a leader to form a government; make appointments, give honors, issue pardons; and formally command the armed forces. Queen Elizabeth is also Head of the Church of England, Head of the Commonwealth, and queen of 17 other independent nations, former colonies that retained the British monarchy as their formal head of state. Except in rare instances, the monarch's powers are exercised by the government, and the monarch acts on the advice of the ministers, which cannot be ignored. The formal role of the monarchy is seen in the following instances: The last time a monarch refused to sign a bill was in 1707 (Queen Anne); and the last time a monarch dismissed a government that had the confidence of Parliament was in 1834 (George III). Because the political party system usually provides a single leader for the majority in the House of Commons, the monarch's choice of prime minister is also determined by the dominant politicians. Although the real powers of the office are controlled by the government, the monarchy performs a number of useful functions in the British political system. The queen symbolizes the unity of the nation and provides a continuity that cabinets lack. Members of the royal family attend many public functions, and the queen performs a large number of ceremonial and formal duties such as receiving ambassadors. These duties remove a burden from the policy-making ministers. The queen's official title is "Elizabeth the Second, by the Grace of God of the United Kingdom of Great Britain and Northern Ireland and of the other Realms and Territories Queen, Head of the Commonwealth, Defender of the Faith." *See also* CROWN, p. 13; HOUSE OF WINDSOR, p. 31; PARLIAMENT, p. 47.

Significance   From the point of view of his or her role within the nation, the British monarch is more than a figurehead. Although the real powers of the office are circumscribed by tradition and the constitution, the monarch has the right "to be consulted, to encourage, and to warn." A conscientious monarch with long experience, especially in times of crisis or parliamentary confusion, may become more influential than is commonly believed to be the case. But it is in the intangibles that the British monarchy greatly benefits the system. The monarchy is criticized at times for its cost, its symbolic perpetuation of an undemocratic social system, and for the occasional unseemly behavior of some members of the royal family. But republicanism in Britain is very weak, and the institution of the monarchy is strongly supported by the people.

Northern Ireland A province of the United Kingdom, often called Ulster. Northern Ireland was established in 1921 under the Government of Ireland Act of 1920, which partitioned the island. In the partition, six of the historic counties of Ulster formed Northern Ireland, which was granted home rule status with a parliamentary form of government. Twenty-six southern counties became the independent Irish Free State in 1922. The division of Ireland was unacceptable to Irish nationalists, who agitated for Irish unification; the Irish Republican Army (IRA) engaged in a large number of bombings, killings, and other violent acts throughout the 1920s and 1930s. The Northern Ireland government, dominated by Protestant Unionists, was adamant in maintaining the union with Britain; it enacted legislation that denied Catholics the same economic, social, and political rights and benefits as Protestants. In 1968 a Catholic civil rights movement agitated against the discriminations; this grew to disruptive demonstrations and clashes with police and Protestant groups. The IRA stepped up its terroristic guerrilla war activity, and Protestant groups did the same. To maintain order, Britain sent in troops in 1969, and when this and other moves failed to bring peace, Britain suspended the Ulster government and assumed direct rule in 1972. In 1973 Britain attempted to create a new power-sharing government between Catholics and Protestants with consultative links to the Irish Republic; it was rejected by Protestant Unionists and workers. Britain reassumed direct rule in 1974, but the violence continued as moderates on both sides were driven from positions of influence. Under direct rule, Northern Ireland is administered under the supervision of a British secretary of state for Northern Ireland. Various British attempts at initiating alternative forms of home rule have been unsuccessful, whether proposed by Labour or Conservative governments. *See also* IRISH REPUBLICAN ARMY (IRA), p. 32; NORTHERN IRELAND: GOVERNMENT, p. 43; NORTHERN IRELAND: POLITICAL GROUPS, p. 45; REPUBLIC OF IRELAND, p. 58; ULSTER, p. 71; ULSTER UNIONISTS, p. 71.

Significance Northern Ireland is not a single community and lacks a central unifying political culture. Although it is part of the United Kingdom, it does not share the constitutional consensus, political values, and pragmatic spirit that is prevalent in England. The province is dominated by descendants of Scottish Presbyterian and English Puritan settlers many of whom were "planted" in Ulster to make Ireland safe for the English. The one-third of the population who are Catholic identify with the Republic of Ireland. Hard-core leaders of either group have not progressed much beyond the religious war mentality of the seventeenth century, and sectarian terrorists of both sides place revenge and hate above humane values. Moderates on both sides have been overcome, as both communities are driven to support a bloody civil war in the name of religious freedom. The tragedy of Northern Ireland today is a problem the English created 300 years ago, but the English today can do little to resolve the matter. They are skewered by their fundamental democratic principle of free elections, which places power in Protestant hands, and their physical inability to control the violence, which places veto power in terrorists' hands. Many observers are convinced that a simple leave-taking by the British would solve nothing because the lessons of Irish nationalism and violence have been well learned by Protestant Ulster extremists. The tragedy of Ireland will continue to be played in Northern Ireland for some years to come.

Northern Ireland: Government   Rule-making bodies for Northern Ireland with devolved authority granted by Britain. In the Government of Ireland Act of 1920, Britain granted local home rule to the government of Northern Ireland, while reserving national and international matters to the British government. The structures established in 1920 consisted of: (1) a bicameral parliament, composed of the House of Commons, chosen by direct elections, and the Senate elected by Commons on a proportional representation basis; (2) a prime minister and cabinet responsible to Parliament; and (3) the governor, representing the crown. The Northern Ireland government was commonly referred to as "Stormont," after its location in Belfast. A substantial number of Catholics were disfranchised by property qualifications and gerrymandering (the demarcation of electoral districts for partisan gain). The authority of the Stormont (or Ulster) government was withdrawn when Britain assumed direct rule in 1972, following several years of civil disorder. Under direct rule a British secretary of state in charge of the Northern Ireland Office exercised authority over the region. In a 1973 plebiscite, 57 percent of the Northern Ireland electorate voted for union with Britain, and less than 1 percent voted for union with Ireland; Catholic parties boycotted the plebiscite, however. Later in 1973 Britain authorized a unicameral Northern Ireland assembly to be elected by proportional representation, and with shared power between Catholics and Protestants in the executive. In the Sunnydale agreement, Britain, Ireland, and an appointed Northern Ireland executive body agreed to establish a tripartite council of Ireland with consultative powers. This plan was brought down after elections in 1974 by a combination of

Unionists who controlled the new shared executive and by a strike of Protestant workers. In 1975 Britain authorized a constitutional convention to be elected, but 59 percent of the elected delegates were Unionists who opposed power sharing. The convention voted for a majority rule governmental system and opposed power sharing. Britain rejected the plan, and subsequent efforts were fruitless. Various other proposals were made in the following six years, but nothing was satisfactory to either Unionist or Catholic parties. In 1982 Britain enacted a plan for "rolling devolution," whereby home rule would be gradually reintroduced to certain administrative departments while the British minister retained control over others. A Northern Ireland assembly elected by proportional representation would constitute committees to supervise departments with devolved powers. Elections to the assembly resulted in a 60 percent vote for Unionists opposed to shared power; the Provisional *Sinn Fein,* the political wing of the Irish Republican Army, participated in the elections. Sinn Fein and the Catholic Social Democratic and Labour party (SDLP) boycotted the assembly. In February 1984 the Official Unionist party (OUP) withdrew from the assembly, leaving only 33 of the 78 seats filled with nonboycotting members. Although there were attempts to revitalize the assembly, this plan of government also appeared to be a failure. *See also* IRISH REPUBLICAN ARMY (IRA), p. 32; NORTHERN IRELAND, p. 42; NORTHERN IRELAND: POLITICAL GROUPS, p. 45; ULSTER, p. 71.

Significance Attempts by the British and moderate Northern Ireland political leaders to construct a viable governmental system for Northern Ireland have foundered on the principle of free elections. Two-thirds of the population are Protestants, most of whom voted in a plebiscite for union with Britain; therefore British governments will not support unification of Ulster with Ireland. Unionists win the elections, and although divided into several parties, they are opposed to power sharing. Unionists agree among themselves that a governmental system for Ulster must be based on majority rule. The broad alternatives for resolving the Northern Ireland impasse have been considered and discussed for many years. These include (1) unification with the Republic of Ireland; (2) a federation with Ireland; (3) independence for Northern Ireland; (4) union with Britain, and a majority rule Ulster government with devolved powers; (5) union with Britain, and a power-sharing Ulster government; and (6) direct rule by Britain. Variations of these ideas have been suggested, some have been tried, but none are acceptable to all the major interests in the region. The problem seems unsolvable either through democratic procedures or by force.

Northern Ireland: Political Groups   Political parties, organizations, and movements that attempt to control or influence the governance of Northern Ireland. Political groups in Northern Ireland show a bewildering variety of forms, purposes, and methods. Current political parties that contest elections are (1) Official Unionist party (OUP), the largest Protestant group, whose leaders have been William Craig and James Molyneaux; (2) Democratic Unionist party (DUP), a slightly smaller and a more militant group, headed by the Reverend Ian Paisley; (3) Social Democratic and Labour party (SDLP), the largest Catholic party of the center-left, which favors unification with Ireland, led by John Hume; (4) Alliance party, a nonsectarian center party, which supports compromise and power-sharing arrangements; and (5) Provisional *Sinn Fein*, the political wing of the Irish Republican Army (IRA). There are a number of smaller parties, particularly among unionists that are able to win seats under a proportional representation system. Paramilitary and guerrilla forces that are responsible for much of the violence in the last 20 years include (1) the Provisional Irish Republican Army (IRA), the most active and oldest Catholic terrorist group; (2) the small but extremely violent Irish Nationalist Liberation Army (INLA), the military wing of the Irish Republican Socialist party (IRSP), groups that split from the Official IRA and the Official Sinn Fein; (3) the Ulster Defence Association (UDA), the largest Protestant paramilitary group; and (4) the Ulster Volunteer Force, a small, extremely militant group. Other groups have attempted to influence public affairs. The Orange Order is a strongly connected Protestant religious and cultural society that vigorously supports union with Britain. The Northern Ireland Civil Rights Association was founded in 1967 by Catholics who protested against discrimination; its demonstrations led to increased civil unrest, but it faded as violence increased dramatically in the 1970s. The Northern Ireland Peace Movement was organized in 1976 by Catholic and Protestant women after the deaths of a family of Catholic children, innocent victims of an IRA-British action. The peace movement demonstrated, marched, and prayed, and it received much media attention and support in Ulster, Ireland, and Britain. Its leaders, Catholic Mairead Corrigan and Protestant Betty Williams, won the Nobel Peace Prize for 1976, but the movement faded shortly thereafter. *See also* IRISH REPUBLICAN ARMY (IRA), p. 32; NORTHERN IRELAND, p. 42; ULSTER UNIONISTS, p. 71.

Significance   Some current Northern Ireland political groups can be traced to Catholic and Protestant forces in the nineteenth century, while others were born in the recurring crises of the last 20 years. Many groups have a short life, are small, and depend on the personality of particular leaders. The largest and lasting groups are those that are based on the irreconcilable goals of unification with Ireland or union with Britain. Moderate movements, peace groups, and compromising politicians are washed away by the emotional responses of the masses, whose prejudices are reinforced by demagogic politicians and terrorist atrocities.

Ombudsman   A public officer who is charged with investigating citizen complaints against a government agency. In Britain, the ombudsman, who is called the parliamentary commissioner for administration, was first created in 1967. The commissioner has the authority to investigate complaints against the administration of government, call for documents, examine files, suggest remedies to the offending agency, and make a report to Parliament if the agency fails to respond. The commissioner is an officer of Parliament and can act only on the request of a member of Parliament (MP). The commissioner has no authority regarding nationalized industries. *See also* CIVIL SERVICE, p. 9.

Significance   "Ombudsman" is a Swedish word and institution that has been widely copied in Western governments, quasi-public agencies, and private institutions. In Britain, the office was created only after much hesitation and fear that it would dilute the authority of Parliament. The commissioner's office became quite popular after its first year, when it uncovered and publicized some notorious cases of maladministration. The sphere of competence of the commissioner was soon extended to the Health Service, and other commissioners were created for Northern Ireland and local governments. Although the powers of the parliamentary commissioner are limited and citizens must first appeal through an MP, the office is popular. It has received, investigated, and resolved many complaints, especially cases dealing with health, social security, and tax matters.

Opposition   The second largest, or minority, party in the House of Commons that stands ready to replace the government with alternative leaders and policies. The group is legally recognized as Her Majesty's Loyal Opposition, and its leader is given an official status and special salary. The opposition comprises the leader, the shadow cabinet (members who would assume particular cabinet posts), and rank and file members of the minority party. The important roles of the opposition are (1) to evaluate and criticize the government's policies; (2) to participate in debates on public policy questions and help organize floor time on debates; (3) to inform and influence public opinion; and (4) to stand ready with identified individuals to step into cabinet posts should the government be defeated in Commons or in an election. *See also* HOUSE OF COMMONS, p. 28; POLITICAL PARTY SYSTEM: BRITAIN, p. 52.

Significance By fulfilling its primary role in opposing the government, the opposition keeps the public informed about impending policy changes and actions of the government. Inasmuch as the Parliament can be dissolved at any time and an election held after three weeks, it is important that the opposition be ever vigilant and ready to step into office. Although criticism and opposition, particularly in debates, can be quite vigorous, it takes place within clearly defined limits. Both majority and opposition parties cooperate in making Parliament run smoothly; mere obstruction is not tolerated. The opposition party must present itself as a respectable alternative to the government to win over the public, and it realizes that when it becomes the majority it too must work with the new opposition. The opposition party, like the government majority party, functions through party discipline and responsibility and usually votes as a bloc on most critical issues.

Parliament The supreme authority and legislative assembly in Britain. In a formal sense, Parliament consists of the crown, the House of Lords, and the House of Commons, but the most powerful element is the House of Commons. Consequently, "Parliament" is commonly used to refer to Commons, less frequently to both houses. Within Commons, the locus of power lies in the party that constructs a government that has the confidence of a majority of the house. This group is the government (prime minister, cabinet, and other executive officers) that acts in the name of the crown. Thus, although Parliament remains the highest legal authority, real policy-making power has passed to the political executive, which is drawn from the House of Commons. Inasmuch as the fundamental principle of the British constitution is the supremacy of Parliament, the powers of Parliament are limited only by political or practical considerations; but these limitations can be quite restrictive because of the operation of the party system. "Parliament," understood as the legislative assembly of Britain, is ofter referred to as "Westminster," because the houses of Parliament are located in the Palace of Westminster in London. *See also* DECLINE OF PARLIAMENT, p. 15; HOUSE OF COMMONS, p. 28; HOUSE OF LORDS p. 30; MONARCH, p. 41.

Significance The "Crown in Parliament" is the source of all constitutional authority in Britain, rather than the people as in a republic. The origins of Parliament, as a body distinct from the crown, can be traced back over 600 years to the Curia Regis, the Great Council of lords that advised the king. The House of Lords developed from this council. In the thirteenth century representatives of knights and burgesses were called to meet at various times; these groups became the House of Commons. The first Parliament as such was called in 1265 by Simon de Montfort, and by the fourteenth century the bicameral nature of Parliament was formalized. A series of dynastic wars, struggles between Parliament and the monarchy followed, including the Civil War of the 1640s. The supremacy of Parliament was established in the Glorious Revolution of 1688. A continuing struggle between the House of Commons and the House of Lords was finally resolved in the twentieth century, when the Parliament Act of 1911 stripped Lords of its power to veto money bills and gave Commons the power to override Lords' legislative veto. As the political party system evolved in the nineteenth and twentieth centuries, strong discipline within the parties resulted in the transfer of political power to the party leaders who could command a majority within the House of Commons. The "decline of Parliament" consequently refers not to a diminution of the authority of Parliament, but to the control over policy making that is exercised by party leaders in the political executive.

Party Government The system in which the majority party in the House of Commons becomes the political executive and plays the major role in making public policy. Party government is based on two important features of the British political system: the constitutional supremacy of Parliament, and the strong party system that usually results in a single-party government with a working majority in the House of Commons. Party government means that the majority party, which has been chosen in free elections, has been given a type of popular mandate to rule the nation. In the parliamentary system the leaders of the majority party become the government—the prime minister, cabinet, and other officers, totaling about 100 persons. This produces a type of "interlocking directorate," in which party leaders and government officials are the same persons. The government is responsible for initiating and seeing through the enactment of a legislative program, and for supervising the bureaucracy. *See also* MANDATE DOCTRINE, p. 39; PARLIAMENT, p. 47; POLITICAL PARTY SYSTEM: BRITAIN, p. 52.

Significance Democratic party government in Britain developed after Parliament wrested power from the monarchy and modern political parties were able to control stable majorities in the House of Commons. The system functions as party government so long as elections result in single-party majorities in Commons. This has been usually true in the twentieth century, except in transitional periods when the two-party system breaks down. Coalition governments are generally rare, being reserved for times of national crisis, like World War II. In the 1920s and 1930s when the Labour and Liberal parties vied with each other for the anti-Conservative vote, minority and coalition governments were constructed. Again, in 1974 to 1979, the Labour party presided over a minority government that relied on uncertain votes and was ineffective in putting through its program. A minority government is one in which the government does not have a majority of all the seats in the House of Commons; it is able to remain in office because small third parties choose to abstain rather than vote against it. The return of strong single-party majority government occurred with the Conservative victory of 1979, which was reinforced in 1983. Although the two-party system in Britain appears to be breaking down, the electoral system still produces strong single-party majorities in the House of Commons, which is the ultimate basis for British party government.

Party Organization The structures used by British political parties to govern party affairs. The Conservative and Labour parties have structural features typical of modern party organizations. These include (1) the leader, who is head of the party and leads the party in Parliament; (2) a central party secretariat or headquarters office; (3) a national executive committee; (4) an annual conference of delegates; (5) parliamentary parties, the organization of each party's members of Parliament (MPs); and (6) constituency parties, the party organization within the electoral districts (constituencies). Both parties have a large number of dues-paying members and volunteer activists. Compared to parties in the United States, both are highly centralized, and their MPs exhibit a very high degree of cohesiveness and are subject to party discipline. Despite their similarities, the two parties function differently and have important organizational differences. The Conservative party has a hierarchical, unitary structure, while the Labour party is a federation of trade unions, constituency parties, and socialist societies; Labour party membership includes regular members and indirect members who belong to affiliated trade unions. The policy-making Annual Conference of the Labour Party is more assertive in attempting to impose its left-wing policy positions on the more moderate Parliamentary Labour party (PLP). The Conservative annual conference of the National Union of Conservative and Unionist Associations is a docile, purely advisory group that rallies behind the party leadership. Before 1965 a new Conservative leader would "emerge" from the top group in a system of leader cooptation; in 1965 Conservatives adopted an older Labour method of election by the party MPs. In 1981 the left wing in the Labour party pushed through a reform whereby the leader is elected by an electoral college of trade unions (40 percent), constituency parties (30 percent), and the Parliamentary Labour party (30 percent). *See also* CONSERVATIVE PARTY, p. 12; IRON LAW OF OLIGARCHY, p. 33; LABOUR PARTY, p. 35; POLITICAL PARTY SYSTEM: BRITAIN, p. 52.

Significance The organizations of the Conservative and Labour parties contribute in different ways to the decision-making processes within the parties and the degree of intraparty democracy. The Conservative party has been traditionally controlled by a few leaders who had upper-class origins and acted in accord with their paternalistic attitudes. When the party moved from a system of leader cooptation to election by the Conservative MPs, the party became more democratic, and this resulted in the elections of Edward Heath and Margaret Thatcher. There is nothing in the Conservative party comparable to the trade union group in Labour. This is true not only regarding the large numbers of affiliated members and contributions to party funds by the unions, but also regarding the role played by the group's leaders. Since the mid-1950s, trade union leaders have moved the Labour party to the left and have exerted great pressure on Labour governments on matters of economic policy. Some authorities have concluded from earlier postwar studies that, despite organizational differences and Labour's federal structure, the two parties are both dominated by a few leaders at the top. The extreme statement of this view is found in older studies of working-class parties and unions, which concluded that democracy was not possible in mass membership organizations and that all societies are ruled by a few. Recent developments in the Labour party, as in the role of the annual conference, the selection of the party leader, and the making of policy, show that whether for good or ill, lower party units have a greater role in party affairs than in the Conservative party.

Plaid Cymru The small Welsh nationalist party that advocates self-government for Wales. *Plaid Cymru* (Welsh for "Party of Wales") was organized in 1925 to promote the language and culture of Wales; in 1932 the organization adopted the policy of self-government for Wales as a means to achieve this goal. The party first elected a member of Parliament (MP) in 1946; it won 3 of 36 Welsh seats in October 1974, and 2 seats in 1979 and 1983. The party's best showing was in October 1974, when it won 10 percent of the Welsh vote. Plaid Cymru supported the Labour government's plan in the mid-1970s for devolution, the creation of regional assemblies in Scotland and Wales. The 1978 devolution act for Wales provided for an elected assembly, but with less authority than was to be granted in Scotland. The act also provided that a popular referendum be taken on the plan and that a favorable vote be carried by at least 40 percent of the eligible voters. In Wales only 20 percent of the electorate cast votes; and only 12 percent of the electorate (20 percent of those voting) supported devolution. Despite this overwhelming rejection of self-government in Wales, Plaid Cymru continued to elect its normal complement of 2 MPs in 1979 and 1983. *See also* DEVOLUTION, p. 17; WALES, p. 74.

Significance Plaid Cymru represents a small portion of the people of Wales, only 20 percent of whom speak Welsh. Most English-speaking Welsh persons clearly feared that devolution would bring the imposition of Welsh, a difficult Celtic language, throughout the country. In Scotland, where devolution won a majority of those voting but failed to surpass the 40 percent minimum, economic issues and demands for full independence were more at issue. Economic concerns were not at issue in Wales, and the vote turned on Plaid Cymru's goals for cultural nationalism, which the people rejected by a large majority.

Political Culture: Britain The system of attitudes, values, and beliefs held by the people of Great Britain about their political system. Important features of British political culture include (1) a high value placed on personal liberty and individuality; (2) strong support for democratic methods, political compromise, and cooperation; (3) widespread consensus on the constitutional system and belief in the legitimacy of governmental institutions; (4) preference for gradualistic reform through piecemeal change rather than abrupt or radical change; (5) an empirical (experimental) and pragmatic approach to problem solving rather than an ideological or doctrinaire approach; (6) a stress on lawful behavior and opposition to illegal actions; and (7) attitudes of trust and confidence in fellow citizens and government officials. Britons have pride in their institutions, defer to the authority of government, and defend the system in times of crisis. These features of the political culture apply only to Great Britain, since Northern Ireland has unique characteristics. British political culture is diffused throughout social classes and party affiliations. Political subcultures are basically variations on the theme, whether they be laissez-faire supporters of the Conservative party or socialists in the Labour party. Although atypical political groups like undemocratic nationalists and communists in Britain do not share the characteristic features, they are small and have little impact on the political system. *See also* SOCIAL DEFERENCE THESIS, p. 62.

Significance The political culture provides a strong base for the successful operation of British political institutions and processes and contributes to their adaptability and survivability. Change is piecemeal and incremental, but this gives rise to contradictions and anomalies within the system, such as monarchical and aristocratic institutions coexisting with democratic ones. Democracy in Britain is moderated by traditional beliefs, and ideals give way to practical necessity. Some observers of the postwar scene argue that, unlike that of other nations on the continent of Europe, British political culture has survived the great international changes brought by the war and the socioeconomic changes within the society. Although policy disputes within Britain are quite noisy and self-interest groups vetoes are disruptive of orderly business, these matters must be placed in the context of widely diffused attitudes and popular beliefs that continue to support the political system.

Political Party System: Britain A system dominated by two major parties with third parties and regional parties playing a subordinate role. Since 1945 the British political party system has been dominated by the Conservative and Labour parties, the only parties able to form governments. Except in the election of February 1974, the single-member district electoral system has produced a majority of seats in the House of Commons for one of the two major parties. The largest minor party is the Liberal party; since 1974 it has received from 14 to 19 percent of the vote, but it wins only 2 to 3 percent of the seats. The Social Democratic party, whose leaders split from the Labour party in 1981, cooperated with the Liberals in an election alliance in 1983; together they won 25 percent of the vote, but only 3.5 percent of the seats. Nationalist parties in Northern Ireland win all the seats in that province. In 1983 the Ulster Unionists, Protestant groups divided into several parties, won 15 seats and two Catholic parties, the Social Democratic Labour party and the Provisional *Sinn Fein* group won 1 each. Other very small parties, including the National Front, a racist group with prewar fascist origins, Communists, Ecologists, and others, run candidates in a large number of districts, but they seldom total 1 percent combined or win any seats. The cohesiveness of the major parties is typically strong in Parliament, but factionalism within the Labour party weakened the effectiveness of Labour governments in the 1960s and 1970s, particularly over domestic economic and European Common Market issues. *See also* ELECTIONS OF 1983: BRITAIN, p. 19; ELECTORAL SYSTEM: HOUSE OF COMMONS, p. 20; NORTHERN IRELAND: POLITICAL GROUPS, p. 45; PARTY ORGANIZATION, p. 49.

Significance From 1945 to the 1970s, the British political party system functioned as a typical two-party system. Two major parties won about 90 percent of the votes and up to 95 percent of the seats; a single party won a majority in Parliament and formed a government; the two major parties alternated in office; and minor parties competed, but they had too few seats to have a bearing on the majority in Parliament. In 1974 the two-party system began to break down, as Liberals improved their percentage of vote and nationalist parties, particularly Unionists in Northern Ireland, drew seats away from the major parties. In the postwar period, some elections have been very close, with only a few seats separating the major parties; in 1976 the Labour government of James Callaghan lost its slim majority through attrition and had to rely on Liberal, Scottish, and Welsh parties for support. In 1979 Callaghan was overthrown by one vote, the first time a cabinet lost a motion of nonconfidence since 1924. In another transition period, the 1920s and 1930s, when the Labour party was replacing the Liberals as the nation's second party, the two-party system did not function. In 1979 and 1983 the Conservative party won substantial majorities in the House of Commons, but these were largely the result of the disparity between votes and seats that is produced by the single-member district system. The two-party system and single-party governments could not exist if the Parliament were to enact a system of proportional representation, but this is unlikely so long as the two large parties retain exclusive control over the government. Interpretations of what has happened to the British party system since 1974 vary. Some observers see the decline of voter support for the two parties as the end of the two-party system; others believe that the drop in party memberships and party identification are indications of "partisan dealignment" in Britain; and others see the birth of the Liberal-SDP alliance and its 25 percent popular vote in 1983 as indications of a continuing transition period in which the Labour party will be replaced by a refashioned two-party system dominated by Conservatives and the Liberal-Social Democratic Alliance.

Prime Minister (PM)   The head of government, the most powerful position within the British political system. The prime minister is formally appointed by the reigning monarch, who is constitutionally bound to select the person who is the leader of the majority in the House of Commons. Since 1945 the political party system has provided the monarch with a clear choice, and the queen has little or no discretion. Like any head of government, the prime minister has extensive powers, which include presiding over the cabinet, appointing and dismissing members of the government, leading the government majority in the House of Commons, making final decisions on matters of public policy, supervising the administration of government departments, and making appointments in military, judicial, and civil branches of government.

The prime minister is in a stronger constitutional position than any other cabinet minister or public official. Only the PM can report to the queen, recommend dissolution of the House of Commons, and guide the cabinet, determine its agenda, and control information provided to it. The prime minister is also the head of the majority party and leads it in election campaigns, when much media attention focuses on the candidates for the PM office. A victory in the election confirms the party's choice and strengthens the PM's position against any rivals for leadership. Since World War II, the prime ministers have been: Clement Atlee, Labour (1945–51); Winston Churchill, Conservative (1951–55); Anthony Eden, Conservative (1955–57); Harold Macmillan, Conservative (1957–63); Alec Douglas-Home, Conservative (1963–64); Harold Wilson, Labour (1964–70); Edward Heath, Conservative (1970–74); Harold Wilson (1974–76); James Callaghan, Labour (1976–79); and Margaret Thatcher, Conservative (since 1979). *See also* CABINET, p. 6; HOUSE OF COMMONS, p. 28.

Significance The prime minister is more than *primus inter pares,* or first among equals. The special constitutional roles and political leadership position make the PM equivalent in some respects to the head of government in a presidential system. This is especially true when the PM has led the party to a resounding victory, as Margaret Thatcher did in 1983. Because the Labour party is more faction-ridden than the Conservative party, Labour PMs can be less dominating. Prime ministers are always limited by their popularity among the voters and the general political environment of the times. Since the 1970s, the breaking down of the strong two-party system has brought about an alternation of parties in office and a quick turnover of party leaders in both the Conservative and Labour parties. The prime minister's powers are not based on specific constitutional or statutory provisions but have emerged in the evolution of the British system of government and are thus based mainly on custom and usage. The PM may serve up to five years before having to seek a new mandate from the voters through an election of the House of Commons. Unlike an American cabinet, however, the British cabinet is collectively responsible for the functioning of the government, but a strong PM can dominate cabinet decision making.

Privy Council A body of royal advisers whose independent powers have been exercised by the cabinet since the eighteenth century. The Privy Council comprises all present and former cabinet ministers, certain high-ranking administrative officials, some Church of England prelates, and other persons of achievement who have been appointed to the council as an honor. The total numbers about 380 persons; the full body gathers only on special occasions, like the coronation of a monarch. The cabinet acts in the name of the Privy Council and at times certain cabinet officials meet in this capacity. These officials issue "orders in council," which are executive orders that have no prior approval by Parliament. Their authority is derived from "royal prerogatives," executive powers that are exercised by the cabinet, or from delegated legislative powers. Of the various committees of the council, a noteworthy one is the Judicial Committee of the Privy Council. This is a body, mostly comprised of the law lords of the House of Lords, that acts like an appellate court that reviews cases appealed to it from the Empire or the Commonwealth. Most Commonwealth nations have abolished the right of appeal to the Privy Council, but the power remains for nonself-governing territories. *See also* CABINET, p. 6.

Significance At one time the Privy Council comprised the main group of advisers to the sovereign, but as it became too large, a smaller group within it retained the confidence of the king. Its origins are traced to the Great Council (Magnum Concilium) that advised the Norman kings, and the Curia Regis that developed from it. When the Curia Regis grew and developed specialized judicial and administrative bodies, royal advisers were confined to a smaller body, the Permanent Council. The Privy Council developed from this group in the fifteenth century, and as it too became unwieldy, the smaller cabinet assumed the role as chief adviser to the sovereign. Today the Privy Council is primarily a ceremonial body, except for a small office that acts in its name.

Profumo Affair A scandal in 1963 with national security implications that involved John Profumo, a cabinet minister. John Profumo was the secretary of state for war in the Conservative government of Harold Macmillan. In 1961 he had a relationship with Christine Keeler, who was also associating with a Soviet naval attaché, who apparently was attempting to use Keeler to solicit defense information. When this was rumored about, Profumo, in a personal statement to the House of Commons, denied having an affair with Keeler, and his word was accepted by Prime Minister Macmillan. As rumors persisted despite his successful suit for libel against a magazine, Profumo finally admitted he had lied and resigned from the government and the House of Commons. While the press engaged in sensationalist publicity, an independent inquiry commission was appointed. The report of Lord Denning, the chairman, was an instant best-seller; it concluded that national security was not compromised and that no secrets were passed to the Soviets. The Macmillan government was severely criticized by the opposition and the press, however, for not being diligent in investigating the rumors. *See also* SPY AFFAIRS, p. 64.

Significance The Profumo affair revealed a scandal in the highest levels of the British government and gave the opposition many opportunities to criticize the Conservative "old boy network," its false code of honor, and the laxity in governmental security procedures. Security measures were tightened, but the public was constantly reminded of the previous spy cases of Guy F. Burgess and Donald D. Maclean in 1951 and Harold (Kim) Philby in 1962. Macmillan's government was able to withstand a Labour motion of nonconfidence despite some defections, but the affair contributed to the growing unpopularity of the Conservative party. Macmillan subsequently retired from public life, but the party and his successor, Alec Douglas-Home, bore the burden of the affair. In the election of 1964, the Labour party continued to exploit the matter, which may have contributed to the victory of Harold Wilson. John Profumo gave himself over to charity work.

Public Corporation A government agency charged with administering a nationalized industry or public enterprise. Public corporations are semiautonomous bodies that are run by a board of directors. They are outside the regular administrative structure of government, and the employees of the corporation are not civil servants. Wages, salaries, and working conditions are determined by the corporation. Public corporations are organized like private corporations and are financially independent in that they can borrow private funds and made expenditures free of Treasury department controls. Parliament has removed public corporations from close supervision, but it has required that annual reports subject to debate be submitted to Parliament. Ministers nominate members of the board of directors, and may work closely with corporations; they can approve the corporation's investments and goals. Public corporations exist in utilities, transportation, communication, and heavy industry. Some important examples of public corporations are the National Coal Board, British Broadcasting Corporation, British Railways Board, and the Post Office (since 1969). *See also* CIVIL SERVICE, p. 9.

Significance Public corporations are created with a large measure of independence and flexibility on the theory that this is necessary to successfully operate an industrial enterprise. These features are sometimes compromised, however, because ministerial concerns, employee demands, consumer interests, and the directors' plans for the industry seldom coincide. Public corporations are not the only method used to manage public enterprise in Britain. Other systems are direct control by a government department; mixed enterprise, in which the government owns a share of the stock; and quasi-autonomous nondepartmental governmental organizations (called "quangos"). Quangos are nondepartmental government agencies that are state-financed but free from daily supervision by a minister. Of the several hundred quangos, two examples are the Arts Council and the University Grants Committee. Quango powers range from purely advisory to regulatory.

Reform Acts Fundamental extensions of voting rights in the nineteenth century that helped change the nature of the British system of government. The reform acts enlarged the electorate, created uniformity in voting qualifications throughout the country, and eliminated electoral corruption. Prior to 1832, some cities, including Manchester and Birmingham, were not represented in the House of Commons; other communities had representatives but very few people ("rotten boroughs"); and some were controlled by the crown or large landowners ("pocket boroughs"). The Reform Act of 1832, adopted by the Whigs, extended the franchise to certain property-holders, eliminated rotten boroughs, and redistributed seats in favor of larger towns. The electorate was increased by about 50 percent, from about 5 to 7 percent of the total adult population. The Reform Act of 1867 extended voting rights to some working groups, made another redistribution of seats, and helped eliminate corrupt election practices. The act was adopted by the Conservative government of Benjamin Disraeli, who attempted to shore up his "Tory democracy" by appealing to working men. The Reform Act of 1884, adopted by the Liberal government of William Gladstone, enfranchised most men, adding about two million voters to the rolls. In 1885 another act reduced the great population discrepancies among districts (constituencies), although some still remained. Secret voting was adopted in 1870, which also helped reduce corrupt election practices. Full adult suffrage was not achieved until 1928. *See also* BRITISH CONSTITUTION, p. 3; PARTY GOVERNMENT, p. 48; REPRESENTATION OF THE PEOPLE ACTS, p. 58.

Significance The great reform acts of the nineteenth century changed the nature of the British political system by redistributing power between the institutions of government. After 1832 power shifted to the House of Commons, which now had the effective voice in the selection of the head of government. Governments thereafter needed the confidence of Commons to remain in office. With an enlarged electorate, the later reform acts encouraged the development of registration societies and modern national party organizations, contributing to party cohesion and discipline and to a preeminent role for party leaders. Power was transferred from Commons to the cabinet as rank and file members of Parliament played their role in supporting party leaders. As stronger party organizations evolved, Britain developed a system of party government.

Representation of the People Acts Acts of the British Parliament in the twentieth century that enlarged the suffrage and made other electoral changes. The Representation of the People Act of 1918 enfranchised women over age 30 and men over 21 who had not been granted voting rights earlier. The act of 1928 extended voting rights to women on the same basis as men. The act of 1949 eliminated plural voting and made all voting personal by removing the votes of universities; it also codified the election laws. The voting age was lowered to age 18 by the act of 1969. Unlike the United States, British law permits certain resident noncitizens to vote in elections. This includes citizens of the Commonwealth and citizens of the Republic of Ireland. Peers, who already have a seat in the House of Lords, are not permitted to vote in elections for the House of Commons. *See also* REFORM ACTS, p. 57.

Significance The representation of the people acts continued the process begun by the great reform acts of the nineteenth century of increasing the suffrage in stages. The process was one of slowly removing property qualifications, enfranchising most adult men, and then women in stages. By the twentieth century, the impact of the reform acts had already been made as effective power was transferred from Lords to Commons to cabinet. The extension of suffrage to women fully democratized the electorate, and 18-year-old suffrage enlarged it further. The impact of these last two developments on the institutions of government is difficult to discern, but they have affected the outcomes of particular electoral contests. Researchers tend to agree that in Britain class is more important than sex or age regarding voting behavior. Women tend to vote slightly more conservatively than men, and the younger people are inclined to be more liberal or leftist and to engage in public demonstrations; Scottish youth tend to vote for the Scottish National party.

Republic of Ireland Official name of the independent state of Ireland. Dominated by the English since the twelfth century through many turbulent periods, Ireland was formally united with Britain on January 1, 1801. The early and middle nineteenth century was marked by various nationalist movements including that of the Fenians, a secret society with a strong wing in the United States that tried to achieve independence by violent means. Irish politicians in the British Parliament agitated for home rule (self-government for domestic affairs) and were supported by the Liberals. This issue divided British politics throughout the last decades of the century, and on two occasions a Liberal-sponsored home rule bill was defeated. In 1914 over the opposition of the Protestants in Ulster, a home rule bill was passed, but it was not implemented because of World War I. Civil war was threatened as armed Irish groups, the Protestant Ulster Volunteers and Catholic *Sinn Fein*, took violent actions. In the Easter Rising of 1916, a rebellion in the Irish capital of Dublin led by the Sinn Fein, who expected aid from Germany, was crushed; most of the leaders were executed, except Eamon De Valera, who had American roots. Civil strife continued as the Irish Republic Army (IRA) engaged in numerous guerrilla actions after 1919, and the Black and Tans, a special branch of the Royal Irish Constabulary, tried to suppress resistance by counterviolence. Britain passed the Government of Ireland Act in 1920, which provided for a home rule government in Dublin for the 26 Catholic counties of Ireland, and one in Belfast for the 9 Protestant Counties of Ulster. The Ulster Parliament accepted the plan and received home rule, but Dublin refused. In December 1921 the British and Dublin governments agreed by treaty to establish the Irish Free State; this gave southern Ireland political independence and dominion status within the British Commonwealth. An internal Catholic civil war ensued between IRA supporters of De Valera, who objected to the partitioning of Ireland, and the Irish Republican Movement of Michael Collins, who accepted the treaty. The Irish Free State was officially proclaimed in 1922. De Valera formed a government in 1932 and continued the claim on Ulster. From 1932 to 1949 the country was named "Eire" under the 1932 constitution. In 1949 the Republic of Ireland was proclaimed, and it withdrew from the Commonwealth. In 1955 Ireland was admitted to the United Nations, and it joined the European Community in 1973. The Irish Republic has a parliamentary form of government, with a prime minister (*Taoiseach*) and a bicameral legislature. The lower house (*Dail Eireann*) is elected by proportional representation; the senate (*Seanad Eireann*), based on functional representation, is composed mostly of representatives of vocational groups and universities. The two largest parties that vie for power in a multiparty system are the *Fine Gael* and the *Fianna Fail*. The population is 3.4 million, of which 94 percent are Catholic. *See also* IRISH REPUBLICAN ARMY (IRA), p. 32; NORTHERN IRELAND, p. 42; ULSTER, p. 71.

Significance The turbulent history of Ireland turns on the interrelated themes of religion and British domination. These themes still characterize Irish affairs. The contrast is stark between English politics, where religion plays a minor role today, and Irish politics, both south and north, where it dominates all other factors. The partitioning of Ireland into a Catholic republic and Protestant Ulster has not eliminated the issue of British control. Ireland still claims Ulster, and the Protestant majority in Ulster refuses to make any substantial concessions to the Catholic minority. The guerrilla war continues and claims hundreds of innocent victims in the name of freedom. Despite Ireland's claim on Ulster, a complete break between Britain and Ireland seems unlikely. About one-third of the population of Northern Ireland is Catholic, and there is a sizable Irish community in English metropolitan centers. Although Ireland is no longer part of the Commonwealth, Irish citizens may freely migrate across an open frontier, and resident Irish may vote in British elections. The Irish and British governments have worked out a *modus vivendi* on many subjects, but the partition of Ireland is an unacceptable solution for Irish nationalists who are prepared to use terrorist violence to bring about Irish unification.

Scotland A territorial division of the British isles that has been formally united with England and Wales since 1707. Before the union, Scotland had a long and turbulent relationship with England. At various times throughout this 800-year history, Scotland was a fiefdom of English kings, an independent monarchy, or at war with England—and it often suffered from internal dynastic wars and civil strife. In 1603 the two kingdoms were dynastically joined on the death of Elizabeth I, when James VI of the Scottish House of Stuart succeeded to the English throne as James I of England. Separate parliaments were maintained until the Act of Union of 1707 united them in a single parliament. Scotland retained its legal system, which is based on Roman law, the Established Church of Scotland, which was Presbyterian, and its distinctive educational system. Since 1885 Scotland has had a separate cabinet minister who heads the Scottish Office, which administers departments dealing with health, housing, agriculture, local government, and other matters. Local government in Scotland is different from that in England and Wales, but it generally follows the same principles and has the same relationships to the central government. In politics, Scotland is a strong center of Labour party support, particularly in the industrialized areas. In a typical election, the Labour party wins about 60 to 65 percent of the seats. The Scottish National party (SNP) has had an impact on the region's politics since the 1970s, when it became the second party on the basis of the popular vote. The SNP seeks independence for Scotland, but this goal received a major setback in 1979 when a devolution proposal to create an assembly with limited powers failed to win a majority of the electorate in a referendum. *See also* DEVOLUTION,

p. 17; SCOTTISH NATIONAL PARTY (SNP), p. 61; UNITED KINGDOM OF GREAT BRITAIN AND NORTHERN IRELAND, p. 73.

Significance   Scotland, like Wales, is part of the "Celtic fringe" in which the Conservative party is weak. Long a safe bastion for Labour, Scotland's sizable number of seats (71 in 1979) became crucial to Labour in the close national elections of the 1970s as the SNP mounted an effective challenge. In the depressed industrial areas, the SNP won strong support with the argument that revenues from North Sea oil would be sufficient to meet Scotland's needs for economic modernization. Labour leaders attempted to ward off the SNP and retain their support in Parliament by enacting the devolution plan for a Scottish assembly. When the plan failed, the SNP helped overthrow James Callaghan's government in 1979, but this helped usher in a Conservative government. From 1974 to 1983, the SNP suffered a 60 percent drop in the popular vote, and fell back to 2 seats in Parliament. Inasmuch as a Scottish assembly would be controlled by the Labour party or the SNP, the Conservatives hold no brief for the idea.

Scottish National Party (SNP)   The nationalist party in Scotland that advocates independence for the region. The Scottish National party (SNP) was founded in 1934, and it first won a by-election in 1945, but this seat was lost in the next general election. The SNP became politically significant in the 1960s, when it again won a by-election in 1967; by 1970 it was winning 11 percent of the vote in Scotland. In February 1974 it won 32 percent of the Scottish vote (7 seats); in October 1974 30 percent (11 seats); and in 1979 it fell to 17 percent (2 seats), where it remained in the 1983 election. The rise of the SNP is attributed to general dissatisfaction with the major parties, the depressed state of the economy, the enfranchisement of 18-year-olds, and the SNP's claim that proceeds from North Sea petroleum would solve the country's economic ills. Although the party promotes full independence for Scotland, it accepted as a first step the devolution plan of 1979 whereby an elected assembly with a separate executive would be created in Scotland. For the plan to be adopted in a referendum, an affirmative vote was required from a majority of those voting and from at least 40 percent of all those entitled to vote. On March 1, 1979, 51.6 percent of those voting cast a "yes" vote, but this represented only 32.8 percent of the electorate, and the devolution plan failed. The SNP insisted that the James Callaghan Labour government institute the plan, but it refused to do so. The SNP then withdrew support from Callaghan's minority government, which, along with an earlier Liberal withdrawal, contributed to his fall on

March 28, 1979. *See also* DEVOLUTION, p. 17; ELECTIONS OF 1983: BRITAIN, p. 19; SCOTLAND, p. 60.

Significance On the basis of popular votes, the Scottish National party in the 1970s attained the rank of second largest party in Scotland after the Labour party. Although the SNP took most of its votes from the Conservatives, it threatened the position of Labour. A major reason that the Labour government proposed the plan for devolution was to prevent the loss of its support in Scotland. The failure of the devolution proposal and the fall of Callaghan's government greatly damaged the SNP. The party dropped from 800,000 votes (October 1974) to 500,000 (1979) to 330,000 (1983), and from a high of 11 seats back to its normal complement of 2 seats in 1979 and 1983. Unlike the Welsh nationalist party, whose themes are primarily cultural nationalism and local self-government, the SNP desires full independence, and it is primarily concerned with economic development achieved through the use of offshore oil revenues. These goals received a big setback with the failure of devolution and the Conservative party victories in 1979 and 1983.

Social Deference Thesis The theory that the working class in Britain has voluntarily yielded political power to conservative, upper-class elites. The social deference thesis attempts to explain the reasons for the substantial number of working class persons who politically support conservative elites rather than leaders of working-class origin. According to the thesis, the "working-class Tory" prefers socially superior leaders and traditional elites over mass-based, lower-class politicians. Conservative workers emphasize the role of leadership in government over policy options, and they believe the Conservative party is more patriotic and inclined to serve the public interest. These attitudes are held by about one-third of the working class, and by persons in the middle class. The thesis uses social deference to explain two related phenomena: (1) the lack of a social revolution in Britain despite the rapid development and large size of the working class after industrialism; and (2) the failure of the Labour party to win the full allegiance of the working class in the twentieth century. *See also* EMBOURGEOISIEMENT THESIS, p. 21; POLITICAL CULTURE: BRITAIN, p. 51.

Significance The social deference thesis has been used in various forms since the nineteenth century to explain working class conservatism. Some observers believe that while social deference does exist, the thesis ascribes too much explanatory power to one factor. Other aspects of the political culture, class system, economic development, and political party history must be taken into account to explain either the general nonrevolutionary approach of the working class or the working-class Tory. The thesis may have reached the end of its intellectual life span because postwar empirical research shows that: (1) the general category of the "working class" has limited research usefulness; (2) economic modernization has reduced the size and importance of specific occupations linked to the working class; and (3) the voting behavior of manual workers is seldom traceable to attitudes of deference to social superiors.

Social Democratic Party (SDP)   A centrist party that was founded in 1981 by leaders who split from the Labour party. The origins of the Social Democratic party (SDP) can be traced to 1972, when the deputy leader of the Labour party, Roy Jenkins, and shadow cabinet member David Owen resigned their positions in protest against the plans of party leader Harold Wilson to hold a referendum on continued British membership in the European Community (EC). Dissatisfaction within the Labour party mounted in the late 1970s. The party moved further to the left and adopted collectivistic, anti-European, and nuclear disarmament positions. When Michael Foot was chosen as Labour leader over the moderate Denis Healey, the "Gang of Four" (Roy Jenkins, David Owen, Shirley Williams, and William Rodgers) founded the Social Democratic party in 1981 and ultimately built a group of 29 members of Parliament by attracting Labour MPs and winning a few by-elections. Jenkins, who was then President of the European Commission in Brussels, won a by-election and became the party leader in 1982. The new party's program stressed continued membership in the European Community and in the North Atlantic Treaty Organization (NATO), maintenance of the nuclear deterrent, no further nationalizations, proportional representation, and economic policies favoring investment, job creation, and social security improvements. The SDP joined forces with the Liberal party in an electoral alliance for the 1983 elections. The Alliance partners agreed on a joint manifesto and not to compete against one another in the elections; they each ran about 300 candidates. In its first national test, the Alliance won 25.4 percent of the popular vote, 2 points behind the Labour party, but the SDP won only 6 seats and the Liberals 17, compared to Labour's 209. Shirley Williams and William Rodgers both failed to be reelected; in June 1983 Jenkins resigned as party leader and was replaced by Owen. *See also* ALLIANCE, p. 1; ELECTIONS OF 1983: BRITAIN, p. 19; LABOUR PARTY, p. 35.

Significance   The creation of the Social Democratic party was one of the most important developments in English party politics in the postwar period. The building of the Alliance with the Liberals gave voters another real choice. Although the single-member district electoral system greatly disadvantaged the Alliance (25.4 percent of the popular vote yielded only 3.5 percent of the seats in the House of Commons), it was clear that large numbers of voters were dissatisfied with the socialist and antinuclear stance of the Labour party. The fortunes of the Social Democratic party are clearly tied to maintaining a solid front with the Liberals in an alliance, and to developments within the Labour party. So long as the electoral system is not changed, the Alliance can succeed only if support for Labour continues to fall. The Labour party, however, retains a large social base of support, and it also has its share of moderate leaders who may recapture the party and lead it back from the doctrinaire left toward the center. The last time a new party succeeded in Britain was when Labour surpassed the Liberals in 1922.

Spy Affairs Events concerning British spies for the Soviet Union that revealed major breaches of security. A number of spy affairs attracted a great deal of attention in the media, raised public awareness, and brought criticisms on British governments. One of the most important cases was that of Klaus Fuchs, a naturalized British citizen from Germany and communist sympathizer. A nuclear physicist, Fuchs worked on the development of the atomic bomb and transmitted secret information to the Soviet Union. His arrest in 1949 led to the uncovering of the Julius and Ethel Rosenberg spy ring in the United States. He confessed and was imprisoned from 1950 to 1959; upon his release he went to East Germany. Other cases that were revealed at different times involved a group of persons at Cambridge University in the 1930s who spied for the USSR in the 1930s and 1940s. In 1951 two of these spies who were foreign service officers, Guy F. Burgess and Donald D. Maclean, fled to the Soviet Union despite being under surveillance. In 1962 an associate, Harold (Kim) Philby, also evaded surveillance and fled to the USSR. A fourth member of the spy ring was publicly identified in 1979: Anthony Blunt, a knighted, distinguished art historian who had served as art adviser to Queen Elizabeth. Blunt actually confessed in 1964, but the matter was kept quiet as he was offered immunity in return for cooperation in security investigations. Other well-known cases were those of John Vassal in the 1950s and Geoffrey Arthur Prime, who was sentenced in 1982 to 35 years in prison for passing communications surveillance secrets to the Soviet Union. The most notorious case because it involved a cabinet minister—although not damaging to security—was that of War Minister John Profumo, who lied to the House of Commons in 1963 about his affair with a woman who had a relationship with a Soviet naval attaché. *See also* PROFUMO AFFAIR, p. 55.

Significance The postwar spy affairs revealed serious weaknesses in British counterintelligence operations and questionable decisions by the

British government. Media reporting was often sensationalistic because some of the cases uncovered sexual indiscretions, which the opposition played on. In 1964 the Labour party failed to overturn the Macmillan government on the Profumo affair, but it used the matter to its advantage in the close election of 1964 to demonstrate the laxity and "old boy network" of Conservative governments. In 1982 Margaret Thatcher had to defend the practice that kept Blunt's treason from the public for 18 years while he served the queen as art adviser. Rumors persisted that a fifth member of the Cambridge spy ring was still at large, probably in the intelligence service.

Suez Crisis of 1956 Joint British-French military operations against Egypt, ostensibly over the issue of Egyptian nationalization of the Suez Canal. The Suez Canal Company was a private French concession whose shares were mainly owned by the British government; Britain and France helped administer the canal zone. In July 1956 the president of Egypt, Gamal Abdel Nasser, nationalized the company to acquire funds from canal revenues to finance the building of the Aswan Dam on the Nile River. This was a project the United States had decided not to support, partly because of Nasser's growing links to East European communist countries. Britain and France undertook the military action in a preplanned operation with Israel. The Israeli government was primarily interested in destroying the buildup of Egyptian forces and Palestinian guerrilla bases on the Sinai peninsula, and in opening the Straits of Tiran to its shipping. Britain and France hoped the military operations would result in the removal of Nasser, whose nationalist revolution threatened their interests in the region. Britain expected thereby to regain the canal, and France sought to strengthen its position in North Africa and stop Egyptian aid to Algerian rebels. When Israel attacked on October 29, 1956, Britain and France, in accordance with the plan, issued an ultimatum that Egypt and Israel withdraw ten miles from the canal. Failing this, Britain and France launched aerial attacks on Egyptian bases and landed military units. The military campaign was poorly executed, however. By this time, Egypt had blocked the canal, and Israel had achieved its objectives in routing Egyptian forces in the Sinai. The British-French action resulted in opposition within their countries, international indignation, threats from the Soviet Union, and criticism and pressure from the American government, which had not been informed prior to the operations. President Dwight Eisenhower threatened to withhold financial backing of the British pound, which had collapsed, unless the British followed a United Nations General Assembly resolution calling for a cease-fire. The government of British Prime Minister Anthony Eden, which had expected the United States to remain neutral, relented, and the French necessarily followed. The United Nations authorized the United Nations Emergency Force (UNEF) to supervise the Israeli-Egyptian cease-fire.

Significance The outcome of the Suez crisis symbolized the end of Britain as a great power; it showed that Britain was not able to undertake independent military actions that are opposed by both the United States and the Soviet Union. The affair greatly strained American-British relations. The Eisenhower government's ultimatum to London to withdraw was successful because of the dependence of Britain on American financial backing when the pound sterling collapsed and petroleum prices rose dramatically. President Eisenhower, who was in the last days of his reelection campaign, was angered at the lack of prior consultation and the potential harm to his projected image as a man of peace. The British-French military operations also distracted world attention from the Soviet military intervention against the Hungarian rising which overthrew a Stalinist government, and it equated Western military actions with communist ones. Israel achieved its objectives in removing hostile forces from the Sinai and opening shipping in the straits. Although the Egyptian army was humiliated by the quick Israeli victory, Nasser's prestige among Arab nations increased, and he became more dependent on Soviet military and financial assistance.

Thatcherism The theories, policies, and political style of Margaret Thatcher, who became prime minister in 1979. When Margaret Thatcher took office, Britain was suffering from a low growth rate, business inefficiency, poor productivity, low investment, high inflation, high unemployment, and perennial industrial strikes. She stated her goals to be producing a change in attitudes toward work, creating a new climate for business, revitalizing industry, and reducing the role of government regulation and intervention in people's lives. Her program for reform was many-sided, including (1) a policy of "monetarism," control of the money supply so as to reduce inflation; (2) "privatization" (denationalization) of government-owned enterprise; (3) reduction in government expenditures; (4) reduction of taxes, elimination of restrictions on private investment, and providing incentives for investment; and (5) restrictions on disruptive union practices. These policies were based on her trust in market economics and her opposition to socialism as being counterproductive and leading to the erosion of democracy. In the first two years Thatcher's program of monetarism to stem inflation caused much opposition; unemployment remained high, strikes continued, and her popularity in the polls fell to the lowest level of any prime minister since Neville Chamberlain. Most observers believed she would lose the next election easily, but a clear turn in opinion came with the British victory in the Falklands War of June 1982. Her image as an anticommunist "Iron Lady" now took on a favorable connotation in public opinion as the nation experienced a burst of patriotic emotionalism. By the time of the June 1983 elections, inflation had been substantially reduced, although unemployment remained high. As the Labour party, split in two and captured by the doctrinaire left, mounted an ineffective campaign, Thatcher led the Conservative party to a landslide victory. With a big 144-seat majority in Parliament and her opponents in the Conservative party routed, she pushed her advantage in 1983 and 1984 against nuclear disarmers, socialists, trade union strikers, and European Community governments that opposed budgetary concessions to Britain. But she also continued popular social welfare programs, like the Health Service, and promoted others like private ownership of government homes. *See also* CONSERVATIVE PARTY, p. 12; ELECTIONS OF 1983: BRITIAN, p. 19; WELFARE STATE, p. 75.

Significance Thatcherism is a blend of market economics, the self-help ethic, "strongman" nationalism, and middle-class populism. In practice Thatcherism is an attack on socialism and *dirigisme* rather than welfarism. Critics see her ideas as simplistic and old-fashioned, and her reduction of inflation bought at the cost of the highest rate of unemployment since the great depression of the 1930s. She also had the good fortune of coming into office as the North Sea fields made Britain self-sufficient in petroleum. Others note that the 1983 landslide in parliamentary seats represented only 44 percent of the popular vote and they question whether her policies are thereby justified. The big parliamentary victory was made possible in part by the three-sided contest between Conservatives, Labourites, and the Liberal-Social Democratic Alliance. Yet the political record is remarkable—the first woman prime minister, and the first Conservative leader to win reelection in the twentieth century, with the greatest landslide since 1945. Some observers believe Thatcherism marks the end of the socialist era in Britain.

Trades Union Congress (TUC) A national association of 105 affiliated employee unions. The Trades Union Congress (TUC) includes most British unions, ranging from very large groups of over a million members to very small unions of less than a hundred. Total membership of the affiliated unions in 1981 was 11 million; the largest 14 unions enroll 75 percent of the total members. The TUC is primarily a coordinating body and has little authority over its affiliated unions, which are autonomous and have much larger budgets and staffs. The TUC holds an annual congress in which delegates representing unions cast crucial votes based on the number of members a union has. The annual congress receives reports, adopts policy motions, and elects the general council and general secretary. The general council is an executive body of 44 members, representing 18 different categories of trade groups, such as mining, transport, professional and clerical, and public employees. The general secretary lacks the power of leaders of the large unions and acts primarily as a coordinator and spokesman. The ideological approach of member unions varies; one finds the guild-like outlook of craft unions, the conservative approach of the General and Municipal Workers (GMWU), the democratic socialism of unions of public employees, and the confrontation style of the National Union of Mineworkers (NUM), which is led by the Marxist Arthur Scargill. *See also* TRADE UNIONS: BRITAIN, p. 69.

Significance Founded in 1868, the Trades Union Congress is the oldest labor organization of its type in the world. The TUC built on the experience of previous labor organizations in the 1830s, which were unsuccessful, and the Chartist movement, which pushed for electoral reforms. In an effort to gain labor representation in Parliament, the TUC played a predominant role in organizing the Labour Representation Committee (LRC) in 1900. When the Labour party developed from the LRC in 1906, trade unions comprised the largest share of the party's affiliated membership. Since the late nineteenth century the labor history of Britain is mostly that of the TUC. This history is marked by stormy and peaceful periods, by gains and losses, and since the 1970s, by an increasing number of confrontations with British Conservative and Labour governments. In February 1974, trade unionists, led by the TUC, helped defeat the government of Edward Heath on economic issues. But the subsequent Labour governments were not effective in solving Britain's problems. In the late 1970s and early 1980s, trade unionists, in association with socialists in the party, pushed through a number of left-wing positions, including (1) a party reform that gave unions 40 percent of the electoral college vote that selects a Labour party leader; (2) increased collectivization of industry; (3) withdrawal from the European Community; and (4) a foreign policy favoring unilateral nuclear disarmament. This leftward drift contributed to a split in the party and a drastic decline in voter support in the 1983 elections. The TUC has been influential in promoting international trade union organizations, including the International Labor Organization. After World War II, it helped organize the World Federation of Trade Unions (WFTU), but when communists became a disruptive force, the TUC with other groups founded the International Confederation of Free Trade Unions (ICFTU) in 1949.

Trade Unions: Britain Organizations of employees that engage in economic and political activity on behalf of their members. Most British trade unions are affiliated with the Trades Union Congress (TUC), a national federation that was first organized in 1868. The TUC comprises 105 affiliated unions that enroll 11 million of the 11.5 million trade union members in Britain (1981). The three largest unions have 40 percent of the TUC membership; they are the Transport and General Workers Union (TGWU), the Amalgamated Union of Engineering Workers (AUEW), and the General and Municipal Workers (GMWU). Two smaller but very active unions are the National Union of Mineworkers (NUM) and the National Union of Teachers (NUT). The NUT enrolls about 85 percent of the teachers in state-run schools. (In British usage, "public schools" are private, nongovernmental schools.) Most British unions are craft unions, which organize workers with particular skills, and general unions, which organize employees of all kinds. Industrial unions, which organize all workers in a particular industry, are less typical in Britain; two of the most important are the National Union of Mineworkers and the National Union of Railwaymen. The total number of unions has declined from 218 in 1918 to 108 in 1980, but civil service and white-collar unions have risen rapidly. White-collar unions, including office, civil service, teacher, and professional organizations, are as active in protecting jobs and promoting wage increases as general or industrial unions. Some of the more important white-collar unions are the National Union of Public Employees (NUPE), the Association of Scientific, Technical and Managerial Staffs (ASTMS), and the National and Local Government Officers Association (NALGO). Trade unions in Britain enroll about 50 percent of the work force, compared to 20 percent in the United States. *See also* THATCHERISM, p. 66; TRADES UNION CONGRESS (TUC), p. 67.

Significance The trade union movement in Britain is the oldest labor movement in the world and the largest in Western Europe. Unlike French unions, most British trade unions are organized in one national federation and are affiliated with one political party. TUC leaders helped organize the Labour Representation Committee in 1900, which became the Labour party in 1906; the TUC is a constituent part of the Labour party and provides most of its affiliated members and its funds. Always militant, the trade union movement became more active in the 1970s as economic recession, high inflation, and high unemployment seriously damaged worker income and job security. The winter of 1973–74 was especially disruptive as the oil embargo, fuel price rises, a miners' strike, and other protests combined to produce a three-day workweek in industry and plant shutdowns. In February 1974 Conservative Prime Minister Edward Heath focused his reelection campaign against unions on the theme "Who Shall Govern Britain?" He lost to the Labour party, which rescinded his restrictive industrial relations act of 1971. Labour governments under Harold Wilson and James Callaghan (1974–79) restored union rights and other measures favorable to employees. Labour worked out a cooperative scheme with the TUC called the "social contract," in which unions would hold down wage demands as part of an inflation-control program, but this ultimately broke down. When the Conservatives returned to power in 1979 under Margaret Thatcher, some labor legislation was repealed, and the Employment Act of 1980 was adopted. It restricted trade union practices such as mass picketing and reduced certain rights of employees. In 1984 the Thatcher government was again besieged by very disruptive strikes by mineworkers and dockworkers who protested against modernization plans that further curtailed jobs in a period of high unemployment. Despite the popular conception of the great power of unions in Britain, unions mostly have "negative power," the ability to prevent adoption of certain policies. Their "guild mentality," where job security is foremost over the public interest, has produced numerous strikes, but it has failed to prevent massive layoffs and high unemployment. One-third of the working class usually votes Conservative, and this was increased when unions and other groups moved the Labour party to doctrinaire left-wing positions in the 1983 elections.

Treasury Control The power of the Treasury department to regulate the expenditures and coordinate the programs of other government departments. The system of Treasury control and coordination is based on its authority to approve or disapprove proposed budgets (called "estimates"), new programs, and the transfer of money within departmental budgets. Major projects require prior approval by Treasury. By closely scrutinizing expenditures, Treasury exercises a type of interdepartmental coordination that prevents duplication of services and waste of resources. Other major functions of the Treasury department include controlling the collection of revenue and making payments from the Consolidated Fund in accordance with strict guidelines. The head of the department is the chancellor of the exchequer, who is usually the second-ranking officer in the cabinet after the prime minister. *See also* CABINET, p. 6; CIVIL SERVICE, p. 9.

Significance Because of its power to control expenditures, the Treasury department is the most powerful department within the British government. Disputes between other departments and Treasury must be taken to the cabinet if not reconciled beforehand. Prior to 1968, Treasury was also charged with the management of the civil service, and although part of this function has been transferred, it still maintains control over most public employees through its financial powers. For a period of time in the 1960s, the role of Treasury in coordinating national economic policy was transferred to a new agency, but this experiment failed. Treasury then resumed its role as the dominant department in the British system on all matters dealing with financial and economic policy.

Ulster In contemporary times, the northeastern portion of the island of Ireland that forms the province of Northern Ireland, which is a constituent part of the United Kingdom. Traditionally Ulster was the northern province of Ireland, comprising nine counties. In 1920 Ulster was split by Britain in the Government of Ireland Act, a home rule bill; three southernmost counties were awarded to southern Catholic Ireland, and the northernmost six counties to Protestant Ulster; both parts were to receive local self-government. In 1921 the Ulster parliament accepted the plan and the six counties formed Northern Ireland and remained united with Great Britain. The Irish government rejected this home rule plan; the three southern counties of Ulster were later incorporated into the Irish Free State when it was granted dominion status in 1922. For most practical purposes, "Ulster" is commonly used today to refer to Northern Ireland. *See also* NORTHERN IRELAND, p. 42; REPUBLIC OF IRELAND, p. 58.

Significance Britain divided the historic province of Ulster between Northern Ireland and the Irish Free State to maintain a secure Protestant majority in the north. The partition of Ulster was an integral part of the partition of Ireland, a plan acceptable to Ulster Protestants but not to Catholics. Despite the reduction in size of Ulster a substantial number of Catholics remained in the north, now constituting one-third of the population of Northern Ireland. Discriminations by the Ulster government against Catholics after 1922 provided additional fuel for Irish national movements that aimed to bring Ulster into the Republic of Ireland by peaceful or violent means. In 1937 Ireland was declared to be a sovereign state within the Commonwealth and in 1949 an independent republic. Although Ireland claims all of Ulster, it incorporates only the three southern counties as its province of Ulster, and the bulk of Ulster remains within the United Kingdom as Northern Ireland. In 1974 the Northern Ireland government collapsed in the face of increasing sectarian violence, and Britain assumed direct control over the province.

Ulster Unionists Protestant political groups that favor the union of Northern Ireland with Great Britain. Ulster Unionists have passed through various formations since the government of Northern Ireland was created in 1922. The Ulster Unionist party (UUP) dominated the government and enjoyed a measure of unity until the late 1960s, when its various factions split over concessions to Catholics. In 1975 most Unionists joined the United Ulster Unionist Coalition (UUUC), which contested the election for seats in a constitutional convention. The UUUC groups brought about the convention's demise with their opposition to a British proposal for a Protestant-Catholic power-sharing government. Currently, the largest Unionist party is the Official Unionist party (OUP) headed by James Molyneaux; the OUP is opposed to any power-sharing arrangement with Catholic parties and pushes hard for a strict majority rule system of government for Northern Ireland. William Craig, who in the mid-1970s headed the Vanguard Unionist party (VUP), which supported power sharing, disbanded the VUP and joined the OUP. The second-largest party in Northern Ireland is the Democratic Unionist party (DUP), which is led by the fundamentalist preacher the Reverend Ian Paisley of the evangelical Free Presbyterian Church. The DUP split from the UUP in 1971; it is strongly anti-Catholic and right-wing in its policy positions and has ties to the Ulster Workers' Council (UWC) and the Ulster Defence Association (UDA), the largest Protestant paramilitary group. Small unionist groups that contested the elections of 1982 are the United Ulster Unionist party (UUUP), and the Ulster Popular Unionist party (UPUP). The relative size of popular support for political parties is seen in the 1982 election for the Northern Ireland Assembly, which was based on proportional representation. With a 60 percent turnout, the results were: Official Unionist, 26 seats; Democratic Unionist, 21 seats; Social Democratic and Labour party (Catholic), 14 seats; Alliance party (nonsectarian), 10 seats; Provisional *Sinn Fein* (Catholic), 5 seats; Ulster Popular Unionist, 1 seat; and 1 seat to an independent Unionist. In the 1983 elections to the British parliament, using a single-member district plurality system, Official Unionists won 11 seats; Democratic Unionists, 3; Ulster Popular Unionist, 1; Social Democratic and Labour, 1; and Provisional Sinn Fein, 1. *See also* NORTHERN IRELAND, p. 42; NORTHERN IRELAND: POLITICAL GROUPS, p. 45.

Significance Ulster Unionists are the largest political force in Northern Ireland. They disagree over details of various plans for devolution of authority to Ulster, in their leadership style, relations with the United Kingdom government, and possible association with the Republic of Ireland. But they vary little from the fundamental principle that Northern Ireland be united with Britain and that an Ulster government be based on majority rule, not power sharing with Catholic groups. Those Unionists like former Ulster prime ministers Terence O'Neil, James D. Chichester-Clark, and Brian Faulkner, who attempted to adopt compromising policies or move Unionists to a power-sharing position, were driven from power. Before the troubles of the 1970s, Unionists associated with the Conservative party in United Kingdom affairs, but this ceased when Conservative governments continued Labour-initiated policies, such as direct rule from London and power-sharing constitutional proposals.

United Kingdom of Great Britain and Northern Ireland

The official name for the state commonly called Britain, Great Britain, or England. The United Kingdom of Great Britain and Northern Ireland (UK) comprises the historic kingdoms of England and Scotland, the principality of Wales, and the province of Northern Ireland. "Great Britain" is a geographic term for the large island of the British isles, which includes England, Scotland, and Wales. Northern Ireland, also called Ulster, is the northeastern part of the island of Ireland that remained united with Great Britain when Ireland became an independent republic in 1920. Although the constituent parts of the United Kingdom have separate identities, the UK has a unitary, not a federal, form of government, with all constitutional authority vested in the national parliament in Westminster. England and Wales are administered as a single unit, but Scotland has incorporated differences into its legal, educational, and local government systems. From 1920 until 1972, Northern Ireland had local home rule with a separate parliament, but it came under direct rule from London because of the sectarian violence that broke out in the late 1960s. An attempt at "devolution," creating separate parliaments for Scotland and Wales, failed when the plan was rejected in a popular referendum in 1979. The Channel Islands and the Isle of Man are distinct from the UK and are considered to be fiefdoms of the crown. The 13 remaining dependencies of the UK include Gibraltar, Bermuda, various islands in the Indian and Pacific Oceans, and the British Antarctic Territory. Most of the former colonies in the old British Empire are members of the Commonwealth, an intergovernmental association of independent states that includes the UK. The population of the United Kingdom in 1981 was about 56 million distributed as follows: England, 46.2 million; Scotland, 5.1 million; Wales, 2.8 million; and Northern Ireland, 1.2 million. *See also* BRITISH CONSTITUTION, p. 3; COMMONWEALTH, p. 11; NORTHERN IRELAND, p. 42; SCOTLAND, p. 60; WALES, p. 74.

Significance The United Kingdom is dominated by the culture, institutions, and traditions of the people of England, who comprise about 80 percent of the total. Although England is one of the oldest nation-states in the world, the political community that comprises the

United Kingdom is under strain, particularly over the issue of Northern Ireland. Additionally, several important developments have greatly affected the United Kingdom as a state in world affairs. These include its relative decline as a world diplomatic, military, trading, and financial power, the breakup of the British Empire after World War II, and the government's decision to join the European Community in 1972. Although the United Kingdom suffers from these internal pressures and international challenges, the state continues to show the stability and adaptability that has contributed to its success over centuries.

Wales   A principality that is an integral part of the United Kingdom. Wales was politically integrated with England in 1536, but it retained its distinctive language and folk culture, primarily in rural areas. The politics of Wales in the late nineteenth and early twentieth centuries was much affected by the growth of a nationalist spirit and the move to disestablish the Anglican Church of Wales. This was partially achieved in 1914 and fully in 1920. Nonconformists, especially Methodists and Baptists, are strong in Wales, particularly among the Welsh-speaking minority. In party politics, Wales supported the Liberal party strongly to 1922, when it shifted to Labour; Conservatives do poorly in the region. *Plaid Cymru* ("Party of Wales"), the nationalist party that first won a seat in Parliament in 1966, reflects the cultural and linguistic nationalism of the rural areas. Its goal is devolution—the transfer of local self-government powers to a regional assembly in Wales. This idea was seriously defeated in 1979 in a referendum when only 12 percent of the Welsh electorate supported the proposal. Wales has essentially the same local government and judicial system as England. There is a cabinet minister in charge of the Welsh Office, which administers functions for the region that are performed separately by several other departments for England. *See also* DEVOLUTION, p. 17; PLAID CYMRU, p. 50; UNITED KINGDOM OF GREAT BRITAIN AND NORTHERN IRELAND, p. 73.

Significance   In the electoral geography of Britain, Wales is part of the "Celtic fringe" that has strongly supported the Liberal and Labour parties. Although the Labour proposal for devolution of power to a Welsh assembly was overwhelmingly defeated, Plaid Cymru continues to retain the support of its rural constituents and win its normal complement of two seats. In 1979 Wales had only 36 of the 635 seats in Parliament, but the Welsh seats won by Labour are important in very close elections, such as those in 1964 and 1974. In 1983, the Conservative landslide, which amassed a majority of 144 seats, completely obscured the Welsh vote.

Welfare State A state in which the government directly provides the people with a substantial number of goods, services, and benefits. A welfare state has a wide range of public programs in areas such as education, health, housing, unemployment, occupational safety, disability, old-age pensions, and child, maternity, and family benefits. While most Western governments provide some or most of these benefits, a welfare state is commonly defined as one in which the cost of the public portion of the gross national product ranges from at least one-third to one-half of the total. Welfarism is often distinguished from socialism, which is defined as public ownership of the means of production in industry and agriculture, and in distribution, banking, and finance. A state may also choose to manage the economy in various degrees without nationalizing the means of production; the most extreme form of state management of the economy is called *dirigisme*. In practice, many Western states have a complex and shifting mixture of free enterprise, welfarism, socialism, and dirigisme, usually called a mixed economy. A welfare state goes far beyond providing relief for the poor and destitute; its goal is to improve the standard of living and provide opportunities for advancement for all the people. The welfare state brings government into people's daily lives as it provides programs "from the cradle to the grave." Government becomes large and complex, regulations abound (as, for example, determining eligibility for benefits), taxation is increased dramatically, and relationships between interest groups and government agencies become interlinked and mutually dependent. Only rich, industrialized states like Britain have the capacity to operate meaningful welfare state systems. *See also* LABOUR PARTY, p. 35; LIBERAL PARTY, p. 36; THATCHERISM, p. 66.

Significance In Britain the origins of the welfare state are found in the mid-nineteenth century, when the Liberal party enacted a number of social welfare measures; these were expanded in later decades to include measures dealing with housing, public health, workers' compensation, and regulation of the working hours of women and children. In the early twentieth century, Liberals added old-age pensions, health insurance, and unemployment insurance, and these programs were expanded by later Conservative governments. A major step toward a comprehensive welfare state was the 1942 Beveridge Report (of William Beveridge, a Liberal) that documented the need for substantial progress in combating "want, ignorance, idleness, squalor, and disease." When the Labour party assumed power in 1945, a host of new programs was adopted, including the National Health Service, which nationalized hospitals and provided for medical care and family allowances. The Labour government also nationalized some utilities and "sick" industries, such as coal and steel; it also attempted to regulate the economy to provide for full employment by utilizing Keynesian methods. Keynesianism is named after economist John Maynard Keynes, who called for government manipulation of taxes, credit, and public spending to maintain full employment. Since 1951, despite alternations of Conservative and Labour governments, welfare services have been maintained, but some industries, like steel, have gone through two full cycles of nationalization and denationalization. When Conservative Margaret Thatcher became prime minister in 1979, she attacked socialism and disruptive trade union practices, denationalized some industries, and attempted to use free market forces to regulate unemployment. But she retained welfare programs, defended the Health Service, and provided for increased benefits in at least ten social security and housing programs. The welfare state in Britain is very expensive, and has been criticized for stifling personal initiative and self-reliance. But it is politically popular, and, judging from most reports, has dramatically improved the health, education, housing, and income security of the people. The term "welfare state" is often used in a derogatory manner, but in Britain, public welfare services are considered by the people to be part of the normal functions of government.

Whigs and Tories   The two major English political groups that contested for power from the seventeenth to the early nineteenth centuries. Whigs favored parliamentary supremacy against royal absolutism and supported the Glorious Revolution of 1688 against James II. Tories defended royal absolutism, the doctrine of divine right of kings, and the Stuart kings. With the accession of William and Mary, whom some Tories supported, and the defeat of James II, Tories reverted to their role as strong defenders of the established monarchy and the Church of England. In the 150 years that followed, the two groups, both led by nobles, dominated Parliament in a system of greatly restricted suffrage. Tories were the more conservative group and were strengthened in their resolve after the French Revolution; they drew their support primarily from the landed gentry. The adoption of the electoral reform of 1832 greatly weakened the Tories, and the remaining adherents became the Conservative party. Whigs drew their support from religious dissenters and industrial interests. In the early nineteenth century, Whig leaders promoted parliamentary and electoral reform, which some of its aristocratic leaders resisted, however. Electoral reforms also affected the Whigs, although somewhat later. By the mid-1860s, Parliament was much changed by the newly enfranchised voters; the Whigs declined, and the last supporters were absorbed into the new Liberal party. *See also* CHARTERS AND ACTS, p. 8; CONSERVATIVE PARTY, p. 12; LIBERAL PARTY, p. 36.

Significance The historic Whigs and Tories were primarily two factions in Parliament; both were drawn from the upper classes, and both faded from existence when suffrage was extended to common people. Neither group was a political party in the modern sense. While the modern Liberal and Conservative parties can trace their origins to these parliamentary groups, the origins of the Labour party are much later and outside Parliament. The words "Whig" and "Tory" were originally terms of abuse. "Whig" first referred to Scottish ecclesiastical rebels and then to English Protestant nonconformists; and "Tory" first referred to Irish robbers, and later to English defenders of a Catholic heir to the English throne. "Whig" has fallen into disuse, but members of the modern Conservative party are often referred to as "Tories."

2. France

Action Français A rightist political movement that was founded in 1898 and was active until 1944. Organized by the literary figure Charles Maurras, *Action Français* was antidemocratic and opposed to the Third Republic, supporting monarchy and traditional Catholicism. An extremely nationalistic and anti-Semitic organization, it strongly supported the army in the Dreyfus Affair. Although Action Français was condemned by the pope in 1926, the movement was backed by some French churchmen. In the 1930s the organization became fascistic and its militant, uniformed wing, the *Camelots du Roi*, engaged in street fighting. Although Action Français was originally anti-German, after France's defeat in World War II, it strongly supported the Vichy Regime. The movement declined after the war, and in 1945 Maurras was condemned to life imprisonment for collaborationism. *See also* POPULAR FRONT, p. 130; THIRD REPUBLIC, p. 148.

Significance Action Français was one of several antirepublican groups hostile to the Third Republic, but it never had much popular backing. The movement gained notice because of the intellectual appeal of the traditionalist, Catholic, anti-Semitic, and nationalistic writings of its ideologist, Charles Maurras. In the 1930s, it was one of several protofascist and nationalistic organizations, like the *Jeunesses Patriotes* (Young Patriots) and *Croix de Feu* (Fiery Cross), that tried to bring down the government through street fighting. This helped to unite the leftist parties into the Popular Front. The history of Action Français exposes the dissensual nature of French society, but given its anti-Semitism, fascist-like activities, and pro-Vichy support, it could not survive World War II.

Algerian Crisis of 1958   Events leading to the demise of the Fourth Republic following the taking of power by European extremists and the French military in Algeria. The Algerian Crisis was precipitated when French settlers in Algeria rioted and elements of the French army under the paratroop general Jacques Massu staged a coup d'etat in Algiers on May 13, 1958. With the cooperation of the army commander in Algeria, Raoul Salan, and the former minister, Jacques Soustelle, the settlers and the army organized a committee of public safety and called for Charles de Gaulle to take power in France. Paratroopers soon flew to Corsica, the island joined in the revolt, and a civil war in metropolitan France was threatened. The French premier, Pierre Pflimlin, unable to control the situation and unwilling to accept Communist votes for resisting the revolt, resigned. This prompted President René Coty to threaten to resign unless the National Assembly chose de Gaulle as premier, which it did on June 1, 1958. Taking office on his own terms, de Gaulle demanded full powers and the right to draft a new constitution, which were granted. The Assembly then adjourned, and the rebels in Algeria accepted de Gaulle's government. As the last premier of the Fourth Republic, de Gaulle ruled for six months with a nonpartisan cabinet that included former ministers. The new constitution of the Fifth Republic was ratified by the people in September 1958. *See also* ALGERIAN WAR, p. 80.

Significance   The Algerian Crisis of 1958 exposed the inherent weaknesses of the Fourth Republic and thus led to its demise. The French government, crippled with instability and political immobility, had reached an impasse over Algeria; it could neither win the war against the Algerian Arab nationalists, nor could it give Algeria independence. When Pflimlin's government was voted into power in May 1958, it was after a series of short-lived cabinets and a governmental crisis lasting one month. The identification of the army with the European settlers in Algeria and their revolt against established authority showed the shallowness of loyalty to the Fourth Republic. Although the revolt succeeded in overthrowing the governmental system in France, the Algerian war continued, and the major aim of the rebels to keep Algeria French was ultimately frustrated.

Algerian War   The war for Algerian independence fought by France against Arab nationalists from 1954 to 1962. The Algerian War broke out in 1954 after Arab nationalists formed the National Liberation Front (FLN), and its military arm, the National Liberation Army (ALN), began attacking government and army posts. French settlers in Algeria (*colons*), who made up 10 percent of the Algerian population, wanted

Algeria to remain integrated with France; this was reflected in their war cry, "*Algérie français.*" The French army became increasingly identified with the settlers; high-ranking officers opposed government concessions to the Arab community or to the nationalists. The FLN set up a government-in-exile in Tunisia and was aided by Tunisia and Morocco. As the guerrilla war became increasingly brutal and violent, outrageous acts of terrorism, atrocities, torture, and cruelty were committed by both sides, particularly after the army was granted police powers. In May 1958 the settlers and army units staged a coup d'etat in Algiers; this led to the downfall of the Fourth Republic, the coming into power of Charles de Gaulle, and the creation of the Fifth Republic. De Gaulle's Constantine Plan for the social and economic development of Algeria had little impact. Believing that integration with France was not a viable solution, and supported by a 75 percent favorable referendum vote, he moved to give the Algerian people a choice between independence and autonomy within the French Community. A revolt by European settlers and army units was put down in January 1960. De Gaulle survived plots and attempts on his life by the terrorist Secret Army Organization (OAS) of the European extremists led by General Raoul Salan. The "Generals' Revolt" of April 1961 in Algeria was also put down, and Salan and other high-ranking officers were arrested. In March 1962, after negotiations with the Algerian nationalists, France in the Evian Accords agreed to Algerian independence. The Evian Accords were ratified by a 99 percent favorable vote in Algeria and an 80 percent vote in France. Algeria became independent on July 3, 1962. *See also* ALGERIAN CRISIS OF 1958, p. 80.

Significance No other postwar problem had such important repercussions for France as the Algerian War. The war ripped French society apart, particularly as the terrorism and atrocities committed by both sides became widespread. Most importantly, the war led directly to the fall of the Fourth Republic and the installation of a new constitutional system. At its height, a half-million French troops were stationed in Algeria; over 100,000 Arab fighters and civilians were killed along with 10,000 French soldiers. The French army was again disgraced, this time by its brutalities and the disloyalty of its highest officers. When Algeria became independent, over 750,000 European settlers left the country for France; they were eventually followed by the remaining 250,000 Europeans. The war also led to the peaceful liquidation of the French empire in Africa as other territories made demands for full independence. The old French ideal of establishing a large community of self-governing territories integrated with France died. After 132 years of French rule, Algeria became independent, and France had a new constitutional system that enabled it to move forward on other problems.

Ancien Régime The monarchical system that was destroyed by the French Revolution of 1789. In the *ancien régime,* controlled by the Bourbon dynasty since the sixteenth century, the king had absolute authority and governed by a claim of divine right. The king was supported by two social classes, the clergy and the nobility, both of which had special privileges. The entire society was divided into three classes: the First Estate (clergy), the Second Estate (nobility), and the Third Estate, comprising peasants, workers, and the middle class (bourgeoisie) of commercial, professional, and artisan groups. Prior to the revolution, the Third Estate included about 97 percent of the population of 25 million, four-fifths of whom were peasants. A general assembly, the Estates General, was summoned occasionally by the king, but it had no independent power, and it did not meet from 1614 to 1789. The power of weak kings was checked at times by the *Parlement* of Paris, which was a law court with advisory powers. See also REVOLUTION OF 1789, p. 139.

Significance In its final 100 years, the ancien régime brought France under a centralized political authority and established a hierarchical administrative system. The Bourbon kings destroyed early moves to constitutionalism, delayed social reform, and lived an extravagant life. The administrative system was wasteful, inefficient, and corrupt. The government intervened into all sectors of economic life (*étatism,* or statism), and imposed an inequitable taxation system on the people. Unwilling to evolve into a constitutional monarchy, the ancien régime effectively prepared the ground for the great Revolution of 1789.

Bonapartism A political system that is based on strong executive power, a personalistic political movement, loyalty to the chief of state, and the use of plebiscites. In Bonapartism, a strong personality, often with a military background, establishes a mass-based political movement and takes control of government. The assembly continues to be popularly elected, but it is weak. The chief of state (a king, emperor, or president) at crucial times stages plebiscites to establish his legitimacy, confirm his policies, and defeat his opponents. See also GAULLISM: POLITICAL DOCTRINE, p. 116.

Significance Bonapartism and republicanism have struggled against one another in France since the Revolution of 1789. Whereas Bonapartism stresses strong executive government and plebiscitary democracy, republicanism would forego plebiscites, strengthen the assembly, and recognize the deputy as the true representative of the people. Napoleon Bonaparte initiated Bonapartism when he took executive power and had himself confirmed as emperor by a popular vote. In the mid-nineteenth century, the term was used to identify the political system and supporters of Napoleon III. After World War II, "Bonapartism" has been used to describe the political ideas, personal style, and governmental system of Charles de Gaulle. Even though de Gaulle retained the republican form of government, his push for a strong presidency and the use of referenda made him a Bonapartist in his opponents' eyes. The term "Bonapartism" is also used by theorists to categorize the Gaullist-type system, but when used in political discourse, it has pejorative connotations.

Bourbon Restoration The rule of the House of Bourbon after the defeat of Napoleon, from 1814 to 1830. The Bourbon Restoration was accomplished by the allied powers that defeated Napoleon, and it was confirmed as part of the reestablishment of the "legitimate" dynasties and territories at the Congress of Vienna in 1815. The first Bourbon king, Louis XVIII, agreed to a constitutional order and retained many of the reforms of the revolutionary and Napoleonic periods. But eventually he fell under the influence of the ultraroyalists, reactionaries who wanted to purge republicans and Bonapartists, to return property to former owners, and to reestablish former privileges of the nobility. The second king, Charles X, tried to restore the absolute, divine monarchy and reestablish the authority of the Catholic church. When he dissolved a liberal assembly, further restricted the suffrage, and imposed censorship, the people of Paris rose in the July Revolution of 1830. The new moderate assembly called Louis Phillipe of the House of Orléans to reign as a constitutional monarch. *See also* JULY MONARCHY, p. 120.

Significance The Bourbon Restoration failed either to return France to the governmental and social systems of the *ancien régime* or to adapt to the bourgeoisie's desire for a constitutional monarchy. The restoration did little to bring social peace to France, and its prochurch policies contributed to strong anticlericalism and religious controversies later in the nineteenth century. The government's assertive foreign policy was largely successful, taking Algiers in 1830, but this did not save the regime, and no Bourbon ruled after 1830. In the end, the regime was overthrown because, as history records, "the Bourbons learned nothing and they forgot nothing."

Business Associations: France Organizations of commercial and industrial employers in the private sector. The largest business association is the National Council of French Employers (*Conseil National du Patronat Français*, CNPF), often referred to as the *patronat*. This is an umbrella organization, primarily representing big business interests. It includes some 5,000 commercial and industrial geographical groups and about 400 national trade associations. Individual firms are not direct members, but through their associations about 900,000 firms are included. Before the nationalizations of 1982, the patronat firms employed about six million persons. Smaller and middle-sized employers are organized by the General Confederation of Small and Medium-Sized Enterprises (CGPME, or usually, PME). PME is affiliated with the patronat, but it is primarily concerned with defending the interests of the family-owned company. Radical associations in defense of the small shopkeeper and artisan have surfaced in the postwar period with notorious results. In the mid-1950s, the Poujadists, followers of a shopkeeper leader of the Association for the Defense of Shopkeepers and Artisans (UDCA), organized a political party and won a large bloc of seats in the assembly. In the 1970s, the same interests were organized into the CID-UNATI (Committee of Information and Defense–National Union of Artisans and Independent Workers). Led by the cafe owner, Gérard Nicoud, the group engaged in raids on government offices, demonstrations, street battles with police, and kidnappings of tax collectors. Although Nicoud was arrested, the organization won some concessions in its fight against bigness and modernization. *See also* NATIONALIZATIONS OF 1982, p. 127; POUJADISM, p. 132.

Significance Associations of businesses are fragmented according to product, size, and degree of modernization. Although all are defenders of private enterprise, the CID-UNATI has protested against the "technocapitalist" class of big business interests. The CNPF is extremely well financed and powerful; its various trade associations employ 7,000 staff members. Although the CNPF was generally sympathetic to the modernizing and business-oriented governments of presidents Charles de Gaulle, Georges Pompidou, and Valéry Giscard d'Estaing, it sometimes opposed their policies. The patronat took a strong position against the plans of the Socialist government of François Mitterrand in 1981 to nationalize large sectors of industry and finance. When the nationalization bill was adopted in 1982, the association became less hostile; some of the executives of the nationalized firms were retained by the government to continue administering the nationalized companies. Despite the nationalizations, 70 percent of the sales of industrial products are still in the private sector.

Center of Social Democrats (CDS) A small democratic center party that coalesces with the parliamentary alliance of Republicans, centrists, and Radicals called the Union for French Democracy. The

Center of Social Democrats (*Centre des Démocrates Sociaux,* CDS) is the current expression of the politicians who reorganized the center following the collapse of the Popular Republican Movement (MRP) in the early 1960s. In 1966, MRP leader Jean Lecanuet joined with other centrists to form the Democratic Center party to counter the socialist-communist left and the Gaullist right. The attempt was not successful, and after de Gaulle resigned the presidency in 1969, the center split into pro-Gaullist and anti-Gaullist parties. The anti-Gaullist left wing organized the Progress and Modern Democracy party (PDM) and the pro-Gaullist deputies followed Jacques Duhamel into the Center for Democracy and Progress (CDP). Later another alliance of centrists and Radicals, called the Reformers' Movement, backed Valéry Giscard d'Estaing's successful bid for the presidency in 1974. In 1976 the Center of Social Democrats was formed by the merger of Lecanuet's Democratic Center and Duhamel's Center for Democracy and Progress. The CDS party has a pro-European, social reform program; it favors worker self-management in industry and is opposed to unregulated free enterprise. The CDS joined the government majority of President Giscard d'Estaing, 1974–81, and it is part of the electoral and parliamentary alliance, the Union for French Democracy (UDF), also known as the Giscardians. Along with other UDF parties, the CDS suffered from the Socialist victories in the presidential and parliamentary elections of 1981. In the National Assembly, the CDS group fell from 36 to 19 deputies. *See also* FIFTH REPUBLIC: POLITICAL PARTY SYSTEM, p. 100; POPULAR REPUBLICAN MOVEMENT (MRP), p. 131.

Significance   The Center of Social Democrats is the latest manifestation of a secularized Christian Democratic movement in France. In the European Parliament the CDS associates with the Christian Democratic group, the European People's Party. In France, the Christian Democratic movement has been surpassed by political developments, and its social base of support has been lost to the Gaullists and to the Republican party. The bipolarization of French politics into the socialist-communist left and the Gaullist right has practically eliminated any possibility that an independent center, even combined with the Republicans and right-wing Radicals in the Union for French Democracy, can play an important role. In the Giscard presidency, the UDF needed the larger Gaullist party to make a majority.

Code Law System   The legal system of France, which is based on compilations of enacted laws classified by subject matter called codes. The code law system, sometimes called a civil law system, contrasts with the common law system of judge-made law that is used in Great Britain and the United States. In France the codes regulate all spheres of life and serve as the basis for judicial decisions. Typical codes deal with such civil matters as commercial law, criminal procedures, family relations, property, and maritime law. In the code law system, the law is readily accessible and is uniform throughout the nation. The disadvantages of the system are that the codes must be periodically revised by the legislature or the rules will become outmoded, and that the codes can be inflexible when confronted by circumstances unforeseen by the lawmakers. Another revision of the codes was undertaken in the Fifth Republic. *See also* JUDICIAL SYSTEM: FRANCE, p. 119.

Significance The French code law system is based on the great modernization and consolidation of the Roman law codes that was undertaken by Napoleon. The *Code Napoléon* was very influential and was widely imitated throughout Europe, Latin America, and other regions of the world. In France the code law system provides uniformity of treatment of citizens, protection of rights, and an inexpensive and speedy administration of justice.

Commune of Paris The revolutionary government of the city of Paris in 1871, which refused to accept the new French national government after the fall of the Second Empire of Napoleon III in the Franco-Prussian War. Dominated by republicans, the Commune of Paris objected to the harsh peace terms agreed to by the national government of Adolphe Thiers, which was supported by a monarchist national assembly. Paris rebels refused to disarm as ordered by French troops, and the city council declared the Commune of Paris in March 1871. Thiers ordered the army to lay siege to the city, and Paris was retaken in very bloody and destructive street fighting in May 1871. About 20,000 Communards were killed or executed, and thousands were jailed, deported to penal colonies, or went into exile. The Communards, in turn, burned public buildings and shot hostages, including the archbishop of Paris. *See also* FRANCO-PRUSSIAN WAR, p. 109.

Significance The suppression of the Commune of Paris resulted in the bloodiest civil war in French history, and Paris suffered more destruction than in any national war. The membership of the Commune government was dominated by radical republicans, socialists, and anarchists who lacked sufficient unity to make major social reforms. Their insurrection and suppression, however, served as symbolic acts and created a set of martyrs that has been used by the revolutionary left in France and abroad ever since.

Constituent Assembly The popularly elected body that drafted the constitution of the Fourth Republic and approved the presidents of the Provisional Government. The Constituent Assembly was chosen in the first postwar election of October 1945 by a system of proportional representation, and it came to be dominated by the three mass parties that fought in the Resistance—the Communists, the Popular Republic Movement (MRP, Christian Democrats), and the Socialists. Charles de Gaulle was approved as the head of the government, but he resigned in January 1946 when partisan politics in the Assembly blocked his proposals. The first constitution drafted by the Assembly featured a single-chamber legislature and a weak presidency; this was rejected by the people in a national referendum in October 1946. A second Assembly was elected; the MRP increased its seats, and its leader George Bidault became the head of the government. The second Assembly produced a constitution essentially similar to the first, again rejecting de Gaulle's proposals for a strong presidency. This draft was approved by the voters in October 1946 and became the constitution of the Fourth Republic. *See also* PROVISIONAL GOVERNMENT p. 133.

Significance The political parties that controlled the Constituent Assembly reflected the same constitutional preferences that predominated in the Third Republic. Although the Radicals declined and were replaced by the MRP, the constitutional ideas of the republican left that placed power in a popular assembly prevailed. The attempt by de Gaulle to use his postwar popularity and prestige to bring about a change in the constitutional structures or in political party influence failed. The constitutional system generated by the Assembly lasted but 12 years, from 1946 to 1958, to be replaced by the constitution of the Fifth Republic, which was based on de Gaulle's ideas. During this period of 12 years, 23 governments were instituted under the constitution of the Fourth Republic.

Constitutional Council A major government organ that exercises quasi-judicial review powers and performs other functions. The Constitutional Council was authorized by the Constitution of 1958 to rule on the constitutionality of "organic laws," which relate to the organization of the public powers, and of standing orders (rules of procedure) of the two houses of Parliament before they are promulgated. Laws and treaties may also be submitted to the council before they are promulgated for a definitive ruling on their constitutionality. Appeals to the council may only be made by the president of the republic, the prime minister, the president of the National Assembly, the president of the Senate, or (since 1974) by 60 members of the National Assembly or 60 members of the Senate. Provisions declared unconstitutional may not be promulgated nor appealed to any other body. The council also performs other functions. It supervises presidential elections and referenda and proclaims the results, and it decides disputes concerning the election of deputies and senators. The council must be consulted by the president whenever he intends to declare a state of emergency under Article 16 of the Constitution, and it is also consulted by the president on the measures he intends to take in the emergency. When petitioned by the government, the council may also certify whether the president is physically incapable of performing the functions of the office. The Constitutional Council consists of nine appointed members who serve nine-year terms. One-third of the council is renewed every three years, and members may not be reappointed. Three members are appointed by the president, three by the president of the National Assembly, and three by the president of the Senate. In addition to the appointed members, former presidents of the republic are *ex officio* members for life. See also JUDICIAL SYSTEM: FRANCE, p. 119.

Significance The most important function of the Constitutional Council is its authority to rule on the constitutionality of pending legislation. The council was not intended to be a court of last resort with full powers of judicial review similar to the West German Constitutional Court. Private citizens may not appeal to the council; the council may rule on proposals only before they are promulgated, and its members need not be lawyers. In the first decade of its existence the council was ineffectual and usually supported the government's interpretation of the Constitution in legislative-executive jurisdictional disputes. The council has acted more independently since 1971, when it declared unconstitutional a bill restricting the right of association for groups alleged to be subversive. The 1974 constitutional change permitting either 60 deputies or 60 senators to appeal to the council has in effect given the opposition the power to challenge the legislative acts of the government. An increasing number of bills, especially those concerning civil liberties, have been referred to the council by opposition legislators and nominal government supporters. Since 1978, the council has ruled all or part of a law unconstitutional in seven instances. In 1982 the council ruled that the extensive socialist nationalizations were constitutionally permissible but the government's bill was unconstitutional in several respects, including its failure to provide adequate compensation to the former shareholders. The government repassed an amended bill and increased the compensation by over one billion dollars. Generally, however, the council has practiced judicial restraint, and has recently approved bills permitting abortion, and decentralization and regionalization of government. Although France has no tradition of judicial review and the authority of the Constitutional Council is limited, this constitutional innovation in the Fifth Republic has established an additional method whereby legislators and political minorities can effectively challenge the government.

Constitutional Dissensus Widespread disagreement over the form of government by which the society should be ruled. French politics has been characterized by a perennial constitutional dissensus since the Revolution of 1789. Three major constitutional forms have contested for power: (1) the monarchical or imperial type, which is headed by a king or emperor; (2) the republic, in which power is located mainly in the assembly; and (3) the Bonapartist type, which may be either a monarchy or a republic, but is always dominated by a strong chief of state who often turns to the people for support through plebiscitary democracy. Since 1789, France has had at least 16 different regimes; some writers, preferring to count every constitution and provisional government, have a larger total. One can, for example, enumerate five different "constitutions" in the period from 1789 to 1804. A simplified listing of the major periods in constitutional history since 1789 includes the following: House of Bourbon, to 1792; First Republic, 1792–1804; First Empire, 1804–14, and in 1815; Bourbon Restoration, 1814–30; House of Orléans, 1830–48; Second Republic, 1848–52; Second Empire, 1852–70; Third Republic, 1870–1940; Vichy Regime, 1940–44; Provisional Government, 1944–46; Fourth Republic, 1946–58; Fifth Republic, since 1958. *See also* SOCIOECONOMIC THEORY: CONSENSUS THESIS, p. 144; SOCIOECONOMIC THEORY: STALEMATE SOCIETY THESIS, p. 147.

Significance The French constitutional dissensus is often cited by political analysts as the fundamental cause for the lack of a continuous, effective governmental system in France. Underlying reasons for this dissensus have been traced to (1) the political culture, which promotes civic irresponsibility and ambivalence to authority; (2) the uneven development of the economy, which has retained large numbers of unmodernized socioeconomic groups; (3) the unwillingness of traditional and conservative forces to yield power to the bourgeoisie or the working class; and (4) the inability of reformist or revolutionary forces to agree on constitutional forms and public policy. Despite the constitutional dissensus, France has displayed remarkable national unity in certain periods. Since the mid-1970s, the constitutional system of the Fifth Republic, which was unacceptable to many people when Charles de

Gaulle was president, has been accepted by parties of the republican left as a means to achieve their socialist goals.

Council of State   A multifunctional institution that acts as the nation's highest court of administrative law and as an advisory body to the government on legislative and administrative matters. The Council of State (*Conseil d'État*) is composed of about 200 members, each of whom is assigned to one of its five sections. The judicial section acts as the high court on cases concerned with administrative law, a branch of law which deals with the proper use of legal authority by administrative officials. Citizens may challenge the arbitrary use of power or the legality of administrative decisions by appealing to the administrative law courts. These questions are not considered by the regular court system, but are handled in a separate network of administrative courts. The Council of State stands at the apex of the system and takes cases on appeal and has original jurisdiction in certain types of important cases. The other functions of the council, which are performed by other sections, are to give advice to the government on such matters as: the language of draft bills; the legality of bureaucratic regulations and executive decrees; and the constitutionality of the government's interpretation of the constitution. This advice does not need to be followed by the government, but given the prestige of the Council, it usually is. *See also* CODE LAW SYSTEM, p. 85; JUDICIAL SYSTEM: FRANCE, p. 119; GRAND CORPS, p. 117.

Significance   The Council of State is one of the most prestigious bodies that make up the *grand corps* of powerful, elite administrative agencies. In its role as the high court of administrative law, the council has developed a reputation for integrity, impartiality, and independence from government interference. It rules by case law, not code law, and has established an impressive body of law that protects the citizen against arbitrary government action. Although cases take a long time to be resolved, the process is simple and inexpensive. In its advisory role to the government, its recommendations are usually but not always followed. In 1962 President de Gaulle refused to accept the council's view that the referendum process he was using to amend the Constitution for the direct election of the president was an unconstitutional procedure. In other cases, however, he accepted the council's opinion.

Declaration of the Rights of Man and Citizen   The historic statement of natural rights adopted by the National Assembly in 1789 during the French Revolution. The Declaration of the Rights of Man and Citizen proclaims the doctrines of natural rights, popular sovereignty, the legal equality of all citizens, and government by consent of the governed. The "natural and imprescriptible rights of man" are listed as "liberty, property, security, and resistance to oppression." The document guarantees freedom of speech, press, opinion, and religion. The rights of a person accused of crime are also delineated. *See also* REVOLUTION OF 1789, p. 139.

Significance The Declaration of the Rights of Man and Citizen was influenced by the American Declaration of Independence and by the French intellectuals of the Enlightenment (*philosophes*). The Declaration ranks as one of the great documents of the natural rights philosophy and has greatly influenced liberal thought in the nineteenth century and contemporary human rights philosophy. The document is a clear statement of the principles of the French Revolution. It was incorporated into the Constitution of 1781, and it became a continuing reference for republicans in later periods. The Declaration was "reaffirmed" in the Preamble of the Constitution of 1946 (Fourth Republic), which listed other rights, and it was "proclaimed" along with the 1946 Preamble in the Constitution of 1958 (Fifth Republic). Along with the Declaration of Independence, the Declaration of the Rights of Man and Citizen stands as one of the two great documents that have influenced the course of modern history.

Economic and Social Council An advisory body created by the constitution that is consulted by the government on economic and social matters. Members of the Economic and Social Council are chosen by labor, business, farm, and other economic, social, and cultural groups, and by the government. The government consults the council on relevant bills in the parliament, the national economic plan, and other economic and social matters.

Significance The Economic and Social Council has existed under various names since 1924; in the Fourth Republic it was called the Economic Council. Although reports of the council have been of a high quality, the body has not been effective in influencing the government. The creation of the council reflects the continuing desire in France to establish a type of interest group representation in government, known as functional representation or corporatism. In 1969 a proposed constitutional amendment failed that would have merged the Senate with the council and had the senators appointed by interest groups and the government.

Elections of 1981: France Presidential and parliamentary elections that resulted in the transfer of government power to the Socialists for the first time in the Fifth Republic. In the presidential election of May 1981, the Socialist leader François Mitterrand defeated incumbent President Valéry Giscard d'Estaing in the runoff ballot by 52 percent to 48 percent of the popular votes cast. Other major candidates in the first-round balloting were the Gaullist leader Jacques Chirac and the Communist leader Georges Marchais. The voter turnout was very high at 86 percent of the registered electorate. Following his taking office, President Mitterrand dissolved the National Assembly and called for legislative elections in June. The parties organized themselves into the following electoral alliances: (1) the Union for the New Majority, the alliance of the former government majority parties, i.e., the centrists (UDF) and the Gaullists (RPR); (2) the Socialists and the Leftist Radical Movement (MRG); and (3) for the second round of balloting, the Socialists and the Communists. At the conclusion of the second round, the Socialists emerged with an absolute majority in the National Assembly; the Gaullist, UDF centrists, and the Communist parties lost seats. President Mitterrand refashioned a coalition government of the leftist parties, although a coalition was not necessary to make a majority. The Socialist prime minister, Pierre Mauroy, was reappointed, and four Communists were brought into the cabinet in less important posts, along with several representatives of the Leftist Radical Movement and the Movement of Democrats, a small center-left party. The Communist party and the Socialist party issued a joint statement as part of an agreement whereby Communists would receive cabinet posts. The statement called for social and economic reform, defended foreign policy principles that showed continuity with the previous government, and supported the European Community. It also called for the withdrawal of Soviet troops from Afghanistan and expressed the hope that the people of Poland without interference would complete their program of economic, social, and democratic renewal. *See also* ELECTORAL SYSTEM: PRESIDENT, p. 94; ELECTORAL SYSTEM: TWO-BALLOT SYSTEM, p. 96; FIFTH REPUBLIC: POLITICAL PARTY SYSTEM, p. 100.

Significance The Socialist victories in the presidential and parliamentary elections of 1981 represented a major change in the politics of the Fifth Republic. Although Socialists had been premiers in the Third and Fourth Republics, their power was limited by the weak executive system and unstable legislative coalitions. In control of a strong executive and a large assembly majority, President Mitterrand proceeded to do what the Socialist party had promised: nationalize the large industrial and financial companies; reform the local government system; and adopt other social programs. The Communists, no longer isolated in

French politics, entered the government for the first time since 1947. This was done with much debate within the party, for the leadership essentially agreed to support the pro-Western and nationalistic foreign policy of President Mitterrand, which was not much different from that of previous presidents. The 1981 elections also eliminated the Gaullists from the government for the first time in the 23-year history of the Fifth Republic, although they had previously lost the presidency to Giscard d'Estaing in 1974. The constitutional system gained more legitimacy because it made possible the transfer of effective power peacefully to the former opponents of the regime. The French people themselves acted in a responsible fashion in the assembly elections in June, for having elected a Socialist president, they prevented a political impasse by giving the Socialists a strong legislative majority.

Electoral System: Party List System   A system of proportional representation used in the Fourth Republic that provided a relatively close ratio between the percentage of the popular vote received by a political party and the percentage of seats won in the Assembly. The party list system was used in two elections for the Constituent Assembly (1945 and 1946) and in the 1946, 1951, and 1956 elections for the Chamber of Deputies. In the party list system of proportional representation (PR), the voter casts a ballot for a list of candidates of a political party. Candidates are elected from the party list in priority order (topmost first) according to a formula for determining proportionality. In France, under the Fourth Republic, the electoral district size was small, usually the department, with each electing about three to five members of the Assembly. In the first three postwar elections, the "highest average" formula for allocating seats was used, and this formula combined with small-size districts slightly benefited the larger parties. In the 1951 and 1956 elections, a less proportional, highly complex, modified party list system was used. Electoral alliances between parties (called *apparentements*) were permitted, and the method of allocating seats was changed to the "largest remainder" formula, which tends to benefit smaller parties. A different system was used in the Paris region. Voters were also given the right to use *panachage*, the opportunity to delete names from a party list and add names from other party lists. The party list system was also used in three elections in the Third Republic. *See also* ELECTORAL SYSTEM: TWO-BALLOT SYSTEM, p. 96; FOURTH REPUBLIC: POLITICAL PARTY SYSTEM p. 108.

Significance   The party list system of proportional representation emphasizes political party philosophy or program over individual candidates. Although it provides a system of fair representation (understood as proportionality) that may coincide with the people's idea of "representative justice," it gives power to leaders who prepare the party list. The *panachage* system that gave voters the option in 1951 and 1956 to rearrange the official lists was not used much by voters. Of more importance in these two elections was the shift to permit electoral alliances, whereby smaller parties would submit joint lists and then split the winnings after the election. This change was engineered by the Third Force (Socialist, Radicals, MRP, and Independents) to preserve their power against the Communists and the Gaullists. Although proportional representation tends to perpetuate a multiparty system and contribute to cabinet instability, multipartyism in France was more evident in the Third Republic, which used a nonproportional system in most elections. Manipulation of the electoral system has been a constant feature of French politics since the Third Republic, but when the Third Force shifted to a less proportional system in 1951 it did not lessen cabinet instability. The party list system was dropped in the Fifth Republic for the two-ballot system.

Electoral System: President A direct popular election that uses the majority runoff system. In the presidential election system used since 1965, the president of the republic is elected directly by universal suffrage for a seven-year term. Candidates must be at least 23 years of age and must be sponsored by at least 500 national legislators, local councillors, or members of the Economic and Social Council from at least ten departments. A candidate winning an absolute majority of the votes cast on the first ballot is elected. If none has a majority, a runoff election is held two weeks later between the two candidates with the greatest number of votes. In the runoff ballot the candidate receiving the majority is elected. A candidate eligible for the runoff may withdraw in favor of another candidate, but no one has yet done so. The direct popular method of election was adopted by constitutional amendment in 1962 and was used in the elections of 1965, 1969, 1974, and 1981. In the first election for president of the Fifth Republic that was held in 1958, an indirect election system was used. In that election, an electoral college composed of about 80,000 national legislators and local councillors chose the president using the majority runoff system. The presidents of the Fifth Republic have been: Charles de Gaulle, 1959–69; Georges Pompidou, 1969–74; Valéry Giscard d'Estaing, 1974–81; and François Mitterrand, elected in 1981. Senate president Alain Poher twice served as acting president when the office fell vacant: in 1969 when de Gaulle resigned, and in 1974 when Pompidou died in office. *See also* FIFTH REPUBLIC: PRESIDENT, p. 101; REFERENDUM POWER, p. 136.

Significance The direct election method for choosing the president has increased the legitimacy of the office and has received widespread popular support. The constitutional amendment of 1962 that provided for a popular vote was adopted by 78 percent of the voters; voter turnout in presidential elections has been high, as much as 86 percent of the eligible voters. Although parties of the republican left opposed the 1962 amendment because a popular election of the president would damage their claim that the deputy was the only true representative of the people, they came to accept the system. The majority requirement using the runoff principle assures that the winner has broad popular support, but it also gives the voter a chance to express a protest against an incumbent knowing that the voter can have a second chance to vote for that person on the second ballot.

Electoral System: Senate An indirect election system in which Senators are chosen by departmental electoral colleges composed primarily of municipal councillors. The total number of electors in the electoral system for the Senate of the Fifth Republic is about 110,000. Ninety-seven percent of the electors are members of municipal councils, the other electors being members of departmental general councils and national deputies. Each department has at least one senator, and large departments have several, depending on size. The electoral college within each department is composed of municipal and general councillors and national deputies from the department, with the size of the college varying with the population. Larger municipalities have more electors. Senators are elected by a majority runoff system in most departments, but the 7 large departments having 5 or more senators use a proportional representation party list system. Senators have a nine-year term and one-third are elected every three years. *See also* FIFTH REPUBLIC: SENATE, p. 103.

Significance The electoral system for the Senate results in overrepresentation of rural areas at the expense of urban areas. Electors from small towns and villages often have a majority in the departmental electoral colleges; large cities do not have as many senators as their population warrants on a proportional basis. In the first decade of the Fifth Republic, this system consequently resulted in the political composition of the Senate being similar to that of the Fourth Republic. The Senate was anti-Gaullist and often used its powers against the government. This in turn led President Charles de Gaulle to propose a constitutional amendment in 1969 to reduce the Senate's powers, which was defeated.

Electoral System: Two-Ballot System The single-member district runoff system that is used to elect members of the National Assembly in the Fifth Republic. In the two-ballot system, the French Republic (including five overseas departments and four overseas territories) is divided into 491 electoral districts, each having one member (deputy) of the National Assembly (lower house). Deputies are elected for a five-year term by universal suffrage. Candidates must be French nationals at least 23 years of age; they do not need to live in the district they compete in. In the first ballot, those candidates are elected who receive an absolute majority of the votes cast and at least 25 percent of the registered electorate. If there is no such majority, a second ballot (*ballotage*) is taken one week later. Only candidates receiving votes greater than 12.5 percent of the registered voters may continue in the second round, but any otherwise eligible candidate may withdraw. In the second round, the candidate receiving the most votes (plurality) is elected. Each candidate runs with an alternate or substitute (*suppléant*) who takes the deputy's seat if he dies or resigns. *See also* FIFTH REPUBLIC: POLITICAL PARTY SYSTEM, p. 100.

Significance Coupled with the constitutional changes of the Fifth Republic, the two-ballot system has contributed to the bipolarization of French politics. Unlike the proportional representation system of the Fourth Republic, the runoff system with the plurality rule in the second ballot produces disproportional results. Small and isolated parties are especially hurt by the plurality rule. In 1958, for example, the isolated Communist party won 19 percent of the popular vote but only 2 percent of the seats. The small center parties, Radicals and Catholics, were much damaged by the left-right confrontations and their own divisions over whether to join the government coalition. The left and center parties soon learned to make alliances on the second ballot to match the power of the Gaullists and their allies. By 1967 the Communist and Socialist parties had made a binding agreement not to oppose each other on the second ballot. As a result of these coalitions, the National Assembly came to be organized as the government majority versus the opposition. In 1978, over 95 percent of the second-round ballots were straight two-candidate runoffs between the left and the right. The first ballot has become a kind of primary for party alliances, a test of which party's candidates are the strongest. This has led to the typical situation whereby the voter makes his personal choice on the first ballot and then votes for the least undesirable candidate on the second ballot.

Enlarged Sanctuary The defense policy of President Valéry Giscard d'Estaing, which held that France would defend a wider area than the traditional "sanctuary" of the French homeland. The doctrine of enlarged sanctuary (*sanctuarisation élargie*) expanded the previous basic principle of French defense policy that national territory was a sanctuary that would be defended regardless of what happened elsewhere. The new policy recognized that serious threats to French security or to its supplies of vital resources might have to be met outside the confines of national territory. Having implications for both nuclear and conventional warfare, the doctrine implied an increase in the defense budget, closer cooperation within NATO, and the expansion of military capabilities for overseas operations. See also MONDIALISME, p. 125; NUCLEAR WEAPONS STRATEGY, p. 128.

Significance The doctrine of enlarged sanctuary was devised by the chief of staff, General Guy Méry, and adopted by President Giscard in 1976. By expanding the zone of defense, French policy became more realistic in Europe and more expansive overseas. Although not rejecting the fundamental principle that France would always practice an independent foreign policy, the new policy led to full French participation within NATO's joint strategic planning operations. This in turn lent some credibility to France's nuclear deterrent that was previously lacking. Overseas, sanctuarisation élargie was partly linked to Giscard's foreign policy principle of globalism (*mondialisme*), whereby France would take an active role in stabilizing friendly governments in Francophone Africa and in protecting supply lines and access to raw materials and petroleum. In practice, the doctrine of enlarged sanctuary justified an expansion of naval forces in the Indian Ocean and military intervention in a number of Francophone African states. President François Mitterrand continued many of the doctrine's policies, as, for example, in the French involvement in the civil war in Chad in 1983.

Farmers' Associations: France Organizations of independent farmers and agricultural workers. The largest farmers' association is the National Federation of Farmers' Unions (FNSEA), which claims 700,000 members. FNSEA is an umbrella association of 30,000 local organizations, 36 specialized produce groups, chambers of agriculture, and affiliated groups. A noteworthy affiliate is the National Center of Young Farmers (CNJA), a militant, progressive group that developed out of a Catholic youth association. There is also a right-wing farmers' association, the French Federation of Agriculture (FFA), which split from the FNSEA in 1969. Of the several left-wing groups, the Movement for the Coordination and Defense of Family Farms (MODEF), is the most prominent. It is affiliated with the Communist party and claims 200,000 members, mostly small farmers in the south. A Socialist affiliate, the

National Movement of Agricultural and Rural Workers (MONATUR), was founded in 1975.

Significance Farmers' associations have been traditionally fragmented along ideological lines, and this is still true, but differences of product, farm size, region, and degree of modernization seem to be more important. The FNSEA is by far the strongest association; it includes about half of all French farmers. A conservative organization, it has numerous contacts with the government in the *concertation* system of consultation between government and interest groups, and it is influential in the making of agricultural policy. Its progressive affiliate, the Young Farmers, is more inclined to public protest. In the 1960s the Young Farmers helped organize rural protests and demonstrations in favor of agricultural modernization programs. The left-wing organizations affiliated with the Communist and Socialist parties are small and represent different interests from the dominant FNSEA.

Fifth Republic: Constitution The fundamental law of France that was promulgated on October 6, 1958. The authority to draft a new constitution was granted by the last parliament of the Fourth Republic to the government of Charles de Gaulle, who had assumed office as prime minister following the insurrection in Algeria in May 1958. The document was drafted by a committee headed by Michel Debré, and it was approved by a 79 percent vote of the people in a referendum on September 28, 1958. Based largely on de Gaulle's ideas, the Constitution combines features of presidential and parliamentary forms of government. Constitutional principles include: republicanism, universal suffrage, a strong presidency, a "government" (prime minister and cabinet) responsible to the popular house, a bicameral legislature, the incompatibility of a ministerial office with a parliamentary office, a separate and independent judiciary, and institutional arrangements uniting the republic with overseas territories. The Constitution has no separate bill of rights, but rather proclaims its attachment to the Rights of Man of 1789 as set forth in and further expanded by the Preamble of the Constitution of the Fourth Republic. Important changes from the previous system include provisions for a strong presidency, a weakened National Assembly, a strengthened Senate, a new Constitutional Council with authority to rule on the constitutionality of bills, and provisions for popular referenda. Since 1958 several important constitutional amendments have been adopted; these provide that (1) overseas territories that become independent may remain within the French Community; (2) the office of president is directly elected; and (3) 60 deputies or 60 senators may submit bills to the Constitutional Council. In 1969 the people rejected a combined constitutional proposal that would have weakened the power of the Senate and would have created regional governments, whereupon President de Gaulle resigned. *See also* FOURTH REPUBLIC: CONSTITUTIONAL SYSTEM, p. 107; GAULLISM: POLITICAL DOCTRINE, p. 116.

Significance The Constitution of the Fifth Republic has established in just over 25 years one of the most successful French constitutional systems since the Revolution of 1789. Although the system is based largely on the principles of one man and his movement, the Gaullist constitution has come to be accepted by most of the people and most political parties. Adopted after the revolutionary circumstances that led to the fall of the Fourth Republic, the constitution lacked legitimacy in its first decade even though it was ratified by a large number of voters. In the 1970s, however, the system came to be accepted by the democratic left. Combined with the simplified political party system brought about by electoral law changes, the governmental system provided an effective means to overcome the immobility that marked the Fourth Republic. The election of François Mitterrand in 1981 and his subsequent legislative majority gave the Socialists and their allies the constitutional means whereby they might enact major economic and social reforms. Although the strong presidential system provides a powerful instrument for social change, the combination of presidential and parliamentary institutions does create the possibility of a constitutional crisis unsolvable by regular processes. The good sense of the French people has prevented this from happening by giving the president strong legislative majorities. Although it may be too soon to conclude that France's perennial constitutional dissensus has been completely eliminated, the Constitution of the Fifth Republic has helped reconcile the traditional left-right divisions over the form of government.

Fifth Republic: National Assembly The popularly elected and constitutionally more powerful house of parliament. The National Assembly has all the constitutional powers typical of a lower chamber in a parliamentary system, but these have been circumscribed under the 1958 constitution. The National Assembly may enact laws, approve budgets, ratify treaties, declare wars, and propose constitutional amendments. It approves prime ministers and may censure governments. But, compared to the Fourth Republic, parliamentary prerogatives and powers have been curtailed in the following ways. Parliament meets only six months a year (two sessions of three months each) unless called into emergency session by the president. It may legislate only on enumerated matters, and its rules of procedures and bills may be examined for constitutionality by the Constitutional Council. The government controls the agenda, and committees have been reduced in number and in power. Regarding its own legislative proposals, the government can reject all amendments and separate votes on parts of the bill, and require a vote on the entire bill. This is called the "package vote," or *vote bloqué*. Censure of the government by the National Assembly was made more difficult to propose or to accomplish. Although new cabinets are approved by a simple majority, a vote of censure requires an absolute majority. The government may also "engage its responsibility" on a bill or resolution; this is a procedure whereby the bill or resolution is adopted unless the government is rejected by an absolute majority. The government also has decree and budgetary powers, and combined with the Senate, it can prevent enactment of a bill. Members of the National Assembly (called deputies) are elected for a five-year term, but the Assembly may be dissolved by the president after one year. The term "National Assembly" has been used for different structures in French history. In the Fourth Republic, it was the name of both houses meeting jointly, and the lower house was called the Chamber of Deputies. *See also* ELECTORAL SYSTEM: TWO-BALLOT SYSTEM, p. 96; FIFTH REPUBLIC: CONSTITUTION, p. 98; FIFTH REPUBLIC: SENATE, p. 103.

Significance The authority of the National Assembly has been limited by the increased prerogatives of the government and the increased legislative authority of the Senate. Although the Assembly retained sufficient constitutional authority for a national legislative body, effective power passed to the executive branch. With the changes in the political party system that have occurred in the Fifth Republic, parliament seems to retain only enough power to harass the government. Only once, in 1962, has the government been censured, and since 1968 very few censure motions have been introduced. In the first three years of the Fifth Republic, the government was forced to use the package vote more than 20 times, but this too is less necessary. So long as the presidential majority retains its cohesion, the decline of parliament that has occurred in other European states will continue to exist in France.

Fifth Republic: Political Party System The ideologically bipolarized multiparty system that has characterized French politics since the late 1960s. In the political party system of the Fifth Republic, most parties in the National Assembly are organized into the government majority or the opposition. Four parties or parliamentary groups have come to dominate the political scene: Communist, Socialist, Union for French Democracy (a coalition of the Republican party and other center parties), and the Gaullists (since 1976 called Rally for the Republic). Most small parties in the parliament affiliate with these groups. Although the number of parties that run in national elections remains large (from 10 to 20), the party system is changed from that of the Fourth Republic. These changes are primarily the result of (1) the return of Charles de Gaulle to power and adoption of the new constitutional system that placed power in the presidency; (2) the move away from proportional representation to the two-ballot runoff system of election; and (3) modernization of the socioeconomic system. Important developments in the party system include the following: the bipolarization of political parties into two broad left-right coalitions; the immediate rise to the rank of first party by the Gaullists; the decline of the center parties; the end of the isolation of the Communists and the electoral alliance of the Communists and Socialists; the breakup of the conservatives of the Fourth Republic; the liberalizing of the Republican party and its alliance with the center group; and a reduction in the number of important parties. Party cohesion in the parliament has increased, and government majorities have been strong; only once in the Fifth Republic has a cabinet lost a vote of confidence, in 1962. *See also* ELECTORAL SYSTEM: TWO-BALLOT SYSTEM, p. 96; FIFTH REPUBLIC: CONSTITUTION, p. 98; FOURTH REPUBLIC: POLITICAL PARTY SYSTEM, p. 108.

Significance The bipolarized political party system and the constitutional changes of the Fifth Republic have resulted in strong, stable governments. Inasmuch as power in the parliament has declined, parliamentary groups are not as important as they were in the Fourth Republic. The government and parliament are dominated by the new system of presidential politics and the presidential majority. The legislative impasses that marked the Fourth Republic have been overcome because the presidential majority has maintained a cohesive front. In 1981 a dramatic change occurred in the presidential and parliamentary elections. The Gaullist-centrist majority gave way to a new left-wing majority headed by the new president, the Socialist leader, François Mitterrand. Although multipartyism in France is a permanent feature of French politics, there seems to be little likelihood that the stable bipolarized coalition system of the Fifth Republic will revert to the undisciplined multipartyism of the Fourth Republic.

Fifth Republic: President The head of state and chief executive, which is the most powerful office in the government. The president of the republic has extensive constitutional powers including the authority to: appoint the prime minister; confirm cabinet appointments; dissolve the National Assembly; send messages to parliament; promulgate laws; issue decrees; negotiate treaties; declare a state of emergency; call a referendum; preside over the Council of Ministers; make civil and military appointments; appoint one-third of the Constitutional Council; preside over high national defense and judicial councils; and act as commander-in-chief of the armed forces. The president has the broad responsibility to see that the Constitution is respected, and to ensure the functioning of the institutions of government and the continuance of the state. He is the guarantor of national independence, territorial integrity, and respect for Community agreements and treaties. Since 1962 the president is elected by popular vote for a seven-year term. *See also* ELECTORAL SYSTEM: PRESIDENT, p. 94; FIFTH REPUBLIC: CONSTITUTION, p. 98; FIFTH REPUBLIC: PRIME MINISTER, p. 102; REFERENDUM POWER, p. 136.

Significance The powers of the office of president of the republic were increased dramatically over the powers of the figurehead chief of state of the Fourth Republic. Although some powers of the office are shared, the president dominates the executive branch and exercises strong influence over the National Assembly. The president's choice of prime minister must be confirmed by the National Assembly, and the president cannot dismiss the prime minister. Nor can the president dissolve the National Assembly until it has been in office for at least one year. Despite these and other formal limitations, the presidents of the Fifth Republic have had complete control over the prime minister and cabinet and have engineered their removal whenever desired. The National Assembly has been dominated by a presidential majority that has sapped its independence. Because the constitutional system is a formal hybrid of presidential and parliamentary structures, it is possible for the president to be at odds with a prime minister who has the support of an opposition-controlled assembly. This has not happened, for the French voters have consistently given the president a strong majority in the National Assembly.

Fifth Republic: Prime Minister The head of the government, which consists of the prime minister and the Council of Ministers. The prime minister, also called the premier, is the weaker part of the dual executive system of the Fifth Republic, which is dominated by the president. The Constitution provides that the government determines and directs national policy, and that the prime minister directs the operation of the government. The prime minister is responsible for national defense and the execution of the laws; he also has regulatory and appointment powers. The government, which constitutionally does not include the president of the republic, is responsible to the National Assembly. The prime minister is nominated by the president and must be confirmed by the National Assembly, which can also censure the government. Under the Incompatibility Rule, no minister may at the same time hold a seat in parliament or in any other public or national-level office in business, professional, or labor organizations. In the first 25 years of the Fifth Republic, there have been only 8 men who have served as prime minister, compared to the 20 cabinets in the period of the Fourth Republic, 1946–58. Under President Charles de Gaulle, the prime ministers were: Michel Debré, 1959–62; Georges Pompidou, 1962–68; and Maurice Couve de Murville, 1968–69. Under President Pompidou, the prime ministers were: Jacques Chaban-Delmas, 1969–72; and Pierre Messmer, 1972–74. Under President Valéry Giscard d'Estaing, the prime ministers were: Jacques Chirac, 1974–76; and Raymond Barre, 1976–81. Under President François Mitterrand the prime ministers have been Pierre Mauroy, 1981–84, and Laurent Fabius, since 1984. *See also* FIFTH REPUBLIC: CONSTITUTION, p. 98; FIFTH REPUBLIC: PRESIDENT, p. 101.

Significance The Constitution of the Fifth Republic substantially strengthened the government in its relations with parliament. But, although the prime minister and government share executive powers with the president, the formal heads of government have been dominated by the chief of state. The amount of independence and discretion that a prime minister has depends on his relationship with the president and the policy areas with which the president concerns himself. Presidents de Gaulle and Giscard d'Estaing paid a great deal of attention to foreign policy and left domestic matters to their prime ministers, but prime ministers who began to show significant political power that might challenge the president were forced from office; examples of this are Debré in 1962, Pompidou in 1968, and Chirac in 1976. The stability of the governments of the Fifth Republic has been remarkable, as compared to the previous two republics. Only one government has been censured, that of Pompidou in 1962 on a proposal to call a referendum for the popular election of the president. This stability is ultimately traceable to the president's political support among the people, which has resulted in strong legislative majorities.

Fifth Republic: Senate The second or upper house of the parliament. The Senate shares full legislative authority with the National Assembly, but it cannot initiate finance bills or call for special sessions. The government is responsible only to the National Assembly, and the Senate has no authority to approve prime ministers or censure governments. In legislating, the two houses must agree on an identical text, and if they do not, the bill is not adopted. In case the two houses disagree on a bill that the government wants adopted, a joint committee can be authorized by the government to prepare an identical text. If the two houses still disagree, the government can ask the National Assembly "to rule definitely," that is, to vote again and adopt the bill without Senate consent. In this manner the government can legislate through the National Assembly but not through the Senate. The Senate is a continuing body and is not dissolved along with the National Assembly. Senators have a nine-year term, and one-third are elected every three years by electoral colleges primarily composed of local government representatives. The Senate president becomes acting president of the republic in case of the death, resignation, or permanent incapacity of the president. The term "Senate" was also the name of the upper house in the Third Republic. In the Fourth Republic the second chamber was called the Council of the Republic and was virtually powerless. *See also* ELECTORAL SYSTEM: SENATE, p. 95; FIFTH REPUBLIC: CONSTITUTION, p. 98; FIFTH REPUBLIC: NATIONAL ASSEMBLY, p. 99.

Significance The authority of the Senate was increased by the 1958 Constitution over that of the second chamber in the Fourth Republic in order to place additional limitations on the National Assembly. But given its indirect method of election, the Senate retained a center-left majority that was characteristic of the Fourth Republic. The center-left orientation of the Senate results from the strength of these political forces in local elections in which most members of the departmental electoral colleges are chosen. Thus, while there were progovernment majorities in the National Assembly, the Senate was staunchly anti-Gaullist. It often voted down Gaullist measures, which then had to be repassed in the Assembly. The first president of the Senate, Gaston Monnerville, used his authority to bring Gaullist bills to the Constitutional Council for a determination of their constitutionality. In 1969 President Charles de Gaulle, wanting to end this harassment and renew his popular mandate, proposed a constitutional amendment through the referendum process that would have changed the Senate. The power of the Senate would have become advisory, and the senators would have been selected by occupational, professional, and other associations, and by the government. The proposal failed, de Gaulle resigned, and the Senate continued as before.

First Empire The rule of Napoleon I as the emperor of the French, from 1804 to 1814 and again in 1815. Although Napoleon Bonaparte did not proclaim the Empire until 1804, he had been in control of France since he overthrew the Directory government in 1799. Napoleon's rule was that of an absolute dictatorship, marked by authoritarian methods, rigid police control, and censorship. Although he overturned the republic and established a new noble class of family and supporters, he was very popular. Apart from his military conquests in Europe, his domestic reforms, some of which were initiated when he was First Consul, were lasting and substantial. Napoleon established an efficient bureaucracy, created the Council of State (*Conseil d'État*), centralized the judicial system, appointed prefects in departments to guide local governments, and established new police organizations. The legal system was completely revised and a great series of law codes (*Code Napoléon*) were adopted. Other reforms include the promotion of industry, commerce, trade, and agriculture; the extension of public education; a concordant with the Catholic church that lasted until 1905; the establishment of the Bank of France and a sound fiscal policy. His spectacular successes in foreign policy, however, were followed by defeat and exile. Napoleon's attempt to have the European states forbid trade with England (known as the Continental System) was not successful and damaged his domestic economic program. After conquering much of Europe and establishing vassal states throughout the region, he was defeated by a coalition of powers. His return from exile in 1815 was frustrated by his defeat at Waterloo and the reestablishment of the Bourbon monarchy in France. *See also* BONAPARTISM, p. 82; CODE LAW SYSTEM, p. 85; REVOLUTION OF 1789, p. 139.

Significance Napoleon's domestic and international achievements during and before the First Empire have been unmatched in French history. He consolidated the gains of the Revolution of 1789, such as the abolition of feudalism, the elimination of special privileges for the old nobility and the church, and the transfer of land to the peasants. Power in France passed to the bourgeoisie. The governmental system of France today is based on many of the Napoleonic reforms, especially in administration, local government, education, and military training. The Napoleonic civil and penal codes form the basis of the French legal system and were adopted in other nations. Napoleon promoted revolution, reform, liberalism, and national unification in Europe, and his influence was also felt in South America. Although the First Empire ended in defeat, the glory and achievements of the Napoleonic period were indelibly etched in the minds of the French. Later in the nineteenth century, a Napoleonic legend developed that contributed to the rise of Napoleon III and the Bonapartists.

Force de Frappe The independent French nuclear striking force. The decision to build the *force de frappe* was announced by President

Charles de Gaulle in 1959, but preparations to build an atomic bomb had been taken earlier during the Fourth Republic. The first nuclear test explosion was held in 1960, and a small nuclear force became operational in 1965. First consisting of atom bombs carried by Mirage IV airplanes, the nuclear force was continuously modernized and developed by subsequent governments. In 1984 it included intermediate-range land-based missiles, submarine-launched missiles, and tactical nuclear weapons. A multiple independently targetable warhead missile (MIRV) was expected to be deployed on the sixth nuclear-powered submarine in 1985, and plans for developing cruise missiles and newer tactical weapons and delivery systems were also being developed. *See also* EUROMISSILE CONTROVERSY, p. 251; NUCLEAR WEAPONS STRATEGY, p. 128.

Significance The decision to build the force de frappe touched off a long-standing national debate concerning the usefulness, dangers, and benefits of French nuclear weapons. Arguments defending the system include (1) France cannot depend on American nuclear forces because the Soviet-American nuclear stalemate prevents only global nuclear war and has left small and medium states vulnerable; (2) French nuclear weapons would serve as a deterrent (*dissuasion*) against attacks from major powers; (3) it is not necessary to build nuclear forces equal in size to those of the superpowers because nuclear weapons are so destructive that a small force would threaten potential aggressors with unacceptable levels of damage; (4) the French nuclear force would act as a trigger for American nuclear forces, which might remain uncommitted in a European conflict; and (5) the development of nuclear weapons has important technical and economic spillover benefits for the nuclear energy industry that the nation must have. Arguments against developing and deploying the force de frappe include (1) French nuclear forces will always be too modest to deter any major nuclear power; (2) any use of nuclear weapons against the Soviet Union would be suicidal; (3) the mere possession of nuclear weapons is dangerous in the context of a major European war because they invite attack; (4) nuclear warfare strategies that call for independent French operations lack credibility, and those that integrate French nuclear actions with NATO operations are unnecessary; and (5) there are no real political benefits resulting from French membership in the "nuclear club" that would outweigh the dangers and the economic costs of maintaining a national nuclear striking force. Despite the strong arguments presented by the opponents and the continual need to revamp nuclear warfare strategies to justify the force de frappe, all French governments, including Gaullist, Giscardian, and Socialist, continued to improve and modernize the system. Although Socialists were for many years opposed to the system,

President François Mitterrand maintained continuity, and even the French Communists ceased their opposition once they entered his government. In 1983, Mitterrand was quite insistent that France would not dismantle or reduce its nuclear forces no matter what agreements resulted from the American-Russian negotiations over the deployment of NATO intermediate missiles in Europe. In the context of European international politics in the second half of the twentieth century, French nuclear forces seem to have little military utility. The widespread national support for the force de frappe continues, however, because it is symbolic of French independence, it contributes to the myth of French national greatness, and it creates prestige among other states in the world.

Fourth Republic: Constitutional System   The system of government under which France was ruled from 1946 to 1958. The Constitution of the Fourth Republic was drafted by the popularly elected Constituent Assembly in 1946 and accepted by the people by a 52 percent vote, although one-third of the electorate did not vote. The constitutional system was similar to that of the Third Republic in that it emphasized republican values and assembly government, despite an earlier referendum in which the people called for a new constitution. Power was located in the Chamber of Deputies, to which the prime minister (called the president of the Council of Ministers) was responsible. The second chamber, now called the Council of the Republic, was much weaker than the Senate of the Third Republic. Practically powerless at first, the Council of the Republic was given the right in 1954 to delay legislation for 100 days. The president of the republic was elected by parliament for a seven-year term. The two presidents, Vincent Auriol (1947–53) and René Coty (1953–58), were primarily figureheads, although their formal powers were extensive. Vocational groups were represented in the Economic Council, which had the right to be consulted on social and economic legislation. Overseas territories were associated with France in the French Union, which had appropriate institutions but no real powers. The Preamble of the Constitution was noteworthy in proclaiming an extensive list of political, economic, and social rights. This comprehensive statement of human rights, however, was not backed up by any institutional guarantor, such as the Constitutional Council in the Fifth Republic. *See also* ALGERIAN CRISIS OF 1958, p. 80; CONSTITUENT ASSEMBLY, p. 87; FOURTH REPUBLIC: POLITICAL PARTY SYSTEM, p. 108.

Significance   The constitutional system of the Fourth Republic lasted but 12 years. Because it was combined with the undisciplined multiparty system, cabinets were unstable, lasting on the average six months. The longest-lived government, that of the Socialist Guy Mollet, endured for one and a half years. There were 23 governments in the 12 years of the republic. The office of prime minister was constitutionally stronger than that of premier in the Third Republic, but the "regime of parties" in the National Assembly kept the office politically weak and ineffective. Although prime ministers had the authority to dissolve the National Assembly and call for new elections in certain circumstances, this power was exercised only once, over great criticism. A constitutional provision requiring extraordinary majorities for the passage of most legislation contributed to legislative immobilism. Although the constitutional system of the Fourth Republic in the context of another political setting might have been successful, in postwar France it was disastrous. Unable to cope with the problems associated with the Algerian War, the system was in effect overthrown in 1958.

Fourth Republic: Political Party System   The multiparty system from 1946 to 1958, which was composed of five major party groups and several smaller parties. The largest parties and party groups in the Fourth Republic were the Communist, Socialist, Radicals, Popular Republican Movement (Christian Democrats, MRP), and Independents (Conservatives). The Radicals and Independents were names for groups of several similar parties. Two "flash" parties that made a brilliant but brief showing in the Fourth Republic were the first Gaullist party (Rally of the French People, RPF) in the 1951 election and Poujadists in the 1956 election. The party system that emerged in the first postwar election of 1945 was dominated by three mass-based movements, Communist, Socialist, and MRP. The Radicals, who were a large force in the Third Republic, were reduced in their various parties to a total of about 12 percent of the vote. The Communist party was the largest vote-getter, winning as much as 28 percent of the vote. It participated in coalition governments with the Socialists and MRP until 1947. Coalitions thereafter tended to be dominated by the Third Force parties: Socialist, MRP, and Radicals, who stood between the Communists and Gaullists. The electoral system used in the first three postwar elections (1945 and two in 1946) was a proportional representation party list system that slightly benefited larger parties. In 1951 and 1956 a complex, modified list system was adopted that permitted electoral alliances (*apparentements*) that benefited the Third Force parties. Except for Communists and Socialists, the parties often showed little discipline or cohesion; factions and *ministrables* (potential ministers ambitious for a cabinet post) would often maneuver to bring down governments. Government coalitions were short-lived, and cabinets lasted on the average six months. *See also*

ELECTORAL SYSTEM: PARTY LIST SYSTEM, p. 93; FIFTH REPUBLIC: POLITICAL PARTY SYSTEM, p. 100; FOURTH REPUBLIC: CONSTITUTIONAL SYSTEM p. 107.

Significance The undisciplined multiparty system of the Fourth Republic was combined with a constitutional system that placed power in the Assembly. This contributed to cabinet instability and an inability to break out of legislative impasses. The electoral system was manipulated by the Third Force parties, particularly in 1951 and 1956, to benefit themselves, and this brought more disrepute to the system. The multiparty system reflected the social cleavages in France, but it was also exacerbated by the proportional system and electoral system manipulations. In the Fifth Republic, the party system became simpler and more responsible because of political, constitutional, and electoral system changes.

Franco-Prussian War A conflict between France and Prussia in 1870 that resulted in the overthrow of the French Second Empire. The origins of the Franco-Prussian War are traced to their rivalry for European leadership and to Prussian support for a Hohenzollern prince as the candidate for the Spanish throne. The prince was related to the Prussian royal house, and the issue inflamed the war spirit in both nations. After the prince's candidacy was withdrawn, France demanded further assurances from King William I of Prussia, who refused. The report of the French ambassador's meeting with the king in the famous Ems Dispatch was shrewdly edited and publicized by the Prussian chancellor, Otto von Bismarck, who desired war with France. This report appeared to insult France and thus provoked Emperor Napoleon III to declare war on Prussia on July 19, 1870. France was ill prepared for war, while Prussia quickly mobilized and was supported by southern German states. Prussia defeated the French armies, and Napoleon himself was captured in the disastrous defeat at Sedan. When this news reached Paris, the people demonstrated against the Empire and a republic was proclaimed on September 4, 1870. Other French military defeats followed, and Paris finally surrendered in January 1871. *See also* COMMUNE OF PARIS, p. 86; SECOND EMPIRE, p. 141.

Significance The Franco-Prussian War was disastrous for France and had long-term consequences for Europe. The Treaty of Frankfurt of May 1871 imposed harsh terms on France: Prussian occupation, heavy reparations, and the cession of Alsace and a large part of Lorraine to the new German Empire, which had been proclaimed at Versailles in January 1871. The war put an end to Bonapartism and established the Third

Republic by means of a bloodless revolution. But Paris refused to accept the new French national government and declared the independent Commune of Paris, which was later brutally crushed. Diplomatic and military power flowed to the German Empire, as France lost influence. The Franco-German rivalry continued, however, now made worse by the French memory of national humiliation, German occupation, heavy reparations, and the loss of Alsace-Lorraine. These issues in turn provided some of the background for the Great War, World War I.

French Bureaucracy Model   A model of the French bureaucracy developed by Michel Crozier that attempts to explain the rigidity and lack of innovation in the system. According to Crozier's French Bureaucracy Model, permanent French cultural traits concerning interpersonal and intergroup relations play an important role in the policy-making process in France. These traits are: the isolation of the individual, the predominance of formal over informal activities, the isolation of the levels in the hierarchic system (the strata), and a constant struggle among the strata for rank and privilege. Individuals are apathetic, lack initiative, and avoid conflict and dependency relationships. There is a lack of contact between strata and an avoidance of direct face-to-face relations with established authority. These cultural traits result in a bureaucracy characterized by a high degree of centralization and stratification, poor communication, and a wide gulf between superiors and subordinates. Power in the system tends to recede from below and rigidities develop that are difficult to adjust gradually. Although the system provides stability, regularity, and predictability, it is flawed by defensiveness, inflexibility, and favoritism. There is a heavy emphasis on formal rules. Change can only be made by writing new rules, and this is viewed as a crisis, but it is only through crisis that change occurs. *See also* SOCIOECONOMIC THEORY: STALEMATE SOCIETY THESIS, p. 147.

Significance   The French Bureaucracy Model developed by Crozier after World War II was very influential among French social scientists and was used to guide a number of case studies that seemed to confirm the thesis. Crozier also used his theory to support the concept of the "stalemate society," which argued that modernization and innovation in France is blocked by its preindustrial cultural traits, rigid bureaucratic system, and archaic administrative style. Critics of the bureaucratic model point out that the factor of political culture, which has been used to explain everything, is too broad to explain the policy-making process in

France. Although attitudes toward authority are related to the stability and social progress of a political system, a policy-making model must recognize the intentions of policy-makers and their informal networks. Moreover, in recent periods, the French bureaucracy has not only provided the stability that the political executive lacked, it also guided the remarkable progress that the nation has made in social programs and economic modernization.

French Communist Party (PCF)   The large Marxist party of the revolutionary left that receives much working class support. For most of its history since it was first organized in 1920, the French Communist party (PCF) has been isolated in French politics because of its revolutionary Leninist approach, its criticism of the Socialists as bourgeois revisionists, and its loyal support of the policies of the Soviet Union. In the Fifth Republic, however, the PCF moved from a position of isolation to one of cooperation with the Socialist party in electoral alliances; from 1981 to 1984 it was a participant in the Socialist government of Pierre Mauroy under President François Mitterrand. In 1972 the PCF joined Socialists and left-wing Radicals in a statement, called the Common Program, which detailed the legislative program the parties would enact if elected to power. In 1977, however, the PCF, apparently fearing the rise of popular support for the Socialist party, prevented the renewal of the pact by insisting on a much larger measure of nationalization of industry than the Socialists or Radicals would accept. Also at that time the Communist party seemed to break away from statements it had made in 1976 which declared its independence from Moscow, affirmed its acceptance of a constitutionalist route to power, and proclaimed its support for the pluralist, bourgeois system as the best way to bring "socialism" to France. In 1979, for example, the PCF supported the Soviet military intervention in Afghanistan. Socialists and Communists continued their electoral alliance, however, and the PCF supported Mitterrand on the second ballot of the 1981 presidential election. In the 1981 elections for the National Assembly, Communist support fell to 14 percent of the vote, a postwar low, and the Communist assembly delegation declined from 86 to 44 deputies. President Mitterrand brought Communists into the government in four relatively unimportant ministries on the basis of a joint statement of the two parties. The statement called on the USSR to pull its forces out of Afghanistan, demanded nonintervention in Poland, and approved the pro-Western foreign policies of France. In the PCF party congress of February 1982, Georges Marchais was reelected as secretary general, and the delegates papered over the controversies that troubled the party by adopting ambiguous and contradictory positions. The Soviet Union and its Eastern European allies were warmly praised for adopting "correct" global policies, and the pro-Russian Polish and Afghanistan Communist delegations were warmly received. But Stalinism was again condemned, the 1976 policy of seeking to adapt socialism to French conditions was reaffirmed, and the commitments to NATO were supported. In July 1984 the PCF left the government of Prime Minister Laurent Fabius, condemning Socialist economic policies that eliminated jobs. *See also* ELECTIONS OF 1981: FRANCE, p. 92; EUROCOMMUNISM, p. 250; FIFTH REPUBLIC: POLITICAL PARTY SYSTEM, p. 100; TRADE UNIONS: FRANCE, p. 153.

Significance The French Communist party is the second largest Communist party in the West after the Italian party. The PCF emerged in the postwar period as the largest and best organized party in France. It obtained the allegiance of the working class, dominated the largest trade union, the General Confederation of Labor (CGT), and its popular support stabilized at 20 percent of the popular vote until it fell drastically in the 1981 elections. Party membership numbers about 600,000 persons, and the party is tightly disciplined, cohesive, and well financed. The large size of the popular vote for the PCF has been analyzed as resulting from: (1) a protest vote of noncommunists against the governmental and social system; (2) the disaffection caused by the opportunistic policies of the Socialist party under Guy Mollet; and (3) the continuing support of the working class. The working-class vote is evident in the high support the party receives in the "Red Belt," the industrial suburbs of Paris. The PCF's history as an antisystem, Stalinist, revolutionary party always loyal to Moscow has limited its success in the past. The party's move in 1976 to a type of Eurocommunist approach is not convincing to many observers, because, although it has on several occasions criticized the USSR, its loyalty has never wavered. In 1968 the party criticized the Soviet Union for invading Czechoslovakia, but in 1979 it defended the intervention in Afghanistan when it first occurred. Upon entering the government in 1981, the party's public positions again seemed to be confusing and contradictory. Although the PCF has dropped the Marxist idea of the dictatorship of the proletariat, it has retained the principle of democratic centralism, which in practice has meant absolute party discipline and purges of critics. The PCF's participation in the government in 1981–84 lent credibility to its constitutionalist line, and added votes to the reform of French society along lines chosen by President Mitterrand. But this compromise proved untenable in the face of domestic economic crises that threatened working-class jobs. And it was also unbearable in international crises, such as the deployment of NATO intermediate range missiles in Europe, in which Mitterrand's nationalistic and pro-Western foreign policies confronted the Soviet Union.

French Community The abortive association of the French Republic and its self-governing colonies created by the 1958 Constitution. The French Community was the successor to the French Union of the Fourth Republic, which gave the colonies limited authority. The Constitution of the Fifth Republic created an extensive set of executive, legislative, and judicial organs to handle Community affairs; the president of France was the president of the Community. In 1958 Charles de Gaulle gave the voters in the colonies the option to accept the constitution and thereby gain autonomy status within the Community. Only Guinea voted against the constitution and was immediately given full independence. Within a few years the pressures for complete independence mounted within the African colonies and by 1961 all but one— French Somaliland (Djibouti)—opted for complete sovereignty. The French Constitution consequently had to be amended to permit fully independent members to remain within the Community, and more than half chose to do so. Since that time, the Community has ceased to have meaning, and the institutions have no practical use. Most relationships between France and its former colonies are governed by bilateral agreements. *See also* FRENCH REPUBLIC, p. 113.

Significance The French Community was the last effort of France to maintain a modified type of colonial empire in a period of rapid decolonization. The traditional French goals of establishing and maintaining a worldwide French-led union of nations and of integrating colonial people into French society died very rapidly in the late 1950s. President de Gaulle's policy of autonomy and union could not save it. The ideal, however, still lives in the notion of *Francophonie* (French-speaking states and subnational areas), in which France would continue to exert its influence.

French Republic The official name for France, which represents the victory of republican principles, institutions, and values over monarchical and imperial ones. As a state, the French Republic comprises metropolitan France, overseas departments, and overseas territories, each with distinctive governmental institutions. There are 22 regions in metropolitan France, including the island of Corsica, comprising 96 departments. The five overseas departments, which are Guadeloupe, Guiana, Martinique, Reunion, and St. Pierre and Miquelon, are administered like metropolitan departments as integral parts of France. There are four overseas territories: French Polynesia, New Caledonia, Wallis and Fortuna, and the French Southern and Antarctic Islands. The island of Mahoré (formerly Mayotte), which voted in 1976 to remain within the French Republic when the other Comoro islands opted for independence, has a special status as a territorial collectivity, which is intermediate between an overseas department and an overseas territory. France also possesses a number of other small islands that are not included as constituent parts of the French Republic. The population of metropolitan France, including Corsica, was 53,840,000 in 1981, 10 percent of whom are foreigners. Although at 211,208 square miles France is the largest nation in Western Europe, its population is smaller than that of West Germany, Italy, or Great Britain. *See also* FRENCH COMMUNITY, p. 113; POLITICAL CULTURE: FRANCE, p. 129.

Significance The term "French Republic" is at once a name, a symbol, and a political system. The words express much more than a preference for the republican form of government; they reflect deeply held convictions for certain political values, such as popular sovereignty and the political and legal equality of the citizen. The "Republic" stands for a complex system of emotions, beliefs, and values that are held by the vast majority of the French people, and it has come to be identified with the French nation. The term has such strong emotional overtones that it is favorably used by all contemporary political forces of the left, center, and right, and no group will permit the "Republic" to be identified exclusively with one constitutional system or political regime. As a symbol, the "French Republic" inspires national pride, personal sacrifice, and extreme patriotism, while at the same time it justifies partisanship, opposition, and rebellion against governments that allegedly threaten the existence of the "Republic."

Gaullism: Bayeux Speech A major address of Charles de Gaulle in the town of Bayeux in Normandy on June 16, 1946, in which he set forth his ideas for a new constitutional system for France. In the Bayeux Speech, de Gaulle condemned "the regime of parties" of previous republics that created unstable and ineffective governments that led ultimately to dictatorships. He called for a new constitutional order in which a popularly elected assembly would be supplemented by a second chamber that represented different interests, i.e., local governments, economic and social groups, and overseas territories. The executive power would not emanate from the parliament, but would be vested in a constitutionally strong chief of state (president) who would appoint and control the prime minister and cabinet. The independent chief of state, chosen indirectly by an electoral college of national and local legislators, would stand above partisan interests and guarantee the independence of the nation. *See also* GAULLISM: POLITICAL DOCTRINE, p. 116; CONSTITUENT ASSEMBLY, p. 87.

Significance The Bayeux Speech had little immediate effect, but it became the basis upon which the constitutional system of the Fifth Republic was established. De Gaulle chose to speak in Bayeux because it was the first liberated French town he had visited after the Normandy landings. When de Gaulle made the speech in Bayeux, he was not in the government, having resigned as president of the Provisional Government in January 1946 because he objected to the return of the "regime of parties." In May 1946 the voters rejected the constitution that had been drafted by the first Constituent Assembly; this draft constitution called for a parliamentary system with a figurehead presidency and a single-chamber legislature. De Gaulle's speech was an attempt to influence the Popular Republican Movement, a large Catholic party, to promote his ideas in the next Constituent Assembly. Although the second Assembly made some minor changes in the Constitution, it rejected de Gaulle's proposals and the people approved the second draft over de Gaulle's opposition. This became the Constitution of the Fourth Republic. Within 12 years, however, the Fourth Republic fell, de Gaulle was called back to power, and the Bayeux principles became the foundation for the Constitution of the Fifth Republic.

Gaullism: Foreign Policy The strategies and courses of action taken by Charles de Gaulle in pursuing the interests of France in international affairs. De Gaulle's foreign policy was based on principles and goals in his political doctrine, such as the importance of the nation-state, the greatness, independence, and world mission of France, and the pervasive role of power in international politics. After de Gaulle took power in 1958, his foreign policy passed through several phases, but always with certain objectives foremost. Generally, these objectives were to place France in the first rank with the superpowers, to give France freedom of action and independence in its foreign relations, to break up the East-West power blocs in Europe, and to remove the United States as the predominant power in Western Europe. Some of the important ideas he pursued but failed to achieve were (1) a proposal for an "Atlantic Directorate," in which the United States, Great Britain, and France would jointly make decisions on all worldwide security matters including the use of nuclear weapons; (2) a "Grand Design," in which a "Europe of Fatherlands" or a "Europe from the Atlantic to the Urals" would replace the power blocs; (3) a special relationship with West Germany, whereby Germany would reject dependence on American forces for its security in favor of the French nuclear deterrent; (4) a "Third Force," or a neutralist West Europe under French leadership that would act as the arbiter between the Soviet Union and the Anglo-Americans; (5) an agreement with the Soviet Union whereby the two states would settle European problems; and (6) the maintenance of the French empire through a community of self-governing states associated with France. These objectives failed, but de Gaulle was able to solve the Algerian war, liquidate most of the empire, and retain influence in most of the former colonies. He constructed an independent atomic striking force (*force de frappe*) and removed French military forces from NATO commands. He vetoed British membership in the European Economic Community and prevented the community from developing into a political union. In the Middle East he shifted from Israel to the Arab side, and he attempted to exert influence in French Canadian and Latin American affairs. In these and in other economic and diplomatic efforts de Gaulle tried to achieve his foreign policy of *grandeur*. *See also* ALGERIAN WAR, p. 80; FORCE DE FRAPPE, p. 105; FRENCH COMMUNITY, p. 113; GAULLISM: POLITICAL DOCTRINE, p. 116; TOUS AZIMUTS, p. 152.

Significance De Gaulle's foreign policy of *grandeur*, or the spirit and quality of greatness, could not very well succeed given the relative weakness of France as compared to the superpowers. When he left office, some of his policies were reversed by President Georges Pompidou, including the veto of British membership in the European Community, the attack on the international monetary system, and the attempt to extricate the United States from Western Europe. The three presidents after de Gaulle, however, Pompidou, Valéry Giscard d'Estaing, and François Mitterrand, changed little in the security policy he established. French nuclear forces have been expanded, the armed forces have not been placed under NATO command, naval forces are active outside the European region, military units are used to intervene in some former African colonies, and France refuses to be bound by American-Soviet arms control agreements. Although France is more cooperative in Western European affairs, there has been no move toward political union. And French nationalism, which long predated the coming of de Gaulle, has also survived his passing.

Gaullism: Political Doctrine The fundamental principles of Charles de Gaulle concerning political society, constitutional structures, and France's role in world affairs. De Gaulle's political doctrine is built around several core ideas: (1) the great importance of the nation in all aspects of human affairs; (2) the role of the nation-state as the basis for political action and the consequent need for national independence; (3) the greatness of France and its cultural and political mission; (4) the importance of power in international relations and the necessity to build a strong France capable of independent action; (5) the concept of national interest, which stands above local or partisan interests; (6) the role of the chief of state to be the guarantor of the independence and integrity of France; (7) the need for exceptional leaders of strong character and wisdom who can interpret the national interest in a nonsectarian manner; (8) the need to replace the ineffectual assembly government of France and its regime of parties with a strong chief of state; and (9) the need to modernize the industrial and technological facets of French society. In addition to these ideas, de Gaulle declared a commitment to traditional republican and democratic values and institutions, such as popular sovereignty, universal suffrage, representative government, and free elections. *See also* BONAPARTISM, p. 82; FIFTH REPUBLIC: CONSTITUTION, p. 98; GAULLISM: BAYEUX SPEECH, p. 114; GAULLISM: FOREIGN POLICY, p. 115; RALLY FOR THE REPUBLIC (RPR), p. 135.

Significance The political doctrine of Charles de Gaulle provided the foundation upon which the constitutional system of the Fifth Republic was based. Many people who rallied around his leadership in crisis times were also attracted to his ideas which evoked memories and aspirations of French greatness. Critics of de Gaulle point out that his nationalistic ideas were outmoded, that he practiced a peculiar brand of democratic republicanism that was more like a Bonapartist plebiscitary government, and that he identified himself with France while still looking down on the French people when they refused to follow his leadership. Despite his stubborn personality and paternalistic approach, de Gaulle sometimes showed a flexibility in policy, such as giving independence to Algeria, that was not possible in previous governments. The success of the ideas he embodied is witnessed by the widespread acceptance of his constitution, the survival of his political movement, and the continuation of his national security policies.

Grand Corps High-ranking civil servants who administer the powerful and prestigious agencies of the national government. The *grand corps* agencies include the Council of State, the Inspectorate of Finances, the Court of Accounts, the prefectoral corps, and the diplomatic corps. These agencies exercise great power within the French bureaucracy and have much influence over the political executive. The superelite members of the grand corps are highly trained and have usually attended one of the *grand écoles*, prestigious schools of higher education that are separate from the universities. Some of the well-known grand écoles are the *École Nationale d'Administration, École Polytechnique,* and *École Normale Supérieure.* There are a number of other schools, some of which are run by government ministries to train engineers, geologists, tax accountants, and other specialists. The most noteworthy school for training bureaucrats is the

École Nationale d'Administration (ENA), or the National School of Administration. It was created in 1945 and provides high-level training in the social sciences, statistics, and public administration. Graduates of the ENA, who include some of the most powerful men in French government and politics, are popularly known as *enarches*. See also COUNCIL OF STATE, p. 90; FRENCH BUREAUCRACY MODEL, p. 110; PREFECT, p. 133.

Significance The grand corps and the grand écoles are closely related to each other and are integral parts of the French bureaucratic system. This system is characterized by professionalism, centralization, compartmentalization, and independence. The grand corps has been criticized for being elitist and overly powerful, and the grand écoles for drawing their students from the upper classes. Many members of the grand corps sometimes take well-paying jobs in the private sector in a move known as *pantouflage* (putting on soft slippers). Despite the decentralization reforms that were introduced by the Socialist government in 1981–82, it is unlikely that the influence of the grand corps will decline.

Indochina War A colonial war fought by France in 1946 to 1954 against Vietnamese nationalist forces led by the Communists of Ho Chi Minh. The Indochina War broke out in 1946 when Vietnamese nationalists rejected a French plan for a self-governing Federation of Indochina, comprising Vietnam (the union of Annan, Tonkin, and Cochin China), Laos, and Cambodia. Weary of the inconclusive guerrilla war that dragged on for years, the French military planned to entice the Viet Minh (Communist) forces of Ho Chi Minh into a set-piece battle, deep within enemy territory at Dienbienphu. Under siege for two months, Dienbienphu fell to the Viet Minh in May 1954, and the French government of Pierre Mendés-France negotiated a cease-fire in the Geneva agreements of July 1954. Vietnam was partitioned; the northern half controlled by Ho Chi Minh and the south by noncommunist nationalists. French forces withdrew from Vietnam in 1956. South Vietnam declared itself an independent republic in 1956, and Laos and Cambodia became independent monarchies. Guerrilla war in South Vietnam continued, and the United States took the place of France in defending the South Vietnamese government in a losing cause.

Significance The Indochina War was very costly to France in more than an economic sense. France lost influence in the region and any hope of keeping parts of Indochina within the French Union. About 71,000 French soldiers were killed, and many thousands more were casualties. The French army lost prestige, and the Fourth Republic suffered a serious blow. Believing that the army was unsupported by the government, French officers, soon to be fighting another colonial war in Algeria, began to withdraw allegiance to the Fourth Republic. Outside France, the Indochina War became a symbol and a lesson to anticolonial liberation forces elsewhere in the Third World. It emboldened the South Vietnamese Communist guerrillas (Vietcong) and the North Vietnamese Communist government to continue the struggle for national unification under a single communist government. This was finally achieved in April 1975.

Jacobinism　　Extreme leftist radicalism, the term deriving from the Jacobins, who were the most radical group of the French Revolution. Jacobins were the strongest political club in the revolutionary period, and they took their popular name from the convent where they met. In the assembly they sat to the left of the president on raised seats with other radicals (hence, they were called the "Mountain"). They opposed the more moderate republicans, the Girondists, who sat to the right. Jacobins established political clubs throughout France, and they drew much of their support from the working class of Paris. Led by Maximilien Robespierre, they supported the Reign of Terror. Jacobins pushed hard for republicanism, universal suffrage, separation of church and state, popular education, and other major economic and social reforms. Their typical executive-administrative system was government by committee, such as the Committee of Public Safety and the Committee of General Security. In later periods of French history, Jacobins were republicans who opposed royalists and imperialists by revolutionary means if necessary. *See also* POLITICAL CULTURE: FRANCE, p. 129; REVOLUTION OF 1789, p. 139.

Significance　　In contemporary times, the term Jacobinism is often used in a pejorative sense to refer to radical revolutionaries and their leftist programs. Modern Jacobinism derives its support from the urban poor and would use violence to gain power to bring about wholesale political and social change. In a more neutral usage, the term refers to the principles of centralized administration, assembly government, rule by uncontrolled committees, and the domination of the national government over local government.

Judicial System: France　　The organization and operation of the courts in France. The judicial system is composed of a network of regular courts and administrative courts. The regular court system is divided into three types of courts: civil courts, criminal courts, and specialized courts that deal with labor, commerce, social security, children, and other specialized matters. In the civil and criminal divisions, higher-level courts take the more serious cases. Cases from all regular courts may be appealed to the Courts of Appeal, and in certain cases to the Supreme Court of Appeal (*Cour de Cassation*). The ordinary courts apply the law as written and do not entertain questions about the constitutionality of the law. The Cour de Cassation is not an ordinary appellate court, for it reviews only the interpretation of law made by lower courts, not the facts of the case. Alongside the regular courts is a system of courts to handle administrative law cases, headed by the Council of State (*Conseil d'État*). In the Fifth Republic, a new body was created, the Constitutional Council, which was given the authority to examine the constitutionality of bills and legislative rules of procedure. French judges and prosecuting and investigating magistrates are career civil servants; promotions are decided by a committee of high court and government officials. The entire judicial system is supervised by the High Council of the Judiciary, composed of the president of the Republic and high government and judicial officials. *See also* CODE LAW SYSTEM, p. 85; COUNCIL OF STATE, p. 90; CONSTITUTIONAL COUNCIL, p. 87.

Significance The judicial system of France is noted for providing French citizens with easy access to the courts. The administration of justice is relatively inexpensive and is carried out by career professionals. The Supreme Court of Appeal assures uniformity of treatment throughout France by quashing those lower-court decisions that have wrongly interpreted the law. The system has been criticized, however, for being elitist and high-handed, and since 1958 under the influence of the president and the government, who control appointments to the High Council of the Judiciary. Judicial procedure in France differs from that in the Anglo-American states. One important difference is the use of the inquisitorial system, whereby judges take an active role in the trial in the attempt to discover the truth. This compares to the Anglo-American accusatorial or adversarial system, in which the trial judge acts as an impartial umpire in a contest between opposing attorneys.

July Monarchy The reign of Louis Phillipe as king of the French, from July 1830 to February 1848. The July Monarchy was established by a middle-class-dominated assembly following the July Revolution of 1830 against the Bourbon king, Charles X. Coming from the House of Orleans, a wing of the Bourbon family that supported the French Revolution of 1789, Louis Phillipe was installed as a constitutional monarch. Freedoms were honored, and the suffrage was partially extended, but the government came increasingly under the control of wealthy, bourgeois landowners who resisted further change. Louis Phillipe himself was an uninspiring, middle-class "Citizen King," whose own supporters considered him boring. Generally, he pursued a cautious foreign policy, although Algeria was finally conquered under his reign. The king was opposed by Bourbon "legitimists," Bonapartists, republicans, and socialists. His last government opposed popular demands for political reform and universal suffrage. In February 1848, following riots in Paris when the government prohibited a political meeting, the king abdicated, and the assembly proclaimed a republic. *See also* BOURBON RESTORATION, p. 83; SECOND REPUBLIC, p. 141.

Significance The July Monarchy was formally a constitutional monarchy, but it was a government dominated by a single class, the upper bourgeoisie. Although France experienced relative peace and prosperity during most of the period, opposition mounted as times grew bad in the 1840s. By refusing to extend the vote, the conservative government was toppled by a relatively minor incident, and France was led into a new crisis-packed revolutionary period, that of the Second Republic.

Leftist Radical Movement (MRG) A moderate socialist party that split from the Radical party and participated in the Socialist government of President François Mitterrand in 1981. The Leftist Radical Movement (*Mouvement des Radicaux de Gauche,* MRG) was founded in 1973 by the left wing of the Radical party, which had split two years earlier. The original president of the party was Robert Fabre, but he was expelled from the party in 1978 when he cooperated with the government of President Valéry Giscard d'Estaing. The leader in 1984 was Michel Crepeau. The MRG advocates a program of "authentic Radicalism" and "humanistic socialism"; it draws its support of about 2 to 3 percent of the popular vote primarily from the middle class. The party has an electoral alliance with the Socialist party, called the Union of the Democratic and Socialist Left (UGSD), which helps to keep it alive in assembly elections. In the 1981 elections, the MRG increased its seats from 10 to 14 deputies, and it was included in the cabinet of Prime Minister Pierre Mauroy under President François Mitterrand. *See also* FIFTH REPUBLIC: POLITICAL PARTY SYSTEM, p. 100; RADICAL PARTY, p. 134.

Significance The Leftist Radical Movement appears to be the last surviving offshoot of the old Radical party, which has practically disappeared in the Fifth Republic. Like its parent, the MRG is a party of small-town notables that has retained some strength at the local level. The party's program of traditional Radicalism and moderate socialism was visible in 1977 when it contributed to the breakup of a Communist-Socialist-Radical meeting that was called to revise the tripartite Common Program of socialism for France. The MRG opposed the Communist move to extend a nationalization plan to middle-sized companies. The MRG has been able to escape the fate of the Radical party in national elections through its alliance with the Socialists.

Local Government: France   The system of subnational government that acts as a unit of national administration and performs local functions. France is a highly centralized unitary state, and local government has been closely supervised by the national government. A primary unit of local government is the commune, or municipality, which may vary in size from small villages to large metropolitan cities. There are about 36,400 communes, 90 percent of which have fewer than 2,000 inhabitants. Each commune has an elective municipal council, which in turn chooses the mayor. The second basic unit of local government is the department (*département*), which is similar to a county; each department has an elective General Council. There are 96 departments in metropolitan France and five departments overseas. A department is divided into *arrondissements,* which serve as the electoral districts for elections to the National Assembly. The arrondissement is further divided into cantons, which are the territorial units for electing department General Councils; departmental elections are therefore called cantonal elections. Generally, the arrondissement and the canton are only electoral districts; before 1981 they had no elective bodies and provided no local services. In 1981 a major local government reform provided that arrondissement councils be created in Paris, Marseilles, and Lyons, and be given specified local functions. The functions of communes and departments are prescribed by law, and each unit must provide certain specified services, and may choose to provide other services permitted by law. Typical local services include maintaining schools, roads, social services, parks, playgrounds, theaters, and the like. Local governments may levy certain types of taxes to maintain mandatory services. Until the 1981 reforms, local governments were closely supervised by the prefect, a national official in each department who exercised great powers over the department and the commune. Prefects could dismiss councils, prepare budgets, raise taxes, and establish required services. This system of national supervision over local government was called tutelage (*tutelle*). In 1964, as part of a program of "deconcentration" of administration, another level of administration was established, the region. Twenty-two regions were created, which were to be primarily concerned with economic development. The region had no elective officials, but in 1972, regional councils were incorporated, which were composed of national legislators and communal and departmental councillors. The work of the regions was coordinated by a "superprefect." *See also* LOCAL GOVERNMENT REFORMS, p. 123; PREFECT, p. 133.

Significance Local government in France has been traditionally highly centralized, uniform, and under the close supervision of the national government's Ministry of Interior. The prefect played a predominant role in administering local matters in accordance with policies established by the national ministry. This system was very influential outside France, for it was widely imitated in Europe, Latin America, the Middle East, and Asia. The reform laws passed in 1981–82 by the government of President François Mitterrand, however, have formally dropped tutelage and decentralized the system. Although local government structures have not been changed, more authority and resources have been transferred to these units. The prefect is now called the commissioner of the Republic, and his powers have been circumscribed. It is too early to determine how extensive in practice the new decentralization reforms will be.

Local Government Reforms Legislation adopted in 1981–82 that formally decentralized the system of local government in France. The local government reforms, which were proposed by the Socialist government of President François Mitterrand, made changes in the structures, functions, resources, and electoral systems of local authorities. The prefect is now called the commissioner of the Republic, and his formal powers of supervision over local government (called tutelage, *tutelle*) have been curtailed. The reforms partially transfer an impressive list of functions in planning, economic development, education, job training, housing, transportation, social security, and welfare payments to local governments. Additional national resources are also transferred along with power to decide on the allocation of national funds; and regional governments are given authority to levy certain taxes. Little change was made in the structure of local governments, except that elective district councils (*conseils d'arrondissement*) were created in the cities of Paris, Marseilles, and Lyons, and given specific functions. The complex system of local government elections was also changed, but the changes introduced other complexities, and there is no uniform electoral system. A variety of electoral systems have been renewed or introduced, depending on city size. Generally, the two-ballot runoff system is used in smaller communes, a combination of this system with proportional representation in larger cities, and a ward list system in Paris, Marseilles, and Lyons. *See also* LOCAL GOVERNMENT: FRANCE, p. 122; PREFECT, p. 133.

Significance It is too soon to assess the impact on national-local relationships that might be brought about by the local government reforms of 1981–82. The changes do have the potential for transferring real power to local authorities, which would give France a system of local government worthy of its name. The centralized tradition of France is great, however, and the centralizing effects of modernization may circumscribe the effects of the reforms. The prefects, who still use their old title along with the new, have much control over technical services that are essential to small villages and rural areas, which comprise 90 percent of the communes and departments. Some observers note that tutelage had already declined in the larger cities before the reforms were enacted, and that little change is expected. It is foreseen, however, that mayors, deputies, senators, and other notables (local persons of influence) will increase in power as local authorities begin bargaining with national agencies for greater prerogatives and resources.

May Events of 1968 Nationwide strikes, occupations of buildings, and massive demonstrations that followed student riots in May 1968. The May Events were touched off by a protest of students at the suburban Nanterre campus of the University of Paris in March 1968 that spread to the Sorbonne and the Latin Quarter in Paris. In May, students set up barricades, occupied buildings, and battled the police. The demonstrations and riots spread; the Stock Exchange was burned, and other important buildings in Paris were occupied by leftist forces. Demonstrations occurred in the rest of the country, and university and high school students, workers in factories, civil servants, white-collar workers and technical employees in the schools, banks, post offices, stores, and transportation services went on strike. The country was almost paralyzed as 10 million workers, or at least one-third of the work force, participated in the general strike. Most shades of political opinion and social classes participated, but few agreed on the goals of the revolt. Participants included anarchist students led by Daniel Cohn-Bendit, centrist politicians who wanted to bring down President Charles de Gaulle's government, trade unionists who sought wage increases, and middle-class office workers who wanted a greater voice in their worklife. President de Gaulle's initial reaction to the revolt was to call a referendum on the "participation" of workers and students in management decisions. This was rejected, and strikes continued. Finally, order was restored after de Gaulle returned from a secret trip to Germany, where he conferred with French army commanders who promised to support his government in case of a civil war. De Gaulle dissolved the National Assembly and scheduled new elections; he released from prison the generals who had revolted against his government in 1961 over the Algerian issue; and he also permitted political exiles to return to France. Massive Gaullist demonstrations supporting the government then took place in Paris, and the nation prepared for the elections. Prime Minister Georges Pompidou engineered a brilliant election campaign in which the "forces of order" were pitted against "chaos," and "democracy" against "communist totalitarianism." The Gaullist party won a smashing victory in the June 23 elections, winning an absolute majority of seats in the National Assembly, the first time a single party did so in French history.

Significance The May Events constitute the most massive general strike in French history. Although President de Gaulle survived, the mystique of his power was gone, and he resigned in the following year when he lost a referendum. Reforms were enacted after the election; workers received wage increases, and the universities were modernized under the Faure Reforms. Although only two persons were killed in the May Events, the widespread participation in the revolt is considered to be of great importance. Observers have developed various conflicting theories trying to explain the events. Some of the better-known interpretations are that the May Events were (1) a revolt against modernization and the consumer-materialist society of affluence; (2) a revolt in favor of modernization in educational and industrial organizations; (3) an expression of the anomic and revolutionary behavior that characterizes the dissensual French society; (4) a revolt against all authority and a cry for spontaneous self-expression; and (5) a demand for greater democracy and participation of students and workers in making decisions affecting their lives. Given the large-scale participation, the May Events were probably part of all of these things and something more—a desire by opportunists to remove President de Gaulle from office. In the end, the Fifth Republic survived its greatest challenge, and the crisis was resolved by democratic means.

Mondialisme The major principle of the foreign policy of President Valéry Giscard d'Estaing that France should maintain a worldwide presence and practice an assertive role in international affairs. *Mondialisme* or globalism meant that France would follow an active, independent, and distinctive foreign policy toward all major geographic regions of the world and in all important international policy matters. In practice, Giscard took initiatives in the Middle East, Africa, Asia, and Eastern Europe. He gave special attention to nonaligned Third World states and at the same time projected an assertive posture in major Atlantic, European, and East-West problem areas. Examples of the *mondialiste* foreign policy include: (1) engaging in military intervention in various Francophone African states to support friendly but unstable governments; (2) taking an activist role in North-South conferences; (3) establishing special relations with nonaligned and oil-producing states; (4) taking initiatives to bring about peace in the Middle East; (5) making proposals for East-West detente and disarmament; (6) establishing closer relations with West Germany; (7) maintaining a strong and diversified military capability; and (8) promoting the expansion of European Community institutions, such as the European Monetary System, the European Currency Unit, and European summit conferences (called the European Council). *See also* GAULLISM: FOREIGN POLICY, p. 115.

Significance Giscardian foreign policies based on the principle of mondialisme were similar in purpose and partially in content to those practiced under Gaullism. Basic goals of mondialisme were to project France as the predominant power in Western Europe, put the country on a par with the superpowers, and promote French prestige and influence throughout the world. Some of Giscard's policies were successful, particularly in stabilizing friendly governments in Francophone Africa and in maintaining access to resources and markets. But because of the nation's structural economic weaknesses as compared to Germany and its military inferiority as compared to the United States and the Soviet Union, some important policies had no success. For Giscard, however, the domestic political benefits of maintaining the French myth of greatness and independence and of retaining Gaullist support for his government seemed to balance the economic costs, inconsistent application, and essential weakness of mondialisme.

National Center of Independents and Peasants (CNIP) The formerly large conservative party that has declined in the Fifth Republic. The National Center of Independents and Peasants (*Centre Nationale des Independants et Paysans,* CNIP), known as Independents and referred to as conservatives by observers, draws its support from rural, Catholic, farmer, and small business interests. It advocates traditional values, is opposed to government intervention in the economy, and is strongly anticommunist. In the Fourth Republic, it had a large but undisciplined parliamentary group and participated in a number of cabinets. The CNIP supported the coming of Charles de Gaulle to power in 1958 and did very well in the parliamentary elections of that year. In 1962 it split over the issue of whether to back the constitutional referendum on the popular election of the president. The party's leader,

Valéry Giscard d'Estaing, who supported the referendum, organized the Republican Independent party, later called the Republican party. In the 1960s the CNIP declined rapidly, losing most of its conservative supporters to the Gaullist party. During the Giscard presidency, 1974–81, the CNIP was in the parliamentary majority of the president. In the National Assembly elections of 1981, the CNIP dropped from nine to five deputies. It is much stronger in municipal elections and in the Senate, where rural overrepresentation and the indirect system of election benefit the party. *See also* FIFTH REPUBLIC: POLITICAL PARTY SYSTEM, p. 100; REPUBLICAN PARTY (PR), p. 138.

Significance The National Center of Independents and Peasants is a small remnant of the traditional, rural, conservative, prorepublican forces that were important in the Third Republic and part of the Fourth Republic. In 1936 the party, then called National Center of Independents (CNT) won 42.5 percent of the vote. It was much smaller in the Fourth Republic, but in the wake of the Gaullist victory in 1958 it won 22 percent of the vote and 28 percent of the seats. Afterwards its former supporters moved to the Gaullist or Giscardist parties, and the party has ceased to play an important role in national elections.

Nationalizations of 1982 The legislative enactment of a program of collectivization of a large number of industrial and financial firms by the Socialist government of President François Mitterrand. The 1982 nationalizations resulted in the public takeover of 5 industrial groups, 39 banks, and 2 financial holding companies. Included in the nationalizations were the nation's largest private companies in electrical equipment, electronics, computers, building materials, aluminum, petrochemicals, household appliances, and other industries. In addition, two steel companies were nationalized in 1981 by separate legislation, and the government took majority shares in two firms manufacturing military aircraft, armaments, and other equipment. Not affected were foreign-controlled banks, small banks, and small mutual savings institutions. The nationalization bill was originally passed by the National Assembly in December 1981 over the Senate's veto, but the Constitutional Council ruled that portions of the bill were unconstitutional. The Council objected to the exclusion of certain large cooperative banks as discriminatory, and it required parliamentary approval for nationalized concerns to divest themselves of foreign subsidiaries. The most important objection by the Council was that the compensation to be paid to former owners was too little. In January 1982 the government of Prime Minister Pierre Mauroy increased the compensation by about $1.2 to $1.4 billion, thus raising the cost of the takeovers to $7 billion. The revised bill was passed by the National Assembly and signed into law in February 1982. *See also* SOCIALIST PARTY (PS), p. 142.

Significance The 1982 nationalizations fulfilled François Mitterrand's campaign promise in 1981 to seek the public takeover of large industrial and financial companies. These nationalizations, however, are not the first major expansions of the public sector. The Popular Front government of 1936–37 collectivized certain public utilities, and after World War II, the Provisional Government of Charles de Gaulle, in an effort partially aimed at "punitive nationalization" of collaborationist firms, nationalized coal mines, the Renault automobile company, an aircraft motor firm, air transport companies, four commercial banks, and other companies. The 1982 nationalizations increased the number of employees working in the public sector from one to two million, who are distributed among 3,500 companies that are directly or indirectly controlled by the state. Public sector employment accounts for 12 percent of the workforce and 30 percent of the sales in industry. In the banking and finance field, the 1982 nationalizations raised the public sector share to 90 percent of the deposits held and 84 percent of the credit issued by regular banking institutions. Some observers have argued that since the French government has usually followed a policy of *dirigisme*, or state intervention in the economy, the nationalizations will make little change in the manner in which the economy is managed.

Nuclear Weapons Strategy Doctrines pertaining to the use of French nuclear weapons in wartime. Nuclear weapons strategy evolved through various phases depending on the president in power, events in Europe, and the stage of French nuclear weapons development. The main strategies have been (1) in the early 1960s, deterrence of any attack on France or its European allies by threatening "massive reprisals" against the Soviet Union; (2) in the late 1960s, a strategy of *tous azimuts*, whereby national territory would be defended by nuclear forces against attacks coming from any and all directions, presumably including attacks from Western states; (3) since 1969, under the Fourquet Doctrine, strategic defense of French territory would stress deterring attacks specifically emanating from the Soviet Union; (4) since 1969 and especially since the deployment of tactical nuclear weapons in 1976, a doctrine of "graduated, flexible response," which would not require the initial use of strategic weapons; and (5) under President Valéry Giscard d'Estaing, the doctrine of "enlarged sanctuary," whereby France would defend with nuclear weapons not only national territory, but a wider area in northern and southern Europe in the context of joint planning with NATO. Some Socialists advocate a return to the massive retaliation strategy. *See also* ENLARGED SANCTUARY, p. 96; FORCE DE FRAPPE, p. 105; TOUS AZIMUTS, p. 152.

Significance French nuclear weapons strategies have been aimed at making credible the supposed deterrent power of the nation's nuclear forces. The essential weaknesses in the strategies are directly linked to the gross military inferiority that a medium-sized state like France suffers from compared to a nuclear superpower such as the Soviet Union. Those strategies that were based on an independent and neutralistic foreign policy and on a defense policy outside the context of joint cooperation with other NATO powers were so unrealistic that they had to be abandoned. Because French nuclear forces have been created and expanded, a nuclear strategy needs to be devised by the government, but outside NATO, the forces provide no security against attacks from the Soviet Union. Independent French nuclear forces serve more in symbolic and prestige-generating roles than as a deterrent force against possible Soviet attacks on Western Europe.

Political Culture: France The system of attitudes, values, and beliefs that are held by the French people about their political system. French political culture, currently undergoing change, has the following traditional characteristics: (1) a stress on individualism, understood as personal independence; (2) a striving for material self-interest, but without taking risks; (3) apathy and a low level of voluntary participation in political and social associations; (4) social fragmentation and a distrust of members of other social groups; (5) *incivisme,* or a lack of civic responsibility and unwillingness to make sacrifices for the greater social good; (6) an ambivalent attitude toward authority; (7) an ideological style of politics; (8) a cynical mistrust of government; and (9) a strong sense of nationalism, patriotism, and cultural superiority. These features of the political culture contribute to a social and political ethos that is uncooperative, fragmented, uncompromising, dissensual, and conflictual. In the postwar period, however, particularly in the last two decades, economic, social, and political changes may be affecting the traditional political culture. Some of these changes are: the decline in the farm population, rapid industrialization, urbanization, growth in economic competitiveness, and a rise in geographical and social mobility. The increase in affluence and commitment to growth and development seem to be accompanied with a decline in alienation and acceptance of the institutions of the Fifth Republic. *See also* CONSTITUTIONAL DISSENSUS, p. 89; SOCIOECONOMIC THEORY: CONSENSUS THESIS, p. 144; SOCIOECONOMIC THEORY: STALEMATE SOCIETY THESIS, p. 147; SOCIOECONOMIC THEORY: TWO FRANCES THESIS, p. 147.

Significance The political culture provides the means by which the French people evaluate and respond to the leaders, institutions, and policies of government. Major features of French politics are related to the traditional political culture; these include such phenomena as frequent revolutions and massive public protests, a constitutional dissensus, cabinet instability, legislative immobilism, and the traditional slow progress towards socioeconomic modernization. It may be too soon to determine whether the socioeconomic changes in recent years have made a lasting impact on the political culture. Attitudes and values undergo much slower change than the economy or institutional arrangements. The potential for alienation, fragmentation, and revolt remains in France. Some observers dispute the traditional interpretation of French political culture and argue that the society is more consensual than dissensual and that there is strong support for republican and democratic values in France. There seems to be no dispute, however, about the fact that democracy in France has been traditionally weak and that the French people are difficult to govern.

Popular Front The alliance of Socialists, Communists, and Radical Socialists that provided support for several French governments from 1936 to 1938. The Popular Front was formed in 1935 to unite the republican left against the threat of fascism and the extreme right, which had manifested itself in bloody riots in Paris in 1934. In 1936, the Popular Front won a great victory in national elections that had an 85 percent voter turnout. The Socialist leader, León Blum, became premier; the Communists supported but did not enter his government. Blum's Popular Front government enacted a number of labor reforms, such as the 40-hour week, collective bargaining, paid vacations, and improved wages; he also nationalized the munitions industry and reorganized the Bank of France. Regarding the Spanish Civil War, Blum adopted a policy of nonintervention, which was condemned by the revolutionary left. In 1937, unable to win Senate support for his budgetary program in the face of an economic crisis, Blum resigned. Several milder Popular Front governments followed in 1937–38, and the alliance broke up in 1938 as power flowed to center-right governments. *See also* ACTION FRANÇAIS, p. 79; THIRD REPUBLIC, p. 148.

Significance The Popular Front provided France with its first Socialist premier. The labor reforms of Blum's government were remarkable, but some of them were rescinded by later governments in order to deter capital flight and spur economic recovery. Although the more conservative Senate brought down Blum's government in 1937, the alliance itself could not hold together when he moved to conservative economic policies to meet the economic slump. The parties in the alliance coalesced again in the wartime Resistance against the German occupation of France.

Popular Republican Movement (MRP) The Christian Democratic party that was a strong force in the Fourth Republic and that formally dissolved in 1967. The origins of the Popular Republic Movement (*Mouvement Républicain Populaire*, MRP) are in the wartime Resistance against German occupation. In the first postwar election of 1945, the MRP emerged along with the Communists and Socialists as one of the three mass-based parties in France. The party leadership was committed to Catholic social reform principles, sometimes called Christian Socialism, and to an alternate vision of society opposed to Marxist socialism and unregulated liberalism. Its program called for social reform, European integration, and aid to church schools. During the Fourth Republic the party's popular support ranged from a high of 28 percent of the popular vote in 1946 to about 14 percent, depending on whether a Gaullist party was competing. Being in the political center, the MRP supplied many of the premiers and cabinet ministers, including Georges Bidault, Robert Schuman, and Maurice Schumann. Following the 1958 Algerian crisis that brought Charles de Gaulle to power, the MRP supported the new constitution and de Gaulle's government. It broke with de Gaulle in the early 1960s when he turned against European integration. This led to a further decline, and in 1962 MRP support fell to 9 percent of the vote. Although party leader Jean Lecanuet made a good showing in the first ballot of the presidential election of 1965, the MRP had declined so much that it formally dissolved the organization in 1967. The Center of Social Democrats headed by Lecanuet is a secular descendant of the MRP. *See also* CENTER OF SOCIAL DEMOCRATS (CDS), p. 84; CONSTITUENT ASSEMBLY, p. 87.

Significance The Popular Republican Movement was one of the dominant parties in the Fourth Republic, and its contribution to the cause of European integration was very important. The European Coal and Steel Community was created after proposals, called the Schuman Plan, that were made in 1950 by Robert Schuman, the MRP premier. Georges Bidault and Maurice Schumann were foreign ministers of France for almost the entire period of the Fourth Republic. The fate of the MRP was quite unlike the conservative Christian Democratic parties in Western Europe, which continue to enjoy strong voter support. The MRP's program of social reform was popular so long as the party's more conservative Catholic voters did not have a Gaullist party to vote for. The parliamentary allies of the party were to the left, but its voter support came from the right. Also, the government coalitions the MRP would make to the anticlerical left often could not survive its program of aid to church schools. An irony is that when the MRP dissolved in 1967, Christian Democratic parties were in office in the other five nations of the European community.

Poujadism   A right-wing protest movement that was active in the 1950s. Poujadism takes its name from its founder, Pierre Poujade, a small town shopkeeper who organized the Association for the Defense of Shopkeepers and Artisans (UDCA) in 1953. Originally an antitax, antiregulation movement, the organization grew dramatically, and on occasion used violence against officials. In 1955 Poujade organized the Union of French Fraternity (UFF) to contest the January 1956 national elections. Poujadists made a spectacular showing: the party received over 2.8 million votes and won 52 seats in the Chamber of Deputies. With 12 percent of the popular vote, the Poujadists outpolled the Christian Democrats (MRP) and the Radicals, but won fewer seats because of the electoral system. Support came from shopkeepers, farmers, and the lower middle class, primarily in the south, and from others who were disgusted with the Fourth Republic. In the assembly, the Poujadists were obstructionists, voting against liberal and social measures, European integration proposals, and any indications of decolonization. By holding a substantial bloc of seats in the assembly, the party made it difficult for center-right cabinets to retain majority support. With the coming of Charles de Gaulle to power in 1958, the Poujadists disintegrated, and their supporters moved to other right-wing and conservative parties. The party received less than 3 percent of the vote in the 1958 elections, and consequently under the new electoral system, won no seats. *See also* FOURTH REPUBLIC: POLITICAL PARTY SYSTEM, p. 108.

Significance   Poujadism began as a movement of premodern social classes against the forces of modernization and large-scale enterprise. As the movement grew into a general protest against the Fourth Republic, it attracted many who objected to the ineffectual government, the colonial defeats, the partisan bickerings, and other failures of the republic. The party died when the Fourth Republic died, but the premodern Poujadist social groups soon fell to protesting against de Gaulle's government when they observed his modernizing and decolonizing policies. The Poujadists are an excellent example of a "flash party" in the French system, one that grows suddenly, makes an impact, and quickly dies.

Prefect An official of the national government who has traditionally exercised vast powers of supervision over local units of government. The title of prefect was changed to commissioner of the republic in the local government reforms enacted in 1981–82. Before these reforms, prefects had the power of supervision, known as tutelage (*tutelle*), under which a prefect could control the agenda of local councils, dismiss councils, prepare budgets, and raise local taxes to ensure the administration of local services that were mandated by national law. The prefect is assigned to a department and is assisted by subprefects. In the regional level of government, which is primarily concerned with transportation and economic development, the national officer in charge of coordinating regional affairs was popularly called the superprefect. Local government reforms adopted in 1981–82 reduced the tutelage power of the prefect, transferred important functions and national resources to local authorities, and created elective regional councils. The role of the prefect, however, was reaffirmed as the office who has ultimate responsibility to defend national interests, maintain respect for the law, ensure public order, and keep administrative control. *See also* LOCAL GOVERNMENT: FRANCE, p. 122; LOCAL GOVERNMENT REFORMS, p. 123.

Significance Prefects, or commissioners of the republic, are professional civil servants who are members of the prefectoral corps that is controlled by the Ministry of the Interior. They have traditionally been used by national governments, sometimes in a highly partisan manner, to maintain tight control over local government affairs. The new decentralization reforms of local government that formally ended the tutelage system may not have ended the prefects' importance or their power to influence local decisions. Some observers have noted that tutelage had already declined in the larger cities. But the technical services at the disposal of the prefect are essential to the many small communes and rural departments. Although they are now officially called commissioners of the republic, prefects and subprefects also use their old titles.

Provisional Government The temporary government that ruled France from October 1944 to January 1947 during the period of transition from the Third to the Fourth Republic. The Provisional Government of the French Republic developed out of the French Committee of National Liberation, which had combined various forces in the Resistance to German occupation of France in World War II. General Charles de Gaulle, who had organized the Free France group in Britain, emerged as the head of the committee and then as first president of the

Provisional Government. In 1946 a Constituent Assembly was elected to draft a new constitution and to approve the provisional presidents. The presidents were: Charles de Gaulle, 1944–46; Félix Gouin (Socialist), 1946; Georges Bidault (Popular Republican Movement), 1946; and Léon Blum, who served for one month, and who turned over power to the new government of the Fourth Republic in January 1947. *See also* CONSTITUENT ASSEMBLY, p. 87.

Significance The Provisional Government provided France with a governmental system as the country was liberated from German control and as the Vichy government disintegrated. By combining the Resistance parties in a coalition government, it provided a degree of unity, stability, and order. Although the government and the Constituent Assembly were marked by partisanship and disagreement over the new constitution, the transition to the Fourth Republic was orderly and democratic.

Radical Party A party of the center that once dominated the Third Republic, was influential in the Fourth Republic, but has virtually disappeared. In the postwar period, the Radicals (Radical Republican and Radical Socialist party) was a loose amalgam of independent, undisciplined centrist politicians that provided many of the cabinet ministers and 12 of the 27 premiers from 1944 to 1958. The party had no internal cohesion or consistent program, and often made alliances to the left or to the right. Sometimes it linked itself with other small parties of personality, such as François Mitterrand's Socialist and Democratic Union of the Resistance (UDSR). The hopes of the Radicals were raised when Pierre Mendès-France came to power in 1954–55; he settled the Indochina War and made a coalition with the Socialist party, but this also broke apart. In the Fifth Republic the Radical party split into pro-Gaullist and anti-Gaullist groups, and into left and right wings divided over whether to make electoral alliances with Communists. The regular Radical party was revitalized by the anti-Gaullist publisher Jean-Jacques Servan-Schreiber in the early 1970s and adopted a progressive and egalitarian program. Servan-Schreiber also helped organize the Reformers' Movement with the Democratic Center, but neither effort won popular support. Radicals supported Valéry Giscard d'Estaing's successful bid for the presidency in 1974 and were part of his electoral and parliamentary alliance, Union for French Democracy. The Radical party was practically wiped out in the 1981 elections, when its assembly delegation fell from eight to two deputies. The left wing of the party, which split in 1971 and is called the Leftist Radical Movement (MRG), has fared better. *See also* FIFTH REPUBLIC: POLITICAL PARTY SYSTEM, p. 100; LEFTIST RADICAL MOVEMENT (MRG), p. 121.

Significance The Radical party is the oldest party in France, and it once dominated French politics. It was the typical undisciplined, republican, anticlerical party composed of personalities and local notables that participated in most of the unstable governments of the Third and Fourth Republics. The coming of presidential government, the two-ballot electoral system, and the bipolarization of French politics have helped to eliminate the Radicals as a political force.

Rally for the Republic (RPR) The large political party, renamed in 1976, that is the successor of the political movement founded by Charles de Gaulle. The Rally for the Republic (*Rassemblement pour la République*, RPR) is the continuation of the Gaullist movement, which has gone through a number of name changes. The origins of the party are in the first political organization that was founded by de Gaulle in 1947, the Rally of the French People (RPF). De Gaulle wanted to create a political movement of loyal supporters, not another political party of the type that had dominated the Third Republic. The RPF did very well in the elections of 1951, but de Gaulle disassociated himself from the organization when its parliamentary leaders began cooperating with the constitutional system instead of opposing it, and the RPF collapsed in 1952. After the fall of the Fourth Republic in 1958, a new Gaullist organization was formed, the Union for the New Republic (UNR), and it is this group that has changed its name several times. In 1962 the UNR joined with a small leftist Gaullist party, the Democrat Union for Labor (UDT), and the party became the UNR-UDT. In 1967 the name was changed to Union of Democrats for the Fifth Republic (UD-V^{e}Rep.), and for the 1968 elections, to Union for Defense of the Republic (UDR). In 1971, the party kept the same initials but changed the name to Union of Democrats for the Republic (UDR). The former Gaullist prime minister, Jacques Chirac, made a major reorganization of the party in 1976 after he left the government, and the party took on its present name. Under Chirac the RPR retains the broad policy outline that has characterized Gaullism: a nationalistic and global-oriented foreign policy, an independent national security policy, modernization of the economic system, participation of workers in decisions affecting their worklife, and a defense of the institutions of the Fifth Republic. The party has about 760,000 members, most of whom have joined since 1976; 65 percent are professionals, executives, middle-level managers, or white-collar workers; 11 percent are blue-collar workers, and 11 percent are farmers. The party is strong in western, northern, and eastern France and in the last three elections has won from 20 to 25 percent of the popular vote. In the Socialist victories of 1981, Chirac won only 18 percent of the vote on the first ballot for president, and the RPR representation in the National Assembly dropped from 153 to 85 deputies. *See also* ELECTIONS OF 1981: FRANCE, p. 92; FIFTH REPUBLIC: POLITICAL PARTY SYSTEM, p. 100; GAULLISM: FOREIGN POLICY, p. 115; GAULLISM: POLITICAL DOCTRINE, p. 116.

Significance The Rally for the Republic is the latest organization of the continuing Gaullist movement, which has played a predominant role in the Fifth Republic. The constitutional system that de Gaulle initiated and the defense policies that he pursued have been passed on intact to the succeeding governments under Presidents Georges Pompidou, Valéry Giscard d'Estaing, and François Mitterrand. Gaullists supplied all seven premiers from 1959 to 1976, and they had an important part in the government of the Republican prime minister, Raymond Barre. Originally a movement of supporters of one man, the Gaullist party has survived the passing of de Gaulle, the presidency of Giscard, and the Socialist victories of 1981. Although Gaullists are still reluctant to use the word "party" in their title, Chirac has refashioned an amorphous, catch-all movement into a modern cohesive political party. The organization's membership is large, the militants are active, local party structures and intermediate agencies have been strengthened, and power is concentrated at the top. The RPR has returned as the major force opposing the social-communist left, and Jacques Chirac, reinvigorated by his reelection as mayor of Paris in 1983, is the focal point of the opposition to the Socialist government.

Referendum Power The constitutional authority to submit to a popular vote questions regarding the adoption of laws, treaties, policies, or constitutional issues. There have been ten referenda in France since World War II, six of which related to constitutional questions. In 1945 the people approved by 95 percent a Constituent Assembly to draft a new constitution, and by 66 percent limitations on the assembly's governmental powers. In 1946 the first draft of a constitution was rejected by 53 percent, and later that year the Constitution of the Fourth Republic was approved by 54 percent. About one-third of the people abstained in both cases. The Constitution of the Fifth Republic was approved by 79 percent in 1958. During the Fifth Republic the referendum power was used in a controversial manner by presidents Charles de Gaulle and Georges Pompidou. The Constitution provides that the president may submit referenda on a proposal by the government (cabinet) or the two houses of parliament on questions concerning the "organization of the public authorities," on European Community agreements, and on treaties. Although the Constitution provides for a regular constitutional amendment process that passes through parliament, de Gaulle had his government propose several constitutional amendments and policy questions through the referendum process. In January 1961 voters approved by 75 percent the policy of self-determination for Algeria, and in April 1962 voters approved by 91 percent the Evian Accords, which gave independence to Algeria. The most controversial use of the referendum power was the October 1962 question of whether the Constitution should be amended to provide for a popular vote for electing the president; this proposal was approved by 62 percent. In 1969, a combined constitutional amendment that would have restructured the Senate and created a new level of regional government was rejected by 53 percent. President de Gaulle resigned after this defeat. In April 1972 President Pompidou submitted the question of whether the United Kingdom, the Republic of Ireland, Denmark, and Norway should be admitted to the European Communities. The voters approved the expansion by 68 percent, but voter turnout was low. No referenda were submitted in the presidency of Valéry Giscard d'Estaing, from 1974 to 1981, nor in the first three years of François Mitterrand's term. *See also* BONAPARTISM, p. 82; FIFTH REPUBLIC: CONSTITUTION, p. 98.

Significance The use of the referendum power by the executive for partisan reasons is a feature of Bonapartism opposed by the republican left. In the Gaullist period of the Fifth Republic, 1958 to 1974, critics charged that the two presidents used the power in an unconstitutional manner. De Gaulle's presidency is sometimes referred to as an illustration of "plebiscitary democracy," in which people are asked to confirm previously made decisions in a simple vote that in effect amounts to a vote of confidence in the government. The 1962 constitutional amendment on the popular vote for the president was opposed by parliament, the Council of State, and the Constitutional Council because it sidetracked the regular amendment process. Pompidou's use of the referendum on the expansion of the European Community was clearly adopted to reestablish his popular mandate; although the question was approved, he failed in his purpose because many voters abstained. Afterwards the use of the referendum in a plebiscitary manner declined because it did not fit President Giscard's style and is contrary to the republican traditions of the Socialists now in power.

Republican Party (PR)   The neoliberal party founded by Valéry Giscard d'Estaing that participates in the center coalition called the Union for French Democracy. The origins of the Republican party are in the traditional conservative party, the National Center for Independents, which supported the creation of the Fifth Republic. Out of this group, Giscard formed the Independent Republicans (RI) in 1966, and, following losses in municipal elections in 1977, he reorganized the RI as the Republican party (PR). Giscard allied with the Gaullists, but took an independent position on national policy. He criticized excessive presidential power and the nationalistic foreign policy of the Gaullists; he also called for fiscal restraint, less government intervention in the economy, and pro-European and Atlanticist policies. After winning the presidency in 1974, Giscard developed a neoliberal social reform platform that stressed moderate liberal reforms and a pluralist democracy. His policies as president, however, were not too different from Gaullist positions, particularly in foreign affairs, where he practiced a worldwide policy he called *mondialisme*. Giscard helped create the electoral and parliamentary alliance of Republican, centrist, Radical, and other groups called Union for French Democracy, which positioned itself midway between the socialist-communist left and the Gaullist right. The UDF was not strong enough to govern without Gaullist support, however, and French politics continued to show the bipolarization that has marked the Fifth Republic. In 1981 Giscard lost the presidential election to the Socialist candidate François Mitterrand, and the Republican party dropped from 65 to 32 deputies in the subsequent Assembly elections. Current leaders of the party are Michel Poniatowski and Jean-Pierre Soisson. *See also* FIFTH REPUBLIC: POLITICAL PARTY SYSTEM, p. 100; MONDIALISME, p. 125; NATIONAL CENTER OF INDEPENDENTS AND PEASANTS (CNIP), p. 126.

Significance   The Republican party and the centrist coalition, the Union for French Democracy, played an important role during the presidency of Giscard d'Estaing from 1974 to 1981. Although the party's program has been modernized, the PR does not have a strong social base and still relies in large measure on local government notables. The rise and decline of the party has been dependent on the fate of one man, whose future in French politics is uncertain. Following Giscard's defeat in 1981, leadership of the opposition to the Socialist majority passed to Jacques Chirac, leader of the Gaullist party.

Resistance   Various French underground forces that fought against the German occupation of France from 1940 to 1944. The Resistance included a large number of separate groups, overwhelmingly of the center and the left. Communists joined in large numbers after Germany attacked the Soviet Union in 1941. Resistance forces were assisted by the British and increasingly related to the Free France forces of General Charles de Gaulle in Britain. A National Resistance Council was created in 1943 that brought together underground groups, political parties, and labor unions. Participation in the Resistance increased so that by 1944, perhaps over a half-million persons were active. About 50,000 resisters were killed or executed, and many thousands were deported to concentration camps. A number of important postwar politicians including Georges Bidault, Michel Debré, Jacques Chaban-Delmas, and François Mitterrand were active in the Resistance. *See also* VICHY REGIME, p. 154.

Significance The Resistance played important roles in gathering military intelligence, sabotaging equipment, harassing German forces, and fighting in guerrilla operations. An insurrection was initiated in Paris one week before the city was liberated by regular army units on August 25, 1944. As towns were liberated by the allied armies, Resistance forces assumed local government powers and summarily executed perhaps as many as 10,000 collaborators. Although the Resistance alone could never have freed France from German control, its contribution regained some of the national honor that was lost by the ignominious defeat in 1940 and the disgrace of the Vichy episode.

Revolution of 1789 The great French Revolution that convulsed France and had worldwide effects. The origins of the French Revolution have been traced to the unwillingness of the monarchy (*ancien régime*) to make political and social reforms, to recognize the position of the new bourgeoisie that developed under capitalism, or to accept new ideas popularized by the *philosophes* (intellectuals and writers). The immediate cause was the financial collapse of the government; this forced the king to try to raise taxes by summoning the Estates General in 1789, which had not met since 1614. The Revolution passed through various stages, accompanied by popular riots (such as the storming of the Bastille prison on July 14, 1789), plots and counterrevolution by royalists and conservative republicans, violence between revolutionary factions, and a series of international wars (the French Revolutionary Wars, 1792–1802) against monarchist rulers of Europe who opposed the Revolution. The major institutions used in the revolutionary period include (1) the National Assembly, declared by the commoners in the Estates General in 1789, which adopted many reforms and proclaimed the Declaration of the Rights of Man and Citizen; (2) the Legislative Assembly, which retained a limited monarchy and established property qualifications for voting; (3) the National Convention, elected by universal manhood suffrage, which abolished the monarchy and declared a republic in 1792; (4) the Committee of Public Safety and the Committee of General Security, instruments of the Jacobins who defeated the moderate republicans, the Girondists, and installed the Reign of Terror under the leadership of Maximilien Robespierre; (5) the Directory, 1795–99, resulting from a conservative reaction, which had a plural executive of five directors and a cumbersome bicameral legislature; and (6) the Consulate, 1799–1804, established by a coup d'etat by Napoleon Bonaparte, which was ostensibly a republic, but in reality a military dictatorship with Napoleon as first consul. In 1802 Napoleon was named first consul for life and in 1804 a popular plebiscite recognized his title as emperor. Many historians mark 1799 as the formal end of the Revolution. The First Republic is usually dated from 1792 to 1804, but some writers close the period in 1795 with the Directory or in 1799 with Napoleon's coup d'etat. *See also* ANCIEN RÉGIME, p. 82; DECLARATION OF THE RIGHTS OF MAN AND CITIZEN, p. 90; JACOBINISM, p. 119.

Significance The French Revolution of 1789 had important effects in France, Europe, and the Americas, and its influence is still being felt today. In France, the Revolution abolished feudalism, placed limitations on the church, established the bourgeoisie in power, and made a host of political, social, and economic changes. Its proclamation of human rights was very influential both politically and intellectually; and its slogan "Liberty, Equality, Fraternity" became a national motto. Through the revolutionary and Napoleonic wars against European powers, the Revolution successfully challenged royal absolutism. Nationalism throughout Europe and in Latin America was promoted by the French example. The spread of liberalism and the doctrines of popular sovereignty and legal equality of the citizen owe much to the revolution in France. French political culture was affected a great deal, as the notion of revolution became part of the national heritage. Although the Republic was overthrown, the ideals of the Revolution ultimately prevailed over royalist and imperialist ones. In sum, the year 1789 is the beginning of a new period in the political and intellectual history of Europe. In the contemporary theory of revolution, some theorists use the French Revolution as an explanatory model of the process of a social revolution. According to this theory, a revolution passes through the following stages: (1) the failure of prerevolutionary reformism; (2) progress toward political and social change by the first revolutionary government; (3) a conservative reaction; (4) the increasing radicalization and use of violence by extreme revolutionaries; (5) the purge of moderates by revolutionary radicals; and (6) the establishment of a continuing revolutionary dictatorship.

Second Empire The rule of Napoleon III as emperor of the French from 1852 to 1870. The Second Empire was proclaimed in 1852 by Louis Napoleon Bonaparte, the nephew of Napoleon I, one year after he seized power as president of the Second Republic. Ruling as Napoleon III, he established an authoritarian government that had the support of conservatives and local notables. He promoted industrialization, modernization, the building of railroads, public works, and the beautification of Paris. The foreign policy was expansive but not always successful. Wars were fought with little gain in the Crimea and Italy, and an intervention in Mexico (the Maximilian Affair) turned out badly. Napoleon helped promote the building of the Suez Canal, and the empire was extended to Indochina. In the 1860s opposition to Napoleon's rule mounted from groups disaffected by the foreign ventures and his fluctuating economic policy. He therefore permitted more freedoms and gave more power to the weak assembly as he moved to establish a "Liberal Empire." This was confirmed by a plebiscite in 1870, but the Liberal Empire never took hold because Napoleon mishandled France's relations with the growing power of Prussia. In 1870 Napoleon was goaded by the Prussian chancellor, Otto von Bismarck, to declare war on Prussia even though France was unprepared. French armies fared badly, and Napoleon himself was captured in the battle of Sedan. This disaster led to a bloodless revolution in Paris and the proclamation of a republic. *See also* BONAPARTISM, p. 82; FRANCO-PRUSSIAN WAR, p. 109; SECOND REPUBLIC, p. 141.

Significance The Second Empire of Napoleon III contributed much to the economic modernization of France but little to its constitutional development. The move to constitutional government under the Liberal Empire was frustrated by the Franco-Prussian War. Napoleon III used the Napoleonic legend to ride to power, but this led him to questionable foreign ventures and ultimate defeat. The Empire ended in a military disaster, for the Prussians exacted heavy reparations and annexed Alsace and parts of Lorraine. Although the nation was humiliated, Bonapartists continued as a significant force well into the Third Republic. In contemporary usage, the term "Bonapartism" has come to mean a personalistic regime headed by an authoritarian who dominates the assembly and who uses plebiscites to confirm his personal decisions.

Second Republic The period from the Revolution of February 1848 that toppled the July Monarchy of Louis Phillipe to the establishment of the Second Empire of Napoleon III in 1852. The Second Republic was troubled by constant crises, demonstrations, riots, and protests. The provisional government was often under siege as the working class of Paris strove for political reform and jobs in the wake of an economic crisis and rising unemployment. Popular elections established control over the assembly by moderates and conservatives who wrote a constitution providing for the popular election of the president. In the "June Days" of 1848, a working-class revolution in Paris was brutally crushed. Louis Napoleon Bonaparte, the nephew of Napoleon I, returned to France from exile and was elected president in December 1848. Subsequent assembly elections strengthened the power of monarchists and conservatives, who opposed both the Bonapartists and the republicans. In December 1851 Louis Napoleon staged a coup d'etat, which led to further working-class uprisings that were again crushed. Napoleon's assumption of power was overwhelmingly confirmed by a plebiscite in December 1851, and in 1852 he staged another plebiscite that restored the empire with himself as Emperor Napoleon III. *See also* JULY MONARCHY, p. 120; SECOND EMPIRE, p. 141.

Significance Although the Second Republic lasted but four years, it had a considerable impact on France and Europe. The February 1848 Revolution that established the Republic soon turned into a struggle between the revolutionary working class in Paris and the conservative provinces that controlled the assembly. All the unreconciled forces in France joined in the conflict: Bourbon and Orleans monarchists, Bonapartists, liberal and conservative republicans, and socialists. The February Revolution also led to revolutions throughout Europe, which were crushed for the most part.

Socialist Party (PS) The large left-wing party in France that won the presidential and parliamentary elections of 1981. The Socialist party (PS) was first organized in 1905 when it took the name French Section of the Workers' International (SFIO), which it retained until 1971. The SFIO organized several Popular Front governments in 1936–38 and participated in many of the 27 governments in the period 1944–58. It held the premiership on several occasions, including that of Guy Mollet in 1956–58. Popular support for the SFIO steadily declined under the temporizing leadership of Mollet, who led the party from 1946 to 1969, from a high of 23 percent of the vote to 13 percent in 1962. In 1965 its unofficial presidential candidate, Gaston Defferre, won only 5 percent of the popular vote. The SFIO made an electoral alliance with Radicals and other center-left groups called the Federation of the Democratic and Socialist Left (FGDS) in 1965 to 1968, but this did not prevent the decline. Following a poor showing in the 1968 elections, the party organized a number of conferences. At the Epinay Conference in 1971 it changed its name to the Socialist Party; François Mitterrand merged his small Convention of Republican Institutions (CIR) with the PS and became its general secretary. Later Michel Rocard of the small Unified Socialist Party (PSU) also joined the PS. Under Mitterrand's strong and popular leadership the Socialist party was reinvigorated; memberships tripled to about 200,000, the local party organizations (the "federations") were restaffed, party financing improved, and some measure of unity was brought to the feuding factions. Mitterrand's strategy to achieve power had been to make an alliance with the strong Communist party. In 1972 the two parties agreed to a highly detailed Common Program that called for substantial changes in the French economy and social system. The Common Program was abandoned in 1977 when at a meeting of the leftist parties to renew the plan, the Communist party insisted on a great expansion of the provisions calling for nationalization of French industry. Most observers agree that the Communists precipitated the crisis because of their concern over the growing popular support for the Socialists. In subsequent national elections, a first-ballot coalition of Socialists and left-wing Radicals, the Union of the Socialist and Democratic Left (UGSD), was formed along with a second-ballot alliance with the Communists, the Union of the Left. In 1974 Mitterrand lost the presidential election to Valéry Giscard d'Estaing by less than 1 percent of the vote, but he defeated President Giscard in May 1981. The Socialist party then won an absolute majority of the National Assembly a month later. *See also* ELECTIONS OF 1981: FRANCE, p. 92; FIFTH REPUBLIC: POLITICAL PARTY SYSTEM, p. 100; LOCAL GOVERNMENT REFORMS, p. 123; NATIONALIZATIONS OF 1982, p. 127.

Significance The revitalization of the Socialist party and its election victories of 1981 are the most important political developments that have occurred in France since Charles de Gaulle left office in 1969. The Socialist party has not only surpassed the Communist party, it is the largest electoral party in the nation. Although the defense policies of President Mitterrand are not too dissimilar from those of previous presidents, the domestic programs of nationalization, local government reform, and social change are remarkably different. By 1984, however, the structural weaknesses of the economy had not yet been corrected, and the nation had not yet recovered from the economic recession. The social-communist alliance consequently suffered in the municipal elections of 1983. Mass demonstrations occurred in 1983 and 1984 in protest against the government's restrictive fiscal, monetary, and labor policies. The Socialist party still lacks strong support from the working class. Although smaller trade union activists affiliate with the PS, much of the party's membership is drawn from civil servants, white-collar workers, professionals, and local notables. Internal party differences are still present, particularly between the moderate wing of Rocard and the doctrinaire socialists of CERES (Center of Socialist Studies and Research) led by Jean-Pierre Chevènement. The party's platform is a self-contradictory mixture of Marxist socialism, *autogestion* (workers' self-management), government decentralization, citizen participation, economic modernization, improved worker benefits, and enlarged welfare programs. From the point of view of the French political system, however, the renewal and increased strength of the Socialist party have benefited the nation. The Gaullist constitutional system has been legitimated, the Communist party has been coopted and reduced in strength, and the French people have been provided an alternative to the conservatism of the Gaullists and the neoliberalism of the much weakened Giscardians.

Socioeconomic Theory: Consensus Thesis The theory that in French society there is fundamental agreement on political values and continuity of institutions that is more important than the apparent societal dissensus. According to the consensus thesis, the typical manifestations of civic irresponsibility, distrust and criticism of government and anomic behavior of the French people, are not sufficient proof of a societal dissensus. These phenomena also occur in other societies that are said to be consensual, such as the United States. Despite the numerous constitutional and political changes in France, there is a consensus on values, a persistence of administrative, legal, and educational institutions, and a continuity of political personnel. The thesis concludes that the French people are agreed on the republican state and show a continuing commitment to democracy. *See also* CONSTITUTIONAL DISSENSUS, p. 89; SOCIOECONOMIC THEORY: ISSUE PILEUP THESIS, p. 146.

Significance The consensus thesis was developed as a countertheory to the more widespread belief that France suffers from a fundamental societal dissensus. Consensus theorists believe that in the postwar period cabinet instability and ideological rhetoric mask the underlying consensus in the country. They maintain that dissensus theorists overemphasize the social fragmentation and the disfunctional aspects of the political culture. Consensus theorists argue that *incivisme* (lack of civic responsibility) may serve positive goals, distrust in government is counterbalanced by patriotism and municipal pride, and criticism of government is not necessarily evidence of social alienation.

Socioeconomic Theory: End-of-Ideology Thesis The theory that ideology in the Western industrialized democracies has declined in recent decades as the motivating force for left-wing revolutionary movements. According to the end- or decline-of-ideology thesis, there is less passionate attachment to Marxist revolutionary ideals and programs in left-wing working-class movements, and the formerly radical parties of the left have adopted a pragmatic approach to socioeconomic change. Various explanations advanced for this development include (1) the dominant role of the administrative state; (2) exhaustion of ideas among Marxist intellectuals; (3) disillusionment among working classes; (4) vast improvements made in the economic life of the working class; and (5) growth of multiclass "catch-all" parties that have largely replaced single-class parties. The end-of-ideology thesis was advanced in the 1950s by many well-known intellectuals and scholars in Europe and America, such as Daniel Bell and Seymour Martin Lipsett, but it soon came under great criticism by other scholars and left-wing intellectuals. Criticisms have included the arguments that: (1) the term "ideology" should not be confined to left-wing or Marxist approaches; (2) ideas and ideals have always been and will remain a driving force in society; (3) Marxist ideology has not lost its élan, as student activism, growth of the New Left, and the radical activity of the late 1960s demonstrated; (4) although ideology may have declined in some Western nations, it retains motivational power among the Socialist and Communist parties in France and Italy; and (5) the advocates of the thesis are liberal, pluralist, and bourgeois democrats who are opposed to revolutionary Marxism and are merely engaging in polemics rather than analyzing real trends. The advocates of the thesis reply that the concept "decline of ideology" does not mean that ideologically-inspired ideals or standards are no longer relevant, or that class conflict is declining, or that the diminution of Marxist-inspired movements in the postindustrial world implies their demise in the developing countries as well. *See also* CATCH-ALL PARTY THESIS, p. 167; *EMBOURGEOISIEMENT* THESIS, p. 21; FRENCH COMMUNIST PARTY (PCF), p. 111; SOCIALIST PARTY (PS), p. 142.

Significance Although some of the advocates of the end-of-ideology thesis were French intellectuals, such as Raymond Aron, other specialists tried to demonstrate the persistence of ideology within the French Socialist and Communist parties. It was pointed out that, although the French Socialist party took a pragmatic approach in the period 1947 to 1969, the reorganization of the party in 1971 has intensified its ideological fervor, that revisionists within the party are weak, and that the party's program for socioeconomic change has not been curtailed. This view seems to be confirmed by the Socialist rapprochement with the Communist party and the enactment of a program of nationalization of private enterprise, local government reform, and other social changes by the Socialist government of President François Mitterrand. It is also argued that although the Communist party has declined in popular support, the voters have moved to the still ideologically-oriented Socialist party. Further, the Communist party's adoption of a constitutionalist "Eurocommunist" approach is only an admitted tactical change on the road to a communist state. It seems to be clear that the debate over the end of ideology in advanced industrial democracies will continue to engage the energies of intellectuals in these societies as the parties of the left alternate between pragmatic and doctrinaire approaches to socioeconomic problems.

Socioeconomic Theory: Issue Pileup Thesis The theory that the historic French constitutional instability has been caused by an overload on the governmental system that results from the failure to resolve old controversies. In the version of the issue pileup thesis according to Phillip M. Williams, three broad issues were fought out simultaneously in the Third and Fourth Republics: the eighteenth-century struggle between rationalism and Catholicism, the nineteenth-century conflict between democracy and authoritarianism, and the twentieth-century conflict between employer and employee. The nation's inability to resolve these problems is traced to a combination of inflexible political attitudes, an incomplete industrial revolution that retained unmodernized socioeconomic groups, and a political culture characterized by individualism and civic irresponsibility. The old and new struggles are manifested in such postwar political issues as aid to Catholic schools, uneconomic agricultural subsidies, labor relations policy, social welfare programs, the taxation system, and the structure of the government. The society is too divided for the government to cope with these issues simultaneously, and this consequently results in an unstable system and a weak democracy. *See also* CONSTITUTIONAL DISSENSUS, p. 89; SOCIOECONOMIC THEORY: CONSENSUS THESIS, p. 144; SOCIOECONOMIC THEORY: STALEMATE SOCIETY THESIS, p. 147.

Significance The issue pileup thesis is one of several related theories that attempt to explain long-term historical French instability by stressing the underlying societal dissensus. As in the stalemate society thesis, heavy emphasis is placed on the influence of French political culture and the role of social groups. Both theories reject the simple notion that French instability is due to the multiparty system, which instead is viewed as an effect of the broader societal dissensus rather than as a cause. Some critics of dissensus theory argue that there is an underlying consensus in France and that constitutional instability can be directly linked to particular historic circumstances, such as the defeat of the nation in wartime.

Socioeconomic Theory: Stalemate Society Thesis The theory that progress toward socioeconomic modernization in France is blocked by the combination of a centralized administration, a social caste system, and a rigid style of education and models of thinking that oppose experimentation. The stalemate society thesis (*la societé bloquée*) was developed by the French sociologist Michel Crozier, who used this model of French society to explain French instability and the slowness of socioeconomic change. Blockages exist throughout the society wherever collective action is required. The main mechanisms of the blockages are (1) interpersonal and intergroup relations, which are characterized by the isolation of the individual, a lack of communication between groups (the strata), a struggle for group privileges, and an avoidance of face-to-face authority relationships; and (2) a centralized, rigid bureaucracy based on formal rules. The system is inflexible and defensive, and change can occur only through means of a crisis. It is this combination of preindustrial values and obsolete administrative system that retards innovation in France. *See also* FRENCH BUREAUCRACY MODEL, p. 110; SOCIOECONOMIC THEORY: ISSUE PILEUP THESIS, p. 146.

Significance The stalemate society thesis developed by Crozier was widely accepted among scholars, and the expression entered the political vocabulary of intellectuals and journalists. Although the term has been popularized to mean simply a lack of progress in socioeconomic development, Crozier's thesis is a more complex model of French society that attempts to explain constitutional instability, political immobility, and socioeconomic backwardness. Critics of the thesis argue at two levels. First, that in terms of modernization, France has been developing steadily since the nineteenth century, and that significant progress was made in the Fourth Republic despite the high degree of ministerial instability. This modernization is seen in population growth, urbanization, the decline of regional differences, improvements in industrial organization and management style, growing affluence, and changes in social relations. At another level, a second set of criticisms is directed toward the stalemate society thesis as a model of policy making within the French state. Critics point out that the model is heavily rooted in an interpretation of French political culture that is controversial and that is inadmissibly applied to the policy-making process in the French bureaucracy. Although the French bureaucracy is centralized, defensive, and elitist, it has not retarded the modernization of the society, according to the critics.

Socioeconomic Theory: Two Frances Thesis The theory that French society has been divided into two antagonistic blocs that have been in conflict since the Revolution of 1789. The two Frances thesis is an interpretation of French history that stresses the historic struggles between two relatively equal groups, usually called the left and the right. Major examples of these conflicts in French history are the struggles between republicans and monarchists, anticlericals and the church, republicans and Bonapartists, Dreyfusards and the army, Paris and the provinces, antinationalists and nationalists, the Resistance and Vichy, and decolonizers and colonialists. According to the thesis, in times of great crisis, the nation naturally splits in two, with typical sociopolitical forces of the republican left arrayed against typical forces of the conservative right. In more subtle forms of the thesis, it is argued that the two Frances interpretation gives order and meaning to the confusing periods of French history. It is also argued that persistent voting patterns confirm the thesis: the right dominates in particular regions like Normandy, Brittany, Alsace, and parts of Lorraine, while the left typically wins in Paris and its environs, and in the south. *See also* CONSTITUTIONAL DISSENSUS, p. 89; SOCIOECONOMIC THEORY: CONSENSUS THESIS, p. 144.

Significance The two Frances thesis has been argued by respected scholars since the nineteenth century. Although critics have often pointed out that this dichotomous interpretation of French history has serious weaknesses, the thesis still resurfaces in different forms. Its critics say that the two Frances thesis overlooks the diversity within the French social system and the complexity of historical events. It is further argued that it is rare that France has a government exclusively of the left or the right or shows a persistent alternation between the two. Rather, the critics conclude, there is a widely shared consensus in France, which is shown by the more typical domination of center-left and center-right governments.

Third Republic The political system of France from 1870 to 1940. Although the Third Republic is generally dated from 1870, its constitutional system was not finally established until 1875, when the assembly passed several constitutional acts. The governmental system was based on the principles of a parliamentary republic. Legislative power was shared by the Chamber of Deputies and the Senate, which together chose the president of the republic for a seven-year term. The premier and cabinet (the ministry) were responsible to the Chamber of Deputies, but the president and Senate could dissolve the Chamber. In 1877 President Patrice de MacMahon unsuccessfully attempted to establish ministerial responsibility to the president instead of to the assembly. Thereafter the Chamber dominated the governmental system, the presidency became a figurehead office, and the ministry could not dissolve the Chamber. The electoral system most often used for the Chamber of Deputies was the single-member district runoff system (*scrutin d'arrondissement*), but in several elections a modified proportional representation or party list system (*scrutin de liste*) was adopted. The Senate was elected by electoral colleges in each department that were composed of municipal councillors and departmental and national representatives. An uncompromising multiparty system characterized the Republic and contributed to a high degree of cabinet instability. There were 99 cabinets (or "governments") from 1873 to 1940; from 1918 to 1940 there were 44 cabinets headed by 20 different premiers. With the defeat of France by Germany in 1940, the Third Republic was dissolved when the National Assembly (Chamber of Deputies and Senate meeting jointly) convened at Vichy and voted full powers to Marshal Henri Philippe Pétain, who then declared himself head of state. *See also* THIRD REPUBLIC: BOULANGER AFFAIR, p. 149; THIRD REPUBLIC: DREYFUS AFFAIR, p. 150; THIRD REPUBLIC: MACMAHON AFFAIR, p. 151; THIRD REPUBLIC: PANAMA SCANDAL, p. 152.

Significance The Third Republic was the most long-lived French political system since the Revolution of 1789. Its founders expected the system to be only a temporary interlude, for the parliamentary act that authorized a republic was formally approved by only one vote. The Republic's leadership was often weak and its governments unstable and immobilized, yet it survived a large number of crises and scandals. The Republic overcame strong opposition from monarchist, authoritarian, and clerical forces in the nineteenth century, and economic crises, revolutionary forces of the left and right, and World War I in the twentieth century. Coming into being by virtue of a humiliating defeat by Germany in 1870, the Third Republic collapsed in the same fashion in 1940. Yet its republican values, political practices, and institutions somehow survived World War II, the Vichy regime, and the Gaullist Provisional Government. Beyond survival, however, its achievements were modest: the consolidation of the Republic, the separation of church and state in 1905, and a slow pace of economic modernization and development. And in the end the Third Republic bequeathed to its pale carbon copy, the Fourth Republic, a heritage of parliamentary democracy, legislative immobilism, and the regime of parties.

Third Republic: Boulanger Affair The series of events concerning the attempt of General Georges Boulanger to take power in 1887–89. A popular and dashing figure, Boulanger was minister of war in 1886, but he was dropped from the government and sent to an isolated army post in 1887. He soon became the rallying point for dissatisfied workers, peasants, royalists, right-wing politicians, and those seeking revenge against Germany. He formed a political movement, was elected to the Chamber of Deputies in many districts, and was very popular in Paris. In January 1889 it seemed that he was about to stage a coup d'etat, but lacking nerve, he fled the country. He committed suicide in Belgium in 1891 over the death of his mistress. *See also* THIRD REPUBLIC, p. 148.

Significance The Boulanger Affair, like other episodes in the Third Republic, revealed the deep divisions within the nation. Authoritarians, nationalists, antirepublicans, and other frustrated groups for a while strongly supported his movement. In his defense, it can be said that Boulanger probably would not have attempted a coup d'etat but instead was building support to win the elections of 1889. He fled when opponents circulated rumors that he would be arrested and charged with treason. The Boulanger movement collapsed when he left the country, and some of his supporters became more reconciled to the Republic.

Third Republic: Dreyfus Affair The notorious court-martial in 1894 and punishment of Captain Alfred Dreyfus, a Jewish army staff officer, for selling military secrets to the Germans. After a secret trial, Dreyfus was sentenced to solitary imprisonment for life on Devil's Island. The Dreyfus Affair developed into a national crisis of great proportions when it was discovered that trial irregularities, perjury, and false evidence were used by the army to convict Dreyfus and in effect to cover up military inefficiency and corruption. The sensational revelations split the society down the middle, with Radicals, Socialists, anticlericals, and republicans rallying to the side of Dreyfus (the Dreyfusards), and royalists, clericals, extreme nationalists, aristocrats, militarists, and anti-Semites defending the army. A Major Marie Charles Esterhazy was subsequently accused of the crime, but the army found him innocent in a bogus trial. In 1898 proof of forged documents that were used against Dreyfus was uncovered. The army retried Dreyfus and again found him guilty but with extenuating circumstances. Dreyfus received a presidential pardon, but, refusing it, he remained in prison until 1906, when he was finally fully vindicated by a civilian court. He returned to the army, was promoted and decorated, and served in World War I. *See also* THIRD REPUBLIC, p. 148.

Significance The Dreyfus Affair was the most serious crisis that rocked the Third Republic. Its effects were profound, as the case attracted worldwide attention and divided France for over a decade. At stake was more than the fate of one man, but the existence of the republic. A type of bloodless civil war developed, replete with sharp divisions, street clashes, a virulent press campaign, confrontations, and class hatreds. Of the many writers, intellectuals, and politicians that rallied to Dreyfus were the novelist Émile Zola and the Radical party leader Georges Clemenceau. Ultimately the affair united the supporters of the republic, brought the left to power, and contributed to antimilitarism and to anticlericalism that finally resulted in the separation of the church and state in 1905.

Third Republic: MacMahon Affair The events surrounding President Patrice de MacMahon's forced resignation of Premier Jules Simon on May 16, 1877, even though Simon had majority support in the Chamber of Deputies. Sometimes referred to as the Sixteenth of May crisis (*le Seize Mai*), the MacMahon Affair was precipitated by the conflict between the royalists and conservatives who had elected MacMahon in 1873 and the new republican majority that was elected to the Chamber of Deputies in 1876. When MacMahon's designated successor to Simon, a moderate monarchist, was rejected by the Chamber of Deputies, the president, with the Senate's consent, dissolved the Chamber of Deputies and held new elections. MacMahon campaigned hard for his supporters, but he lost the election to the republicans. Forced to compromise, he ultimately appointed an acceptable republican as premier. MacMahon resigned the presidency in 1879 after the republicans also won control of the Senate. *See also* THIRD REPUBLIC, p. 148.

Significance The MacMahon Affair affected the operation of the Third Republic in a major way and significantly reduced royalist strength. A marshal in the French army, MacMahon had a long military and governmental career, which was stained in later years by his defeat at Sedan in the Franco-Prussian War in 1870 and his crushing of the Paris Commune in 1871. As president, MacMahon supported royalist, clerical, and conservative causes. His attempt to establish presidential predominance and control over the premier and cabinet in the Sixteenth of May episode was soundly defeated by the Chamber of Deputies and by the people in subsequent elections. Following this episode, the full power of the presidency was rarely exercised in the Third Republic, the Senate went into decline, and the governmental system came to be dominated by the Chamber of Deputies. The MacMahon Affair illustrates the competitive power positions and tenuous balance between the president and the legislature that have typified the French political system.

Third Republic: Panama Scandal A notorious affair in the 1890s in which deputies and journalists were bribed to secure government financing for the bankrupt Panama Canal Company. The Panama Scandal broke in 1892 following the failure of the company to build a canal through the isthmus of Panama. Headed by Ferdinand de Lesseps, who had won great prestige by building the Suez Canal, the company attracted many small investors. Mismanagement, corruption, poor engineering, and disease in Panama brought about the failure of the project in 1889 and the collapse of the company. Many small investors were wiped out by the company's failure. Investigations followed, and a large number of deputies came under suspicion, but only de Lesseps and a few others were convicted. *See also* THIRD REPUBLIC, p. 148.

Significance The Panama Scandal was one of the most notorious scandals in the nineteenth century. The episode brought disgrace to the Third Republic in that some prominent republican leaders were suspected of complicity, and a large number of parliamentary leaders lost or withdrew in the elections of 1893. Support for the authoritarian right and the socialists increased as a consequence. Because two important Jewish financiers and promoters were deeply implicated in the scandal, the affair also contributed to the anti-Semitism that characterized the period.

Tous Azimuts A doctrine of French defense policy in 1967–69 that the armed forces should be prepared to defend the nation from attacks coming from all directions. Also called the Ailleret Doctrine, *tous azimuts* ("all azimuths" or "all directions") provided that France would use its nuclear weapons against all attacks, presumably even those originating from Western states, including the United States. Proclaimed by the chief of staff, General Charles Ailleret in 1967 and endorsed by President Charles de Gaulle in 1968, the doctrine reflected de Gaulle's independent foreign policy and the neutralism that seemed to pervade his policies. This all-points deterrence doctrine was based on the assumption that the international system was changing from the American-Soviet bipolar stalemate to a more flexible multipolar world of several independent nuclear powers. Lacking credibility, the Ailleret Doctrine was dropped after de Gaulle resigned in 1969. It was replaced by the Fourquet Doctrine (after General Michel Fourquet), which identified the Soviet Union as the likely potential enemy and called for a flexible, graduated response to military threats from the East. *See also* FORCE DE FRAPPE, p. 105; NUCLEAR WEAPONS STRATEGY, p. 128.

Significance The multidirectional doctrine of tous azimuts was enunciated at a time when de Gaulle was on the verge of moving completely away from the NATO alliance. The strategy, however, was eclipsed by two important events in 1968: (1) the May student-worker revolt, which created serious political and economic problems for de Gaulle's government; and (2) the Soviet invasion of Czechoslovakia, which pointed out the unrealistic aspects of a neutralistic foreign policy and multidirectional defense strategy. Subsequent defense doctrines sought to devise a more credible strategy for the nation's nuclear forces.

Trade Unions: France Organizations of wage employees that engage in political activity and collective bargaining with employers. The oldest and largest of the French trade unions is the General Confederation of Labor (*Confédération Générale du Travail*, CGT), which has claimed over two million members. The CGT is the heir to a long tradition of revolutionary syndicalism and Marxism. Although its members are drawn from various shades of opinion, most of its ranking members are members of the Communist party, and the general secretary, Georges Séguy, was a member of the central committee of the party until 1982. The CGT was especially active in the cold war period, agitating against the Marshall Plan and the government. The second largest union is the French Democratic Confederation of Labor (*Confédération Française Democratique du Travail*, CFDT), which was originally part of the Catholic trade union movement, but which split in 1964 and adopted a secular approach. The CFDT is allied to the Socialist party and advocates the adoption of worker participation in the management of plants, called *autogestion*. It has about 700,000 members. In 1948 democratic socialists split from the parent, communist-dominated CGT and formed the *Force Ouvrière,* Workers' Force (CGT-FO, or FO). The FO has about 500,000 members and is noted for pursuing economic unionism, that is, bargaining with employers on wages and working conditions and signing collective bargaining agreements. When the CFDT became secular, the members of the older Catholic labor movement reorganized into the French Confederation of Christian Workers (*Confédération Française des Travailleurs Crétiens,* CFTC). This organization is small, having about 80,000 members. There are also a large teachers' union, National Federation of Education (*Fédération de l'Education Nationale,* FEN) with 500,000 members, and a union of low and middle ranking management employees, the General Confederation of Staffs (*Confédération des Cadres,* CGC).

Significance Trade unionism is not strong in France, for only 20 to 25 percent of the workers are members of unions. Membership claims by the industrial unions are exaggerated, and some observers routinely reduce them by half. A scholarly estimate of the relative strength of the unions showed that in 1980 the CGT had about 40 percent of the total union membership, the CFDT had 22 percent, the Force Ouvrière had 16 percent, and the Catholic CFTC had 6 percent. The history of trade unionism in France is dominated by political unionism, the use of workers' organizations by parties to bring about a transformation of society through political activity. This has contributed to union pluralism, or fragmentation and competition between unions having different conceptions of the ideal society. Occasionally French unions have coalesced or cooperated, but the general picture is one of rivalry. The creation of the Force Ouvrière with economic unionism (also called business unionism) objectives has aided other unions to seek agreements with employers or the same benefits through government action. In the French governmental system, corporatism is sometimes practiced, that is, representing people in government by their economic function. Unions are represented in the Economic and Social Council, which gives advice to the government on legislative proposals. And the government sometimes engages in a process called *concertation,* in which government, industry, and labor representatives attempt to reach agreement on economic questions. In 1982 a law that nationalized large sectors of French industry and finance provided that government, labor, and management experts will be represented on the boards of directors of the nationalized companies.

Vichy Regime The government of unoccupied France and the French colonies from 1940 to 1944. The Vichy Regime was formally established by an overwhelming vote of the National Assembly of the Third Republic on July 10, 1940, in the wake of the defeat of the French army by Nazi Germany. Although some government leaders wanted to continue the fight from the colonies, the Assembly accepted Marshal Henri Philippe Pétain's argument that further resistance was harmful to the French nation and that an armistice was the best course. The Assembly gave Pétain full power to rule and he named himself Head of State. While German forces occupied three-fifths of France, Pétain's government ruled the unoccupied portions and the colonies from the town of Vichy. At first composed of right-wing traditionalists and authoritarians, the regime came to be dominated by collaborationists like François Darlan and Pierre Laval, and later by French fascists. After allied forces landed in North Africa, Germany occupied all of France in November 1942, and the Vichy government was relocated to Germany in 1944 when France was liberated by the allies. Vichy disintegrated when Nazi Germany collapsed in 1945. After the war, Vichy leaders and other officials and collaborationists were tried as traitors; Laval was executed and Pétain's death sentence was commuted to life imprisonment. Darlan had been killed by a royalist in 1942 when he cooperated with the allied landings in Africa. About 50,000 persons were officially punished, and 700 were executed. Resistance forces summarily executed many collaborationists, perhaps as many as 10,000 persons. *See also* RESISTANCE, p. 138.

Significance The Vichy Regime was considered by the French forces that came into power in 1944 to be a disgraceful blot on the national honor. The defeatist generals who argued for an armistice and the Vichy leaders who collaborated with Nazi Germany believed they were acting in the best interest of France. The Vichy government, however, was clearly antirepublican, authoritarian, and corporatist. It showed once again that the nation still disagreed over the form of government, but it contributed nothing that has endured except bitter memories.

3. The Federal Republic of Germany

Anschluss The union of Austria with Germany, brought about by the German Nazi government in 1938. The idea of *Anschluss,* or incorporating Austria into the German Reich, was supported in both countries after World War I, but the union was prohibited by the treaties of Versailles and St. Germain of 1919. A proposal in 1931 to make a customs union of Germany and Austria was opposed by France and some of its allies and ruled to be a breach of the treaties by the World Court at the Hague. Pressure on Austria increased after Adolf Hitler took power in Germany. An attempted Nazi *putsch* in Vienna in 1934 against the authoritarian government of the Austrian Chancellor Engelbert Dollfuss, who was killed, failed when Italy threatened to intervene. In 1938 Hitler demanded that Austrian Chancellor Kurt von Schuschnigg include Nazis in his government. Schuschnigg complied, but when he scheduled a plebiscite on whether Austria should remain independent, Hitler issued an ultimatum forcing the resignation of the Austrian chancellor. He then sent German troops into Austria. Italy, now Germany's ally, decided not to intervene, and a new Austrian Nazi chancellor proclaimed the union on March 13, 1938. Austria became a province of Germany, and the Nazi totalitarian system was installed in Austria. On April 10, 1938, a Nazi-administered plebiscite returned a 99 percent vote in favor of Anschluss. *See also* NAZISM: DOCTRINE, p. 207; NAZISM: MOVEMENT, p. 211.

Significance Anschluss was favored by many Germans and Austrians as an essential part of the traditional goal of uniting all German-speaking people into one state. Hitler's forcible annexation of Austria was a violation of the postwar treaties, but the European powers did not respond except by protesting. The Anschluss was an initial step in

Hitler's foreign policy to expand the Third Reich, and, emboldened by this success, he moved quickly to annex the German-populated Sudetenland of Czechoslovakia. In 1943 the United States, Great Britain, and the Soviet Union declared the Anschluss to be invalid, and they occupied Austria after the war. Austria was established as an independent, neutral state in 1955.

Basic Law   The constitution of the Federal Republic of Germany. The Basic Law was drafted in 1948–49 by the Parliamentary Council, which was composed of state delegates called by the governments of the West German states at the instigation of the Western occupying powers. The document is called a "basic law" instead of a constitution, and the drafting body was not termed a constituent assembly because the German leaders wanted to emphasize that the new system was to be temporary pending the reunification of Germany. The Basic Law was approved by the Western Allied powers and ratified by the West German states; it was promulgated on May 22, 1949. Although the Federal Republic of Germany was created at that time, the Allied occupying powers retained important rights that they exercised under the Occupation Statute that went into effect in 1949; these included such matters as disarmament, foreign policy and trade, and emergency powers. Full sovereignty was granted to the Federal Republic on May 5, 1955. The Basic Law proclaims the Federal Republic to be a "democratic and social federal state," and it provides that the constitutional order within the states (*Länder*) "conform to the principles of republican, democratic and social government based on the rule of law within the meaning of this Basic Law." The political system established by the Basic Law is based on the constitutional principles of popular sovereignty, the rule of law, universal suffrage, democracy, federalism, parliamentary government, and a bicameral legislature. An innovation was also adopted—judicial review, which provides a type of check and balance to the parliamentary fusion of powers. A Bill of Rights specifies an extensive list of political, civil, economic, and social rights. Some rights, such as legal equality and freedom of speech and religion, are guaranteed to "all persons"; other rights, such as freedom of assembly, association, and movement, and the right to choose a profession, are guaranteed to "all Germans." A Constitutional Court is established to ensure the enforcement of these rights and other constitutional provisions. The Basic Law may be amended by a two-thirds vote in both houses of parliament; being a "temporary" and lengthy document of over 160 articles, the constitution has been amended often. There have been 32 amendments by 1982. *See also* FEDERAL CONSTITUTIONAL COURT, p. 182; FEDERALISM: WEST GERMANY, p. 183; OCCUPATION PERIOD, p. 214.

Significance The framers of the Basic Law were strongly influenced by the negative experiences of the Weimar Republic and the Nazi Regime. The "lessons learned from Weimar" and the desire to prevent another totalitarian system are both discernible in the constitutional system of the Federal Republic. Some of the provisions based on past experience include those which (1) concentrate executive power in the chancellor rather than sharing it with the president; (2) provide for an indirectly elected and weak office of federal president; (3) set limitations on the exercise of emergency powers by the government; (4) make it more difficult to censure governments by requiring that a successor government be simultaneously chosen; (5) create a federal system that grants some exclusive powers to the states and gives states an important role in federal legislation; (6) found the entire system on the concept of the rule of law and justice (*Rechtsstaat*) as opposed to arbitrary authority; (7) authorize limitations on undemocratic political parties; and (8) protect the guarantees against unconstitutional governmental actions by establishing an independent Constitutional Court. These and other features of the constitutional system established by the Basic Law have been well adapted to the conditions facing postwar Germany. Combined with the simple and responsible political party system, the Basic Law has helped give West Germans a stable and effective democratic system.

Basic Treaty A watershed treaty signed in 1972 between East and West Germany that normalized relations between the two German states. The Basic Treaty, negotiated in 1972 and ratified in 1973, was part of Social Democratic Chancellor Willy Brandt's *Ostpolitik*, or Eastern policy, which reversed the prior German policy of attempting to isolate East Germany and deny it legitimacy. In Brandt's view, the treaty represented an acknowledgement of his formula: "Two German states in one German nation." In the treaty, the parties agreed to (1) develop normal good-neighborly relations on the basis of equality; (2) abide by United Nations principles; (3) settle their disputes by peaceful means, and promote peace and disarmament in Europe; (4) reaffirm the inviolability of their common border, and respect their territorial integrity; (5) respect each other's independence and autonomy; and (6) exchange diplomatic representatives and conclude a number of agreements in various areas. *See also* OSTPOLITIK, p. 217.

Significance The Basic Treaty was negotiated in an international atmosphere of detente, or relaxation of tensions, that was marked by increased dialogue, trade, and arms control agreements between the great powers. Brandt's Ostpolitik included the Basic Treaty and the

Moscow and Warsaw treaties, which recognized the loss of prewar German territories to Poland and the Soviet Union. The general policy was supported in West German public opinion, but strongly opposed by the opposition Christian Democratic and Christian Social Union parties (CDU/CSU). Critics charged that the Basic Treaty (1) was a moral step backward because it gave Communist East Germany equal status; (2) ended the West German goal of national unity; (3) threatened the Federal Republic's association with the West by a "mad race to the East"; and (4) failed to get concessions, such as freedom for East Germans to emigrate to West Germany, recognition of West Berlin as a part of the Federal Republic, or placing East Berlin on the same international status as West Berlin. Defenders argued that Ostpolitik (1) was simply a recognition of power realities in Central Europe; (2) preserved the status of West Berlin, which was under constant threat; (3) was based on humanitarian considerations because it opened up visitation rights to East Germany; and (4) fostered trade and other agreements that would help East Germans and also permit West Germany to be influential in Eastern Europe. After ratification, the Basic Treaty was challenged in the Federal Constitutional Court by the Christian Social Union, but the pact was held to be valid. The Basic Treaty led to a subsequent number of agreements concerning trade, transit, and visitation rights.

Berlin Blockade The stoppage of surface access across East Germany to West Berlin by the Soviet Union from June 1948 to May 1949. The Soviet Union instituted the Berlin Blockade by first preventing rail traffic across their occupation zone of Germany in late March 1948; road traffic was halted in June. By laying a nonviolent siege to West Berlin by cutting off supplies to the Western garrisons located there and the over two million West Berlin residents, the Soviets expected the Western powers to abandon the city. The Soviet Union did not interdict air traffic, and the United States with British help responded with a massive airlift of food, consumer goods, industrial materials, and fuel, which was especially needed in the harsh winter months. The Berlin Airlift delivered over 12 million tons of supplies in almost 200,000 flights in a ten-month period. At its peak, the airlift, or airbridge as the Berlin residents called it, delivered 8,000 tons a day in airplanes that were flying day and night. After the Russians saw that the airlift succeeded despite the harsh winter of 1948–49, they opened surface routes, but the airlift continued until September 1949 in order to build up stockpiles of materials. *See also* OCCUPATION PERIOD, p. 214; WEST BERLIN, p. 238.

Significance The Berlin Blockade was one of the most dangerous confrontations between East and West in the tension-filled early years of the Cold War, but it also showed that East-West confrontations took place within certain limits. The Russians did not try to interdict the airlift, and the Americans did not try to force their way across the ground surface of the Soviet occupation zone. Although the Russians claimed that the blockade was imposed in protest against Western currency reform, they instituted the rail blockage months before the reform. It began several days after they walked out of the Allied Control Council, the body that was to supervise the miliary occupation of Germany. The Soviets also tried to lure West Berliners with promises of food and fuel, but the inhabitants of the city remained loyal to the West. The Soviet purpose was clearly to force the West from Berlin, and in this aim they failed. But the blockade also strengthened the resolve of the Western Allies, created great prestige for the United States among West Germans, and ensured the loyalty to the West of the inhabitants of West Berlin.

Berlin Wall A physical barrier that separates West Berlin from East Berlin and East Germany. Construction of the Berlin Wall was begun on August 13, 1961, by East Germany to prevent the flow of East Germans to the West. The wall is a 13-foot concrete barrier that snakes through the city, effectively sealing off West Berlin from ground access except on terms that are acceptable to the East German government. In addition to the wall in Berlin, the 858-mile border between East Germany and West Germany is also fortified with barbed wire, electrified fences, mined fields, tank traps, electronic warning devices, watchtowers, and bunkers. East German border guards are instructed to shoot or capture persons trying to "escape" to the West. Since 1961 over 23,400 persons escaped by overcoming the physical barriers. The West German government asserts that East Germany has committed 28,000 acts of violence in border areas; in Berlin over 70 persons have been killed attempting to surmount the wall; over 100 have been wounded and over 3,000 captured. When the wall was first built, the Western Allies did little more than make a verbal protest despite their claim that the action violated wartime agreements with the Soviet Union. Determined to prevent its trained manpower and younger population from fleeing its territory, the East German government, supported by the Soviet Union, ignored these protests. *See also* BERLIN BLOCKADE, p. 160; WEST BERLIN, p. 238.

Significance By building the Berlin Wall and similar barriers separating East and West Germany, the East German government achieved its purpose of preventing its active population from leaving its territory. Prior to 1961, many East Berliners commuted daily to work in West

Berlin, which had become a showplace of Western democracy and a welfare capitalist economy. Fearful that the border would be closed, many East Germans traveled to East Berlin, crossed the border easily through checkpoints, and then were flown to West Germany. The effectiveness of the Berlin Wall is seen in that several days before August 13, 1961, about 2,000 East Germans were fleeing the country daily. About three million people left East Germany after 1945. By building the wall the East German government suffered a great propaganda loss, for it showed its system to be not a communist paradise but a prison. But it also demonstrated that the reunification policy of West Germany was futile and that it could control its own people despite Western propaganda victories. The wall convinced many East Germans to accept their fate and make the best of their lives, a result that helped contribute to the rapid expansion of the East German economy in the 1960s and 1970s. Following the signing of agreements between East and West Germany in the 1970s, many West Germans were permitted to visit their families in the East, and an increased number of pensioners were permitted to leave East Germany, about 12,000 yearly in the early 1980s. But despite the easing of restrictions, many East Germans risk an illegal departure; in 1982, 2,400 persons illegally fled East Germany, including 270 persons who broke through the barriers.

"Bonn Is Not Weimer" The thesis that the socioeconomic environment and the political system of the Federal Republic of Germany are so fundamentally different from that of the Weimar Republic that a stable democracy is assured. According to the "Bonn is not Weimar" thesis, the social system of contemporary Germany is more open, integrated, and less stratified. Refugees and expellees from Eastern Europe have been quickly assimilated into the West German system. Instead of being faced with a harsh peace treaty like that of Versailles, West Germany was helped by the United States through a generous program of economic assistance after World War II. The political culture of West Germany is less authoritarian and more democratic than Weimar: a substantial number of Germans have moved from a pragmatic acceptance of the democratic system to a sincere adoption of democratic values. The revised federal system also strengthens the democratic system by balancing the states and increasing state powers. Although 95 percent of the people formally belong to a church and pay the church tax, the secularization of society and the decline of religious controversies have removed some areas of strife. The economic problems that contributed to the rise of extremist groups in Weimar have not been a major problem in the Bonn Republic. The defects in the Weimar constitutional system have been corrected, in that executive power is concentrated in the chancellorship and made responsible to the popular house, the use of emergency powers is strictly circumscribed, and unconstitutional government actions can be voided by a constitutional court. Although proportional representation has been retained, the political party system has been simplified and made more responsible. Communists and neo-Nazis have been unable to win 1 percent of the vote. Germany is fully integrated with other Western European states in an economic community, a factor that strongly binds them together. The international system that emerged after World War II and the integration of Germany in the North Atlantic Treaty Organization greatly reduce the possibility that Germany may develop an independent or aggressive foreign policy. The presence of American, British, and French military forces in Germany not only helps make the nation secure, they are also a protection against internal upheavals. In sum, the social system, political culture, economic prosperity, worker affluence, the constitutional structure, political leadership, the political party system, economic and military integration with Western democratic states—all these factors combine to create a strong viable democracy in West Germany. *See also* POLITICAL CULTURE TRANSFORMATION THESIS, p. 218.

Significance According to the "Bonn is not Weimar" thesis, nothing short of a major war could shake the democratic system in the Federal Republic. Critics have pointed out, however, that the thesis has not been fairly tested. Because the security crisis requires the presence of Western forces in the country, Germany cannot independently evolve according to its own natural bent. Moreover, despite West German acceptance of East Germany as a separate state and the ratification of the postwar status quo in the Helsinki Accord, the traditional German drive for unification has not disappeared from the German mind. This historical German force and the peculiar status of West Berlin, which is both dangerous to international peace and a hindrance to a permanent solution of the German problem, remain as potential destabilizing factors. Although West Germany is economically prosperous and many people affluent, wealth is not equitably distributed, nor is the prosperity guaranteed. The presence in West Germany of four million foreign workers may become the focus for the rise of undemocratic forces in hard times. Defenders of the thesis reply that most criticisms depend on speculation about the future, whereas the thesis relies on real developments within Germany. They point out that the Weimar Republic lasted only 14 years, while the Bonn Republic is still strong after almost four decades.

Bundesrat The upper or second house of the bicameral parliament of the Federal Republic of Germany. The Bundesrat, sometimes called in English the Federal Council, is composed of 41 delegates from the constituent states in the Federal Republic. States have 3, 4, or 5 delegates according to population; the West Berlin parliament sends 4 delegates who do not have voting rights. Bundesrat delegates are appointed by state governments from among state cabinet members, headed by the chief executive officer of the state (minister-president), but very often civil servants are sent to do most of the work of the ministers. State delegations vote as a bloc and under instructions from the state government. The Bundesrat cannot be dissolved, and delegates have no fixed term of office. The legislative process in the Federal Republic is a complex one, with bills passing back and forth between the two chambers. All government bills are first sent to the Bundesrat for comment and then forwarded to the Bundestag, the lower house. The constitutional powers of the Bundesrat are equal to those of the Bundestag on constitutional amendments, national emergencies, and questions affecting state interests, such as state boundaries, education, finances, and police matters. On these matters it has an absolute veto. On other questions, called "ordinary" legislation, the Bundesrat has a suspensive veto that can be overcome by a second vote in the Bundestag. To overcome the veto, the Bundestag needs to pass the bill by a majority vote or a two-thirds vote, depending on the size of the rejection vote in the Bundesrat. The Bundesrat has no power to elect the chancellor or to entertain confidence motions against the government. *See also* BASIC LAW, p. 158; BUNDESTAG, p. 165; FEDERALISM: WEST GERMANY, p. 183.

Significance The Bundesrat is one of the most powerful second chambers in the parliamentary democracies, and it is a strong guarantor of the West German federal system. In the first decade of the Federal Republic the Bundesrat used its veto power sparingly, but in the 1960s and 1970s it expanded the scope of its absolute veto from about 10 percent of federal legislation to 50 percent. Because state governments in the West German federal system have the authority to administer many federal laws, the Bundesrat claims that, under this dual responsibility principle, it has authority to veto any federal bill states would have to administer if the bill became law. Attempts to make the Bundesrat completely coequal with the Bundestag have failed, however. The Bundesrat is less representative than the Bundestag. Small states are overrepresented according to population, and the political minority within a state legislature is not represented in the state's delegation to the Bundesrat. The composition of the Bundesrat is made up of partisan state executives who do not always agree with the national leaders of their parties in the Bundestag. Also, state and national politics do not coincide, and the Bundesrat may be dominated by a different group than that which controls the Bundestag. During most of the period of Social

Democratic governments from 1969 to 1982, the Bundesrat was controlled by the Christian Democrats. Acting as a party bloc, Christian Democrats voted against important tax, finance, and social legislation and the *Ostpolitik* treaties of Chancellor Willy Brandt. They also vetoed other bills in subject areas where the Bundesrat had coequal power.

Bundestag   The lower or popular chamber of the bicameral parliament of the Federal Republic of Germany. The Bundestag, sometimes rendered in English as the Federal Diet, has all the constitutional powers normally delegated to a popular house in a parliamentary system. It can pass laws, levy taxes, approve budgets, ratify treaties, elect the chancellor, censure the government, question ministers, debate policy, and investigate issues. The Bundestag also participates in the election of the federal president and the enactment of constitutional amendments. Most of the chamber's legislative powers are shared with the second house, the Bundesrat, which represents the interests of the states. In case of a disagreement between the two houses on "ordinary" legislation, the Bundestag is dominant, but both houses share equal power in legislation affecting state interests and on constitutional amendments, which require a two-thirds vote in both chambers. The Bundestag is composed of deputies who are elected for a four-year term by universal suffrage by means of a mixed electoral system that is based on the principle of proportional representation. West Berlin sends delegates to the Bundestag who have no voting rights on legislation. Parliamentary groups or party caucuses are organized into *Fraktionen* (sing. *Fraktion*), which control the legislative process and are represented in the committees, the government group always having a majority. The Council of Elders is a type of legislative steering committee that makes committee assignments and controls legislative business. It is composed of Fraktion leaders and their oldest members in proportion to their party strength in the house. The Bundestag may remove a chancellor from office only by a procedure called the constructive vote of nonconfidence, in which the Bundestag simultaneously elects a new chancellor by majority vote. The term of office of the deputies is four years, but the Bundestag may be dissolved earlier by the federal president if a chancellor requests and fails to receive a vote of confidence in the house. *See also* BASIC LAW, p. 158; BUNDESRAT, p. 163; CONSTRUCTIVE VOTE OF NONCONFIDENCE, p. 174; ELECTORAL SYSTEM: BUNDESTAG, p. 177.

Significance   The Bundestag is a much more effective body compared to the Reichstag, its counterpart in the Weimar Republic. But the Bundestag suffers from the same conditions that limit the political power of other parliaments in the industrialized democracies in the twentieth century: the growing power of the executive branch of government, the expanding role played by the bureaucracy, and the dominant position of party leaders in states that have a simple, disciplined political party system. The framers of the Bonn constitution were confronted with a complex problem, for they tried to fashion a parliamentary democracy in an age in which parliaments are in decline, in a nation which has a tradition of strong executive and authoritarian government, and with the knowledge that the nation's single national experiment with parliamentary democracy, the Weimar Republic, was a disastrous failure. The constitutional system they fashioned in these circumstances does limit the legislative power of the Bundestag in several respects. These include granting exclusive legislative powers to the states, giving the government prerogatives in budget making, and providing for judicial review of legislation. Yet the Bundestag has avoided the instabilities, legislative impasses, and reliance on emergency procedures that transferred legislative powers to the executive branch in the Weimar Republic. In these ways the Reichstag helped bring about the downfall of the Weimar Republic. In the Bonn Republic, the Bundestag plays a circumscribed role, but one that is part of a parliamentary party-government system that has provided West Germans with a stable, responsible, and effective democratic order.

Business and Industrial Associations: West Germany Organizations of employers in the fields of business, industry, and commerce in the Federal Republic of Germany. There are three peak organizations of business and industrial employers, each a federation of regional or trade associations. The largest and most influential is the Federation of German Industry (BDI) an organization of 39 national industrial associations, whose membership includes over 90,000 firms, which account for 98 percent of all firms in Germany. The Federation of German Employers Association (BDA) has a larger clientele and is primarily concerned with labor relations. The third peak association, in which membership is compulsory, is the Diet of German Industry and Commerce, the national association of chambers of industry and trade. The three national associations are well financed, have professional staffs, and maintain extensive operations in publicity and lobbying; some are directly represented on various government boards and commissions in the modified German system of functional representation. The memberships of the associations overlap, and they often collaborate in seeking certain public policy goals. Generally the associations agree on policy goals, such as maintaining a favorable business climate, holding down wage increases and social programs, promoting exports, resisting the extension of codetermination (labor participation in management), and opposing anticartel legislation. Beyond these general goals, business and trade associations do not always agree on specific policy issues because of the competition between industries and the different nature of the enterprises. *See also* CODETERMINATION. p. 172; FUNCTIONAL REPRESENTATION, p. 188.

Significance   Business and industrial associations have been very influential in maintaining the free enterprise system that was reestablished in the postwar period. The initial Allied goal of breaking up German big business failed, and large-scale enterprises and cartels came to be the characteristic form of enterprise in Germany. In addition, trade unions have been moderate in their goals, engage in few strikes, and do not seek to nationalize industry. The peak associations have direct links to the leadership and deputies of the Christian Democratic and Free Democratic parties, and, since the Social Democrats dropped their collectivization goals, business organizations also have been influential with SPD governments. Although some observers have noted that the influence of big business is limited, this must be placed in the context of a society that has an economy characterized by large-scale capitalism modified in part by social welfare policies.

Catch-All Party Thesis   The theory that attempts to explain the transformation of the political party systems in the industrialized democracies of Europe by emphasizing the changes in the socioeconomic system. According to the catch-all party thesis, the socioeconomic systems in postwar Europe have undergone a significant change, as the farmer, artisan, self-employed, and industrial worker classes have declined and given way to the increasingly large middle class of managerial, technical, and clerical white-collar workers. The new middle class has different interests from the older bourgeoisie of industrial, financial, and commercial property-owners. Accompanying these changes is the growth of affluence and "consumerism" among middle and lower classes and the decline of religious disputes. Consequently, the formerly narrowly based, single-interest, and ideologically oriented political parties in Western Europe have been replaced by catch-all parties that try to appeal to the new middle class and to all social groups. Those parties that have retained a single-interest focus have declined or disappeared. Because the dominant parties appeal to the same social groups, they have become moderate and programmatically similar. The theory argues that this transformation is widespread in Europe, although less so in the smaller democracies; but it is especially evident in West Germany, particularly in the Christian Democratic and Social Democratic parties. Along with the moderation and the convergence of large parties is a "waning of opposition" in Western Europe, again most evident in West Germany. The number of competing parties has declined, antisystem parties are disappearing, and two parties have come to dominate the political scene. *See also* EMBOURGEOISIEMENT THESIS, p. 21; POLITICAL PARTY SYSTEM: WEST GERMANY, p. 220; SOCIOECONOMIC THEORY: END-OF-IDEOLOGY THESIS, p. 144.

Significance The catch-all party thesis was developed by Otto Kirchheimer as a general theory for all of Western Europe, but it relied a great deal on developments in the Federal Republic of Germany. When the theory first appeared, the idea was accepted by many observers as a "seminal work," but it increasingly came under criticism. Although West Germany seemed to be a good example of the theory, the notion of a catch-all party did not appear to apply to France, Italy, and other states, where prewar multipartyism, ideological confrontation, and single-class parties still predominated. In Germany, the catch-all party idea corresponded to the development of the *Volkspartei* (pl. *Volksparteien*), a mass-based party of the whole people. The Christian Democrats originated this approach, and it was later adopted by the Social Democrats, who abandoned their socialist doctrine for the pro-Western, moderate, welfarist Godesberg Program. Critics pointed out that the catch-all party thesis was a variant of the "end-of-ideology" theory, which argued that ideology was no longer a driving force in Western politics. These critics dismissed the theory as superficial and not consistent with the rebirth of radicalism in the late 1960s and 1970s. Other observers have argued that the transformation of the German party system should be explained by factors peculiar to Germany, such as: (1) the Nazi disruption of the traditional party system, and the limitations placed on postwar competition by the Allies (Gerhard Loewenberg); and (2) the postwar rejection of Nazism and Communism by the people, and the development of the Volkspartei, which does attempt to appeal to all groups, but which still retains a traditional ideological bias (Gordon Smith).

Christian Democratic Union (CDU) The large center-right party that has controlled the government of the Federal Republic for much of the postwar period. The Christian Democratic Union was founded in 1945 as a new party of Catholics, Protestants, conservatives, liberals, workers, farmers, and business groups into a multiclass people's party. Although the party's name is typical of Catholic parties in Europe, the CDU was formed as a nondenominational, nonideological union of Christians and other groups; it specifically included Protestants in leadership positions. Under its first leader, Konrad Adenauer, the CDU pursued conservative and centrist goals, such as reconstruction of

Germany, strong ties to the Western Allies, rapprochement and economic integration with Western Europe, and the establishment of a free market economy. In Bavaria, the Christian Democrats, more Catholic in membership but still separate from the church, organized a separate party organization, the Christian Social Union (CSU). The CDU and CSU do not compete against one another, run on the same platform in national elections, and form a single group in parliament known as the CDU/CSU. In the first national election, the CDU/CSU won 30 percent of the vote, but this rapidly increased and stabilized at about 45 to 48 percent. About 10 to 11 percent of the Union's total is supplied by the CSU. Adenauer's strong, authoritarian-style leadership dominated the party and the government until 1963. Two subsequent chancellors, Ludwig Erhard (1963–66) and Kurt Georg Kiesinger (1966–69), were less effective. The party was out of power from 1969 to 1982, but returned in 1982 under Chancellor Helmut Kohl. For most of its history, the CDU had a loose confederal style of organization and few party members, but when it fell from power in 1969, the party reorganized at the grass roots and increased its membership to 800,000. This revitalization helped it in the 1983 elections, when the CDU/CSU won 48.8 percent of the vote. With their Free Democratic allies the CDU/CSU formed a large majority in the Bundestag. In 1984 the Christian Democrats were in power in state governments either alone or with the Free Democrats in six of the ten states and also in West Berlin, a traditional Social Democratic stronghold. *See also* CHRISTIAN SOCIAL UNION (CSU), p. 170; ELECTIONS OF 1983: WEST GERMANY, p. 176; POLITICAL PARTY SYSTEM: WEST GERMANY, p. 220; *SPIEGEL* AFFAIR, p. 229.

Significance The Christian Democratic Union dominated the government during the first 20 years of the Federal Republic. The major policies it adopted in that period established the parameters within which subsequent Social Democratic governments moved, except for policy concerning East Germany. These include the free enterprise system modified by social welfare programs, rearmament and participaton in the North Atlantic Treaty Organization, strong ties with the United States, and West European economic integration. The Social Democrats (SPD) came into power only after the party abandoned its doctrinaire socialism, imitated the CDU in becoming a catch-all party, and adopted the same military-security policy as the CDU. The major change made by the SPD was in the *Ostpolitik*, or eastern policy, in which the CDU hard line was dropped in favor of detente and the acceptance of the status quo in East Europe and East Germany. The CDU opposed Ostpolitik, but later came to accept the new legal situation as regards the former eastern territories of Germany and the existence of the East Germany. In the late 1970s and early 1980s, the CDU returned from a position of weak leadership and internal strife to control a majority of state governments and the federal government. It appears that the CDU under Kohl may have entered another long period of electoral domination in the Federal Republic, providing the unpredictable Free Democrats remain loyal to the coalition.

Christian Social Union (CSU) The Christian Democratic party in the state of Bavaria, which joins with the larger Christian Democratic Union in national politics. The Christian Social Union (CSU) was founded in 1949 as a successor to the Bavarian People's party, and it soon came to dominate politics in that Catholic state. The CSU maintains a separate organization and officers, but it forms a single parliamentary group (*fraktion*) with the Christian Democratic Union (CDU/CSU). The two parties are not organized in one another's territory, do not compete against one another, and run in national elections with a joint platform and a single candidate for chancellor. The CSU has been dominated by its forceful chairman, Franz Josef Strauss, who has been a deputy since 1949, the deputy chairman of the CDU/CSU fraktion, a cabinet minister, the minister president of Bavaria, and the Christian Democratic candidate for chancellor in 1980. Under Strauss the CSU is more conservative and nationalistic than its larger sister party, and Strauss has often had a falling out with other national leaders. In 1962 he was forced to resign as minister of defense for having ordered the arrest of editors of the newsmagazine *Der Spiegel* for allegedly publishing defense secrets. Relations between CDU leaders and Strauss deteriorated in the mid-1970s, and in 1976 Strauss threatened to run candidates in CDU's territory, but he withdrew when the CDU threatened to run in Bavaria. After the CDU parliamentary leader Helmut Kohl lost the election of 1976, the fraktion with CDU votes agreed to make Strauss the candidate for chancellor in the 1980 elections. He lost in a period when the CDU was making a resurgence. The CSU usually wins Bavarian government elections by about 60 percent of the vote, and it consistently contributes about 20 percent of the combined CDU/CSU vote in national elections. After the 1983 elections, which the CDU Chancellor Helmut Kohl won, Strauss remained as minister president of Bavaria, while four other CSU members entered the cabinet. *See also* CHRISTIAN DEMOCRATIC UNION (CDU), p. 168; ELECTIONS OF 1983: WEST GERMANY, p. 176; POLITICAL PARTY SYSTEM: WEST GERMANY, p. 220; *SPIEGEL* AFFAIR, p. 229.

Significance The Christian Social Union is indispensable to the Christian Democratic Union, for it consistently wins 10 to 11 percent of the national vote and 50 seats in the Bundestag. It is this margin that makes the CDU/CSU the largest parliamentary group in the Federal

Republic. Since the two parties do not compete against one another and remain cohesive in the Bundestag, they may be viewed as one unit. But the CSU's separate organization and controversial leader does place limitations on the direction the larger party may take. Under Strauss the CSU buttresses the conservative and nationalistic wing of the Union and prevents it from moving to the left. The Bavarian organization has been so dominated by Strauss for the last two decades that it is difficult to estimate the direction the party might take in his absence.

Church-State Relations The close association between organized religion and the government in the Federal Republic of Germany. The relationship between church and state is very close in Germany even though there is no established church. The Basic Law incorporated provisions of the Weimar constitution that provide for freedom of religion, prohibit civil disabilities based on religious belief, and prohibit the establishment of a state church. But the constitution also gives churches a corporate status in law and permits them to levy taxes on members according to state law. In addition, a number of ecclesiastical agreements, *Land* concordats, and the 1933 Concordat between Germany and the Vatican are also used to govern church-state relations. A "church tax" is assessed by churches on all members whether they practice the faith or not, and it is collected and distributed by Land governments. The tax is usually 8 to 10 percent of the income tax collected through employee payroll deductions. A person may avoid the tax by a difficult procedure of opting out, but he then has no claim on church services such as baptisms, marriages, or funerals. Other church-state links include additional state grants to church educational, medical, and charitable institutions, church representation on Land and federal boards and advisory commissions, and church representation in the consultative Senate of the Bavarian parliament. Also, church property is not taxed. The two largest churches in West Germany are the Evangelical church in Germany (EKD), an alliance of regional Lutheran, Reformed, and United churches, and the Roman Catholic church. Other Protestants are organized in the Free Protestant churches; the total number of Protestants comprise about 49 percent of the population. Catholics constitute about 45 percent; a small Jewish community numbers about 30,000 persons. Catholics and Protestants have equal representation on the various government boards and commissions. *See also* FUNCTIONAL REPRESENTATION, p. 188.

Significance The church-state relations that were authorized in the postwar period are a continuation of the close traditional association between church and state in Germany. Anticlericalism is not strong, and traditional religious strife has disappeared. Only the Free Democratic party advocates the complete separation of church and state. In 1959 the Social Democratic party dropped its opposition to religion in its attempt to become a multiclass people's party. The distance the SPD travelled from its previously strong anticlerical views is seen in the election campaign of 1980, when Chancellor Helmut Schmidt bitterly condemned the CDU/CSU candidate Franz Josef Strauss for alleging that the SPD would stop collecting the church tax. Both the Evangelical church and the Catholic church are active in trying to influence public policy through lobbying and public pronouncements, and, in the Catholic church, through efforts to rally its members through pastoral letters and sermons. The church tax has made German churches relatively affluent and secure by providing them with a guaranteed and inflation-proof source of income. Regular Protestant church attendance stands only at 15 percent, however. The influence of the large churches has been declining. But despite criticisms of the churches for their conservatism, it is unlikely that a full break in church-state relations will occur soon.

Codetermination The system of worker participation in management decisions that is required by law in West German private industry. Codetermination (*Mittbestimmung*) in West Germany takes place at two levels: (1) on the shop floor; and (2) on supervisory boards (similar to American boards of directors) and on management boards (similar to American management committees). Every third year, workers select representatives to works councils in nationwide shop floor elections in companies with over five employees; about 200,000 representatives are chosen in about 30,000 firms. Although employees and representatives need not belong to a trade union, over 80 percent of the councillors are members of the German Trade Union Federation (DGB). Works councils have equal rights with management regarding matters directly affecting workers, such as employment policies, working hours, holidays, shop floor conduct, and the like. In large companies, works councils have economic committees that are entitled to manufacturing, production, and financial information, and must consent to plant closings and staff and pay cuts. When disagreement betwen works councils and management occurs, the law requires arbitration; final settlement is determined by a labor court. At the highest levels of codetermination, workers have representatives on supervisory and management boards in one of three ways: (1) in the coal and steel industries, workers have an equal number of directors as shareholders on supervisory boards, and a labor director on management boards; (2) workers have equal representation in firms employing over 2,000 persons; and (3) workers have one-third of the directors in firms employing from 500 to 2,000 persons. Generally, worker directors have equal rights and responsibilities with shareholder and management directors in controlling the firm's activities, except that they are in a minority in small firms and shareholder directors prevail in tie votes in the coal and steel industries. *See also* TRADE UNIONS: WEST GERMANY, p. 230.

Significance The laws providing for codetermination have established one of the most extensive systems of worker participation in the management of private enterprise in the Western world. Codetermination has a long labor tradition in Germany; works councils were first established during the Weimar Republic in 1920. After World War II, trade unions pushed for the extension of industrial democracy rather than the nationalization of private enterprise. Important codetermination acts were adopted in 1951 and 1976. The practical results of the laws are mixed, but they may well have contributed to the high degree of labor harmony in West Germany as compared to France and Italy. At the shop floor level, works councils are important regarding matters touching on employment and the organization of work, and unions are influential in plant bargaining. At board levels unions object that workers lack parity with management, that white-collar workers are separated from manual workers, and that shareholders prevail in tie votes. Employers complain that unions have become too powerful, that profits are reduced, and that the private property system has been eroded. Codetermination laws have been upheld by the Constitutional Court, but the extension of the system in the 1970s helped to widen disagreements between the Social Democratic party and the Free Democratic party, which ultimately led to their split in 1981. Despite the continuing controversy over the extension and application of the law, particularly in the coal and steel industries, the system of codetermination has created an important form of industrial democracy in West Germany.

Confederation of the Rhine An association of German states under French tutelage from 1806 to 1813. The Confederation of the Rhine was created by Napoleon after his defeat of Austria at Austerlitz in 1805. Comprised of refashioned German states and territories except Austria and Prussia, the Confederation accepted French protection and influence and was obliged to provide an army under French command. The Confederation disintegrated following Napoleon's retreat from Moscow in 1813 when its members joined Austria, Prussia, and Russia to defeat the French at the battle of Leipzig. *See also* GERMAN CONFEDERATION, p. 189.

Significance The Confederation of the Rhine marked the end of the Holy Roman Empire and served as a transition to the German Confederation that was established in 1815. Some member states came under French influence as Napoleonic law codes and French-style administration were adopted. When Napoleon's enemies guaranteed the sovereignty of the members of the Confederation, they shifted sides in the war and contributed to the French defeat in Germany.

Constructive Vote of Nonconfidence A constitutional procedure in which the Bundestag may remove a chancellor from office by choosing another chancellor by majority vote. The purpose of the constructive vote of nonconfidence is to reduce cabinet instability by thwarting parliamentary groups that can engineer the overthrow of a chancellor but cannot provide a stable alternative. The maneuver has been rarely used in the history of the Federal Republic because government coalitions have usually remained united. In 1972, the Christian Democratic (CDU) leader Rainer Barzel introduced the motion against the government of the Social Democratic (SPD) Chancellor Willy Brandt, but the motion failed by two votes. In 1982, however, the Free Democratic (FDP) leaders resigned from the cabinet of the SPD Chancellor Helmut Schmidt, and the FDP allied itself with the Christian Democrats. A constructive vote of nonconfidence in October 1982 was successful for the first time; CDU leader Helmut Kohl became chancellor, and FDP leader Hans-Dietrich Genscher returned to the government as the vice chancellor and foreign minister, the position he held under Schmidt. In another constitutional procedure concerning a confidence motion, a dissolution of the Bundestag can occur if the chancellor requests a vote of confidence from the Bundestag and fails to receive majority support. In these circumstances, the chancellor may request the president to dissolve the Bundestag and call new elections. This maneuver was used by Chancellor Willy Brandt in 1972 to resolve a parliamentary impasse in which a budget bill could not be adopted and Barzel failed to replace him by the constructive vote of nonconfidence. A more controversial use of this procedure occurred in December 1982 when Chancellor Kohl purposely lost a confidence motion so that he could request the president to dissolve the assembly. President Karl Carstens deliberated before doing so because some people believed that the maneuver was unconstitutional. The president decided to dissolve the Bundestag, explaining that all the parliamentary parties had agreed to the dissolution, that the new CDU-FDP coalition was only temporary, and that the minority would not be injured. Several Bundestag deputies challenged the constitutionality of the president's dissolution of the assembly and took the question to the Constitutional Court. In a six-two vote the Court approved the president's actions and permitted the elections to occur. *See also* BUNDESTAG, p. 165; ELECTIONS OF 1983: WEST GERMANY, p. 176; FEDERAL CHANCELLOR, p. 180.

Significance The two confidence motion procedures provided for in the Basic Law lay dormant for many years in the Federal Republic. In 1982 the constructive vote of nonconfidence and the maneuver of a chancellor purposely losing a confidence vote in order to dissolve the assembly were both used successfully. These intricate political maneuvers generated a great deal of controversy, bitter recriminations, and charges of unconstitutionality. The Free Democrats, who had been elected as coalition partners of the Social Democrats in 1980, were much criticized for deserting the SPD government and bringing about its downfall by jumping to the side of the opposition party. Before the new CDU-FDU coalition was established, however, SPD Chancellor Schmidt had also wanted to use the procedure of purposely losing a confidence motion to call new elections. Ironically, he could not convince the CDU opposition to vote against his government in this case, and he lacked sufficient votes to bring about his own downfall. In 1982, the CDU saw the opportunity to take power through the constructive vote of nonconfidence procedure by making a coalition with the Free Democrats, who feared early elections. In the end, the public sided with the new CDU-FDP coalition, for it gave the new government a substantial majority in the March 1983 elections. Combined with the postwar simplified political party system, the constructive vote of nonconfidence has achieved its purpose of reducing cabinet instability in the Bonn Republic.

Economic Miracle The rapid rise in economic development, industrial production, and personal affluence that occurred in West Germany after World War II. The economic miracle was promoted by a combination of economic recovery assistance from the United States, the reduction of trade barriers in Western Europe, an economic policy promoting industrial expansion and investment in a free market economy, and labor discipline and cooperation. Beginning in the 1950s, levels of industrial production rose dramatically along with increases in international trade and the accumulation of foreign currency reserves. Accompanying this dramatic increase in economic growth was a rise in the standard of living and increases in disposable income and the consumption of luxury goods. Full employment levels were reached, and Germany admitted immigrant "guest workers" to meet industry's demands for labor. The public revenues created by the economic miracle enabled the government to expand educational and social welfare programs, especially in the areas of health care, income maintenance, unemployment compensation, retirement, housing, and accident insurance. *See also* GUEST WORKERS, p. 197; SOCIAL MARKET ECONOMY, p. 228.

Significance The West German economic miracle created the strongest economy in Europe, except for that of the Soviet Union. Today the nation's economy ranks fourth in the world, second to the United States in foreign trade and per capita income. The transformation of the economy hastened the pace of modernization of the occupational and social structure. There has been a decline in the number of persons employed in agriculture, a leveling off of employees in industry, and a rapid growth in white-collar and service occupations. The economic miracle brought about political consequences as well, for it contributed to the popular acceptance of the political system of the Federal Republic and the democratization of the political culture. Although the highly industrialized economy helped produce a strong economy and mass consumption, it also exacerbated problems of congestion, environmental pollution, and resource depletion. In the late 1970s, the high cost of imported petroleum and competition from Japan ended the trade surplus. And, although the economy was relatively strong in the 1980s, it suffered, like other Western industrial states, from recession, inflation, and rising unemployment.

Elections of 1983: West Germany   Parliamentary elections in the Federal Republic of Germany in which the Christian Democrats and their Free Democratic allies won a sweeping victory. The elections for the Bundestag (lower house) were precipitated by the overthrow of the government of Social Democratic (SPD) Chancellor Helmut Schmidt in October 1982. Schmidt fell after the coalition partner, the Free Democratic party (FDP), resigned from the government and joined the Christian Democrats to elect Helmut Kohl (CDU) chancellor through the nonconfidence procedure. After two months in office Kohl deliberately lost a confidence motion in December 1982 so that the president could dissolve the Bundestag and schedule national elections. This controversial procedure was tested in the Federal Constitutional Court, which ruled it to be valid, and national elections took place on March 6, 1983. Following his overthrow, Schmidt resigned as the SPD parliamentary leader, and the party selected Hans-Jochen Vogel as its candidate for chancellor. Fourteen parties presented candidates for Bundestag seats, but 87 percent of the popular vote typically went to the Christian Democrats (CDU/CSU) and the Social Democrats. The Free Democrats were returned as the small third party, but a fourth party (the Greens) won seats for the first time since the 1957 elections. A typically high voter turnout of 89 percent produced the following results: CDU/CSU, 48.8 percent of the popular vote and 226 seats; SPD, 38.2 percent and 193 seats; FDP, 6.9 percent and 34 seats; and the Greens, 5.6 percent and 27 seats. The National Democratic party (NPD) and the German Communist party (DKP) each won 0.2 percent of the vote and no seats. Following the election, Chancellor Kohl reconstructed his coalition with the Free

Democrats, and Hans-Dietrich Genscher, the FDP leader, remained as vice chancellor and foreign minister. *See also* CONSTRUCTIVE VOTE OF NONCONFIDENCE, p. 174; ELECTORAL SYSTEM: BUNDESTAG, p. 177; POLITICAL PARTY SYSTEM: WEST GERMANY, p. 220.

Significance The German elections of 1983 confirmed the change in German politics that occurred in October 1982 when Helmut Kohl became chancellor through a vote in parliament. Christian Democrats improved their position as the first party by an increase of 4 percentage points in the popular vote. This increase in the CDU/CSU vote occurred because over two million voters switched from the SPD to the Christian Democrats. The Social Democrats and the Free Democrats lost votes in all states, but the Free Democrats remained above the 5 percent minimum that is required to win seats in the Bundestag. They consequently maintained their traditional position as the holder of the balance of power. The election results supported the FDP's decision in 1982 to resign from the Schmidt government and switch to the Christian Democrats. The Greens, an environmentalist, antinuclear "peace" party, became the first new party since 1957 to enter the Bundestag. Although a fourth party now joined the other three in parliament, the elections of 1983 maintained the simplified multiparty system that took shape in the late 1950s.

Electoral System: Bundestag A type of proportional representation system in which the voter casts one vote for a district representative and a second vote for a list of party candidates. The electoral system used to select deputies for the Bundestag (lower house) is a type of "personalized" proportional representation in which one-half of the 496 seats are elected by plurality vote in single-member districts and the other half are filled from party lists. The voter casts one vote for a district (constituency) representative, who needs only a plurality to win, and a second vote for a list of candidates presented by the parties within the state. This is sometimes called a "mixed" system, but it is basically proportional representation because the size of a party's vote in the second vote determines the number of seats the party is awarded. The d'Hondt system of proportional representation (also called the highest-remainder formula) is used to determine the total number of seats to be awarded to a party. Seats are filled first with the candidates who won in district elections, and then the remaining seats are awarded to candidates on the party list. In addition, there is a minimum hurdle that a party must overcome to enter the Bundestag. The "5 percent clause," also called the "five-three rule," requires a party to win at least 5 percent of the total national vote or win at least three district elections to be awarded any seats. Because of the plurality rule in the district elections, small parties cannot win district seats; they consequently must receive at least 5 percent of the national vote, which has been difficult to achieve. The delegates to the Bundestag from West Berlin are not chosen by this method but are elected by the city's parliament. Voter turnout in national elections is very high, at about 90 percent of the electorate. *See also* BUNDESTAG, p. 165; POLITICAL PARTY SYSTEM: WEST GERMANY, p. 220.

Significance The peculiar features of the electoral system for the Bundestag were adopted in the postwar period to overcome the anonymity that usually results in a pure system of proportional representation. Germans wanted to retain the principle of proportionality but introduced the district elections so that voters could become familiar with their district representatives. Thus, by providing for district representatives, the system of proportional representation was "personalized." The apparent mixture of the two systems works well so long as the voter does not "split the ticket," that is, vote for a candidate of one party in district elections and for a different party list in the second vote. If sufficient numbers of voters do this, extra parliamentary seats beyond the 496 may need to be created. This is because, since seats are awarded first to the district winners, extra seats may need to be created so that a party will receive its correct proportion. This is rare, but one extra seat was created in 1980 and two in 1983. Of more importance is the 5 percent clause, which has eliminated very small parties and regional parties from the Bundestag. This provision was introduced in the postwar period to avoid the splintering of the assembly that characterized the Weimar Republic. Two parties that have disappeared are the German Party (DP) and the All German Bloc/Federation of Expellees and Dispossessed (GB/BHE). Some politicians have proposed that Germany move completely to a form of the district system. This idea has been opposed strongly by the Free Democratic party because the FDP receives all of its seats by virtue of the proportional representation rule. Since the FDP holds the balance of power between the Christian Democrats and the Social Democrats, it has been able to bargain the retention of the proportional system. In the 1983 elections the Greens party was able to break the 5 percent barrier and entered the Bundestag for the first time.

Electoral System: Federal President An indirect election by a national convention composed of national and state legislators. The federal president is elected in the Federal Assembly, which comprises all members of the Bundestag (popular house) and an equal number of delegates elected by state legislatures. Delegates from the states are chosen on a proportional basis in accordance with the strength of the party within the state assembly. There are 1,036 delegates, including a delegation from the city of West Berlin. Although West Berlin is not a constituent state in the Federal Republic and its delegation has no voting rights in the national parliament, the city's delegation does vote in the Federal Assembly. Presidential candidates are nominated by political parties. In voting in the Assembly, no more than three ballots are taken; an absolute majority is required on the first two ballots and a plurality (leading candidate) wins on the third ballot. Presidents have a five-year term and may be reelected once. Six men have served as federal president: Theodor Heuss (Free Democratic party), 1949–59; Heinrich Luebke (Christian Democratic party), 1959–69; Gustav Heinemann (Social Democratic party), 1969–74; Walter Scheel (Free Democratic party), 1974–79; Karl Carstens (Christian Democratic party), 1979–84; and Richard von Weizsäcker (Christian Democratic party), who was elected in 1984. *See also* FEDERAL PRESIDENT, p. 185.

Significance The indirect election system for the federal president is a change from the Weimar Republic system in which the president was popularly elected and held important constitutional powers. The framers of the Bonn constitution reduced the powers of the office and provided for its election by the convention system. The structure of the Federal Assembly comprising state and national deputies ensures that state interests will be equally represented with national ones, and that the majority in the Bundestag will not necessarily dominate the convention. Partisan politics plays its role in the election, however. National and state delegates affiliate by party, are cohesive, and back the party's candidate. Given the multiparty system, it often happens that a coalition of two parties is necessary to elect a candidate; thus the Social Democrats and Free Democrats combined to elect Scheel in 1974. National and state politics are similar but do not always coincide, and state delegations may represent parties not found in the Bundestag, or may distribute party votes in different proportions. In the 1979 convention, the Christian Democrats were stronger in the states, and the party's Federal Assembly delegation of state and national deputies was able to elect Carstens on the first ballot. Although Heuss was an elder statesman, some candidates have been elected while at the peak of their partisan careers, such as Scheel and Carstens, who were both party leaders at the time. Like other presidents, these men acted in a nonpartisan fashion after the elections. Von Weizsäcker, the Christian Democratic candidate, was elected overwhelmingly in 1984, for he was also supported by the Social Democratic leadership.

Farmers' Associations: West Germany Organization of farmers in the Federal Republic of Germany. The major farmers' associations are the League of the German Farmers, the League of Agricultural Chambers, and League of German Cooperatives and Agricultural Banks. All farm owners are required to belong to the agricultural chamber, and many voluntarily join the other associations. The three peak organizations represent different aspects of agriculture and cooperate to protect the interests of the 2.5 million German farmers in an informal union called the Green Front. Traditionally Germany has not been self-sufficient in agriculture; farms were small, not modernized, and suffered from low productivity. Postwar agricultural policy goals have been to increase production and increase farmers' income through various programs of price supports and agricultural subsidies. Some of the programs include promoting farm consolidation and modernization, establishing regional production and marketing cooperatives, making improvements in rural infrastructure, such as new roads and electricity, and adopting social measures such as retirement and training schemes. Since Germany is a member of the European Community, German farmers benefit from the Common Agricultural Policy, which guarantees prices. *See also* COMMON AGRICULTURAL POLICY (CAP), p. 245.

Significance German farmers' associations have been very effective in advancing the interests of farmers. Although the agricultural community is typically conservative and the powerful agricultural lobby won many benefits from Christian Democratic governments, it was also able to extract important benefits from Social Democratic governments in the 1970s. Important changes have occurred in the agricultural sector in the postwar period. These include the elimination of many small farms and the reduction of the agricultural labor force from 25 percent to 7 percent of the national labor force, and a tripling of production. But many inefficiencies and structural problems remain that have been only partially relieved by agricultural policies. Although there are indications of oppositon to the high subsidies which drive up food costs and manufacturers' export prices through taxes, the Green Front retains a powerful position in German politics.

Federal Chancellor The head of government in the Federal Republic of Germany, who exercises strong executive powers. The federal chancellor is the equivalent of a prime minister in a parliamentary system, but in some respects he is in a stronger position vis-à-vis the assembly. The chancellor alone is responsible to the Bundestag (popular house), and he can choose and dismiss cabinet members. The chancellor chairs cabinet meetings, decides the direction of government policy, and supervises the work of the government. He is in charge of the Federal Chancellery, a central office that coordinates the work of the entire federal government. The government includes a deputy to the chancellor, called the vice chancellor, cabinet ministers, parliamentary secretaries, who are deputies, and state secretaries, who are senior career civil servants. The chancellor is chosen by the parliamentary parties that have majority control in the Bundestag. Following an election, the federal president consults with party leaders and nominates a person for chancellor. In the Bonn Republic, party alignments and majority support for a candidate for chancellor have been unambiguous, and the president's choice is clear. The president's nominee must be accepted by a majority of the Bundestag, or the Bundestag may choose another person by majority vote. If a majority is not possible, the Bundestag may select a person by plurality vote. The president is bound to appoint a chancellor who has majority support. But if a candidate has been chosen by the Bundestag by a plurality vote, the president has the option of appointing the Bundestag's choice or of dissolving the Bundestag and calling for new elections. If a chancellor loses a motion of confidence in the Bundestag, he may ask the president to dissolve the house and call new elections. The Bundestag in turn may, in a procedure called the "constructive vote of nonconfidence," elect a new chancellor by a majority vote and request the president to appoint the new chancellor and dismiss the previous one. The president must comply with this decision. There have been six chancellors in the Federal Republic: Konrad Adenauer (CDU), 1949–63; Ludwig Erhard (CDU), 1963–66; Kurt Georg Kiesinger (CDU), 1966–69; Willy Brandt (SPD), 1969–74; Helmut Schmidt (SPD), 1974–82; and Helmut Kohl (CDU), who took office in 1982. Except for the period of the Grand Coalition, 1966 to 1969, the vice chancellors have always been Free Democrats. *See also* BUNDESTAG, p. 165; POLITICAL PARTY SYSTEM: WEST GERMANY, p. 220.

Significance The federal chancellor is one of the strongest chief executive officers in the Western European democracies. This position comes from the increase in the chancellor's constitutional powers provided by the Bonn constitution and the rather cohesive majorities that chancellors have been able to command in the Bundestag. For the most part, governments have been stable. Only one government has been overthrown in the history of the Federal Republic by a constructive vote of nonconfidence, that being Helmut Schmidt's in October 1982. He was replaced by Helmut Kohl when the Free Democratic party shifted from supporting the Social Democrats to the Christian Democrats. On two other occasions, chancellors purposely lost nonconfidence motions, so that the Bundestag could be dissolved and new elections called; this was done by Willy Brandt in 1972 and Kohl in December 1982. The domination of the chancellor in the Federal Republic has given rise to the term "chancellor democracy." Under this interpretation, the combination of strong constitutional powers and stable majorities has made the office of chancellor equivalent to that of a strong president in a presidential system. The popular confirmation of the new Christian Democratic–Free Democratic coalition under Chancellor Kohl in the March 1983 elections again provided a chancellor with a solid majority.

Federal Constitutional Court The high national court that exclusively exercises the power of judicial review of legislation and performs other functions. The Federal Constitutional Court stands apart from the regular court system and is primarily concerned with questions involving the interpretation of the Basic Law. Its jurisdiction, which is enumerated in the constitution and organic laws, includes (1) concrete jurisdiction, or actual cases in which an injured party challenges the constitutionality of a law; and (2) abstract jurisdiction, in which federal or state governments or one-third of the Bundestag may challenge the constitutionality of a law before it is applied. The most important types of issues that come before the Court are such matters as (1) judicial review cases that resolve issues of whether federal or state laws are compatible with the Basic Law; (2) citizen-initiated "constitutional complaints," involving charges that federal or state actions infringe on constitutional rights; (3) disputes between state and federal governments, between states, or between federal organs; (4) cases concerning the banning of political parties that have been charged with unconstitutional activity; and (5) other matters, such as presidential impeachment cases, disputed Bundestag election contests, the removal of federal judges, and the acceptability of international law. The Constitutional Court comprises two senates or panels of 8 judges each (formerly 12 each). Each panel acts separately within its assigned responsibilities; one panel generally considers cases involving civil rights and civil liberties, and the other panel considers other matters, such as jurisdictional disputes between different levels and units of government, political parties, and international law questions. Judges are selected by parliament for a 12-year term and cannot be reelected. One-half of the Court is elected by the 12-member Judicial Selection Committee of the Bundestag (lower house); the other half is elected by the Bundesrat (upper house). A two-thirds vote is required to elect the judges. The selection process ensures that minority parties will have a voice and that state governments are equal to the national deputies in these judicial appointments. Although politics is involved in their selection, judges have been highly qualified persons, a significant number of whom come from the civil service or the executive branch, as well as from the regular judiciary. *See also* JUDICIAL SYSTEM: WEST GERMANY, p. 201; RECHTSSTAAT, p. 223; UNCONSTITUTIONAL PARTIES, p. 231.

Significance The Federal Constitutional Court is a postwar innovation that has been used by opposition parties to try to invalidate laws and treaties. But the Court has high prestige with the German people, and its decisions have been accepted by the government. Well over 35,000 cases have been brought before the Court, many of which have been filed by citizens using the "constitutional complaint" procedure, alleging the infringement of basic rights. Over 350 cases have concerned the constitutionality of federal or state laws, and the Court has declared over 50 federal and 35 state laws unconstitutional. In some of the landmark cases the Court protected exclusive state rights in education and cultural affairs (television programming); defended the civil, economic, and social rights of citizens; and approved treaties that acknowledged the loss of prewar eastern territories to Poland and the Soviet Union. Concerning political parties, the Court approved clauses in federal and state electoral laws that effectively deny seats to small parties, but it invalidated a federal law that denied public financing to minor parties. A communist party was declared unconstitutional as well as a neo-Nazi party. The Court disapproved a liberal abortion law, but established standards under which a more conservative abortion law was adopted. In 1983, the Court approved by a six-two vote the constitutionality of the president's controversial early dissolution of the Bundestag, following the chancellor's deliberate loss of a confidence motion. In sum, the Federal Constitutional Court has played an active role in the Federal Republic as an arbiter of federal-state jurisdictional disputes, the guardian of constitutional institutions and procedures, and the protector of the basic rights of citizens.

Federalism: West Germany The system of government in West Germany in which constitutional authority is divided between the national government and state governments. The West German system of federalism is based on a complex division of constitutional authority between the two levels of government. The national or federal government has exclusive authority in such areas as foreign affairs, foreign trade, defense, citizenship, the economy, currency, rail and air transportation, and postal and telecommunications. The ten states (*Länder* or *Laender,* sing., *Land*) have exclusive authority in the areas of education, cultural and religious affairs, police, and local government. The Basic Law establishes a long list of concurrent powers in which either government may legislate, although for some areas the federal government may only establish broad guidelines. Federal legislation has priority in matters on the concurrent list, and the government in Bonn has preempted most fields. The constitution created a number of institutional arrangements that help to guarantee the continuation of the West German federal system. The Federal Constitutional Court has authority to rule on the constitutionality of national government actions that may encroach on state prerogatives, and to settle other federal-state or state-state disputes. The Bundesrat, the upper house in the national parliament, comprises delegates from state governments, who share equal powers with lower-house deputies on matters directly affecting state interests, the creation of states, and constitutional amendments. Land governments in effect have veto rights in about 50 percent of all federal legislation that is enacted. Additionally, many federal laws are administered by state agencies, some of which entail very little federal supervision. The regular court system in the Federal Republic is also integrated; the highest appellate courts are federal courts, and all the lower courts are state courts, which apply both state and federal law. *See also* BASIC LAW, p. 158; BUNDESRAT, p. 163; *LAND* GOVERNMENT, p. 202.

Significance The West German system of federalism grants more authority and prerogatives to the Länder than did previous German systems. Prussia dominated the other states in the German Empire, and the Weimar Republic was only nominally a federation because the central government had been granted much authority. Although the states in the Federal Republic have few exclusive powers, their authority to administer federal law gives states a great deal of discretionary power. This has created certain weaknesses in the federal system. The states are not equal in size, population, or resources, and their methods and policies of handling common problems differ. Some states are not economically viable and cannot cope with many current problems such as economic development, environmental pollution, and health care. The Basic Law requires the federal government to maintain "unity of living standards" among the states. This has consequently led to a complex system of revenue sharing, whereby federal tax revenues are distributed to the states in various programs. Poorer states receive "equalization payments," which in effect are paid by richer states. The methods for distributing federal revenues are a constant source of controversy because all states depend on federal revenues. Some observers have noted that the federal system in Germany needs to be revised and made more centralized, but states are reluctant to agree to a larger federal role in policy making, administration, or law enforcement.

Federal President The formal head of state of the Federal Republic of Germany. The federal president is a nonpartisan, ceremonial officer who acts as head of state in a standard parliamentary system. Executive power is exercised by the chancellor and cabinet. Although the president signs laws, decrees, and treaties, and makes civil, judicial, and military appointments, all his public acts must be countersigned by the chancellor or other cabinet minister. The president may give advice to the government, but it need not be followed, and only in certain ambiguous parliamentary situations may he be able to exercise his reserve powers with some degree of discretion. If the Bundestag (lower house) is unable to agree on a chancellor or on a replacement, the president's choice for chancellor or his decision to call for new elections may be binding, but this has never happened. Although a president may refuse to sign a bill, it is doubtful that he possesses an independent veto power. The federal president is elected for a five-year term by a convention composed of national and state legislators. *See also* ELECTORAL SYSTEM: FEDERAL PRESIDENT, p. 178.

Significance In the Federal Republic of Germany the office of federal president is quite different from the head of state in the Weimar Republic. The dual executive system used in Weimar, whereby the president exercised independent executive authority and was directly elected by the people, gave the president strong constitutional authority and a popular mandate. The framers of the Bonn constitution decided to concentrate executive authority in the office of chancellor and make it directly responsible to the popular assembly. Although the reserve powers of the federal president are a fallback in case of a breakdown in parliamentary government, there has been no occasion to use them. The simplified multiparty system of the Bonn republic has provided stable majorities and unambiguous choices for the president. Some presidents have disagreed with the government and have tried to exercise influence on the making of public policy, but in the face of determined and politically strong chancellors they have retreated into a nonpartisan role.

Federal Republic of Germany (FRG) The official name for West Germany. The Federal Republic of Germany (*Bundesrepublik Deutschland*) was created in 1949 from the union of the three western zones of Germany that were occupied by the United States, Great Britain, and France. A constitution (Basic Law) for the Federal Republic of Germany (FRG) was approved by the Allied powers, and the national capital was moved to Bonn. For this reason the Federal Republic is sometimes referred to as the "Bonn Republic." Full sovereignty was not granted in 1949, however, for the Western Allies retained important rights in disarmament matters, foreign trade, foreign relations, and emergency powers under an Occupation Statute that came into force in the same year. Full sovereignty was granted to the Federal Republic on May 5, 1955, by the Western Allies on the basis of a series of agreements that removed all Allied controls, authorized German rearmament, and admitted the FRG into the North Atlantic Treaty Organization. West Germany is a federation comprising ten states (*Länder*): Schleswig-Holstein, Hamburg, Lower Saxony, Bremen, North Rhine-Westphalia, Hesse, Rhineland-Palatinate, Baden-Württemberg, Bavaria, and Saarland. The city of West Berlin is not a constituent state of the Federal Republic and is officially under the ultimate authority of the occupying powers. Much of this authority is not exercised, however, and in many economic, political, and legal respects West Berlin is part of the FRG. The Federal Republic is about half the size of prewar Germany. The official name for East Germany, the former occupation zone of the Soviet Union, is the German Democratic Republic (GDR). *See also* BASIC LAW, p. 158; GERMAN DEMOCRATIC REPUBLIC (GDR), p. 191; OSTPOLITIK, p. 217; WEST BERLIN, p. 238.

Significance The Federal Republic of Germany was to be a provisional state with a temporary constitution and capital until the former occupation zones of Germany could be united and the capital moved again to Berlin. But because of the postwar international political situation, which could not be remedied short of war, the provisional arrangements have become permanent. Under agreements made by the government of Willy Brandt with East Germany, the Soviet Union, Poland, and Czechoslovakia, the FRG has recognized the de facto partition of Germany and the loss of the Eastern Territories (parts of prewar Germany east of the Oder-Neisse rivers) to Poland and the Soviet Union. The status quo in Europe was also affirmed in the Helsinki Accord of 1975, a diplomatic agreement signed by the nations of Europe and the United States. The Federal Republic of Germany has existed as long as the Weimar Republic (1919–33) and the Nazi Regime (1933–45) combined. The same is true of the German Democratic Republic, although the existence of East Germany as a separate state was not recognized by the West until the 1970s. At that time, both West and East Germany were admitted to membership in the United Nations. Barring a major war in Europe, the continued existence of these two states with their different political systems seems assured.

Free Democratic Party (FDP) The liberal party in the Federal Republic of Germany, which holds the balance of power in the parliament. The Free Democratic party (FDP) was reorganized in the postwar period as the successor to several liberal parties that existed in the Empire period and in the Weimar Republic. Thus it brought together various regionally based parties and movements, those of classic, free enterprise liberals, conservative business interests, anticlericals, nationalists, and progressive liberals. The FDP emerged in the first national elections of 1949 with 12 percent of the vote and a conservative leadership and program that made it a natural ally to the Christian Democrats (CDU). Never a cohesive party, the FDP suffered from factionalism and volatile leadership as it participated in several cabinets under Konrad Adenauer and Ludwig Erhard in the 1950s and 1960s. Having brought about the downfall of Erhard's government in 1966, the party was out of power during the time of the Grand Coalition, from 1966 to 1969. Walter Scheel and younger members then took control of the party and refashioned its program into that of progressive liberalism; and conservatives, such as the former leader, Erich Mende, left the party for the Christian Democrats. From 1969 to 1982 the FDP participated in the Social Democratic governments of Willy Brandt and Helmut Schmidt. Walter Scheel was elected federal president in 1972; the new party leader, Hans-Dietrich Genscher, continued the party's cabinet position as vice chancellor and foreign minister. In October 1982 the FDP resigned from Schmidt's government and joined the Christian Democrats to form a coalition government under the CDU leader Helmut Kohl. In the March 1983 elections, the FDP received 7 percent of the vote; it renegotiated a new coalition agreement with the Christian Democrats, and continued to play a pivotal role in German politics. *See also* ELECTIONS OF 1983: WEST GERMANY, p. 176; POLITICAL PARTY SYSTEM: WEST GERMANY, p. 220.

Significance The Free Democratic party is a relatively small party, but by holding the balance of power in the political center, it has been able to play an important role in the German political system. Decisions made within the FDP determine whether the Christian Democrats or the Social Democrats will control the government. Because of this parliamentary position, the FDP has been out of power only from 1956 to 1961 and from 1966 to 1969. In the first 35 years of the Federal Republic, the party was in the cabinet for 27 years. But the party is vulnerable to any change in the electoral law, for it receives all of its seats through the system of proportional representation. Moreover, because of its factionalism and lack of discipline, the FDP gained a reputation in the 1950s and 1960s as an unreliable coalition partner. In 1982 it was bitterly condemned by the Social Democrats as an untrustworthy partner for shifting to the Christian Democrats. Intraparty squabbles characterized the 1984 party convention, which reelected Genscher as party chairman for a two-year term. Party fortunes have been steadily declining at the state level; in 1984 the FDP had representation in only five of the ten state legislatures and West Berlin. Yet, so long as proportional representation is retained for the Bundestag and the FDP can win the minimal requirement of 5 percent, it seems likely that it will continue to exercise power far beyond what its small size would indicate.

Functional Representation The direct representation of economic and social interest groups in advisory government bodies. In West Germany functional representation is used to supplement the basic system of territorial or political representation. The peak organizations of business, labor, agriculture, and church interests have representatives on consultative bodies, commissions, regional planning councils, and the supervisory boards of the radio and television networks of the states. These and other organized interests have direct formal contact with government ministries, which must consult with the relevant organizations when drafting bills. In addition, there has been a system of regular conferences called "Concerted Action," in which government ministers, top civil servants, and the leaders of peak organizations meet to discuss economic conditions and try to establish guidelines for economic policy. In the state of Bavaria, the only state that has a bicameral legislature, the second chamber is chosen by various organized interests in the state. *See also* BUSINESS AND INDUSTRIAL ASSOCIATIONS: WEST GERMANY, p. 166; CHURCH-STATE RELATIONS, p. 171; FARMERS' ASSOCIATIONS: WEST GERMANY, p. 180; TRADE UNIONS: WEST GERMANY, p. 230.

Significance Functional representation in the Federal Republic is an instance of the political doctrine called corporatism. In this typical European idea, society is understood to be a union of functional groups rather than an aggregate of free individuals. Economic interests are to be organized into publicly authorized hierarchical associations that are given rights to represent and regulate persons who are members of the group. In the West German political system, this idea is partially used, only as an additional form of representation to the prevailing system of political or territorial representation. In addition to their representation on advisory boards, major pressure groups, including churches, are very active in promoting their interests through political parties and trying to influence public opinion. Yet the formal aspects of functional representation, even though it occurs at the advisory level, has had the effect of directing the power to the leaders of the peak organizations and away from the rank and file, thus strengthening the hierarchical character of the system. But functional representation has also helped integrate groups within the political system by giving them a direct voice in government before policy is made.

German Communist Party (DKP) The small Communist party (DKP) that was legalized in the late 1960s as the successor to the former Communist Party of Germany (KPD), which had been banned in 1956. The KPD had been a large group in the Weimar Republic, winning 17 percent of the popular vote in 1932. It was suppressed by the Nazis, but it emerged in the first postwar elections in West Germany with 5.6 percent of the popular vote and representation in the Bundestag. In 1953 its vote fell to 2.2 percent, and it won no parliamentary seats. In 1956 the Federal Constitutional Court declared the party to be an unconstitutional group within the meaning of the Basic Law. In 1967 a Communist party was legalized in some states and established itself as a national party in 1968 with a new name and a new program. The German Communist party (DKP) deemphasizes the revolutionary approach and associates with other leftist groups in order to meet constitutional standards. The party has about 30,000 members, mostly younger persons, and has been able to win a few seats in municipal councils. In national elections it has won no more than 0.3 percent of the popular vote; in the elections of 1980 and 1983 it received only 0.2 percent of the vote. *See also* POLITICAL PARTY SYSTEM: WEST GERMANY, p. 220; UNCONSTITUTIONAL PARTIES, p. 231.

Significance The German Communist party has played a very minor role in the politics of the Federal Republic. Much of the prewar Communist vote was located in the eastern parts of Germany, territory not incorporated into the Federal Republic. West Germans reacted negatively to the Communist takeover in East Germany, and by the time the KPD was declared unconstitutional in 1956, the party had already lost its seats in parliament. The government's decision to permit the party to organize under a new label relieved a source of embarrassment. West German Communists had very little popular support and posed no threat to the West German democratic system. By permitting the Communists to compete in elections, the government revealed the Communists' weakness as it prepared to negotiate some type of settlement with East Germany.

German Confederation A loose union of German states from 1815 to 1866 that included Austria and Prussia. Following the Napoleonic Wars, the German Confederation was created in 1815 by the Congress of Vienna as a replacement for the Holy Roman Empire. The establishment of the Confederation was linked to the goals of the Congress to make territorial settlements in Europe, to restore the legitimate dynasties to their thrones, and to establish a balance of power that would preserve the peace. The Confederation was comprised of 35 German principalities and 4 free cities, with the seat at Frankfurt. Austria acted as the permanent president of a powerless Diet composed of ambassadors who represented the sovereign member states of the Confederation. The first two decades of the Confederation were dominated by the Austrian statesman, Prince Clemens von Metternich, who, supported by Prussia, opposed the liberalism, nationalism, and reformism that was growing in parts of Germany. The Carlsbad Decrees of 1819 instituted rigid censorship and banned reformist groups. In 1834 Prussia, much enlarged by territorial settlements, initiated a customs union (*Zollverein*) throughout much of Germany that promoted free trade and contributed to the growing industrialism. In 1848 as a result of the Liberal Revolution that swept Vienna, Berlin, and many parts of Germany, an elected assembly, the Frankfurt Parliament, replaced the Diet of the Confederation. The work of the Parliament was delayed by the conflict between liberals and radical democrats and between those who advocated the union of all German states (the great German solution) and those who wanted a union under Prussian leadership without Austria (the small German solution). The Parliament proclaimed the Declaration of Fundamental Rights and adopted a liberal, federal constitution for a greater Germany, and attempted to choose an emperor. This latter plan failed because the Austrian emperor demanded that his eastern territories be included in the union, and the Prussian king rejected the offer because it came from an elective assembly. The Parliament was dispersed in 1849 after a conservative reaction restored the power of the legitimate princes in the German states, but the German confederation was reestablished in 1850. The growing rivalry between Prussia and Austria broke wide open in the 1860s over issues concerning the Zollverein, the reformation of the Confederation, and the administration of the area of Schleswig-Holstein, which had been taken in the Danish war. Under the brilliant leadership of its chancellor, Otto von Bismarck, Prussia challenged Austria and established itself as the leading German state. In 1866 Prussia quickly defeated its rival in the Austro-Prussian war (Seven Weeks War), declared the German Confederation at an end, and replaced it with the North German Confederation. *See also* HOLY ROMAN EMPIRE, p. 199; NORTH GERMAN CONFEDERATION, p. 212.

Significance The German Confederation was founded on the principles of legitimacy and state sovereignty for the constituent units. These principles prevented it from evolving into an effective instrument for the unification of the nation. Within the context of the Confederation several important struggles took place among the following forces: (1) nationalists who desired the unification of Germany; (2) petty German states that wanted to retain the system of state sovereignty; (3) commercial and industrial interests that wanted to establish a national economy and end internal barriers on trade and economic development; (4) liberals who tried to establish a limited democracy under a constitutional monarchy; (5) radical democrats and socialists who pushed for egalitarian social and economic goals; and (6) monarchists and conservatives who fought to retain the traditional system of absolutism. Participating in these struggles were the two large states of Austria and Prussia, each pursuing sometimes coinciding but increasingly conflicting goals. It was only after defeating Austria and breaking the Confederation that Prussia was able to bring about the unification of Germany under its control. The failure of the Liberal Revolution of 1848 meant that this unification would be under authoritarian leadership.

German Democratic Republic (GDR) The official title for the state of East Germany. The German Democratic Republic (GDR) was founded on October 7, 1949, as a separate political entity. Created from the Soviet occupation zone, the GDR was originally a nominal federation comprising five states (*Länder*). East Germany adopted the unitary form of government in 1952 and replaced the states with 15 districts including East Berlin, the nation's capital. In 1958, it abolished the bicameral legislature in favor of a single chamber. The constitution of 1968 declared the GDR to be a "socialist German state"; since 1974 the constitution no longer proclaims the goal of reunification with the territory and people of the Federal Republic of Germany. The governmental system features a unicameral legislature, the People's Chamber (*Volkskammer*), which is the supreme organ of state power. The chamber elects the Council of State and its chairman, who is the head of state, and designates the chairman of the Council of Ministers, who is the head of government. The Supreme Court is responsible to the People's Chamber; the judicial system and civil and criminal codes are modeled after the Soviet system. The GDR is a one-party Communist state dominated by the Socialist Unity Party of Germany (SED), which has a structure typical of Communist parties. The SED was created in 1945 by a Soviet-forced amalgamation of the Communist party and the larger Social Democratic party. The National Front of the German Democratic Republic is an umbrella organization controlled by Communists that incorporates the SED and four other Communist-controlled parties; the Front presents a single list in elections. East Germany is a member of the Warsaw Treaty Organization, the Council of Mutual Economic Assistance, and the United Nations. *See also* BASIC TREATY, p. 159; BERLIN WALL, p. 161; FEDERAL REPUBLIC OF GERMANY (FRG), p. 185; OCCUPATION PERIOD, p. 214; ODER-NEISSE LINE, p. 216.

Significance The German Democratic Republic was founded three weeks after the establishment of the Federal Republic of Germany. Hard-line German Communist leaders cooperated with the USSR in creating a Stalinist system in East Germany. Outnumbered by West Germany's population, 60 million to 16 million, and fearing Bonn's oft-stated goal of reunification, East German communists presented an antagonistic and uncooperative attitude toward the West. In 1953 the GDR brutally crushed a workers' revolt that began in East Berlin; in 1961 the GDR built a wall in Berlin that prevented East Germans from freely leaving the territory. The East German economy began to develop rapidly in the 1960s, and it became the strongest economy of the East European Communist states. In the 1970s with the *Ostpolitik* of Federal Chancellor Willy Brandt, East Germany was accepted by the West Germans as another state of the German nation. Emigration from the GDR remained strictly controlled, however, as the Berlin Wall and border fortifications prevent the active population from fleeing the country. Although the goal of reunification is still a long-run West German goal, the existence of the GDR as a separate German state seems assured, barring a major convulsion in central Europe.

German Empire The unified German state from 1871 to 1918. The German Empire (*Reich*) was proclaimed in Versailles after the victory of Prussia over France in the Franco-Prussian War, with the Hohenzollern king, William I of Prussia, as emperor (*Kaiser*). Popularly called the Second Reich, the Empire was a successor to the North German Confederation, and it comprised 24 (later 25) states, including monarchies, grand duchies, principalities, and free cities. The Empire thus included the southern German states previously not in the Confederation, but not Austria. The governmental system continued features of the Confederation: the German emperor, who was also the king of Prussia, appointed the federal chancellor, who was responsible to the emperor, not to the parliament. The Federal Council (Bundesrat), or upper house of the parliament, represented the states of the union and consisted of delegates instructed by state governments. The Reichstag (lower house) was elected by universal manhood suffrage, but its constitutional powers were few, and it was further weakened by an extreme multiparty system. The Empire government was dominated by Prussia, which had a large share of Bundesrat votes enabling it to veto constitutional amendments. From 1871 to 1890, the Federal chancellor was Otto von Bismarck, who was also the chancellor of Prussia and president of the Bundesrat, and who had great influence over Kaiser William I. Bismarck pursued an expansive foreign policy, strengthened Germany militarily, and introduced some social reforms. From 1871 to 1877 Bismarck adopted strict anti-Catholic measures in the Empire and Prussia in the belief that the church was opposed to the Empire; this was called the *Kulturkampf,* or struggle for civilization. Afterwards he practiced a more even domestic policy that tried to balance the various social, economic, political, and regional groups in the nation. Bismarck was dismissed by William II in 1890, and the young emperor took a more active role in government. In the twentieth century the Empire pursued an ineffectual overseas imperial policy, and it made few concessions to the rising power of working classes. The Reich remained under the control of the landowners, nobility, Junkers (Prussian landed aristocracy), army, high civil service, industrialists, and upper middle classes. Following military defeat in World War I, the government collapsed as revolutions broke out in Germany; Kaiser William II fled the country in November 1918, and a republic was proclaimed by revolutionary forces. The new republican government under the Social Democrats, who had the loyalty of the workers, joined with the military to put down left-wing revolutionaries led by the Spartacists (Spartacus League), who wanted to establish a Soviet-style system. A republican constitution for the successor system, the Weimar Republic, was adopted in 1919. *See also* FRANCO-PRUSSIAN WAR, p. 109; NORTH GERMAN CONFEDERATION, p. 212; VERSAILLES TREATY, p. 232; WEIMAR REPUBLIC p. 234.

Significance The German Empire was the first successful effort that unified most Germans into a single national state. This unification was brought about by the forceful and expansive policies of the state of Prussia under its chancellor Bismarck, who successfully used a policy of "blood and iron." In wars against Denmark (1864), Austria (1866), and France (1870), Bismarck expanded the territory of Prussia, defeated Prussia's major German rival, and incorporated the southern German states into a Reich that Prussia controlled. Although the Empire united the German states and hastened the industrialization of the nation, it resisted the general European trend toward constitutional democracy. The Second Reich was an authoritarian state that centralized power in the emperor and his closest advisers, and it primarily reflected the interests of the army, landed aristocracy, industrialists, and upper middle classes. Although this closed system achieved a remarkable series of international successes in the nineteenth century, it eventually led to the downfall of the regime. The Reich brought Germany to the rank of first powers, and it taught the lesson that unification and international status are achieved by power politics. Given the disastrous failures of its successor, the Weimar Republic, this lesson was well learned by the Nazis who followed and, under Adolf Hitler, created a short-lived Third Reich.

Godesberg Program versus Neosocialism The debate over party program that took place within the Social Democratic party following its defeat in the March 1983 national elections. The fundamental issue in the debate was whether to continue the 1959 Bad Godesberg Program that had rejected Marxist socialism and opted for free market economics, or to adopt a modified version of socialism that stressed state intervention in the economy. Having simmered for several years, the debate broke wide open when the new party leader, Hans-Jochen Vogel, moved to the left and appointed the socialist Wolfgang Roth as the party's economic spokesman. Roth advocated a program calling for state-financed and state-directed restructuring of industry, concentration on high-technology enterprises, adoption of "environmentally oriented" public works projects, shortening of the workweek to 35 hours, and extension of the codetermination policy that would give public interest groups a voice in management. Although Roth stopped short of calling for the nationalization of industry, other left-wingers in the party argued for a fuller extension of socialist principles and programs. *See also* SOCIAL DEMOCRATIC PARTY (SPD), p. 227.

Significance The Godesberg Program versus Neosocialism debate was propelled by the party's need to develop an alternative to the new Christian Democratic Chancellor Helmut Kohl's economic policy, which stressed supply side economics. SPD party leaders argued that Kohl's policies would provide only short-term relief, that private banks and firms would not substantially restructure German industry, and that the high unemployment caused by the recession would continue. The failure of former Social Democratic Chancellor Helmut Schmidt's economic policies to deal with the recession, which brought the new postwar problem of high unemployment to Germany, highlighted the need for a different policy. The defection of substantial numbers of industrial workers in the 1983 election to the Christian Democrats, and the growth of the environmentalist, antinuclear Greens party gave added impetus for the SPD to develop policies that would appeal to these groups. The debate on socialism within the party is expected to continue until the next national election, which is scheduled for 1987.

Grand Coalition The government coalition of the two large parties, the Christian Democrats and the Social Democrats, from 1966 to 1969. The Grand Coalition was formed in December 1966 by Kurt Georg Kiesinger after the resignation of Christian Democratic (CDU) Chancellor Ludwig Erhard, who had lost support within the party and the nation. Erhard fell because, following an economic decline, the Free Democratic (FDP) coalition party refused to support a tax increase and resigned from the government. Erhard was left with a minority government, and his position became untenable when the Social Democrats (SPD) won a surprising victory in state elections in North Rhine–Westphalia. Kiesinger, who was minister-president of Baden-Württemberg, brought in Willy Brandt, the SPD leader who was mayor of West Berlin, as the vice chancellor and foreign minister. The new government commanded 447 of the 496 seats in the Bundestag, a fact that led many to question whether there could be an effective opposition. The Grand Coalition used its 90 percent majority to enact some overdue legislation and constitutional amendments, which required a two-thirds majority. The legislative program of the Grand Coalition included passage of a constitutional amendment providing for executive government during a state of emergency, a major tax reform, and measures to boost the economy. In foreign affairs, the government instituted a new policy toward Eastern European Communist nations. The Hallstein Doctrine, which called for a boycott of any nation that recognized East Germany, was abandoned, and the government recognized Romania. Kiesinger's eastern policy stopped short of recognizing East Germany, however, an idea that had stronger support within the SPD than in the CDU/CSU. The Grand Coalition was dissolved when, following SPD gains in the 1969 elections, a new government was formed by the SPD and FDP under Willy Brandt as chancellor. *See also* HALLSTEIN DOCTRINE, p. 199; POLITICAL PARTY SYSTEM: WEST GERMANY, p. 220.

Significance The Grand Coalition of the two major parties had a considerable impact on West German politics. It enacted some needed legislation and constitutional reforms, and it brought the Social Democratic party into the government for the first time. This experience reinforced its new image as a moderate social democratic party and contributed to its increase in popular support in the 1969 elections. The Free Democrats reinforced their image as an undisciplined party and unreliable coalition partner when they resigned from Erhard's government. An ineffective opposition, their popular support continued to decline, and they barely survived the election of 1969. But, under the new leadership of Walter Scheel, they were able to make a government coalition with the Social Democrats, which continued until 1982. Although the Grand Coalition made important changes in domestic policy and took initiatives toward the East, it primarily served as a transition to the new period of Social Democratic governments.

Greens A left-wing environmentalist and antinuclear political party that won seats in the parliament for the first time in 1983. The

Greens (*Die Grünen*) developed out of disparate groups with various names that advocated causes such as the protection of the environment, the elimination of nuclear energy plants, improvement in local housing, and opposition to the stationing of nuclear missiles in Germany. These groups, sometimes calling themselves "the Alternative," protested against the policies of the established parties and gained notoriety with street demonstrations, public protests, and acts of civil disobedience. In the early 1980s, the Greens began to receive from 3 to 8 percent of the popular vote in state elections; by the end of 1982 they had representation in five state legislatures and in the West Berlin parliament under the name, the Alternative List. The Greens won only 1.3 percent of the popular vote in the 1980 national elections, but in 1983 the party received 5.6 percent of the vote and won 27 seats in the Bundestag (federal lower house). In addition to their primary concern with nuclear, ecological, and peace questions, the party also advocated a new economic order, socialization of the means of production and finance, and assistance to the less-developed world. Although they are a type of antiparty and espouse left-wing causes, they were seated in the center of the Bundestag chamber, between the Socialists and the Christian Democrats. One of the leaders of the movement, Petra Lehmann Kelly, who was educated and first became an activist in the United States, has become an internationally recognized personality. *See also* ELECTORAL SYSTEM: BUNDESTAG, p. 177; POLITICAL PARTY SYSTEM: WEST GERMANY, p. 220.

Significance The Greens were the first nonestablishment party to win seats in the Bundestag since 1957. Although they made a remarkable showing in the 1983 elections, the question remains as to whether the organization has lasting power. The party may lose support as its ecological and antinuclear program is picked up by larger parties, or the Social Democratic party (SPD) rediscovers its socialist roots. Most of the votes the Greens received in 1983 came from new, younger voters and former SPD voters. In late 1983, in an effort to capture the support of the growing antinuclear movement, the Social Democrats reversed their position and rejected the emplacement of American cruise and Pershing II missiles. The Greens' unorthodox style and antiestablishment stance, however, may limit its activities to nothing more than harassment. The 1983 party conference required that the "rotation principle" be followed—that the party's deputies resign their Bundestag seats in favor of their substitutes after two years, in March 1985. In 1984 the Greens suffered resignations of some prominent figures, fighting broke out among the factions, and the parliamentary leaders, including Petra Kelly, were replaced. But the party continued to do well in elections—it won 8.2 percent of the popular vote in the June 1984 elections to the European Parliament.

Guest Workers The term for foreign workers who are part of the West German labor force. Guest workers were recruited in the 1950s and 1960s by the West German government to meet the labor shortage caused by the expanding economy. Active recruitment ceased in the 1970s, but immigration has continued because family members of guest workers may enter Germany under the family reunification policy. In 1983 there were 4.5 million foreigners in the country, constituting 7.5 percent of the population. The major ethnic groups are: Turks, 1.6 million; Yugoslavs, 632,000; Italians, 602,000; and Greeks, 301,000. Over one million foreigners are children under 16, and half of these are Turkish. It is estimated that by 1985 one of every ten schoolchildren will be Moslem. Foreign workers fill important manpower needs in certain industries and in restaurants, and they take menial jobs that few Germans want. They have a higher rate of unemployment than Germans, live in slums, have a higher crime rate, and less education and vocational training. Foreign workers receive the same unemployment, welfare, housing, and other social benefits as other workers. Because foreigners have become a large and permanent part of the German scene, the federal government has adopted a three-part policy: (1) integrating long-term foreign residents by special programs in education for the second generation, and by promoting naturalization; (2) placing limits on immigration by stopping recruitment of workers outside the European Community and by controlling illegal entry; and (3) promoting repatriation by giving relocation assistance to workers from non–European Community nations who are out of work. The government also attempts to curb the influx of persons who seek political asylum under the country's liberal asylum laws. Over 200,000 persons, a majority of whom are Turks, have sought political asylum in recent years. *See also* CODETERMINATION, p. 172; ECONOMIC MIRACLE, p. 175.

Significance For Germans, "guest worker" implied a temporary status, with the guests leaving in time. The term, however, has become a misnomer because many foreigners have become permanent residents of the Federal Republic. The government's attempt to curb immigration may have only limited success because persons from European Community countries may enter Germany without visas or work permits. Since many foreign workers have come from the less-developed parts of southern Europe, they, particularly the Turks, constitute a culturally distinct and alien minority. The potential for ethnic conflict may increase, especially in hard economic times when foreign workers hold jobs Germans want. Cultural adaptation among the Turks is very slow, and only a small percentage have become naturalized. Yet demands that foreign workers "go home" can have little effect because for permanent residents and their second-generation children, Germany is home.

Guillaume Affair An espionage scandal that led to the resignation of Social Democratic Chancellor Willy Brandt in 1974. Günter Guillaume, who was Brandt's appointment secretary for party affairs, was arrested in April 1974 for being a spy for East Germany. Two weeks later, Chancellor Brandt resigned, citing his personal responsibility for negligence in allowing Guillaume to remain employed in the Federal Chancellery after he had been warned that Guillaume was under suspicion. Günter Guillaume was an officer in the East German State Security ministry. In 1956, he and his wife and child entered West Germany from East Germany, posing as refugees. He took a position as a functionary in the Social Democratic party and after 14 years was promoted to a position in the Federal Chancellery, where he became Brandt's personal assistant for Social Democratic party (SPD) affairs. Warnings from the security service about Guillaume's East German origins went unheeded. Guillaume came under investigation in 1973; he and his wife were arrested in April 1974, and he was charged with running a six-man spy ring. While he was employed in the Chancellery, Guillaume allegedly had access to classified information, NATO documents, cabinet meeting reports, and other secret information. After a trial, Guillaume and his wife were found guilty; he was sentenced to thirteen years and his wife to eight years in prison. Both were released to East Germany in an exchange of prisoners in 1981. Although some of Brandt's advisers asked him to stay on as chancellor, he resigned on May 6, 1974, citing his negligence and other personal reasons. *See also* SOCIAL DEMOCRATIC PARTY (SPD), p. 227.

Significance The Guillaume affair brought about Brandt's resignation, but some observers have noted that Brandt was ready to step down because his domestic reform program had not been going well. The Social Democratic party had been losing in state elections, and Brandt did not want to play the role of a domineering leader in order to hold the coalition with the Free Democrats together to meet the economic challenges caused by the increase in petroleum prices. Brandt remained chairman of the Social Democratic party, however, and he continued to speak out on domestic social reform matters and on economic development in the less-developed societies. The finance minister, Helmut Schmidt, replaced Brandt as chancellor, a position he maintained until the Free Democrats resigned from his government in 1982. The Guillaume Affair confirmed the views of Brandt's critics that his detente policy, which gave East Germany diplomatic recognition and international status, was a mistaken one.

Hallstein Doctrine   The policy that West Germany would withhold diplomatic relations from states that recognized East Germany, except the Soviet Union. Named for Walter Hallstein, state secretary in the Foreign Ministry of Konrad Adenauer's government, the doctrine was proclaimed in 1955 as part of Bonn's attempt to deny legitimacy to the German Democratic Republic (GDR). The policy was applied in the 1950s and early 1960s, and diplomatic relations were withdrawn from several Third World countries and Yugoslavia when these countries engaged in official relations with the GDR. In 1967 the policy was quietly shelved when the government of Chancellor Kurt Georg Kiesinger recognized Romania and sent a trade mission to Czechoslovakia. Diplomatic relations were resumed with Yugoslavia in 1968, but it was not until Chancellor Willy Brandt negotiated the Basic Treaty with the GDR that the doctrine was fully abandoned. *See also* BASIC TREATY, p. 159; ODER-NEISSE LINE, p. 216; OSTPOLITIK, p. 217.

Significance   The Hallstein Doctrine was successful until the mid-1960s in that it influenced a large number of Third World countries not to open relations with the GDR. The attempt of the Adenauer and Ludwig Erhard governments to isolate East Germany and deny legitimacy to the status quo in East Europe ultimately failed as subsequent Bonn governments realized the desirability of opening relations with Eastern European states. The original exception to the Hallstein Doctrine, the Soviet Union, was a curious anomaly, because this necessary exception was made to the most powerful supporter of the GDR. The *Ostpolitik* of Willy Brandt was grounded on the assumption that the Federal Republic's attempt to be the sole representative of the German people had failed, and that a new Eastern policy was necessary. In 1973, both Germanies were admitted to the United Nations, and most states entered into full diplomatic relations with both.

Holy Roman Empire   A loose union of Germanic states and territories that formally existed from 962 until 1806. The Holy Roman Empire was the eastern successor state to the empire that was established by Charlemagne in 800, and it was formally established when a German Saxon king was crowned emperor in 962. Only later did the empire come to be called the Holy Roman Empire of the German

Nation; in modern times it is sometimes referred to as the First Reich. The emperors were German kings who were chosen by electors, a small group of secular and ecclesiastical princes, and confirmed by popes; although the position of emperor was elective, in the fifteenth century it came to be dominated by the Austrian Habsburg dynasty. The empire provided some unity until the thirteenth century, but thereafter it consisted of a large number of independent cities, small territories, principalities, and kingdoms, which only nominally acknowledged the authority of the emperor. The empire was often in conflict or at war with the papacy, German kings, and other European powers over church control, territory, and succession rights to the throne. In addition to dynastic wars, the Lutheran Protestant Reformation in the sixteenth century further divided the German people along religious lines, with Protestant princes pitted against Catholic emperors. The extremely destructive Thirty Years War (1618–48), a religious war of Catholics versus Protestants in which foreign powers played an important role, resulted in the deaths of one-fifth to one-third of the German people. The Peace of Westphalia further weakened the empire because, although the form of the empire was retained, the individual states that comprised it were recognized as independent states, and the empire became identified with Austria. In the sixteenth century, Germany had over a hundred principalities, fifty free cities, and well over a thousand lesser territories. The empire was formally dissolved in 1806 when, after Austria was defeated by Napoleon in the battle of Austerlitz in 1805, the Habsburg King of Austria renounced the imperial title. *See also* CONFEDERATION OF THE RHINE, p. 173.

Significance The Holy Roman Empire provided an ideal and symbol of unity for Christendom in a Germanic empire that was effective in its first 200 years, but which was extremely weak afterwards. When other European kings in France, Spain, and England were creating nation-states, the German people remained divided in small, particularistic entities. Throughout most of its history the empire was nothing more than a loose collection of feuding free cities, church states, minor principalities, and kingdoms that effectively retarded the creation of a single German nation. The weak empire contributed to German provincialism, the continuation of a multiplicity of political institutions and loyalties, intra-German conflict, and international intervention. Although Martin Luther's translation of the Bible into German brought a measure of linguistic unity, the Reformation and the religious wars divided the people according to the religion of the dominant local princes. This division is still visible today, with Protestants generally located in the north and the east and Catholics in the south and the west. The Holy Roman Empire bequeathed to modern Germany an ideal of national unity, but also a history of division, particularism, civil war, and weakness in the face of foreign intervention.

Judicial System: West Germany The organization and operation of the court system in the Federal Republic of Germany. The judicial system in West Germany is composed of an integrated network of state and federal courts and a separate Federal Constitutional Court, which exercises the power of judicial review. State courts are organized at the local, district, and appellate levels, and only the highest courts of appeal are federal courts. The regular court system considers civil and criminal cases, but there are specialized state courts that consider questions concerning administrative law, social security, labor, and fiscal matters. Six regular federal appellate courts receive cases from the lower state courts. The Federal Appeals Court (Supreme Court) is the court of last resort for regular cases; other federal appellate courts are the administrative, labor, social, fiscal, and patent courts. Neither lower-level state courts nor federal appellate courts consider matters concerning the interpretation of the constitution. The Federal Supreme Court also does not take constitutional issues; its main task is to ensure the uniformity of law throughout the Federal Republic. When issues are raised regarding the interpretation of the Basic Law, the question is referred to the Federal Constitutional Court, which decides the constitutional issue and remands the case to the appropriate lower court for final disposition. Most of the states also have a state constitutional court that decides whether state government actions are compatible with the state constitution. Judges take an active role in a trial and are assisted by several lay judges drawn from the citizenry or from knowledgeable groups in certain types of cases. *See also* CODE LAW SYSTEM, p. 85; FEDERAL CONSTITUTIONAL COURT, p. 182; *RECHTSSTAAT*, p. 223.

Significance The heritage of the German judicial system is one of heavy-handed legalism and authoritarianism. Since the days of the German Empire, judges applied an extensive body of law in accordance with the concept of the *Rechtsstaat*, a state governed by the rule of law unquestioned by the courts. In the Weimar Republic many judges were antidemocratic and openly hostile to the Republic. In the Nazi period, most judges applied Nazi laws and presided over Nazi prosecutions in an acquiescent manner, with the belief that a judge must not question the law of the state. Attempting to counter this legacy, the framers of the Basic Law sought to found a federal republic on a richer meaning of the concept of the Rechtsstaat, now understood as the rule of law and justice. The regular court system emerged in traditional form, but the framers provided, under the prompting of the Western Allies, that a

Federal Constitutional Court would enforce the democratic protections provided in the constitution. Germans are a very litigious people, and there are more judges per capita than in other industrialized nations. Although the regular court system still suffers from its authoritarian past, the citizen has easy access to courts, which generally provide simple, speedy, and inexpensive justice. Additionally, Germans now enjoy an additional protection against arbitrary and unconstitutional government in the Federal Constitutional Court.

***Land* Government**   The governmental system of the ten constituent states of the Federal Republic of Germany. *Land* (pl. *Länder* or *Laender*) or state government is generally based on some form of the parliamentary system. The Basic Law of the Federal Republic of Germany provides that the "constitutional order in the Länder must conform to the principles of republican, democratic and social government based on the rule of law, within the meaning of this Basic Law." Beyond this requirement, each Land can specify any framework of government it chooses. Each Land has a constitution, a parliament (*Landtag*) elected by the people every four years (five years in the Saarland). The Landtag elects the chief executive officer, who is called the minister-president (*Ministerpräsident*, pl. *Ministerpräsidenten*) who heads a cabinet. The state political party system is similar to the national system, and most governments are coalitions of two parties. All states have a unicameral parliament, except Bavaria. This state has an advisory second chamber called the Senate that is based on the corporative principle or interest group representation. In the city states of Hamburg and Bremen, the terminology is different: the head of government is called the mayor (*Bürgermeister*), and the government is called the Senate. Although the exclusive authority of state governments to enact legislation is limited to the areas of education, cultural and religious affairs, police, and local government, the states administer about 50 percent of all federal laws. State bureaucracies therefore are large, accounting for 90 percent of all civil servants in West Germany. Land governments choose and instruct the state's delegation to the Bundesrat, the upper house in the federal parliament, and state legislators are elected to serve in the Federal Assembly, which elects the federal president. State courts are integrated with the appellate federal courts in a unified judicial system; each state also has a constitutional court that interprets the state constitution. The city of West Berlin has a governmental framework similar to those of the other city states, but not being a state, its authority is different. *See also* FEDERALISM: WEST GERMANY, p. 183; *LAND* POLITICAL PARTY SYSTEM, p. 203; LOCAL GOVERNMENT: WEST GERMANY, p. 204; WEST BERLIN, p. 238.

Significance   The state constitutions that created Land governments were written and put into effect before the Basic Law was adopted in 1949. Most postwar German states are creations of the Western occupying powers, who established units based on political, administrative, or military considerations. Only Hamburg, Bremen, and Bavaria emerged in 1949 with prewar boundaries that show historical continuity. In 1952 three states were joined into one new southwest state, Baden-Württemberg; the Saar, integrated into the French economy in the postwar period, did not become a Land in the Federal Republic until 1957. The parliamentary structures of the Länder are based on German tradition, but the authority that was granted to the states in the Basic Law enlarged the sphere of state power from that in the Weimar Republic. The effectiveness of Land governments depends in large measure on resources available to individual states. Some states are small and lack sufficient resources to be economically viable. In the West German system of federalism, poorer states are assisted by "equalization payments" made by the national government under a constitutional requirement to maintain "unity of living standards" among the states. All states benefit from an extensive revenue sharing program that is essential to their well-being.

Land Political Party System   The simple multiparty system that exists within the constituent states of the Federal Republic of Germany. The *Land* political party system is similar to the national party system. Two large parties dominate state politics, the Christian Democratic party (CDU), and the Social Democratic party (SPD); the smaller third party, the Free Democratic party (FDP), is able to win seats in most state parliaments. In the state of Bavaria, the Christian Democrats are organized in the Christian Social Union (CSU). At times a fourth party has been able to win seats or to replace the Free Democrats. In the mid-1960s the fourth party was the National Democratic party; in the 1980s the fourth group is the Greens, a left-wing environmentalist and pacifist party. Other parties run but seldom win any seats. The electoral system used in the states is similar to the personalized system of proportional representation used in national elections, but there are a few states that use a single-member district system. In states using proportional representation, parties that receive less than 5 percent (10 percent in Bavaria) of the popular vote win no seats. In some states, a single party is able to win a majority and can form a government without a coalition partner. This is usually the case in Bavaria with the Christian Social Union, the Christian Democrats in Rhineland-Palatinate, and the Social Democrats in Hamburg. In 1983 there were six Christian Democratic governments, two Social Democratic governments, two SPD-FDP coalitions, and one CDU-FDP coalition. In 1981 a Christian Democratic government was formed in West Berlin for the first time in that city in the postwar period. *See also* ELECTORAL SYSTEM: BUNDESTAG, p. 177; LAND GOVERNMENT, p. 202; POLITICAL PARTY SYSTEM: WEST GERMANY, p. 220.

Significance Since the 1960s Land politics have paralleled national politics: regional parties have disappeared (except the CSU in Bavaria), and the only parties able to win seats in state elections are those that can generate a national following. New national political movements, such as the National Democratic party in the 1960s and the Greens in the 1980s, begin to make their mark and win seats first in state parliaments. This nationalization of state politics has had several effects. State elections, which occur at various times between Bundestag elections, have become barometers of national trends. National political leaders campaign in these elections to defend or criticize the leadership and policies of the federal government. State elections have become tests of the public's support for the federal chancellor, and have been part of the opposition's campaign against a weak or faltering government. On several occasions, particularly in the early 1970s, state elections have contributed to maneuvers or changes in national leadership or policy. Party coalitions in state governments do not coincide with national coalitions, but a shift in alignments following a state election sometimes signals a forthcoming change at the national level.

Local Government: West Germany The system of substate government in the Federal Republic of Germany. The Basic Law guarantees self-government to the local authorities, but the forms of local government are established by state (*Land*) law. There is consequently a variety of types between states, but uniformity within a state. The two basic units of local government are (1) the local community (*Gemeinde*, pl. *Gemeinden*), which are incorporated municipalities that vary in size from small villages to large cities; and (2) the county or district (*Kreis*, pl. *Kreise*). Each municipality and county has an elective council and other structures, but their terminology varies with size, complexity, and state traditions. Typical forms of municipalities include the mayor-council government with a strong mayor, the dominant council type, and a type in which the city council chooses a commission that delegates administrative matters to a manager (*Stadtdirektor*). The mayor (*Bürgermeister*) is directly elected in some cities and chosen by the council in others. The county council (*Kreistag*) is elective; urban or city counties are known as *Stadtkreis*, and rural counties are called *Landkreis*. The chief executive officer of a Kreis is the *Landrat*, who is usually chosen by the council, but who is elected in some places. The functions of local government are extensive and fall into three broad types: (1) compulsory responsibilities, or services required by law, such as school buildings, fire protection, and public utilities; (2) delegated responsibilities, such as health care, housing, and tax collection, which are transferred, supervised, and financed by the federal or state government; and (3) voluntary services, such as parks, recreation, and cultural activities. Local government services are financed by local taxes and fees, federal and state grants, federal revenue sharing, and industrial taxes. Unlike state politics, the politics of local government is less affected by national politics. Social Democrats control most of the larger cities, but in many places local personalities, local machines, or nonpartisan citizen groups dominate the elections. See also FEDERALISM: WEST GERMANY, p. 183; LAND GOVERNMENT, p. 202.

Significance Germany had a strong tradition of local self-government that was reestablished in the Federal Republic. In the Nazi period, most authority was centralized. In the postwar period, however, the costs and pressures to keep up the large measure of local services grew too great for many small authorities. Consequently, consolidation of local government has proceeded very rapidly in the last two decades, particularly in rural areas. In 1968 there were about 24,000 local authorities; there were 11,000 in 1975 and about 8,000 in 1983. At least 10,000 villages of less than 1,000 inhabitants have been amalgamated into larger units. Despite this rapid consolidation, German cities suffer from the same urban problems that occur in other industrialized nations. These include rapid population growth, inadequate housing, poor transportation, insufficient resources, and political conflicts concerning regional and urban redevelopment schemes.

Munich Agreement The settlement reached at the Munich Conference of 1938, in which Czechoslovakia was forced to cede its German-speaking territories, the Sudetenland, to Germany. The Munich Agreement was made by the heads of government of Germany (Adolf Hitler), Great Britain (Neville Chamberlain), France (Edouard Daladier), and Italy (Benito Mussolini); neither Czechoslovakia nor its ally the Soviet Union was present. The conference was called at the initiative of Mussolini in order to avert a war that was being threatened over the Czech crisis. The Sudenten Germans, encouraged by a local Nazi party and supported by Germany, had been causing disorders and making demands on the Czech government. In March 1938 Czech President Edward Beneš ordered a partial mobilization when German intervention appeared imminent. Chamberlain's conciliatory intercession failed to resolve the crisis, and when agitations and fighting within Czechoslovakia broke out in the summer, Hitler demanded that Sudetenland be integrated with Germany. Britain, following a policy of appeasement, and France, unwilling to go to war to defend its ally, Czechoslovakia, agreed to Hitler's demands in Munich on September

29, 1938. The terms of the agreement were (1) Sudenten territories be ceded to Germany; (2) plebiscites be taken in other districts; (3) Poland and Hungary be granted their ethnic districts in Czechoslovakia; and (4) the four powers would guarantee the boundaries of the new Czechoslovakia. In addition, Hitler signed a conciliatory statement prepared by Chamberlain, which Chamberlain believed would secure "peace in our time." Although not present at the conference, Czechoslovakia was forced to accept the terms of the pact; German troops occupied the Sudetenland on October 1, 1938. *See also* VERSAILLES TREATY, p. 232.

Significance The Munich Agreement resulted in the immediate transfer of three million German-speaking persons to Germany, which was about one-third of the population of prewar Czechoslovakia. The frontier Czechoslovakia had fortified against Germany was lost, and the new rump state lay defenseless. In March 1939 Hitler eliminated the Czechoslovak state by establishing a German Protectorate of Bohemia and Moravia; Slovakia was declared to be independent. The Munich Agreement is often cited as a prime example of the policy of appeasement, which in the end fails to bring peace but leads to greater disasters. After Munich, Hitler forced Lithuania to cede Memel, and he made territorial demands on Danzig and Poland. Britain did not discern Hitler's designs until Bohemia and Moravia were occupied; it later made an alliance with Poland. The Russians, seeing the concessions the West made to Hitler and fearing a Western alliance with Germany, agreed to urgent German requests for a mutual nonaggression treaty. In the nonpublished portions of the Nazi-Soviet Pact of August 1939, the Germans and Russians divided Poland and East Europe into two spheres of influence. Britain and France finally declared war on Germany when Hitler invaded Poland on September 1, 1939. After World War II, Czechoslovakia expelled the three million German-speaking people from the Sudetenland and resettled the area with Czechs.

National Democratic Party (NPD) A small right-wing party that won seats in state legislatures in the late 1960s but quickly declined after 1969. The National Democratic party (NPD) was founded in 1964 by nationalists and former members of the Nazi party to rally the many small right-wing groups for the 1965 elections. The party won only 2 percent of the popular vote in 1965, but in subsequent state elections it earned from 5.8 to 9.8 percent of the vote. By 1968 the NPD had elected deputies in seven of the ten states; in Bavaria, the NPD replaced the Free Democrats as the third party. Because it had state representation, the NPD was entitled to send delegates to the Federal Assembly that elected the federal president in 1969. Although the leadership of the party under Adolf von Thadden was overwhelmingly drawn from former members of the Nazi party, the NPD denied that it was a neo-Nazi, undemocratic, or anti-Semitic organization. The platform of the party included provisions calling for: all foreign troops to leave Germany; curtailing American influence in Europe; refashioning NATO into a strictly European defense organization; building a German nuclear force; ending the prosecution of German war criminals; and stopping reparation payments to Israel. In 1968 the Grant Coalition government of Chancellor Kurt Georg Kiesinger decided not to petition the Constitutional Court to outlaw the NPD as an unconstitutional party. The government declared that the NPD was not acting in an unconstitutional manner and that such a move might prove to be counterproductive. In the subsequent national elections of 1969, the NPD won only 4.3 percent of the total vote and consequently was denied any seats in the Bundestag for failing to win more than the minimal requirement of 5 percent. The party's popular support within the states then declined rapidly, and by the early 1970s the NPD had lost all state representation. In the national elections of 1980 and 1983, the NPD received only 0.2 percent of the popular vote. *See also* POLITICAL PARTY SYSTEM: WEST GERMANY, p. 220; UNCONSTITUTIONAL PARTIES, p. 231.

Significance The National Democratic party is the successor to similar right-wing groups that flourished in the 1950s, such as the German Reich party and the Socialist Reich party, which was declared unconstitutional in 1952. The NPD received a great deal of media attention and comment when it was consistently winning seats in state legislatures in the late 1960s. Some observers, including the philosopher Karl Jaspers, concluded that the rise of the NPD was proof that authoritarianism was an irremediable element in the German national character. After the party's decline, more astute observers saw the rise of the NPD as a conservative reaction to the Grand Coalition of Christian Democrats and Social Democrats, for the NPD declined rapidly when the coalition broke up after the 1969 elections.

Nazism: Doctrine The body of ideas advocated by Adolf Hitler that formed the ideological basis for the Nazi movement. The doctrine of National Socialism or Nazism was popularized in large measure by Hitler in his book, *Mein Kampf* (*My Struggle*, 1928), and in his many speeches. The central theme in this doctrine is the concept of race. Based in large measure on the racial theories of Arthur de Gobineau and Houston Stewart Chamberlain, Hitler posited a hierarchy of races in which the Aryan (Germanic or Nordic) race was superior to other races and the creator of civilizations. Latin and Slavic races were inferior and could only maintain civilizations, provided they were not racially mixed with even more inferior races, such as blacks and Jews. History is a struggle between races, and Germany, the home of pure Aryans, must resist the corrupting influence of the Jews. Hitler argued that the *Volk* (the German nation or people) must create a Folkish State, in which all Germans would be united. The state would protect racial purity, promote national culture and power, and develop a master race of supermen. The doctrine of National Socialism originally advocated a mixed economy of partial state socialism of large-scale industry, business, and landholdings, and private enterprise of small firms. This collectivist idea was abandoned after 1928 in favor of rigid state controls over the economy. National Socialism considered both communism and bourgeois democracy as ideological enemies. Government in the ideal Nazi state was not based on democracy, but rather on the leadership principle (*Führerprinzip*). A single national leader, the *Führer*, would make decisions that would express the best interests of the Volk. The Führer would preside over a government that would exercise total control over all state, political, social, economic, and cultural institutions. The Folkish State would need to expand, seeking *Lebensraum* (living space) to relieve overcrowding, conquer inferior peoples, and spread its culture. The Volk could only achieve its destiny of carrying civilization to other parts of the world by an act of will, using force, power, and war. The great empire they would establish, the Third Reich, would last a thousand years. *See also* NAZISM: INSTITUTIONS, p. 209; NAZISM: INTERPRETATIONS, p. 210; NAZISM: MOVEMENT, p. 211.

Significance Nazi doctrine was largely derivative from earlier themes developed by German thinkers, nationalists, and racial theorists. It reflected the irrationalist ideas of philosophers who placed emphasis on the will rather than on the intellect, and it followed a long history of German nationalist thinking. The racist ideas and anti-Semitism, which were commonplace in central Europe, however, were pushed to the extreme by Hitler both in theory and in practice. Nazi doctrine primarily emphasized two interrelated concepts, racialism and folkish nationalism; consequently, it was much less developed than the ideology of Italian Fascism. Except for the core members of the Nazi movement, the doctrine won few adherents, although it did express traditional themes many Germans could support. In practice, the main ideas provided little guidance for economic policy making, but the leadership principle, the aggressive nationalism, and racism were the ideological foundations Hitler used to justify the totalitarian state, the annexation of Germanic territory, the war against Poland and Russia, and the destruction of the Jews.

Nazism: Institutions   The instrumentalities Adolf Hitler used to take power in Germany and establish a totalitarian state. At the apex of the Nazi institutional system stood Adolf Hitler, the *"Führer* (leader) of the German Reich," a position that combined head of state, head of government, and commander-in-chief. All party, government, judicial, and military officers were required to give an oath of loyalty to Hitler. A core Nazi institution was the National Socialist German Workers' party (NSDAP), or Nazi party, which had a central political organization, various party formations, and affiliated organizations. The main territorial unit of the central party organization was the *Gau* (district), which was headed by Gauleiters who controlled district and local units. Two important party formations were the SA (*Sturmabteilung*) and the SS (*Schutzstaffel*). The SA Storm Troopers, or Brown Shirts, were at first a uniformed paramilitary force of street fighters, which later grew to a large army in 1932 under Ernst Röhm, who was purged in 1934. The SS, the Protective Formation or Security Squad, or Black Shirts, were an elite party police force that developed out of the SA and were commanded by Heinrich Himmler. After the war broke out in 1939, the SS organized a large number of military units, called the *Waffen-SS* (Armed-SS). The Gestapo, or Secret State Police (*Geheime Staatspolizei*), the main instrument of Nazi terror, was charged with eliminating political opponents and Jews and administering concentration and extermination camps. Special Task Formations (*Einsatzgruppen*) were mobile units that liquidated Jews in occupied countries; they killed about two million of the six million Jews who were exterminated. The SD (*Sicherheitsdienst*), or Security Service, the intelligence and security branch of the SS, was responsible for the security of Hitler and top party and government leaders. The Propaganda Ministry in the Nazi government was headed by Joseph Goebbels, who controlled all media of communication and culture. The activities of the millions of people in the affiliated economic, professional, cultural, and social organizations were supervised by the Nazi party. About 60 percent of all German youth were organized in the Hitler Youth (for boys) and the League of German Girls. *See also* NAZISM: DOCTRINE, p. 207; NAZISM: MOVEMENT, p. 211; NUREMBERG WAR CRIMES TRIALS, p. 213.

Significance   The central institutions of Nazism came to dominate the regular administrative, military, and judicial organs of the German government. Through a combination of brute force, propaganda, and mass appeals based on emotionalism and prejudice, Nazis took control of the German state and established a monopoly over weapons, communication, culture, and law making. They created a totalitarian state that did not fall until it was defeated by external military forces in World War

II. Learning from the Nazi period, the framers of the constitutional system of the Bonn Republic created institutions that placed limitations on antidemocratic movements, protected individual rights, and checked the power of the central government. These included such provisions as the bill of rights, the constitutional court, the banning of undemocratic parties, exclusive rights granted to the states in cultural and educational affairs, and provisions guaranteeing responsible parliamentary government.

Nazism: Interpretations   Theories that attempt to explain the nature and causes of the Nazi movement of Adolf Hitler in Germany. The major theoretical interpretations of Nazism consider it to be a species of the more generic form of right-wing authoritarianism called fascism. A wide range of interpretations has been suggested, ranging from theories that stress very general factors dealing with human nature to those that concentrate on the historical peculiarities of Germany or the psychopersonality of Adolf Hitler. Some of the more general theories are those that state that fascism, particularly its Nazi variant, is the embodiment of evil, or the manifestation of the moral decline of the West. Other theories find the root causes in the revolt of the "amorphous masses," in which undifferentiated groups of urban mass society provide the base for irrationalist and antiintellectual fascist movements. Some theorists see fascism as the radicalism of the middle classes or of the political center, primarily the professionals, civil servants, and small property-holders, who are denied status and access to power by traditional elites. Marxists see fascism as the consequence of the class struggle in history and its leaders as the agents of bourgeois capitalism. Some theorists link fascism to the reaction against demands for modernization. One group of theorists believes fascism to be an expression of antimodernity, of social groups opposed to the economic, intellectual, and social consequences of modern industrialization. Others believe that fascism is the product of political movements that attempt to overcome delayed industrialization through a system of forced development through mass mobilization and class collaboration. *See also* NAZISM: MOVEMENT, p. 211.

Significance   Theoretical interpretations of Nazism and fascism first advanced in the prewar period were more inclined to stress more general and normative factors than those developed recently, which tend to stress more narrow economic and social factors. Some observers offer explanations that can be applied to quite different political phenomena, including fascism, communism, and revolutions in less-developed countries. The general theory of totalitarianism asserts that fascist and communist political systems are subspecies of the twentieth-century form of extreme authoritarianism called totalitarianism. The systems established by Hitler and Josef Stalin are the best examples of modern totalitarianism. Although postwar theories are intellectually stimulating, they do not provide satisfactory explanations for the successes and failures of fascist movements in different countries. Recent research shows profound differences in fascist movements, and some observers deny that a generic definition of fascism can be developed. Worse still, the words *fascism* and *Nazism* have become terms of opprobrium in political discourse, which makes the theoretical task more difficult.

Nazism: Movement The extreme right-wing political movement of Adolf Hitler that ruled Germany from 1933 to 1945. A main organizational arm of the Nazi movement was the National Socialist German Workers' party (NSDAP), a small party that Hitler took control of in the early 1920s. Using his exceptional oratory skills, propaganda, and control over party newspapers, he developed the party into an effective political instrument. The term *Nazi* is the acronym for the German words for National Socialism; the party's emblem, the swastika (*Hakenkreuz*, hookcross), was an ancient East German symbol of folkish nationalism. On November 8, 1923, Hitler failed in an attempt to take over the government of Bavaria in the Munich *Putsch*. During the ten months he spent in prison for this affair, he wrote *Mein Kampf* (*My Struggle*, 1928), a political tract in which he laid out his anti-Semitism, his criticisms of the Versailles Treaty, and his program for a new Germany. The Nazi party grew tremendously after the economic depression of the early 1930s by drawing support from veterans, disaffected nationalists, middle-class supporters, anti-Semites, and workers; Hitler also won the backing of industrialists and conservatives who hoped to use him in their struggle against the Weimar Republic. Receiving no more than 3 percent of the vote in the 1920s, the party became the largest group in the Reichstag in 1932; Hitler was appointed chancellor by President Paul von Hindenburg in January 1933. Hitler used the burning of the Reichstag building in February 1933 to pass the Enabling Act, which gave him dictatorial powers; he then banned all parties (except the Nazis who were called a "movement"), and instituted a one-party state. Threatened by the rising power of Ernst Röhm, who commanded the SA Brown Shirts, originally groups of street fighters who had grown to a large army, Hitler moved against him and other Nazis in a blood-purge in June 1934. This action eliminated the left-wing of the Nazi movement and won the sympathy of the German military, who feared and resented the power of the SA. The Nazi system of terror and propaganda was used to crush opponents, liquidate racial and ethnic groups, and impose obedience on the bureaucratic, judicial, and military branches of government. Millions of Germans joined voluntarily or were forced into the affiliated professional, occupation, industrial, cultural, and social organizations. Their activities were "coordinated" (that is, supervised and controlled) by the Nazis. Hitler's foreign policy successes—in rearming Germany, winning a plebiscite in the Saar, remilitarizing the Rhineland, ending Germany's isolation, annexing Austria and the Sudetenland—brought increased popular and military support. In the last free election, one week after the Reichstag fire in 1933, the Nazi party won 44 percent of the vote. Over a million persons joined the party, and 13 million were affiliated in economic, professional, youth, leisure, and occupational organizations. *See also* NAZISM: DOCTRINE, p. 207; NAZISM: INSTITUTIONS, p. 209; NAZISM: INTERPRETATIONS, p. 210; WEIMAR REPUBLIC, p. 234.

Significance The Nazi movement was originally one of many small radical parties that emerged in Weimar Germany. It grew to become the largest party in 1932 primarily due to the political skills, determination, charismatic qualities, and good fortune of Adolf Hitler, who used and benefited from the political, economic, and social environment of postwar Germany, particularly after the Great Depression. Although some analysts consider Nazism to be a middle-class movement, it drew support from all social classes. At its height in the early years of World War II, Nazism commanded the allegiance of most Germans when it drew on wartime patriotic sentiment fanned by the emotional appeals of official state propaganda. The movement was a complex phenomenon whose interpretation and understanding is still subject to dispute. Its importance lies in its remarkable rise to political power, its capture of the social, cultural, economic, and military institutions of the nation, and its winning the allegiance of millions of German citizens. Although it did not fall until it was defeated by the Allies of World War II, its demise has been equally remarkable, given its wide prewar backing. Neo-Nazism in Germany exists only in very small groups that have no popular support.

North German Confederation The union of Prussia and northern German states from 1867 to 1871. The North German Confederation was established by Prussia following its victory over Austria in the Austro-Prussian War (Seven Weeks War) of 1866. It consisted of Prussia and its 21 northern allies that fought in the war against Austria. Although the union was named a confederation, it was constitutionally a new state, a federation with Prussia in control. The parliament consisted of the Federal Council (Bundesrat), comprising instructed delegates from state government, and the Diet (Reichstag), which was elected by universal manhood suffrage. The executive power was located in the president of the Confederation, the king of Prussia (William I), who in turn appointed the federal chancellor (Otto von Bismarck). Southern German states, such as Bavaria, Baden, Württemberg, and Hesse, were not part of the Confederation, but remained members of the customs unions (*Zollverein*) that had been established by Prussia 30 years earlier. The Confederation ceased to exist when the German Empire (Reich), now including the southern states, was proclaimed in 1871 following the victory of Prussia in the Franco-Prussian War of 1870. *See also* GERMAN CONFEDERATION, p. 189; GERMAN EMPIRE, p. 192.

Significance   The North German Confederation was controlled by the Prussian government, which was the largest and most powerful member of the union. In effect, the Confederation was an interim solution to Prussia's goal of German unity, for it did not include the southern states. The constitutional system of the Confederation with modifications was used as the basis for the governmental structure of the new German Empire.

Nuremberg War Crimes Trials   Trials of the principal surviving Nazi leaders and Nazi organizations that were held in 1945–46. The Nuremberg war crimes trials were conducted by a special International Military Tribunal comprised of American, British, French, and Soviet judges. Defendants were accused of "crimes against peace" (such as planning and waging aggressive war), "war crimes" (such as maltreatment and murder of prisoners of war), and "crimes against humanity" (such as enslavement and extermination of civilian populations). Of the organizations brought to trial, the Leadership Corps of the Nazi party, the Gestapo, the SS, and the SD were convicted, which meant that individuals could be prosecuted for membership in a criminal organization. The general staff of the armed forces, the Reich cabinet, and the SA were acquitted. Of the principal surviving leaders, 12 were sentenced to death, 7 to prison terms, and 3 were acquitted. Adolf Hitler, Heinrich Himmler, and Joseph Goebbels had committed suicide earlier. Following the Nuremberg trials, many individuals were tried by military and civilian courts of the wartime Allies in their respective zones of occupation. After 1949 West Germany and East Germany also tried and convicted a large number of war criminals. *See also* NAZISM: INSTITUTIONS, p. 209; NAZISM: MOVEMENT, p. 211.

Significance   The Nuremberg war crimes trials established a legal precedent in that individuals as opposed to nations could be punished for "crimes against peace," such as launching aggressive war. Critics charged that the trials violated the principle forbidding ex post facto punishments in that the Kellogg-Briand Pact of 1928, which banned war as an instrument of national policy, did not imply personal criminal responsibility for national actions. It was also charged that the Allies practiced "victor's justice" because they did not punish their own war criminals. The evidence adduced against the defendants, however, was overwhelming and established new legal precedents. The trials that followed in national courts were concerned with the acceptable practice of punishing persons for violating specific national and international laws of warfare. Although principal Nazi leaders and lesser war criminals argued the "doctrine of superior orders," i.e., that they were compelled to commit these acts, this defense generally was not acceptable to the courts. The novel charge of "crimes against humanity" was generally welcomed as an appropriate reaction to the holocaust—Hitler's plan to exterminate European Jews and other groups such as Gypsies. This charge helped lay the foundation for a 1951 United Nations convention that banned the crime of "genocide," the killing of a population because of its racial, religious, national, or ethnic origins.

Occupation Period   The period from 1945 to 1949, when Germany was ruled by the military governments of the wartime Allies, i.e., the United States, Great Britain, France, and the Soviet Union. During the occupation period, Germany was divided, according to decisions made in the Yalta and Potsdam conferences, into four zones of military occupation. Each zone was put under a separate military administration, but the whole of Germany was to be treated as a single economic unit that would be supervised by a joint Allied Control Council. Greater Berlin was likewise divided into four sectors with a separate joint administration called the Berlin *Kommandatura*. The territory east of the Oder-Neisse rivers came under Polish administration, but was soon absorbed as part of Polish territory. Cooperation among the Allies broke down quickly after the war; the Allied Control Council was never effective, as France and the Soviet Union pressed hard to achieve national objectives within their zones. France, not being a party at the Yalta and Potsdam agreements, was uncooperative, and it absorbed the Saarland into the French economy. The Soviet Union refused to ship food to the West as required under the agreements, while taking heavy reparations from East Germany; it also refused to treat all of Germany as one economic unit. Municipal and state governments were elected in the three Western zones in 1946 and 1947. In January 1947 the Americans and British joined their two zones into one economic unit, called the Bizone, and an advisory German Economic Council was established for the Bizone. The United States also announced plans to treat Germany as one unit and to aid all of Europe in a massive program of economic reconstruction assistance called the Marshall Plan. Two four-power conferences were held in Moscow and London in 1947, but they failed to resolve the differences between the occupying powers. Relations between the East and the West deteriorated rapidly in 1948 as the Cold War became very tense. France joined its zone (without the Saarland) to the Bizone in January 1948, and the German states were asked to draft a plan for a constitution for Germany. The Soviet Union boycotted the Allied Control Council and the Berlin Kommandatura, and in June 1948 the Western states introduced a major currency reform in their zones. The Russians in turn blockaded ground access to West Berlin. The draft constitution for West Germany, called the Basic Law, was completed and approved by the Western powers and the West German states, and it was promulgated in May 1949. Thus was born the Federal Republic of Germany. The Soviets responded by creating the German Democratic Republic in their zone. *See also* BERLIN BLOCKADE, p. 160; ODER-NEISSE LINE, p. 216; POTSDAM CONFERENCE p. 221; YALTA CONFERENCE, p. 241.

Significance It was during the occupation period that specific policies were adopted that brought about the establishment of the two German states and their integration into the rival camps of the Cold War. West Berlin survived the Berlin Blockade by means of an American airlift, was granted a city government of its own, and increasingly became integrated into the West German system. The initial policies the Western Allies had adopted for the treatment of Germany in the occupation period were only partially successful. These policies called for the demilitarization of Germany, the denazification of the government and society, the reeducation of Germans to the democratic way of life, the punishment of war criminals, and the decentralization of the government and industry. As the occupation proceeded, however, the economic problems of administering a shattered country and the political problems of reconciling the different objectives of the Allies became more important. Germany was beset with the influx of millions of refugees from Eastern Europe, food shortages, lack of housing, black markets, and the like. Although many major war criminals were punished, others escaped punishment. The denazification program broke down because of unclear objectives, changing criteria, and poor administration. Germany was disarmed, but less than ten years later it was rearmed and brought into NATO. A centralized national government was established, and German industry was reconstructed and came to be dominated by large firms. Given the power realities and the conflicting objectives of the four Allies, there probably was little that could have been done to prevent the partitioning of Germany in the occupation period. In the long run, both Germanies have prospered, with West Germany's success due in part to the policies adopted by the Western Allies in the occupation period.

Oder-Neisse Line The boundary line between East Germany and Poland, which is formed by the Oder and Neisse rivers. The Oder-Neisse line was tentatively established in wartime agreements made at Yalta and Potsdam. Under these agreements the Soviet Union acquired East Prussia and portions of prewar Poland, and other western boundaries of Poland were extended to the Oder and Neisse rivers. Poland was provisionally to administer the former German territory pending the signing of a peace treaty with Germany, but the arrangement became permanent when Poland expelled about eight million ethnic Germans. Although the line was recognized in the 1950s as permanent in various agreements between Poland and East Germany, and by the Soviet Union, the West German government refused to acknowledge its legitimacy. Under the reunification policy of the Konrad Adenauer and Ludwig Erhard governments, Bonn asserted that the "Eastern Territories" that were annexed by Poland and the Soviet Union would ultimately be joined to a united Germany. In the 1970s, the West German government of Willy Brandt accepted the Oder-Neisse frontier as the permanent boundary between East Germany and Poland in the various agreements that comprised his *Ostpolitik,* or eastern policy. The line was also acknowledged as legitimate in the Helsinki Accord of 1975. *See also* HELSINKI ACCORD, p. 263; OSTPOLITIK, p. 217; POTSDAM CONFERENCE, p. 221.

Significance The Oder-Neisse line served as the de facto border between East Germany and Poland until the 1970s, when West Germany and the Western wartime Allies accepted its legitimacy. The postwar history of the issue shows how a controversial provisional wartime agreement became the basis for a legitimated resolution of the problem. The original reunification policy of West Germany received public support from the Western powers, but there was little expectation that Germany could be reunited short of a major upheaval in central Europe or that a reunited Germany would regain its prewar territories in the east. West Germany's policy of refusing to accept the line ultimately failed, and it raised fears and bred solidarity among its eastern neighbors. An essential prerequisite for the acceptability to the East of Brandt's Ostpolitik was West Germany's recognition of the East German–Polish frontier. The wide acceptance of the Oder-Neisse line among the signatories of the Helsinki Accord legitimated the status quo created by World War II in Europe. Also, the admission as members of the United Nations of the two sovereign states of East and West Germany in 1973 gave a de facto global recognition to the division of Germany and the legitimacy of the Oder-Neisse boundary.

Ostpolitik West German foreign policy toward the communist countries of Eastern Europe based on initiatives undertaken in the early 1970s by Chancellor Willy Brandt. The *Ostpolitik* of Brandt was primarily a series of treaties and agreements that opened diplomatic relations with East European nations, accepted the international status of the German Democratic Republic (GDR), and recognized the annexations of prewar German territory by Poland and the Soviet Union after World War II. The major treaties and agreements that comprise Ostpolitik include the following. In the Moscow Treaty signed in August 1970, the Federal Republic of Germany (FRG) and the USSR renounced the use of force in their mutual relations and recognized the Oder-Neisse boundary line between East Germany and Poland, and the FRG-GDR boundary. In the Warsaw Treaty of December 1971 Bonn recognized the Oder-Neisse line, Poland agreed to repatriate ethnic Germans to the FRG, and both renounced all territorial claims against the other. In the Basic Treaty between the FRG and the GDR, signed in December 1972, the two German states agreed to recognize each other's independence and borders, and normalize diplomatic relations. The Basic Treaty was concluded after the 1971 Quadripartite Agreement on Berlin, which was signed by the United States, Great Britain, France, and the Soviet Union. In this agreement, the four powers renounced the use of force to settle their disputes and reaffirmed their responsibility for Berlin. The Soviet Union guaranteed civilian transit traffic through the GDR to West Berlin, and the Western powers declared that West Berlin had special ties to the FRG, and that it would "continue not to be a constituent part of the Federal Republic of Germany and not to be governed by it." In April 1972 the two Germanies negotiated transit and visitation agreements pertaining to Berlin within the framework of the four-power agreement. In 1973 Bonn signed a treaty with Czechoslovakia in which the parties declared the Munich Agreement of 1938 to be void, renounced any territorial claims, and reestablished diplomatic relations. As part of Ostpolitik both Germanies were admitted to the United Nations in 1973. A capstone was placed on Ostpolitik by the 1975 Helsinki Accord, signed by 35 nations at the Conference on Security and Cooperation in Europe, which recognized the status quo in Europe. *See also* BASIC TREATY, p. 159; HALLSTEIN DOCTRINE, p. 199; HELSINKI ACCORD, p. 263; ODER-NEISSE LINE, p. 216.

Significance Willy Brandt's Ostpolitik represented a fundamental change in West Germany's foreign policy toward the East. Although some initiatives had been undertaken in the prior government of Kurt Georg Kiesinger, such as the recognition of Romania, it was Brandt, aided by Federal State Secretary Egon Bahr and Foreign Minister Walter Scheel, who negotiated and secured the ratification of the treaties. For his efforts Brandt won the Nobel Peace Prize in 1971. Although there was some concern that Brandt was "racing to the East," Ostpolitik had strong support among the Western powers. The policy was also strongly supported in German public opinion, even though Christian Democratic leader Rainer Barzel came within two votes of overturning Brandt's government in 1972 over the Moscow and Warsaw treaties. In the subsequent 1972 election Brandt's Social Democratic party won 46 percent of the vote, the most it has ever received in the history of the Federal Republic. In an atmosphere of detente, quite unlike the earlier Cold War period, Ostpolitik led to a series of subsequent agreements with East European countries, the emigration of German nationals in Poland to West Germany, a substantial increase in trade, and millions of West Germans visiting relatives in East Germany. By the late 1970s, however, the great expectations raised by Ostpolitik vanished as East Germany hardened its currency exchange requirements for FRG visitors, the Soviet Union threatened to intervene in Poland, and the issue of intermediate nuclear missiles reemphasized the basic split between East and West.

Political Culture Transformation Thesis   The theory that the political culture of Germany has changed from a prewar authoritarian orientation to a democratic one. The political culture transformation thesis argues that public support for the principles and institutions of the Empire or Nazi periods has declined dramatically in the Federal Republic, and that support for the postwar political system is very high. Empirical evidence shows near-unanimous support for the Federal Republic among the public at large, political elites, and special interests. Public opinion polls indicate large-scale support for democratic values, high levels of political awareness and participation, the acceptance of civic responsibility, and widespread feelings of political efficacy. Civic attitudes in West Germany compare favorably with those of people in the older, established Western democracies. According to the thesis, the sources for the remarkable change in German political culture have been traced to (1) the association of West Germany with the democratic nations of West Europe and North America; (2) the dramatic "economic miracle," which brought about a rapid economic transformation and raised the standard of living of all German classes; (3) the entry into the political system of younger generations who have been socialized to the democratic way of life; and (4) the acceptance and promotion of unifying and moderate policies by political elites in the dominant political parties. *See also* BONN IS NOT WEIMAR, p. 162; POLITICAL CULTURE: WEST GERMANY, p. 219.

Significance The political culture transformation thesis attempts to document and explain the changes that have taken place in the typical attitudes, values, and beliefs of the people of West Germany. The empirical evidence adduced by the proponents of the thesis supplies ample proof that a remarkable transformation has occurred. There exists a national consensus on the values of democracy and on the governmental institutions and processes of the Federal Republic. The Bonn system is stable, and has, through peaceful constitutional processes, successfully handled the postwar strains of economic reconstruction, large-scale immigration, economic recessions, alternation of political parties in office, and national security crises. Simpler explanations provided by some forms of the transformation thesis typically trace changes in political behavior to underlying socioeconomic causes. More complex analyses show the interrelated causes and effects of changes in the economic system, the social structure, and political institutions and processes. It is this combination of factors that has helped transform Germany into a strong democratic nation.

Political Culture: West Germany The system of political attitudes, values, and beliefs of the people of West Germany. Traditional German political culture emphasized authoritarian, statist, and nondemocratic values. There was high respect for law, rules, and authority figures; personal discipline, hard work, and orderliness were practiced and valued. An ideal of national unity, achieved and maintained through statist policies and power politics, was mixed with a legacy of localism and particularism. Although liberty, equality, individualism, and humanitarianism ideals were influential in German political thinking, the predominant mode of thought stressed hierarchy, society, order, the state, law, and authority. Traditional political culture reinforced the political system of the German Empire and contributed to the social environment that provided fertile ground for the growth of Nazism. The Western Allies and the Bonn government attempted through denazification, reeducation, and democratization to strengthen the rudimentary democratic themes in German history and society. These policies promoted a system of law based on justice, legitimacy defined by democratic republicanism, and authority limited by institutional checks and human rights. Ideology and doctrine have given way to pragmatism, and traditional idealism has been replaced in large measure by materialism and the desire for economic well-being. The institutions and processes of the Federal Republic are widely accepted, not only because they are successful, but also for the values they represent. *See also* BONN IS NOT WEIMAR, p. 162; POLITICAL CULTURE TRANSFORMATION THESIS, p. 218.

Significance The political culture of a nation is one of the slowest and most difficult factors in a political system to undergo change. Postwar West German attitudes and values, however, are substantially different from prewar ones. These attitudes, primarily pragmatic, and values, primarily democratic, provide a strong social base of support for the political system of the Bonn Republic. Aspects of the traditional political culture remain and are manifested in various ways in law, politics, and social relations. But the typical authoritarian traits have been balanced, and in some areas replaced, by the values of a modern, democratic, postindustrial society.

Political Party System: West Germany The simple multiparty sytem of the Federal Republic, which has two large parliamentary parties and one or two small parties holding the balance of power. About 12 parties compete nationally, but the number of groups able to win seats in the Bundestag (lower house) declined from 10 in 1949 to 3 in 1961. This situation continued until 1983 when a fourth party, the Greens, won some seats. The largest group is the Christian Democratic Union and its smaller sister party, the Christian Social Union (CDU/CSU). The two parties do not compete against each other in elections and form one cohesive parliamentary group (*fraktion*). The second party is the Social Democratic party, which has always run second to the Christian Democrats, except in 1972. These two large parliamentary parties win from 85 to 90 percent of the popular vote and an equivalent number of seats. Liberals are organized in the Free Democratic Party (FDP), which wins only about 6 to 8 percent of the popular vote but has held the balance of power and is usually the second party in a government coalition. Christian Democrats and Social Democrats have alternately controlled the government since 1949. The CDU held the chancellorship from 1949 to 1969, the SPD from 1969 to 1982, and the CDU again since 1982. The Basic Law recognizes the role of political parties in "forming the political will of the people." It also requires that parties be democratic, and it establishes a standard by which undemocratic or subversive parties may be banned. Although political debates may be vituperative, the prewar ideological style of politics has declined. Party politics dominates lawmaking. The two dominant parties are well organized, appeal to all social classes, and are cohesive in the parliament. The parties play such an important role in governance that West Germany has been considered one of the best examples of a "party state" in the Western democracies. *See also* CATCH-ALL PARTY THESIS, p. 167; ELECTIONS OF 1983: WEST GERMANY, p. 176; ELECTORAL SYSTEM: BUNDESTAG, p. 177; GRAND COALITION, p. 194; *LAND* POLITICAL PARTY SYSTEM, p. 203; UNCONSTITUTIONAL PARTIES, p. 231.

Significance The simplification of the German political party system has contributed in large measure to the cabinet stability that has characterized German politics in the postwar period. Explanations for this simplification have relied on the following factors: (1) the limitations placed on party competition, such as the electoral law that requires political parties to win 5 percent of the national vote in order to earn any seats in the Bundestag; (2) the modernization of the socioeconomic system and the assimilation of social, religious, and refugee groups into the larger society; (3) the economic prosperity that the nation has experienced; (4) the postwar rejection of extremist parties by the German people; and (5) the development of peoples' parties (*Volksparteien*, sing. *Volkspartei*) that appeal to all classes. Both the Christian Democrats and the Social Democrats tried to become Volksparteien, and, as catch-all parties, they have helped transform the German political party system into one that provides stable and responsible party government.

Potsdam Conference A meeting of the leaders of the United States, the Soviet Union, and Great Britain at Potsdam outside Berlin in July and August 1945 that resulted in agreements concerning the occupation and boundaries of Germany, the war against Japan, and other postwar matters. The leaders of the Big Three who attended the Conference were Harry S Truman, Josef Stalin, and Winston S. Churchill, who was replaced during the Conference by Clement Attlee following British elections. Although France was to be an occupying power of Germany, it was not invited to the Conference. Under terms of the Potsdam Agreement, the parties decided to (1) divide Germany into four zones of occupation, but to treat it as a single economic unit under the administration of a joint four-power Allied Control Council; (2) establish the eastern border of Germany at the Oder and Neisse rivers; (3) divide Greater Berlin into four zones (called sectors) of occupation under the administration of a separate Allied *Kommandatura;* (4) provide for the transfer of ethnic Germans from Poland, Czechoslovakia, and Hungary to Germany; (5) award the northern part of East Prussia including the port of Königsberg (later called Kaliningrad) to the Soviet Union; (6) postpone a final decision on reparations, but permit each party to take reparations from its own zone; and (7) demilitarize

Germany, punish war criminals, denazify German society and reeducate Germans, destroy the German armaments industry, and break up the monopolies and cartels in German industry. Because the Soviet Union had not yet entered the war against Japan, the British and American governments issued a joint Potsdam Declaration establishing the terms for Japanese surrender. The Big Three could not agree on other matters regarding the postwar world, and these were referred to a Council of Ministers comprising the Big Three, and France and China. *See also* OCCUPATION PERIOD, p. 214; ODER-NEISSE LINE, p. 216; YALTA CONFERENCE, p. 241.

Significance The decisions made at the Potsdam Conference were very much structured by previous decisions made at the Yalta Conference in February 1945 and the power realities of that time. The two conferences in effect established the political structure, geographic boundaries, and economic systems of the states of Central Europe for the postwar period. Germany suffered severe consequences, although the Allies rejected an earlier American idea, called the Morgenthau Plan, which would have deindustrialized Germany and made it an agricultural state incapable of launching another aggressive war. The three western occupation zones of Germany became the territory of the Federal Republic of Germany, and the Soviet zone became the German Democratic Republic. West Germany developed a political system similar to the constitutional democracies of the West, and East Germany and the Eastern European states were established as Communist states under the control or influence of the Soviet Union. The three western sectors of Berlin became a single city, West Berlin, an island of Western-style democracy surrounded by East Germany. The eastern sector of Berlin was annexed by East Germany. The parts of Germany east of the Oder-Neisse line that were to be "administered" by Poland became an integral part of Poland. Ten million Germans were expelled from East Europe, most of whom ultimately ended up in West Germany, which absorbed them in a territory one-half the size of prewar Germany. The Potsdam Conference and its consequences were much affected by the suspicions created by the failure of the Soviet Union to live up to the Yalta agreements. The British accused the Russians of not holding free elections in Poland and imposing a Communist government on that nation; Russians accused the British of similar domination in Greece. The reparations policy was never satisfactorily resolved. The West, wanting to prevent a reenactment of postwar German bitterness similar to that after World War I, sought to hold back on reparations, while the Russians were stripping industrial equipment from Eastern Europe and East Germany to rebuild the wartorn Soviet economy. The Allied

Control Council for Berlin was soon to be ineffective and stymied by vetoes. Thus, within a short time, the suspicions and conflicting interests of the wartime Allies broke out into a full-scale Cold War.

Rechtsstaat A state based on the rule of law and justice. *Rechtsstaat* is a traditional German legal concept that incorporates the notions of the supremacy of law and the impartial administration of justice. As the concept developed in the nineteenth century, a Rechtsstaat was not to be an example of democratic constitutionalism or limited government, but rather a state based on the rule of law in which the assumption was that the law was fair and just. Judges were an integral part of the state and were to apply the law without question. This notion was combined with the theory of legal positivism, which accepted the enacted law as proper and acknowledged no higher authority or moral standards above the law. In the Nazi period, this understanding of the Rechtsstaat was pushed to the extreme, and judges applied Nazi laws as proper because they were enacted by legal authority. The framers of the Basic Law attempted to reintroduce the notion of justice into the concept of Rechtsstaat, for they based the entire constitutional system on this idea. The Basic Law states: "Legislation shall be subject to the constitutional order; the executive and the judiciary shall be bound by law and justice." An extensive list of civil and political rights was provided for and a Constitutional Court was given the authority to use these constitutional standards of law and justice to rule on the permissibility of government actions. *See also* FEDERAL CONSTITUTIONAL COURT, p. 182; JUDICIAL SYSTEM: WEST GERMANY, p. 201.

Significance The legalistic and authoritarian practices whereby a Rechtsstaat becomes merely a rule of law, any law, no matter how arbitrary or unjust, reached its zenith in the Nazi regime. After World War II, the concept of Rechtsstaat was resurrected, redefined as the rule of law and of justice, and made the foundation of the constitutional order of the Federal Republic. The first judges to be appointed to the new Constitutional Court took the new idea of Rechtsstaat and pushed it to the opposite extreme. They devised the notion of "unconstitutional constitutional norms," the idea that above the constitution lay a higher law that could be used to invalidate provisions in the supreme law of the land. With this understanding of Rechtsstaat, the Court's concept of justice could be substituted for an obvious intention provided in the Basic Law. This theory has faded, however, and the concept of Rechtsstaat, understood as a state based on both law and justice, seems to be the foundation of postwar German jurisprudence.

Red Army Faction (RAF)   A small group of radical left-wing terrorists that has been active since the 1970s. The postwar origins of the Red Army Faction (RAF) are found in the German Socialist Student Alliance (SDS), originally a large and powerful affiliate of the Social Democratic party (SPD). When SDS leaders became increasingly radicalized in the 1960s, they were expelled from the SPD; Rudi Dutschke became the acknowledged spokesman of the terrorist strategy for making a revolution. The SDS broke up into various terrorist factions after a near-fatal assassination attempt against Dutschke. By the end of the 1960s, Andreas Baader, Ulrike Meinhof, Gudrun Ensslin, and Gustaf Mahler emerged as leaders of terrorist groups variously known as the Weathermen, the Baader-Meinhof Group, and the Red Army Faction. These groups engaged in a series of spectacular bank robberies, bombings, kidnappings, hijackings, murders, and attacks on American installations in Germany. A number of RAF leaders were captured and convicted in 1977 after a three-year trial. Meinhof was found hanged in her cell, an apparent suicide in 1976; Mahler died through a hunger strike; Baader, Ensslin, and Jan-Carl Raspe were sentenced to life imprisonment. Terrorist leaders were able to make contact with outside parties while in prison and apparently planned some operations. In September 1977 the prominent industrialist and president of the industrialists' (BDI) and employers' (BDA) associations, Hanns-Martin Schleyer, was kidnapped and held for ransom and release of the prisoners. A month later, a German airliner was hijacked by the RAF, and the 91 passengers and crew members were also held hostage for release of the prisoners. Baader, Ensslin, and Raspe apparently committed suicide in their cells a few hours after a German commando unit stormed the aircraft, then in Mogadishu, Somalia, and rescued the hostages. Schleyer was murdered by the Red Army Faction shortly thereafter. Responding to these and earlier events, the German Social Democratic government enacted antiterrorist legislation, increased security measures. and made numerous arrests, thus breaking the back of the movement. In the 1980s the Red Army Faction has been reduced to a few hundred persons and occasionally carries out an operation.

Significance   Red Army Faction members were drawn primarily from the educated middle class and were supported in part by radical lawyers and professors. Advocating revolution through terrorism, RAF members saw themselves as part of an international organization that included similar groups abroad and the Palestine Liberation Organization. These other groups often aided the RAF with finances, weapons, and participation in operations. Terrorist organizations in Germany were unsuccessful in recruiting members from the working class, despite their goal to seize power from "monopolistic capitalists, landowners, and imperialists" in the name of a "free society." The booming economy and the consensual political situation in West Germany provided a hostile environment for terrorists, and public opinion strongly supported the government's measures to quash terrorist activity. The deaths of RAF leaders and arrests of many lesser figures greatly hurt the movement. Although terrorist operations occur occasionally, the Red Army Faction has little impact on the political system of the Federal Republic.

Refugees, Expellees, Escapees   Ethnic Germans primarily from Eastern Europe and East Germany who relocated in West Germany after World War II. The term "refugees" refers to those displaced persons from various parts of prewar Germany who were rendered homeless and dislocated by the war. "Expellees" are those ethnic Germans who were living in areas of Eastern Europe, primarily East Prussia, Poland, and the Sudetenland, which were annexed by Poland and Russia or returned to Czechoslovakia after the war. Numbering about 8 to 10 million, they were expelled from their traditional homelands as the new local governments moved their nationals into the territories. About 3 million expellees were also relocated in East Germany. "Escapees" are East Germans who fled that Communist state. They number about 3 million persons. Since the building of the Berlin Wall in 1961, the number of escapees has slowed to only a few thousand per year because the action of leaving East Germany for most persons is illegal and dangerous. Generally, the total number of refugees, expellees, and escapees who relocated in the Federal Republic is well over 13 million, not including their children born in West Germany. *See also* BERLIN WALL, p. 161.

Significance   Refugees, expellees, and escapees dramatically increased the population of the Federal Republic, particularly at a time when the nation was recovering from the devastation caused by the war. The federal government welcomed these persons, gave them economic assistance, and enacted policies favoring their quick integration and assimilation. In the first decade of the Federal Republic, many refugees and expellees supported the All German Bloc/Federation of Expellees and Dispossessed party (GB/BHE). It is a mark of the political integration of the Easterners into the West German system that these parties have disappeared. Generally conservative in their foreign policy position, refugees supported the anticommunist and reunification policies of the Konrad Adenauer government. Since the *Ostpolitik* policy of Willy Brandt, Easterners favor the recognition of the Communist governments in the East and the adoption of agreements providing for family visits.

Saar Question The issue of whether the Saar would be returned to Germany after World War II or be given an international status under French influence. At first, the Saar was made part of the French zone of occupation of Germany, but in 1946 the French government separated the territory from its zone of occupation. In 1947 France integrated the Saar's economy with its own and took charge of its foreign and defense policies. The Saar remained separated from Germany when the Federal Republic was established in 1949, and it continued under French control despite West German protests until the mid-1950s. In 1954 France rejected a proposal for the European Defense Community (EDC) that would have integrated the military forces of the six West European states, including those of West Germany. As part of a substitute plan whereby West Germany would become a member of the North Atlantic Treaty Organization, Bonn and Paris agreed to a plebiscite in the Saar. In October 1955 Saarlanders voted on a charter that would have given the territory a European status within the context of the Western European Union. Saarlanders rejected the charter by a 68 percent vote, thereby indicating their wish to be returned to Germany; France and Germany agreed the following year that the territory should be politically united with the Federal Republic. On January 1, 1957, the Saar became the tenth state (*Land*) in the Federal Republic, and its economy was fully integrated with West Germany three years later. *See also* FEDERAL REPUBLIC OF GERMANY (FRG), p. 185; OCCUPATION PERIOD, p. 214.

Significance The Saar question after World War II illustrated the continuing desire of France to remove the territory from German control and the Saarlanders' wish to remain part of Germany. A highly industrialized area, rich in coal deposits, the Saar is culturally German. After World War I, the territory was placed under the jurisdiction of the League of Nations, which permitted France to administer the territory from 1919 to 1935. In a 1935 plebiscite, Saarlanders voted overwhelmingly to be returned to Germany, which contributed to Adolf Hitler's popularity. After World War II, France again attempted to annex the Saar or to keep control of its economy. When this met great opposition, it tried to prevent Germany from controlling the land by promoting the plan for an independent free territory that would become the focus of European economic integration. Following the overwhelming rejection of this idea by the Saarlanders, France agreed to the return of the territory to Germany. The potentially explosive issue was resolved by applying the principle of self-determination.

Social Democratic Party (SPD) The large party of the democratic left that controlled the government of the Federal Republic of Germany from 1969 to 1982. When the Social Democratic party (SPD) was founded in the 1860s, it was a doctrinaire party that advocated an evolutionary road to socialism. Basing its support on the working class, the SPD was the largest party in the parliament before 1914. A strong defender of democracy, the SPD was one of the founding parties of the Weimar Republic, and it supplied the first president and chancellors of the regime. Crushed by the Nazi government, the SPD emerged after World War II with a clean reputation, a socialist program, and uncompromising leadership under Kurt Schumacher. An anti-Nazi who had suffered greatly in Nazi prisons, Schumacher was also an anticommunist who opposed the fusion of the SPD with the Communists, which took place in Berlin and in the Soviet zone of occupied Germany. SPD voting strength had been traditionally located in eastern Germany, but in the first postwar election in 1949 in West Germany, the party gained 29 percent of the vote, only 2 points behind the Christian Democrats (CDU/CSU). Under Schumacher, the party advocated a worker's state, the adoption of socialism, and the reunification of Germany; it opposed Western European economic integration and strong ties to the West as a hindrance to reunification. This program made no headway with the voters, while the CDU/CSU jumped to 45 and then to 50 percent of the vote in the 1953 and 1956 elections. Although the SPD had a mass membership of about a million members, reform-minded socialists, such as Herbert Wehner, Fritz Erler, Willy Brandt, and Carlo Schmidt, were fearful that the party would become a permanent 30 percent minority. They decided to refashion the SPD into an all-people's party (*Volkspartei*) that would discard doctrinaire socialism, anticlericalism, and neutralism. This new approach was formalized in a party convention in the city of Bad Godesberg in 1959. In the Godesberg Program the SPD proclaimed itself to be a national party, not a single-class party, dropped its hostility to religion, and declared that freedom was more important than collectivism and economic planning. The SPD endorsed German participation in NATO, accepted the necessity of military conscription, and supported Western European economic integration. Under party chairman Willy Brandt, the pro-Western mayor of West Berlin, the party's popular support increased steadily in the 1960s, and in 1966 the SPD entered the government for the first time as a junior partner in the Grand Coalition headed by the CDU Chancellor Kurt Georg Kiesinger. Willy Brandt became Chancellor in 1969, heading a government coalition with the Free Democratic party (FDP). In his foreign policy of detente toward the East, called *Ostpolitik*, he made treaties with the Soviet Union, Poland, Czechoslovakia, and East Germany, which recognized the status quo in Europe. For this Brandt won the Nobel Peace Prize in 1971, and the German people made the SPD the first party with 46 percent of the popular vote in the 1972 elections. Helmut Schmidt was elected chancellor in 1974, keeping the SPD in power until 1982, when the Free Democrats switched their support to the Christian Democrats. In the March 1983 elections, the SPD fell to 38.2 percent of the vote under its new leader, Hans-Jochen Vogel, and the party was forced to reexamine its program in the postelection period. *See also* ELECTIONS OF 1983: WEST GERMANY, p. 176; GODESBERG PROGRAM VERSUS NEOSOCIALISM, p. 194; GUILLAUME AFFAIR, p. 198; POLITICAL PARTY SYSTEM: WEST GERMANY, p. 220.

Significance The Social Democratic Party was in the government for almost half of the first 33 years of the Federal Republic, and it controlled the chancellorship for 13 consecutive years from 1969 to 1982. Although it lost its traditional base of support in eastern Germany after the war, the party made a remarkable recovery from 29 percent of the vote in 1949 to 46 percent in 1972. This popular support can be attributed to its new multiclass appeal, its acceptance of the social market economic policy, and Brandt's Ostpolitik. In the late 1970s, however, the SPD began a decline at the state level that increased in the early 1980s as the economy worsened. The Young Socialists (Jusos), comprising one-third of the party members, demanded more attention to social reform and a return to socialist principles; they were supported in these goals by Willy Brandt, who had retained the chairmanship of the party. Outside the SPD, a new force, the Greens and the Alternatives, gained attention and votes for their environmentalist, antinuclear, and pacifist program. In 1983 the party's fortunes were at the lowest level since the 1950s as it faced a possibly damaging factional struggle over policy questions dealing with the extension of socialization and the deployment of medium-range NATO missiles in Germany.

Social Market Economy An economic strategy or philosophy based on the principles of a free market, limited state intervention, and social welfare programs. The social market economy approach was promoted by Ludwig Erhard, the Christian Democrat minister of economics in Konrad Adenauer's government from 1949 to 1963 and chancellor from 1963 to 1966. The purpose of the social market economy was to promote economic growth and the efficient use of resources by relying on free market forces. The government would intervene only to prohibit abuses, such as the concentration of economic power by monopolies. It would give aid to small businesses and adopt social welfare programs that would aid the disadvantaged. The policy attempted to avoid the extremes of both laissez faire economics and economic planning by a minimal regulation of the free market coupled with social programs. See also CODETERMINATION, p. 172; ECONOMIC MIRACLE, p. 175.

Significance Economic policies enacted by the Federal Republic in its first 15 years were based in part on the principles of the social market economy. Erhard's attempt to retard the growth of trusts was not successful, but the policies were held to be responsible for the "economic miracle" of that period. The economy was reconstructed, production greatly increased, full employment achieved, labor strife reduced, and inflation remained at low levels. Erhard, the champion of the free market, came to be called the "father of the economic miracle," and he succeeded Adenauer to the chancellorship. Erhard was forced to resign in 1966, however, when the country's first serious postwar recession occurred. The Christian Democrats fared poorly in state elections, and the Free Democratic party withdrew from the government coalition. After Erhard, subsequent governments introduced policies providing for economic planning, direct government attempts to regulate business cycles, and increased social welfare programs.

***Spiegel* Affair** A sensational affair in 1962 in which the offices of the newsmagazine *Der Spiegel* were raided and its editors arrested for allegedly publishing secret defense documents. The article in *Der Spiegel*, a newsweekly often critical of the government, charged that national defense preparations were in a poor condition, and it sharply criticized Franz Josef Strauss, the defense minister in Konrad Adenauer's government. The magazine's offices in Hamburg and Bonn were subsequently raided by federal authorities, and the editor, Rudolf Augstein, and staff members were arrested. One editor was arrested at midnight while he was on vacation in Spain by the German military attaché. The magazine's editors were charged with treason for procuring and publishing secret military information. These actions by the government led to an immediate public outcry and charges that the government was using Gestapo-like methods. Bitter debates took place in the Bundestag, with the Social Democratic opposition loudly criticizing the government. The liberals in the Free Democratic party, a coalition partner with the Christian Democrats, also demanded that Strauss resign. Strauss admitted responsibility and vigorously defended his actions, and was supported by Chancellor Adenauer. In the end, however, Strauss resigned. The defendants were brought to trial, and the case dragged on for several years, but eventually all defendants were acquitted; *Der Spiegel* lost a countersuit for damages.

Significance   The *Spiegel* affair demonstrated that both traditional German authoritarian methods and popular support for new democratic values existed side by side in the Federal Republic. Despite the arrests, *Der Spiegel*, a sensationalistic newsweekly, continued its harassment of the government; its circulation and influence continued to grow. After Strauss resigned, he returned to Bavarian politics, retained control of the Christian Social Union, and eventually reentered the national government. He was the losing CDU/CSU candidate for chancellor in the 1980 federal elections. The affair contributed to the mounting criticisms of Adenauer's authoritarian manner and his insensitivity to democratic norms; it also reinforced popular demands that he resign. In the end, the government's methods were repudiated, and the popular and parliamentary outcry demonstrated that authoritarian-style government was incompatible with the new Germany.

Trade Unions: West Germany   Associations of workers and employees in the Federal Republic of Germany. The largest trade union is the German Trade Union Federation (DGB), an association of 17 industrial, white-collar, and civil servant unions, which had a total of 8 million members in 1984. One of its constituent unions, I. G. Metall, the metalworkers union, represents 2.5 million workers in the iron and steel, automobile, shipbuilding, and engineering industries. Other independent unions are: the German Federation of Civil Servants (DBB), an organization of about 730,000 middle- and upper-level government employees; and the German Salaried Employees' Union (DAG), about 450,000 white-collar workers. These three peak organizations include most of the 30 percent of the workforce that is unionized. In the early postwar period, the DGB first called for the nationalization of industry, but this goal was dropped in favor of collective bargaining, direct benefits for workers, and codetermination (worker participation in management). Although many DGB activists are affiliated with the Social Democratic party, the organization was founded as a nonpartisan group and is not directly linked to any party. Since its founding in 1949, the DGB has exercised restraint and called few strikes, preferring to achieve its goals through cooperation with the social market policy of government, and pushing for the adoption of a strong codetermination law. The union participates in various government boards and commissions and takes part in the process called "concerted action" in which government, business, and labor representatives meet and discuss general economic policy. In the 1970s, however, with the rise of unemployment and inflation and a decrease in economic growth, the DGB became increasingly hostile toward the government. Many workers, including unionists, voted for the Christian Democratic party in the March 1983 elections. On Labor Day (May 1, 1983), with unemployment at 9 percent (14 percent for foreign workers), the DGB called for the "democratization of the economy and society," a shorter workweek, early retirement to create job opportunities, and the extension of codetermination to full parity between workers and management. *See also* CODETERMINATION, p. 172; FUNCTIONAL REPRESENTATION, p. 188; GUEST WORKERS, p. 197.

Significance By combining into one large nonpartisan trade union federation, German industrial workers avoided the counterproductive competition among rival unions that occurred in France and Italy in the postwar period. The DGB became large and financially secure, and the nation benefited from the absence of industrial strife and political strikes. The DGB's acceptance of the democratic pluralist system and social market philosophy, and its moderate goals and cooperative attitude all contributed to the economic miracle that occurred in Germany. But the DGB's power has been relatively weak within the German political system compared to industrial and agricultural associations, and its achievements, such as codetermination rights, have been limited. With the recession in full force and a large number of unemployed foreign workers present in Germany, the decade of the 1980s may well see the DGB move to a more militant style and a socialistic program.

Unconstitutional Parties Political parties that have been banned for violating constitutional standards of political activity. The Basic Law provides: "Parties, which by reason of their aims or the behavior of their adherents, seek to impair or abolish the free basic democratic order or to endanger the existence of the Federal Republic of Germany are unconstitutional." The Federal Constitutional Court is given the authority to decide the question of constitutionality, but this is done only on petition of the government or either house of parliament. In 1952 the Court ruled a neo-Nazi group, the Socialist Reich party (SRP), to be unconstitutional. Some of the SRP members then formed a less extreme party, the German Reich party (DRP), but it received little national support. After a lengthy case, the Court declared in 1956 the Communist Party of Germany (KPD) to be unconstitutional. In theory West German law applies to all of Germany, but in this case, the Court specifically confined its ruling to the territory of the Federal Republic, leaving open the possibility of reunification and all-German elections in which Communists would participate. Rulings of unconstitutionality do not apply to West Berlin, which is not a constituent part of the Federal

Republic. In 1969 a successor Communist party with a similar name to the former KPD was permitted to organize in West Germany. It is called the German Communist party (DKP), and it claims to follow constitutional standards. In the late 1960s, a question was raised whether the government should petition the Court to ban the right-wing National Democratic party (NPD). The government announced that it decided not to do so because it probably could not prove that the NPD was violating the constitution and that it did not wish to make a martyr of the party. *See also* GERMAN COMMUNIST PARTY (DKP), p. 189; NATIONAL DEMOCRATIC PARTY (NPD), p. 206; POLITICAL PARTY SYSTEM: WEST GERMANY, p. 220.

Significance Although the Basic Law establishes standards whereby undemocratic and subversive parties may be banned, it is a political decision whether to prosecute a party before the Constitutional Court. The banning of the two extremist parties seemed appropriate to the governments in the 1950s. Some observers have noted that although the Constitutional Court was probably correct that the old Communist party (KPD), a Stalinist group linked to East Germany and the Soviet Union, violated constitutional norms, it was unnecessary to ban the party. The KPD had won 5.6 percent of the popular vote in 1949, but it had fallen to 2.2 percent in the 1953 elections and had no seats in the Bundestag when it was banned in 1956. In the 1970s the government, confident of the security of the West German democratic order, made the successful political decisions to permit a new Communist party to organize and to refrain from prosecuting the National Democratic party. Neither of these parties has been able to win more than one-third of one percent of the popular vote in the three national elections since 1976.

Versailles Treaty The peace settlement with Germany after World War I, which was signed at the Paris Peace Conference in 1919 and came into force in 1920. The Treaty of Versailles dealt primarily with German questions, but it also contained the Covenant of the League of Nations. Drafted by the heads of government of the United States, the United Kingdom, France, and Italy, the treaty was imposed on a defeated and demobilized Germany under a threat of the resumption of hostilities. Regarding Germany, the treaty provided for (1) transfers of German territory, some to be confirmed by plebiscites, to France, Belgium, Poland, Denmark, and Lithuania; (2) German overseas colonies to be ceded to the Allied powers as mandates under the League of Nations; (3) the Rhineland to be occupied by Allied powers for 15 years and to remain demilitarized; (4) major limitations on German armed forces, including a prohibition of an air force and general staff, an army limited to 100,000 men, and restrictions on armaments and naval ships; (5) the payment of heavy reparations, later established at $33 billion; (6) the War Guilt Clause, in which Germany accepted sole responsibility for the war and liability for all Allied losses and costs; (7) the release of certain Germans to be tried as war criminals, and the request that the Netherlands release the former emperor, William II, to be tried for crimes against humanity. In the major territorial transfers, Alsace-Lorraine was ceded outright to France; Poznan and West Prussia were ceded to Poland, which gave Poland direct access to the Baltic Sea (the Polish Corridor); Danzig was made a Free City; and the Saar was put under French administration for 15 years. The Versailles Treaty was opposed by all political groups in Germany, many of which were willing to reject the treaty and accept further hostilities because its harsh terms went far beyond the spirit of Woodrow Wilson's Fourteen Points on whose basis Germany had requested the armistice of November 11, 1918. They particularly objected to the "honor clauses," that is, the War Guilt Clause, and the requirement to turn over alleged war criminals. The Social Democratic government accepted the treaty, believing it had no other practical choice. Because it also contained the Covenant of the League of Nations, the United States refused to ratify the treaty. The American government later formally ended the war with Germany. *See also* MUNICH AGREEMENT, p. 205.

Significance The Treaty of Versailles brought to a close a terrible war that had caused 10 million deaths, but the treaty has been much criticized for being overly harsh on Germany, counterproductive to Western interests, and contributing to tragedies of greater magnitude than those of the First World War. Critics of the treaty have argued that it (1) was vengeful and unjust, and that the War Guilt Clause especially humiliated Germany; (2) brought disrespect to the Weimar Republic and to those governments that tried to fulfill the obligations of the treaty; (3) contributed directly to the rise of aggressive nationalism and indirectly to left-wing radicalism; (4) was a major factor in the rise of Nazism and Adolf Hitler, who used every occasion to condemn the "dictate of Versailles"; (5) reinforced the stab-in-the-back legend that the military had not lost the war but was betrayed by the government; (6) permitted self-determination for some regions, but prohibited the union of Austria and Germany, which was desired by both countries; and (7) established a reparations policy that was impossible to fulfill. Defenders of the treaty usually point out that although the spirit of the Fourteen Points was ignored regarding Germany, the self-determination principle was generally applied; that many British and French citizens believed the treaty to be too lenient; and that the treaty was no more severe than the Treaty of Brest-Litovsk the Germans had imposed on Russia in 1918. They also note that, apart from Germany, the treaty provided for the League of Nations, which was an important initial step in establishing a global community. However, in the two decades following Versailles, German domestic and international politics were played out within the context of the treaty in an increasingly tragic fashion. When France and Belgium occupied the Ruhr in 1923 for German nonpayment of reparations, German nationalism and embittered feelings greatly increased. With the coming of the economic depression, the reparations payments became an impossible obligation; they were suspended and not resumed after 1931. After Hitler came into power in 1933, the terms of the treaty were consistently abrogated in a fashion that gave him increasing stature within Germany and power in international affairs. Hitler repudiated the disarmament provision in 1935, remilitarized the Rhineland in 1936, annexed Austria in 1938, annexed, with Western consent, the Sudetenland of Czechoslovakia in 1938, and absorbed the remainder of Czechoslovakia in 1939. The attack on Poland in 1939 that began World War II was another major act by which Hitler tried to revise the treaty by force.

Weimar Republic The political system of Germany from 1919 to 1933. Weimar Republic is the popular designation for the republic proclaimed in the German Revolution of 1918, which overthrew the monarchy of Kaiser William II. The name is derived from the city where the National Constituent Assembly met in February 1919 to draft the constitution for the new republic. The constitution established a federal, parliamentary democracy, with an elected president, responsible chancellor, and a bicameral legislature. The lower house was chosen by universal suffrage on the basis of proportional representation, which contributed to an extreme form of multipartyism and unstable cabinets. In its first five years, the republic was troubled by a succession of crises that almost toppled the regime. These included (1) widespread hunger in 1918–19; (2) attempts by the Spartacists (Spartacus League, later called Communists), to capture the revolution in 1918; (3) the unsuccessful right-wing Kapp *Putsch* of 1920 in Berlin; (4) the French occupation of the Rhineland in 1923, which led to massive resistance and economic disruption; (5) the hyperinflation of 1922–23, which wiped out the savings of the middle class; (6) Hitler's unsuccessful Munich Putsch (revolt) of 1923 (Beer Hall Putsch); and (7) a Communist revolution in Saxony in October 1923. From 1924 to 1929 the republic seemed to overcome its troubles, as economic recovery, agreements on reparations payments, and rapprochement with Western and Eastern European powers took place. The great economic depression that began in 1929, however, brought massive unemployment, business failures, increased government instability, large-scale support for the Nazis and Communists, and the breakdown of the democratic coalition. The Weimar Republic was overthrown by Adolf Hitler, who was appointed chancellor in January 1933 and was voted dictatorial powers by the enabling act of March 1933. This action was used by Hitler to subvert and in time to destroy the Weimar system. *See also* VERSAILLES TREATY, p. 232; WEIMAR REPUBLIC: CONSTITUTIONAL SYSTEM, p. 235; WEIMAR REPUBLIC: POLITICAL PARTY SYSTEM, p. 237.

Significance The Weimar Republic was the first national experiment with parliamentary democracy in German history. Since World War II, the failure of the republic has attracted much analysis and attempts to derive lessons from its experience. Explanations for the fall of Weimar emphasize a variety of historical, cultural, social, economic, and political factors. Some of the most often mentioned reasons are the following: (1) the revolutionary origins of the republic, which contributed to the persistence of antistate activity; (2) the Treaty of Versailles, whose harsh terms and "dishonorable" provisions brought disrepute to the republic and to those governments that tried to fulfill its terms; (3) the lack of a national democratic tradition and the absence of a strong middle class committed to democracy; (4) German political culture, in which the premises of democracy were little understood and which emphasized authoritarianism and statism; (5) social groups, such as the Junkers (Prussian landlords), the military, and revolutionary working classes opposed to parliamentary democracy; (6) the economic privation, hyperinflation, and depression, which successively contributed to antirepublican movements; and (7) the constitutional system and political party system, which contributed to government instability and excessive reliance on emergency powers. After World War II, the Allies and the founders of the Bonn Republic attempted to apply the "lessons" of Weimar. These included making a less punitive peace settlement; attempting to democratize German society and political culture; removing defects in the constitutional system; and creating stable governments by limiting the impact of splinter and unconstitutional political parties.

Weimar Republic: Constitutional System The governmental system of Germany from 1919 to 1933. The constitution of the Weimar Republic was adopted by the popularly elected National Constituent Assembly, which met in Weimar in 1919. The assembly was controlled by the more moderate forces of the German Revolution of 1918, the Majority Socialists (Social Democrats), Democrats (liberals), and Centrists (Catholics). The constitution reflected their democratic orientation and was based on the principles of republicanism, federalism, parliamentarism, and democracy. There were 18 (later 17) states (*Länder*) in the federal union, and each state was required to have a republican constitution. The federal system was unbalanced, however, as Prussia controlled 40 percent of the votes in the upper house. The upper house of the legislature (Reichsrat) represented state governments; its powers were reduced from that of the upper house in the Empire. The lower house, the Reichstag, which was chosen by universal suffrage on a proportional representation basis, had full legislative powers and the authority to overturn governments. The executive power was divided between the president and the chancellor. The president, who was popularly elected for a seven-year term, had the authority to dissolve the Reichstag, to declare a state of emergency under Article 48, and to rule by decree. The chancellor headed the government; although chosen by the president, he was responsible to the Reichstag. The constitution provided for a long list of democratic liberties of the people and for direct democracy through the use of plebiscites. *See also* WEIMAR REPUBLIC, p. 234; WEIMAR REPUBLIC: POLITICAL PARTY SYSTEM, p. 237.

Significance The constitutional system of the Weimar Republic was solidly based on democratic principles, but it functioned poorly in the political, economic, and social environment of postwar Germany. Its special features, such as the unbalanced federal system, the provision for plebiscites, and the famous Article 48 authorizing constitutional dictatorship, came to be used by enemies of the republic. It was through the application of Article 48 that Adolf Hitler established his dictatorship. Because of the failure of the Weimar Republic, the framers of the Bonn Constitution of 1949 attempted to cure the "defects" in the constitutional system. Constitutional "lessons" used to strengthen the governmental system of the Federal Republic include (1) reducing the number of states in the federal union and equalizing the size of the larger states: (2) increasing the constitutional authority of the states; (3) providing that the presidency become a figurehead office and that the president not be directly elected but chosen by a convention comprised of federal and state legislators; (4) improving government stability by requiring that the lower house elect a new chancellor before it can dismiss the one in office; (5) placing strong limitations on the exercise of emergency powers, which were not permitted until 1968; (6) establishing a constitutional court with power to declare laws unconstitutional, thus giving meaning to the bill of rights; and (7) establishing limits on political parties, in the attempt to improve government stability. Many political observers have concluded that, although the constitutional system of the Weimar Republic may have functioned well in a different environment, the defects of the system contributed to the fall of the republic.

Weimar Republic: Political Party System The extreme multiparty system of Germany from 1919 to 1933. The political party system of the Weimar Republic included from 6 to 8 large parties and about 25 very small parties that were active at various times. The system went through an evolution in its early years in which the Reichstag (lower house) was dominated by a group of parties known as the Weimar Coalition. These parties, the Social Democrats (socialists), Democrats (liberals), and Center party (Catholics), soon cooperated with the People's party (democratic conservatives). The democratic forces were overcome by the rising power of the antirepublican and antidemocratic right, the Nationalists and the National Socialist German Workers' party (Nazis). In the election of 1919 the Social Democrats emerged as the largest party, with 38 percent of the vote. That party supplied the first president and the first four governments of the new republic. By 1930, however, the Weimar Coalition had broken up, the Democrats and People's party were in decline, the Communist party had grown to 13 percent of the vote, and the Nazis replaced the Nationalists as the most significant force on the antirepublican right. The electoral system of proportional representation contributed to the multitude of splinter parties and government instability. In the 14 years of Weimar there were 21 different cabinets, 12 different chancellors, and 9 separate national elections. Two men served as President of the Republic: the Social Democrat, Friedrich Ebert, from 1919 to 1925, and the monarchist sympathizer, Field Marshall Paul von Hindenburg, from 1925 to 1934. The Weimar party system was brought to a close after President Hindenburg appointed Hitler chancellor in January 1933. In the last relatively free but violence-prone election of March 1933, which followed the burning of the Reichstag building, the Nazis received 44 percent of the vote; the Socialists, 18 percent; Communists, 12 percent; Centrists, 12 percent; and Nationalists, 8 percent. With Communists disqualified for their alleged conspiracy in setting fire to the Reichstag building, and only Socialists in opposition, Hitler pushed the enabling act of March 1933 through the legislature, and proceeded to establish a one-party state. The Nazis received 92 percent of the vote in the election of November 1933. *See also* POLITICAL PARTY SYSTEM: WEST GERMANY, p. 220; WEIMAR REPUBLIC, p. 234; WEIMAR REPUBLIC: CONSTITUTIONAL SYSTEM, p. 235.

Significance The political party system of the Weimar Republic reflected the serious divisions in postwar German society. The lack of consensus on the new political system was aggravated by the newly adopted system of proportional representation and reinforced by a constitutional system that encouraged the use of emergency powers and unchecked executive authority. The democratic parties of Weimar were eventually overwhelmed by the myriad economic, social, and political emergencies Germany faced in the postwar period and by the antirepublican and antidemocratic forces they engendered. After World War II, the Federal Republic of Germany adopted constitutional and legal measures that were designed to overcome the deficiencies of the party system of Weimar. These included curbing the influence of very small parties and antisystem parties in the attempt to create stable and responsible governments. In the Federal Republic, parties with less than 5 percent of the national vote are denied any seats in the lower house, and undemocratic parties may be banned from political competition.

West Berlin The common name for those sectors of Greater Berlin that were occupied by the United States, Great Britain, and France after World War II and that were united under one city government that is associated with the Federal Republic of Germany. The governmental system of West Berlin is based on a constitution that was adopted in 1950, which was to apply to all four sectors of Greater Berlin, including the Soviet-occupied sector (East Berlin). In 1948, however, the Soviets had walked out of the *Kommandatura* (the four-power Allied Control Council for Berlin) and established a separate city government in their occupation zone. Later the Soviet Union permitted East Berlin to be incorporated into the German Democratic Republic (East Germany), a development the Western powers do not recognize as legal. Although the constitution of the Federal Republic of Germany (FRG) considers Berlin to be a part of the FRG, the Western Allies do not acknowledge this, and, while conceding local self-government, have retained rights of intervention in Berlin. The laws of the FRG do not automatically apply to West Berlin, and must be reenacted by the city parliament. Although West Berlin sends delegates to the federal parliament, they have no voting rights on legislative matters. The city's delegates to the Bundestag (lower house) are not popularly elected, but are chosen by the West Berlin parliament. The governmental system of West Berlin is similar to that of other city states in the Federal Republic. The important institutions are: a directly elected unicameral parliament (the House of Representatives); a chief executive officer, called the governing mayor (*Regierender Bürgermeister*), who is elected by the House of Representatives; and a cabinet, called the Senate, which exercises the executive power. West Berlin political parties are similar to those in the FRG. The Social Democratic party had always been in power, either alone or in coalition with the smaller Free Democratic party, until 1981, when a financial scandal brought down the government. The Social Democratic–Free Democratic majority then elected Hans-Jochen Vogel to be mayor; Vogel had been a federal minister and was later to become the leader of the national Social Democratic party. Early elections were called for May 1981. The Christian Democrats became the leading party for the first time with 48 percent of the popular vote, and the Free Democrats fell to fourth position behind the Alternative List, a left-wing antinuclear and environmentalist group. The Christian Democrats were able to construct a minority government under Governing Mayor Richard von Weizsäcker; the mayor was elected federal president in 1984. *See also* BERLIN BLOCKADE, p. 160; BERLIN WALL, p. 161; FEDERAL REPUBLIC OF GERMANY (FRG), p. 185; OCCUPATION PERIOD, p. 214.

Significance West Berlin holds an anomalous position. In a legal sense, it is at once a self-governing city, an integral part of West Germany, an area occupied by three Western powers, and part of Greater Berlin still under four-power authority. The reality is that West Berlin is an island 100 miles inside East Germany surrounded by a wall. It is highly vulnerable to East German pressures, relies on West German subsidies for its economic viability, and exists by virtue of the East-West stalemate and status quo in Central Europe. In the 1971 Quadripartite Treaty, the Soviet Union agreed that the four powers still have continuing responsibilities in West Berlin. The USSR permits the Federal Republic limited rights to represent the interests of the city in international affairs, but it has objected successfully to the FRG government's conducting important federal business in the city, such as holding the election of the federal president there. The West's view that East Berlin has the same status as West Berlin does not square with reality. In 1981, for example, East Berliners for the first time voted directly for candidates to the East German parliament; the Western powers objected unsuccessfully that the Quadripartite Treaty could not be changed unilaterally. Thus, despite Western claims that there is only one city of Berlin, it is a fact that East Berlin has been absorbed into East Germany and that West Berlin continues to occupy an anomalous position. The Western Allies are not willing that the Federal Republic completely absorb West Berlin for fear of losing any rights they have in all of Berlin. West Berlin is a symbol of freedom and a showplace of free enterprise, but it is also an extreme irritant to East Germany and an unsolved problem. Yet it has survived the darkest days of the Cold War—the Berlin Blockade, the Berlin Crisis of 1958, the Berlin Wall, and numerous economic, social, and political problems. The city is likely to continue to exist as it has so long as the West remains steadfast, the Soviet Union controls East Germany, and peace prevails in Central Europe.

West German Bureaucracy The administrative system in the Federal Republic of Germany. The main features of West German bureaucracy include a hierarchical but decentralized administrative system, an efficient, merit-based civil service, and close links between top civil servants and the political executive. In the West German federal system, most national laws are administered by state officials; for this reason about 85 to 90 percent of all civil service officials work for state or local governments. The civil service is a classified and stratified system, highly regulated by law. German civil servants are known as *Beamte* (sing. *Beamter*) and are organized into three classes: official, clerical, and manual workers. Special training and education, typically a legal education, is required for entrance into the official class; and because of the education requirement, there is little movement between classes. The German civil servant has traditionally been a person who carried high prestige and social status, and the service has a reputation for efficiency and incorruptibility. Civil servants have typically been meticulous, disciplined, and respectful of the law, but also hierarchical, rule-minded, conservative, and elitist. At the top level of the service, linkages with the government are both formal and informal. The subcabinet position of state secretary in the government is held by a career official; some officials become very close advisers to the chancellor or other cabinet ministers. Civil servants may take leaves and run for elective office, returning to their former position whenever they wish. Many elective council positions in local government are held by civil servants. *See also* FEDERALISM: WEST GERMANY, p. 183; *LAND* GOVERNMENT, p. 202.

Significance The reputation of the German civil service for efficiency, integrity, and adherence to law was established in the Empire period and was generally maintained in the Weimar Republic. The Nazi government, however, centralized the service, purged democratic critics, and required a loyalty oath. Many civil servants consequently joined the Nazi party. In the postwar period, the Western Allies at first tried to denazify the civil service completely by eliminating any person who had been a member of the party. This attempt failed because, in their haste to reestablish a working German government, the Allies had to rely on experienced personnel. Although activist Nazis were discharged, most nominal members of the party were rehired or regained their civil service rights. Almost all of these persons are now retired, but the civil service still bears traditional German characteristics. Most officials are recruited from the upper class and upper middle class; one-half of the civil servants come from civil service families. Efficiency still is high although traditional prestige and status has declined somewhat. The bureaucratic system of the Federal Republic remains typically German, but observers note that the government employees have now become loyal servants of the democratic order.

Yalta Conference A meeting during World War II of the leaders of the United States, Great Britain, and the Soviet Union at Yalta in the Soviet Crimea in February 1945 that produced major agreements concerning wartime strategy, postwar arrangements in Europe and Asia, and decisions pertaining to the proposed United Nations organization. The Yalta Conference was attended by the leaders of the Big Three, Franklin D. Roosevelt, Winston S. Churchill, and Josef Stalin; France and China were not represented. Regarding Europe, the conference proclaimed a Declaration on Liberated Europe, whereby the parties reaffirmed the principles of the Atlantic Charter, that is, respect for national sovereignty, self-government, and democracy. They agreed to jointly assist the liberated peoples of Eastern Europe to establish broadly representative interim governments, and to base their future governments on the principle of free elections. The boundaries of Poland were to be established in the east at the former Curzon Line proposal, under which Poland would lose territory to the Soviet Union. Poland was to be compensated by territory in the west and north at the expense of Germany. Regarding Germany, the parties agreed to a strategy of unconditional surrender, the swift punishment of war criminals, the payment of reparations, the demilitarization of Germany, and the denazification of German government and society. France was to be given a zone of occupation of Germany along with those assigned to the Big Three. Other decisions made at Yalta were: the Soviet Union agreed to enter the war against Japan within three months after the European war ended in return for territorial compensations in Asia; the USSR was assigned three seats in the General Assembly of the United Nations; the veto power in the Security Council of the UN was restricted to certain uses; and a UN trusteeship system would replace the mandates system of the League of Nations. *See also* OCCUPATION PERIOD, p. 214; POTSDAM CONFERENCE, p. 221.

Significance Decisions made at the Yalta Conference greatly affected certain features of the postwar world. These include the establishment of a United Nations system with its special membership and veto provisions; the expansion of Soviet territory and influence in the Far East and Europe; the establishment of Communist states in East Europe under Soviet hegemony; the movement of millions of people in Europe; and the partition of Germany. The outbreak of the Cold War and the creation of military alliances in Europe are indirect effects of decisions made at Yalta. Critics of the Yalta agreements argue that, because of concessions made by the United States and Britain, the USSR became a Far Eastern power, even though it did not declare war against Japan until a few days before Japan surrendered, and that the arrangements for creating independent governments in Eastern Europe were so vague that they permitted the USSR to establish satellite Communist regimes there. Defenders of the Western powers reply that the Red Army had already liberated and occupied Eastern Europe, and that the USSR was thus able to violate the spirit of the Declaration on Liberated Europe by imposing its will on the peoples of Eastern Europe. Throughout Eastern Europe, the Soviets were able to bring Communist parties to power by manipulating elections and controlling political decisions. One political device used effectively by the Soviets was that of forcing left-wing and center parties to join a Communist-controlled national front that assumed power. As a result, by 1948, all of the countries of Eastern Europe except Finland—Albania, Czechoslovakia, Hungary, East Germany, Poland, and Romania—had come under Communist rule. Other observers point out that each party went into Yalta with different goals. The United States sought to create a strong United Nations system, to establish a free, noncommunist Poland, to bring the USSR into the war against Japan, and to raise China to great power status. Britain wanted to preserve its empire, establish an independent Poland, and create a zone of occupation for France in Germany. The Soviet Union wanted reparations, control over Poland, a powerless Germany, and Asian possessions. The compromises the parties reached were much affected by the realities of February 1945. The Western Allies were bogged down in fighting in Belgium at the Battle of the Bulge; the Soviet armies had overrun Eastern Europe, controlled Poland, and were in a position to take Berlin; and Japan was far from being defeated. Britain was concerned that the United States would quickly pull out of Europe once the war was ended; and the American goal of creating a strong, universal United Nations system to keep world peace was not yet established. In this view, the Yalta decisions and the postwar arrangements in Europe are the direct consequences of conflicting national interests of the wartime Allies and the power realities of early 1945.

4. Western European Regionalism

Benelux   An acronym formed from the first syllables of Belgium, Netherlands, and Luxembourg that refers to the joint activities of these nations. The term "Benelux" is primarily applied to the customs union of these states that was established in 1948. Officially known as the Benelux Economic Union, the organization's governing body is the Committee of Ministers; there are also a full range of supervisory and advisory councils, a dispute-settling court, and a secretariat. The Benelux Economic Union aims to establish the free movement of labor, capital, goods, and services among member states. It has abolished internal tariffs, greatly reduced trade quotas and other trade restrictions, and eliminated labor permits and passport controls. Benelux is a member of the European Economic Community (EEC), and its members follow Community policies. Toward non-EEC states, Benelux has a common external tariff, trade and immigration regulations. *See also* ECONOMIC INTEGRATION TYPES, p. 249; EUROPEAN ECONOMIC COMMUNITY (EEC), p. 257.

Significance   The origins of Benelux are traced to the customs union that was established between Belgium and Luxembourg in 1922. This union negotiated an agreement with the Netherlands in 1932 for a modified customs union, but little was done because of protectionist pressures in recession years and growing international tensions. A Customs Convention was signed in 1944 by wartime governments-in-exile; it went into effect on January 1, 1948. The Treaty of 1958, which went into effect in 1960, codified these and subsequent agreements, and pushed Benelux beyond a customs union toward an economic union. Common policies regarding labor regulations and social benefits have been adopted, and budgetary, planning, and economic policies of member states are reviewed. In the 1958 treaty, the three states projected an eventual merger of their fiscal and monetary systems, but this and other integration plans were set back by the recession of the early 1980s.

Commission of European Communities The common executive arm of the three organizations of the European Community (EC). The Commission of the European Communities acts as an independent executive and administrative body for the European Coal and Steel Community (ECSC), the European Economic Community (EEC), and the European Atomic Energy Community (Euratom). The Commission consists of 14 members appointed for renewable four-year terms by common agreement of member governments. There are two members each from France, Federal Republic of Germany, Italy, and the United Kingdom, and one each from Belgium, Denmark, Greece, Ireland, Luxembourg, and the Netherlands. Commissioners may not be removed from office by the Council, but the European Parliament can force the Commission as a body to resign by adopting a motion of censure. This has never occurred. The Commission exercises a wide range of executive and administrative powers including (1) initiating policies and defending Community interests and Community rules; (2) implementing the provisions of the basic treaties; (3) preparing decisions and proposals for Council action; (4) administering funds and controlling the borrowing and lending operations of Community; and (5) supervising the management of Community policies. From its headquarters in Brussels, the Commission supervises the "Eurocrats," about 11,300 civil servants in the employ of the EC. Recent presidents of the Commission are Roy Jenkins (United Kingdom), 1977–80; Gaston Thorn (Luxembourg), 1980–84; and Jacques Delors (France), since 1985. *See also* COUNCIL OF MINISTERS OF THE EUROPEAN COMMUNITIES, p. 247; EUROPEAN COMMUNITY (EC), p. 254; EUROPEAN PARLIAMENT, p. 261.

Significance The European Commission acts as an independent group of executive specialists that has promoted the fuller integration of the European Community. When the institutions of the three communities were merged in 1967, the Commission succeeded to the position of the High Authority of the European Coal and Steel Community. Under the Paris Treaty of 1951 that established the ECSC, the executive has more independent authority in its relations with the Council of Ministers than was granted to the Commission in the 1957 Rome Treaties that created the EEC and Euratom. The Council of Ministers assumed more authority in 1958, and this continued when the institutions were merged in 1967. Generally in recent years, heads of government and the Council are making decisions, and the European Parliament has assumed a policy-making role. In these circumstances the Commission tries to promote policies that in its view best advance the interests of the Community as a whole.

Common Agricultural Policy (CAP)   The unified agricultural market and system of agricultural price supports established by the European Economic Community (EEC). The Common Agricultural Policy (CAP) includes (1) a common market with free trade among the ten member states of the EEC for most agricultural products; (2) a common external trade policy with protection from imports; (3) a price support system coupled with subsidies based on production; and (4) a program to increase efficiency, promote modernization, and give help to disadvantaged farmers. The price support system is a very complex arrangement involving "target" prices, or a guaranteed price support level; somewhat lower "intervention" prices, which the Community uses to purchase surpluses to drive up prices; and a system of subsidizing exports to maintain intervention-level prices. The central aim of the CAP is to raise income for farmers by keeping prices artificially high to consumers, thus maintaining a steady rate of production and avoiding the need to import vast quantities of food into the Community. The policy has achieved these aims, but at great cost and much criticism; CAP now consumes over 70 percent of the European Community budget; about 90 percent of CAP costs go to price supports and only 10 percent to agricultural modernization. Critics of CAP charge that it is extremely costly to consumers and taxpayers, encourages inefficiency, and promotes overproduction at subsidized prices. The CAP results in huge surpluses of foodstuffs, which must be "dumped" abroad at cheap rates while European consumers pay high prices. Further, the cost burden is not spread equitably among member states, for Britain is seriously disadvantaged. Defenders of CAP point out that it has reduced the rate of small-farm closings, provided a ready and sufficient quantity of agricultural produce, and increased the income of farmers. It has made the Community self-sufficient in food, reduced food imports, and stabilized prices. *See also* EUROPEAN COMMUNITY (EC), p. 254; FARMERS' ASSOCIATIONS: BRITAIN, p. 26.

Significance   The Common Agricultural Policy is in many respects the only fully developed common policy of the European Economic Community. It is also the most expensive, most controversial, and most liable to hinder further integration of the European Communities. In Britain, which has borne much of the burden of CAP, the Labour party and many consumers have advocated withdrawal from the EEC. On the continent, farmers vigorously protest against any attempt to establish production controls or reduce subsidies or price levels. The European Parliament has become a strong defender of CAP against any attempts of the Council of Ministers or heads of government to make changes or give Britain Budgetary relief. In the meantime, overproduction has produced costly surpluses, which are dubbed the "mountain of butter," "mountain of meat," the "milk lake," and the "wine lake." Yet CAP has achieved many of its original aims, to ensure an adequate supply of foodstuffs, to compensate farmers, and to eliminate the fluctuations in supplies and prices caused by nature or world market conditions. The next decade will test the EEC on how well it can cure the side effects caused by the CAP.

Council of Europe   A regional organization of 21 member states established in 1949 to promote economic, social, and political cooperation and unity among the European democracies. The Council of Europe—not to be confused with the European Council, the summit meeting of the ten European Community states—has the largest membership of all Western European organizations, including all European democratic states. Its purpose is to promote greater unity among members, safeguard democratic ideals, and facilitate economic and social progress. The organization is excluded from considering matters of national defense. It functions primarily by making recommendations to member states and by approving conventions (treaties) that are submitted to members for ratification. The Statute of the Council of Europe provides for two major institutions: (1) the Consultative Assembly, which has deliberative and recommending power, consists of 170 deputies chosen by national parliaments; and (2) the Committee of Ministers, composed of the foreign ministers of member states, has the power to make decisions. In addition there are a number of committees of experts and a secretariat at Strasbourg. *See also* EUROPEAN COUNCIL, p. 256; EUROPEAN COURT OF HUMAN RIGHTS, p. 256.

Significance   The Council of Europe was proposed at the Congress of Europe of 1948 to help Europe maintain its democratic heritage and move to unity. Membership includes the major European powers in the North Atlantic Treaty Organization, neutral states, and small entities like Malta, Cyprus, and Liechtenstein. The Council has proposed about 80 conventions on a wide variety of matters dealing with such things as human rights, commerce, public health, education, and social security. The Council proposed the European Convention on Human Rights in 1950, which established machinery to investigate alleged violations of human rights. Many of the conventions have been ratified, and in this fashion the Council promotes cooperation and advances democracy in the region. The original ideal of some of its founders, however, that the organization would move to a united, federal Europe, is nowhere in sight.

Council of Ministers of the European Communities The body that represents governments of member states in the merged institutional framework of the European Community (EC). The European Council of Ministers exercises its powers in the European Coal and Steel Community (ECSC), the European Economic Community (EEC), and the European Atomic Energy Community (Euratom). It consists of representatives of national governments, normally the foreign ministers, but other ministers often attend meetings, depending on the topic under review. The Council's main duty is to approve proposals presented to the Council by the Commission, the executive arm of the EC. The Council and the Commission work together closely in a "dialogue" between representatives of governments expressing the views of member states, and the Commission, which represents the Community as a whole. The Council has the authority to issue (1) *regulations,* which are binding and applicable to all member states; (2) *directives,* which allow affected states to choose means to achieve a mandatory objective; and (3) *decisions,* which obligate the parties concerned, either governments, enterprises, or individuals. *Recommendations* and *opinions* of the Council are not binding. The terminology of similar orders issued for the European Coal and Steel Community is different. In the typical year of 1980, the Council of Ministers adopted about 300 regulations, 50 directives, and 130 decisions. Voting procedures in the Council of Ministers vary with the issue. Important decisions require a unanimous vote, but others may be taken by an extraordinary majority, or by a simple majority. In light of its infrequent meetings, the Council established a Committee of Permanent Representatives (COREPER) of senior officials to represent government interests in its relations with the Commission. *See also* COMMISSION OF EUROPEAN COMMUNITIES, p. 244; EUROPEAN COMMUNITY (EC), p. 254; EUROPEAN PARLIAMENT, p. 261.

Significance The role of the Council of Ministers within the decision-making framework of the EC increased when the major institutions of the three communities were merged in 1967. Under the Paris Treaty that established the ECSC, states had created a supranational institution that would function primarily by qualified majority vote; the rule of unanimity was required only for a "manifest crisis" or to adopt a treaty provision. When the EEC was established in 1958, a unanimous vote requirement became normal practice in the EEC. In 1967, when the institutions of the three communities were merged, the unanimous rule, now commonplace, was continued in an atmosphere of crisis over voting procedures. By the mid-1970s, however, the member states permitted more decisions to be made by qualified majority vote. At the same time, the heads of government began meeting as the European Council thrice yearly with the foreign ministers of the Council of Ministers. It is at the meetings of the European Council that most important decisions are made on major budget questions, community membership, and future direction of the Community. The heads of government, acting by unanimous rule in the European Council, establish guidelines that are followed by their representatives in the Council of Ministers. In this fashion, member governments have retained a large measure of control over the policies and direction of the Community.

Court of Justice The supreme judicial authority of the European Communities (EC). The Court of Justice is common to all three EC organizations, superseding the Court of Justice of the European Coal and Steel Community. It is not to be confused with the European Court of Human Rights, which hears cases concerning the European Convention on Human Rights. The Court of Justice consists of 11 judges, who are appointed by common agreement of the governments of member states; judges have a renewable term of six years; although there is no nationality requirement, currently there is one judge from each member state. The judges are assisted by five advocates-general, who present cases to the Court in an impartial and independent manner. The Court has the authority to interpret and apply Community law, which includes three basic treaties and the regulations and directives issued by the Commission and the Council of Ministers. The three basic treaties that established the European Communities are the Treaty of Paris of 1951 for the European Coal and Steel Community (ECSC) and the two Treaties of Rome of 1957 for the European Economic Community (EEC) and European Atomic Energy Community (Euratom). The Court also has limited jurisdiction regarding national law; it rules on cases involving the failure of a member state to fulfill an obligation and on the conformity of national law to Community law. Since national courts also apply Community law, the Court of Justice also hears requests from national courts for preliminary rulings on the interpretation of Community law, and on the validity of actions of the Council of Ministers or the Commission. *See also* EUROPEAN COMMUNITY (EC), p. 254; EUROPEAN COURT OF HUMAN RIGHTS, p. 256.

Significance Since 1952 the Court of Justice of the European Communities has considered almost 2,000 cases, excluding administrative actions concerning staff regulations. The great bulk of these cases relates to the application of the EEC treaty. This reflects the basic economic purpose of the Court; thus its major contributions have been in the field of business law. The Court has also developed case law in the areas of social welfare and agriculture. An increasing number of cases involve requests for preliminary rulings from national courts; this results from the growing and complex interrelationships between Community law and national law. In the 30-year history of the Court, two fundamental principles have been established in Community law: (1) the direct applicability of Community law to individuals within member states, and (2) the supremacy of Community law over national law. The Court's enforcement of these two principles and the impressive body of case law it has developed have had a major impact in making the Community a legal union as well as an economic one.

Economic Integration Types Forms and levels of economic collaboration between independent states. Economic integration is usually classified according to types of organizations whose members are increasingly interdependent. In a *free trade area*, tariffs and other trade restrictions are eliminated on most of the trade that passes between member states. There is no agreement among the members concerning third-party countries and no common external tariff. Nonmembers may avoid the high barriers of a member state by passing their exports first through a low-barrier member state. This possibility can be prevented by the high-barrier member state's imposing differential tariffs and requiring certificates of origin, but this increases administrative costs. A *customs union* abolishes trade barriers between member states and adopts a common trade policy and common external tariff to nonmember states. This is often called a *common market* or *tariff union*. This form of economic integration handles the problem of trade with nonmember states, but avoids decisions on other factors of production clearly related to trade. An *economic community* is a common market with an external tariff that allows for the free movement of capital and labor between member states as well as goods. An *economic union* is formed when member states of an economic community jointly coordinate their monetary policy (value of the currency), fiscal policy (taxation), economic policy (levels of private and public enterprise), and social policy (social security benefits). When economic union is fully achieved, central institutions will have adopted common policies in financial, economic, and social matters and harmonized the laws and regulations of member states. Beyond this level of integration, a *political union*, most likely a federation, will integrate all aspects of the economy into a single economic system. At the other extreme of economic cooperation and economic integration are states that pursue a policy of *autarky*, relying solely on national resources and avoiding international economic interdependence as much as possible. *See also* BENELUX, p. 243; EUROPEAN COMMUNITY (EC), p. 254; EUROPEAN FREE TRADE ASSOCIATION (EFTA), p. 259.

Significance Economic cooperation and integration in Europe has proceeded through various levels but has stopped short of an economic union. The European Free Trade Association (EFTA) is an illustration of a free trade area that has eliminated barriers regarding industrial products, but not on agricultural commodities. An older example of a simple customs union or tariff union is the Prussian *Zollverein* of 1833. Belgium, Netherlands, and Luxembourg established a customs union in 1948, known as Benelux. The European Economic Community (EEC) began as a customs union and is still popularly referred to as the European Common Market, even though it has progressed to the level of an economic community. The European Community has adopted a number of common policies, for example, in tariffs, transport, agriculture, the environment, and the movement of workers, but progress toward a full economic union was halted when the region was struck by chronic economic recession after the mid-1970s.

Eurocommunism The doctrine that the Communist parties of Western Europe have renounced the Leninist revolutionary road to power in favor of a democratic constitutionalist approach. In the fullest application of the doctrine of Eurocommunism, the Communist parties of Western Europe would (1) choose a "national road to socialism," rather than follow the Soviet model; (2) break away from the control of the Communist Party of the Soviet Union; (3) renounce the Marxist doctrine of dictatorship of the proletariat, which would eliminate liberal democracy after the party seizes power; (4) renounce the Leninist violent revolutionary approach as a means to gain power; (5) accept democratic elections and work within a pluralist political party system; (6) retain democratic liberties, free elections, and majority rule once in power; and (7) make common cause with Western European Communist parties, rather than with the Eastern European bloc, because of the commonality of Western interests. The ideas of Eurocommunism are not accepted or applied uniformly or consistently by the Communist parties of Western Europe. The movement is strongest in the Spanish Communist party (PCE) and the Italian Communist party (PCI); the French Communist party (PCF) has proclaimed Eurocommunist ideas, but its adherence is less credible. *See also* FRENCH COMMUNIST PARTY (PCF), p. 111; POLYCENTRISM, p. 270.

Significance Eurocommunism was strongly promoted by Santiago Carrillo, the head of the Spanish party in the 1970s. The doctrine built on previous ideas advocated by Palmiro Togliatti of the Italian party and Josip Broz Tito of Yugoslavia that stressed the necessity for separate paths to socialism. Togliatti also publicized the notion of "polycentrism," which denied a guiding role to the Soviet Union and recognized the plurality of Communist centers of power and influence. The Italian party, the largest Communist party in the West with over 30 percent of the popular vote, continues to promote an "historic compromise" with the slightly larger Christian Democratic party, whereby the two parties would coalesce to rule Italy jointly. In France, the PCF's sporadic espousal of Eurocommunism makes it less credible than that of the Spanish and Italian parties. Even though the PCF participated in the Socialist government of President François Mitterrand in 1981–84 and accepted France's participation in the Atlantic alliance, its motives are still suspected by many French citizens. Eurocommunism was strongly opposed by the Soviet Communist party. Concerned that these ideas would spread to the East European parties and fearful of losing influence among Western parties, Russians used world Communist party meetings in Moscow in the early 1960s to condemn Eurocommunism. Since the 1970s most Communist parties in Western Europe reject the interference of the CPSU in their affairs, and many have condemned Soviet intervention in Hungary in 1956, Czechoslovakia in 1968, and Afghanistan in 1979. But no party has broken completely with Moscow, renounced membership in the world Communist movement, or abandoned the principle of "democratic centralism," which is applied as strict party discipline for internal party decision making. Unless Communist parties take over Western governments, there seems to be no practical method to resolve the continuing debate over the credibility of Eurocommunist claims. If Eurocommunism is indeed a permanent phenomenon, it represents a fundamental change in the nature of Western Communism, making it similar to democratic Marxist socialism. The domestic politics and international linkages of Western European states, however, preclude the possibility that Communist parties will be able to dominate their national political systems and put Eurocommunist ideas fully into practice.

Euromissile Controversy The major foreign policy issue over whether American-built intermediate-range nuclear missiles should be deployed in Western Europe to counter the threat from Soviet intermediate-range missiles targeted on Western Europe. The Euromissile controversy erupted throughout Europe following a unanimous 1979 decision of the North Atlantic Treaty Organization to deploy 572 Pershing II and ground-launched cruise missiles in West Germany, Britain, Italy, Belgium, and the Netherlands. The NATO plan, originally prompted by Western European governments, was intended to provide a balance against an increasing force of over 600 Soviet intermediate-range missiles (SS-20s, SS-4s, and SS-5s). The deployment of the NATO missiles was to take place beginning in December 1983 if the American and Soviet governments were not able to negotiate any reductions in the number of intermediate-range missiles in Europe. In the context of a growing antinuclear peace movement and second thoughts by some Western governments, the American-Soviet negotiations on intermediate nuclear forces in Geneva produced a number of proposals and counterproposals but no agreement by December 1983. Consequently, NATO missiles were deployed in 1984, and the Soviet Union responded by breaking off most arms control negotiations and by deploying intermediate missiles in East Germany and Czechoslovakia. *See also* CAMPAIGN FOR NUCLEAR DISARMAMENT (CND), p. 7; INTERMEDIATE NUCLEAR FORCES TALKS, p. 265.

Significance The East-West confrontation sparked by the Euromissile controversy was reminiscent of the darker days of the Cold War period. Large-scale public involvement in the foreign policy issue threatened to bring down a number of Western European governments. Massive antinuclear demonstrations and rallies, a growing "peace movement," and major opposition registered in public opinion polls, particularly in Britain, the Netherlands, and West Germany, forced these and other governments to reconsider the original NATO plan and pressure the United States away from its hard-line position in the Geneva negotiations. A number of local governments declared their areas to be "nuclear-free zones" and refused to accept deployment of nuclear missiles. By playing on popular fears in Western and Eastern Europe that the region would become a wasteland in a nuclear war, the Soviet Union exploited this opportunity to drive a wedge within the Western alliance and to rally support among the peoples of Eastern Europe and Russia for its position. The Euromissile controversy exposed several primary weaknesses of the Western alliance: the preponderant position of the United States within the alliance, the conflicting national interests of member states, and the differing domestic political exigencies that face member governments.

European Atomic Energy Community (Euratom) A European Community organization that is concerned with developing the peaceful use of nuclear energy in Europe. The European Atomic Energy Community (Euratom) was established by the Treaty of Rome of 1957; at the same time the European Economic Community (EEC) was established under a separate treaty. Euratom's membership of ten states is the same as that of the other two European communities, the EEC and the European Coal and Steel Community (ECSC). In July 1984 the members were Belgium, Denmark, France, Germany (West), Greece, Ireland, Italy, Luxembourg, the Netherlands, and the United Kingdom. Portugal and Spain were expected to be admitted in late 1984 or 1985. In 1967 the institutions of Euratom were merged with the other two communities into the common institutional framework of the European Community (EC). On nuclear energy matters, the EC Commission receives advice from the Economic and Social Committee and the Scientific and Technical Committee. Euratom is charged with creating a common market in nuclear materials, products, investment capital, and technical specialists; coordinating peaceful nuclear research and pooling information; establishing safety standards; and promoting the building of nuclear power stations. *See also* EUROPEAN COMMUNITY (EC), p. 254.

Significance The European Atomic Energy Community has achieved some of its purposes, but it has not been as successful as the European Economic Community. Euratom has built and operates four nuclear research centers, created a common market in the civil nuclear industry, and helped the building of nuclear power plants. The organization was established before its members were aware that a serious international energy crisis would develop in the mid-1970s, but when oil shortages and price increases burst on the scene, the typical reaction of EC members was to rely on national solutions. Although Euratom-promoted cooperation in the civil nuclear energy industry has been useful, the EC did not develop a comprehensive energy policy. In the late 1970s, the nuclear energy industry also came under attack from environmentalists. The full potential of Euratom will be realized only if the EC develops and vigorously pursues a comprehensive energy policy.

European Coal and Steel Community (ECSC) The first European Community established in 1952 to create a common market in the coal and steel industries in Western Europe. The European Coal and Steel Community (ECSC), also known as the Schuman Plan after French Foreign Minister Robert Schuman, who proposed the idea in 1950, had six original members, Belgium, France, Federal Republic of Germany, Italy, Luxembourg, and the Netherlands. Since 1958 the ECSC has had the same membership as other European Community (EC) organizations; in early 1984 this included the original six members and Denmark, Greece, Ireland, and the United Kingdom. The Treaty of Paris of 1951 defined the purposes of the ECSC to take common actions to expand the coal and steel industries, harmonize production and trade policies, and improve the standard of living of the labor force. A common market would be created by eliminating customs duties, quotas, and price and trade restrictions on coal, steel, iron ore, and scrap metal. The organization was also authorized to adopt policies regarding labor, research, and industrial development. The institutional structures of the ECSC included a Council of Ministers (representing governments), the High Authority (the executive arm), the Assembly, and the Court of Justice. These institutions were merged with those of the European Economic Community (EEC) and the European Atomic Energy Community (Euratom) in 1967. The detailed plan for ECSC was drafted by Jean Monnet, the first president of the High Authority (1952–55), who is considered to be the founder of the European Community. *See also* COMMISSION OF EUROPEAN COMMUNITIES, p. 244; COUNCIL OF MINISTERS OF THE EUROPEAN COMMUNITIES, p. 247; EUROPEAN COMMUNITY (EC), p. 254.

Significance The European Coal and Steel Community was the first major instance of successful sector integration in Europe. Originally, under terms of the Paris Treaty, the ECSC acted as a true supranational organization in which state sovereignty and the single-state veto were superseded by qualified majority vote. The ECSC was very successful in its aims: it established a common market in the coal and steel industry by 1953, helped raise production, promoted capital investment, and established rules for competition. The organization also adopted a novel social policy by helping retrain 400,000 miners who were displaced by production cutbacks. An essential purpose of the founders of ECSC was to end traditional Franco-German rivalry and fears; it was hoped that by integrating their economies the unity of Europe would become a reality. The ECSC achieved the first of these goals and its success in sector integration provided the basis for the adoption of the wider common market of the EEC. The supranational institutions of the ECSC, however, have been pretty much replaced by the intergovernmental emphasis of the common institutions of the European Community. Also, in the 1980s when economic recession struck Europe, the ECSC moved to production controls and quotas, which are designed to protect particular national enterprises at the expense of the free market. In 1984 attempts to remove quotas to revitalize the steel industry were stopped by governments that insisted on deciding the issue by unanimous vote.

European Community (EC) The collective name for the European Coal and Steel Community (ECSC), the European Economic Community (EEC), and the European Atomic Energy Community (Euratom). Sometimes refereed to as the European Communities, the EC includes the original members, Belgium, France, Federal Republic of Germany, Italy, Luxembourg, and the Netherlands (the "Six"); Denmark, Ireland, and the United Kingdom, which joined in 1973 (the

"Nine"); and Greece, which joined in 1981 (the "Ten"). In 1967, the institutions of the various governing bodies of the three organizations were merged into single executive, administrative, parliamentary, and judicial bodies. The major institutions of the EC are (1) the Council of Ministers, 10 representatives of member governments that make broad policy; (2) the Commission, 14 expert executives who manage EC affairs; (3) the European Parliament, 434 deputies directly elected by the people; (4) the Court of Justice, 11 judges who settle disputes and interpret the treaties; and (5) the Court of Auditors, 10 members who supervise audits and financial investigations. Of the many EC committees, two stand out as most important. The Economic and Social Committee is an advisory body composed of representatives of employers, trade unions, and other special interests, such as consumers, the professions, and agriculture. This body must be consulted by the Commission before it makes decisions pertaining to matters of concern to the EEC and Euratom. On coal and steel matters, the Commission must consult the Consultative Committee, which is composed of representatives of labor, producers, dealers, and consumers. *See also* COMMISSION OF EUROPEAN COMMUNITIES, p. 244; COUNCIL OF MINISTERS OF THE EUROPEAN COMMUNITIES, p. 247; COURT OF JUSTICE, p. 248; EUROPEAN ATOMIC ENERGY COMMUNITY (EURATOM), p. 252; EUROPEAN COAL AND STEEL COMMUNITY (ECSC), p. 253; EUROPEAN COUNCIL, p. 256; EUROPEAN ECONOMIC COMMUNITY (EEC), p. 257.

Significance The European Community functions under the Paris Treaty, which established the ECSC, the Rome Treaties, which established the EEC and Euratom, and the 1967 agreement, which merged the central institutions. Proposals that a single treaty codify the current arrangements have not been successful. The achievements of the European Community are collectively those of its separate constituent bodies. In addition the EC represents a major step toward a full economic union that goes far beyond the sector integration of the ECSC or the early customs union approach of the EEC. By merging the decision-making organs of the three organizations, the EC accelerated European integration to the highest level yet achieved among major states in the modern world. Yet, although majority votes can carry many questions, the large states have in effect exercised single-nation veto power on important questions. It is expected the EC will be enlarged in the near future with admission of Spain and Portugal. Increased membership, as in the case of Ireland, Denmark, Britain, and Greece, extended the customs union idea to a wider area, but it places limits on movement toward fuller economic union. Large membership effectively prevents any real possibility of political union. The community of Europe is an ideal that is supported by many Europeans. A common political culture is evolving, which is promoted by free movement of people, and common institutions, and the creation of vested interests. But expectations that a political federation of the United States of Europe will be created from the Six, the Ten, or the Twelve in the foreseeable future are very unrealistic.

European Council The summit meeting of the heads of government of member states of the European Community (EC). The European Council—not to be confused with the Council of Europe, an organization of all the European democracies—was formalized in 1974 to meet three times a year. Although the European Council may meet as the Council of Ministers of the European Community, it tends rather to be concerned with broader political matters. Topics for the summit meeting range from routine matters to major questions such as the expansion of the community, budgetary questions, economic and social policies, and political relations with other states. *See also* COUNCIL OF EUROPE, p. 246; EUROPEAN COMMUNITY (EC), p. 254.

Significance Meetings of the European Council have been very important, for it is here that decisions are made that affect the functioning and future development of the EC. Generally, the heads of government establish guidelines that are then followed in subsequent meetings of the Council of Ministers. The rule of unanimity prevails, and in this respect the EC functions as an intergovernmental association whose members have retained national sovereignty, rather than as a supranational organization operating by qualified majority rule. Illustrations of important decisions made at European Council meetings include approval for direct elections of the European Parliament, the creation of the European Monetary System, members' contributions to the EC budget, and declarations on political developments in other areas of the world, such as Afghanistan, Lebanon, Poland, and the Middle East. Disappointed in the poor turnout in the European Parliament elections of June 1984, the European Council took a number of decisions in late June 1984 to revitalize the EC and promote greater unity. These decisions included agreeing to a plan to resolve the five-year-old problem of Britain's contribution to the EC budget, setting final guidelines for the admission of Portugal and Spain, simplifying customs procedures, promoting increased technological cooperation, adopting a European passport, and initiating plans for a European flag, anthem, and currency.

European Court of Human Rights A judicial body established in 1959 to decide cases arising out of the European Human Rights Convention. The European Court of Human Rights—not to be confused with the Court of Justice of the European Community—is the final court of appeal for those parties who have exhausted other remedies under the European Convention for the Protection of Human Rights and Fundamental Freedoms of 1950. The Convention defined a wide range of political, civil, economic, and social rights and established mechanisms for states or individuals to file cases. The Convention was drafted under the auspices of the Council of Europe, but only 15 of the 21 Council members have accepted the treaty, and only 12 states have recognized the compulsory jurisdiction of the Court. Alleged violations of the Convention are first examined by a Commission on Human Rights; the Commission makes recommendations concerning admissible cases to the Committee of Ministers of the Council of Europe. Some cases may then go to the Court, which is the final appeal for persons whose states have accepted its jurisdiction. The Court makes judgments, but its decisions are not enforceable, for they depend on the voluntary compliance of affected states. *See also* COUNCIL OF EUROPE, p. 246; COURT OF JUSTICE, p. 248.

Significance The Convention and the European Court of Human Rights were established by the Council of Europe to provide mechanisms for states and citizens to take appeals beyond national courts. Several thousand petitions have been filed before the commission, involving all types of cases, including alleged violations of traditional civil liberties as well as economic and social rights. Only a few cases have reached the Court, however, because the Commission has found most to be without merit or they do not involve states that have accepted the Court's mandatory jurisdiction. The Court's impact lies primarily in the negative publicity its decisions bring to governments charged with violating the Convention.

European Economic Community (EEC) The central organization of the European Community established in 1958 to create a common market and economic union among member states. The European Economic Community (EEC), also called the Common Market, was established by the Treaty of Rome of 1957 to provide for the free movement of goods, services, labor, and capital among its members; to establish a common external tariff; and to adopt common economic, social, and political policies for the Community. Members of the EEC include the original six states of the European Coal and Steel Community (Belgium, France, Federal Republic of Germany, Italy, Luxembourg, and the Netherlands), and Denmark, Ireland, and the United Kingdom (since 1973) and Greece (since 1981). Portugal and Spain were expected to be admitted to the Community in late 1984 or 1985. The EEC has three associate members, Cyprus, Malta, and Turkey; and 63 affiliated states under the Lomé Convention—the African, Caribbean, and Pacific countries (ACP). The main institutions of the EEC are those common to the three European Communities: the Council of Ministers, the Commission of the European Communities, the European Parliament, and the Court of Justice. Principal activities of the EEC have been directed toward creating a large, unified market and increasing the productive capacity of member states. To this end, the EEC has adopted a Common Customs Tariff (CCT) toward external states, promoted the use of the value-added tax (VAT), eliminated internal trade barriers, and required the free movement of workers and capital. Much of the Community's attention and resources have been devoted to the establishment of a Common Agricultural Policy (CAP), a complex mechanism of price supports and marketing arrangements. Although the CAP constitutes the EEC's principal common policy, other measures include the industrial policy, which tries to limit monopolistic practices that stifle competition, and which regulates state assistance to enterprises; and the energy policy and the research policy, which have had little success. Another principal area of activity concerns attempts to harmonize economic policies of member states and establish an economic and monetary union. Achievements here have been limited, the principal institution being the European Monetary System (EMS), with its mechanisms to control fluctuations in the exchange rates of members' currencies. EEC has adopted a social policy to help improve working conditions, pay standards, social security benefits, and living conditions of workers. The Social Fund is used to retrain and redeploy workers and help reduce unemployment in less-developed areas. The regional policy, assisted by the Regional Development Fund, attempts to remove economic disparities by supplementing national aid to regions that have been identified as less developed. In its external relations, the EEC has adopted a common trade policy and participates in the General Agreement on Tariffs and Trade (GATT) to reduce global trade restrictions. Customs barriers between EEC and the European Free Trade Association (EFTA) have been abolished, and trade, financial, and development assistance agreements have been made with the African, Caribbean, and Pacific states. Important aspects of its relations with ACP states include providing aid through the European Development Fund (EDF) and helping prevent wide fluctuations in ACP agricultural export earnings by a transfer mechanism called the Stabex. The Treaty of Rome also established the European Investment Bank (EIB), a nonprofit development bank. The EIB makes development loans for projects in Community and associated states, for industrial modernization and conversion projects in the Community, and for joint industrial projects of member states. *See also* COMMON AGRICULTURAL POLICY (CAP), p. 245; EUROPEAN

COMMUNITY (EC), p. 254; EUROPEAN MONETARY SYSTEM (EMS), p. 260; VALUE-ADDED TAX (VAT), p. 271.

Significance   The European Economic Community is the most far-reaching and important instance of economic integration among independent states in recent history. The EEC serves a population of 270 million people and accounts for 20 percent of world exports, making it the world's leading trader. In light of the history of European rivalry, the EEC has shown remarkable success in eliminating trade barriers, adopting common policies, and going beyond the requirements of a common market. The Community also has at times adopted common foreign policies. The EEC, however, has not yet established an economic union, and has made only modest progress in establishing common economic, fiscal, and monetary policies. The rapid progress of its first ten years was slowed dramatically when fuel shortages, oil price rises, high inflation, and economic stagnation destabilized the economies of member states in the 1970s and 1980s. The recent period has been marked by demands by some states for emergency relief through protectionist policies; an increasing competition for influence between governments and parliamentarians within the political institutions of the Community; and lack of agreement on how to solve the high costs and overproduction created by the Common Agricultural Policy. Yet the EEC, as the backbone of the European Community, is not likely to fall apart, for the eonomic benefits it has made possible in the last 25 years far outweigh the disadvantages to particular regions or sectors.

European Free Trade Association (EFTA)   A regional organization of six states originally established to reduce trade barriers among its members, to promote a customs union in Europe, and to increase world trade. The members of the European Free Trade Association (EFTA) are Austria, Iceland (since 1970), Norway, Portugal, Sweden, and Switzerland; Finland is an associate member (since 1961). The EFTA was created by the Stockholm Convention of 1959 under the initiative of Britain as a response to the establishment of the European Economic Community (EEC). Original members also included Britain and Denmark, and EFTA was therefore dubbed the "Outer Seven," in contrast to the "Inner Six" of the EEC. Britain and Denmark withdrew in 1973 to join the EEC; Iceland joined the EFTA in 1970. The EFTA has a simple organizational structure consisting of a Council of Ministers, six standing committees, and a small secretariat in Geneva, Switzerland. *See also* ECONOMIC INTEGRATION TYPES, p. 249; EUROPEAN COMMUNITY (EC), p. 254.

Significance By the end of 1966 the European Free Trade Association achieved its goal of eliminating tariffs and quotas on industrial goods among its members. Trade within EFTA more than doubled with the first ten years. As a free trade area, not a customs union, the EFTA does not have a common external tariff. To control the problem of imports from nonmembers entering high-tariff member states through low-tariff members, the organization required certificates of origin. After Britain and Denmark joined the EEC, the European Community and EFTA eliminated tariffs between members of the two organizations. Thus a free trade area exists among the 16 states of EFTA and EEC. Britain decided to forego membership in EFTA and join EEC because the Outer Seven market was too small and the pattern of trade with the Commonwealth was changing as Commonwealth states began exporting more manufactured goods. In the early 1980s Spain began a series of tariff reductions with EFTA in anticipation of its joining the European Community (EC). With the accession of Portugal to the EC, the EFTA will be reduced to five states (Austria, Iceland, Norway, Sweden, Switzerland) and the associate member, Finland. The free trade agreements EFTA has established with the EEC, however, give it access to the largest market in Europe.

European Monetary System (EMS) Mechanisms established by the European Council in 1979 to create monetary stability within the European Community. The European Monetary System (EMS) has three basic purposes. First, it helps states maintain their currencies within certain limits of fluctuation by establishing funds from which they can borrow to intervene on the money exchanges. The limits of fluctuation of exchange rates are plus or minus 2.5 percent for all currencies except the Italian lira, which is 6 percent. Second, it provides for a means of settlement and adjustment by defining currencies according to a central accounting unit, called the European Currency Unit (ECU). Third, it assists states with "less prosperous" economies by making low-interest loans for financing investment projects; the economies of Italy and Ireland have been defined as less prosperous. The EMS includes only eight of the ten European Community states, for Britain and Greece have chosen not to join. The European Currency Unit is a central feature of the EMS and is used as a standard unit of accounting for bookkeeping and budgetary purposes. The value of the ECU is the sum of fixed amounts of currencies of nine EC states (excluding Greece). The value of the ECU in other currencies is calculated daily by the market exchange rates of the various currencies. *See also* EUROPEAN COMMUNITY (EC), p. 254; EUROPEAN COUNCIL, p. 256.

Significance The European Monetary System is not a monetary union, but a combination of mechanisms to maintain stability in the exchange rates of currencies of EC states. This is done mainly by controlling fluctuations through EMS-assisted interventions in the exchange market. A true monetary union would require a central supranational body with power to control all aspects of economic, fiscal, and monetary policy, and a central bank and single currency. A monetary union would imply a large measure of political unification. These ideas were rejected by EC members in the mid-1970s when the region was hit by economic recession and inflation. The EMS that was created by the heads of government in 1979 was a more limited plan to control exchange rate fluctuations. Some observers see it as a first step toward greater integration, and the ECU as an eventual European currency. Other observers, especially noting the nonparticipation of Britain and Greece, view it as another useful exchange rate mechanism and the ECU merely as a convenient accounting device. Recent uses of the ECU by the private sector, however, show that it is no longer a mere accounting device. By 1983, the ECU was the third most frequently used currency (after the dollar and the German mark) in the European financial markets.

European Parliament The popularly elected assembly of the three organizations of the European Community. The European Parliament acts as a consultative and decision-making body for the European Coal and Steel Community (ECSC), the European Economic Community (EEC), and the European Atomic Energy Community (Euratom). Originally called the Assembly in the treaties, the European Parliament is a single body composed of 434 members distributed among the Community states as follows: France, the Federal Republic of Germany, Italy, and the United Kingdom have 81 each; the Netherlands, 25; Belgium and Greece, 24 each; Denmark, 16; Ireland, 15; and Luxembourg, 6. Since 1979 members of the European Parliament are elected directly by the people in separate national elections. Members affiliate in Parliament in multinational political groups, such as Socialist and Christian Democrat, rather than in country blocs. Parliament has the authority to debate policy, to request information from the Commission in oral or written questions, to express its opinion on proposals for Community legislation, and to adopt resolutions on policy matters. It has the power to censure the Commission by two-thirds of at least a majority of its members; in this case the entire Commission must resign. The budgetary authority of the Parliament was increased by treaties in 1970 and 1975 from consultative to decision-making powers. The budget is adopted jointly with the Council of Ministers, but Parliament has the right to control all noncompulsory expenditures (i.e., not required by law, about 23 percent of the total), and it may reject the entire budget. Since direct elections, the presidents of the Parliament have been Simone Veil of France, 1979–82, and Pieter Dankert of the Netherlands. The European Parliament meets at its headquarters in Strasbourg, France, or in Luxembourg, while some of its committees meet in Brussels. *See also* COMMISSION OF EUROPEAN COMMUNITIES, p. 244; COUNCIL OF MINISTERS OF THE EUROPEAN COMMUNITIES, p. 247; EUROPEAN COMMUNITY (EC), p. 254; EUROPEAN PARLIAMENT: 1984 ELECTIONS, p. 262.

Significance The role the European Parliament plays within the European Community has increased substantially since the late 1970s. This can be attributed mainly to (1) the direct election of its members, which has increased their prestige and independence; (2) the increase in its budgetary powers; and (3) the independent financial resources the Community has acquired. Prior to 1979 the EC relied on contributions from its member states. Since 1979 the Community is financed by its own resources, mainly customs duties from nonmember states, agricultural levies on imports, and up to 1 percent of the value-added tax revenues of member states. The European Parliament has been aggressively exercising its budgetary powers. In 1980 it rejected a draft budget by an overwhelming vote; and in July 1984 after new elections, it voted to block payment on a $600 million budget rebate the European Council (heads of governments) agreed to grant Britain. The exercise of this independence against the Council of Ministers can be attributed to the facts that voter turnout is lower in Community elections; that most members are not national parliamentarians; and that different political combinations are possible in the Parliament.

European Parliament: 1984 Elections Separate direct elections in the states of the European Community in June 1984 to choose members of its common assembly. The 1984 elections to the European Parliament were conducted separately in the ten EC countries according to their respective electoral systems; this was mainly some form of proportional representation, although Britain used its single-member district plurality system. Over 4,600 candidates competed throughout the Community for the 464 seats in the Parliament, which are apportioned to the states roughly according to their population size. Voter participation was generally low by European standards and disappointing to supporters of the EC. Averaging about 60 percent of the electorate, 2 points lower than in 1979, the turnout ranged from a high of 89 percent in Belgium to 32 percent in Britain. In EC elections candidates run under separate party labels in their countries, but elected Members of the European Parliament (MEP) then organize themselves in multinational political groups. The main groupings after the 1984 elections (compared with 1982 figures, which include Greece, given in parentheses) are: Socialists 132 (124); European Peoples' party (Christian Democrats) 109 (117); European Democrats (Conservatives) 50 (63); Communists and allies 42 (48); Liberals 32 (38); European Progressive Democrats (Gaullists and allies) 29 (22); extreme right 16 (5); Ecologists 11, and others 13. *See also* EUROPEAN COMMUNITY (EC), p. 254; EUROPEAN PARLIAMENT, p. 261.

Significance The 1984 elections to the European Parliament were generally analyzed as an unofficial negative referendum on the national governments in office and a popular show of dissatisfaction in the work of the European Community. In most instances, the parties in power lost support compared to previous national elections, and opposition and newer groups improved. In Britain, a very low turnout of 32 percent reflected the public disappointment in the EC; the Labour party improved its percentage over 1983 national elections, but the Liberal-Social Democratic Alliance won no seats despite receiving 20 percent of the vote. In France, the Socialist party lost support, and Communist party support fell to a low of 11 percent; a newer group, the right-wing, anti-immigrationist National Front won 11 percent of the vote and was elected for the first time. In West Germany, the Christian Democrats lost some support, and its coalition partner, Free Democrats, failed to win a seat; the ecologist Greens party was the only group to improve its position. In Italy the Communists for the first time were returned as the leading party, edging out the Christian Democrats; observers believed this increase was in part a sympathy vote because the party leader, Enrico Berlinguer, died shortly before the election. Most observers conclude that the voters, knowing the limited authority of the European Parliament, used the occasion to express dissatisfaction with the parties in power without having to turn them out of office. Given the low voter turnout, however, the results are not a necessary indication of future national returns. Only 20 percent of the MEPs have a "dual mandate," that is, are also elected members of national parliaments. When the new European Parliament met in its first session in July 1984, it continued to assert its independence of national governments. One of its first actions was to reject by a wide margin a decision by the European Council (heads of government) that Britain be granted a substantial rebate in its payment to the EC budget. The 1984 elections showed that the government-parliament differences within the EC would continue for some time to come.

Helsinki Accord An agreement signed in August 1975 by 35 nations at the Conference on Security and Cooperation in Europe

(CSCE). The Helsinki Accord, formally called the Final Act, was concluded after two years of discussions dealing with matters relating to the security of Europe, recognition of postwar European boundaries, economic and trade matters, human rights, and the free flow of people and information. The Final Act was signed by members of the North Atlantic Treaty Organization, the Warsaw Treaty Organization, and 13 neutral and nonaligned (NNA) European states. The agreement is divided into four sections, called "Baskets." The first Basket pertaining to security in Europe contains a statement of ten basic principles guiding relations among states, such as sovereign equality, territorial integrity, peaceful settlement of disputes, nonintervention, and respect for human rights and international law. The signatories also agreed to certain "confidence-building measures," such as giving prior notification of military maneuvers. Basket II called for cooperation in the fields of economics, science and technology, and the environment. This includes such matters as providing economic statistics, removing trade barriers, and sponsoring joint programs in science and technology. Basket III promoted cooperation in humanitarian and other fields; these included family reunification and visitation rights, personal and professional travel, religious contacts, freer dissemination of information, improved working conditions for journalists, and educational and cultural exchanges. In Basket IV, the signatories also pledged to continue the Helsinki process with periodic conferences to review implementation of the Final Act. Two review conferences have been held: at Belgrade, from 1977 to 1978, and in Madrid, from 1980 to 1983. As called for in the Madrid meeting, a Conference on Confidence and Security Building Measures and Disarmament in Europe (CDE) opened in Stockholm in January 1984. Expected to last over two years, the first stage of the Stockholm conference is concerned with confidence and security-building measures, such as supplying information on military forces and exercises, and communication in times of crisis. Another CSCE review conference is scheduled for Vienna in 1986. *See also* OSTPOLITIK, p. 217.

Significance The Helsinki Accord was the beginning of a continuing process that attempts to deal comprehensively with the interrelated political, military, economic, and humanitarian issues that divide Europe. Although the Final Act was not a treaty, it in effect legitimated the political status quo in Europe. Adopted by 35 nations at a time when detente was at its height, the Helsinki Accord produced some achievements, such as increases in human contacts, increased emigration from the Soviet Union, and adoption of agreements in subsidiary areas. International tensions were very high at the Madrid Conference, however, which ended in 1983 after 34 months of difficult negotiations. The conference was filled with East-West criticisms over events like the Soviet invasion of Afghanistan in 1979, the banning of the labor union Solidarity and the declaration of martial law in Poland, the maltreatment of Soviet political dissidents and religious minorities, the forced disbanding of the Moscow Helsinki monitoring group, the shooting down of a South Korean airliner by Soviet military aircraft, and the proposed deployment of NATO intermediate-range missiles in Europe. Attempts by the neutral and nonaligned nations (NNA) were partially successful in getting agreement on a final document. It was this agreement that called for the CDE conference in Stockholm in 1984 and the 1986 review conference in Vienna. Although the initial aspirations of the CSCE have been greatly reduced, the Helsinki process represents the continuing desire of the signatories to resolve the interrelated political, military, economic, and humanitarian problems of Europe by peaceful means.

Intermediate Nuclear Forces Talks Negotiations in Geneva from November 1981 to December 1983 between the United States and the Soviet Union over the deployment of intermediate nuclear missiles in Europe. The intermediate nuclear forces (INF) talks were prompted by the 1979 NATO plan to deploy 572 American-built Pershing II and cruise missiles in Western Europe to counter Soviet intermediate missiles. Deployment of NATO missiles would occur unless agreement was reached in the INF talks. Proposals and counterproposals included (1) President Ronald Reagan's "zero option," which would forego the NATO missile deployment if the USSR would dismantle its intermediate missiles; (2) the West German suggestion adopted by the United States for an "interim solution" that would equalize the number of NATO and Soviet missiles at a low level; and (3) Soviet leader Yuri Andropov's proposal to reduce the number of Soviet SS-20 missiles to 162, the number of missiles independently held by France and Great Britain, an idea strongly opposed by France. The United States argued that (1) the deployment of the newer triple-warhead SS-20s created an imbalance that needed to be redressed by the single-warhead Pershing II and ground-launched cruise missiles; (2) Soviet SS-20s presently stationed in Soviet Asia are highly mobile and could be shifted to Europe in a crisis; and (3) the independent French and British nuclear missiles were not sufficiently accurate or powerful enough to threaten Soviet hardened missile silos or airbases. Soviet arguments included (1) NATO missiles could strike at the heart of Russia, including Moscow, whereas the SS-20s posed no threat to American territory; (2) French and British missiles must be included in the NATO count because of their threat to Russian territory; (3) Soviet missiles in Europe are balanced out by the many American nuclear bombers that are based in Europe and on aircraft carriers; and (4) the deployment of NATO missiles would so seriously disrupt the global nuclear balance that the Soviet Union would have to respond by deploying medium-range missiles close to American territory. In the spring and summer of 1983 some progress away from the original hard-line negotiation positions was made in the talks, but no agreement was reached by the cutoff date of December 1983. NATO missiles were deployed in 1984 over the protests of the Soviet Union, which then withdrew from INF negotiations and moved intermediate missiles into several countries of Eastern Europe. *See also* EUROMISSILE CONTROVERSY, p. 251.

Significance The Intermediate Nuclear Forces Talks were the most serious attempt to place limitations on the nuclear arms race since the failure to ratify the SALT II agreement in 1979. The INF negotiations took place in a period of hostility and superpower confrontation, and both parties perceived the deployment of theater missiles by the other side as serious threats to national security. The talks were much affected by the growing antinuclear peace movement, which threatened a breakup of the Western alliance, and by a general Soviet distrust of the Reagan administration. Although the initiative for the NATO plan to deploy the American-built missiles originated in West European governments, the Euromissile controversy came to be seen as an American-Russian superpower confrontation over the future of Europe. The talks showed the futility of separating theater nuclear forces from the broader strategic nuclear balance, the difficulty of balancing different weapons systems despite their apparent similarity, and the limitations placed on negotiators by the conflicting political objectives of major government leaders and alliance partners.

Nordic Council An organization established by treaty to promote economic, social, and cultural cooperation among the five Scandinavian states. Member states of the Nordic Council are Denmark, Finland, Iceland, Norway, and Sweden. The Nordic Council assembly consists of 78 elected members and about 45 appointed members. The elected members are selected by national parliaments, as follows: Norway and Sweden, 18 each; Finland, 17; Denmark, 16; and Iceland, 6; the legislature of Faroe Islands elects 2, and the county council of Aland 1. In addition, national governments and the executive bodies of the Faroe Islands and Aland appoint about 45 nonvoting members. The Council meets in one plenary session a year; its Presidium supervises the Council's work between meetings and presides over meetings. The Nordic Council makes recommendations on all matters of concern to the organization. Other important structures are (1) the Council of Ministers, which has decision-making authority on all Nordic affairs; (2) five subject-matter standing committees of the Nordic Council; and (3) two secretariats—one in Oslo, Norway, serving the Council of Ministers, and one in Copenhagen, Denmark, which administers matters concerning cultural cooperation.

Significance The origins of Nordic Council are traced to a postwar attempt to create a Scandanavian defense organization. This idea failed, but cooperation in nondefense matters took hold. First established by identical national laws, the Council's legal basis, functions, and institutions were codified by the supplementary Treaty of Cooperation of 1962, which was amended in subsequent agreements. Serving primarily as a forum for the parliaments and governments of member states, the Nordic Council's recommendations have been very influential in facilitating cooperation in legal, economic, and cultural fields. A substantial number of agreements have been made in harmonizing commercial laws, granting reciprocal social security benefits, and in creating a common labor market. Visas have been abolished, and citizens have been granted reciprocal voting rights. A Nordic Investment Bank has been established. The organization also promotes close collaboration on transportation, communication, and environmental matters.

North Atlantic Treaty Organization (NATO) The organizational structure of the military alliance established in 1949 for the collective defense of Western Europe and North America. The 16 members of NATO are: Belgium, Canada, Denmark, France, Federal Republic of Germany (since 1955), Greece (since 1952), Iceland, Italy, Luxembourg, the Netherlands, Norway, Portugal, Spain (since 1982), Turkey (since 1952), United Kingdom, and the United States. NATO was created under the authority of the North Atlantic Treaty signed in Washington on April 4, 1949, which states that an attack on any member in Europe or North America is considered to be an attack against them all. The alliance has a complex civil and military institutional structure. On the civil side, the North Atlantic Council, the highest decision-making body, makes basic policy, either through meetings of foreign ministers, heads of governments, or the permanent representatives (ambassadors). The Council is assisted by the secretary-general and the international staff with headquarters in Brussels, and a large number of political, economic, social, and military committees. Two other important groups are the Defense Planning Committee and the Military Committee, the highest military body in the alliance, which makes recommendations to the Council and Defense Planning Committee. The military structure of NATO includes three strategic commands for Europe, the Atlantic, and the English Channel. The military commanders of these areas are best known by their military acronyms: SACEUR, the Supreme Allied Commander Europe, whose headquarters in Belgium is known as SHAPE, the Supreme Headquarters Allied Powers Europe; SACLANT, the Supreme Allied Commander Atlantic, with headquarters in Norfolk, Virginia; and CINCHAN, the Allied Commander-in-Chief Channel, with headquarters in Britain. Another NATO body of importance is Eurogroup, an informal association of defense ministers of European member governments, which promotes closer European military cooperation and improvements in European defense contributions. The North Atlantic Assembly is an interparliamentary organization of 184 deputies chosen by national parliaments that acts as a forum for the expression of views. In June 1984 Lord Carrington (Britain) succeeded Joseph Luns (Belgium) as the secretary-general of NATO. *See also* ATLANTICISM, p. 2; EUROMISSILE CONTROVERSY, p. 251; INTERMEDIATE NUCLEAR FORCES TALKS, p. 265.

Significance The North Atlantic Treaty Organization was created in the immediate postwar period to defend Western Europe from possible Soviet aggression. Although the region has undergone vast economic and social changes in the last 35 years, the member states continue to believe that NATO and American forces are necessary to the defense of Europe. In the 1960s President Charles de Gaulle withdrew French military and naval units from NATO commands, and NATO headquarters moved from Paris to Brussels. France remains within the alliance, however, and cooperates in joint NATO exercises and uses the NATO radar network. Iceland threatened to withdraw because of a dispute with Britain, and Greece because of a dispute with Turkey, but they have not done so. A continuing issue is the American desire to have the European powers increase defense spending, which has not been successful. In 1983 and 1984 NATO's plans for the deployment of American intermediate-range nuclear missiles in Europe (Euromissiles) to counter a similar Soviet force led to a bitter controversy. As negotiations with the USSR proved fruitless, many groups protested in European capitals. Some communities declared themselves to be nuclear-free zones, and some political groups, including the Annual Conference of the British Labour party, opted for unilateral nuclear disarmament. The governments of all the large NATO states, however, are convinced that the nuclear deterrent is necessary for European defense. NATO controversies seem to go in cycles, often depending on the independent actions of the Soviet Union and the United States in other areas of the world. Many Europeans, fearful that Europe will become a nuclear battleground and convinced that NATO is necessary, continue to have ambivalent feelings about the alliance.

Organization for Economic Cooperation and Development (OECD) An association of 24 advanced industrial states, mostly in Europe, that promotes economic growth and development. The Organization for Economic Cooperation and Development (OECD) was established in 1961 as the enlarged successor to the Organization for European Economic Cooperation (OEEC). The membership includes 17 Western European states, Australia, Canada, Iceland, Japan, New Zealand, Turkey, and the United States. The purposes of the OECD are (1) to promote economic growth, employment, and improved standards of living within member states; (2) to promote the sound development of the world economy; and (3) to help the economies of less-developed countries. The OECD functions through a ministerial council, an executive committee, a secretariat, and a large number of functional committees concerned with a wide variety of economic matters. *See also* ORGANIZATION FOR EUROPEAN ECONOMIC COOPERATION (OEEC), p. 269.

Significance The establishment of OECD in 1961 with an expanded membership and functions shows the success of the preceding OEEC in achieving its goals for Europe. Within the context of its limited authority and much broadened scope of concerns, the OECD has been useful to member states and third parties. This is done through the publication of statistics, research, and reports, and serving as a forum for analyzing and debating policies. The OECD assists members and developing states in planning projects, and encourages the development and use of new techniques and methods of production. It promotes economic modernization and free trade by encouraging states to adopt cooperative economic policies.

Organization for European Economic Cooperation (OEEC) The European agency that coordinated the administration of the European Recovery Program (ERP) from 1948 to 1961. The original membership of the OEEC included 14 nations of Western Europe, Iceland, and Turkey; Germany became a full member after it gained sovereignty in 1949; the United States and Canada became associate members in 1950. The prime function of the OEEC was to help coordinate the distribution of American economic assistance granted in the European Recovery Program (ERP). Also known as the Marshall Plan (after American Secretary of State George C. Marshall), the ERP dispensed over $12 billion of loans and goods from 1948 to 1952 to be used for the industrial recovery of Europe. A second major purpose of OEEC was to foster economic cooperation among member states, a function that concerned the agency after the task of distributing recovery assistance was completed in 1952. In 1961 the OEEC was transformed into the Organization for Economic Cooperation and Development (OECD), which included the United States, Canada, and others as full members. *See also* ORGANIZATION FOR ECONOMIC COOPERATION AND DEVELOPMENT (OECD), p. 269.

Significance A major factor in the creation of the OEEC was the American desire not to have recovery assistance wasted because of European restrictive trade practices. The original American invitation to participate in ERP was made to all European states, but the Communist nations refused to participate. Beyond coordinating the distribution of ERP assistance, the achievements of the OEEC in promoting economic cooperation were considerable. Intraregional tariffs were lowered, and quotas and other restrictive practices were eased. In 1950 the European Payments Union (EPU) was established to facilitate trade through an automatic multilateral system of payments that offset monthly surpluses and deficits. The EPU also promoted trade liberalization policies by helping finance intraregional trade for members with balance-of-trade deficits. It was replaced by the European Monetary Agreement (EMA) in 1958 to further promote the convertibility of European currencies. The OEEC was the first major instance of economic cooperation on a regional scale in postwar Europe. By 1961 it had achieved important improvements in regional cooperation; it was then broadened geographically in its successor organization, the OECD. The more complex tasks of integrating the economies of Europe were assumed by the European Coal and Steel Community and the European Economic Community.

Polycentrism In the world Communist movement, the doctrine that there are a number of centers of power and policy making. The doctrine of polycentrism developed in 1956 by Palmiro Togliatti, the head of the Italian Communist party, denied a guiding role to the Soviet Union in the international Communist movement. It asserts that other centers of Communist power, particularly in China, have been established, and national Communist parties should not be dominated by the Soviet party. The world Communist movement is a free union of autonomous national Communist parties that are agreed on general goals; it is not an organization of subservient parties under the direction of the Soviet party. There are no "general laws for the construction of socialism" as claimed by the Soviet party, but each party should be free to choose its own national strategies to achieve socialism. *See also* COMINTERN, p. 281; DE-STALINIZATION, p. 305; EUROCOMMUNISM, p. 250.

Significance The doctrine of polycentrism as developed by Togliatti came in the wake of the de-Stalinization movement following Nikita Khrushchev's criticisms of the crimes of Josef Stalin in 1956. Togliatti, reflecting traditional Italian Communist party independent thinking and its doctrine of "separate paths to socialism," posited a pluralist model of communism that was contrary to orthodox Soviet policy. Soviets considered polycentrism to be deviationist and revisionist. In the mid-1970s, the doctrine of polycentrism was developed into a more liberal viewpoint, that of Eurocommunism. As primarily expounded by Santiago Carrillo, the head of the Spanish Communist party, Eurocommunism not only asserts the autonomy of Western Communist parties, it also rejects the Leninist doctrine of revolution and the dictatorship of the proletariat. Eurocommunism supports the idea of a pluralistic and democratic political system as the means to build socialism, and it asserts that Western European Communist parties have a commonality of interests that are different from those of the Soviet bloc in Eastern Europe.

Value-Added Tax (VAT)   A levy applied on the increase in value of a product at each stage of production and distribution. Although the value-added tax is paid at each stage of the manufacturing process, and is collected from manufacturers and merchants, the tax burden is passed on to the final consumer. Consequently VAT is a general turnover tax that is in effect a type of general sales tax collected in stages. In the European Community (EC), VAT rates vary from several percent on items like food to 35 percent on luxury items. The standard tax throughout the Community ranges from 15 to 25 percent. VAT produces up to 25 percent of the total revenue collected by EC countries. Since 1979 up to 1 percent of the revenues EC countries receive from their VAT goes directly to the EC budget.

Significance   The value-added tax was first adopted by France, where it is known as TVA; it was promoted by the EC Commission and later adopted by all EC countries. Supporters of the tax argue that VAT is competitively neutral because it does not discourage expansion, savings, or investments; that it raises high amounts of revenue; and that it promotes productivity and modernization. Critics point out that unless low rates are placed on necessities, the tax is regressive, and that VAT is inflationary, for it drives up prices across the board. Unlike the income tax, VAT is hidden from view in the purchase price, and being a good revenue producer, it is consequently supported by policy-makers. In the EC, VAT revenues, combined with customs duties on nonmember imports, permit the Community to rely on its own resources rather than on contributions from its members.

Western European Union (WEU)   A military alliance established in 1954 that expanded the Brussels Pact alliance of 1948 to incorporate West Germany and Italy into the defense of Western Europe. The members of the WEU include the original members of the Brussels Pact, Belgium, Britain, France, Luxembourg, the Netherlands, and the two former enemy states, Germany and Italy. The Brussels Pact, which predates the North Atlantic Treaty Organization (NATO), and WEU were European responses to the perceived security threat from the Soviet Union. WEU was created in light of the American desire to have Europeans, including Germany and Italy, increase their contribution to the defense of the region. The French, concerned about German revanchism, responded to this problem by proposing the European Defense Community (EDC). This would have created an integrated European army composed of units from France, Germany, Italy, and Benelux (but not Britain). EDC was defeated by the French Parliament in 1954 even though a French government had initiated the proposal. Germany and Italy were then brought into WEU and NATO, and their forces were incorporated in the NATO framework. The institutional structure of WEU includes the Council of Ministers, an assembly of delegates, and a secretariat. The Council meets irregularly and may be called into session by any member when a threat to security is perceived. *See also* NORTH ATLANTIC TREATY ORGANIZATION (NATO), p. 267.

Significance The Western European Union was created at a time when West German rearmament was believed to be crucial to the defense of Western Europe. The French rejection of the EDC showed that Europeans—particularly the French—were not ready to move to a political union and a uniform foreign policy, which would be required to control an integrated military force. By creating WEU and operating within the NATO framework, Europeans solved the problem of German rearmament. In recent years, WEU has been inactive, its members functioning as part of the NATO system. In June 1984, however, the Council of Ministers decided to revitalize WEU to assert European interests more strongly within NATO.

5. The Soviet Union

Bolshevik The Russian word for "member of the majority," the title given to the followers of Vladimir Lenin's version of Marxism. Originally a minority within the tiny Russian Marxist movement, the Bolsheviks eventually emerged as the Communist Party of the Soviet Union (CPSU), the ruling institution of the Soviet state. Russian Marxism developed in the nineteenth century, in part in reaction to the peasant-based agrarian socialism of the Russian Populist movement (*Narodnichestvo*). As with all parties and trade unions in czarist Russia before 1905, the Marxist movement was illegal. Russia's first Marxist party, the Russian Social Democratic Labor party (RSDLP), was founded in 1898. Its leaders were immediately arrested, and Lenin, then in forced exile, demanded that the party reorganize itself as a clandestine, tightly disciplined band of professional revolutionaries controlled by an inner-core leadership. His opponents within the Marxist movement, the Mensheviks, advocated a more gradualist approach through a mass, worker-based party and trade union activity. The RSDLP split on this issue. The moderates walked out of the 1903 RSDLP Congress in protest, and Lenin could thus claim a majority, dubbing his opponents the Mensheviks, or "members of the minority." The names stuck, although for several years afterwards the Bolsheviks actually remained a minority within the Marxist movement. Lenin insisted on a party comprised of a self-selected elite vanguard, dedicated to any available means, including violence. Because Russian capitalism was not yet fully developed, and the masses could not accomplish a revolution by themselves, Lenin argued for leadership by the "vanguard" party, the Bolsheviks. Lenin's argument implied that for a long period the masses would require leadership, a role he assigned to the Bolsheviks. However, by acting in the interests of and in the name of the proletariat, the

Bolshevik vanguard would avoid dictatorship. Lenin's use of the term Bolshevik, or majority, enabled the party to claim the leadership of the working class. The more gradualist Mensheviks refused to compromise Marxist doctrine with Russian realities, maintaining that the revolution could occur only when Russia had achieved full capitalism. When the Czar reluctantly granted Russia its first parliament in 1905, the Mensheviks participated. The Bolsheviks remained opposed to all such incremental, bourgeois reforms. By 1912 Russian Marxism had formally divided into two parties. Refusing to concede, Lenin adopted the name RSDLP-Bolshevik for the party that was to carry out the Russian Revolution in the name of Bolshevism. *See also* BOLSHEVIK REVOLUTION, p. 274; LENINISM, p. 330.

Significance The tactics of the Bolsheviks and the political dynamics upon which a communist dictatorship was erected were determined by Lenin's insistence on a self-selected elite, disciplined party. Lenin's organizational plan proved decisive. When the czarist system collapsed in February 1917 under the accumulated strains of heavy war losses, economic disaster, and royal ineptitude, a hastily convened Provisional Government replaced it. The Mensheviks joined the Provisional Government and were compromised by its inability to arrest Russia's descent into anarchy. Support for the Bolsheviks grew. In October 1917 the Bolsheviks deposed the Provisional Government, and Lenin's elite vanguard of professional revolutionaries became Russia's new leaders. Menshevik became a term of opprobrium, the particular target of the CHEKA, Lenin's secret police, during the ensuing civil war. Lenin's heirs portray the Mensheviks as the chief traitors to the new socialist order. Opponents of Bolshevism paint them as true democrats. They were neither. Both the Bolsheviks and the Mensheviks were committed to a Marxist revolution that would destroy capitalism and czardom. They differed in their interpretations of Marxism and in their timing. Such is the power of the success of Lenin's organizational tactics and doctrinal additions to Marxism that today the term Bolshevik has become almost synonymous with Communist. In the West it is used pejoratively, to describe Marxists who pursue undemocratic and illegal tactics. In the Soviet Union it is a term of honor.

Bolshevik Revolution The uprising that brought the Bolsheviks to power in Russia, transforming czarist Russia into a Communist state that established the Union of Soviet Socialist Republics. The Bolshevik Revolution overthrew the Government on October 25, 1917. It is sometimes called the October Revolution to distinguish it from the February Revolution of eight months earlier, which deposed Czar Nicholas II, thus ending three centuries of Romanov rule. The guiding spirit of the Bolshevik Revolution was Vladimir Lenin, leader of the small Marxist Bolshevik party. Amid deepening chaos and military failures in World War I, Czar Nicholas dissolved Russia's first parliament, the Duma, in February. A group of liberal and moderate Duma politicians formed the Provisional Government and forced Nicholas to abdicate. The February Revolution, unlike the Bolshevik Revolution, was essentially unplanned and spontaneous. The Provisional Government proved unable to construct a workable government and from the beginning was forced to share power with the Petrograd (Leningrad) Soviet of Workers' and Soldiers' Deputies, a loose federation of delegates from worker-elected soviets (councils) in the capital city. The most immediate problem was Russia's war involvement. Brought into being by the failures of the czarist war effort, the Provisional Government remained committed to Russia's participation despite the widespread cry for peace. Lenin seized on this and began a drive for power, concentrating on securing control of the soviets, initially dominated by Mensheviks and left-wing Social Revolutionaries. In July, the Galician front in Poland collapsed. Peasant conscripts deserted en masse as strikes, food crises, and peasant insurrections erupted. The liberals resigned from the Provisional Government, the regular army dissolved, and Alexander Kerensky became Prime Minister. Kerensky, in order to stave off the attempt by General Lavr Kornilov to restore conservatism, rearmed the Bolshevik Red Guards. Thus the Provisional Government had no credible military support. It was unable to stem the growing anarchy, contained only by the soviet militia who controlled the streets and much of the military ranks. In September, Leon Trotsky, who emerged as the strategist of the Revolution, became head of the Petrograd Soviet. The final act came on October 24, when troops stationed in Petrograd and the nearby Kronstadt naval fortress acknowledged the Petrograd Soviet as sole leader. Bolsheviks occupied key points in the capital city and seized the Winter Palace, the site of the Provisional Government. The Revolution was timed to coincide with the Second All-Russian Congress of the Soviets, where the Bolsheviks enjoyed a majority. The Congress voted to vest all governmental power in the Council of People's Commissars (*Sovnarkom*), headed by Lenin, and the Bolshevik Revolution was accomplished. *See also* BOLSHEVIK, p. 273; DUMA, p. 309; SOVIET, p. 355.

Significance Possibly no other event has had more impact on the twentieth-century world than the Bolshevik Revolution. From what was initially more of a coup than a revolution, a drastically different state emerged. The immediate issue the Bolsheviks faced was how to consolidate power amid chaos. For this Marxism provided no guide. Lenin immediately reinstated the secret police, reimposed censorship, dissolved the Constituent Assembly, and redistributed the land. The Constituent Assembly was Russia's first and last democratically elected parliament, one in which the Bolsheviks had won a bare quarter of the seats. The Sovnarkom, under tight Bolshevik control, continued to rule and carried out a bloody and successful three-year civil war against all opponents. The Bolshevik Revolution was unique in its degree of success but not in its central dilemma of reconciling ideals with power realities. The Revolution, ostensibly carried out in the name of socialist democracy by a small band of disciplined radicals, had to consolidate control over a backward, conservative, and heterogeneous society that had little or no experience in democracy.

Brezhnev Doctrine A doctrine proclaimed in 1968 by Leonid Brezhnev and the Soviet leadership that declares that the Soviet Union and Eastern European states are committed to defend, by force of arms if necessary, the integrity of the existing socialist order whenever and wherever it is threatened. The Brezhnev Doctrine was invoked as an after-the-fact rationale to justify the Soviet-led invasion and occupation of Czechoslovakia in August 1968 by troops of the Warsaw Treaty Organization. The definition of a "threat to socialism" rests with the Soviet leadership, as the Czechoslovak Communist leadership was not attempting to jettison socialism but to institute reforms and moderate Soviet hegemony. In effect, the doctrine stipulates internal liberalization of socialist states as well as intervention by the West as policies that are not permissible in socialist states. *See also* WARSAW TREATY ORGANIZATION (WTO), p. 365.

Significance The Brezhnev Doctrine was developed as a justification for intervention in Communist states by the Soviet Union. Asserting the concept of "socialist internationalism," the doctrine proclaims the principles of solidarity and unity among socialist nations, implicitly under the guidance of the Soviet Union. Accordingly, all socialist states are obliged to protect and preserve socialism. The Brezhnev Doctrine clearly limits the sovereignty of the East European states. Since the end of World War II, the Soviet leadership has insisted on unilaterally determining what policies and actions are politically acceptable in the Communist bloc states of Eastern Europe, distinguishing between socialist and capitalist states. In the case of socialist states, the interests of the socialist movement take precedence over the sovereignty of individual states. Thus, Soviet intervention in a socialist state is a domestic matter; Western criticisms of violations of sovereignty are rejected. As the Soviets were promoting a policy of detente with the West in 1968, the Brezhnev Doctrine emphasized the enduring priorities of the Soviet leadership. It articulated a major power's determination to maintain hegemony within its regional sphere of influence. In 1979, the doctrine was given new meaning with the Soviet invasion of Afghanistan, when the principle of "socialist solidarity" was extended to a nonbloc country.

Budget of the State The financial instrument by which the funds of the Soviet Union are collected and disbursed according to the planned distribution determined by the national economic plan. The budget of the state is thus the means by which the government finances and controls the entire economy and all other government operations. The national budget is prepared yearly by the Ministry of Finance, advised by the State Planning Committee (Gosplan), approved by the Council of Ministers, and promulgated as law by the Supreme Soviet. It is therefore legally binding. It is comprised of the budgets of some 50,000 subordinate units, from local villages to republics. Each higher-level budget includes all subordinate units. Expenditures cover five categories: economic, social and cultural, administrative, defense, and debt service. The largest portion finances the economy (an estimated 50 percent), which in turn provides about 90 percent of all revenues, the remainder deriving from direct taxes on citizens. Soviet state budgets are never in deficit. A slight surplus is maintained to form a reserve fund that enables Gosbank, the national bank of issue, to issue currency without inflating. Gosbank, operating through about 4,000 regional and local branches, acts as the principal financial officer for the state, executing the budget. Each enterprise or farm must keep its accounts with Gosbank, which is also charged with collecting the turnover (sales) tax, a major source of budgetary funds. Gosbank and its institutions are the chief sources of credit and are part of the state budget. *See also* GOSPLAN, p. 321; PLANNING, p. 340; SOCIALIST OWNERSHIP, p. 354.

Significance The budget of the state functions as the major instrument for redistributing the national income according to the interests of the state. It provides a powerful means of centralized control over the economy. Critics point out that Gosbank grants credits on the basis of the plan fulfillment, rather than on marketability or economic rationality. As long as an enterprise has met its production targets, even if the goods are not saleable, it can obtain the necessary credits to pay workers and suppliers. Because the USSR state budget embraces practically all economic activity, it is far larger than the budgets of Western states in terms of percentage of national income. The principle of socialist (i.e., state) ownership of all means of production provides the legal basis for the state's right to the profits of enterprises and cooperatives. The state determines by law what percentage of profits accrue to the state budget; the remainder is available for operating expenses and worker benefits. The state budget is the instrument by which hundreds of thousands of economic units are placed under the control of the state. Although the state budget indicates the priorities of the Soviet state, it is by no means a complete guide. Published budgetary statistics, particularly in the area of defense expenditures, are usually incomplete.

Capitalist Encirclement   The concept that the Soviet Union is a socialist state surrounded by hostile capitalist states dedicated to destroying it. Spurred by the Allied intervention on the side of the anti-Bolsheviks during the Civil War (1918–21), capitalist encirclement became the guiding principle of Soviet foreign policy. The concept of an outside world implacably hostile to the "first workers' state" was adopted and refined by Josef Stalin during the power struggle after Vladimir Lenin's death in 1924. Stalin maintained that capitalist encirclement could only be blunted through rapid industrialization, by "building socialism in one country," without the aid of Communist revolutions elsewhere. His chief opponent, Leon Trotsky, argued that the only way to escape capitalist encirclement was by supporting revolutions in capitalist states. With Stalin's victory over his rivals in the late 1920s, the Soviet Union embarked on a massive program of rapid industrialization. Stalin's program of "building socialism in one country" necessitated a strong and powerful state apparatus, which could not "wither away" as long as capitalist encirclement existed. After World War II, with the establishment of Communist governments in China and Eastern Europe, Stalin announced that the "two camps" doctrine had replaced capitalist encirclement. The two camps doctrine, however, merely posited a rough balance of power, not a lessening of the innate antagonisms between socialism and capitalism. *See also* PEACEFUL COEXISTENCE, p. 339.

Significance   Until the late 1940s, Soviet foreign and domestic policy was based on the concept of capitalist encirclement. Stalin used the concept to justify the ruthless internal policies he pursued. Industrialization and the building of a massive military force were regarded as the means of survival for a Soviet state surrounded by hostile enemies. After the rise of fascism, which the Soviets described as the highest stage of capitalism, many observers accepted the idea that Soviet behavior was conditioned by the hostility of capitalism. The postwar change to the "two camps" doctrine ultimately did little to improve East-West relations, as it was also based on the idea of innate differences between socialism and capitalism that projected the future victory of the former over the latter.

Citizen Participation The involvement of individual citizens in collective activities that relate to the functions of the political system. Citizen participation in the Soviet Union is directed by the Communist party through myriad citizens' organizations designed to give each citizen a sense of participation in the system. As no group is permitted to organize without official permission, be it a sports club or a literary discussion group, the Soviet definition of citizen participation is broader than the Western construct. Soviet participatory modes may be divided roughly into four categories: (1) job-related activities such as in trade unions; (2) administrative support; (3) monitoring officials; and (4) participating in hobby, social, and peer groups. The last category provides officially approved leisure activities and serves as an agent of official socialization. The second and third categories include citizens' groups ranging from the quasi-judicial Comrades' Courts and self-governing residence committees to the seven million volunteer militia (*Druzhiny*) who patrol the streets and maintain public order. Participatory modes are designed to permit citizens a role in the implementation and monitoring of policy. The maintenance of civil authority and "socialist" mores is delegated to the residence committees and Comrades' Courts, while millions of citizen inspectors monitor the activities of all government agencies and enterprises. *See also* DEPUTY, p. 303; DOSAAF, p. 307; KOMSOMOL, p. 328; MASS ORGANIZATIONS, p. 334.

Significance Although Soviet citizen participation does not meet the Western definition of articulation of interests and influence over policy decisions, some observers argue that Soviet participatory activities fall within the general understanding of citizen participation as both personally efficacious and as an instrument of citizen input. Soviet authorities expend much energy in soliciting the opinions of myriad citizens' groups. Marxist doctrine includes a strong commitment to citizen governance. Although the party refuses to dilute its control over policy making, much of day-to-day life is regulated by citizens' groups. Involvement is impressive, estimated at over 30 million adults. By involving so many persons, the party seeks to build a sense of grassroots participation and community, perhaps mitigating the anomie of a large-scale industrial society. The party, however, still controls and defines the scope of participation.

Civil Rights According to Marxist-Leninist doctrine, those individual rights, such as liberty, property, and security, that first appear with the class struggle. Marxist legal theorists maintain that in a bourgeois political system, workers are denied most civil rights—only under communism will they possess them in full. Soviet legal theory separates socialist civil rights into four categories: (1) Socioeconomic rights, such as the rights to pensions, medical care, and education. Soviet law emphasizes these above all other rights. (2) The uniformity of rights and duties, including ethnic and sexual equality. Since the Bolshevik Revolution the Soviet system has maintained a strong commitment to equal protection. (3) Personal rights, such as the rights to property and security. These rights are protected only insofar as they do not impinge on the interests of the state. (4) Individual political rights, such as freedom of speech and assembly. These individual rights of conscience may be exercised only in conformity with the interests of the socialist system; otherwise they are not legally protected. Soviet legal theory recognizes two types of speech: "socialist" speech, which springs naturally from the socialist order and is supportive of it, and "nonsocialist" speech, which must be curtailed to protect socialism. Soviet legal theory rejects the concept of natural law and innate natural rights. State-created socialist law is the only source of nonbourgeois civil rights. The Soviet treatment of all civil rights stems from these assumptions. If the exercise of a civil right is deemed a threat to socialism, it is not protected. The emphasis, in all but socioeconomic rights, is on the responsibility of the citizen to the state. *See also* CRIMINAL OFFENSES: ANTI-SOVIET AGITATION AND PROPAGANDA, p. 299; DISSENT AND OPPOSITION, p. 306; SOCIALIST LEGALITY, p. 353.

Significance In the area of what Soviet doctrine defines as civil rights, the material guarantees and equal protection are the most well developed. The 1977 Soviet Constitution expanded these areas, in particular protecting equal rights for women. Protection of civil rights depends on the state, as all are considered privileges granted by the state. Although a handful of dissidents have publicly called for the meaningful implementation of the rights guaranteed by the Constitution and by the Helsinki Accord of 1975, they have been systematically suppressed by the authorities. Marxist legal theory aside, the dynamics of a centralized one-party Communist state preclude the idea that civil rights constitute a limitation on state action.

Collectivization The process that transformed Soviet agriculture from private farming to state-controlled collective farms. Collectivization was imposed by Josef Stalin in 1929–35 through force and terror. Immediately after the Bolshevik Revolution 96 percent of the land was distributed to the peasants. Landholdings were fragmented, and agriculture remained primitive. Despite the free market permitted by Vladimir Lenin's New Economic Policy (1921–28), the subsistence-style agriculture produced only minimal marketable surpluses. Once Stalin consolidated power over the party in 1928, he turned to the twin problems of imposing communism on the countryside and securing an agricultural base for rapid industrialization. Abrogating the reforms of the New Economic Policy, he set the nation on the path of massive, forced-draft industrialization. The instrumentality chosen was the collective farm (*kolkhoz*), a "voluntary" cooperative in which the peasants pooled labor and resources while the state took title to the land. Collectivization was both swift and brutal. Those peasants who resisted were summarily executed or sent to the prison labor camps. The toll is estimated at some five million. The severe disruptions in agriculture caused widespread famine in 1932–33, in which millions more peasants perished. In 1932, the internal passport system was reinstated, and most peasants were denied passports, thus tying them to the collective farm. Ultimately, 25 million small peasant farms were amalgamated into 250,000 collectives, and Soviet agriculture was permanently transformed. *See also* GREAT PURGE, p. 322; KOLKHOZ, p. 327; SOVKHOZ, p. 356; STALINISM, p. 357.

Significance In political terms, collectivization can be considered a success, for it enabled Stalin to Sovietize the countryside and appropriate food for the cities. The tight control exercised over the movement of peasants permitted the government to regulate the flow of new labor into the cities. Political control secured through terror became highly centralized and authoritarian. Soviet agriculture paid a heavy price. The better-off and more productive peasants, whom Stalin labeled *kulaks* ("fist," implying that they had squeezed the poorer peasants) were destroyed as the "class enemy," thus robbing Soviet agriculture of its more productive members. Living standards declined precipitously. The iron control exercised by the chairman placed over each collective farm discouraged any innovation. Collectivization marks the turn of the Stalinist system to mass terror as an instrument of political control. It revoked the worker-peasant alliance forged by Lenin and once again bound the peasants to the land as in the days of czarist serfdom.

Comintern The Soviet-dominated international organization of Communist parties that was founded in 1919 by Vladimir Lenin and operated until 1943. The Comintern (Communist International) served chiefly as an instrument of Soviet foreign policy. Through the Comintern, the Soviet leadership dominated the Communist parties of the world, dictating their policies and tactics. The Comintern was organized into national sections that functioned as subunits of the international Communist movement, headquartered in Moscow. Bound by the Soviet-inspired doctrine of socialist internationalism, foreign Communists were subject to total acceptance of Soviet policy and Soviet interpretations of Marxism-Leninism. In the 1930s, the Comintern became a tool of Josef Stalin's personal dictatorship, and was repeatedly purged by Stalin's secret police. Foreign Communists who incurred Stalin's distrust were executed in the Soviet Union or tracked down abroad by Comintern assassins. During World War II the Comintern became an embarrassment to the Soviets, who were now fighting with the Western Allies, and it was dissolved in 1943. A much more limited successor agency, the Cominform (Communist Information Bureau) was created in 1947 to maintain Soviet control in those countries where Communist parties had come to power, or were expected to. Its membership included the parties of Albania, Bulgaria, Czechoslovakia, France, Hungary, Italy, the Soviet Union, and Yugoslavia. Its most momentous decision was to expel the Yugoslav Communist party in 1948 for refusing to accept Soviet domination. With the death of Stalin, the Cominform declined and was quietly dissolved in 1956. *See also* EUROCOMMUNISM, p. 250.

Significance The Comintern crystallized the division between radical Marxists and the mass-based socialist parties of Europe, which pursued socialism through the parliamentary process. Most of the Communist parties of Europe were born out of this conflict between social democracy and revolutionary Marxism. Lenin founded the Comintern partly out of the fear that Soviet Communism could not long survive unless revolutions in Europe created friendly Communist regimes. The founding document of the Comintern enjoined all Communists to support the Bolsheviks and to struggle not only against capitalism but also against all leftist rivals—European socialists, Mensheviks, trade unionists, the German Social Democrats, and the British Labour party. Much of the Comintern's efforts in the 1930s were devoted to destroying its leftist rivals. It played a fateful role in the rise of Hitler's Germany by splitting the left-wing opposition to Hitler that, if united, would have probably possessed enough votes in the 1932 Reichstag elections to overrule the Nazis. Similarly, during the Spanish Civil War, Comintern supervisors of the International Brigades divided their efforts between fighting Francisco Franco and exterminating Trotskyites and other rivals within the international Communist movement. The Comintern introduced the concept of externally directed, Soviet subversion into world politics. In the long run, the Comintern succeeded neither in overthrowing governments nor in stopping Fascism, nor, as Yugoslavia's ouster demonstrated, in dominating all Communist movements. Subsequently, Albania, the People's Republic of China, Romania, and other Communist parties have refused to subordinate national goals to Soviet policy. The Eurocommunists of Western Europe, led by the Italian Communist party, have explicitly rejected Soviet hegemony. The most lasting effect of the Comintern occurred in 1921 when Lenin dictated the organizational structure for all member parties, a structure that is still followed by most Communist parties.

Command Economy A state-administered economy in which the role of the market and private ownership is replaced by administrative bodies that make all economic decisions. The command economy is essentially a developmental strategy that relies on administrative control and the mobilization of all resources under state direction. The interests of the state take precedence over all other interests; there is no competition and no free market in prices or wages. The system was initiated by Josef Stalin in 1928 as a means of achieving rapid industrialization. Stalin's command economy model is characterized by (1) state ownership of all means of production; (2) state-determined allocation of resources; (3) mandatory, long-range economic planning; (4) high rates of capital investment; and (5) administrative enforcement of the economic plans. The state planning organs determine production; profits and losses accrue to the state budget. The economy is organized along branch lines. Each economic sector is directed by a state ministry that receives directives ("commands") from the planning authorities that they must enforce upon the enterprises under their jurisdiction. The command economy is a supply-dominated system rather than a demand system. Only in the area of defense production, where the planner and the consumer are the same (that is, the state), is there any consumer sovereignty. The centrally administered, state-owned economy produces, in essence, a single state monopoly. *See also* CAPITALIST ENCIRCLEMENT, p. 278; PLANNING, p. 340; SOCIALIST OWNERSHIP, p. 354; STALINISM, p. 357.

Significance The command economy model rests on Stalin's argument that rapid industrialization, and thus national security, could be created only from above. By placing the state in total control of the economy, Stalin sought to shortcut the lengthy industrialization undergone by Western capitalist systems. He argued that, given the Soviet Union's isolation in a largely hostile world, it was necessary to "build socialism in one country" and secure the industrial base necessary to defend socialism from the "capitalist encirclement." He was largely successful—the Soviet Union today is the world's second industrial power—but at tremendous human costs. While in theory the command economy model is not totally incompatible with political democracy and individual liberties, in practice it has proven inherently intolerant of both. The record also suggests that it is more successful in a developing state than in complex industrial systems. It depends on extensive development: growth is dependent on increases in outputs rather than on productivity, technology, or modernization of existing facilities. While the state can mobilize and control all resources, it cannot enforce efficiency. Nonetheless, the successes of this revolution from above continue to make it attractive to developing nations that face conditions similar to or more difficult than those of the Soviet Union in 1928.

Council of Ministers: USSR The highest executive and administrative organ of the Soviet government. According to the Constitution, the Council of Ministers is "the government of the USSR." As such, it is the apex of a vast government bureaucracy that supervises the economic, political, and social activities of the state. It also supervises the republican councils of ministers and can void any act of a republican government. In theory the Council of Ministers is appointed by and responsible to the Supreme Soviet, as with Western parliamentary governments. In reality the Council of Ministers acts independently. Its members are selected by the party leadership, and all hold high party positions as well as top government posts. Its membership currently includes: a chairman (or premier), 2 first deputy chairmen, 11 deputy chairmen, about 12 chairmen of interdepartmental state committees, the 3 heads of national administrative agencies, and over 60 ministers, each the head of a powerful ministry. The chairmen of the republican councils of ministers serve ex officio. Its most important function is to draw up and implement the national economic plan. Additional statutory functions include directing monetary and fiscal policy, administering foreign policy, and supervising the immense bureaucracy necessary to implement all this. It is empowered to issue legally binding decrees (*postanovlenie*) and orders (*rasporyazhenie*) to all under its jurisdiction. The most important of these decrees are usually issued jointly with the party Central Committee and later translated into law (*zakon*) by the Supreme Soviet. *See also* MINISTRY, p. 335; PRESIDIUM OF THE COUNCIL OF MINISTERS, p. 343; SUPREME SOVIET, p. 360.

Significance In terms of the scope of its jurisdiction, the Council of Ministers is unique. Few if any governments attempt to regulate so much of national life. Although sometimes compared to an all-powerful parliamentary cabinet, it is far too large to act as a working cabinet. Probably most of its assigned functions are delegated to a smaller inner body, the Presidium of the Council of Ministers. The full Council of Ministers meets only quarterly. Thus it is not a collective decision-making or policy-making body. Key members are believed to report directly to the party Politburo and Secretariat, directly implementing party policy in their respective areas of jurisdiction. Although constitutionally its only legislative role is to elaborate already existing law, many of the decrees issued by the Council are far broader, reflecting the party's self-perceived need to translate party policy into action. Decrees do not have to be published unless they are normative (lawmaking), a determination made by the Council itself. Some analysts believe that this "secret" legislation outnumbers published laws. Of the legislation that is published, an estimated three-fourths originates in the Council of Ministers. The post of chairman, or premier, has been held by various party leaders, the first being Vladimir Lenin. Josef Stalin first assigned the premiership to lesser party officials, then held it himself from 1941 to 1953, as did Nikita Khrushchev from 1958 to 1964. Since 1964 the premiership has been occupied by a Politburo member, but not the general secretary. The incumbent in 1984 was N. A. Tikhonov. Thus, since 1917 the Soviet system has followed Lenin's dictum, first enunciated at the Tenth Party Congress, of fusing the "party and government summits."

Council of Mutual Economic Assistance (COMECON or CMEA)   An East European–Soviet group organized in 1949 by the Soviet Union to promote trade and economic integration. COMECON originally included Bulgaria, Czechoslovakia, the German Democratic Republic, Hungary, Poland, and Romania. Its members now include Cuba, Mongolia, and Vietnam; it also maintains trade links with North Korea, Finland, and Yugoslavia. COMECON is headed by a Council that functions as the chief decision-making body except on matters of basic policy, where it can only make recommendations. A permanent Executive Committee implements decisions, a Secretariat headquartered in Moscow is directed by the Council, and more than 20 standing commissions carry out planning and operations. Originally designed to enhance Soviet control over Eastern Europe, COMECON's impact for the first decade was minimal. Until the death of Josef Stalin, COMECON operated on the basis of bilateral trade agreements imposed unilaterally by the Soviet Union. In the late 1950s Nikita Khrushchev revived COMECON and sought to build a "socialist commonwealth" based on economic specialization and integration. *See also* WARSAW TREATY ORGANIZATION (WTO), p. 365.

Significance   Although the ideal of an integrated world socialist economy has never materialized, COMECON has accomplished much since its revitalization under Khrushchev. It has fostered intrabloc trade and permits both the Soviet Union and the East European states access to each other's raw materials and products without requiring payment in hard currencies. Particularly until the oil price crisis of the 1970s, it insulated the COMECON countries from fluctuations in the world economy. It serves as the vehicle for joint investment projects such as the Orenburg-Uzhgorod gas pipeline and for intrabloc projects such as the East European power grid and common freight car pool. Member states have retained economic sovereignty, which has impeded coordination. In particular, Romania refused to accept its designated role as supplier of raw materials and agricultural products. As each nation's economic plan must provide for foreign trade and allocate the necessary inputs, central economic planning and national economic autonomy also impede integration. Much interbloc trade operates on the basis of material balances—surplus items will be exported. Although the Soviet Union does not completely dominate COMECON, the other members are disadvantaged by the sheer economic and political power of the Soviet Union. An additional calculation is that the Soviet Union supplies most of the energy requirements to the energy-poor East European states, until recently at preferential prices. A major question for the 1980s is whether the Soviet Union can, or is willing to, guarantee energy supplies to the COMECON states, perhaps at the sacrifice of much-needed hard currency earnings.

Communist Party of the Soviet Union (CPSU) The ruling institution and sole political authority in the Soviet Union. Although the USSR Constitution sets forth an elaborate parliamentary system and administrative structure, in effect the Communist Party of the Soviet Union (CPSU) is the governing organ of the state. The over 17 million CPSU members are bound by party discipline to obey all decisions of the central party leadership, who control the Soviet party-state. In a party-state, all institutions are subordinated to the party through duplication of office: important personnel, be they government ministers, trade union officials, or factory managers, are always party members. The party is organized as a vast pyramid controlled by a single, unified leadership. All decisions are transmitted downward, and thence outward to the subordinate institutions of the state. The CPSU operates under party statutes that delineate its organizational structure and fundamental principles; in effect these constitute the basic law of the state. Monolithic unity and a monopoly of control form the basis of the party's power. The most salient party principle, democratic centralism, includes the basic ideas that (1) monolithic unity is fundamental to Marxism-Leninism; (2) all party decisions are irrevocably binding on party members; and (3) any restriction or questioning of party policy is considered revisionism, contrary to the party's role as the only legitimate interpreter of Marxism-Leninism. All the means of production are state-owned and party-controlled, thus enabling the party to allocate the resources of the state according to its goals. The CPSU is organized according to Leninist principles. Every member must belong to a primary party organization (PPO) formed in the workplace. Above the PPO level the party is organized into territorial units that replicate the administrative structure of the state: county or city districts; cities, provinces; territorial units within the republics; republics; and national. Party organs above the PPOs are composed of members delegated from the preceding level; in actuality preselected by the higher party leadership. Party organs supervise the lower party units on their territory; for example a district party typically monitors 150–200 PPOs. Each party unit is composed of a conference (at republican and national levels, the congress); a permanent committee (at republican and national levels, the central committee); and an inner executive organ, the bureau (at the national level, the CPSU Politburo). Although according to party statutes the ruling bodies are the congresses or conferences, when not in session replaced by the committees, in reality the inner executive organs, the bureaus, have largely usurped the committees' statutory functions. The bureaus, including the CPSU Politburo, are assisted by a permanent administrative organ, the secretariat. Above the PPO, secretariats are headed by the secretary of each party unit (at the top, the CPSU general secretary), assisted by one or more deputy secretaries. Each secretary is responsible for supervising a functional area in the party unit's territory—agriculture, heavy industry, ideology, and so forth. The secretariats and their full-time staffs comprise the party apparatus, whose estimated 250,000 members are referred to as the *apparatchiks*. The party's power is buttressed by its control of the military and secret police (KGB), which enforce conformity and treat any perceived deviation from party policy as betrayal of the socialist state. See also OTHER CPSU ENTRIES, pp. 288–298; DUPLICATION OF OFFICE, p. 310; LENINISM, p. 330; *NOMENKLATURA*, p. 337; TERRITORIAL DIVISIONS, p. 362.

Significance Through a unified command structure, monopoly of power, and penetration of all sectors of society, the Communist Party of the Soviet Union has created a party-state in which no intervening institutions between citizen and state are permitted. Although all Soviet constitutions—1924, 1936, 1977—carefully prescribe the organization and functions of the governmental system, in reality Soviet constitutionalism is a fiction. There are no institutionalized limits on the CPSU, and within the party, on the central leadership itself. The 1977 USSR Constitution describes the CPSU as the "leading and guiding force of society, the nucleus of its political system and of all state and public organizations," thus legally endorsing the party's monopoly of power. Despite the immense changes since the 1920s, most of them wrought by the party, there have been few subsequent changes in the CPSU. Lenin's small band of revolutionaries has been transformed into a permanent ruling body, in the process becoming rigidly centralized, increasingly bureaucratized, and all-powerful. The CPSU members who "lead society in the name of the proletariat" are now dominated by the intelligentsia ("mind-workers") who comprise about half of the total membership and almost all of the top-level party organs. Overall, the membership is predominately male, educated, and urban; workers and peasants are underrepresented. Although 25 percent of party members are women, there is little female representation at the top. Women are also excluded from the organs of control. Consequently, the Soviet power structure is overwhelmingly male. As there is no limitation on terms of party office and no intraparty democracy, the leadership is essentially self-selected, and the state is ruled by an aging male oligarchy. The party *is* the state; any change must come from within the party itself.

CPSU: Central Committee   A committee of over 300 members that is the most important continuing party body according to party statutes. The Central Committee is formally responsible for directing the party between party congresses and for supervising all party activities. In theory, the Politburo and Secretariat report to the Central Committee. In reality, the power of the Central Committee is severely limited by its infrequent meetings and large membership. The true power rests with the Politburo and the Secretariat. The major function of the Central Committee is to provide a sense of legitimacy and national consensus for decisions of the Politburo. Thus most important decisions are issued in the name of the Central Committee. Since Josef Stalin's death in 1953 a second function, that of representation, has evolved. The membership of the Central Committee and its allied body, the Party Control Commission, now comprises a carefully worked out balance of all important party, government, national, and social elements. Central Committees are formally elected at each party Congress every five years, the membership selected in advance by the party leadership. The Central Committee elected in 1981 totaled 319 full members and 151 candidate (nonvoting) members. It usually meets twice a year, in sessions of one to three days. Plenary (full) sessions may also be held before major events, such as the introduction of the five-year plan, or to formally announce the selection of a new general secretary. The Central Committee shares many functions with the government, specifically in the legislative process, where the decrees issued in its name jointly with the Council of Ministers are binding on all legislative organs. A permanent staff of around 1,500, divided into departments and sections, provides administrative support for the Secretariat of the Central Committee. Although largely shorn of its policy-making power, the Central Committee fulfills an important role as legitimator for decisions taken by the party leadership, while its representational character makes it the most truly national of party institutions. *See also* CPSU: POLITBURO, p. 294; CPSU: SECRETARIAT, p. 297; *OBLAST'*, p. 337.

Significance Since its inception at the first Bolshevik Party Congress in 1898 the Central Committee has been the most visible part of the party structure. Originally the governing body of the party, the Central Committee evolved into the instrument through which Vladimir Lenin wielded power. By 1919 Lenin had enlarged its membership and created two inner organs, the Organizational Bureau (Orgburo) and Political Bureau (Politburo). Lenin's creation of functionally specific inner bodies set the pattern whereby party power increasingly devolved to a small, inner elite. During the first decade of Bolshevik rule, however, the Central Committee was not totally subordinate, even as late as 1932 occasionally outvoting Stalin. Stalin repeatedly purged the Central Committee membership, installing his own supporters, and reduced its role to that of formal ratification of his policies, a function it retains to this day. In the final years of Stalin's dictatorship, the Central Committee met infrequently. Since his death, the Central Committee has regained its function as legitimator of policy, and its membership is now carefully selected so as to represent all leading elements in the system. Appointment to many important positions carries almost automatic membership in the Central Committee. The first secretaries of the 14 republican parties, heads of major government ministries and state committees, members of the Presidium of the Supreme Soviet, leading representatives of the military and security forces, and preeminent scientific and cultural figures are all coopted into the Central Committee. Provincial (*oblast'*) party secretaries form the largest single grouping. If an oblast' secretary holds Central Committee membership, it is indicative of the political and economic importance of that oblast'. Many other important figures are accorded representation on the Party Control Commission, the organ attached to the Central Committee charged with ensuring party discipline. Since the 1960s, the Central Committee has been characterized by increasing stability of membership. The national elite represented on the Central Committee has become an aged elite, a gerontocracy reflected in the Politburo, whose ages now average around 70. The representational nature lends further legitimacy to the resolutions of the Central Committee, conveying a sense of national consensus and reinforcing the party's self-acclaimed role as the leading element of society.

CPSU: Congress The party body originally intended to be the supreme organ of the Communist party, charged with determining long-range policy and electing a Central Committee to direct party work between congresses. In actuality the national (or all-union) congress has become a ceremonial body, meeting only once every five years. Its policy-making and elective functions, as with those of the Central Committee, have been usurped by the inner party bodies, the Politburo and Secretariat. Thus the flow of power is the reverse of that mandated by the party statutes, which designate the congress as the highest authoritative body. The agenda, the delegates, and the Central Committee it "elects" are predetermined by the party leadership. The large number of delegates—almost 5,000—and infrequent convocations preclude any meaningful role. Democratic centralism and mandatory party discipline make any debate impossible, as all decisions taken by the leadership are binding on all members. The party congress functions as an instrument of legitimation for the leadership. Its ceremonial functions include formally endorsing the party platform, issuing a comprehensive statement of party goals for the next five years, and adopting the party statutes, the governing rules for the party. The major event is the report of the Central Committee, delivered by the general secretary. Although important pronouncements may be made, there is no open dabate since the agenda is set in advance by the party leadership. Thus, the party congress has become a ceremony whose main function is to convey unity with the leadership and publicly endorse its policies. National party congresses are preceded by congresses of the local and regional party bodies, all similarly orchestrated by the party leadership. At each level, preselected central committees, or party bureaus as they are termed at the local levels, are approved. Under careful supervision, the congress approves a list of delegates to the next party congress, on up to the national congress. Thus, at each level of party organization, the party congress functions mainly to publicly endorse the decisions of the higher party authorities. *See also* BOLSHEVIK, p. 273; CPSU: CENTRAL COMMITTEE, p. 288; DE-STALINIZATION, p. 305.

Significance The party congress dates from the early days of the Bolsheviks, when according to the statutes first adopted in 1898 the congress wielded considerable power over the small, illegal party. Between 1917 and 1925, congresses were held annually, and open debate over party policy was permitted. Josef Stalin first breached party statutes by delaying the Fifteenth Party Congress until 1927; by 1952 he had not convened a congress for 14 years. Since then, Stalin's successors have convened congresses every four to five years, but have used them as legitimating devices rather than as policy-making bodies. At times party congresses have been crucial. Soviet intransigence toward intraparty democracy was determined by the Resolution on Unity passed by the Tenth Party Congress of 1921, when Vladimir Lenin suppressed the Workers' Opposition movement and decreed that factions within the party would not be tolerated. It was this resolution that, coupled with Stalin's seizure of undisputed power, doomed intraparty democracy and eventually rendered the congress and most other party bodies meaningless. Until 1927 open debate was still permitted. After Stalin achieved power, the congress as a functional body atrophied. The 1934 Party Congress, called the "Congress of the Victors," was orchestrated by Stalin to praise the success of central planning and agricultural collectivization. The most dramatic post-Stalin Congress was the Twentieth Party Congress of 1956, when Nikita Khrushchev stunned delegates by publicly revealing the scope and inhumanity of Stalinist terror in a "secret speech." Despite the suppression of intraparty democracy, absence of any genuine debate, and ritualistic unanimous votes, the party congress does fulfill some functions. By endorsing policy pronouncements and personnel changes, it provides legitimacy for the leadership. The party statutes, adopted at a congress, in effect the governing constitution of the party, provide the clearest public guide to party organization and practice. The party platform lays out the programmatic and ideological priorities of the party for the next five years. National party congresses are also attended by foreign Communist delegations, and the composition and actions of these delegations can illuminate relations between the Soviet Union and other states. For example, at the Twenty-fourth CPSU Congress in 1971 the Italian Communist party openly criticized the Soviet-led invasion of Czechoslovakia of 1968, a clear signal that the USSR could no longer control the Communist parties of Western Europe. Thus, while the party congress bears little resemblance to the original Bolshevik institution, it remains a useful aid in political analysis.

CPSU: General Secretary   The head of the Communist Party of the Soviet Union and the acknowledged leader of the state. The general secretary is the single most powerful figure and the symbol of national authority. His formal position is head of the party Secretariat. As chief administrative officer of the party, the general secretary oversees the implementation of party policy, determines key appointments, and controls the party apparatus. The general secretary is also head of the Politburo—although party rules make no explicit provision for this—and thus controls the policy-making process. As all government institutions are in practice subordinate to the party, the general secretary also functions as head of state, whether or not he holds the formal position as chairman of the Supreme Soviet. Since Josef Stalin was named general secretary in 1922, the party leader has been selected in a highly secret process from among the three to six men who hold membership on both the Politburo and Secretariat. There are no limitations on terms of office, nor any institutionalized method of removing or replacing a general secretary. Although according to party statutes the general secretary is elected by the Central Committee, his selection is the prerogative of the small oligarchy who actually wield power in the Soviet system; the Central Committee merely ratifies their decision publicly. Whatever limitations apply to his actions are the result of internal politicking and the competition between party groups rather than from any statutory checks. Only in 1964, when the Politburo (then called the Presidium) determined to oust Nikita Khrushchev, was the decision deferred to and confirmed by a vote of the Central Committee. In over 60 years, only six men have permanently held the post: Stalin (1922–53), Khrushchev (1953–64), Leonid Brezhnev (1964–82), Yuri Andropov (1982–84), Konstantin Chernenko (1984–85), Mikhail Gorbachev (1985–). Stalin used the party apparatus to seize and exercise dictatorial control; most evidence indicates that his successors have operated far more consensually, as chief conciliators responsible for effecting acceptable compromises. Particularly in foreign affairs the general secretary probably does not possess enough power to unilaterally determine foreign policy, although his is the final voice. Periodically the general secretary delivers reports to the Central Committee, thus making public issues of import. The policies announced in the name of the general secretary are in effect binding upon the state. The dynamics of Soviet politics, with its subordination of government to party, strict hierarchical flow of power, and mandatory obedience to party decisions, almost necessitates the existence of a supreme party leader. The general secretary has thus come to symbolize the authority of the Communist party and its dominance over the state. *See also* CPSU: CENTRAL COMMITTEE, p. 288; CPSU: POLITBURO, p. 294; CPSU: SECRETARIAT, p. 297; DEFENSE COUNCIL, p. 303; PRESIDIUM OF THE SUPREME SOVIET, p. 343.

Significance The fact that the position of general secretary is determined secretly by the leading figures on the Politburo and Secretariat illuminates the true locus of power in the Soviet system. The intense speculation that develops whenever a change in the secretaryship impends attests to the power of the position. The actual selection process remains a political mystery. Few Western analysts picked Chernenko as Andropov's successor. What factors may be weighed into the selection process may be apparent only after the succession is announced. For example, it is now believed that the 1984 selection of the then 73-year-old Konstantin Chernenko, once passed over in favor of Yuri Andropov, indicated that the equally aged ruling oligarchy was reluctant to turn over the reins of power to a new generation. The lack of an institutionalized method of succession to the highest post in the Soviet Union constitutes a major weakness of the system, stripping it of a regularized means of handling a transfer of power. It contributes heavily to the ossification and conservatism of the system. Only Khrushchev was replaced by a means other than death. His downfall may have resulted from the threat his proposed administrative reforms posed to party bureaucrats, themselves the occupants of posts with unlimited tenure. Lacking true elections and any legal, constitutional claim to national leadership, the general secretaries have traditionally pursued two methods of legitimating power: (1) by manipulating the symbols of office so that the polity accepts him as national leader and (2) by creating a power base of local and national officials who owe their positions to him. The position also naturally lends itself to legitimation through charisma, or what Khrushchev criticized as the Stalinist "cult of personality." Since Khrushchev's revelations about Stalin's brutality, party leaders have eschewed terror, preferring to base their legitimacy on economic and foreign policy achievements. The power of the general secretary as national leader lies not in legal institutions but in his control over the party and the policy process. Party control means control over the nation, thus making it clear who rules the Soviet state.

CPSU: Main Political Administration (MPA)   The chief organ of party supervision over the military, responsible for supervising and directing all political work in the Soviet armed forces. The Main Political Administration reports directly to the Central Committee and is supervised by the Politburo. The MPA evaluates the political reliability of all military personnel and directs the party and Komsomol units based in the armed forces. Members of the MPA hold military rank and are trained in military party schools, the highest being the Lenin Military Political Academy. At each level of operation, from the company to the division, the chief MPA official is the *zampolit,* or political officer. In addition to political supervision, the MPA is responsible for political indoctrination (agitprop) and for the military press. The MPA's work is coordinated by the Main Military Council, charged with supervising overall national party policy in the armed forces. *See also* DEFENSE COUNCIL, p. 303; NOMENKLATURA, p. 337.

Significance   The Main Political Administration is the major instrument by which the party hierarchy maintains ideological control over the military and ensures that only the politically reliable advance in rank. The zampolit can be the key determinant of a young officer's career. The origins of the MPA lie in the Civil War period, when the Bolsheviks instituted a system of political commissars as a means of surveillance over the many former czarist officers who served with the Red Army. The MPA thus continues the tradition of civilian control over the military. The MPA also recruits promising members into military party units, creating a self-generating pool of politically reliable officers who owe their positions to the party. For young Soviet males, the MPA's agitprop work forms the capstone in the socialization of Soviet youth that begins in preschool. Rather than contending for power, the party and the military have traditionally maintained a symbiotic relationship.

CPSU: Politburo The Political Bureau of the Central Committee, the supreme policy-making organ and dominant political institution in the Soviet Union. Although technically its mandate extends only over the party, in reality the Politburo sets policy for both party and state. Its decisions are translated into law by the Supreme Soviet and other government bodies, and are implemented by a vast array of government and party officials, all of whom are ultimately subordinate to the Politburo. The Politburo is composed of up to two dozen of the most powerful national leaders and is headed by the general secretary of the party, the acknowledged leader of the nation. Membership includes both full and candidate (nonvoting) members. Membership is self-selected, through cooptation. All Politburo members sit on the Central Committee, which functions chiefly to legitimate Politburo policy. Although it is the dominant political institution, only two concrete facts are known about the Politburo: its membership and the fact that all important policy decisions are made there. According to party statutes, the Politburo is responsible for the work of the party when the Central Committee is not in session. Because the Central Committee meets infrequently, the Politburo has become the chief policy-maker. Much of its work is concerned with international affairs, the economy, and national security. The Politburo has no set size, no formal selection process, and no set agenda; it operates without formal institutional restraints. Although it has no designated head, in practice the general secretary is the leading figure and thus the ultimate repository of political power. Disagreements or changes in policy can frequently be ascertained only through rumor or sudden shifts in membership. Under Josef Stalin's dictatorship the power of all party organs, including the Politburo, atrophied; his successors have restored its power and emphasized the consensual nature of its decision making. The Politburo constitutes a self-selected elite that has arrogated major decision making power to itself, operates without restraints, and makes policy decisions for the entire country. This emphasizes the fusion of power and oligarchic nature of the Soviet system. *See also* CPSU: CENTRAL COMMITTEE, p. 288; CPSU: GENERAL SECRETARY, p. 291; CPSU: SECRETARIAT, p. 297; SUPREME SOVIET, p. 360.

Significance First constituted by Vladimir Lenin in October of 1919 to consolidate Bolshevik power, the Politburo has been the true locus of power throughout much of Soviet history. Politburo membership is the most tangible sign of power, ranking above even a position on the Secretariat. Membership can offer some clues to Soviet priorities. When Yuri Andropov, then head of the KGB, and Andrei Grechko, minister of defense, were named to the Politburo in 1973, it was taken as evidence of the increased emphasis on national security and the military. The Politburo usually contains an inner group of three to six members who also sit on the Secretariat and are assumed to be the top rulers of the state. Thus, Andropov's accession to the Secretariat in 1982 was a signal that he had joined the inner ruling elite and was in line to succeed Leonid Brezhnev. The secretive nature of the Politburo makes political analysis difficult, but it may be safely assumed that any substantive change in priorities, reallocation of resources, or important policy change has originated in the Politburo.

CPSU: Primary Party Organization The basic organizational unit of the Communist Party of the Soviet Union, commonly called the party cell. Every party member, regardless of rank, must be a member of a primary party organization (PPO). The major functions of a PPO are (1) selecting and training new members, usually on recommendation from the local Komsomol unit; (2) mobilizing support and explaining party policy (agitprop); (3) assessing public opinion; (4) recommending people for promotion in their workplaces; and (5) supervising the administration of the work unit in which the PPO is based. The last, verification (*pravo kontroyla*), is a key function. It gives the party the right to supervise the management of all economic enterprises, as well as government agencies. Unlike higher party units (county, city, province, territory, and republic), which are territorially based, PPOs are based on the place of work or economic function. PPOs, which now number about 420,000, are found in factories, farms, schools, hospitals, military units, government agencies—in short, wherever Soviet citizens carry out their daily duties. Only a PPO can accept candidate (nonvoting) members, admit new members, or expel them. Candidate members must serve a probationary period of one to three years. PPOs range in size from 3 to over 1,000 members; about 95 percent have less than 100. On the farms, the collective farm party organization (or PPO) is usually subdivided into functional party groups headed by the organizers (*partgruporgs*). Similarly, large industrial PPOs are subdivided at the shop floor or department level. All PPOs with over 15 members are directed by an inner body, the executive committee or the party bureau. PPO officials are selected through cooptation, which means preselection by higher party bodies. All decisions of higher party bodies are binding on the PPOs. Every party member is given a party assignment, such as leading a mass organization, doing agitprop work, or serving in a government post. How well a member performs the party assignment may largely determine advancement through party ranks. See also COMMUNIST PARTY OF THE SOVIET UNION (CPSU), p. 288; DUPLICATION OF OFFICE, p. 310; KOMSOMOL, p. 328; LENINISM, p. 330; NOMENKLATURA, p. 337.

Significance   The primary party organization evolved from Vladimir Lenin's organizational plan, first explained in "What Is to Be Done" (1902), as the direct link between the worker and the vanguard party. Originally a decentralized, secret cell system in which only a few members would know the entire network and thus be liable to betray it to the czarist police, the functions of the modern PPO have changed. It is still the major mobilizational device at local levels. The verification function has become especially important, providing both surveillance over the bureaucracy and a means of applying party policy to concrete situations. PPOs can question all administrative and managerial decisions, and review how party policy is implemented. As practically everything in the Soviet system is in the public sector, there is very little that is not subject to party verification. The PPO is the primary instrument through which the party ensures penetration of all society. For over 17 million Soviet adults, the PPOs are the major mode of political participation, thus encouraging millions of citizens to perceive themselves as part of the decision-making process.

CPSU: Purge   Periodic review of members of the Communist party aimed at removing all unreliable or unworthy members. The original meaning of the term purge (*chistka*) refers to the practice of "purifying" the party by periodically reviewing the dedication and accomplishments of all members. The purge, as practiced by pre-Stalin and post-Stalin Soviet leaderships, is an exchange of party cards. Members are interviewed, their qualifications assessed, and new party cards are issued for all those who pass the review. Josef Stalin debased both the term and the practice in the 1930s when he used it to weed out all real and potential rivals for power. The term, purge, became synonymous with Stalinist terror, as the hundreds of thousands of Communists whom

Stalin purged were summarily imprisoned or executed. The period of terror, which has become known as the Great Purge (1934-38) affected millions of Soviet citizens, both party and nonparty. Since Stalin's death his successors have returned the mechanism to its original function, and confined such periodic reviews to an exchange of party cards with the aim of stripping the party of unworthy elements. An exchange of party cards today is an administrative procedure, carried out by the basic party organs, the primary party organizations, which are respsonsible for issuing new party cards. *See also* GREAT PURGE, p. 322.

Significance The purge, or exchange of party cards, enables the party periodically to review members' qualifications and to reinforce its image as the vanguard of society. Such reviews are used to weed out those who refuse to carry out their assigned party duties as well as those who refuse to live by the rules of the party. Purges may be local, as in the Republic of Georgia in 1972-74, when revelations of widespread corruption prompted the Brezhnev leadership to tighten discipline there. Or they may be national, as in 1974. Unlike Stalinist times, such national reviews are limited in scope; it is estimated that the 1974 membership review affected only about 1 percent of the total party membership. Both the meaning of the term and the method of implementation have changed drastically since Stalin. Stalin essentially used the purge to create a revolutionary movement, under his undisputed control, that would build the perfect communist society. Post-Stalin leaderships have largely given up on the pursuit of ideological perfection through terror, preferring to create stable and secure bureaucracies where only a tiny minority are threatened by an exchange of party cards.

CPSU: Secretariat The central executive body of the Communist Party of the Soviet Union. The Secretariat of the Central Committee is responsible for supervising the vast party apparatus and ensuring that party decisions are implemented by the government and all other officials. It thus controls all sectors of national life and is the most influential and pervasive organ of the party. A key component of the Secretariat's power is its control over the *nomenklatura* system, through which appointment to all important posts, party and nonparty, can be made only with party approval. By virtue of party membership and strict party discipline, government officials are subordinated to the control of the Secretariat. Party directives are thus binding upon the government, as well as on all other institutions. The Secretariat consists of several party secretaries, headed by the general secretary, who also heads the Politburo, the chief policy-making body. Each secretary is responsible for a specific sector or group of related sectors of national life. Although nominally elected by and responsible to the Central Committee, the Secretariat is a self-elected body. Members are selected by the top leadership through cooptation and confirmed ex post facto by the Central Committee. A small inner elite of three to six members, including the general secretary, sits on both the Secretariat and Politburo and in effect constitutes the ruling oligarchy of the Soviet state. The Secretariat also operates as a policy-planning group, providing the Politburo with specialized information and frequently participating in Politburo meetings. The major functions of the Secretariat include (1) monitoring the implementation of party policy as determined by the Politburo; (2) researching and proposing policy; (3) approving all important appointments; and (4) overseeing the activities of all party units, each of which, from the 14 republican secretariats to the local party bureaus, possesses a similar executive body subordinate to the all-union CPSU Secretariat. Staff support is provided by the apparatus of the Central Committee, estimated at around 1,500. The staff is divided into 24 functionally specific departments (*otdely*). Departments are further divided into sections, estimated at 150–175. The responsibilities of the Secretariat include ensuring that the various economic ministries and planning organs implement the legally binding economic plans. Other responsibilities cover most of the activities of the nation, from the supervision of schools to foreign policy, defense and ideology. The general secretary possesses a permanent staff that prepares speeches and policy statements and assists him in exercising general leadership over the country. *See also* CPSU: CENTRAL COMMITTEE, p. 288; CPSU: GENERAL SECRETARY, p. 291; *NOMENKLATURA,* p. 337; STALINISM, p. 357.

Significance The all-pervasive supervisory power of the Secretariat is key to understanding how the Communist party penetrates and controls all aspects of Soviet life. Ultimately, no one, neither government official nor factory worker nor school teacher, can operate outside the purview of the CPSU Secretariat. It constitutes a de facto cabinet, one which wields far more power than the putative cabinet, the Council of Ministers. The Secretariat developed from the 1919 party reorganization that created the Politburo and an Orgburo, staffed by the original Secretariat. After Vladimir Lenin's death Josef Stalin used his position as the only party leader on both Politburo and Orgburo to achieve power and used his power over the party apparatus to eventually destroy his rivals, thus achieving undisputed control. Stalin's successors have followed a comparable although far less bloody path to supreme power. The Secretariat epitomizes the monolithic nature of communist party-systems whereby all important decisions are made by party leaders rather than by elected officials.

Criminal Offenses: Anti-Soviet Agitation and Propaganda

The legal charge under which dissidents and those who openly question any aspect of the Soviet system are usually prosecuted and punished. Anti-Soviet agitation and propaganda is defined by Article 70 of the RSFSR criminal code as any speech or expression that slanders or defames the Soviet state, any propaganda with the same intent, or any activities intended to weaken the state, including participation in a group with such goals. The charge, as defined by Article 70, is thus the basic law used to control speech and expression in the Soviet Union. The definition of Article 70 rests with the authorities; it is broad enough that it covers expressions as well as actions and permits the authorities to suppress any activities they view as dissent. Since the legal reforms of 1958–60, most Soviet citizens arrested and convicted for political reasons have been charged under Article 70 and two newer provisions, Articles 190-1 and 190-3, added in 1966. These latter provisions made it a crime to prepare or circulate statements supposedly slandering or defaming the Soviet system even if direct anti-Soviet intent on the part of the perpetrators could not be proved. This made it possible for the authorities to legally prosecute those whose views were politically unacceptable but not in outright opposition, by charging that such activities can be used by the enemies of the Soviet Union. A 1984 addition to the criminal code further extended the control over citizens by making it a crime to discuss any state activities, including a citizen's job, with a foreigner. *See also* CIVIL RIGHTS, p. 279; DISSENT AND OPPOSITION, p. 306; KGB, p. 326; SOCIALIST LEGALITY, p. 353.

Significance Defining and punishing what the authorities view as anti-Soviet agitation and propaganda has been a major concern of the party since the Bolshevik Revolution. During the Civil War (1918–21), the Bolsheviks usually labeled their opponents "counter-revolutionaries" and executed them. Under the new Bolshevik legal code of 1922, any action the authorities defined as being counter to the goals of socialism became a criminal act. Under Josef Stalin's dictatorship, millions of Soviet citizens were exectued or sentenced to almost sure death in the prison labor camps for any actions the dictatorship chose to define as antisocialist. The postwar abolition of the Stalinist terror left the Soviet leadership with the problem of how to suppress those who question the system. With the codification of the legal codes in 1958–60, the leadership turned to a legalistic approach, using the charge of anti-Soviet agitation and propaganda as their main instrument. The charge is elastic enough for anti-Soviet intent to be inferred from almost any questioning of policy or suggestion for change, be it in religion, art, or law. Although some of the most publicized political trials during Leonid Brezhnev's leadership involved convictions for anti-Soviet agitation and propaganda, the record is immeasurably better than during the Stalinist period. In recent years the authorities have used three methods of punishing dissent: (1) punishment under Articles 70 and 190; (2) extrajudicial punishments, such as denial of better housing or jobs; and (3) administrative confinement to psychiatric hospitals. In the mid-1970s, in cases of the most prominent dissenters, the authorities began to supplement judicial and administrative punishments with forced deportation abroad. The legal charge in effect negates the constitutional protection of civil rights, since any criticism of authority can be treated as a criminal act.

Criminal Offenses: Crimes Against Socialist Property

Illegal acts committed in reference to state-owned property. Soviet legal codes distinguish between offenses committed against socialist (state) property and those committed against privately owned property. The three general categories of crimes against socialist property are (1) theft of socialist property; (2) criminal enrichment through the use of socialist property; and (3) the destruction, damage, or loss of socialist property. Some actions, such as negligence, are crimes only if committed with reference to socialist property. By law, all major resources and means of production are state-owned. Socialist property also includes public property, such as the land and equipment of the collective farms. Misuse or theft of socialist and public property, and embezzlement or fraud, are viewed as crime directed against the state itself. Such crime may range from petty pilfering to establishing illegal factories with stolen socialist property. Conviction carries heavier penalties than similar crimes against private property. The death penalty can be, and is, applied to severe cases. *See also* CRIMINAL OFFENSES: CRIMES AGAINST THE STATE, p. 301; SECOND ECONOMY, p. 350; SOCIALIST LEGALITY, p. 353; SOCIALIST OWNERSHIP, p. 354.

Significance Crime against socialist property probably ranks as the second largest category of crime committed in the Soviet Union—the first being minor social offenses such as public disorderliness ("hooliganism") and alcoholism. Much crime against socialist property is also minor, involving petty theft or carelessness. Soviet criminal codes treat such crime as second in seriousness only to crimes against the state. The more restricted protection accorded to socialist property is consistent with Marxism-Leninism, which elevates the interests of the state above all else.

Criminal Offenses: Crimes Against the State In the Soviet criminal codes, the most serious category of crime. Crimes against the state comprise a wide range of actions that the authorities view as a threat to the maintenance of the socialist system. Soviet law is characterized by an emphasis on the protection of the state, and in particular, its political and economic interests. These actions, many of which would not be considered criminal under Western legal codes, are defined as crimes because they impinge on the interests of the socialist state. Major state crimes are (1) treason (including flight abroad); (2) espionage; (3) murdering a public official; (4) sabotage; (5) subverting the economy; (6) anti-Soviet agitation and propaganda; and (7) participating in an anti-Soviet (i.e., not approved by the state) organization. The charge is both the most serious and the most flexible in its legal application. Any expression the authorities choose to construe as weakening the party's ideological and political monopoly is viewed as a crime against the state. The Russian (RSFSR) Criminal Code (although there is not yet a uniform federal code, the 15 republican codes seldom diverge) clearly states this priority. The first article reads "... the RSFSR criminal code has as its task the protection of the Soviet social and state system...." Conviction for crime against the state carries the most severe penalties, including the death penalty. *See also* CRIMINAL OFFENSES: ANTI-SOVIET AGITATION AND PROPAGANDA, p. 299; CRIMINAL OFFENSES: CRIMES AGAINST SOCIALIST PROPERTY, p. 300; CRIMINAL OFFENSES: ECONOMIC CRIMES, p. 301; CRIMINAL OFFENSES: OFFICIAL CRIMES, p. 302; SOCIALIST LEGALITY, p. 353.

Significance The Soviet legal system has consistently used criminal law for the dual purpose of controlling criminal behavior and buttressing state power. The latter purpose lies behind the concept of state crime, defining as criminal any action that threatens state power. The charge itself carries a special burden. Pretrial investigation is carried out by the KGB rather than by the state attorneys of the Procuracy. Frequently, political considerations weigh more heavily than the actual act itself. Those whom the Western press refers to as "political prisoners" have usually been convicted of crimes against the state. A recent addition to the procedural codes permits the authorities to extend without trial the sentences of political prisoners for "malicious disobedience or opposition to the prison administration."

Criminal Offenses: Economic Crimes Activities related to the production, distribution, and consumption of material goods that are subject to criminal sanctions. Economic crimes range from illegal currency transactions or smuggling to operating flea markets. Soviet legal codes contain long lists of economic activities defined as crime, usually because they in some way impede the functioning of the state economy. They include such things as: buying and selling outside of the state retail establishments, issuing substandard products, moonlighting, falsifying economic reports, feeding state-produced bread to livestock, or distilling *samogon,* home-brewed alcohol. Despite the range in seriousness, the common characteristic of these activities is that they are carried on outside the state economic system. Penalties for conviction range from minor sentences to several years imprisonment or the death penalty. *See also* CRIMINAL OFFENSES: CRIMES AGAINST THE STATE, p. 301; SECOND ECONOMY, p. 350; SOCIALIST LEGALITY, p. 353.

Significance The common element in all the activities designated as economic crimes is that, in a system posited on total state control of almost all economic activity, they in some way violate that control. Thus, the singling out of these activities as criminal is consistent with the doctrine of socialist legality, which elevates the interests of the state above all other judicial concerns. Many relatively minor offenses are tacitly permitted, giving rise to the second economy. The activities of the enterprise "fixer," the *tolkach,* who frequently circumvents the state supply system by making private deals for crucial supplies, may be illegal but are rarely prosecuted. Since Soviet judicial theory holds that such activities may be defined as crime, the criminal codes have become the main legal instrument used to protect the economic monopoly of the state.

Criminal Offenses: Official Crimes Legal infractions committed by state officials in the exercise of their duties. A separate chapter of each republican criminal code is devoted to official crimes, which includes abuse of authority, neglect of duty, offering and taking bribes, and forgery. "Officials" encompass a wide range of persons: soldiers on duty, policemen, enterprise management, teachers, sea captains, and in general, any representative of authority or anyone in the administration of a public or state institution. Since there are for all practical purposes no private institutions, anyone in authority is included. "Substantial" harm must be proved. Official crimes must be intentional and damaging to the interests of the office or the state. They may be committed either by deliberate action or by omission, the nonperformance or improper performance of official duties. *See also* CRIMINAL OFFENSES: CRIMES AGAINST THE STATE, p. 301; CRIMINAL OFFENSES: ECONOMIC CRIMES, p. 301; SOCIALIST LEGALITY, p. 353.

Significance Although most modern legal codes contain provisions directed at official crime, the scope of such crime in the Soviet Union is unique. In effect, it extends criminal responsibility to the entire public sector, which in the Soviet Union is almost all-encompassing.

Defense Council A little-publicized but powerful interdepartmental body headed by the general secretary of the Soviet Communist party. The Defense Council probably functions as the chief body for coordinating military policy with the domestic and international priorities of the state. Its membership includes the top political and military leaders. Analysts assume that, in addition to its coordination functions, the Defense Council may make crucial military decisions. It should not be confused with the Military-Industrial Commission, a subordinate body of the Council of Economic Ministers that coordinates the work of the economic ministries in charge of defense-related production. *See also* CPSU: GENERAL SECRETARY, p. 291; KGB, p. 326; PRESIDIUM OF THE SUPREME SOVIET, p. 343.

Significance The Defense Council is typical of the Soviet pattern of governance, wherein some of the most important decision-making bodies are the least public. Possibly functioning as a secret chancellery for military affairs, it undoubtedly predates by many years the official admission, in 1975, of its existence. The fact that the three key posts in the Soviet system are considered to be the general secretary of the party, the president of the Supreme Soviet Presidium, and the chairmanship of the Defense Council attests to its importance. Presumably the general secretary of the CPSU chairs the Council. It is therefore a crucial element in a system that gives top priority to military interests. All branches of the economy must meet defense needs first; much more rigid quality controls are imposed on military production. The total defense budget of the Soviet Union is not made public, but its proportionate share of investment has continually increased. American CIA estimates place it as high as 16 percent of gross national product, far above the official Soviet figure of 3 percent. Although some analysts point to the Defense Council as proof that the Soviet Union possesses a powerful military-industrial complex, in reality the military and government are fused at the top. In a sense, the Soviet system itself may be described as a military-industrial complex in which military needs traditionally receive top priority. The fusion of civilian and military probably makes economic reform—and a cut in military spending—extremely difficult for the contemporary leadership.

Deputy An elected member of a local, regional, or national legislative body. More than 2.2 million deputies serve in the over 50,000 legislatures (soviets), which range from village soviets to the soviets of the 15 union-republics and the linchpin of the system, the Supreme Soviet. Deputies, who run unopposed, are elected in calendar-determined elections from single-member geographic districts. The crucial stage is the nomination process, which is structured to provide party control over candidate selection. Nominees are selected at general voters' meetings called by the mass organizations—the trade unions, work cooperatives, youth organs, cultural organizations, and party units. The intent is to give each part of society a voice. The key people in the mass organizations are always party members who in prenomination discussions have already agreed upon a slate. Campaigning is conducted with great seriousness, and almost all citizens are contacted personally by an election worker. Voters do not have an alternative choice, but they may reject the party's nominee; only if a candidate fails to poll a majority will a new nominee be presented. Failure to vote is viewed as a political act. Once elected, the role of the deputy is largely ceremonial as most soviets meet for only short periods of time, delegating their work to executive bodies. Their chief function is to validate by promulgating as law the decisions already made by administrative officials. In recent years, however, the deputy has also begun to function as an ombudsman between citizen and state. Deputies are now empowered to request information from any government agency (the *spravka*), file complaints, and render legal aid, all of which actions must be honored by the relevant administrative department. Many deputies now employ a staff of paid help and volunteers; some may handle up to 30,000 spravkas yearly. Deputies protect their constituents against administrative malfeasance, explain government decisions, cut red tape, and answer myriad requests for information and aid. *See also* CITIZEN PARTICIPATION, p. 279; MASS ORGANIZATIONS, p. 334; SOVIET, p. 355; SUPREME SOVIET, p. 360.

Significance The deputy is the focus of an elaborate electoral process that often has been characterized as a charade. The over 2.2 million deputies, however, along with the over 9 million citizens who run nomination meetings, the 1.3 who serve on the electoral commissions that must validate slates, and the over 3 million volunteers who contact voters constitute a major mode of Soviet political participation. The goal of Soviet elections, in which over 99 percent of the electorate votes, is not the selection of representatives but the involvement and mobilization of the citizenry. The widespread participation in the electoral process is a legitimating device; the single-candidate list preserves party control and a sense of universal support. It also provides a means of entry for reliable nonparty members, as over half the local deputies may be nonparty members. At higher levels, many deputy seats are reserved on an ex officio basis—that is, the occupant of a high party or government post is automatically entitled to a legislative seat. Further legitimacy for the system has been created by the expansion of the deputy's ombudsman role. Since the 1972 law that regularized this function, many a deputy has become a servant and mediator for the local community.

De-Stalinization   The renunciation of the Stalinist model of Communist governance of institutionalized terror begun after Josef Stalin's death in 1953. De-Stalinization renounced Stalin's personal dictatorship (1928–53), during which millions were arbitrarily sent to their deaths and party institutions atrophied. The secret police became a government within the government. The post-Stalin struggle for leadership passed through several stages, a crucial first act being the secret execution in 1953 of Lavrenti Beria, Stalin's head of the secret police. The Soviet Supreme Court then quietly rehabilitated many party members who had been executed in the Stalinist purges of the 1930s. Eastern Europe was immediately shaken by revolts in 1953 in Czechoslovakia and East Berlin. The East Berlin uprising spread throughout East Germany and was quelled only with Soviet military aid. In 1956, Nikita Khrushchev, who had emerged as first (general) secretary of the party, fueled the de-Stalinization campaign in a "secret speech" before the Twentieth Party Congress. Khrushchev's public admission at the Congress of Stalin's inhumanity irrevocably changed Soviet politics. Party organs, which Stalin had circumvented and controlled through terror, were restored to power. The prison labor camps were emptied, and a massive reform of the legal codes was undertaken. Internationally, the Soviet Union shifted from the "two camps" policy of confrontation with the capitalist nations to one of pursuing peaceful coexistence. De-Stalinization also spurred opposition in Eastern Europe, where unpopular and rigidly doctrinaire Stalinists remained in power. The opposition culminated in large-scale riots against the Polish Communist party and outright rebellion in Hungary in 1956. The "Polish October" was resolved with the installation of Wladyslaw Gomulka, recently released from a Polish prison, as leader, and the Soviet troops withdrew. In Hungary, the revolt quickly spun out of party control. Communism was restored only by a massive Soviet military intervention. Krushchev's de-Stalinization campaign may have also contributed to his own ouster. As all top party leaders, including Khrushchev, rose to power through Stalin's apparatus, his insistence on continuing de-Stalinization questioned the very nature of the Soviet system. In the only time that a general secretary has been replaced by a vote rather than through death, in 1964 Leonid Brezhnev replaced Khrushchev, and halted further liberalization. Since Khrushchev's ouster, the Soviet leaderships have refused to reopen the issue, but have also abjured any return to Stalinist terror. *See also* COLLECTIVIZATION, p. 280; GREAT PURGE, p. 322; PEACEFUL COEXISTENCE, p. 339; POLYCENTRISM, p. 270; SOCIALIST LEGALITY, p. 353; STALINISM, p. 357.

Significance De-Stalinization remains Khrushchev's most lasting contribution. The abandonment of the massive use of terror as a method of governance permanently changed the Soviet system. Party institutions revived. One of Khrushchev's chief criticisms was that Stalin had erected a "cult of personality" that undermined the role of the party and Marxist-Leninist collective leadership. De-Stalinization also meant the end of what the world until then had perceived as a monolithic Communist movement. It shattered the myth of Soviet infallibility and encouraged the rise of various "national" communisms that placed national interests over the interests of the Soviet Union. In 1962 China severed relations with the Soviet Union, hastening the development of a polycentric Communist world in which Communist parties no longer automatically tendered their allegiance to Moscow. In the Soviet Union, although liberalization has been curtailed, there has been no return to mass terror.

Dissent and Opposition The term applied to activities that either implicitly question the policies of the Soviet Communist party or that directly advocate change. Western constructs are imprecise in the Soviet context; Soviet authorities treat dissent and opposition as virtually indistinguishable. Essentially, any questioning of the party's monopoly of control, whether or not it posits systemic change, is treated by the authorities as oppositon. Overt dissent and opposition emerged in the Soviet Union only after the subsequent dismantling of the Stalinist terror system. For a brief period until the early 1960s, known as the Thaw, it appeared that a within-system evolution might be possible. Artistic censorship was relaxed, the labor camps emptied out, and works such as Aleksandr Solzhenitsyn's *One Day in the Life of Ivan Denisovich* were permitted publication. However, controls were soon tightened, although never to the Stalinist level. By the mid-1960s demands for the creative freedom promised by the Thaw had expanded into a broadbased spectrum of demands for religious freedom, national cultural identity for non-Russians, and implementation of meaningful civil liberties—in short, the right to question party policies. In 1970 the Fifth Directorate of the KGB, charged specifically with suppressing internal dissent, was created. Nonetheless, as the Soviet leaderships have been unwilling to reinstate the Stalinist terror system, they have relied on repressing what they define as dissent through legalistic means, sentencing offenders to prison for anti-Soviet propaganda (Article 70), incarcerating them in psychiatric hospitals to avoid public trials, or forcing them into exile abroad. *See also* CIVIL RIGHTS, p. 279; CRIMINAL OFFENSES: ANTI-SOVIET AGITATION AND PROPAGANDA, p. 299; SAMIZDAT, p. 349; SOCIALIST REALISM, p. 354.

Significance   Suppression of dissent and opposition has been embedded in the Soviet system since Vladimir Lenin outlawed intraparty factions in 1921. The Leninist policy was carried to extremes by Josef Stalin. Post-Stalinist dissent differs in that the authorities have been unable to compel total conformity. It also is characterized by two differences: (1) dissenters have publicized their causes abroad, and (2) dissenters have made common cause across national and social boundaries. The causes are varied. The Human Rights Movement, many of whose adherents remain avowed Marxists, focuses on civil liberties and the failure of the Soviet government to observe its treaty obligations under the Helsinki Accord of 1975 as well as the liberties guaranteed by the 1977 Soviet Constitution. The adherents grouped around the suppressed journal *Veche* espoused the most conservative, if not reactionary, Great Russian nationalism. A broader community, including the human rights activists, various artistic groups, dissenting religious groups, advocates of ethnic autonomy, and free trade unionists, is frequently referred to as the Democratic Movement. Loosely grouped around the *samizdat* journal, the *Chronicle of Current Events,* the Democratic Movement looked to physicist Andrei Sakharov as leader until the authorities forcibly exiled Sakharov to Gorky. Others have focused on the cause of the Crimean Tatars and other dispossessed minorities driven from their traditional homelands by Stalin. Another manifestation is the *Refuseniks,* those who have applied for permission to emigrate and have been refused exit visas, mainly Jews seeking to emigrate to the West and to Israel. Although during the 1970s over 250,000 Soviet Jews were permitted to leave, the return of the Cold War atmosphere slowed emigration to a trickle in the 1980s. Essentially, anything that lacks official sanction, from religion to folksongs, will be treated by the authorities as potential dissent. In the Soviet context, in particular those who press for human rights and greater democracy are advocating a political form that contradicts much of Russian and Soviet political culture and threatens party control. In the last decade, the Brezhnev leadership, followed by the Adropov and Chernenko leaderships, increasingly tightened control of Soviet dissent. By the early 1980s, the activists were a scattered, silenced handful, largely isolated from the masses.

DOSAAF   The Voluntary Association for the Assistance of Army, Air Force, and Navy, a mass organization that provides paramilitary training and recreation for civilians. First set up in the 1920s as *Osoaviakhim*, DOSAAF's membership is estimated at some 80 million persons. Operating independently of formal military control, it provides paramilitary training for youth, trains men and women to serve in the volunteer militia, home guard, and civil defense, and serves as the medium for sports activities such as glider training, parachute jumping, amateur radio broadcasting, and pilot training, which are otherwise not permitted in the civilian sector. DOSAAF also operates the mandatory preconscription military training for all young men between 14 and 17 that is part of the regular Soviet school curriculum. See also CITIZEN PARTICIPATION, p. 279; MASS ORGANIZATIONS, p. 334.

Significance DOSAAF provides the Soviet Union with an immense ready reserve of trained manpower and reinforces the image of a nation in arms, ready to defend itself against outside threat. Because so many of its activities are intrinsically appealing, DOSAAF attracts a sizable proportion of the active population. Military conscripts with DOSAAF experience are usually promoted more rapidly and, in general, the result is a militarily trained population.

Dual Subordination The administrative principle that all soviet organs are responsible to the next highest analogous government body and to the appropriate soviet (elected assembly). The principle of dual subordination mandates both vertical and horizontal subordination. Thus, the administrative departments and agencies of the soviets, from local soviets to the Supreme Soviet, are responsible to both their parent soviet and to the corresponding government organ at the next highest level, creating a hierarchical system of responsibility. For example, a district (*raion*) executive committee is responsible to the district soviet and to the provincial (*oblast'*) executive committee. At the topmost level, a republican Ministry of Education is responsible to its republican Council of Ministers and to the USSR Ministry of Education. See also DUPLICATION OF OFFICE, p. 310; PRESIDIUM OF THE COUNCIL OF MINISTERS, p. 343.

Significance Dual subordination enjoins the strict subordination of all lower organs of government to the superior organs in the government hierarchy, while providing responsibility to the local electoral body. In practice it means that final or important decisions are made by higher authorities while issues of local import are left to the local bodies. Two key institutions, the KGB and the Procuracy, are exempt from the principle of dual subordination, being responsible only to the central authorities. As the party and government hierarchies overlap, dual subordination reinforces party control. It tends to erode local authority, since government organs can always appeal upwards.

Duma   The lower house of the czarist legislature, established in 1906 as Russia's first representative national assembly. The Duma represents the major concession forced upon Czar Nicholas II by the abortive Revolution of 1905. The competence of the Duma was severely limited from its inception. The Cabinet and prime minister were responsible only to the crown, which retained control of the budget, foreign affairs, and the military. The upper house, the State Council, half of whose membership was selected by the czar, could veto any legislation passed by the Duma. The czar also could circumvent the Duma when it was not in session by issuing Orders in Council (*Ukazes*) although these had to be submitted for ex post facto approval at the next Duma session. Voting was multistage and indirect, heavily weighted in favor of the urban wealthy and the landowning gentry. Despite this, Nicholas illegally dissolved the first two Dumas as too "radical." A new electoral law, tailormade by Nicholas, produced an even more biased body, which lasted through two Dumas, from 1907 to 1917. Despite this, Nicholas still refused to cooperate with the Duma. That the third and fourth Dumas managed to pass some meaningful legislation and to provide an occasional oppositional voice is less a testimony to any royal cooperation than to the increasing bankruptcy of the czarist system as an agent of governance. In 1917 the Duma, along with other czarist institutions, was swept away by the Revolution. *See also* BOLSHEVIK REVOLUTION, p. 274; REVOLUTION OF 1905, p. 347.

Significance   Any possibility that the Duma might guide Russia toward democracy was aborted by Nicholas's stubborn commitment to royal absolutism. The skewed electoral rules were designed to disenfranchise peasants, urban workers, liberals, and non-Russian minorities. The deputies themselves were hampered by a lack of parliamentary experience and by Nicholas's refusal to establish a working relationship with the Duma. Furthermore, both leftists and rightists sought to bring down the Duma. Only the Kadets (Constitutional Democrats) were truly committed to a working parliament. Thus, by 1917, the chances for both constitutional reform and parliamentary democracy had been stymied by Nicholas's implacable absolutism and the lack of any institutionalized means of change. The abrupt fall of the monarchy in March 1917 was far less the result of an organized political opposition than of the simple recognition that the czarist order could no longer function. Its successor, the Provisional Government, disintegrated with equal rapidity in the Bolshevik Revolution.

Duplication of Office   The practice whereby party leaders simultaneously hold both party and government positions. Duplication of office is a major element in the Communist party's dominance over all of Soviet society. All party members, whether acting as government officals or not, are bound by party discipline to observe party decisions. The result is a series of interlocking party-government directorates where functional lines are blurred and the party is supreme. Duplication of office is all-pervasive, enabling the party to penetrate all levels of society. At the top, Politburo and Secretariat members hold positions on the Central Committee, the Supreme Soviet, the Council of Ministers, and the Presidium of the Supreme Soviet. At each level of administration in the Soviet federation, party committees possess departments that parallel the functions of the state bodies and share many of the personnel. At the local level, key members of the local soviet (assembly), enterprise managers, trade union heads, local police chiefs, and judicial procurators inevitably will be party officials. The top personnel of all nongovernmental organizations, such as youth groups and trade unions, are always party members. Because the party controls nominations to the elected assemblies and, through the *nomenklatura* system, determines appointments to all important positions, party members occupy all important positions. The only meaningful separation of party-government functions is in the generally accepted principle that the party determines the policies that the government executes. *See also* DUAL SUBORDINATION, p. 308; *NOMENKLATURA,* p. 337.

Significance   The effects of the interlocking party-government structure produced by duplication of office are far-reaching. Overall, the dominance of the party is ensured and the monolithic nature of the Soviet system preserved. Government initiative is stifled, local administrative bodies weakened, public confidence eroded, and large sections of the Constitution rendered meaningless. Since duplication of office was first instituted by Vladimir Lenin immediately after the Bolshevik Revolution, as consistent with the party's prerogative to lead society, party officials have consistently usurped the functions of government. Separation of powers, or *any* division between party and government, is dismissed by Soviet theorists as a bourgeois device. Nonetheless, *Podmena*, the substitution of party for government, is recognized as a problem even by Soviet commentators. The party, however, has thus far refused to dilute this key element of control. The tight interlock of party and government is maintained by party discipline, and no nonparty institution is permitted any measure of independence.

Enterprise   The basic unit of production in the state-owned and state-controlled Soviet economy. The enterprise is the instrument through which the state operates the economy. It is a legal entity—it can enter into contracts, sue and be sued, and receive legal remedies. Its legal personality begins when it is granted operational management over the state property allocated to it. Comparable to a factory in a capitalist system, the enterprise is set up by a state charter defining its scope of operations and allocating the necessary capital equipment. The state retains ownership of all assets and decides what percentage of the profits accrue to the state, the remainder being allocated for operational expenses and worker benefits. The primary responsibility of the enterprise is to fulfill the production targets set by the central planning organs. It is thus the basic unit in the state economic plan. As economic plans are legal enactments, they are legally binding upon the enterprises. The government determines production targets, product mix, wages, levels of profit, introduction of new technologies, and supply of materials. Each enterprise is economically accountable and must keep its account with Gosbank, the state bank. The enterprise manager is appointed by and responsible to the state. Unless it is part of an industrial association, the enterprise is directly supervised by the government ministry responsible for its particular branch of industry. At present, there are about 50,000 enterprises. *See also* COMMAND ECONOMY, p. 283; PLANNING, p. 340; SOCIALIST OWNERSHIP, p. 354.

Significance The enterprise functions as an agency of the state, fulfilling specific legally mandated economic activities. It is held economically accountable for the proper utilization of the assets of the state. Its role as the implementator of the economic plan limits its activities; management is paid on the basis of plan fulfillment, not on sales. For all practical purposes then, the enterprise is a subordinate unit for the administration of state property in a system where almost all property is owned by the state. It is, however, also a key unit in the social structure of the nation. The enterprise is the base for several important organizations, such as party and trade unions, and many social activities are carried out through the enterprise structure. It is also responsible for administering many worker benefits. Although it controls little of the production process, the enterprise must compete for workers, as Soviet workers are not legally bound to a specific job.

Explanatory Theory: Autocracy A theory that stresses the continuities in the czarist and Soviet systems as an explanation for the nature of Soviet politics. Autocracy is an absolutist form of government, with all power vested in one ruler, unrestricted by any institutional restraints on the exercise of power. It is characterized by personalized political authority, a centralized state apparatus, a lack of representational institutions, and the intolerance of dissent. In the Russian autocratic system the czar ruled without any legal constraints on the power of the crown. Czarist autocracy developed when Ivan the Terrible (1533–84) unified the state around the Grand Duchy of Moscow and assumed the title of Czar (Caesar) and Autocrat of all Russia. Ivan's methods, which included breaking the power of the nobles, imposing centralized control, and the use of terror, protected the new state but also set it on an absolutist course. The rule of law and representational institutions, as they evolved in the West, were stifled, as was the development of an independent middle class. The Autocrat was the symbol of the state; all persons and possessions were viewed as possessions of the crown. The nobles were dependent on the crown, 80 percent of the Russian people were bound to the landowners or crown as serfs, and the small middle class was virtually powerless. By the mid-eighteenth century, when England was 50 percent urbanized, only 7 percent of the Russian population lived in cities. All were subject to the absolutist rule of the crown. As the Basic Law of the Russian Empire (1832) asserted, the powers of the czar were bestowed by God himself—and thus could be changed only at his will. *See also* DUMA, p. 309; POLITICAL CULTURE: USSR, p. 341; REVOLUTION OF 1905, p. 347; SERFDOM, p. 351.

Significance Autocracy as an explanatory theory holds that Soviet communism endures because it is so compatible with Russian political culture. Proponents point out that both czarist autocracy and Soviet communism exhibit similar political dynamics. These include (1) personalized authority (the czar or general secretary); (2) decision making by a very few or by one man; (3) rigid centralism; (4) a lack of institutional restraints on the exercise of power; (5) state dominance over property relationships; (6) a strong military and secret police; (7) intolerance and repression of dissent; and (8) an expansionist drive. In particular, the theory emphasizes Russia's lack of experience with democratic institutions. The argument that czarist autocracy has been reborn in the Soviet system has powerful attractions. The parallels are numerous—many explain the Soviet Union's determination to control Eastern Europe and the 1979 invasion of Afghanistan as the old czarist expansionism in new ideological clothing. The theory is, however, a single-factor analysis, which blurs the many distinctions between the Russian Empire and the modern Soviet state. It ignores the postrevolutionary explosion in education and the drastic changes in the class system and presents the Soviet system as irrevocably bound to its Russian roots.

Explanatory Theory: Bureaucratic Model A theory that attempts to explain the Soviet system in terms of the institutionalization of bureaucratic power. As applied to the Soviet polity, the bureaucratic model describes a sociopolitical system in which the Communist party directs all activities from the center, operating through a vast complex of appointed officials. It is characterized by (1) a single central command system; (2) the absence of any mediating institutions between citizen and state; and (3) the administration of all aspects of life. The party's control, through bureaucratic administration, of all sectors of society is seen as the hallmark of the Soviet system. The Soviet bureaucracy exhibits the identifying features of modern bureaucracies, including specialization and division of labor, advancement based on seniority and expertise, prudent decision making, institutionalized rules, and a hierarchical chain of command. Where it differs is in its scope; it is responsible for the management of all of society. A major component of the Soviet model is the bureaucratization of all economic activity, where bureaucratic decision making replaces the market mechanism. See also COUNCIL OF MINISTERS: USSR, p. 284; EXPLANATORY THEORY: PLURALISM, p. 316; NOMENKLATURA, p. 337.

Significance The bureaucratic model emphasizes the institutionalization of Soviet power, describing it as largely rational, nonideological, prudent, and above all averse to sudden change that might threaten the vested interests of those who administer the all-embracing Soviet state. It is essentially then a conservative, status quo approach. Variants of the bureaucratic model range from Allen Kassof's view of the Soviet Union as the "administered state" where to be a member of society is to be under party management to Alfred Meyer's comparison of the Soviet system to a huge corporation, "USSR Incorporated," in which the top management operates through a complex of appointed officials whose responsibilities and functions are determined by the managers. Meyer and T. H. Rigby point out that the Soviet bureaucracy shares many common administrative patterns, organizational principles, structures, and functions with modern bureaucracies such as multinational corporations or the military. Some analysts maintain that the Soviet bureaucracy is a "sovereign bureaucracy," in which party and state are merged. The bureaucratic model leads to a cautious appraisal of the prospects for change in the Soviet system, as it also emphasizes the endemic inertia and resistance to change found in most established bureaucracies. This is particularly applicable to the question of fundamental economic reform, where a vast bureaucracy may view their well-paid positions as contingent upon the continuation of the central command economy. The bureaucratic model may also lead to the conclusion that the nature of Soviet power—institutionalized, rational, cautious—diminishes the effects of changes in the top personnel.

Explanatory Theory: Convergence   A theory that maintains that the economic, social, and political systems of industrialized states tend to become similar. Convergence theory argues that modern industrial technology imposes certain common imperatives that shape the nature of an industrialized state, regardless of its political system. As applied to the Soviet Union, convergence theory predicts that as the Soviet Union approaches full industrialization, it will increasingly resemble Western industrialized nations. *See also* EXPLANATORY THEORY: AUTOCRACY, p. 311; POLITICAL CULTURE: USSR, p. 341.

Significance   Convergence theory is a form of technological determinism that assumes that as convergence proceeds, ideological differences between the superpowers will diminish. Critics of convergence theory point out that the content of Soviet political culture and Western political culture differ enough that parallel technological development, without sociopolitical convergence, appears more likely. They also point out that modern industrial technology is politically neutral, having been used to support systems as divergent as fascism, capitalism, and authoritarian military dictatorships. Although the Soviet Union is a first-class industrial power, there is little evidence to date that the tensions between the USSR and the West have been abated by technological parity.

Explanatory Theory: Developmental Model   A theory that seeks to explain Soviet communism in a developmental perspective. The developmental model holds that many features of the Soviet system are the result of the imperatives of modernizing a backward peasant state. Although the commitment to economic planning and nationalization was held by the leaders who made the Bolshevik Revolution, the major features of the Soviet model were provided by Josef Stalin in 1928 when he embarked on the program of forced-draft industrialization that transformed the Soviet state. These are (1) centralized party control over all resource allocation; (2) the mobilization of the entire population; (3) strict discipline, exacted through persuasion, coercion, or any feasible combination; (4) party monopoly over political power; (5) mandatory central economic planning; and (6) a priority on heavy industry. The Soviet leadership shared with Peter the Great the belief that forced draft modernization in a backward state required drastic (if not dictatorial) methods by which the leadership could direct every resource of the state. In addition, industrialization was ideologically necessary in order to build the proper conditions for full communism. Thus, the Soviet Communist party effected a marriage of Marxism with modernization. The imperatives of the methods they developed meant total mobilization of all resources, with the party as leader and coordinator. *See also* COMMAND ECONOMY, p. 283; GREAT PURGE, p. 322; NEW ECONOMIC POLICY (NEP), p. 336; PLANNING, p. 340.

Significance As with any single explanatory theory, the developmental model is not adequate by itself to explain the almost 70 years of extremely complex Soviet politics. Nor does the presumed subordination of all decisions to economic goals explain such cases as the consistent refusal to revamp the agricultural system, despite its dismal record. The Soviet developmental model evolved out of the interaction of a specific developmental approach with a unique political system that felt itself threatened from all sides by hostile capitalist nations. Some of the impetus may have been reactive, the determination to overcome the humiliations suffered in the Crimean War (1853–56), The Russo-Japanese War (1904–05), and the Treaty of Brest-Litovsk (1918), by which Vladimir Lenin ended Russia's participation in World War I but was forced to cede much Russian territory. Nonetheless, even if the Soviet developmental model is *sui generis*, it continues to hold attractions for developing nations simply as a method by which a modernizing, national elite can industrialize.

Explanatory Theory: New Class A critique applied to the rulers of a Soviet-style system that describes them as an oligarchic, privileged elite. Through its control over the centralized state economy, this "new class" exercises a monopoly of power. The term is taken from a book of the same title by the Yugoslav dissident Milovan Djilas. Djilas, the first vice-president of postwar Yugoslavia, argues that the communist-party states are ruled by a new class composed of the top party bureaucrats who arrogate all power to themselves. This new class is an elite identified not by direct ownership of the means of production, but by its control of and access to special privileges stemming from its monopoly power. Once in power, according to Djilas, the revolutionary leadership gives way to a privileged elite whose morality is constantly eroded by the privileges it enjoys. Djilas sees the party's monopoly over the economic process as the foundation of a new ruling class. He vividly described the life-style of the new elite, the access to special stores, cars, vacation villas, and all the appurtenances of power so in contrast to the life of the workers in whose name they claim to rule. His critique therefore is moral as well as ideological. *See also* EXPLANATORY THEORY: STATE CAPITALISM, p. 317; *NOMENKLATURA*, p. 337.

Significance Djilas's *New Class* is the first systematic political and sociological analysis of communism in power by a member of the party elite. Some Western critics of communism have come to use the term new class as synonymous with the ruling party leadership. The term implies the arrogance, venality, and corruption that Djilas attributes to those who betray the ideals of the revolution. A key component of Djilas's critique is the identification of the centrally controlled economy as the source of elite monopoly power and as a form of state socialism, as alienating as capitalism. Although methodologically weak, particularly in its imprecise definition of the elite, Djilas's scathing description of Communist elitism is rooted in the political facts of life in a centrally controlled, one-party state.

Explanatory Theory: Pluralism An approach to understanding the dynamics of Soviet politics that centers on the role played by contending interest groups in the policy process. Pluralism as applied to Soviet politics postulates the existence of various interest groups that contend for policy decisions favorable to their own interests. This approach stresses within-system political competition and conflict resolution rather than political control. It developed as a corrective to the totalitarian model, which assumes a single, monolithic leadership operating free of external political pressures. In contrast, adherents of pluralist theory view the Soviet polity as a body in which various elites compete and bargain for favorable policy decisions. The theory rests on the recognition that the goods and resources of any system are limited. *See also* COUNCIL OF MINISTERS: USSR, p. 284; EXPLANATORY THEORY: BUREAUCRATIC MODEL, p. 312; MINISTRY, p. 335.

Significance The application of pluralist theory has expanded the analysis of the Soviet policy process by identifying demand sectors and potential political groupings. Some analysts, such as Vernon Asparturian, have identified broad demand sectors within the society, such as (1) ideological; (2) security; (3) producers; (4) consumers; (5) agriculture; and (6) public service. Others concentrate on political groupings within the bureaucracy, such as the military, heavy industry, and consumer goods, pointing out that the investment decisions that determine their relative importance are made by the party-government bureaucracy. Pluralist theory does not necessarily predict an eventual diffusion or devolution of power within the system, but has proved a useful corrective to the totalitarian model. Whereas the totalitarian model examines only the outputs of the system, pluralist theory examines the inputs as well. Since the totalitarian model posits a static, closed system impervious to outside factors, pluralist theory provides a more adequate explanation of shifts in Soviet policy.

Explanatory Theory: State Capitalism A critical model of the Soviet system that asserts that, rather than building socialism, the Soviet Communist party has created a bureaucratized dictatorship in which the workers control neither the means of production nor their working conditions. The state capitalist critique asserts that the party elite has replaced the deposed bourgeoisie and, acting as a state capitalist ruling class, exercises monopoly control over all economic and political activities. State capitalism theorists point out that rather than occurring in a developed capitalist state as Karl Marx had predicted, the revolution took place in a semifeudal, developing state that lacked a large working class. Thus the necessary conditions for a socialist revolution were not present. In order to build the base for socialism, the Bolshevik leaders were forced to carry out capitalistic economic development. Under the slogan of the dictatorship of the proletariat, they nationalized all property and controlled its utilization. In the process the party elite became an exploitative class, basing its power on its control over the centralized state economy. As in the capitalist state, power is rooted in economic power, which is the prerogative of the ruling elite of the Communist party. *See also* EXPLANATORY THEORY: BUREAUCRATIC MODEL, p. 312; EXPLANATORY THEORY: NEW CLASS, p. 315; SOCIALIST OWNERSHIP, p. 354.

Significance The state capitalist model utilizes a Marxian class approach to analyzing the Soviet system. As Marxist theory, the approach has flaws. Marx defined class as determined by the relationship to the means of production—it is not at all certain that control is tantamount to ownership. According to Marx, the capitalist ruling class derives its wealth and power from its exploitation of the surplus value of production, that which remains after costs and the workers' wages are deducted. Although the Soviet party leaders are identifiable by their power and special privileges, they are salaried and there is no equity stock ownership. The party leaders do not enjoy wealth created by dividends; nor can their children directly inherit their positions or privileges. An earlier, related critique was proposed by Leon Trotsky, Josef Stalin's chief rival for power. Trotsky's critique, the "degenerate workers' state," declares that, while the Soviet system differs from capitalism, the revolution was only half-completed, as the Bolsheviks substituted the dictatorship of the party for the dictatorship of the proletariat. Trotsky charged that although the Bolsheviks abolished the capitalist class system, they established a new form of elite dominance over the workers and ignored international socialism and the worldwide revolution.

Federalism: USSR A system in which governmental authority is distributed between constitutionally defined units and the national government according to the Soviet Constitution. Soviet federalism is based on the multinational composition of the state, a mosaic of over 100 recognized nationalities. The major administrative units correspond to the territories occupied by the largest nationalities. These units are divided into four groups: the union-republics, the Autonomous Soviet Socialist Republics (ASSRs), the autonomous provinces, and the national areas (*okrug*s). The 15 union-republics, each of which is the homeland of a major historic nationality, are the most important units of the federation. In theory, the union-republics are sovereign states, possessing constitutions, the rights of citizenship and succession, control over their boundaries, supreme courts, and ministerial structures. Soviet federalism, however, is cultural and administrative in content; the national government has exclusive jurisdiction over all important areas of decision making. The extremely broad enumerated powers of the national government are reinforced by the constitutional provision that any question of "all-union significance" is within national purview. Soviet federalism actually operates on two levels, the federal to republic level, and the republics' relationships with their own constituent territorial units. The ASSRs are the homeland of 20 smaller nationalities within the union-republics and in structure are similar to the union-republics but are not considered sovereign. The eight autonomous provinces and ten okrugs, most located within the huge Russian republic, are the homelands of smaller, scattered national groups. They have the power to delineate the boundaries of the local administrative units (*raion*s) on their territory. As with the republics and ASSRs, they use the language of the titular nationality for most official activities, and are represented in the national parliament. An exception to the language rule is the Jewish Autonomous Province, Biro-Bidzhan, an artificial creation on the Chinese borderlands, where only 5.4 percent of the population is Jewish. Federal law is supreme: democratic centralism and the party's monopoly control give the national government virtual veto power. Only the USSR Supreme Soviet or its Presidium can amend the USSR Constitution; the Presidium can also override any decision of a republican Council of Ministers. Republican constitutions and legal codes seldom vary, the differences usually being accommodations to national traditions. Nonetheless, the republics in particular possess substantial administrative powers. They determine the use of investment funds, draw up republican economic plans, and must be consulted on any economic decision that affects their territory. *See also* DUAL SUBORDINATION, p. 308; *RAION*, p. 346; RUSSIFICATION, p. 348; UNION-REPUBLIC, p. 364.

Significance The key to understanding Soviet federalism is to recognize that it is cultural rather than political in nature, posited on the premise that the many diverse nationalities will retain their ethnic identifications within a unified proletarian culture. Originally, both Karl Marx and Vladimir Lenin opposed federalism as perpetuating "bourgeois nationalism." Marx, however, never envisioned the revolution occurring in a semideveloped, multinational empire. Caught up by the reality of imposing control over a heterogeneous state, Lenin conceded the inevitability of federalism as a means of preventing the dissolution of the state. Thus, Marx to the contrary, federalism helped establish Bolshevik power while curbing the centrifugal tendencies implicit in the Leninist principle of national self-determination. As the Bolsheviks consolidated their power, other nationally constituted Soviet republics were joined by treaties to the Russian republic, created in 1918. Although the treaties recognized the republics as sovereign states, truly independent republics, as in Georgia and the Ukraine, were broken by the Red Army. The 1924 USSR Constitution established the Union of Soviet Socialist Republics. Despite its limitations, Soviet federalism does have important consequences. Because the territorial units are ethnically based, the major nationalities possess an organizational base, which is especially important as party doctrine permits no other legitimate form of interest aggregation. The USSR state budget is divided into republican budgets, and the federal principle is observed in numerous ways, from careful attention to nationality representation on the CPSU Central Committee and USSR Council of Ministers to nationality quotas in university admissions. The first secretaries of the most important republican parties (generally, Azerbaidzhan, Kazakhstan, Uzbekistan, and the Ukraine) customarily sit on the CPSU Politburo or the Secretariat. The most important effect of federalism may lie in the preservation and enhancement of ethnic consciousness and its role as a counterbalance to Russian dominance.

Five-Year Plan The key component in the system of state-directed economic planning that forms the linchpin of the Soviet economic system. The first five-year plan was initiated by Josef Stalin in 1928 as a blueprint for the state-directed program of rapid industrialization. It set forth the essentials of the system: (1) state ownership of all land and production; (2) state control over all markets and production; (3) mobilization of all resources; (4) state control over all economic activities; and (5) centralized economic planning that identified priorities and determined capital investment. Almost all surpluses were channeled back into development; agriculture contributed disproportionately, and consumer needs were assigned low priority. Since 1928 the Soviet economy has operated on the basis of five-year plans that subject almost all productive forces to direct, mandatory physical planning under tight central control. The five-year plans set expected growth rates by economic sector and indicates major capital investments. They are supplemented by one-year operational plans that detail how the goals are to be reached and disaggregate the plan by enterprise. The priorities set by the five-year plan are policy decisions made by the party leadership, in consultation with Gosplan, the government planning agency, and are transformed into mandatory production targets by the five-year plan. *See also* COMMAND ECONOMY, p. 283; EXPLANATORY THEORY: DEVELOPMENTAL MODEL, p. 314; GOSPLAN, p. 321; PLANNING, p. 340; STALINISM, p. 357.

Significance The five-year plan approach to development changed the nature of the Soviet system, transforming it from a semi-industrialized state into the world's second industrial power. It also created a powerful state apparatus charged with implementing the plan, tight central control that brooked no opposition or even questioning, and a reliance on coercion to achieve the targets of the plan. The five-year plan assumes a powerful state bureaucracy with the power to enforce the commands of the plan. Since direction and control are the essence, the role of the party is paramount. Despite the brutalities of the Stalinist years, in economic terms the period of the first three plans (1928–40) must be judged a success, producing an estimated sixfold increase in industrial output. It remains a major contribution to theories of development; most developing countries have adopted some form of the five-year plan, albeit with far less brutality and coercion. Such programs are posited on Stalin's argument that, in a situation of scarce resources, it is crucial to plan their use. Soviet five-year plans in recent years have exhibited the systemic constraints that negate some of the value of long-range planning: overcentralization, a top-heavy bureaucracy resistant to change, the stifling of innovation, inflexibility, and a bias toward heavy industry. The Soviet five-year plans continue to illuminate the long-range policy goals of the leadership. Thus, Western analysts interpreted the tenth five-year plan (1976–80), which assigned heavier emphasis to defense-related industries, as indicative either of the increased aggressiveness of Soviet foreign policy or of a growing fear of American power. Soviet planners have developed longer-range plans, spanning 10 or 20 years, but the five-year plan remains the key component in the system.

Gosplan   The State Planning Committee, which plans and coordinates the vast state economy of the Soviet Union. As almost all the means of production are state-owned and state-controlled, the plans developed by Gosplan determine the economic development of the entire state. As a powerful state committee, Gosplan's responsibilities cut across the lines of many different sectors of the system. Its responsibilities include drawing up the short-term (yearly) plans, the five-year plans (intermediate), and the long-term or perspective (10-20 year) plans. The chief goal of all these is to create a uniform framework within which the entire economy of the Soviet Union will operate. Gosplan undoubtedly works closely with the party leadership, which will determine which economic sectors have priority status. Gosplan then coordinates these policy decisions with the resources available to the state, formulates projected growth rates, and determines the allocations necessary. The major objective is to create the material conditions necesary for the attainment, within a specific time period, of the goals set by party leadership. The resulting plans are then used to issue mandatory production targets to the various government ministries that control the economy. Currently, at the national level Gosplan allocates production requirements for about 2,000 production sectors; below that the subordinate republican Gosplans and government ministries allocate needs for smaller production sectors. Gosplan is assisted by several other powerful committees and agencies, such as the State Committee for Building (*Gosstroi*), the State Committee for Supply (*Gossnab*), the State Committee for Science and Technology, and the USSR Academy of Sciences. Gosplan was created in 1921 by Vladimir Lenin. It became a primary organ of party control when Stalin placed the entire economy under state control, embarked on a program of rapid industrialization, and instructed Gosplan to draw up the first five-year plan in 1928. Since then the Soviet economy has functioned under the plans drawn up by Gosplan. *See also* EXPLANATORY THEORY: PLURALISM, p. 316; FIVE-YEAR PLAN, p. 319; PLANNING, p. 340; STATE COMMITTEE, p. 359.

Significance   Gosplan's basic function is to operationalize the priorities and goals of the central leadership. It therefore occupies the pivotal position in the vast planning bureaucracy. Once Gosplan's plans are enacted as law by the Supreme Soviet, they are legally binding. As Gosplan is charged with coordinating party goals with economic reality, and with maintaining the material balances of the economy, it is assumed to be a major arena for within-system competition. Each ministry and economic sector may act as a pressure group, competing for favorable decisions. The plans issued by Gosplan may therefore indicate which sectors of the Soviet system are increasing their influence, such as military-heavy industry, or which sectors are of particular concern, such as agriculture.

Great Purge   The name given to the period of mass terror and repression of the 1930s by which Josef Stalin reshaped Soviet society. The Great Purge denotes the period 1934–38, although the use of mass terror as an instrument of political control began in the 1920s and continued until Stalin's death. Initially, the Great Purge, or Great Terror, was directed at members of the Communist party whom Stalin viewed as possible competitors. It soon developed into a nationwide system of arbitrary terror from which no one was safe. There were two major components: the staged public "show trials" of party leaders and the concomitant terror exercised over all of society, wherein millions of ordinary citizens were sent to almost certain death in the *Gulag*, the prison labor camps. The party was decimated. Included among the victims were the Old Bolsheviks, whose membership dated to prerevolutionary days, ten close associates of Vladimir Lenin, six Politburo members, half of the 1934 Party Congress, and 70 percent of the Central Committee. All were accused of a wide range of crimes, from plotting with Hitler to supporting Leon Trotsky, Stalin's chief rival for power after Lenin died. In a purge that swept the military, three marshals, half the generals, and from 15,000 to 30,000 officers perished. Other particular targets were the intellectuals, non-Russian nationalities, Jews, and religious believers. The commonality was that all in some way might pose a threat to Stalin's all-pervasive power. The terror was applied to the population by the secret police (NKVD), which operated under Stalin's sole control. Special NKVD boards (OSSO) sentenced millions in secret proceedings from which there was no appeal. Many simply disappeared into the camps or the grave. Most analysts place the toll at around 10 to 12 million (approximately 5 percent of the population), although some maintain that as many as 30 million people eventually perished. The Gulag became an integral part of the economic system, providing prison labor on order for massive construction projects. In the end, Stalin possessed a terrorized society and a party whose members owed their positions and lives solely to him. *See also* COLLECTIVIZATION, p. 280; DE-STALINIZATION, p. 305; KGB, p. 326; STALINISM, p. 357.

Significance   For many, the Great Purge symbolizes the nature of communism and the ultimate totalitarian society. It was preceded by the drive to collectivize agriculture, which marks Stalin's turn to terror as an instrument of political control. It is said that no one can understand Soviet society without considering the Great Purge, which may have eventually directly affected one of every two Soviet families. A crucial element of the purge was the arbitrary, extralegal nature of the terror, creating a society in which the fate of every individual ultimately rested with the leader. Stalin did achieve his apparent goal: control over the party, the military, the economy, and all of society. A new party elite arose as an entire generation of officials was replaced by Stalin's men. Some analysts maintain that only when the Andropov-Chernenko generation passes from the scene will the party be rid of the heritage of the Great Purge. The terror ended only with Stalin's death in 1953. Stalin's successors have abjured the ubiquitous terror of the Great Purge. Nikita Khrushchev, who succeeded Stalin, attempted to come to terms with this heritage in his de-Stalinization campaign, an admission of past atrocities. However, this may have contributed to his ouster in 1964. Since then, the Soviet party has refused to reopen the issue.

Industrial Association A large factory or group of factories, frequently established through a merger of several enterprises. The number of industrial associations (*obedinenie*) has increased markedly since the 1970s, now accounting for at least 50 percent of Soviet production. Certain key economic sectors, such as paper and mining, are organized entirely by industrial associations. Frequently the associations replace the department (*glavk*) of the ministry to which they were responsible, thus streamlining administration. They usually are financed from the profits of their constituent units and, unlike the ministerial departments, are held economically accountable. Many Soviet planners advance this organizational form as offering administrative efficiency, economies of scale, specialization, and control over supplies. *See also* ENTERPRISE, p. 310; PLANNING, p. 340.

Significance Industrial associations have not changed the principle of central economic planning. They have, however, removed an intervening layer of bureaucracy and relieved the planning organs of the task of disaggregating plans down to the smallest enterprise. As this represents a redistribution of power, from ministerial administrators to industrial managers, there apparently has been some resistance to the reform despite the fact that the announced goal is that by 1990 almost all production will be carried out by the industrial associations.

Internal Passport The personal identity document that every citizen over the age of 16 is required to carry. The internal passport system enables the authorities to control the movement and residence of citizens. Issued by the Ministry of Internal Affairs (MVD) and the local police, the passport records personal data, nationality, marital status, dependent children, military service, occupation, work record, and place of residence. Permanent residence in most major cities requires a permit (*propiska*), usually contingent upon marriage to a local resident or proof of a job there. Citizens must present their identity papers when applying for a job, changing residence, getting married or divorced, applying for institutes of higher education, registering children in school, traveling, and upon numerous other occasions. *See also* COLLECTIVIZATION, p. 280.

Significance The internal passport system is a major instrument of control over Soviet citizens, enabling the state to maintain a stable agricultural population and to allocate manpower to developing areas. The Soviet Union has been largely spared the problems of developing countries whose cities are strained beyond their resources. Internal passports existed in czarist Russia, were abolished in 1917, and were reinstated by Josef Stalin in 1932 to keep the peasants from fleeing the collective farms; collective farmers did not regularly receive passports until 1974. Those who hold residence permits to "closed" cities whose population is limited by the authorities can usually move at will to another city or to the countryside. The wages in closed cities, such as Leningrad, are typically higher, as these workers enjoy true job mobility. In the case of Jews, Soviet law requires that what is essentially a religion be listed rather than ethnic origin or area of birth. Soviet law treats the Jews as a nationality, although a Georgian Jew may have little in common, including language and religious identification, with a Ukrainian Jew. Many Soviet Jews claim the intent is discriminatory, singling them out for potential surveillance as possible dissidents.

Judicial Structure and Administration The complex Soviet judicial system, which implements the legal codes and maintains public order. Soviet judicial structure and administration is anchored in the Marxist concept of socialist legality, which maintains that the primary responsibility of the judiciary is to protect the interests of socialism. All courts, judicial officials, and lawyers are thus closely monitored by party and government organs. The concept of an independent judiciary is contrary to Marxist legal doctrine. The base of the system is the local district courts (people's courts), followed by the regional courts (city courts, province, territory, autonomous province, national district, autonomous republic), the supreme courts of the 15 union-republics, and the USSR Supreme Court. Other than the USSR Supreme Court there are no federal courts. All courts have jurisdiction over both civil and criminal cases and possess both original and appellate jurisdiction, except for the local people's courts, which have only original jurisdiction (and which handle over 95 percent of all violations of law). Judges of the USSR Supreme Court, the supreme courts of the union-republics and autonomous republics, and the regional courts are selected by the corresponding soviet (assembly). The judges of the people's courts are elected by district election for five-year terms. Judges may be recalled (and some have been). People's courts are presided over by a judge and a rotating panel of two lay assessors, or lay judges, who are elected by citizens at their workplaces. In higher courts, a three-judge panel presides unless the trial is one of original jurisdiction, in which case two of the judges are replaced by lay assessors from a panel selected by the appropriate soviet. As is common in code (civil) law systems, there are no juries. The Soviet legal system does not clearly delineate original jurisdiction. The Procuracy (states' attorneys) or the court itself may send a case to a higher court for first trial. Such cases usually involve serious crimes against the state or issues that the authorities wish to publicize for educative purposes. Trials of original jurisdiction are open unless state secrets are involved (although this has been breached in cases involving political dissidents). All parties involved—the courts, the defendants, the Procuracy, the defense attorney, or the victim—may appeal decisions; defendants are permitted only one appeal. Decisions may also be reviewed by higher courts as part of their supervisory responsibility. Cases also may be reopened on the basis of newly discovered evidence. The appellate court may leave the decision unchanged, modify the decision, annul it, or remand the case for retrial. Common reasons for remanding cases include errors in investigatory work or application of the law, inappropriateness of punishment, errors by the trial court, and the presentation of new facts. The appellate court may not increase the severity of punishment, although if the case is remanded the next trial may do so. The courts must follow three goals in levying punishments: (1) punishment for the crime, as prescribed by the legal codes; (2) rehabilitation of the convicted; and (3) education of the public. In addition to the regular court system, there are a number of specialized judicial organs, such as the panels that handle economic disputes between enterprises (arbitration), maritime arbitration, foreign trade arbitration, and factory commissions that handle labor disputes. *See also* CODE LAW SYSTEM, p. 85; PROCURACY, p. 345; SOCIALIST LEGALITY, p. 353; SUPREME COURT, p. 359.

Significance The Soviet judicial structure and administration operates under tight supervision, implementing party policy and the law. Since Soviet law is code law, rather than common law, judges have little autonomy. Therefore, judicial precedent is not used; Soviet judges can only apply existing law to specific cases as specified by the comprehensive legal codes. Any necessary interpretations are handed down by the

Procuracy and the USSR Supreme Court. Thus, the judiciary is relatively inflexible. On the other hand, changes in policy may be applied quickly by the courts through revision of the codes. In general, Soviet courts act more as agencies of enforcement than as agencies of adjudication.

KGB Abbreviation for *Komitet Gosudarstvennoi Bezopasnosti*, the Committee for State Security, the secret police agency charged with preserving state power and maintaining surveillance over the Soviet population. The KGB is a dual-function agency, responsible for both foreign and domestic security. Its responsibilities include (1) foreign and domestic espionage; (2) intelligence gathering and analysis; (3) counterintelligence; (4) political control over the population; (5) protecting the borders; and (6) covert activities and disinformation. It has over 200,000 border guards, numerous security troops, and a secret service, totaling perhaps 500,000. Although nominally subordinate to the Council of Ministers as a state committee, in reality the KGB is responsible solely to the Communist party. Its subordinate agencies operate at all republican, regional, and local levels. KGB officials sit on all government bodies, party organs, army units, enterprise boards, and mass organizations. Leading KGB officials hold positions on the CPSU Central Committee, the Secretariat, and since 1973, on the Politburo. The KGB is divided into main directorates, independent directorates, and departments, all with their subordinate agencies. The main directorates include: the First Directorate, responsible for clandestine foreign activities and counterintelligence; the Second Directorate, domestic intelligence; and the Fifth Directorate, control of dissent. During World War II the Third Directorate, then in charge of military counterespionage, became known as SMERSH. An independent directorate, Armed Forces, maintains surveillance over GRU, the military intelligence-gathering agency. Dating from 1954, the KGB is the latest in a long line of Soviet state security agencies, beginning with the CHEKA (All-Russian Extraordinary Committee to Combat Counterrevolution and Espionage), created in 1917. Its later incarnations, in order, were the GPU, OGPU, NKVD, NKGB, MGB, and MVD. Through all these transmutations the secret police have functioned as the major instrument of party control. *See also* DISSENT AND OPPOSITION, p. 306; GREAT PURGE, p. 322; STATE COMMITTEE, p. 359.

Significance The KGB represents a constant in Russian and Soviet political history. It is the lineal heir of both the CHEKA and the *Okhrana*, the czarist secret police that enforced political conformity. During the Civil War and the 1920s, the CHEKA carried out a "Red

Terror," mass executions by revolutionary tribunals that operated outside the law to punish those suspected of opposing the Bolsheviks. Under Josef Stalin the secret police became an instrument of personalized terror and the epitome of the totalitarian police state. As Stalin's chosen instrument to carry out purges, they were responsible for sending millions to their deaths. Although Stalin's successors circumscribed the powers of the secret police, the goal was to subordinate the KGB to the party, not to curb its role as the "action arm" of the party. KGB influence has increased since the early 1960s, and it is now represented on all major party bodies. The former head of the KGB, Yuri Andropov, served as party leader from 1982 to 1984. The KGB probably controls the counterpart secret police services of the East European states (excluding Yugoslavia), using them to mount covert operations and maintain Soviet control. Some observers believe that the KGB and two Central Committee organs, the International Department and the International Information Department, are major actors in foreign policy. Reportedly, the KGB head is a member of the secretive Defense Council, thus placing the KGB in a central position in the system.

Kolkhoz The abbreviation for the Russian term for the collective farm. *Kolkhoz* land is owned by the state but allocated in perpetuity to the kolkhoz, which operates under state charter. All other assets are the collective property of the kolkhoz. Kolkhoz peasants are not state employees, as on a state farm (*sovkhoz*), but are members of a self-managing collective (*artel'*) under state direction. In theory the kolkhoz membership elects a manager and admits and expels new members. In practice, the manager is appointed by the party and functions under direct state control. State procurement plans dictate what the kolkhoz produces; many are assigned up to 60 different procurement targets. The typical kolkhoz is a multiproduct unit, averaging 6,700 hectares (16,214 acres) with a workforce of 500–600, scattered over several small villages. The kolkhoz operates on a profit and loss basis (*khozrachet*). It must finance investment expenditures out of revenue as well as maintain intrafarm roads, schools, and other amenities that elsewhere (including sovkhozes) are provided by the state. Although since 1970 kolkhoz workers have received cash wages and state insurance, their wages and benefits lag behind those of other workers. Many kolkhozes are constantly in debt. Although substantial improvements have been made since Josef Stalin's death, the kolkhoz remains the least-favored form of Soviet production. *See also* COLLECTIVIZATION, p. 280; SOVKHOZ, p. 356.

Significance The kolkhoz became the dominant agricultural organization in the 1930s when Stalin seized the land and forced the peasants into collective farms. Collectivization, accomplished with much brutality and the death of perhaps five million peasants, was designed to ensure the delivery of food to the state at minimum cost. Undercapitalized and exploited, agriculture became the problem child of the Soviet economy. Stalin's successors have done much to improve the lot of the collective farmer, but the underlying problems remain. Overcentralized economic planning and control create diseconomies and are most evident in agriculture. Farm management must operate under detailed administrative supervision that is poorly suited to consideration of local conditions or long-range improvements. Private plots, small garden plots allocated to peasants and state employees, account for over one-quarter of the gross agricultural output. The produce of these private plots, which average 0.3 hectares (.72 acres) and comprise 3 percent of all farmland, may be sold on the free peasant markets, consumed, or sold to the collective. The result is an unofficial division of labor, with private plot farming concentrated on crops requiring intensive labor inputs. The post-Brezhnev leadership inherited substantial commitments that include: (1) state funding of kolkhoz improvements and schools; (2) increasing mechanization; (3) forgiving loans to debt-ridden kolkhozes; and (4) increasing agricultural investment to one-third of all state investment (up from 24 percent in 1973). Whether the new leadership can implement these provisions remains problematical. The collective farm economy is plagued by undercapitalization, undermechanization, an aging, unskilled, and feminized workforce, overcentralized administrative control, and the USSR's short growing seasons, lack of assured rainfall, and infertile soils. Most of all, it is plagued by the problem of productivity, of the difficulty of relating agricultural performance to the result.

Komsomol The official mass organization for Soviet youth that serves as a major agent of political socialization for young adults. The Komsomol (Young Communist League) enrolls those between 14 and 28 and serves also as the youth wing of the Communist party. Komsomol units, which are under direct party supervision, are organized in all places of work, schools, farms, and military units. Its organizational structure duplicates the hierarchy of the party itself. At each level, Komsomol units are closely supervised by the analogous territorial unit of the party. Komsomol leaders are always party members. The Komsomol is preceded by similar state-directed organizations for younger children, the Octobrists for 7 to 10-year olds, and the Pioneers, for 10 to 14-year olds. The children's units, however, are mainly recreational in nature, stressing sports and good citizenship, while the Komsomol units typically concentrate more on political activities. As with the Pioneers, many Komsomol units enjoy attractive meeting places, access to recreational facilities, planned trips, and holiday camps. Members are encouraged to volunteer for community work, which may include directing Octobrist and Pioneer units. Although membership is voluntary, it runs at about 70 percent of all eligible youth (about 40 million), but not all are by any means activists. As Komsomol membership is a major path to career advancement, frequently determining university admission and professional advancement, many Soviet youth apparently approach their membership with more cynicism than commitment. Komsomol units frequently are used by the party to carry out official campaigns, such as the recent effort to suppress the black market in smuggled Western music. Komsomol activists comprise many of the volunteer citizens' militia, (*druzhiny*), the citizen inspectorate corps, and other citizens' groups. *See also* CITIZEN PARTICIPATION, p. 279; COMMUNIST PARTY OF THE SOVIET UNION (CPSU), p. 286; MASS ORGANIZATIONS, p. 334.

Significance The Komsomol serves as the main avenue of recruitment for the Communist party and is the primary training ground for future party members. Up to age 23, all candidate party members must be Komsomol members. Thus, those who are asked to join the party have been preselected in a process that begins in their teens. In addition, the Komsomol is a primary agent of official socialization. Close party supervision enables the party to identify promising candidates for nonparty posts as well. For many Soviet youth, the secret personnel file (*Kharakteristika*) kept by the party may begin with their local Komsomol unit. The extremely high levels of Komsomol membership in the military provide the party with a built-in control mechanism. An estimated 80 percent of all military officers have been Komsomol members. University applicants are required to submit a reference from either their workplace or their Komsomol unit. Thus, for many, Komsomol membership is the minimum political requirement for higher education or career advancement. At the very least, membership signifies external compliance with socialist norms, but for the ambitious, Komsomol activism is a major path to upward mobility.

Legal Enactments The laws, decrees, regulations, and administrative orders that constitute the legally binding acts that regulate the Soviet polity. Soviet legal enactments emanate from several sources. Party decisions by themselves are not law; they must be translated into a legal enactment by a state authority. Legal enactments are hierarchically ranked by their source and scope of administrative mandate. These are, with their promulgating bodies (1) statutes or laws (*zakons*), the federal

Supreme Soviet and the republican soviets; (2) edicts (*ukazes*), Presidium of the Supreme Soviet and the republican presidiums; (3) decrees (*postanovlenie*), Supreme Soviet, USSR Council of Ministers, individual ministries, state committees, and analogous republican and territorial organs; (4) regulations (*razporyzhenie*), USSR Council of Ministers, individual ministries, state committees, and analogous territorial organs; (5) orders (*prikazy*), state committees, territorial and local soviets, courts; and (6) decisions (*reshenie*), courts and local soviets. Ministries and their administrative departments also issue instructions (*instruktsiya*) to internal agencies, and *polozhenie*, which delineate the scope and authority of subordinate agencies. All are legally binding. The most important are ukazes and zakons, which are "normative" acts, creating fundamental law. *See also* PRESIDIUM OF THE SUPREME SOVIET, p. 343; SUPREME SOVIET, p. 360.

Significance As the Supreme Soviet meets only briefly, most normative law is initially promulgated as ukazes by the Presidium, later translated into zakons by the Supreme Soviet. Both the practice and the title derive from Russian history when the czar ruled largely by unilaterally declared ukazes. Legal enactments other than zakons and ukazes may be annulled by the Presidium of the Supreme Soviet. Therefore, the heart of the Soviet legislative process is the Presidium of the Supreme Soviet. At the territorial and local levels the regulatory powers vested in the local assemblies and administrative agencies must conform to the laws of the federation, i.e., in the main, to the Presidium of the Supreme Soviet.

Leninism The theoretical interpretations and modifications to Marxist philosophy made by Vladimir Lenin, the leader of the Russian Revolution. Leninism permitted the adaptation of classic Marxism to Russian realities. Since Marxism is a Western philosophy, rooted in nineteenth-century Western experience, much of the Russian situation did not conform to Marxist givens. Essentially Leninism proposes that Russia, which lacked a fully developed capitalist system, a strong bourgeoisie, and a large working class, could nonetheless achieve socialism. Marxism proposes a unilinear historical development, contending that the socialist revolution would occur only under mature capitalism; Leninism alters this. Lenin's major contributions include the following: (1) The theory that capitalism had not succumbed to its "internal contradictions," as predicted by Marx, because the European nations secured colonial markets for surplus investment and production, and cheap sources of raw materials and labor. In what Lenin then termed "the highest and final stage of capitalism," that of imperialism, the focus of the class struggle shifts to the colonialized nations, as the entire undeveloped world becomes the exploited. (2) The theory that as the result of imperialistic competition for colonies, war among capitalist states is inevitable. (3) The theory of "combined development," which holds that the revolutionary potential is greatest in those developing societies that include both feudal and capitalistic institutions. According to Lenin, these weak links of capitalism may be the first to break. (4) The belief that, in the above conditions, only a tightly disciplined party of professional revolutionaries, acting as the vanguard of the oppressed, could effect the revolution. (5) The application of mandatory party discipline, in particular the principle of democratic centralism. Lenin substituted the vanguard party, bound by democratic centralism to obey all decisions of the leaders, for the spontaneous mass workers' movement of classic Marxism; he argued that, by itself, the Russian working class could not develop class consciousness. Lenin also compressed the lengthy stage of bourgeois democracy and capitalism. In the Russian context, this meant the eight months between the fall of the czar and the Bolshevik Revolution. (His lieutenant, Leon Trotsky, argued that the two revolutions, bourgeois and proletarian, could occur simultaneously.) Whereas Marx believed that the necessary conditions for socialism could only be attained in a fully developed capitalist system, Lenin argued that the vanguard party could carry out the revolution and acting in the name of the proletariat build the base for socialism. Lenin also modified Marx's disdain for the peasantry, advocating a worker-peasant alliance (*smychka*). Lenin's major contributions are explained in his published works, especially in *What Is to Be Done* (1902), *Imperialism—The Highest Stage of Capitalism* (1917), and *State and Revolution* (1918). *See also* BOLSHEVIK REVOLUTION, p. 274; MARXISM, p. 332; SERFDOM, p. 351.

Significance The applications of Leninism to Marxist philosophy created Marxism-Leninism, the official ideology of the Soviet Union and other states that claim to be building communism. Lenin's organizational theory has supplied an operational plan for many political movements, while the ideology provides a justification for seizing power. The party structure and tactics contained in *What Is to Be Done* are the organizational basis for all Communist parties. Leninism changes the focus of Marxism from economic to political, transforming historical determinism into historical activism. In particular, Leninism appeals to many newly independent nations that view capitalism as exploitative, yet wish to industrialize. The Leninist support of wars of national liberation seemingly predicted the current struggles in Central America and Africa, where the opposition to these movements centers in the capitalist states. A primary function of Lenin's vanguard party is to train the masses to respond positively to all decisions made by the leadership as they carry out their ideological mandate to lead the state to communism. Thus, from its inception the Soviet Communist party has emphasized explanation and education, or what is termed agitation and propaganda, agitprop. The use of the ideology to justify party rule should not conceal the fact that it does shape the priorities of the Soviet state, as for example the propagation of atheism, the involvement of the citizenry, and the emphasis on heavy industry. However, despite its name, democratic centralism has strangled intraparty democracy and restricted the party's ability to innovate, as members cannot question party policy once effected, no matter how conditions may change. In the process of directing the state, Lenin's small vanguard party has been transformed into a tightly disciplined bureaucracy governed by a self-selected oligarchy.

Marxism The theory of social change developed by Karl Marx, a nineteenth-century German philosopher and economist, and his collaborator, Friedrich Engels. Marxism attempts to scientifically explain and predict the economic, social, and political forces that move human history. Marx insisted that human society results from the interaction of these forces, not from the actions of "great men," abstract ideas, sheer chance, or divine providence. His most important concepts are the materialist conception of history, the dialectical process of class conflict that produces new social orders, the critique of capitalist society, and the laws of social change that will culminate in socialism and the final stage, communism. Marx maintained that the most fundamental aspect of human existence is labor, through which all social orders are created. In each stage of human history labor creates a distinct mode of production (primitive, slave, feudal, capitalist, socialist) that determines the social order. One's relationship to the means of production determines class: the owners (slave-owners, feudal lords, capitalist bourgeoisie) and the exploited (slaves, serfs, workers). According to Marx, all societies have two elements: the substructure or economic forces and the superstructure, the other institutions of society, such as government, religion, and law, which are determined by the economic base (economic determinism). History evolves through stages; the inherent conflicts and contradictions in each stage determine the nature of the next stage that replaces it, through the dialectical process of class struggle. This dialectical process, the unity arising from contradiction, is embodied in the class struggle, which is the motive force of change. The dominating class (the thesis) exploits the subordinate class (the antithesis) until that class finally prevails and creates a new social order (the synthesis). The Marxian dialectical process, or the ultimate union of opposing forces, is based on material ideas, and is termed historical materialism. As *The*

Communist Manifesto (1848) states, "the history of all hitherto existing society is the history of the class struggle." Thus, under feudalism, the conflict between the nobility and the serfs created a new order, capitalism. In turn, capitalism engenders two opposing classes, the bourgeoisie (owners) and proletariat (workers). Marx's major concern was with capitalism, which he viewed as the most exploitative and alienating system, but which in his theory of development is a necessary precondition for the transition to communism. Marx identified certain inherent flaws in capitalism (the contradictions of capitalism) that will doom it. His analysis begins with his theory of surplus value, the value added to the product by the labor of the worker, which the owner takes in the form of his profits. Most of the surplus value is expropriated by the owner; wages in a capitalist system are kept as low as possible. The workers are thus alienated from their labor, and from their essential being, becoming mere "wages slaves." The downward wage spiral creates underconsumption and overproduction. Thus, capitalism breeds continual crises: ceaseless competition, economic depression, and war over markets. As small competitors are bankrupted by large firms, oligopolies and monopolies are created, and capital becomes concentrated in a few hands. The increasing impoverishment of the workers (immiseration) coupled with the rise in education necessary to a developed capitalist economy will create a united, class-conscious proletariat. Acting as a revolutionary force, the proletariat will overthrow capitalism and usher in socialism. For Marx, socialism is a transitory stage in which, as social ownership of the means of production is instituted, society builds the base for the final stage, communism. The process will be carried out by what Marx termed the dictatorship of the proletariat. As private ownership disappears, the class struggle ceases. Government, which Marx viewed as a coercive instrument of the dominant class, will "wither away," and a new classless, stateless society of pure communism will emerge. Human alienation will end, and the society will provide "from each according to his ability, to each according to his need." Communism is the end of social change, since class conflict disappears and a new cooperative human society emerges. Marx also envisioned the process on an international scale, as the workers come to identify worldwide rather than with their nation, a concept Marx considered along with governments as a bourgeois artifact. Thus, Marxism is at once a scientific explanation of social change, a guide for action, and a utopian vision. Marx's theories are developed in *The Communist Manifesto,* a revolutionary call for action, and in his principal work, *Das Kapital,* first published in 1867. *See also* BOLSHEVIK, p. 273; BOLSHEVIK REVOLUTION, p. 274; LENINISM, p. 330; STALINISM, p. 357.

Significance   The Bolsheviks justified their overthrow of the Provisional Government in the name of Marxism and rationalized their monopoly of power as necessary to the building of communism, taking the name the Communist Party of the Soviet Union. Many other states have since established Communist regimes that claim to be building communism according to the tenets of Marxism. Much of the international political dialogue today is carried out in terms of Marxist socialism versus capitalism. Marxism's major appeal lies in the developing world, which looks to the Soviet Union as proof that a society can shortcut, or bypass, a lengthy capitalist development. Marx's critique of capitalism has been accepted by many, revolutionaries and democratic reformers alike, and deeply influences the political parties of both left and right. In practice, Marxism has not led to the classless state, let alone to an international socialist order; nor has the all-powerful Soviet state begun to wither away. Twentieth-century Marxism is national in content, and conflict exists between Communist states as well as between Communist and capitalist states. Marx himself was ambivalent as to whether Russia could move directly into socialism. The argument was rendered moot by the Bolsheviks' adaptation of Marxism to Russian realities, the combination of Marxist philosophy and Vladimir Lenin's operational methods now known as Marxism-Leninism, the official ideology of the Soviet Union.

Mass Organizations Volunteer associations open to both nonparty and party members that encourage the masses to become involved in the system. The party controls the mass organizations, in Josef Stalin's term using them as a "transmission belt" for party policy, but they are also a means of soliciting public opinion and offer a major mode of participation for many citizens. Mass organizations are granted sizable independence in nonpolitical areas, although the party maintains supervision (*rukovodstvo*). The trade unions, youth groups, people's control committees (citizen inspectors), volunteer militia, and paramilitary groups (DOSAAF) are leading examples of mass organizations. Their by-laws must be approved by the government, which can dissolve any organization it deems injurious to the interests of the state. Party members form the active nucleus of all mass organizations; frequently such work is part of a member's party assignment. The preeminent mass organization is the Communist party, which according to the Constitution is "... the leading and directing force in Soviet society." *See also* CITIZEN PARTICIPATION, p. 279; DOSAAF, p. 307; KOMSOMOL, p. 328.

Significance Belonging to a mass organization is the minimum requirement for participation in Soviet public life. Since party membership is selective, totaling about 10 percent of the adult population, without the mass organizations most citizens would have no formal affiliation with the state. The party carefully delegates certain responsibilities to the mass organizations, as the trade unions are responsible for developing the collective agreement with enterprise management, which establishes work rules and labor norms. The mass organizations are also responsible for the nomination process. Although the modes of participation are structured by the party, membership is voluntary.

Ministry An executive unit responsible for administering a specific department of the government. Comparable to a cabinet-level department, the ministry is headed by a minister and is responsible to the Council of Ministries. Ministries exist at three levels: all-union, union-republic, and republic. All-union ministries exercise direct control from Moscow. Most administer a specific branch of the centralized economy, such as the Ministry of Machine Building, and may directly supervise key industrial enterprises. Others direct areas of federal responsibility, such as foreign affairs or defense. Union-republic ministries exist at both federal and republican levels, in areas such as agriculture, finance, education, and social services, and are responsible to both the republican Council of Ministers and their federal counterparts. Republican ministries exist only in the republics and autonomous republics; they administer such areas of government as road construction, local housing, and small industry. The territorial and local administrative agencies subordinate to a ministry are called executive departments. Ministries set their own internal rules and personnel policies and are empowered to issue legally binding orders (*prikazy*) and instructions (*instruksiya*) to all departments under their jurisdiction. Each ministry is headed by a minister, one or more first deputy ministers, several deputy ministers, and a coordinating collegium (*kollegiya*) of the leading officials, who are always party officials. Ministries are divided into functionally specific departments (*otdely*) and chief administrations (*glavki*). Each ministry has an educational institute that trains personnel in public administration. *See also* COUNCIL OF MINISTERS: USSR, p. 284; EXPLANATORY THEORY: BUREAUCRATIC MODEL, p. 312; PLANNING, p. 340; PRESIDIUM OF THE COUNCIL OF MINISTERS, p. 343.

Significance As the Soviet economy is state-directed, and almost every social or cultural activity is directed by the state, the ministry is the key element in an all-pervasive system of bureaucratic control, ensuring that practically every Soviet citizen ultimately is supervised by a ministry. The bulk of the law that governs the Soviet polity originates as regulations and orders issued by the over 100 federal ministries. The concentration of federal ministries devoted to heavy industry and defense production reflects an enduring priority of the Soviet economy. Ministries are thought to play an important role as bureaucratic interest groups, representing the interests of their bureaucratic constituencies in the allocation of state resources. For example, the Ministry of Agriculture may press for greater agricultural investment, while the representatives of heavy industry—commonly called the "metal eaters"—push for investment in heavy industry. The sheer scope and size of the Soviet ministerial system, covering almost all the activities of the society, leads to the description of the Soviet Union as "the administered society."

New Economic Policy (NEP) Economic reforms initiated by Vladimir Lenin in 1921. The New Economic Policy, which lasted until 1928, abrogated much of the radicalism of war communism (1918–21) and permitted limited private production and individual freedom. The NEP was initiated amid widespread peasant revolts, urban riots, and the revolt of the Kronstadt sailors, all of which convinced Lenin that the rising opposition to Bolshevik economic policies endangered Bolshevik control itself. The NEP abandoned the forced-draft policies of war communism, in particular the mandatory grain requisitions that so incensed the peasantry. It created a mixed economic system of private agriculture and trade with state control over banking, foreign trade, and heavy industry. The currency was stabilized, cash wages reinstated, and the consumer sector freed from control. Private traders, known as Nepmen, flourished and by 1923 controlled 50 percent of the wholesale trade and 78 percent of the retail trade. The chief goals of the NEP—to conciliate the peasants and restore the economy to prewar levels—were achieved, and with this, increased support for the Bolsheviks. Although the state continued to control the bulk of investment capital, the low level of coercion distinguishes the NEP from both war communism and the Stalinist command economy, which succeeded the NEP in 1928. *See also* COLLECTIVIZATION, p. 280; SOCIALIST REALISM, p. 354; WAR COMMUNISM, p. 365.

Significance The New Economic Policy represents the high point of Soviet liberalism. For the peasants in particular, the NEP years were their best. The relative liberalism of the NEP also constitutes a golden age of Soviet creativity. Artistic expression was relatively free of party censorship, and innovation flourished, only to be stifled by Josef Stalin's demand for total conformity. The later NEP years, 1924–28, coincided with the intense power struggle after Lenin's death in 1924. Stalin's accession to absolute power in 1928 meant the end of the NEP and the defeat of all those who argued that Lenin had intended the NEP to last for decades. Stalin announced the first five-year plan and forcibly collectivized agriculture, thus ending the relative liberalism of the NEP.

Nomenklatura The list of top government, industrial, and other prestigious positions, appointment to which requires confirmation by the Communist party. Each party organization, from the Central Committee in Moscow to local (*raion*) party committees, maintains a specific list (*nomenklatura*) of posts for which it is responsible. The more important the position, the higher the party organ responsible for confirming appointment. Nomenklatura positions constitute the elite of Soviet society and embrace all sectors, from government ministries and financial institutions to schools, farms, factories, cultural and scientific institutions, local government, and mass organizations. Candidates for nomenklatura posts are selected from lists of promising and politically reliable citizens, information obtained from the *kharakteristika*, the personal information file each party unit maintains on all party members and citizens of potential importance in its territory. Thus, no position of any importance will be occupied by anyone whom the party does not consider politically reliable. Although nonparty members may receive party approval for posts requiring high levels of competence, in particular in the hard sciences, the careers of all Soviet citizens, party and nonparty alike, are thus ultimately determined by the party. *See also* CPSU: SECRETARIAT, p. 297; DUPLICATION OF OFFICE, p. 310; EXPLANATORY THEORY: NEW CLASS, p. 315.

Significance The nomenklatura system is crucial to understanding the maintenance of the party's dominant position in society. Through its control over the staffing of the top posts in all sectors of society, the party ensures that a reliable and uniform elite functions under its supervision. At any level, those party members who sit on the various party bureaus and secretariats control personnel policy and thus wield substantial power over society. Because much of the nomenklatura system is kept secret, it is difficult to estimate the number of nomenklatura positions; each of the 14 republican central committees may control about 2,000 each. Appointment to a nomenklatura position means not only prestige and power but frequently includes such fringe benefits as access to special state-run stores and scarce consumer goods, better housing and medical care, and pay bonuses. The occupants of the nomenklatura positions thus constitute the elite of Soviet society, an elite that operates under party supervision.

Oblast' An important territorial administrative unit, similar to a province or region. The *oblast'* occupies a crucial position in the Soviet administrative hierarchy, as the intermediate unit between the union-republic and the *raion,* the local unit of administration. The smaller union-republics (Azerbaidzhan, Armenia, Estonia, Georgia, Latvia, Lithuania, and Moldavia) are not divided into oblasts; there the raion is directly responsible to the republic. Typically, an oblast' has a population of between one to four million, a territory of 7,700 to 38,000 square miles, and supervises 10 to 40 raions. Each of the 121 oblasts has an elected soviet of between 100 and 300 deputies, an executive committee that handles the day-to-day business of the oblast', an extensive administrative structure, a judiciary, and the oblast' Communist party organization. One of the most important functions of the oblast' is implementing its annual budget and economic plan, in addition to supervising the raions on its territory. A related administrative-territorial unit is the *krai* (territory), a large administrative subdivision of the Russian republic (RSFSR). The six krais are located in the far reaches of the vast RSFSR in areas of ethnically mixed populations and provide a means of uniting several small ethnic groups into an administrative unit. Two cities, Moscow and Leningrad, are also accorded oblast' status. *See also* COMMUNIST PARTY OF THE SOVIET UNION (CPSU), p. 286; TERRITORIAL DIVISIONS, p. 362.

Significance Oblast' politicians have become key personnel in the Soviet system. It is at the oblast' level that much federal policy must be coordinated with regional interests and implemented, thus requiring that oblast' officials resolve conflict over resource allocation. The oblast' system has its roots in the administrative reforms of Peter the Great, which divided the empire into *gubernii* (governments)—the 119 czarist gubernii were not too different from the 121 Soviet oblasts, particularly in central Russia. The party secretary of the oblast' executive committee (*obkom*), sometimes described as the "wheelhorse of Soviet politics," is an important political figure. Many top party leaders have begun their careers as obkom secretary. About one-fourth of the CPSU Central Committee are oblast' secretaries; analysts propose that a major way for a general secretary to consolidate his power is by placing his people in the obkom secretaryships and on the CPSU Central Committee.

Party Schools The extensive system of party-run adult schools that train Soviet citizens for political and community work. Party schools are divided into three levels of increasing rigor: primary, intermediate (the Schools of Marxism-Leninism), and advanced (the Universities of Marxism-Leninism). The capstone of the system is the Academy of Social Sciences, attached directly to the party Central Committee. The higher-level schools train future government and party functionaries in public administration, while the Academy of Social Sciences and the universities prepare the elite. Ordinary citizens, many of them nonparty members, can prepare for volunteer community work and *agitprop* responsibilities at the lower-level schools. Currently, an estimated 20 million Soviet citizens, including about 8 million nonparty members, are enrolled in the party schools. *See also* CPSU: MAIN POLITICAL ADMINISTRATION (MPA), p. 293; *NOMENKLATURA*, p. 337.

Significance The party schools originally were developed in 1919 to prepare a substantially illiterate Soviet citizenry for building communism. They still retain much of the early focus on popularizing Marxism-Leninism, especially at the lower levels, with a heavy dose of party history and ideology. The lower-level schools function in particular to train citizens for agitation and propaganda (agitprop) work in their local communities. Most adults in any position of authority—teachers, factory foremen, local officials—have received training in agitprop activities through the party schools. Future party leaders, selected by their party units, attend regional or republican schools that offer more politically specialized, full-time instruction. Although many graduates privately confess that the political instruction, expecially at the lower levels, is frequently boring, attendance is viewed as a means of upward mobility.

Peaceful Coexistence A policy initiative that represented a major shift in postwar Soviet policy toward the West. First articulated in the postwar period by Georgi Malenkov in August 1953, the policy of peaceful coexistence was strongly reaffirmed by Nikita Khrushchev in 1956, when it became the cornerstone of Soviet foreign policy. Khrushchev changed the thrust of Soviet foreign policy from the confrontational hostility of the Stalinist "two camps" theory to detente and cooperation. The policy does not renounce ideological competition between socialism and capitalism but, recognizing the suicidal nature of war in a nuclear world, rejects the inevitability of war. As Khrushchev stated, only two ways exist: peaceful coexistence or mutual nuclear annihilation. Peaceful coexistence is viewed as a form of the international class struggle that permits the communist-party states to carry out normal relations with the developed capitalist states while encouraging revolutionary movements in the less-developed world. The policy then focuses, as first set forth by Lenin, on the weakest link in the capitalist system, the exploited and dependent developing countries. In November 1960, 81 Communist parties of the world (not including China) affirmed the policy. *See also* CAPITALIST ENCIRCLEMENT, p. 278; DE-STALINIZATION, p. 305.

Significance Peaceful coexistence enabled the post-Stalin leaderships to dismantle the rigid foreign policy of Stalin and move to a global strategy. Although it ushered in a period of detente under Leonid Brezhnev, peaceful coexistence did not rule out Soviet support for wars of national liberation and revolutionary movements in the Third World. This far-flung involvement first culminated in the Cuban missile crisis of 1962 and has since brought Soviet support to revolutionaries around the world. In essence, peaceful coexistence rests on the belief in the inherent superiority and inevitable eventual success of communism, but in the short run tries to avoid the danger of mutual nuclear annihilation. However, by the 1980s conflicts and misunderstandings between the Soviet Union and the West had shattered detente and led to a major escalation in the arms race.

Planning The fundamental principle of the Soviet economic system. Central economic planning, state ownership of the means of production, and management by administrative bodies has created a unified state economy that the party controls. Planning is the responsibility of Gosplan, the state planning committee. Gosplan coordinates the economic priorities determined by the party leadership with the resources of the state. Economic plans cover several time spans: long-range (10 to 20 years), medium (five-year plans), and one-year (operational plans), which at the enterprise level are divided into quarterly and monthly plans. Although many governments practice economic planning, Soviet planning differs in being not indicative but imperative—enterprise managers are legally compelled to fulfill the plans. Plan fulfillment, not profit maximization, is the goal. The party leadership makes the most important decision, the planned rates of increase by key economic sector, which determines investment allocation. These indices are transmitted to the economic ministries, which disaggregate them to the enterprises under their control. Enterprises prepare draft plans that are passed upward through the hierarchical planning system and, after adjustments at each level, are coordinated by Gosplan into the national economic plan and enacted into law. Each enterprise is assigned specific production targets by its ministry and then develops a technical-production-financial plan (*tekpromfinplan*), its operational plan. Plan targets must be quantified—in tons, rubles, dozens, etc.—meaning that enterprises frequently produce whatever most easily meets the measure selected. As the state determines levels of profits, they are not a useful measure of productivity. In short, planning is a system of centrally controlled allocation. The state determines what shall be produced, at what cost, by whom and with what technology, what its final price will be, and to whom it will be delivered. The role of the market as manager and determinant of supply and price is fulfilled by the planners. *See also* COMMAND ECONOMY, p. 283; ENTERPRISE, p. 310; GOSPLAN, p. 321; SECOND ECONOMY, p. 350.

Significance   Central economic planning has become the hallmark of the Soviet system and, many analysts maintain, a major source of party power. Planning is consistent with the regime-proclaimed goal of building communism through industrialization. Since its inception Soviet communism has been a developmental strategy as well as a method of governance. Planning enables the leadership to identify priorities and direct resources. It is also a legitimating device, certifying the party's monopoly rule as necessary. In practice, Soviet planning falls short of the promise. The number of decisions required are mind-boggling, as the Soviet economy now produces an estimated 12 million products. The attempt to plan and administer every economic activity creates diseconomies of scale, bottlenecks when key suppliers lag behind, and endemic shortages, especially in consumer goods. While physical production can be quantified, efficiency, innovation, and productivity cannot be so easily planned. The system has created a huge bureaucracy devoted to enforcing the plans, an entrenched elite that some view as the major obstacle to change. The planning process is undoubtedly a major arena for pressure politics as each sector, region, and bureaucratic group competes for favorable decisions. Soviet planning permits crucial policy decisions to be made and implemented centrally—a key element in the party's power. Whatever its flaws, central economic planning has been the instrument by which the Soviet Union rebuilt the nation after the devastation of World War II and achieved world power while protecting the workers from unemployment and the boom-bust cycles of capitalist economies.

Political Culture: USSR   The prevailing political values, beliefs, and expectations held by the Soviet people. Any analysis of Soviet political culture must consider both the regime's massive effort to resocialize the citizenry and the retention of traditional political values. A major question is whether the political culture of the modern Soviet state represents a distinct break with the past. In addition the many Soviet nationalities have differing historical experiences, levels of development, and traditional value systems. To speak of a uniform Soviet political culture, despite the party's efforts to promote such, may be an oversimplification. Since the Communist party does not permit the publication of value-free attitudinal research, political culture must be deduced from observed behavior, which is difficult in a closed society.

The shared values of the Soviet population are usually assumed to include (1) pride in the successes of the system, especially economic development; (2) a commitment to socialism; (3) support of federalism, which preserves ethnic identities; (4) acceptance of the Communist party's authority; and (5) pride in the USSR's world-power status. To these many observers add patriotism, a general decline in the salience of ideology, and a sense of isolation from the governing elite. No other political system has devoted so much effort to resocializing the citizens. The all-pervasive official socialization emphasizes collectivism, party-directed volunteerism, atheism, belief in the exclusive truth of Marxism-Leninism, and the superiority of the Soviet state. In the view of many Western analysts, Soviet political culture has also been shaped by such constants of the Russian-Soviet political experience as (1) autocracy; (2) the lack of democratic experience; (3) acceptance of state coercion; (4) political passivity; (5) social fragmentation; and (6) reliance on military prowess and expansionism. A dualist thesis proposes that Soviet political culture is conflictual, oscillating between Byzantine and Western traditions, anarchism and obedience, egotism and collectivism, passivity and rebellion. Others hold that the changes wrought by economic development are the major determinants of Soviet political culture. These include urbanization, rapid industrialization, universal literacy, social and geographic mobility, and a vastly altered class structure, all of which serve to legitimate the rule of the Communist party. *See also* CITIZEN PARTICIPATION, p. 279; CIVIL RIGHTS, p. 279; DISSENT AND OPPOSITION, p. 306; EXPLANATORY MODEL: AUTOCRACY, p. 311; SERFDOM, p. 351; STALINISM, p. 357.

Significance Analyzing Soviet political culture illustrates the difficulties of applying Western constructs to the Soviet context. The party's control of communications prevents the spread of opposing values; through its ideological and political monopoly it directs the process of political socialization. Studies of postwar Soviet emigres, including those who oppose the system, demonstrate a common allegiance to such values as respect for discipline and order, fear of the outside world, patriarchal attitudes, political passivity, and belief in progress under socialism. However, the existence of ethnic tensions, crime and corruption, and religious beliefs all belie the official claim to the creation of a homogeneous Communist culture. The existence of some 30 to 50 million Christians and perhaps 40 million Moslems underlines the persistence of traditional values. Ethnic divergencies are apparent. The less-developed areas, especially Moslem Central Asia, exhibit much lower rates of citizen participation, female education and activism, and social and geographic mobility. Whether or not Soviet political culture is viewed as a distinct, modern form, a cluster of attitudes built on Russian traditions, or different patterns based on diverging ethnic traditions, the authority and legitimacy of the Communist party has been sufficient to maintain its power for over 60 years.

Presidium of the Council of Ministers　　The permanent executive committee of the USSR Council of Ministers, which acts as the collective head of government of the Soviet Union. The Presidium of the Council of Ministers probably exercises most of the functions of the much larger Council of Ministers, which totals over 100 members. The term Presidium derives from the Latin, to preside, and in the Soviet system signifies a body that has the power to act for a larger governing body. These small inner bodies, or presidiums, are common throughout Soviet party and government structures. Most operate out of public view; little, for example, is known about the Presidium of the Council of Ministers. It is headed by the chairman, or premier of the Council of Ministers, who is the official head of government. Its membership includes the first deputy chairman and about 12 deputy chairmen, including the heads of important government economic ministries and state committees. The 1977 Constitution refers to it as "the working organ of the Council of Ministers," empowered to decide "all urgent questions" and to "speak in the name of the government." Translated, this means that the Presidium of the Council of Ministers (not to be confused with the Presidium of the Supreme Soviet) is probably the most important organ of government authority. Its major function appears to be coordination of economic planning with party policy. *See also* COUNCIL OF MINISTERS: USSR, p. 284; MINISTRY, p. 335; PRESIDIUM OF THE SUPREME SOVIET, p. 343.

Significance　　The Presidium of the Council of Ministers is typical of the Soviet pattern of delegating government and party responsibility to small inner bodies. How responsibilities are divided is not clear. The legislation issued in the name of the Council of Ministers is most probably the work of its Presidium, as the full Council meets only quarterly. The chairman and first deputy chairman have usually been members of the party Politburo (which under Nikita Khrushchev was called the CPSU Presidium). The other members inevitably sit on the Secretariat and/or Central Committee. The composition of its membership, mainly top economic officials, indicates that it may function as a council of economic advisers to the Politburo. Despite its obscurity, the Presidium of the Council of Ministers is undoubtedly a major institution, reporting directly to the party leadership.

Presidium of the Supreme Soviet　　According to the 1977 Constitution, the "permanently functioning organ of the Supreme Soviet," which acts as a collective head of state. The Presidium of the Supreme Soviet is the highest organ of state authority whenever the Supreme Soviet is not in session. Since the Supreme Soviet, or federal parliament, meets only a few days each year, in effect its Presidium is also the highest legislative body. The Constitution describes it as a collegial body, with its powers vested in the entire collective body. As head of state, the Presidium (1) represents the USSR internationally; (2) ratifies treaties; (3) appoints and receives ambassadors; and (4) exercises the ceremonial functions of state. The chairman of the Presidium of the Supreme Soviet is titular head of state. He therefore is sometimes referred to as the president of the USSR. (This should not be confused with the chairman, or premier, of the Council of Ministers, who is head of government.) The delegation of legislative authority to the Presidium gives it far-reaching legislative powers. It issues legally binding edicts (*ukazes*), which differ from laws (*zakons*) only in that they are not promulgated by the Supreme Soviet. It also issues decrees (*postanovlenie*) binding on all government organs. *Ukazes* cover all areas, from economic policy to judicial affairs. The Presidium is "elected" from among its membership by the Supreme Soviet, although in actuality the Supreme Soviet merely ratifies the Presidium selected by the party leadership. It numbers about 37 members, most of them powerful party leaders as well as high government officials, and includes the 15 chairmen of the republican presidiums. In addition to its ceremonial functions, the powers of the Presidium are extensive. It may (1) issue binding edicts and decrees; (2) set up or abolish government ministries; (3) appoint key government officials; and (4) change republican borders. Its executive powers as military supervisor include the authority to (1) declare war; (2) mobilize the armed forces; (3) proclaim martial law; and (4) appoint military commanders. Its judicial functions include the power to (1) issue orders to the judicial organs; (2) supervise the federal Supreme Court; (3) grant pardons and amnesties; and (4) interpret existing laws. It is therefore the only source of judicial review. The Presidium also grants and revokes citizenship, and is the only body that can grant permission to emigrate. This vesting of legislative, executive, and judicial powers in one body is consistent with Soviet doctrine, which treats separation of powers as a bourgeois device. *See also* CPSU: GENERAL SECRETARY, p. 291; PRESIDIUM OF THE COUNCIL OF MINISTERS, p. 343; SUPREME SOVIET, p. 360.

Significance Although the precise role of the Presidium of the Supreme Soviet is not known, analysts assume it to be the major instrument through which party policy is transmitted into government action. Given its size, it is unlikely that it acts collectively. Most probably the work is carried out by an inner core of top officials, working closely with the

Politburo and, in some cases, sitting on the Politburo itself. The chairman of the Presidium, and thus titular head of state, in recent years has been the Communist party general secretary, thus providing him with the legal right to participate in state and international functions as the head of state. The practice of combining these two offices has varied throughout Soviet history. Nikita Khrushchev headed both party and state between 1958 and 1964. The two posts were then kept separate until 1977, when Leonid Brezhnev became chairman of the Presidium, to be succeeded by Yuri Andropov in 1983 and by Chernenko in 1984. Other party secretaries, as with Vladimir Lenin and Josef Stalin, have at times preferred to occupy the position of chairman of Council of Ministers, or head of government. Whatever the arrangement, in actuality the head of state is the general secretary, whether or not he bears the official title, chairman of the Presidium of the Supreme Soviet.

Procuracy The centralized legal institution that oversees and enforces the uniform compliance of all courts and state agencies with the law. Headed by a procurator-general, who is appointed by the Supreme Soviet, the Procuracy is the key organ of judicial control. Its broad responsibilities include involvement in every stage of the judicial process as well as the supervision of all government actions. The functions of the Procuracy include (1) criminal investigation and prosecution; (2) supervision of all courts, penal institutions, and police; (3) supervision over all administrative bodies; and (4) acting as ombudsman for citizens' complaints. In the courtroom the Procuracy is empowered to detain, arrest, conduct pretrial investigations, determine cause, indict, initiate trial, transfer a case, release the accused, recommend sentence, appeal decisions, and supervise detention. The procurator-general appoints the chief military procurator, the procurators of the republics and higher territorial units, and confirms all lower-level appointments. Every administrative level of government includes a Procuracy. Thus, the *raion* (county) Procuracy oversees the raion executive committee, administrative departments, and raion courts; in Moscow the federal Procuracy monitors the work of the Council of Ministers and the USSR Supreme Court. The Procuracy is exempt from the principle of dual subordination to both local and higher government organs. Although in theory responsible to the Supreme Soviet, in reality it operates essentially under the direction of the Administrative Organs Department of the CPSU Central Committee and is responsible only to the central party leadership. *See also* DUAL SUBORDINATION, p. 308; JUDICIAL STRUCTURE AND ADMINISTRATION, p. 324; SOCIALIST LEGALITY, p. 353; SUPREME COURT, p. 359.

Significance The Procuracy is a unique institution, both administrative and judicial in its function. It exercises far more control over the judicial process than do the courts. Since all economic enterprises, collectives, and public welfare institutions are controlled by a government ministry, ultimately the Procuracy monitors all aspects of public life. The Soviet Procuracy is the heir of the czarist Procuracy, established in 1722 as a means of creating a centralized administrative control system. Abolished in 1917, it was reinstated by Vladimir Lenin in 1922. Although European legal systems based on code law frequently include a procuratorial institution, the Soviet Procuracy is distinguished by its extensive powers and freedom from administrative control. In the judicial process, because there is no equivalent to *habeas corpus*, the actions of the Procuracy are critical. Although it is charged with ensuring the legality of all state actions as well as acting as state attorney, the major function of the Procuracy is to protect the interests of the state.

Raion The basic unit of Soviet local government, similar to a county or municipal borough. In the smaller union-republics, the *raion* is directly subordinate to the union-republic administration; in the larger union-republics, which are divided into *oblast*s (provinces), the raion is subordinate to the oblast' in which it is located. Cities with a population of more than 100,000 are divided into urban raions, similar to a city borough; smaller cities have raion status. Each raion has its own elected assembly (soviet), courts, police, and administrative structure. The lowest administrative subunit is the rural village or settlement, which possess a small soviet and a rudimentary administrative apparatus, responsible for local public services. The functions of the raion administrations vary with their degree of industrialization, population concentration, and location. Remote rural raions may delegate many responsibilities to higher administrative units, while a municipal raion may administer a wide variety of economic enterprises and public services. The raion administers the local budget, is responsible for the fulfillment of the local economic plan and for maintaining public order, supervises the delivery of most social services, and directs subordinate administrative units of any villages and settlements on its territory. Its extensive administrative apparatus is divided functionally into departments (*otdely*) and administrations (*upravleniia*). Each is responsible both to the raion soviet and executive committee and to the analogous administrative body at the oblast' or republican level, thus ensuring tight central control. *See also* OBLAST', p. 337; TERRITORIAL DIVISIONS, p. 362.

Significance The range of raion responsibilities is extensive; over 60 percent of all Soviet government employees are employed in raion administrative organs. Because above the primary party organizations (PPO) level the Communist party is territorially organized, the raion party unit is a critical instrument for maintaining political conformity. It supervises all PPOs on its territory. The *raikom,* the executive committee of the raion party (the municipal equivalent is the *gorkom*) is the major supervisory instrument. Raikom and gorkom party secretaries are the workhorses of local politics, dispensing political favors and selecting proteges. In general, although the raion's administrative powers may be abridged by higher authorities, it remains important as the basic unit of government and party, and is the most visible component of the complex system for most Soviet citizens.

Revolution of 1905 The uprising against the czarist autocracy that culminated in a broad-based attempt to force reforms on Czar Nicholas II (1894–1917). Frequently called the "first bourgeois revolution," the Revolution of 1905 occurred in the context of peasant violence, military mutinies, student demonstrations, industrial strikes, and defeat in the Russo-Japanese War. On January 9, 1905, a large delegation of workers gathered to peacefully petition the czar. Without any provocation, they were fired upon by czarist troops. The tragedy, known as "Bloody Sunday," catalyzed the opposition. Finally, in October 1905 an unprecedented general strike crippled the country, and Nicholas was forced to promise reforms. He promulgated the October Manifesto, which promised limited civil liberties and a representative parliament, the Duma. Having then defused the revolutionary momentum, Nicholas almost immediately welched on the promised reforms. He dissolved the first two elected Dumas, permitting the Duma to meet only after the election laws had been rewritten so as to provide a highly conservative majority. By 1906, repression of political dissidents and non-Russian nationalities was reinstated. Nicholas's implacable insistence on maintaining royal absolutism doomed the reforms promised by the October Manifesto. By 1912, industrial strikes and demonstrations had erupted once again, ended only by Russia's entry into World War I. *See also* BOLSHEVIK REVOLUTION, p. 274; DUMA, p. 309.

Significance The Revolution of 1905 has been called "Russia's unfinished revolution." The promise of any evolution toward democracy and parliamentarianism was thwarted by Nicholas. The Russian state thus entered the twentieth century with no experience in democratic institutions. Until 1905, all political parties and trade unions were illegal, hunted down and persecuted by the *Okhrana,* the czarist secret police. After 1905 repression was applied selectively, but the Okhrana was used to infiltrate unions and political movements, thus driving most meaningful political activity underground. Russia had begun to industrialize under czarist direction, but she differed from many developing nations in that most industrial workers were employed in huge state-run factories employing 1,000 or more workers. The newly urbanized workers had no means of lodging grievances or peacefully resolving disputes. The major effects of the 1905 Revolution were (1) Bloody Sunday destroyed the centuries-old bond between the czar as "Little Father" and the people; (2) the moderates split, between the Octobrists who accepted the limited concessions and the Kadets (Constitutional Democrats) who pressed for continued reform; (3) many liberals and moderates were disillusioned and turned to radicalism; (4) the growing middle and professional classes felt increasingly alienated; (5) the czar became even more isolated; (6) Russia entered the war without the support of many non-Russian nationalities; (7) as hope for evolutionary reform waned a pattern of violent rebellion emerged; and (8) a workers' soviet, or council, formed in St. Petersburg to direct the 1905 general strike. Although the czar arrested all its members in December 1905, the soviet reemerged in 1917 to become the cutting edge of the Bolshevik Revolution. In the long run, the chief effect of the Revolution of 1905 was the destruction of czardom.

Russification A policy that attempts to assimilate non-Russians into Russian culture. As the czarist empire expanded into Siberia, Central Asia, and Europe during the seventeenth and eighteenth centuries, Russification became the official policy of the crown. Occupants of any position of importance had to speak Russian. Those who practiced a religion other than Russian Orthodox Christianity frequently were persecuted, especially Russia's five million Jews, who by a series of decrees were confined to the Pale of Settlement in Western Russia, the Ukraine, and Poland. Under the formula of "autocracy, orthodoxy, and nationality," the crown attempted to inculcate loyalty for czardom, support for the official state religion, and devotion to the Russian nation. The effect was to drive many non-Russians, who constituted the majority of the population, into opposition to the crown. The Bolsheviks came to power with the promise of equality for all nations, a promise they implemented by establishing a federal system based on nationally constituted units. Russians, however, continued to dominate the new state. Their domination increased with Josef Stalin's accession to power in 1928. Stalin repeatedly purged the non-Russian leaderships for "bourgeois nationalism" and propagated Russian as the language of socialism. Although Russians now constitute only 52 percent of the population, party membership is 60 percent Russian, and Russian domination of the top party organs is even more pronounced. The language of military command is Russian, and a preponderant majority of officers and KGB officials are Russian. Although education in non-Russian languages is carefully preserved, Russian is taught as a second language everywhere and is still regarded as crucial to upward mobility. *See also* DISSENT AND OPPOSITION, p. 306; FEDERALISM: USSR, p. 318; POLITICAL CULTURE: USSR, p. 341; UNION-REPUBLIC, p. 364.

Significance The extent of a deliberate policy of Russification under Soviet communism is difficult to gauge. In a centralized one-party state that contains over 100 nationalities, the dynamics of control favor the majority nationality, which in this case is three times the size of the next largest nationality, the Ukrainians. Furthermore, with the exception of the Baltic peoples, the Russians and their co-Slavs, the Ukrainians, have historically been the most educated ethnic grouping. Federal representatives in the non-Russian republics and autonomous republics tend to be Russian; frequently the second secretary of the republican party, who controls important appointments, is a Russian. If there is a portion of the party who advocate Russification, they may receive reinforcement from the fact that the most serious cases of nationalist outbreaks have occurred in Armenia, Azerbaidzhan, Georgia, and the Ukraine—all republics administered mainly by nationals. Some analysts make a distinction between Russianization, non-Russians' adoption of Russian as a second language, and Russification. Much of what may be carelessly labelled Russification may be more the result of modernization, in which the Russians have undeniably played the leading role. The argument may deepen as better education creates cadres of well-trained nationals in the non-Russian republics and territories. A looming problem is the fact that, due to differential birth rates, by the year 2000 the bulk of army conscripts and new labor force supply will come from the Central Asian republics. In addition, some analysts fear that if the aging leadership faces increasing crises, it will turn openly to Russification to preserve its power, as did the czars.

Samizdat The reproduction and person-to-person circulation of uncensored written material, usually operating on the chain letter principle. *Samizdat* is a contraction of *sam* (self) and *izdatel'stvo* (publishing house), a word play on *Gosizdat*, the government publishing house and sole printer in the Soviet Union. Since any published work must be approved by the state censors (*Glavlit*), samizdat is the only way of evading censorship. Most samizdat relies on typed carbon copies or photographs of manuscripts; the police control photocopying and duplicating machines. The production of samizdat itself is not a crime, but the authorities generally assume that samizdat material is inherently suspect and therefore punish its disseminators under the charge of circulating anti-Soviet propaganda. Samizdat is especially prevalent among religious believers and dissident nationalists who reject Russification—the Baptists, Seventh-Day Adventists, Baltic Roman Catholics, Ukrainians, Jews, and others. The civil rights activists have used samizdat extensively, the major samizdat journal being *The Chronicle of Human Events*, which has detailed the repression of free thought. The Communist party has treated samizdat as a threat to its ideological monopoly, and accordingly repressed it whenever possible. See also CIVIL RIGHTS, p. 279; DISSENT AND OPPOSITION, p. 306; SOCIALIST REALISM, p. 354.

Significance Much of what the West knows about dissent and its repression in the Soviet Union is due to samizdat that has reached the West. The samizdat form is a constant in the Russian-Soviet experience, as czarist censorship also forced writers to circulate their works illegally. Russian and Soviet writers have a long history of "writing for the drawer," i.e., in secret for their friends and supporters. Modern technology and human ingenuity have created a host of related unauthorized information networks. *Tamizdat*, "over there" (*tam*) publication is the publishing abroad of uncensored, unapproved material. *Magnitizdat* is illegal taping of speeches, poetry readings, nationalist folk songs, and such. *Kinizdat* involves illegal films and *radizdat* the taping of Western radio.

Second Economy The term applied to a wide range of unauthorized economic transactions conducted by many Soviet citizens. The second economy embraces all economic activities conducted for personal gain without government sanction. It thus operates parallel to the official "first economy," where the state controls all production and market operations. The second economy ranges from barter trade, privately contracted repair services, and moonlighting, to outright smuggling and theft. The key to understanding the second economy lies in the all-pervasive nature of the state-controlled centralized economic system, which permits almost no private economic activity. The Russian term, *na levo*, "on the left," describes the situation well, as many of these activities involving trade and exchange of services are considered illegal only because they violate the principle of total state control over the economy. The second economy permits the citizen to circumvent the consumer shortages endemic to the centrally planned Soviet economy, especially prevalent in the repair sector. The second economy frequently involves the exchange of favors and mutual obligations. A sizable portion of the second economy also involves *blat*, the Russian term for the art of using influence and connections. Blat may be used to short-circuit the cumbersome central sypply system or to secure a favorable action from an official. Outright illegalities, such as black market operations, may involve stolen goods, smuggled goods, or goods illegally produced with state-owned equipment. The simple trading of goods among citizens is not considered black market, but is still part of the second economy because the official state retail system plays no role in this redistribution. The state-run hard currency stores that offer high-quality consumer goods and imports for sale to foreign tourists with hard currency influence the second economy by tempting Soviet citizens into illegal currency transactions. All of these activities frequently involve blat and its more serious manifestations, bribery and corruption, in order to secure protection from official action. *See also* COMMAND ECONOMY, p. 283; CRIMINAL OFFENSES: ECONOMIC CRIMES, p. 301; SOCIALIST OWNERSHIP, p. 354.

Significance The growth of the second economy has created an extensive network where goods, services, and favors are traded. Although this unofficial network serves to make the failings of the state economy more tolerable to the citizen, it may also impede economic reform because many have learned how to benefit from it. Illegal currency transactions are attractive because the state permits foreign currency to be exchanged only at state banks, which peg the exchange rates artificially low for hard currencies. The extent of the second economy, estimated at 10 to 20 percent of the official economy, makes it difficult to accurately assess Soviet living standards, since none of it appears in the official statistics. Some analysts maintain that the more serious forms of illegal economic activity are more prevalent in Soviet Asia, Georgia, and Armenia than in the European Soviet Union. Others propose that it has institutionalized graft and bribery at all levels, including the sale of government posts presumably worth money because of access to bribery.

Serfdom A condition of servitude in which a person is bound in perpetuity to the land. Serfdom, which was the dominant socioeconomic institution of the czarist system, lasted until 1861. Serfs enjoyed neither freedom of movement nor protection of the law. Authority over them rested with the crown or with the landlord, who acted as tax collector and draft board for the crown. The landlord did not hold direct title to the serfs; they were essentially chattels on the land, obliged to render taxes (the "soul" tax), labor, or rent to the landlord and military conscripts to fill his quota. Hereditary serfdom developed in the mid-fifteenth century during the consolidation of the Russian state; most of the remaining free peasants were enserfed in the late seventeenth century. In essence, the crown rewarded the gentry for service to the state by protecting their authority over the serfs. Except for a few huge estates, landholding became extremely fragmented. Consequently, Russian agriculture remained backward. Serfdom also created a special group, the Cossacks, free frontiersmen on the border regions who had fled serfdom and in exchange for the obligation to protect the empire's borders were granted land, tax exemptions, and freedom. At the time of the Emancipation Act of 1861, 80 percent of the population was enserfed, half tied to the crown lands and half to the landlords. Emancipation did not completely transform the old system. Despite limited reforms in local government (the *zemstvo* system) and judicial reforms, the freed serfs did not receive full legal equality until 1905. Authority over them was given to the village (*mir*), which retained civil jurisdiction over the former serfs. The serfs also could not move without permission of the mir authorities, who were supervised by the government. Almost half received inadequate land allotments, while the gentry retained the best land. The remaining land was transferred collectively to the mir, which was charged with the periodic reallotment (*peredel*) of communal lands. The peasants were subject to heavy redemption payments to the government, while the landlords were overcompensated through government credits. The combination of impossibly high redemption payments, peasant overpopulation, recurring famine, and the retention of the medieval communal system froze Russian agricultural productivity. Russia remained a land of greatly maldistributed wealth, with an increasingly impoverished, rebellious peasantry. *See also* BOLSHEVIK REVOLUTION, p. 274; EXPLANATORY THEORY: AUTOCRACY, p. 311; POLITICAL CULTURE: USSR, p. 341; REVOLUTION OF 1905, p. 347.

Significance The legacy of serfdom persisted into the twentieth century. Emancipation satisfied few, neither the gentry, many of whom went bankrupt, nor the land-hungry peasants. The long centuries of serfdom created a society divided into a small landowning gentry dependent on the crown, a miniscule and powerless middle class, and the vast peasantry, who were largely isolated from the state. Emancipation did spur the growth of a small urban working class, totaling about three million by 1900, which provided a base for Marxism. Peasant violence and czarist repression increased throughout the late nineteenth and early twentieth centuries. Despite some later reforms, by 1905 the peasants still owned only 15 percent of the land. Thus Russia entered World War I with an unsolved peasant problem. As the war dragged on, peasant insurrections and the dissolution of the largely peasant imperial army contributed heavily to the revolutionary atmosphere that brought down czardom. In October 1917, Vladimir Lenin forged an alliance with the peasants, who rallied to the Bolsheviks' slogan of "bread, land, and peace."

Socialist Legality   The Marxist theory that the law of a socialist system differs from all other law. The concept views socialist legality as a force that supports the building of socialism, in contrast to bourgeois legality, which protects capitalism. Marxism maintains that law is determined by the economic system; each class structure, from slavery to capitalism, has given rise to a specific type of law. All but socialism are based on private ownership, and all but socialist law are designed to protect it. Socialist law expresses the will of the people and thus preserves the socialist order. Socialist legality also emphasizes the role of law as a means of public education in the norms of socialist behavior. As well as maintaining public order, socialist law is designed to regulate behavior, channeling it into officially approved socialist modes, and elevating the interests of the state over those of the individual. Soviet law therefore is distinguished by a long list of political offenses that are defined as crimes against the state—behavior that threatens the socialist order or that doesn't conform to "socialist community standards." Marxist political theory also rejects the concept of separation of powers as a bourgeois device; law must further the interests of socialism, not act as an independent check. *See also* CIVIL RIGHTS, p. 279; CRIMINAL OFFENSES, p. 299; DE-STALINIZATION, p. 305; DISSENT AND OPPOSITION, p. 306; PROCURACY, p. 345.

Significance   The concept of socialist legality rescued the Bolsheviks from an ideological dilemma. Marxism maintains that once socialism is instituted, the needs for courts and laws will begin to "wither away" with the state as class conflict diminishes. Crime, an artifact of capitalist ownership, will disappear. The Bolsheviks immediately dismantled the czarist courts and were then faced with the problem of maintaining public order and securing the revolution. Vladimir Lenin instituted the Revolutionary Courts, whose main purpose was to punish suspected opponents of the Revolution. During the Civil War period (1918–21) these revolutionary tribunals frequently acted arbitrarily. All operated extralegally, as no Soviet legal codes were published until 1922. The tribunals did establish the precept that the goal of socialist legality is to safeguard the socialist order and to educate the populace. Legal codes and a court system were then established according to the doctrine of socialist legality. During the 1930s the concept of socialist legality was gravely compromised by Josef Stalin's use of the term to justify the mass destruction of the Great Purge. After Stalin's death in 1953, an important part of Nikita Khrushchev's de-Stalinization campaign was the restoration of socialist legality and the codification of the legal codes. The legal reforms of the late 1950s brought Soviet law into conformity with modern civil (code) law systems. Soviet law is now set by comprehensive legal codes containing a systematic outline of general principles and specific crimes, procedures, and punishments. The Stalinist category of "social danger," under which the mere suspicion of supposedly anticommunist tendencies was sufficient for drastic punishment, was dropped. Also dropped was the principle of analogy, inherited from czarist legal codes, under which a person could be convicted of a crime not specifically enumerated in the codes if a court determined it to be analogous to another specific crime. Soviet legal doctrine, however, still retains the major thrust of socialist legality, the use of the law as a means of directing the power of the socialist state and protecting the socialist order.

Socialist Ownership   Ownership of the means of production by the society. The ideology of Marxism-Leninism holds that just as private ownership creates capitalism, socialist ownership creates socialism, and this is necessary to a socialist system. In the Soviet Union, socialist ownership means both ownership and control by the state, and, in reality, by the party, which controls the state apparatus. Socialist property includes almost all land, resources, and property. It is legally superior to all other property (collective, cooperative, or private); the state is subject to no restrictions in its use. *See also* CRIMINAL OFFENSES: CRIMES AGAINST SOCIALIST PROPERTY, p. 300; ENTERPRISE, p. 310; PLANNING, p. 340.

Significance   Socialist ownership has become the base upon which the Soviet Communist party has erected a system of all-pervasive control, ideologically justifying the state's control over all economic activities. Enterprises, institutions, and farms act as managers of the state's assets; the goods and services produced are state property and may be allocated only as stipulated by the state. Critics of Soviet statism maintain that socialist ownership means that all control is vested in the state, creating a form of "state capitalism" that exploits surplus value from the workers as much as does capitalist ownership and control. Their critique focuses on the almost universal socialist ownership of property as the basis for the party's monopoly of power over all aspects of Soviet life.

Socialist Realism   The doctrine imposed by Josef Stalin in the early 1930s that subordinates all artistic creativity to the political aims of the party. Socialist realism values artistic expression only as a means of inculcating what the party views as socialist values. A constant theme is the glorification of the system. Josef Stalin set up professional associations, such as the Writers Union, which are the sole means by which creative artists can publicly exercise their professions. The party determines what forms of artistic expression are permissible, and through control of the professional associations bans all that does not accord with the official precepts. Under Stalin any Western influence was immediately suspect, Stalin going so far as to ban saxophones and to incarcerate jazz musicians in the prison labor camps. The outpouring of avantgarde creativity that so distinguished the Soviet cultural scene in the 1920s was stifled. Artistic creativity was perverted into a vulgar glorification of the system. Under Stalin, Soviet culture was reduced to a sterile conformity, from which it has yet to recover. *See also* CRIMINAL OFFENSES: ANTI-SOVIET AGITATION AND PROPAGANDA, p. 299; DISSENT AND OPPOSITION, p. 306, SAMIZDAT, p. 349.

Significance   Although the doctrine of socialist realism is applied less rigidly today, the original strictures and intent remain. The chief instruments of control are the state censorship agency, *Glavlit*, its analogous institutions, and the professional associations. Glavlit regulates all public information and literature, while *Glavrepertoire* controls all entertainment from ballet and the theater to radio, phonograph records, and television. The professional associations enforce the party line on their creative artists, while the party determines admissions and expulsions. If a creative work breaches the code of socialist realism, the artist is denied membership. As all citizens are required to work, an expelled dissident artist who persists in his work may be charged with "parasitism" and imprisoned. The straitjacket of socialist realism has created a long line of dissident creative artists. Some have elected to stay within their country, but many others have emigrated in search of the artistic freedom their country denies them. Since Stalin's death the system has relied on self-censorship as much as on outright repression. The original intent of Stalin's policy, however, remains in place: socialist realism is essentially a tool of party control over all creative expression, ensuring that its sole purpose is to support the regime.

Soviet   The Russian word for council or assembly. The term *soviet* was first applied to the workers' councils that arose in czarist Russia during the revolutionary period of the early 1900s. It is now the formal title for the over 50,000 local and regional legislative bodies, the parliaments of the 15 union-republics, and the national parliament, the Supreme Soviet. All but the bicameral Supreme Soviet are single-chamber bodies. Each soviet is responsible to the authorities at the next highest level as well as to its own constituents, according to the principle of dual subordination that extends throughout Soviet party and government organs and ensures that hierarchical control is maintained. Most of the work of a soviet is delegated to an inner working body, the executive committee or presidium. Although only half of the deputies to local soviets may be party members, party control over nominations and the delegation of most responsibilities to inner bodies ensures party control. The soviets function mainly as instruments of public legitimation for party decisions, which are transmitted to the soviets for formal legislative approval. See also BOLSHEVIK REVOLUTION, p. 274; DEPUTY, p. 303; REVOLUTION OF 1905, p. 347; SUPREME SOVIET, p. 360.

Significance The initial slogan of the Bolshevik Revolution was "all power to the soviets." Soviets, or workers' councils, first emerged spontaneously during the 1905 Revolution, which forced Czar Nicholas II to grant limited constitutional reforms. In 1917, as the accumulated strains of war losses and czarist ineptitude plunged Russia into near-anarchy, the soviets formed once again. The early soviets were politically heterogeneous, a combination of debate societies, self-governing workers' councils, strike committees, revolutionaries, and action committees. As the Provisional Government, formed in February of 1917, proved increasingly ineffectual, the soviets became more and more powerful. By September the Bolsheviks had won the soviets. In October of 1917, Vladimir Lenin toppled the Provisional Government and seized power in the name of the soviets. The Bolshevik dominance of the soviets was the key to the bloodlessness of the Revolution that brought communism to Russia. The soviets provided the Bolsheviks with a ready instrument of legitimacy. The importance the party attaches to maintaining both the revolutionary heritage of the soviets and the ideal of representative democracy is indicated by the title they chose for the federated state that succeeded Imperial Russia, the Union of Soviet Socialist Republics (USSR). Such is the ideological value ascribed to the soviets that the name has come to stand for a citizen, or collectively the people of the USSR or the state itself, surely one of the few times that a political institution has lent its name to an entire people.

Sovkhoz The abbreviated Russian term for the Soviet state farm, a large, state-owned agricultural operation. The *sovkhoz* is organized and operated like an industrial enterprise. The state retains direct ownership of all sovkhoz assets and land. The management is appointed by and is responsible to the relevant ministry of agriculture. Sovkhoz workers are considered employees of the state and, unlike collective farm peasants, are entitled to full welfare benefits, trade union membership, and a set yearly salary. The sovkhoz operates under the same laws as a state enterprise and possesses legal identity. Many sovkhozes are model farms or research institutions; others are devoted to large-scale grain operations. *See also* COLLECTIVIZATION, p. 280; KOLKHOZ, p. 327.

Significance Contemporary Soviet leaders prefer the sovkhoz to the collective farm, the *kolkhoz*, as ideologically closer to the goals of communism. Although by 1953 sovkhozes accounted for only 6–7 percent of all Soviet agricultural output, Josef Stalin's successor, Nikita Khrushchev, embarked on a "sovkhozization" campaign that brought half of the arable land into sovkhozes. By 1971, 15,502 sovkhozes employed one-third of the agricultural population and produced nearly one-third of the total output. The average sovkhoz now contains up to 20,000 hectares (49,420 acres) and employs up to 600 workers. Soviet policy favors the sovkhozes, which receive a disproportionate share of the agricultural investment. Frequently the state covers sovkhoz deficits with subsidies. There is little proof, however, that they are more productive than the ideologically inferior collective farms.

Stalinism The practices and policies of Josef Stalin, general secretary of the Communist party and undisputed leader of the Soviet Union from 1928 to 1953. Although Stalin based his rule on the tenets of Marxism-Leninism, Stalinism itself is not a comprehensive ideology. Rather it denotes the political means by which Stalin secured and maintained power. These include (1) personalized, one-man dictatorship; (2) pervasive terror as an instrument of control; (3) rapid, coerced industrialization; (4) the fostering of a "cult of the individual" through massive, public adulation of the leader; and (5) the subordination of all institutions, including ideology, to the leader. Stalin was named CPSU general secretary in 1922. In the period following Vladimir Lenin's death in 1924, Stalin skillfully used his control over the Secretariat and party apparatus to build a power base from which he eliminated his opposition. By 1928 he had triumphed over his chief rivals, the Left Opposition, led by Leon Trotsky, and the Right Opposition, led by Nikolai Bukharin. His power secured, Stalin abolished the gradualist reforms of the New Economic Program enacted by Lenin and embarked on a crash program to industrialize the state. A key component was the forced collectivization of agriculture. Simultaneously, Stalin instituted central economic planning and the five-year plan system. It is the methods Stalin used to secure total control and to transform the state that are generally called Stalinism. Using the Leninist principle of democratic centralism, Stalin imposed one-man rule and perverted the collective decision-making machinery of the party and government. Opposition was suppressed by a massive secret police system that employed terror as a routine instrument of governance. No sector of society was immune. The party was hit especially hard; Stalin's victims included Lenin's former associates, the "Old Bolsheviks," most of the CPSU Central Committee, and any others who might question his policies. Party organs atrophied, and the party itself was seriously weakened. The central thrust was the creation of a society totally mobilized around the dictator's will. The effort to create the New Soviet Man, that human who would unselfishly labor for communism and the common good, was accompanied by a campaign to socialize the citizenry into believing that anyone was capable of betrayal. In the end, Stalin possessed a subservient party-state in which all owed their existence to him. The "revolution from above" that transformed the state not only destroyed the party and government as independent institutions, it also cost an estimated 12 to 30 million lives, a disregard for human life perhaps unprecedented in the modern world. *See also* COMMAND ECONOMY, p. 283; DE-STALINIZATION, p. 305; EXPLANATORY THEORY: AUTOCRACY, p. 311; GREAT PURGE, p. 322; LENINISM, p. 330.

Significance The characteristics of Stalinism have led to its description as left-wing totalitarianism. All—party and government, peasants and workers—were subordinated to the autocratic will of one man operating through his chosen instrumentality of control, permanent terror. Stalinism shattered the alliance with the peasantry forged by Lenin. Intraparty democracy and the proletariat disappeared as political forces; only the dictator remained. However, Stalinism may also be viewed as a method of governance, a means of rapid industrialization, and a mobilizational system. Stalin's main contributions are seen as the economic development of the state, the defeat of Nazism, and the postwar reconstruction. The all-pervasive terror system also created massive upward mobility as the millions executed or thrown into prison camps during the 1930s were replaced by new loyalists. Some analysts maintain that only when the generation represented by the prewar politicians passes from the scene will the Soviet Union be rid of the legacy carried by those who began their careers under Stalin. Although it stopped short of attaching any blame to other party members, the de-Stalinization process carried out after Stalin's death in 1953 dismantled the terror system and restored most of the Leninist party norms. However, many of the fundamentals of Stalinism remain: rule by a self-selected few, rigid centralism, censorship, intolerance of dissent, central economic planning, collectivized agriculture, and the use of secret police for political control. A major argument centers on whether Stalinism represents a distinct break with Leninism—an aberration based on economism or paranoid dictatorship—or a logical progression from the Leninist principles of democratic centralism and the dictatorship of the proletariat. For some, Stalinism represents the betrayal of the revolution. For others, it validates all their suspicions of Marxist socialism.

State Committee An interdepartmental agency, attached to the federal Council of Ministers. Two critical agencies are state committees: the Committee for State Security (KGB) and the State Planning Committee (Gosplan). State committees plan and coordinate the work of the state in several broad areas, particularly in economic affairs and state security. Unlike the functionally specific ministries, a state committee has responsibilities that overlap the work of several ministries. The administrative powers of a state committee also are far broader. A state committee can issue orders and regulations that are binding on any relevant agency, including another ministry. The orders of a specific ministry, such as the Ministry of Agriculture, are binding only on its subordinate units. A state committee is headed by a chairman rather than by a minister. The most important state committees include: the KGB, Gosplan, the State bank (Gosbank), the State Committee on Labor and Social Questions, the State Committee for Science and Technology, the State Committee for Prices, and the State Committee for Radio and Television. Although since 1978 the state committees have been members of the Council of Ministers, it is likely that they operate under the direct control of the central party organs. State committees function as decision-making and coordinating bodies rather than as line administrative agencies. Because their orders are binding on other ministries, they outrank the ministries. State committees usually have three functions: planning, coordination, and supervision. Comparable subordinate committees exist at republican and territorial levels. *See also* COUNCIL OF MINISTERS: USSR, p. 284; GOSPLAN, p. 321; KGB, p. 326; PLANNING, p. 340.

Significance The state committees, in particular the KGB and Gosplan, are among the most important institutions in the Soviet system. The chairman of the KGB is one of the most powerful politicians in the system; since 1973 the KGB has enjoyed representation on the Politburo. The detailed economic plans that govern the Soviet economy are the work of Gosplan, probably in conjunction with Gosbank and the state committees for labor and social questions, construction, supply, and prices. Such related state committees appear to work together closely, constituting in effect an alternate Council of Ministers with wide-ranging powers. As their policy-making powers are far broader than those of the ministries, state committees probably play a key role in the policy process, translating the priorities set by the party leadership into policies to be implemented by the ministries.

Supreme Court The highest judicial body in the Soviet legal system. The Supreme Court is the only federal court; there are no federal appellate courts. All other courts operate under the jurisdiction of the

15 republican supreme courts. The USSR Supreme Court is headed by a chairman and a vice-chairman and is divided into civil, criminal, and military panels. Membership totals about 31, appointed by the Presidium of the Supreme Soviet for five-year terms. The chairmen of the republican supreme courts are ex officio members. The USSR Supreme Court hears appeals from the republican supreme courts, in rare instances acts as the court of original jurisdiction, supervises the administration of justice, and issues legally binding judicial instructions and interpretations. It operates under the supervision of the Procuracy, which often suggests the judicial instructions issued in the name of the USSR Supreme Court. In appellate cases, appeals are brought to the Supreme Court by the procurator-general or the chairman, but the Supreme Court will accept an appeal against the decision of a republican supreme court only if it possibly violates federal law or the interests of another republic. It also advises the Presidium of the Supreme Soviet on draft legislation. *See also* JUDICIAL STRUCTURE AND ADMINISTRATION, p. 324; PROCURACY, p. 345; SOCIALIST LEGALITY, p. 353.

Significance Through its power to issue binding instructions and interpretations, the USSR Supreme Court imposes uniformity in an otherwise republic-based judicial system. Since Communist legal doctrine rejects the principle of a fundamental law to which the state is subordinate, the Supreme Court cannot rule on the constitutionality of executive and legislative acts, but it can expand and explain their meaning to lower courts that must implement them. Probably its most important function is providing these instructions, which are binding on all lower courts.

Supreme Soviet The bicameral legislature that is the highest organ of state authority according to the constitution of the Soviet Union. The major functions of the Supreme Soviet include (1) enacting basic laws (*zakons*); (2) approving edicts (*ukazes*) issued by the Presidium of the Supreme Soviet; (3) amending the constitution; (4) ratifying state economic plans and budgets; (5) defining the jurisdiction of state organs; (6) appointing high officials, including the Supreme Court and Council of Ministers; and (7) monitoring the work of administrative agencies and all lower legislatures. In reality, the large size (1,500 members) of the Supreme Soviet, extremely brief sessions, and tight party control preclude it from acting as the supreme state authority. Its two chambers are of equal size—750 member deputies each elected for five-year terms. The Soviet of the Union represents the population at large on the basis of equally-proportioned single-member electoral districts of approximately 300,000 voters each. The Soviet of the Nationalities represents the nationality based constituent units of the Soviet federation as follows: union republic, 32 deputies; autonomous republic, 11 deputies; autonomous region, 5 deputies; and national area, 1 deputy. The Supreme Soviet typically convenes for two 2- to 5-day sessions per year. Most of its work is delegated to an inner body, the Presidium of the Supreme Soviet, which is empowered to act for the Supreme Soviet when it is not in session and to issue edicts that carry the force of law. Such edicts are subsequently ratified as law by the Supreme Soviet, a formality accomplished without debate by a unanimous show of hands. The edicts typically form the bulk of the law enacted by the Supreme Soviet. Since the 1960s, the formal work of the Supreme Soviet has increasingly devolved to functionally specific standing committees, which apparently review draft legislation, hear debate, and monitor the government agencies in their specific areas of responsibility. The 30 standing committees (15 for each chamber) are selected by the coordinating body of the Supreme Soviet, the Council of Elders, composed of about 150 top party officials in the Supreme Soviet. The Council of Elders also sets the agenda and approves the standing orders of each formal session of the Supreme Soviet. Frequently, legislative proposals will be initially enunciated by a joint policy declaration of the CPSU Central Committee and the USSR Council of Ministers. Whether a particular legislative proposal originates in the Council of Ministers, the Presidium, the Politburo, or the Secretariat is difficult to ascertain and probably unimportant, given the fact that all high government posts are occupied by top party officials. Formal sessions of the Supreme Soviet are thus ceremonial in nature, setting a constitutional seal of approval on policy initiated elsewhere. *See also* DEPUTY, p. 303; DUPLICATION OF OFFICE, p. 310; LEGAL ENACTMENTS, p. 329; PRESIDIUM OF THE SUPREME SOVIET, p. 343.

Significance Although the Supreme Soviet does not function as a deliberative body in the sense of Western parliamentarianism, its ceremonial role as public legitimator of party policy is important. Its power to amend or reinterpret the Constitution gives it added authority as no independent agency of judicial review exists. As the chief institutional bearer of the federal principle, the Supreme Soviet can also act as a forum for the articulation of ethnic interests, particularly in the economic sphere. Because the party-controlled election process is obviously aimed at creating a socially balanced deputy membership, the Supreme Soviet is probably the most representative body in the Soviet system. Its membership includes many nonparty members, youth, workers, peasants, and women. However, such seats are characterized by a high rate of turnover. Generally only high party functionaries, about 500 in all, are permitted to accumulate much experience, particularly in the committee structure. That the Soviet leaders feel the necesssity for a constitutional organ of state authority is evident, or else it would not be deemed necessary that all important policy decisions are legislatively validated. The acts of the Supreme Soviet thus provide a clue to the priorities of the party and lend legitimacy to the authority of the CPSU leadership.

Territorial Divisions Administrative and territorial units of the Soviet Union that exist to decentralize administrative functions or to preserve the cultural identity of a specific nationality, or both. The territorial divisions are: 15 union-republics; 20 autonomous Soviet Socialist republics (ASSRs); 8 autonomous provinces; 6 territories (*krai*s); 10 national areas (*okrug*s); 121 provinces (*oblast*s); and 3,458 *raion*s, the last being the basic unit of local government. The oblasts and raions are strictly administrative units; the other territorial divisions are constituted as both administrative units and as national homelands. Most of the ethnically based territorial units are located within the Russian republic, which embraces just over half the population and two-thirds of the Soviet territory. *See also* FEDERALISM: USSR, p. 318; *OBLAST'*, p. 337; *RAION*, p. 346; UNION-REPUBLIC, p. 364.

Significance The vast territory of the Soviet state, extending over 8.6 million square miles across 11 time zones, and its complex multinational composition has dictated the intricate structure of territorial divisions. The state has managed to accommodate most of its major nationalities into some sort of territorial unit and decentralize some administrative responsibilities. These divisions are also important politically because each contains its own local party organization and therefore is the locus of politics on its territory.

Union of Soviet Socialist Republics (USSR) The official name of the communist-party state created by the Bolsheviks as the successor to the Russian Empire. Frequently called the Soviet Union, the Union of Soviet Socialist Republics territorially is the largest state in the world and ranks third in population. Its vast territory, over 6,000 miles from the western border to the Bering Straits, spans two continents; the Ural Mountains are the traditional division between Europe and Asia. Most of the Soviet landmass lies north of 50° latitude, above the latitude of Winnipeg, Canada. The average population density is one-ninth that of Western Europe, with most of the population residing in the European USSR. The Russians, by far the most numerous of the 75 percent of the population who are Slavic, have shaped most of the institutions of the state although they constitute only 52 percent of the population. The history of the state is one of constant wars and expansionism. Various northern Slavic tribes emerged as an identifiable nation (*Rus'*) in the ninth century and as Kievan Russia began to develop political institutions. Kiev was later supplanted by the principalities of Novgorod, near Finland, and Vladimir-Suzdal, near Moscow. After subjugation to the Tatar (Mongol) overlordship from 1240 to 1480, a new Slavic state coalesced around the Duchy of Moscow. Over four and a half centuries of czarist absolutism and steady territorial expansion began with Ivan IV (1533–84). The last areas to come under czarist rule were the Caucasus (1860s), Turkestan (1866), Central Asia including part of Afghanistan (1864–65), the Amur River area (1858), Sakhalin Island, and the Far East (1875). Despite the post–World War I territorial losses in Eastern Europe forced upon the Bolsheviks, the new Communist state retained most of the czarist empire, losing Bessarabia (Moldavia) to Romania, and Poland, Estonia, Latvia, Lithuania, and Finland, which were constituted as independent states. The Bolsheviks proclaimed the Russian Socialist Federated Soviet Republic (RSFSR) in July 1918 and during the course of the civil war added several non-Russian autonomous (in name only) republics to the RSFSR. This arrangement was formalized in 1922 as a federated state, the USSR; the USSR Constitution was promulgated in 1924. In September 1939, as part of the Hitler-Stalin Pact, the Soviet Union invaded eastern Poland and annexed western Belorussia and the western Ukraine. In 1940 the Baltic states and Bassarabia were forcibly annexed as union-republics. After invasion by Nazi Germany in June 1941 the Soviet Union fought the remainder of World War II on the Allied side, and at the end of the war retained its territorial acquisitions, in all adding 22 million non-Russians to the USSR. In addition, communist-party states under Soviet control were set up in the newly liberated countries of Eastern Europe, thus forming a solid bloc of Soviet-dominated states on the USSR's western border. *See also* BOLSHEVIK REVOLUTION, p. 274; FEDERALISM: USSR, p. 318; POLITICAL CULTURE, p. 341; SOVIET, p. 355.

Significance The title, the Union of Soviet Socialist Republics, of the world's first avowedly Communist state symbolizes its unique character: a Marxist socialist state, revolutionary in origin, federal in structure, and ideologically united behind the precepts of Marxism-Leninism. The ruling party, the Communist Party of the Soviet Union, bases its legitimacy in its claim to be building communism and permits no political or ideological competition. According to the 1977 USSR Constitution, "The Great October Socialist Revolution, made by the workers and peasants of Russia under the leadership of the Communist Party ... created the Soviet state, a new type of state and ... began the epoch-making turn of capitalism to socialism." With the United States, the USSR is one of the two superpowers, projecting its influence worldwide and claiming to lead the international Communist movement.

Union-Republic The most important constituent unit of the Soviet federal system. The 15 union-republics, each constituted as the homeland of a major historic nationality, are: the Russian Soviet Federated Socialist Republic (RSFSR), Armenia, Azerbaidzhan, Belorussia, Estonia, Georgia, Kazakhstan, Kirgizia, Latvia, Lithuania, Moldavia, Tadzhikistan, Turkmenistan, the Ukraine, and Uzbekistan. Union-republics differ widely in size, population, levels of economic development, and ethnic composition. The RSFSR embraces over two-thirds of the vast Soviet territory and just over one-half of its population; Estonia contains only .55 percent of the population. The RSFSR contains 31 of the 38 nationality-based territorial administrative divisions below the republican level (autonomous republics, autonomous regions, and national areas). The Ukraine, Georgia, and Armenia are also areas of extremely mixed population. The Central Asian republics are substantially less developed and urbanized than the republics of European USSR. All union-republics have constitutions, governments, equal representation in the Chamber of Nationalities of the Supreme Soviet, and in theory are sovereign states with the right to negotiate treaties and to secede. However, the USSR Constitution gives the federation virtually unlimited power over the republics. In 1944 the Soviet leadership demanded United Nations representation for each union-republic. A compromise agreement, essentially the price of Soviet adherence to the United Nations, led to separate UN membership and representation for Byelorussia and the Ukraine. *See also* FEDERALISM: USSR, p. 318; RUSSIFICATION, p. 348; TERRITORIAL DIVISIONS, p. 362.

Significance The union-republics represent the major compromise between Marxism's scorn for "bourgeois nationalism" and the realities of governing a vast multinational empire. Republican autonomy has been constrained by the centralization of the system and the political monopoly of the Communist party, and is thus largely confined to the preservation of cultural identities and administrative decentralization. Union-republic parties have the full array of Communist party structures but are circumscribed by the unitary nature of the party and mandatory party discipline. An exception is the Russian republic. The RSFSR does not possess a separate republican party apparatus, instead operating within the national CPSU structure, where ethnic Russians enjoy a disproportionately large number of high positions. Of the republican parties, only those in Moldavia and Kazakhstan are dominated by ethnic Russians; elsewhere the titular nationality holds up to 90 percent of the leading positions. Nationalism in the USSR is frequently expressed as republican demands for more investment funds, greater cultural autonomy, and protests against perceived Russification. Such dissent has been most evident in the Baltic republics (Lithuania, Estonia, Latvia), Georgia, and Armenia. The party leadership remains sensitive to such dissent; the only political dissenters to be executed in post-Stalin times have been Georgian nationalists.

War Communism The radical economic reform undertaken by the new Bolshevik regime from 1918 to 1921. War communism was the Bolsheviks' effort to reorganize the war-shattered economy and institute total state control. Lasting until 1921, when the anti-Bolshevik forces were finally defeated, war communism was as much a series of emergency measures in conditions of civil war as a comprehensive, long-range program. In 1918 the Bolsheviks under Vladimir Lenin controlled barely one-seventh of the former czarist empire, inheriting an economy largely destroyed by four years of world war and a looming famine. Lenin nationalized all industry, transportation, and banking, forcibly requisitioned food, instituted strict rationing, abolished most cash payments, and conscripted labor. All industry was placed under the control of the Supreme Economic Council, *VSNKh* (commonly called *Vesenkha*). Lenin modeled this centrally directed economy on the German economy during World War I, thus the name war communism. The stringent measures were backed by police action and the Red Army. By 1921, Lenin had defeated his various opponents and, in the face of mounting opposition to the coercion of war communism, instituted a period of relaxation known as the New Economic Policy (NEP). The NEP lasted until 1928, when Josef Stalin turned once again to the principles of war communism and a forced-draft march toward industrialization. *See also* COLLECTIVIZATION, p. 280; COMMAND ECONOMY, p. 283; NEW ECONOMIC POLICY (NEP), p. 336.

Significance War communism, however brutal and drastic, enabled the new Bolshevik regime to gain enough control over the levers of power to marshal the nation's resources and permit it to survive. The policies of war communism shaped much of what have become the fundamentals of the Soviet system—total state control, supremacy of the interests of the state, central economic planning, enforcement by police terror, and party control over all aspects of Soviet life.

Warsaw Treaty Organization (WTO) The regional military alliance established by the Soviet Union and the Eastern European states in May 1955. The original members of the Warsaw Treaty Organization included Albania (withdrew in 1968), Bulgaria, Czechoslovakia, East Germany, Hungary, Poland, and Romania. North Korea and Vietnam have observer status; China terminated its observer status following the Sino-Soviet break in 1962. The treaty that created the WTO structure, entitled the Treaty of Friendship, Cooperation and Mutual Assistance, replaced a series of bilateral treaties between the Soviet Union and Eastern Europe signed in the 1940s. Yugoslavia repudiated these treaties in 1949 and thus did not become a WTO member. Major decisions supposedly are made by a Political Consultative Committee that meets sporadically. The Joint Secretariat, located in Moscow, resolves policy matters. The key organ is the Joint Armed Forces Command, responsible to the Soviet General Staff and headed by a Soviet marshal. Air defenses are integrated into the Soviet air defense system. The treaty obliges all signatories to go to the aid of any member under attack and to resolve outstanding problems by peaceful means. Currently, WTO ground forces, including Soviet troops stationed in Eastern Europe, total 1.7 million. *See also* NORTH ATLANTIC TREATY ORGANIZATION (NATO), p. 267.

Significance The Warsaw Treaty Organization, also known as the Warsaw Pact from the agreement signed in Warsaw in 1955, formalized de facto Soviet control over Eastern Europe. It represents a response to the strengthening of the North Atlantic Treaty Organization (NATO), the counterpart Western military alliance, through the inclusion and subsequent rearming of West Germany in 1954. The creation of the WTO thus formalized the postwar division of Germany. The WTO has enabled the Soviet bloc to standardize military equipment and integrate the bloc states' militaries under a unified, Soviet-led command. It provides a legal rationale for the stationing of over 500,000 Soviet troops in Eastern Europe. Currently, Soviet troops are stationed in all member states except Romania and Bulgaria; Romania has recently been under pressure to sign a new status-of-forces agreement. The Eastern European states (particularly East Germany and Czechoslovakia) have increasingly supplied arms to Third World countries in which the Soviet Union wishes to expand its influence; the East European states have also provided military training facilities for Third World personnel. In general, the WTO functions to protect Soviet interests and military security, and the primacy of what the Soviets perceive as their forward bases. East European dissatisfaction with Soviet domination, although muted, has tended to weaken the WTO. To date, the only collective WTO action is the 1968 Soviet-led invasion of Czechoslovakia, which cut short the attempted liberalization known as the Prague Spring and restored Soviet control and political orthodoxy. In 1984, the Soviet leadership, in response to the emplacement of cruise and Pershing II missiles in Western Europe, undertook to position short-range missiles in East Germany and Czechoslovakia, a move quietly resisted by some in those states.

APPENDIX A: MAPS

A-1 *Western Europe*
A-2 *Union of Soviet Socialist Republics*

Source: © Current History, Inc. December, 1982.

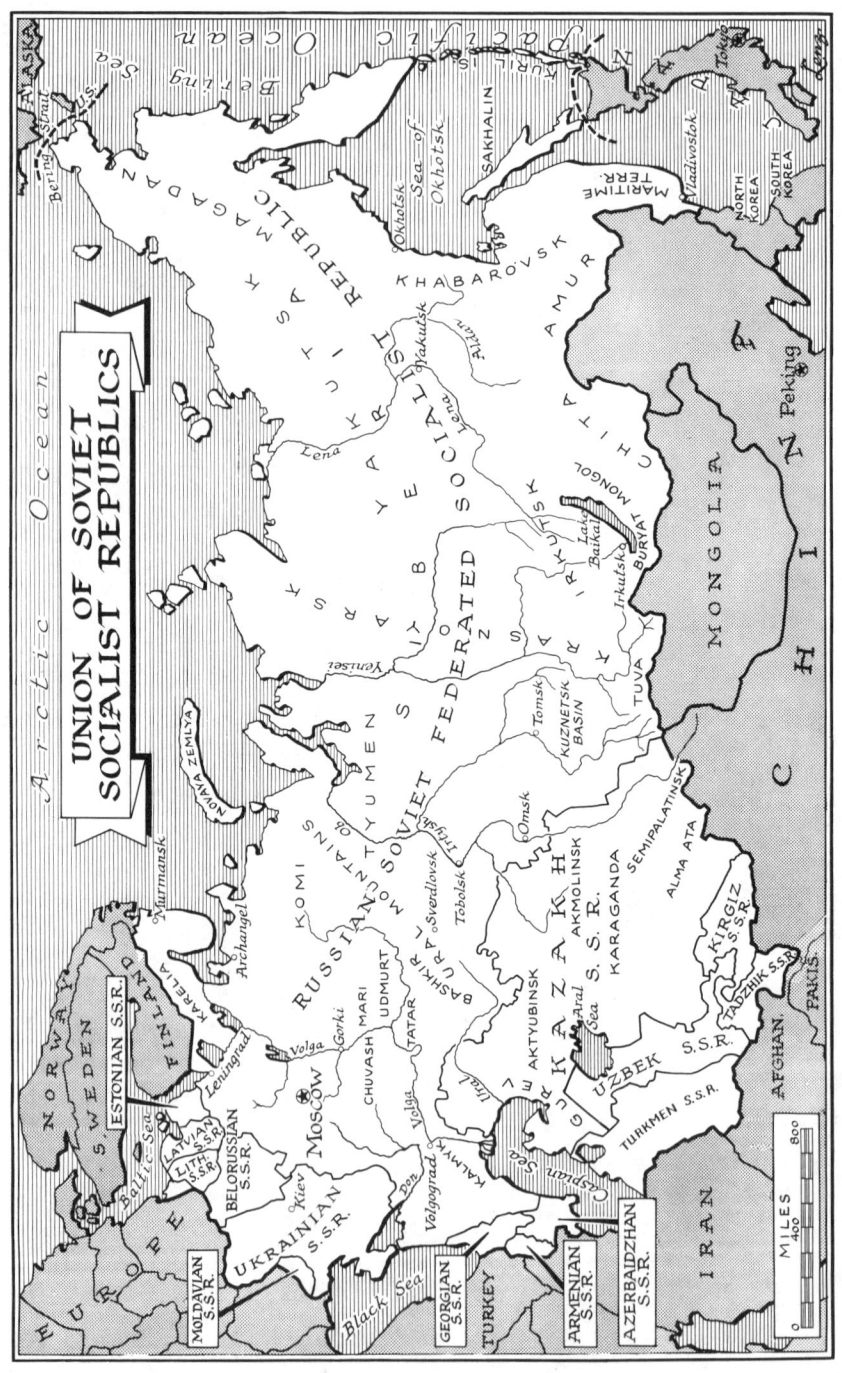

Source: © *Current History, Inc.* October, 1982.

APPENDIX B: TABLES

B-1 *European Community Governments (August 1984)*
B-2 *National Composition of the USSR (1979 Census Figures)*

TABLE 1

European Community Governments (August 1984)

Country	Type of Government	Head of State	Head of Government	Cabinet
Belgium	Constitutional Monarchy	King Baudouin I (since 1951)	Wilfried Martens, CVP (since 1981)	Christian People's Party (CVP) Christian Social Party (PSC) Freedom & Progress Party (PVV) Liberal Reformer Party (PRL)
Denmark	Constitutional Monarchy	Queen Margrethe II (since 1972)	Poul Schlüter, KF (since 1982)	Conservative People's Party (KF) *Venstre* Liberal Party (V) Center Democrats (CD) Christian People's Party (KRF)
France	Presidential– Parliamentary Democracy	François Mitterrand, PS (since 1981)	Laurent Fabius, PS (since July 1984)	Socialist (PS) Leftist Radical Movement (MRG) Unified Socialist Party (PSU)
Germany	Parliamentary Democracy	Richard von Weizsäcker (since July 1984)	Helmut Kohl, CDU (since 1982)	Christian Democratic Union (CDU) Christian Social Union (CSU) Free Democratic Party (FDP)
Greece	Parliamentary Democracy	Constantine Karamanlis (since 1980)	Andreas Papandreou, PASOK (since 1981)	Pan-Hellenic Socialist Movement (PASOK)
Ireland	Parliamentary Democracy	Patrick J. Hillery (since 1976)	Garret FitzGerald, FG (since 1981)	Fine Gael (FG) Irish Labour Party (LP)
Italy	Parliamentary Democracy	Alessandro Pertini (since 1978)	Bettino Craxi, PSI (since 1983)	Christian Democracy (DC) Italian Socialist Party (PSI) Italian Social Democratic Party (PSDI) Italian Republican Party (PRI) Italian Liberal Party (PLI)
Luxembourg	Constitutional Grand Duchy	Grand Duke Jean (since 1964)	Pierre Werner, CSV (since 1979)	Christian Social Party (CSV) Democratic Party (PD)

Continued on next page

TABLE 1—*Continued*

European Community Governments (August 1984)

Country	Type of Government	Head of State	Head of Government	Cabinet
Netherlands	Constitutional Monarchy	Queen Beatrix (since 1980)	Ruud Lubbers, CDA (since 1982)	Christian Democratic Appeal (CDA) People's Party for Freedom and Democracy (VVD)
Portugal*	Parliamentary Democracy	António Ramalho Eanes (since 1976)	Mário Soares, PSP (since 1983)	Socialists (PSP) Social Democrats (PSD)
Spain*	Constitutional Monarchy	King Juan Carlos I (since 1975)	Felipe González Márquez, PSOE (since 1982)	Spanish Socialist Workers' Party (PSOE)
United Kingdom	Constitutional Monarchy	Queen Elizabeth II (since 1952)	Margaret Thatcher, Conservative (since 1979)	Conservative Party

*Portugal and Spain were expected to join the European Community in late 1984 or 1985.

TABLE 2

National Composition of the USSR (1979 Census Figures)

ETHNIC GROUP	POPULATION IN MILLIONS	POPULATION AS PERCENT TOTAL	PERCENT INCREASE/ DECREASE 1970–79	NATIONALITY GROUPING	DOMINANT RELIGION
Russian	137.4	52.4	+6.5	Slavic	Orthodox Christian
Ukrainian	42.3	16.1	+3.9	Slavic	Orthodox Christian
Uzbek	12.5	4.8	+35.5	Turkic	Moslem
Byelorussian	9.5	3.6	+4.5	Slavic	Orthodox Christian
Kazakh	6.6	2.5	+13.7	Turkic	Moslem
Tatar	6.3	2.4	+6.5	Turkic	Moslem
Azerbaidzhani	5.5	2.1	+25.0	Turkic	Moslem
Armenian	4.2	1.6	+16.0	Caucasian	Armenian Christian
Georgian	3.6	1.4	+10.0	Caucasian	Orthodox Christian
Moldavian	3.0	1.1	+10.0	Romanian	Orthodox Christian
Lithuanian	2.9	1.1	+7.0	Baltic	Roman Catholic
Tadzhik	2.9	1.1	+35.7	Iranian	Moslem
Turkmen	2.0	0.8	+33.0	Turkic	Moslem
German	1.9	0.7	+4.9	Germanic	Lutheran
Kirgiz	1.9	0.7	+31.3	Turkic	Moslem
Jewish*	1.8	0.7	-16.0	Jewish	Jewish
Chuvash	1.8	0.7	+3.4	Turkic	Orthodox Catholic
Latvian	1.4	0.5	+0.6	Baltic	Lutheran
Bashkir	1.4	0.5	+10.6	Turkic	Moslem
Mordvinian	1.2	0.4	-5.6	Finno-Ugrian	Christian
Polish	1.2	0.4	-1.4	Slavic	Roman Catholic
Estonian	1.0	0.4	+1.3	Finno-Ugrian	Lutheran
Others	9.8	3.7	—		
Total Population	262.1				

Source: Soviet statistics.

*Soviet nationality policy treats Jews as a single homogeneous nationality, although in actuality the Soviet Jews are comprised of several different ethnic groups, i.e., Ukrainian Jews, Georgian Jews, Russian Jews, and so forth, who do not share a common language.

INDEX

Cross-references to dictionary entries are located in the text at the end of each definition paragraph. Page references in bold type indicate dictionary entries. For individual countries of Europe, consult the *Guide to Countries* on p. xvii.

Abdication crisis (1936), 31
Absolutism, czarist Russia, 311–312, 347
Academy of Social Sciences, USSR, 338–339
Accountability, dual. *See* Dual accountability
ACP. *See* African, Caribbean, and Pacific countries (ACP)
Action Français, **79**
Acts. *See* Charters and Acts
Adenauer, Konrad
  as chancellor, 181
  as Christian Democratic Union leader, 168–169
Administration, Soviet
  all-union ministries in, 335
  bureaucratic model of, 312
  and Council of Ministers, USSR, 284
  deputies as ombudsmen in, 304–305
  dual subordination in, 308
  and duplication of office, 310
  economic bureaucracy in, 320
  judiciary, 325
  Oblast', 337–338
  and official crime, 302
  regulations, 330, 335
  republican and local, 318, 335
  as structure party-government, 287
  Supreme Soviet, role of, 360
  and union-republic, 335
Administrative class, Britain, 9–10
Administrative law, 90, 120
Administrative Organs Department, CPSU Central Committee, 345

Adversarial system, 120
Afghanistan, 112, 312, 363
Africa, 331
African, Caribbean, and Pacific countries (ACP), 258
Agitprop, 293–294, 332, 339
Agriculture, Soviet
  and collectivization, 280–281
  and czarist conditions, 352
  farm debts, 328
  Kolkhoz, 327
  private plots in, 328
  Sovkhoz, 356
  undercapitalization of, 328
Agriculture, West Germany, 180
Ailleret, Charles, 152
Ailleret Doctrine, 152
Aland, 266
Albania, *See* Guide to Countries
Albert, Prince (Britain), 32
Alfonsín, Raúl, 26
Algerian crisis of 1958, **80**
Algerian War, **80–81**
"*Algérie français*," 81
All German Bloc/Federation of Expellees and Dispossessed (GB/BHE), 178, 225
Alliance, Liberal-Social Democratic parties, **1–2**
Alliance party, Northern Ireland, 45
Allied Commander-in-Chief Channel. *See* CINCHAN, Allied Commander-in-Chief Channel
Allied Control Council, 161, 214–215

377

Allies, Western. *See* Western Allies
"All power to the soviets," 356
All-Russian Congress of the Soviets, Second, 275
All-Russian Extraordinary Committee to Combat Counterrevolution and Espionage. *See* CHEKA (All-Russian Extraordinary Committee to Combat Counterrevolution and Espionage)
ALN. *See* National Liberation Army (ALN)
Alsace, 148
Alternative List, 196
Amalgamated Union of Engineering Workers (AUEW), 69
Ancien régime, **82,** 139
Andrew, Prince (Britain), 31
Andropov, Yuri
  as general secretary, 292, 293, 327
  KGB, as head of, 295, 327
  on Politburo, 295
  suppresses dissent, 307
Anglican Church of Wales, 74
Annan, 118
Anne, Princess (Britain), 31
Anne, Queen (Britain), 41
Annual conference, Labour party, 49
Anschluss, **157–158**
Antarctic Islands. *See* Southern and Antarctic Islands
Antarctic Territory, British, 73
Antinuclear groups
  in Britain, 7–8
  in Western Europe, 252
  in West Germany, 196
Anti-Semitism
  in Dreyfus affair, 150–151
  in France, 79
  in Nazism, 208
Anti-Soviet agitation and propaganda, criminal offenses, **299–300,** 301, 306–307
Apparatchiks. See Communist Party of the Soviet Union (CPSU)
Apparentements, 93, 108
Appeasement policy, 206
Arbitration, USSR, 325
Argentina, 25–26
Armed-SS. *See Waffen-SS*
Armenia, 349, 351, 364, 365
Armstrong-Jones, Lady Sarah, 31
Army, French
  in Algeria, 80, 81
  in Dreyfus affair, 150–151
  in Indochina, 118–119
  supports de Gaulle government, 124–125

Aron, Raymond, 145
Arrondissement, 122
Artel', 327
Aryan race, 207
Asparturian, Vernon, 316
Asquith, Herbert, 37
Assembly. *See* Constituent Assembly; National Assembly: Fifth Republic
Association for the Defense of Shopkeepers and Artisans (UDCA), 84, 132
Association of British Chambers of Commerce, 6
Association of Scientific, Technical and Management Staffs (ASTMS), 69
ASSR. *See* Autonomous Soviet Socialist Republic (ASSR)
ASTMS. *See* Association of Scientific, Technical and Management Staffs (ASTMS)
Aswan Dam, 65
Atlantic Charter, 241
Atlantic Directorate, 115
Atlanticism, **2–3**
Atlee, Clement
  as Fabian member, 25
  as Labour party leader, 35
  at Potsdam Conference, 221
  as prime minister, 54
Attitudes. *See* Political culture, specific countries
AUEW. *See* Amalgamated Union of Engineering Workers (AUEW)
Auriol, Vincent, 107
Austerlitz, battle of, 200
Australia, 11
Austria. *See* Guide to Countries
Austro-Prussian War (1866), 212
Autarky, defined, 249
Autocracy, explanatory theory, **311–312**
"Autocracy, orthodoxy, and nationalism," 348
Autogestion, 144, 153
Autonomous province, USSR, 318
Autonomous Soviet Socialist Republic (ASSR), 318, 362
Azerbaidzhan, 319, 349, 364

Baader, Andreas, 224
Baader-Meinhof Group, 224
Backbencher, 29, 40
Baden-Württemberg, 203
Bad Godesberg. *See* Godesberg Program versus Neosocialism
Bahr, Egon, 218
Ballotage, 96
Baltic states, 349, 363, 364
Bank of France, 105

Banks, USSR. *See* Gosbank
BAOR. *See* British Army of the Rhine (BAOR)
Barre, Raymond, 103
Barzel, Rainer, 174
Basic Law, **158–159**
Basic Treaty (1972), **159–160**, 217
Bavaria
  Christian Social Union in, 169, 170, 203
  functional representation in, 188
Bayeux Speech, Gaullism, **114–115**
BDA. *See* Federation of German Employers Association (BDA)
BDI. *See* Federation of German Industry (BDI)
Beamte, 240
Beer Hall *Putsch*. *See* Munich *Putsch*
Belgium. *See* Guide to Countries
Belgrade Conference (Conference on Security and Cooperation in Europe), 264
Bell, Daniel, 145
Belorussia, 363, 364
Benelux, **243–244**
Benelux Economic Union, 243
Beneš, Edward, 205
Benn, Anthony Wedgewood, 31, 36
Beria, Lavrenti, 305
Bering Straits, 362
Berlin, 222. *See also* Berlin Blockade; Berlin Wall; East Berlin; West Berlin
Berlin Blockade, **160–161**
Berlin Wall, **161–162**
Bermuda, 73
Bessarabia. *See* Moldavia
Beveridge Report, 75
Beveridge, William, 75
Bidault, Georges
  as head of government, 87
  as Popular Republican Movement leader, 131
  in Resistance, 139
Bill of Rights, Britain (1689), 3, 8
Biro-Bidzhan, 318
Bizone, 214–215
Black and Tans, 59
Black market, Soviet, 301–302, 350–351
Black Shirts, 209
"Blood and iron," 193
"Bloody Sunday," 347
Blum, León, 130
Blunt, Anthony, 64
Bohemia, 206
Bolshevik, **273–274**
Bolshevik party, 273–274, 275–276, 289–290

Bolshevik Revolution, **274–275**, 309, 355
Bolsheviks
  and civil war, 326–327
  consolidate power, 319
  and Marxism, 333–334
  and nationalism, 348
  and New Economic Policy (NEP), 336
  and Provisional Government, 274–275
  Red Guards, 275
  refuse to cooperate with Duma, 274
  and Revolution of 1905, 348
  and socialist legality, 353
  and soviets (councils), 356
  suppress Mensheviks, 274
  war communism, 365
Bonapartism, 82–83, 141. *See also* Napoleon I; Napoleon III
"Bonn Is Not Weimar," **162–163**
Bonn Republic. *See* Federal Republic of Germany in Index; Germany, West, in Guide to Countries
Book of Common Prayer, 22
Border guards, USSR, 326. *See also* KGB
Boulanger affair, Third Republic, **149–150**
Boulanger, Georges, 149–150
Boundary settlements
  in Eastern Europe, 363
  and Potsdam Conference, 221–222
  Russian losses in World War I, 363
  Saar question and, 226
  from Soviet gains in World War II, 363
  and Treaty of Brest-Litovsk (1918), 315
  and Ulster, 71
  Yalta Conference and, 241
Bourbon, House of, 83
Bourbon Restoration, **83**
"Bourgeois nationalism," 348
Brandt, Willy
  as chancellor, 181
  in Grand Coalition, 195
  and policy toward East, 217–218
  resignation of, 198
  as Social Democratic party leader, 227
  uses nonconfidence procedure, 174–175
  wins Nobel Prize, 218
"Bread, land, and peace," 352
Brest-Litovsk, Treaty of (1918), 315
Brezhnev Doctrine, **276–277**
Brezhnev, Leonid
  and Brezhnev Doctrine, 276–277
  and dissent, 307

as general secretary, 292, 305
tightens discipline, 297, 300
Britain. *See* United Kingdom of Great
Britain and Northern Ireland in
Index and Guide to Countries
Britain, decline of. *See* Decline of
Britain
British Army of the Rhine (BAOR), 2
British Broadcasting Corporation, 56
British Commonwealth of Nations. *See*
Commonwealth
British Empire, **4–5,** 16
British Empire and Commonwealth, 5
British Employers' Confederation, 5
British Railways Board, 56
Brittany, 148
Brown Shirts, 209
Brussels, NATO headquarters, 267
Brussels Pact (1948), 271–272
Budget
of Britain, 70
of European Parliament, 261–262
Budget of the State, USSR, **277–278,** 283, 303
Bukharin, Nikolai, 357
Bulgaria. *See* Guide to Countries
Bundesrat, **163–165**
elects Constitutional Court judges, 182–183
in German Empire, 192
Bundesrepublik Deutschland, 185
Bundestag, **165–166**
and Constitutional Court judges election, 182–183
electoral system, **177–178**
and federal president election, 178–179
Bureaucracy. *See also* Civil service
British, 9–10
French Model, **110–111**
and stalemate society, 147
West Germany, **240–241**
Bureaucracy, Soviet. *See* Communist
Party of the Soviet Union (CPSU);
Administration, Soviet
Bureaucratic model, explanatory theory, USSR, **312–313**
Bürgermeister, 202, 204
Burgess, Guy F., 56, 64
Burma, 11
Business and Industrial Associations:
West Germany, **166–167**
Business Associations
in Britain, **5–6**
in France, **83–84**
Byzantine traditions, USSR, 341

Cabinet, Britain, **6–7**

Callaghan, James
and fall of government, 61–62
as Labour party leader, 35
as prime minister, 54
and trade unions, 70
Cambodia, 118
Cambridge spy ring, 65
Camelots du Roi, 79
Campaign for Nuclear Disarmament (CND), **7–8**
Canada, 11, 267
CAP. *See* Common Agricultural Policy (CAP)
Capitalist Encirclement, **278,** 283
Caribbean. *See* African, Caribbean, and Pacific countries (ACP)
Carlsbad Decrees (1819), 190
Carrillo, Santiago, 250, 271
Carrington, Lord
and Falklands' War, 26
as NATO secretary-general, 268
Case law, 10, 90
Catch-all party thesis, **167–168**
Catholics, 32–33, 131, 171
Caucasus, 363
CBI. *See* Confederation of British Industry (CBI)
CCT. *See* Common Customs Tariff (CCT)
CDE. *See* Conference on Confidence and Security Building Measures and Disarmament in Europe (CDE)
CDS. *See* Center of Social Democrats (CDS)
CDU. *See* Christian Democratic Union (CDU)
CDU/CSU. *See* Christian Democratic Union/Christian Social Union (CDU/CSU)
Cell, communist party. *See* Communist Party of the Soviet Union (CPSU)
Celtic fringe, 61, 74
Censorship, Soviet, 336, 349
Center of Social Democrats (CDS), 84–85, 131
Center of Socialist Studies and Research (CERES), 144
Center party, Weimar Republic, 237
Central America, 331
Central Asia, 341, 348, 349, 351, 363
Central Asian republics, USSR. *See* Central Asia
Central Committee, CPSU, **288–289,** 298. *See also* Communist Party of the Soviet Union (CPSU)
Centre des Democrates Sociaux. See Center of Social Democrats
Centre Nationale des Independants et

Index 381

Paysans. See National Center of Independents and Peasants (CNIP)
CERES. *See* Center of Socialist Studies and Research (CERES)
CFDT. *See* French Democratic Confederation of Labor (CFDT)
CFTC. *See* French Confederation of Christian Workers (CFTC)
CGC. *See* General Confederation of Staffs (CGC)
CGPME. *See* General Confederation of Small and Medium-Sized Enterprises (CGPME)
CGT. *See* General Confederation of Labor (CGT)
CGT-FO. *See Force Ouvrière* (CGT-FO)
Chaban-Delmas, Jacques
  as prime minister, 103
  in Resistance, 139
Chad, 97
Chairman, Presidium of the Council of Ministers, USSR, 343
Chairman, Presidium of the Supreme Soviet, USSR, 344
Chamberlain, Houston Stewart, 207
Chamberlain, Neville, 205–206
Chamber of Deputies, 93, 100, 107
Chamber of Nationalities, 364
Chancellor democracy, 182
Chancellor, federal, **180–182**
Chancellor of the exchequer, 70
Channel Islands, 73
Charlemagne, 199
Charles, Prince of Wales, 31
Charles X (France), 83, 120
Chartered companies, 4
Charters and Acts, **8–9**
CHEKA (All-Russian Extraordinary Committee to Combat Counterrevolution and Espionage), 274, 326
Chernenko, Konstantin, 292, 293, 307
Chevenement, Jean-Pierre, 144
Chichester-Clark, James D., 72
Chief military procurator, USSR, 345
China, 306, 339, 366
Chirac, Jacques
  as leader of Rally for the Republic (RPR), 136
  as presidential candidate, 92
  as prime minister, 103
  reorganizes Gaullist party, 135
Chistka. See Communist Party of the Soviet Union; Purge
Christian Democracy
  in European Parliament. *See* European Peoples Party
  France. *See* Popular Republican Movement (MRP)
  West Germany. *See* Christian Democratic Union (CDU); Christian Social Union (CSU)
Christian Democratic Union (CDU), **168–170**. *See also* Christian Democratic Union/Christian Social Union (CDU/CSU)
  party leaders listed, 169–170
Christian Democratic Union/Christian Social Union (CDU/CSU). *See also* Christian Democratic Union (CDU); Christian Social Union (CSU)
  in elections of 1983, 176–177
  in Grand Coalition, 194–195
  role in party system, 220
Christians in USSR, 341
Christian Socialism, 131
Christian Social Union (CSU), 169, **170–171**. *See also* Christian Democratic Union/Christian Social Union (CDU/CSU)
The Chronicle of Human Events, 350
Churches
  in United Kingdom, 22–23
  in West Germany, 171–172
Church, Established, **22–23**
Churchill, Winston S.
  as Conservative party leader, 12
  at Potsdam Conference, 221
  as prime minister, 54
  at Yalta Conference, 241
Church-state relations, West Germany, **171–172**
Church tax, West Germany, 171–172
CIA estimates of Soviet defense budget, 303
CID-UNATI (Committee of Information and Defense-National Union of Artisans and Independent Workers (CID-UNATI), 84
CINCHAN, Allied Commander-in-Chief Channel, 268
Citizen inspectors, 329
Citizen participation, USSR, **279**, 296, 303–304
"City," London financial district, 6
Civil defense, USSR, 308
Civil rights movement, Northern Ireland, 42
Civil rights, USSR, **279–280**, 300
Civil service. *See also* Bureaucracy
  Britain, **9–10**, 70
  West Germany, 240–241
Civil War, Russia
  CHEKA in, 274

commissars, role of, 294
Main Political Administration and, 276
"Red Terror" in, 326–327
Revolutionary courts and, 353
Sovnarkhom, Lenin heads, 276
and war communism, 365
Class conflict, Marxist theory of, 332, 333
Class enemy, 281
Clemenceau, Georges, 151
Closed cities, USSR, 324
CMEA. *See* Council of Mutual Economic Assistance (CMEA)
CND. *See* Campaign for Nuclear Disarmament (CND)
CNIP. *See* National Center of Independents and Peasants (CNIP)
CNJA. *See* National Center of Young Farmers (CNJA)
CNPF. *See* National Council of French Employers (CNPF)
CNT. *See* National Center of Independents (CNT)
Coal and Steel Community. *See* European Coal and Steel Community (ECSC)
Cochin China, 118
Code law system, 10, **85–86**
Code Napoléon, 86, 105
Codetermination, **172–173,** 230, 231
Cohn-Bendit, Daniel, 124
Coke, Edward, 8
Cold War, 160–161, 215
Cole, G. D. H., 25
Collective agreements, USSR, 335
Collective farm. *See Kolkhoz*
Collective responsibility, 54
Collectivization, **280,** 328
Collegial bodies, USSR, 343–345
Collegium (*kollegiya*), Soviet, 335
Collins, Michael, 32, 59
Colonialism. *See also* Decolonization
British, 4–5, 16
French, 80–81, 113
Colons, 80
COMECON. *See* Council of Mutual Economic Assistance (COMECON or CMEA)
Cominform, 282
Comintern, **281–283**
Command economy, **283–284,** 311, 319, 365
Commissars, 294
Commissioner of the Republic, 133
Commission of European Communities, **244–245,** 255
recent presidents, list of, 244
Committee of General Security, France, 119, 140
Committee of Information and Defense-National Union of Artisans and Independent Workers. *See* CID-UNATI
Committee of Permanent Representatives (COREPER), European Communities, 247
Committee of Public Safety, France, 119, 140
Committee for State Security. *See* KGB
Common Agricultural Policy (CAP), 27, **245–246,** 258
Common Customs Tariff (CCT), 258
Common law, **10–11**
Common market, defined, 249. *See also* European Economic Community (EEC)
Common Program, Socialist-Communist, 111, 143
Commons, House of. *See* House of Commons
Commonwealth, **11–12**
Commonwealth of Nations, 5. *See also* Commonwealth
Communards, 86
Commune of Paris, **86,** 151
Communism
Bolshevik Revolution and, **274–276**
bureaucratization of power, 313
developmental model of, 314
Eurocommunism and, **250–251**
ideology of, 334
and Marxism-Leninism, 331–333
national, 306, 348–349
new class critique of, 315–316
war communism, **365**
wars of national liberation and, 340
Communist Information Bureau. *See* Cominform
Communist International. *See* Comintern
Communist parties, Western Europe, 250–251
Communist party in France. *See* French Communist Party (PCF)
Communist Party of Germany (KPD), 189, 231. *See also* German Communist Party (DKP)
Communist Party of the Soviet Union (CPSU), **286–288,** 310, 325, 343
apparatchiks, 287, 298
bureau, 287, 290, 296, 298
bureaucracy, 313
candidate member of, 295

cell, 295
Central Committee and, **288–289**
as Central Committee apparatus, 298
and collective farm party organization, 296
conference, 287
Congress, **290–291**
Congress of the Victors, 291
control over military, 293–294
Council of Ministers, USSR, Chairman, 285
Defense Council and, **303**
Democratic centralism and, 290
departments (*otdely*) of, 288, 298, 335
dominates state, 298
economic plans of, 340–341
elitism of, 315–316
founding of, 273–274
general secretary, **291–293**
and KGB, 326–327
and Komsomol recruitment, 329
Main Military Council and, 293
Main Political Administration (MPA), **293–294**
mass organizations and, 334
membership composition of, 288, 289
nomenklatura, 337
oblast', 289
Organizational Bureau (Orgburo) and, 289
partgruporgs, 296
party assignment and, 296, 334
Party Control Commission and, 288, 289
platform, 290–291
Politburo and, **294–295**
Primary Party Organization, **295–296**
Purge, **296–297**
reaction to Eurocommunism, 251
Russian domination and, 348, 364
Secretariat, **297–298**
secretaries, 297
and socialist realism, 354
statutes, 286, 290, 291, 292, 294
Tenth Party Congress (1921), 285, 291
and territorial divisions, 362
Twentieth Party Congress (1956), 291, 305
Twenty-fourth Congress (1971), 291
Communists
in European Parliament, 263
Community, French. *See* French Community
Comoro Islands, 114
Comrades' Courts, USSR, 279
Concertation, 154
Concerted action, 188, 230

Confédération des Cadres. *See* General Confederation of Staffs (CGC)
Confédération Française Démocratique du Travail. *See* French Democratic Confederation of Labor (CFDT)
Confédération Française des Travailleurs Crétiens. *See* French Confederation of Christian Workers (CFTC)
Confédération Générale du Travail. *See* General Confederation of Labor (CGT)
Confederation, German. *See* German Confederation
Confederation, North German. *See* North German Confederation
Confederation of British Industry (CBI), 5–6
Confederation of the Rhine, **173–174**
Conference on Confidence and Security Building Measures and Disarmament in Europe (CDE), 264
Conference on Security and Cooperation in Europe (CSCE), 263–264
Confidence-building measures, 264
Congress, CPSU, **290–291**. *See also* Communist Party of the Soviet Union (CPSU)
Congress of Europe (1948), 246
Congress of the Victors, 291
Congress of Vienna (1815), 83, 189–190
Conseil d'État. *See* Council of State
Conseil National du Patronat Français (CNPF). *See* National Council of French Employers (CNPF)
Conseils d'arrondissement, 123
Consensus thesis, socioeconomic theory, **144**
Conservative and Unionist party. *See* Conservative party
Conservative party, **12–13,** 76
and elections of 1983, 19–20
governments, 12–13
Constantine Plan, 81
Constituencies, defined, 20
Constituency party, 49
Constituent Assembly, France, 87, 93
Constituent Assembly, Russia, 276
Constitutional Council, **87–89**
rules nationalization bill invalid, 127–128
Constitutional Court. *See* Federal Constitutional Court
Constitutional Democrats (Kadets), Russia, 309
Constitutional dissensus, France, **89–90**

Constitutional system
 Fourth Republic, **107–108**
 Weimar Republic, **235–236**
Constitutional systems, French, list of, 89
Constitution
 British, **3–4,** 8–9
 East Germany (1968), 191
 France (1958), **98–99,** 103
 France (1946), 91, 107–108
 Germany (1919), **235–236**
 union-republics, USSR, 318
 USSR (1977), 280, 287, 318, 343, 363
 USSR (1936), 287
 USSR (1924), 287, 319
 West Germany (1949), **158–159,** 182–183, 220, 223
Constructive vote of nonconfidence, **174–175**
Consulate, France, 140
Consultative Committee of European Community, 255
Continental System, 105
Contradictions of capitalism, Marxist theory of, 333
Convention Parliament, 8
Convergence, explanatory theory, **314**
Cooperation, Treaty of, Nordic Council (1962), 267
Cooptation, 294, 298
Copenhagen, 267
COREPER. *See* Committee of Permanent Representatives, European Communities (COREPER)
Corporatism, 154, 188
Corrigan, Mairead, 45
Corsica, 80, 113
Cossacks, 352
Coty, René, 80, 107
Council, Defense, **303**
Council of Elders
 USSR, 361
 West Germany, 165
Council of Europe, **245–247,** 257
Council of Ministers
 in European Communities, **247–248,** 255, 256
 in France, 102
 in USSR, 277, **284–285,** 319, 335, 345
Council of Mutual Economic Assistance (COMECON or CMEA), **285–286**
Council of People's Commissars. *See* Sovnarkom
Council of State, France, **90,** 105, 117, 120

Council of the Republic, France, 104, 107
Counterintelligence, USSR, 326
Counter-revolutionaries, 299
Cour de Cassation, 120
Court of Accounts, France, 117
Court of Auditors of European Community, 255
Court of Justice, European Communities, **248–249,** 255
Court structure, USSR, 324–325, 345
Couve de Murville, Maurice, 103
CPSU. *See* Communist Party of the Soviet Union (CPSU)
Craig, James, 45, 72
Crepeau, Michel, 121
Crimean Tatars, 307
Crimean War, 315
Crimes against socialist property, criminal offenses, **300**
Criminal offenses
 anti-Soviet agitation and propaganda as, **299–300**
 crimes against socialist property as, **300**
 crimes against the state as, **301**
 economic crimes as, **301–302**
 official crimes as, **302–303**
Croix de Feu, 79
Crown, **13–14**
"Crown in Parliament," 13
Crozier, Michel, 110, 147
Cruise missiles, 251, 265. *See also* Euromissile controversy
CSCE. *See* Conference on Security and Cooperation in Europe (CSCE)
CSU. *See* Christian Social Union (CSU)
Cuba, 285
Cuban missile crisis, 340
Cult of personality, 293, 306, 357
Curia Regis, 47
Currency transactions, USSR, 351
Curzon Line, 241
Customs union, defined, 249
Cyprus, 257
Czarist Russia. *See* Russia, czarist
Czechoslovakia. *See* Guide to Countries

DAG. *See* German Salaried Employees' Union (DAG)
Dail Eireann, 59
Daladier, Edouard, 205
Dankert, Pieter, president of European Parliament, 262
Danzig, 206
Darlan, François, 154, 155
Das Kapital (1867), 333

Index 385

DBB. *See* German Federation of Civil
    Servants (DBB)
Dealignment, party, 2
Debate, role of, 29
Debré, Michel, 139
    as prime minister, 103
Declaration of Fundamental Rights,
    Germany, 190
Declaration of the Rights of Man and
    Citizen (1789), **90–91**
Declaration on Liberated Europe
    (1945), 241
Decline of Britain, **14–15**
Decline of Parliament, British theory of,
    15–16
Decolonization, **16**
Deconcentration of administration, 122
Defense Council, **303, 327**. *See also*
    Military, Soviet
Defense Planning Committee, NATO,
    267
Defense, Soviet. *See* Military, Soviet
Deference. *See* Social deference thesis
Defferre, Gaston, 142
de Gaulle, Charles, 83. *See also* Gaullism
    entries
    and Algeria, 80
    as head of government, 1944–1946,
        87
    leads Free France, 133
    and nuclear weapons strategy, 152
    as President, 94
    resignation, 104
"Degenerate workers' state," 317
de Gobineau, Arthur, 207
Delors, Jacques, 244
Democracy, support for in West
    Germany, 162–163, 218–219
Democratic centralism, 286, 332, 357.
    See also Leninism
Democratic Movement, USSR, 307
Democratic Unionist party (DUP), 45,
    72
Democrats, Weimar Republic, 237
Democrat Union for Labor (UDT), 135
de Montfort, Simon, 48
Denazification program, 215
Denmark. *See* Guide to Countries
Denning, Lord, 55
Department (*département*), 122
Dependencies
    British, 73
    French, 113–114
Deputies, Soviet, 303–304
Deputy (Soviet), 303–305, 360–361
De-Stalinization, **305–306**, 323, 353,
    358

Detente, 159–160, 218, 276, 340
De Valera, Eamon, 59
Developmental model, explanatory
    theory, **314–315**
Devolution, **17–18**
    Northern Ireland and, 44
    Scotland, referendum on, 61–62
DGB. *See* German Trade Union
    Federation (DGB)
Dialectical process, Marxist theory of,
    332
Dictatorship of the proletariat, Marxist
    theory of, 333
Dienbienphu, 118
Diet of German Industry and
    Commerce, 166
Directorates, KGB, 326
Directory, France, 140
Direct rule
    British colonies and, 4–5
    Northern Ireland and, 43
Dirigisme, 75, 127
Disinformation, Soviet, 326
Disraeli, Benjamin, 12, 57
Dissensus. *See* Constitutional dissensus
Dissent and opposition, **306–307**
Dissidents, Soviet
    and anti-Soviet agitation and
        propaganda, 299
    Crimean Tatars as, 307
    and crimes against the state, 301
    Democratic Movement and, 307
    forced deportation of, 300
    free trade unionists and, 307
    Human Rights Movement and, 307
    judicial process for, 325
    nationalists and, 349, 365
    psychiatric confinement of, 300, 307
    refuseniks, 307
    Sakharov, Andrei as, 307
    Samizdat, 349
    and socialist realism, 354
    and suppression, 307
Dissuasion, 106
Division lobby, 29
Djibouti, 113
Djilas, Milovan, 315
DKP. *See* German Communist Party
    (DKP)
Dollfuss, Engelbert, 157
DOSAAF, **307–308**. *See also* Mass
    organizations, USSR
Douglas-Home, Alec
    as Conservative party leader, 12
    as prime minister, 54
    renounces peerage, 31
DP. *See* German party (DP)

Dreyfus Affair, 79, **150–151**
Dreyfus, Alfred, 150. *See also* Dreyfus Affair
DRP. *See* German Reich party (DRP)
Druzhiny, USSR, 279, 329
Dual subordination, **308–309**, 355
Duchy of Moscow, 363
Duhamel, Jacques, 85
Duma, 275, **309**, 347
DUP. *See* Democratic Unionist party (DUP)
Duplication of office, 284, 286, **310**, 345
Dutschke, Rudi, 224

East Berlin, 222, 238
 status of, 239
 uprising in, 305
Eastern Europe
 and boundary changes, 363
 and Brezhnev Doctrine, 276–277
 and Cominform, 282
 and Comintern, 282
 Communist governments established in, 278
 and Council of Mutual Economic Assistance, 285–286
 de-Stalinization in, 305
 energy requirements in, 285–286
 revolts in, 305
 and secret police control by KGB, 327
 Soviet domination in, 363
 Soviet troops in, 366
 Stalinism in, 305
 and Warsaw Treaty Organization, 365
Eastern territories, 216
Easter Rising, 59
East Germany. *See* Germany, East in Guide to Countries; German Democratic Republic (GDR) in Index
East of Suez, **18–19**
Ebert, Friedrich, 237
EC. *See* European Community (EC)
École Nationale d'Administration (ENA), 117–118
École Normale Supérieure, 117
École Polytechnique, 117
Ecologists, in European Parliament, 263
Economic and Social Committee of European Community, 255
Economic and Social Council, France, **91**
Economic community, defined, 249
Economic conditions
 in Britain, 14, 66
 in West Germany, 174–175
Economic Council, France, 91

Economic crimes, criminal offenses, **301–302**
Economic integration types, **249–250**
Economic miracle, West Germany, **175–176**
Economic planning, USSR. *See* Planning, Soviet
Economic policy, defined, 249
Economic union, defined, 249
Economy, command, **283–284**
Economy, Soviet
 and *blat* (connections), 350
 and budget of the state, 277
 bureaucratization and, 313
 difficulties of reform in, 341
 economic crimes in, 301
 and enterprise, 310
 five-year plan and, 319–320
 flaws of central planning in, 341
 hard currency stores and, 351
 heavy industry and, 320
 and industrial association, 323
 and interbloc trade, 286
 and *Kolkhoz*, 327
 ministry and, 335
 party control of, 320
 planning of, 321–322, 340–341
 priority of military in, 303
 and procurement plans, 327
 and production targets, 321
 second economy in, 350
 Socialist ownership in, 354
 and *Sovkhoz*, 356
 state monopoly in, 283
ECSC. *See* European Coal and Steel Community (ECSC)
ECU. *See* European Currency Unit (ECU)
EDC. *See* European Defense Community (EDC)
Eden, Anthony
 as Conservative party leader, 12
 as prime minister, 54
 and Suez crisis, 65–66
Education, Soviet, 308, 328, 338–339, 349
Edward I (Britain), 8
Edward VII (Britain), 31
Edward VIII (Britain), 31
Edward, Prince (Britain), 31
EEC. *See* European Economic Community (EEC)
EFTA. *See* European Free Trade Association (EFTA)
EIB. *See* European Investment Bank (EIB)

Einsatzgruppen. See Special Task Formations
Eire, 59. *See also* Republic of Ireland
Eisenhower, Dwight, 65–66
EKD. *See* Evangelical Church in Germany
Election manifesto, 39
Elections
  in Britain (1983), **19–20,** 36
  in czarist Russia, 309
  European Parliament (1984), **262–263**
  in France (1981), **92–93,** 125
  in Germany (1933), 237
  in Northern Ireland (1982), 44
  Soviet, 303–305, 360–361
  in West Germany (1983), **176–177**
Electoral districts, USSR, 360–361
Electoral system
  Bundestag, **177–178**
  effects of, 23–24
  and Federal president (West Germany), **178–179**
  House of Commons, **20–21**
  local government (France), 123
  and party list system, **93–94**
  and President (France), **94–95**
  and Senate (France), 95
  two ballot system, **96**
  West German states, 203
Elitism in USSR, 315–316, 317
Elitist theory, 33
Elizabeth I (Britain), 60
Elizabeth II (Britain), 31, 41–42
EMA. *See* European Monetary Agreement (EMA)
Embourgeoisiement thesis, **21–22**
Emigration, USSR, 307, 344
Empire
  British, **4–5**
  First (French), **104–105**
  French, 104–105, 113, 141
  German, **192–193**
  Holy Roman, **199–201**
  Second (French), 141
Employment Act (1980), Britain, 70
EMS. *See* European Monetary System (EMS)
EMS Dispatch, 109
ENA. *See* École Nationale d'Administration (ENA)
Enarches, 118
Encirclement, capitalist, **278**
End-of-ideology thesis, socioeconomic theory, **144–146,** 168
Engels, Friedrich, 332

England. *See also* United Kingdom in Guide to Countries
Church of, 31
local government, 38
population of, 73
Enlarged sanctuary, **96–97**
Enlightenment, 91
Ensslin, Gudrun, 224
Enterprise, **310–311,** 340, 354. *See also* Planning, Soviet
Epinay Conference (1971), 142
EPU. *See* European Payments Union (EPU)
Equalization payments, 184
Equity law, 10
Erhard, Ludwig
  as chancellor, 181
  social market policy of, 228–229
Erler, Fritz, 227
ERP. *See* European Recovery Program (ERP)
Escapees, 161–162, **225.** *See also* Refugees, expellees, escapees
Established Church, **22–23**
Established Church of Scotland, 60
Estates General, 82, 139
Esterhazy, Marie Charles, 150
Estimates, 70
Estonia, 363, 364, 365
Étatism, 82
Euratom. *See* European Atomic Energy Community (Euratom)
Eurocommunism, 112, **250–251,** 271, 282
Eurocrats, 244
Eurogroup, 268
Euromissile controversy, **251–252,** 268
European Atomic Energy Community (Euratom), 244, 247, **252–253,** 254
  members, 253
European Coal and Steel Community (ECSC), 244, 247, **253–254**
  members, 253
European Communities. *See* European Community (EC)
European Communities Commission. *See* Commission of European Communities
European Communities, Council of Ministers. *See* Council of Ministers of the European Communities
European Community (EC), 23, **254–256**
  members, 254
  and value-added tax revenues, 271
European Convention for the Protection

of Human Rights and Fundamental
  Freedoms (1950), 246, 257
European Council, 248, **256**
  budget rejected by European
    Parliament, 263
  creates European Monetary System,
    260
European Court of Human Rights,
  256–257
European Currency Unit (ECU), 260,
  261
European Defense Community (EDC),
  272
European Economic Community (EEC),
  244, 247, 254, **257–259**
  agricultural policy, 245–246
European Free Trade Association
  (EFTA), 258, **259–260**
  members, 259
European Investment Bank (EIB), 258
European Monetary Agreement (EMA),
  270
European Monetary System (EMS), 256,
  258, **260–261**
  members, 260
European Parliament, 261–**262**
  elections (1984), **262–263**
  members, 261
European Payments Union (EPU), 270
European Peoples' party, 85, 263
European Progressive Democrats, 263
European Recovery Program (ERP),
  269
European referendum, Britain, **23–24**
Europe, Council of. *See* Council of
  Europe
Europe, Eastern. *See* Eastern Europe
"Europe of Fatherlands," 115
Evangelical Church in Germany (EKD),
  171
Evian Accords, 81, 137
Exchange of party cards, 296
Exchange rates, 260–261
Expellees. *See* Refugees, expellees,
  escapees
Explanatory theory, Soviet politics
  autocracy and, **311–312**
  bureaucratic model of, **312–313**, 336
  and convergence, 314
  development model of, **314–315**
  New Class, **315–316**
  and pluralism, **316**
  and state capitalism, **317**

Fabian Society, **24–25**, 35
Fabius, Laurent, 103
Falklands' War, **25–26**
  and British elections (1983), 19

Famine
  czarist Russia, 275, 352
  USSR, 281, 365
Far East, 363
Farmers' associations
  in Britain, **26–27**
  in France, **97–98**
  in West Germany, **180**
Faroe Islands, 266
Fascism. *See also* Nazism
  in France, 79
  interpretations of, 210–211
  in Vichy, 154
Faulkner, Brian, 72
Faure Reforms, 125
FDP. *See* Free Democratic Party (FDP)
February Revolution, Russia, 275
Federal Assembly, 178
Federal Chancellor, **180–182**
  list of, 181
Federal Constitutional Court, **182–183**,
  201
  declares parties unconstitutional, 189,
    231
Federal Diet, 165
Federalism, Germany
  Federal president and, **185**
  Federal president electoral system
    and, **178–179**
  Federal presidents, list of, 179
  Weimar Republic and, 236
  West Germany and, **183–184**, 203
Federalism, USSR, **318–319**. *See also*
    Constitution, USSR (1977)
  creation by Bolsheviks, 363
  and federal supremacy, 330
  and nationalism, 348–349
  and preservation of nationalism, 318
  Supreme Court and, 359–360
  Supreme Soviet and, 359–360
  territorial-administrative units and,
    318
  and union-republic, **364–365**
Federal Republic of Germany (FRG),
  185–186. *See also* Germany in
  Index; Germany, West, in Guide to
  Countries
Fédération de l'Education Nationale. See
  National Federation of Education
  (FEN)
Federation of British Industries, 5
Federation of German Employers
  Association (BDA), 166
Federation of German Industry (BDI),
  166
Federation of the Democratic and
  Socialist Left (FGDS), 142
FEN. *See* National Federation of

Education (FEN)
Fenians, 58
FFA. See French Federation of Agriculture (FFA)
FGDS. See Federation of the Democratic and Socialist Left (FGDS)
Fiery Cross. See Croix de Feu
Fifth Directorate, KGB, 306, 326
Fifth Republic
  Constitution, **98–99**
  National Assembly, **99–100**
  Political party system, **100–101**
  President, **101–102**
  Prime Minister, **102–103**
  Senate, **103–104**
Final Act. See Helsinki Accord
Finland. See Guide to Countries
First Directorate, KGB, 326
First Empire, France, **104–105**
First Estate, 82
"First-past-the-post," 20
First Reich, 200
First Republic, France, 140
Fiscal policy, defined, 249
Fitt, Gerald, 19
Five percent clause, 177–178
Five-three rule, 177
Five-Year Plan, **319–320,** 321, 340
Flash party, 108, 132
FLN. See National Liberation Front (FLN)
FNSEA. See National Federation of Farmers' Unions (FNSEA)
FO. See Force Ouvrière (FO)
Folkish state, 208
Foot, Michael, 20, 35
Force de frappe, **105–107**
Force Ouvrière (CGT-FO, or FO), 153
Foreign policy, Soviet
  Afghanistan and, 277, 312
  and arms sales, 366
  and Brezhnev Doctrine, **276**
  capitalist encirclement as, **278**
  Comintern, use of, 281–282
  and de-Stalinization effects, 305
  expansionism as, 312
  General secretary's role in, 292
  Helsinki Accord and, 280, 307
  intervention in Hungary (1956) as, 305
  KGB, role of, 327
  major actors in, 327
  and national communism, 282, 306
  Peaceful coexistence as, **339–340**
  and socialist internationalism, 276, 281
  Spanish Civil War and, 282
  and sphere of influence, 277
  and trade with Eastern Europe, 285
  two camps doctrine as, 278
  and Warsaw Treaty Organization (WTO), 365
Foreign workers. See Guest workers
Fortuna. See Wallis and Fortuna
Fourquet Doctrine, 152
Fourquet, Michel, 152
Fourteen Points, 233
Fourth Republic
  Constitutional system of, **107–108**
  fall of, 80–81
  and political party system, **108–109**
Fraktion, 165, 220
France. See French Republic in Index; Guide to Countries
Franco, Francisco, 282
Francophonie, 113
Franco-Prussian War, 86, **109–110**, 141, 151
Frankfurt Parliament, 190
Frankfurt, Treaty of (1871), 109
Franks commission, 26
Free Democratic Party (FDP), **186–188**
  in elections of 1983, 176–177
  and proportional representation, 178
  quits Schmidt cabinet, 174
Free France, 133
Free trade area, defined, 249
French bureaucracy model, **110–111**
French Committee of National Liberation, 133
French Communist party (PCF), **111–112**
  enters cabinet, 92
  as Eurocommunist party, 250–251
French Community, **113**
French Confederation of Christian Workers (CFTC), 153
French Democratic Confederation of Labor (CFDT), 153
French Federation of Agriculture (FFA), 97
French Republic, **113–114**
French Revolutionary Wars, 139
French Section of the Workers' International (SFIO), 142
French Union, 107, 113
FRG. See Federal Republic of Germany (FRG)
Friendship, Cooperation and Mutual Assistance, Treaty of (1955), 366
Fuchs, Klaus, 64
Führer, 208
Führerprinzip, 208
Functional Representation, 166, **188**
Fusion of powers, 7

Gaitskell, Hugh, 25, 35

Galtieri, Leopoldo, 25, 26
Gang of Four, Britain, 63
Gau, 209
Gauleiters, 209
Gaullism, 85. *See also* de Gaulle, Charles
  Bayeux Speech, **114–115**
  foreign policy of, **115–116**
  political doctrine of, **116–117**
GB/BHE. *See* All German Bloc/
  Federation of Expellees and
  Dispossessed (GB/BHE)
GDR. *See* German Democratic Republic
  (GDR) in Index; Germany, East, in
  Guide to Countries
Geheime Staatspolizei. See Gestapo
Gemeinde, 204
General and Municipal Workers
  (GMWU), 68, 69
General Confederation of Labor (CGT),
  112, 153
General Confederation of Small and
  Medium-Sized Enterprises
  (CGPME or PME), 84
General Confederation of Staffs (CGC),
  153
General Secretary, CPSU, **291–293**, 303,
  355. *See also* Communist Party of
  the Soviet Union (CPSU)
Generals' revolt (1961), 81
Geneva agreements (1954), 118
Genocide, 214
Genscher, Hans-Dietrich, 177, 187
Gentry, Russia, 392
George III (Britain), 41
George V (Britain), 32
George VI (Britain), 31
Georgia, 297, 319, 364, 365
  corruption in, 351
  nationalism in, 349
  nationalists executed in, 365
German Communist party (DKP), **189.**
  See also Communist party of
  Germany (KPD)
German Confederation, **189–191**
German Democratic Republic (GDR),
  191–192. *See also* Germany, East, in
  Guide to Countries
German Empire, 109, 110, **192–193**
German Federation of Civil Servants
  (DBB), 230
German party (DP), 178
German Reich party (DRP), 207, 231
German Revolution (1918), 235
German Salaried Employees' Union
  (DAG), 230
German Trade Union Federation
  (DGB), 172, 230–231
Germany. *See also* Index entries: Federal
  Republic of Germany; German
  Democratic Republic; Guide to
  Countries entries: Germany, East;
  Germany, West
  Confederation of the Rhine and,
    173–174
  and German Confederation, **189–190**
  German Empire and, **192–193**
  in Holy Roman Empire, **199–200**
  occupation period of, **214–215**
  political forces, 19th century, 190–191
  Potsdam Conference on, 221–223
  union with Austria, **157–158**
  and Vichy regime, 154–155
  as Weimar Republic, **234–235**
Gerrymandering, in Northern Ireland,
  43
Gestapo (*Geheime Staatspolizei*), 209, 213
Girondists, 119, 140
Giscard d'Estaing, Valery
  as leader of Republican Party, 138
  loses election (1981), 92
  Mondialiste foreign policy of, 125–126
  nuclear weapons policy of, 96–97
  as president, 94
Gladstone, William, 36, 57
Glavit, 349, 355
Glavk, 323, 335
Glavrepertoire, 355
Glorious Revolution (1688), 48
GMWU. *See* General and Municipal
  Workers (GMWU)
Godesberg program, 168, 227
Godesberg program versus
  neosocialism, **194**
Goebbels, Joseph, 209
Gomulka, Wladyslaw, 305
Gorbachev, Mikhail, 292
Gorkom, 347
Gosbank, 277, 311, 359
Gosizdat, **349**
Gosplan, 277, **321–322**, 340, 359
Gossnab. See State Committee, USSR
Gosstroi. See State Committee, USSR
GPU, 326
Graduated response, 128
Grand Coalition, **194–195**
Grand corps, 90, **117–118**
Grand Design, 115
Grand écoles, 117
Grandeur, 116
Great Britain. *See* United Kingdom of
  Great Britain and Northern Ireland
  in Index; United Kingdom in
  Guide to Countries
Greater Berlin, 238
Greater London Council (GLC), **28**, 30
"Great German solution," 190

Great Purge, 281, 289, **322–323**, 353
Great Terror. *See* Great Purge
Grechko, Andrei, 295
Greece. *See* Guide to Countries
Greeks, in West Germany, 197
Green Front, 180
Greens, **195–197**
   in elections of 1983, 176–177
Grimond, Jo, 37
GRU, 326
Grünen, 196
Guadeloupe, 113
Gubernii, 338
Guest workers, **197–198**
Guiana, 113
Guillaume affair, **198–199**
Guillaume, Günter, 198
Gulag (prison labor camps), **322**

Habeas corpus, 10
   act of 1689, 8
   writ of, 10
Habsburg dynasty, 200
Hailsham, Lord. *See* Hogg, Quentin
Hakenkreuz, 211
Hallstein Doctrine, 195, 199
Hannibal, 25
Hanover, House of, 31
Hard currency stores, USSR, 351
Head of government, USSR. *See* Presidium
Head of state, USSR. *See* Presidium
Healey, Denis, 63
Heath, Edward, 18
   as Conservative party leader, 13
   as prime minister, 54
Helsinki Accord (1975), 217, **263–265**, 280, 307
   review conferences, 265–266
   signatories, 264
Henry, Prince (Britain), 31
High Authority, European Coal and Steel Community, 244
High Council of the Judiciary, France, 120
Highest average formula, 93
Himmler, Heinrich, 209
Historical materialism, Marxist theory of, 332
"Historic compromise," 251
Hitler, Adolf, 205–206, 282. *See also* Nazism
   doctrine of, 207
   organizes Nazi movement, 211–212
Hitler-Stalin Pact (1939) (Nazi-Soviet Pact), 206, 363
Hitler Youth, 209
Ho Chi Minh, 118

Hogg, Quentin, 31
Hohenzollern royal house, 192
Holy Roman Empire, **199–201**
Home, Lord. *See* Douglas-Home, Alec
"Honor clauses," 233
Hooliganism, 300
House of Commons, **28–29**
   decline of, 15
   electoral system in, **20–21**
   members in cabinet, 6
   as unit of Parliament, 47
House of Lords, **30–31**
   as high court, 34
   and London government bill, 28
   members in cabinet, 6
   as unit of Parliament, 47
House of Windsor, **31–32**
Human Rights Court. *See* European Court of Human Rights
Human Rights Movement, USSR, 307
Hume, John, 45
Hungarian revolt of 1956, 305
Hungary. *See* Guide to Countries
Hunger strike
   in Britain, 33
   in West Germany, 224

Iceland. *See* Guide to Countries
ICFTU. *See* International Federation of Free Trade Unions (ICFTU)
Ideology. *See also* Communism; Leninism; Marxism; Nazism: Doctrine; Socialism; Stalinism
   end of ideology thesis, **144–145**
   Soviet decline of, 341
   in the USSR, 332
ILO. *See* International Labor Organization
Imperialism—The Highest Stage of Capitalism, 331
Incivisme, 129, 144
Incompatibility rule, 103
Indirect rule, 4
Indochina, Federation of, 118
Indochina War, **118–119**
Industrial association, **323**
INLA. *See* Irish National Liberation Army (INLA)
"Inner Six," 259
Inquisitorial system, 120
Inspectorate of Finances, 117
Instruktsiya, 330, 335
Integration types, economic, **249–250**
Interest group representation, France, 91
Interest groups. *See* individual countries in Guide to Countries
Interlocking directorate, Britain, 48

Interlocking directorates, USSR. See Duplication of office
Intermediate nuclear forces talks, **265–266**
Internal passport, 281, **323–324**
International Brigades, 282
International class struggle, 339
International Department, USSR, 327
International Federation of Free Trade Unions (ICFTU), 68
International Information Department, USSR, 327
International Labor Organization, 68
International socialism, 317
IRA. See Irish Republican Army (IRA)
Ireland. See Republic of Ireland in Index; Ireland in Guide to Countries
Ireland, Northern. See Northern Ireland
Irish Free State, 42, 59, 71
Irish National Liberation Army (INLA), 33, 45
Irish Republican Army (IRA), **32–33**, 42, 45
Irish Republican Socialist party (IRSP), 45
Iron Law of Oligarchy, **33–34**
IRSP. See Irish Republican Socialist party (IRSP)
Isle of Man, 73
Issue pileup thesis, socioeconomic theory, **146**
Italian Communist Party (PCI), 250–251, 291
Italians, in West Germany, 197
Italy. See Guide to Countries
Ivan the Terrible, 312, 363
Izdatel'stvo, 349

Jacobinism, 119
Jacobins, 140
James I (Britain), 60
James II (Britain), 8
James VI (Britain), 60
Japan, in Yalta Conference, 241
Jaspers, Karl, 207
Jazz, in USSR, 355
Jenkins, Roy, 63, 244
Jeunesses Patriotes, 79
Jewish Autonomous Province, 318
Jews, Soviet, 307, 318, 322, 324, 350
Joint Armed Forces Command, Warsaw Treaty Organization (WTO), 366
Joint Secretariat, Warsaw Treaty Organization (WTO), 366
Judicial Committee of the Privy Council, 17, 34, 55
Judicial review
in France, 87–89
in West Germany, 182–183
Judicial system
in Britain, **34–35**
in France, **119–120**
in USSR, **324–326**
in West Germany, 182–183, **201–202**
July Monarchy, **120–121**
July Revolution (1830), 83
"June Days," 142
Junkers, 193
Jusos. See Young Socialists
Justice, Court of. See Court of Justice

Kadets (Constitutional Democrats), Russia, 309, 348
Kaiser, 192. See also William II (Germany)
Kapp *Putsch* (1920), 234
Kassof, Allen, 313
Kazakhstan, 319, 364
Keeler, Christine, 55
Kellogg-Briand Pact (1928), 213
Kelly, Petra Lehmann, 196
Kerensky, Alexander, 275
Keynesianism, 76
Keynes, John Maynard, 76
KGB, **326–327**
  Andropov, Yuri and, 287, 327
  and crimes against the state, 301
  directorates, 306, 326
  and dissent, 306
  exempt from dual subordination, 308
  representation on Politburo, 287
  and Russian dominance, 349
  as state committee, 359
Kharakteristika, 329, 337
Khozrachet, 327
Khrushchev, Nikita
  codifies Soviet law, 353
  and de-Stalinization, 305
  heads both party and state, 345
  ousted from leadership, 292, 305
  and peaceful coexistence, 339
  proposed party reforms, 293
  revives COMECON, 285
  secret speech of (1956), 291, 305
  and sovkhozization, 357
Kiesinger, Kurt George
  as chancellor, 181
  as Christian Democratic leader, 169
  in Grand Coalition, 194
Kievan Russia, 363
Kinizdat, 350
Kinnock, Neil, 20, 35
Kirchheimer, Otto, 168
Kirgizia, 364
Kohl, Helmut

Index 393

as chancellor, 174
 in 1983 elections, 176
 in 1976 elections, 170
 uses nonconfidence procedure, 174–175
Kolkhoz, 280–281, **327–328**, 356–357
Komitet Gosudarstvennoi Bezopasnosti. See KGB
Kommandatura, 214–215
Komsomol, 293, 295, **328–329**
Kornilov, General Lavr, 275
KPD. See Communist Party of Germany (KPD)
Krai, 338, 362
Kreis, 204
Kreistag, 204
Kronstadt, 275, 336
Kulaks, 281
Kulturkampf, 193

Labor norms, USSR, 335
Labour party, **35–36**, 282
 in elections of 1983, 19–20
 and Fabian Society, 24
 leaders, list of, 35
 and party system, 1–2
 and Scotland, 60–61
Labour Representation Committee, 35
Land, 183
 government, **202–203**
 list of, 186
 and political party system, **203–204**
Landkreis, 204
Laos, 118
Largest remainder formula, 93
Laski, Harold, 25
Latvia, 363, 364, 365
Laval, Pierre, 154
Law, USSR
 Bolshevik legal code of 1922, 299
 code law, Soviet, 325
 codification Soviet law, 299
 and death penalty, 302
 goals of, 325
 lay assessors, 325
 RSFSR Criminal Code, 299, 301
 socialist, 280
Law, Western Europe. See also Code law system; Common law
 British, 10–11
 European community, 247, 248–249
 French, 85–86
 West German, 182, 201, 223
Lay assessors, USSR, 325
League of Agricultural Chambers, 180
League of German Cooperatives, 180
League of German Girls, 209
League of the German Farmers, 180

Lebensraum, 208
Lecanuet, Jean, 85, 131
Leftist Radical Movement (MRG), 92, **121–122**
Left Opposition, USSR, 357
Legal enactments, USSR, **329–330**, 361
Legal system. See Code Law system; Common law system; Judicial system; Law
Legal theory, Soviet
 and civil rights, 279
 and crimes against the state, 301
 and natural rights, 280
 and socialist legality, 353
 and socialist ownership, 354
 and socialist speech, 280
Legislative process
 in Britain, 29, 30
 in France, 87–89
 in USSR, 329, 344, 360–361
 in West Germany, 164, 165
Legislature. See individual countries in Guide to Countries
Leningrad, 338
Leninism, **330–332**
 adaptations of Marxism to Russian conditions, 330–331
 combined development in, 331
 and Communist Party of the Soviet Union, 286–288
 creation of Marxism-Leninism, 331
 democratic centralism and, 331
 and dictatorship of the party, 331
 duplication of office in, 310
 imperialism, theory of, 330
 and party organization, 331
 rejected by Eurocommunism, 250
 and Socialist ownership, 354
 and Stalinism, 358
 vanguard party, 331
 and worker-peasant alliance, 331
Lenin Military Political Academy, 293
Lenin, Vladimir
 Bolshevik party, founder of, 273
 Comintern founder, 281
 ends Russia's participation in World War I, 315
 exiled, 273
 and federalism, 319
 Gosplan, and creation of, 321
 institutes duplication of office, 310
 Marxism-Leninism, 330–332
 nationalizes industry, 365
 and New Economic Policy (NEP), 281–282, 336
 Politburo, and creation of, 295
 and secret police, 275
 seizes power, 356

Sovnarkhom, as head of, 275
and War Communism, **365**
"What Is to Be Done," 296
and worker-peasant alliance, 281, 331
Lesseps, Ferdinand de, 152
Liberal Empire, France, 141
Liberalism, 190. *See also* Free Democratic party; Liberal party; Liberals; Neoliberalism
Liberal party, **36–37**
in elections of 1983, 19
leaders, list of, 37
origins of, 76–77
Liberal Revolution (1848), 190
Liberal-SDP Alliance. *See* Alliance
Liberals, in European Parliament, 263
"Liberty, Equality, Fraternity," 140
Lib-Lab pact, 37
Life Peerages Act of 1958, 30
Linly, Viscount David, 31
Lipsett, Seymour Martin, 145
Lithuania, 206, 363, 364, 365
Lloyd George, David, 37
Local government
in Britain, **37–39**
in France, **122–123**, 133
in USSR, 277, 303–304, 346–347, 362
in West Germany, **204–205**
Local government reforms
in Britain, 38–39
in France, **123–124**
Loewenberg, Gerhard, 168
Lomé Convention, 258
London. *See* Greater London Council
London County Council, 28
Long-range plans, 340
Lord Home. *See* Douglas-Home, Alec
Lords, House of. *See* House of Lords
Lorraine, 148
Louis Napoleon Bonaparte, *See* Napoleon III
Louis Phillipe, 83, 120
Louis XVIII (France), 83
Loyal Opposition. *See* Opposition
Luns, Joseph, NATO secretary general, 268
Luther, Martin, 200
Luxembourg. *See* Guide to Countries

MacDonald, Ramsay, 25, 35
Maclean, Donald D., 56, 64
MacMahon affair, Third Republic, **151**
MacMahon, Patrice de, 148, 151
Macmillan, Harold
as Conservative party leader, 12
as prime minister, 54
in Profumo affair, 55

Madrid conference, Conference on Security and Cooperation in Europe, 264
Magna Charta (1215), 3, 8
Magnitizdat, 350
Mahler, Gustaf, 224
Mahoré, 113
Main Political Administration (MPA), CPSU, **293–294**. *See* Communist Party of the Soviet Union (CPSU); Military, Soviet
Malenkov, Georgi, 339
Malta, 257
Malvinas, 25–26
Mandate doctrine, **39–40**
Manifesto, 39
Marchais, Georges, 92
Margaret, Princess (Britain), 31
Market economy. *See* Social market economy
Marshall, George C., 269
Marshall Plan, 153, 214, 269
Martinique, 113
Marx, Karl, 332–334
Marxism, **332–334**. *See also* Leninism
and civil rights, 279
class theory of, 317, 332
contradictions of capitalism, 333
critique of capitalism, 334
decline of, in West, 145
and developing countries, 334
and dialectic process, 332
and dictatorship of the proletariat, 333
and European socialism, 282
in France, 111, 153
and historical materialism, 332
interpretations of fascism by, 210
Lenin's additions to, 330–331
in Russia, 273–274
and socialist ownership, 354
and socialist property, 300
substructure, 332
superstructure, 332
and surplus value, 317, 333
and withering away of the state, 333, 353
Massive reprisals, 128
Mass organizations, USSR, **334–335**
and citizen inspectors, 279
Comrads' Courts and, 279
DOSAAF, 307–308
Druzhiny, 279
Komsomol, **328–329**
nature and use of, 334–335
Octobrists, 328
Pioneers, 328
residence committees as, 279

Index 395

role in nominations, 304
Massu, Jacques, 80
Mauroy, Pierre, 111
 and nationalization bill, 127
 as prime minister, 92, 103
Maurras, Charles, 79
Maximilian affair, 141
May Events of 1968, **124–125**
Mayotte. *See* Mahoré
Maze prison, 33
Meinhof, Ulrike, 224
Mein Kampf (1928), 207, 211
Member of Parliament (MP), 40
Member of the European Parliament (MEP), 262
Memel, 206
Mende, Erich, 187
Mendes-France, Pierre, 118, 134
Mensheviks, 273, 274, 282
MEP. *See* Member of the European Parliament (MEP)
Mery, Guy, 97
Messmer, Pierre, as prime minister, 103
Mexico, 141
Meyer, Alfred, 313
MGB, 326
Michels, Robert, 33–34
Military Committee, NATO, 267
Military-Industrial Commission, USSR, 303
Militant Tendency, Britain, 36
Military, Soviet
 conscripts, 349
 defense budget, 283, 303
 Defense Council and, **303**
 estimates of defense budget, 303
 GRU, 326
 invasion of Czechoslovakia (1968), 366
 invasion of Hungary (1956), 305
 KGB role in, 326
 language of command, 348
 and Main Military Council, 293
 and Main Political Administration (MPA), **293–294**
 membership on Politburo, 295
 and military-industrial complex, Soviet, 303
 and military training in schools, 308
 party control of, 293–294
 purged by Stalin, 322
 Russian dominance of, 349
 troops in Eastern Europe, 365–366
 and Warsaw Treaty Organization (WTO), 365–366
 zampolit, 293–294
"Milk lake," 246
Ministerpräsident, 202
Minister-president, 202

Ministrables, 108
Ministry of Internal Affairs, USSR. *See* MVD (Ministry of Internal Affairs), USSR
Ministry of the Interior, France, 123, 133
Ministry, Soviet, 277, 311, 323, **335–336**
Miquelon, 113
Mir, 352
MIRV (Multiple independently targetable missile), 106
Missiles in Europe, 367. *See also* Euromissile Controversy; Intermediate Nuclear Forces Talks
Mittbestimmung, 172
Mitterrand, François, 111
 in elections of 1981, 92–93
 and nationalization laws, 127
 as president, 94
 in Resistance, 139
 unites socialists, 142–143
Mobilization tactics, USSR, 283, 304, 314, 334–335
MODEF. *See* Movement for the Coordination and Defense of Family Farms (MODEF)
Model Parliament, 8
Modernization
 in Britain, 66–67
 in France, 146, 147
 in USSR, 314
 in West Germany, 175–176
Mogadishu rescue, 224
Moldavia (Bessarabia), 363, 364
Mollet, Guy, 108, 112, 142
Molyneaux, 45, 72
Monarch, Britain, **41–42**
Monarchy
 British, 41–42
 French, 82, 83, 120
 German, 192–193, 200
MONATUR. *See* National Movement of Agricultural and Rural Workers (MONATUR)
Mondialisme, 97, **125–126**
Monetarism, 66
Monetary policy, defined, 249
Monetary system. *See* European Monetary System (EMS)
Monetary union, 261
Mongolia, 285
Monnerville, Gaston, 104
Monnet, Jean, 254
Moravia, 206
Morgenthau Plan, 222
Moscow, 338
Moscow Treaty (1970), 217
Moslems

in USSR, 341
in West Germany, 197–198
"The Mountain," 119
"Mountain of butter," 246
"Mountain of meat," 246
Mountbatten, Lord Louis, 33
Mountbatten, Philip. *See* Philip, Prince
Mountbatten-Windsor, House of, 32
Mouvement des Radicaux de Gauche. *See* Leftist Radical Movement (MRG)
Mouvement Republicain Populaire. *See* Popular Republican Movement (MRP)
Movement for the Coordination and Defense of Family Farms (MODEF), 97
Movement of Democrats, 92
MP. *See* Member of Parliament (MP)
MPA. *See* Communist Party of the Soviet Union (CPSU)
MRG. *See* Leftist Radical Movement (MRG)
MRP. *See* Popular Republican Movement (MRP)
Multiparty system
 in France, 100, 108
 in Germany, 220
Munich Agreement, **205–206**, 217
Munich *Putsch* (1923), 211, 234
Mussolini, Benito, 205
Mutual Economic Assistance, Council of (COMECON), **285–286**
MVD (Ministry of Internal Affairs), USSR, 324, 326
My Struggle (1928). *See Mein Kampf*

Na levo, 350
NALGO. *See* National and Local Government Officers Association (NALGO)
Nanterre, 124
Napoleon Bonaparte. *See* Napoleon I
Napoleon I (Emperor)
 and Bonapartism, 82
 and Consulate, 140
 and First Empire, 104–105
 reforms of, 105
Napoleon III (Emperor), 83, 86
 in Franco-Prussian War, 109
 Second Empire and, 141
Narodnichestvo (Russian Populist movement), 273
Nasser, Gamal Abdel, 65
National and Local Government Officers Association (NALGO), 69
National Assembly
 Fifth Republic, **99–100**
 Fourth Republic, 100

in revolutionary period, 139
National Center of Independents (CNT), 127
National Center of Independents and Peasants (CNIP), **126–127**
National Center of Young Farmers (CNJA), 97
National Coal Board, 56
National communism, 282, 306, 334
National Convention, France, 140
National Council of French Employers (CNPF), 83–84
National Democratic Party (NPD), **206–207**, 232
National Farmers' Union (NFU), 27
National Federation of Education (FEN), 153
National Federation of Farmers' Unions (FNSEA), 97–98
National Front, Britain, 263
National Front, East Germany, 191
National Health Service, 75
Nationalism
 in Algeria, 81
 in Britain, 20
 Crimean Tatars and, 307
 in France, 79, 116–117
 Great Russian, 307
 preservation of through USSR federalism, 318
 and republican dissent, USSR, 365
 revolution theory and, 140
 and Russian dominance in USSR, 364–365
 and Russification, 348–349
 and Soviet historical and cultural differences, 341
 and Soviet patriotism, 342
 in West Germany, 206
Nationalizations of 1982, France, 84, **127–128**
National Liberation Army (ALN), 80
National Liberation Front (FLN), 80
National Movement of Agricultural and Rural Workers (MONATUR), 98
National Resistance Council, 139
National School of Administration (ENA), 118
National Socialism, *See* Nazism: Doctrine
National Socialist German Workers' party (NSDAP), *See* Nazi party
National Union of British Manufacturers, 5
National Union of Conservative and Unionist Associations, 49
National Union of Mineworkers (NUM), 68, 69

National Union of Public Employees
    (NUPE), 69
National Union of Railwaymen, 69
National Union of Teachers (NUT), 69
NATO (North Atlantic Treaty
    Organization), **267–268**
  British support of, 2–3
  French relations with, 116
  members sign Helsinki pact, 264
  missiles in Europe, 251–252,
    265–266
  weakness of, 252
Natural rights, 90–91
Nazi party, 209, 211–212
  and election of 1933, 237
  tried at Nuremberg, 213
Nazism
  constitutional lessons of, 210
  doctrine, **207–208**
  institutions, **209–210**
  interpretations of, **210–211**
  movement, **211–212**
Nazi-Soviet Pact (1939) (Hitler-Stalin
    Pact), 206, 363
Neoliberalism, 138
Neo-Nazism, 207, 231
Neosocialism. *See* Godesberg Program
    versus Neosocialism
N.E.P. *See* New Economic Policy
Nepmen, 336
Netherlands. *See* Guide to Countries
Neutral and nonaligned (NNA)
  members sign Helsinki pact, 264
New Caledonia, 113
New Class, explanatory theory, **315–316**
New Economic Policy (NEP), 280,
    336–337, 357, 365
New Soviet Man, 358
New Zealand, 11
NFU. *See* National Farmers' Union
    (NFU)
Nicholas II, Czar, 274–275, 309, 347
Nicoud, Gerard, 84
"The Nine," 254
NKGB, 326
NKVD, 322, 326
NNA. *See* Neutral and nonaligned
    (NNA)
Nobel Peace Prize
  1971, 218
  1976, 45
Nomenklatura, 297, 310, **334**
Nomination process, USSR, 303–304
Nonconfidence motion procedure
  in Britain, 53
  in France, 100
  in West Germany, **174–175,** 181
Nonconformist conscience, 23

Nordic Council, **266–267**
Nordic Investment Bank, 267
Normandy, 148
North Atlantic Assembly, 268
North Atlantic Council, 267
North Atlantic Treaty (1949), 267
North Atlantic Treaty Organization. *See*
    NATO (North Atlantic Treaty
    Organization)
Northern Ireland, **42–43.** *See also*
    Ulster; United Kingdom of Great
    Britain and Northern Ireland
  elections of 1982 in, 72
  government of, **43–44**
  political groups in, **45–46**
Northern Ireland Civil Rights
    Association, 45
Northern Ireland Peace Movement, 45
North German Confederation, **212–213**
North Korea, 285, 366
North Sea oil, 14
Norway. *See* Guide to Countries
Notables, 124
Novgorod, Russia, 363
NPD. *See* National Democratic party
    (NPD)
NSDAP. *See* Nazi party
"Nuclear club," 106
Nuclear forces talks. *See* Intermediate
    nuclear forces talks
Nuclear-free zones, 252
Nuclear war, Soviet attitudes about, 339
Nuclear weapons, France, 96–97,
    105–107
Nuclear weapons strategy, France,
    106–107, **128–129**
NUM. *See* National Union of
    Mineworkers (NUM)
NUPE. *See* National Union of Public
    Employees (NUPE)
Nuremberg war crimes trials, **213–214**
NUT. *See* National Union of Teachers
    (NUT)

OAS. *See* Secret Army Organization
    (OAS)
Obedinenie. See Industrial Association
Obkom, 289, 338
Oblast', 289, **337–338,** 346, 362
Occupation period, **214–215**
Occupation Statute, Germany, 186
October Manifesto, Russia, 347
October Revolution, 363. *See also*
    Bolshevik Revolution
Octobrist party, Russia, 348
Octobrists, 328
Oder-Neisse Line, **216,** 217, 221
OECD. *See* Organization for Economic

Cooperation and Development (OECD)
OEEC. *See* Organization for European Economic Cooperation (OEEC)
Official crimes, criminal offenses, **302–303**
Official IRA. *See* Irish Republican Army (IRA)
Official Unionist party (OUP), 44, 45, 72
OGPU, 326
Okhrana, 326, 347
Okrug, 318, 362
Old Bolsheviks, 322, 358
"Old boy network," 56
Oligarchy, Iron Law of. *See* Iron Law of Oligarchy
Ombudsman, **46**
  in USSR, 304
One Day in the Life of Ivan Denisovich, 306
O'Neil, Terence, 72
One-year plan, 320, 340
Opposition, 46–47
  parliamentary role of, 167–168
  theory on waning of, 168
Opposition and dissent. *See* Dissent and opposition
Orange Order, 45
Orders in council, Britain, 55
Orders in council, czarist Russia, 309
Orenburg-Uzhgorod gas pipeline, 286
Organic law, 87
Organization for Economic Cooperation and Development (OECD), **269**
Organization for European Economic Cooperation (OEEC), **269–270**
  and European Monetary Agreement, 270
  and European Payments Union, 270
Orgburo, 289, 298
Orléans, House of, 83, 120
Oslo, 267
Osoaviakhim, 308
OSSO, 322
Ostpolitik, 159, 216, **217–218**
Otdely. *See* Departments, Communist Party of the Soviet Union
OUP. *See* Official Unionist party (OUP)
"Outer Seven," 259
Owen, David, 63
"Oxbridge," 10

Pacific. *See* African, Caribbean, and Pacific countries (ACP)
Package vote, 100
Paisley, Ian, 72
Pakistan, 11

Pale of Settlement, 348
Palestine Liberation Organization, 224
Panachage, 93
Panama Canal Company, 152
Panama Scandal, Third Republic, **152**
Pantouflage, 118
"Parasitism," 355
Paris
  local government reforms and, 123–124
  in revolution of 1848, 142
  votes left, 148
Paris Commune. *See* Commune of Paris
Paris Peace Conference (1919), 232
Paris, Treaty of 1951 (European Coal and Steel Community), 253, 255
Parlement of Paris, 82
Parliament
  of Britain, **47–48**
  of France, 99–100, 103–104
  of West Germany, 163–166
Parliament Act
  of 1911, 9, 30
  of 1949, 3, 9, 30
Parliamentary commissioner, 46
Parliamentary Labour party (PLP), 49
Parliament, decline of. *See* Decline of Parliament
Parliament, European. *See* European Parliament
Partgruporgs, 296
Participation, citizen, USSR, **279**, 296, 303–304
Partisan dealignment, Britain, 53
Party Control Commission, 288
Party government, **48–49**
Party list system, electoral system, **93–94**
Party of Wales. *See Plaid Cymru*
Party organization, **49–50**
Party schools, 293, **338–339**
Patronat, 83–84
PCE. *See* Spanish Communist party (PCE)
PCF. *See* French Communist party (PCF)
PCI. *See* Italian Communist party (PCI)
PDM. *See* Progress and Modern Democracy
Peaceful coexistence, 305, **339–340**
Peace of Westphalia (1648), 200
Peerage Act of 1963, 30
Peasants
  in CPSU, 288
  in Russia, 351–352
  Soviet, 336
People's Chamber, 191
People's courts, USSR, 324–325
People's party, Weimar Republic, 237

People's Republic of China. *See* China
Peredel, 352
Pétain, Henri Philippe, 149, 154–155
Peter the Great, 314, 338
Petition of Right (1628), 3, 8
Petrograd (Leningrad) Soviet of Workers' and Soldiers' Deputies, 275
Pflimlin, Pierre, 80
Philby, Harold (Kim), 56, 64
Philip, Prince (Britain), 31
Phillips, Peter, 31
Phillips, Zara, 31
Philosophes, 139
Pioneers, 328
Plaid Cymru, 17, 19, **50–51,** 74
Planning, Soviet, **340–341**
   and budget of the state, 277
   and command economy, 283
   and disaggregation, 320
   draft plans in, 340
   and enterprise, 310, 340
   and five-year plan, 319
   and Gosplan, 321
   indices, 340
   and industrial associations, 323
   as legally mandatory, 321
   long-range, 320, 321
   and *oblast'* responsibilities, 338
   production targets, 311
   and regional implementation, 338
   and second economy, 350–351
   structure and process, 340–341
   and union-republics, 318
Plebiscitary democracy, 82, 137
Plebiscite
   in Austria (1938), 157
   in Saar (1955), 226
   in Saar (1935), 226
PLP. *See* Parliamentary Labour Party
Pluralism, explanatory theory, **316**
Plurality system, 21
PM. *See* Prime Minister (PM)
PME. *See* General Confederation of Small and Medium-Sized Enterprises (PME)
Pocket boroughs, 57
Podmena, 310
Poher, Alain, 94
Poland. *See* Guide to Countries
Policy process, Soviet
   Defense Council, role of, **303**
   economic planning, role of, 340–341
   and Gosplan, 321–322
   interest groups in, 316
   Politburo, role of, 294–295
   and state committees, 359
Polish October (1956), 305

Politburo, CPSU, 288, **294–295,** 343. *See also* Communist Party of the Soviet Union (CPSU)
Political Bureau. *See* Politburo, CPSU
Political Consultative Committee, Warsaw Treaty Organization, 366
Political Culture
   in Britain, **51–52**
   in France, **129–130,** 144
   and transformation thesis (West Germany), **218–219**
   in USSR, 307, 311–312, **341–343,** 348
   in West Germany, 162, **219–220**
Political party system
   in Britain, **52–53**
   in czarist Russia, 274, 275, 309, 348
   Fifth Republic, **100–101**
   Fourth Republic, **108–109**
   and *Land* (West German states), **203–204**
   and Weimar Republic, **237–238**
   in West Germany, 167–168, **220–221**
Political prisoners, USSR, 301. *See also* Dissent and Opposition
Political socialization, USSR, 294, 328–329, 339, 341–342
Political union, defined, 249
Polozhenie, 330
Polycentrism, **270–271,** 306
Polynesia, 113
Pompidou, Georges
   as president, 94
   as prime minister, 103
Poniatowski, Michel, 138
Popular Front, **130–131**
Popular Republican Movement (MRP), 85, 115, **131–132**
Portugal, *See* Guide to Countries
Postanovlenie, 284, 330, 344
Potsdam Conference (1945), **221–223**
Potsdam Declaration, 222
Poujade, Pierre, 132
Poujadism, 84, 132
PPO. *See* Primary Party Organization (PPO)
PR. *See* Proportional representation (PR)
PR. *See* Republican Party (PR)
Prague Spring, 276, 366
Pravo kontrolya. *See* Verification
Prefect, 133
Prefectoral corps, 117
Premier, USSR, 343, 344
President
   and Electoral system for France, **94–95**
   and Electoral system for West Germany, **178–179**
   of France, **101–102**

French, list of, 94
of USSR, 344
West German, list of, 179
of West Germany, **185**
Presidium, 292, 343
of the Council of Ministers, 284, **343**
of the Supreme Soviet, 330, **343–345,** 360–361
Prikazy, 330, 335
Primary party organization, CPSU, 287, **295–296,** 347. *See also* Communist Party of the Soviet Union (CPSU)
Prime, Geoffrey Arthur, 64
Prime minister
of Britain, **53–54**
British, list of, 54
of France, **102–103**
French, list of, 103
West Germany. *See* Federal Chancellor
Primus inter pares, 54
Prison labor camps, 281, 305, 322
Private members, 40
Private plots, Soviet, 328
Privatization, 66
Privileges, Soviet, 337
Privy Council, **54–55**
Judicial Committee of, 17, 34, 55
Procuracy, 308, 325, **345–346,** 360
Procurator-general, USSR, 345
Professional associations, USSR, 354
Profumo Affair, **55–56**
Profumo, John, 55, 64
Progress and Modern Democracy (PDM), 85
Proletariat, 273, 331, 333
Propaganda Ministry (Nazi), 209
Proportional representation (PR)
in European Parliament, 261, 262
in France, 93
in Northern Ireland, 72
proposed for Britain, 21
in West Germany, 177, 203
Protective Formation, 209
Province, Soviet. *See oblast'*
Provisional government, France, 87, **133–134**
presidents, list of, 134
Provisional government, Russia, 274–275, 309, 356
Provisional Irish Republican Army, 32, 45
Prussia, 109
in German Confederation, 189–190
in German Empire, 192–193
in North German Confederation, 212–213
PS. *See* Socialist party (PS)
PSU. *See* Unified Socialist party (PSU)

Public administration, USSR, 335, 339, 347
Public Corporation, Britain, **56–57**
Public school, 9–10
Punitive nationalization, 128
Purge, CPSU, **296–297.** *See also* Communist Party of the Soviet Union (CPSU)
Putsch
Kapp (1920), 234
in Munich (1923), 211, 234
in Vienna (1934), 157

Quadripartite Agreement (1971), 217, 239
"Quango," 57
Quintus Fabius Maximus, 25

Racism, in Nazism, 207–208
Radicalism, French, 121–122
Radical party, 134–135
Radical Republican party, 134
Radical Socialist party, 134
Radizdat, 350
RAF. *See* Red Army Faction (RAF)
Raikom, 347
Raion, 338, 345, **346–347,** 362
Rally for the Republic (RPR), **135–136**
in elections of 1981, 92
Rally of the French People (RPF), 108
Raspe, Jan-Carl, 224
Rasporyazhenie, 284, 330
Rassemblement pour la République, 135
Rates (taxes), 38
Reagan, Ronald, 235
Rechtsstaat, 201, 223
Red army, 294, 319
Red Army Faction (RAF), **224–225**
Red Belt, France, 112
Red Guards, Bolshevik, 275
Red Terror, 326–327
Referendum. *See also* Plebiscite
on Britain in European Community, 18
on devolution to Scotland, 17–18, 61
on devolution to Wales, 17–18
European, **23–24,** 137
use of in France, 136–137
Referendum power, **136–137**
Reform Acts, 3, 9, **57–58**
Reformers' Movement, 85
Reforms, local government. *See* Local government reforms
Refugees, expellees, escapees, **225**
Refuseniks, 307
Regierender Bürgermeister, 238
Regime of parties, 108, 114
Reich. *See* German Empire

Reichsrat, 236
Reichstag, 192, 212, 236, 282
Reichstag fire, 237
Reign of Terror, 119, 140
Religion in the USSR, 307, 341, 348, 350
Representation, functional. *See* Functional representation
Representation of the People Acts, 58
Representative justice, 94
Republican Party (PR), **138**
Republican presidiums, USSR, 330
Republic
   Federal (West Germany), **185–186**
   Fifth (France), **98–103**
   Fourth (France), **107–109**
   French, **113–114**
   German Democratic (East Germany), **191–192**
   of Ireland, **58–60**
   Second (France), **141–142**
   Third (France), **148–149**
   Weimar, **234–235**
Republics, USSR. *See* Union-Republic
Reshenie, 330
Residence committees, USSR, 279
Resistance, **138–139**
Restoration, Bourbon. *See* Bourbon Restoration
Retail consortium, 6
Reunion, 113
Revolutionary courts, Bolshevik, 353
Revolutionary tribunals, Bolshevik, 327
Revolutions
   Bolshevik Revolution (1917), **274–275**
   Commune of Paris (1870), **86–87**
   February Revolution, France (1848), 141
   February Revolution, Russia (1917), 274–275
   French Revolution of 1789, **139–140**
   German (1918), 234
   July Revolution, France (1830), 120
   June Days, France (1848), 142
   Liberal, Germany (1848), 190
   Russian of 1905, 309, **347–348**, 356
Revolution, theory of, 140
Rhine, Confederation of the. *See* Confederation of the Rhine
Rhineland, 212, 234
Rhodesia, 16
Rigby, T. H., 313
Right Opposition, 357
Rights of Man and Citizen. *See* Declaration of the Rights of Man and Citizen
Robespierre, Maximilien, 119, 140
Rocard, Michel, 143

Rodgers, William, 20, 63
Röhm, Ernst, 209, 211
Romania. *See* Guide to Countries
Romanovs, 275
Rome Treaty (1957)
   established European Investment Bank, 258
   for European Atomic Energy Community, 252, 255
   for European Economic Community, 252, 255, 257
Roosevelt, Franklin D., 241
Rosenberg, Ethel, 64
Rosenberg, Julius, 64
Rotation principle, Greens party, 196
Roth, Wolfgang, 194
Rotten boroughs, 57
Royal Irish Constabulary, 59
Royal prerogatives, 55
RPR. *See* Rally for the Republic (RPR)
RSDLP. *See* Russian Social Democratic Labor party (RSDLP)
Rule of law
   in Britain, 4
   in Germany, 223
Rus', 363
Russia, czarist
   agriculture in, 352
   autocracy in, 311–312
   and Basic Law of the Russian Empire (1832), 312
   class system in, 312, 330, 348
   censorship in, 350
   czar deposed in, 274
   and development of the State, 363
   Duma, 309
   elections of, 309
   Emancipation Act of 1861 in, 352
   expansionism in, 348
   and February Revolution, Russia, 274
   internal passport system in, 324
   legal codes in, 354
   land ownership in, 352
   Marxist movement in, 273
   mir, 352
   and persecution of non-Russians, 347
   and Populist movement (*Narodnichestvo*), 273
   procuracy in, 346
   Russification in, 348
   secret police in, 312, 326
   serfdom in, 351
   state religion in, 348
   urbanization in, 312
   and World War I, 274–275
Russian civil war. *See* Civil War, Russia
Russianization, 349
Russian language, 348, 349

Russian Orthodox Christianity, 348
Russian Populist Movement (*Narodnichestvo*), 273
Russian republic. *See* Russian Socialist Federated Soviet Republic (RSFSR)
Russians, 349, 362–363
Russian Social Democratic Labor party (RSDLP), 273, 274
Russian Socialist Federated Soviet Republic (RSFSR), 319, 338, 362–364
Russian traditions, 341
Russification, **348–349**
Russo-Japanese War, 347

Saar, 212
  French role in, 203, 226
  joins West Germany, 226
  plebiscites, 226
  Question, **226**
SACEUR, Supreme Allied Commander Europe, 268
SACLANT, Supreme Allied Commander Atlantic, 268
St. Petersburg Soviet, 348
St. Pierre, 113
Sakhalin Island, 363
Sakharov, Andrei, 307
Salan, Raoul, 80, 81
Samizdat, 307, **349–350**
Sanctuarisation élargie, 97
Sanctuary, enlarged. *See* Enlarged sanctuary
Sands, Bobby, 33
SA (*Sturmabteilung*), 209, 211, 213
Saxe-Coburg and Gotha, House of, 32
Scandinavian defense plan, 267
Scargill, Arthur, 68
Scheel, Walter, 187, 218
  as federal president, 179
Schleswig-Holstein, 190
Schleyer, Hanns-Martin, 224
Schmidt, Carlo, 227
Schools of Marxism-Leninism, USSR, 338
Schumacher, Kurt, 227
Schumann, Maurice, 131
Schuman Plan, 131, 253
Schuman, Robert, 131, 253
Schuschnigg, Kurt von, 157
Schutzstaffel. *See* SS (*Schutzstaffel*)
Scotland, **60–61**
  Act of Union (1801) in, 9
  Act of Union (1707) in, 8–9
  devolution to, 17
  Established Church of, 60
  local government of, 38
  population of, 73

Scottish National Party (SNP), 17, 19, 60–61, **61–62**
Scottish Office, 60
Scrutin d'arrondissement, 149
Scrutin de liste, 149
SDLP. *See* Social Democratic and Labour party (SDLP)
SDP. *See* Social Democratic party (SDP)
SDS. *See* Socialist Student Alliance (SDS)
SD (*Sicherheitsdienst*), 209, 213
Seanad Eireann, 59
Second All-Russian Congress of the Soviets, 275
Second economy, 302, 329, **350–351**
Second Empire, France, 86, **141**
Second Estate, 82
Second Reich, 192–193
Second Republic, France, **141–142**
Secretariat, CPSU, 287, 288, 292, **297–298**. *See also* Communist Party of the Soviet Union (CPSU)
Secret Army Organization (OAS), 81
Secret police, USSR, 326–327, 358. *See also* KGB
SED. *See* Socialist Unity Party of Germany (SED)
Sedan, battle of (1870), 109, 141
Séguy, Georges, 153
Seize Mai, 151
Senate, France
  Electoral system of, **95**
  Fifth Republic and, **103–104**
  in Third Republic, 104
Separate paths to socialism, 271
Separation of powers, Soviet doctrine, 344
Serfdom, **351–352**
Servan-Schreiber, Jean-Jacques, 134
Settlement, Act of (1701), 8
Seventh-Day Adventists, 350
Seven Weeks war. *See* Austro-Prussian War (1866)
SFIO. *See* French Section of the Workers' International (SFIO)
Shackleton report, Lord, 26
SHAPE, Supreme Headquarters Allied Powers Europe, 268
Shaw, George Bernard, 25
Show trials, 322
Sicherheitsdienst. *See* SD (*Sicherheitsdienst*)
Simon, Jules, 151
Simpson, Wallis, 31
Sinai, 65
Sinn Fein, 32, 45
Sino-Soviet break, 366
"The Six," 254
Sixteenth of May, 151

Slavs, 362–363
  domination of Russia and USSR, 348–349
"Small German solution," 190
SMERSH, 326
Smith, Gordon, 168
Smychka, 331
SNP. *See* Scottish National party (SNP)
Social contract, trade union, 70
"Social danger," 354
Social deference thesis, **62–63**
Social Democratic and Labour party (SDLP), 19, 44, 45
Social Democratic party (SDP), Britain, **63–64**
  alliance with Liberal party, 1–2
  and Falklands' War, 26
  in 1983 elections, 63
Social Democratic party (SPD), West Germany, **227–228**, 282
  decline of anticlericalism in, 172
  in elections of 1983, 176–177, 228
  in Grand Coalition, 194–195
  leaders of, 227
  in Weimar Republic, 237
  in West German party system, 220
Social Fund, European Economic Community (EEC), 258
Socialism
  in Britain, 24–25, 35
  and civil rights, 353
  in France, 92, 111, 121, 127–128, 142–144
  in Marxism, 333
  in parties of Europe, 282
  and socialist legality, 353
  in Third Republic of France, 130–131
  and Trotskyism, 317
  in West Germany, 194, 227
"Socialism in one country," 278, 283
Socialist and Democratic Union of the Resistance (UDSR), 134.
Socialist internationalism, 276, 281
Socialist legality, 302, 324, **353–354**
Socialist ownership, 277, **354**
Socialist party (PS), France, **142–144**
  nationalizations by, 127–128
  relations with Communist party, 92, 111
Socialist property, 300
Socialist realism, 306–307, **354–355**
Socialist Reich party (SRP), 207, 231
Socialist Student Alliance (SDS), 224
Socialist Unity party of Germany (SED), 191
Social market economy, **228–229**
Social mobility, USSR, 329, 337, 339
Social Revolutionaries, Russia, 275

La societe bloquée, 147
Socioeconomic theory, France
  and consensus thesis, **144**
  and end-of-ideology thesis, **144–146**
  and issue pileup thesis, **146**
  and stalemate society thesis, **147**
  and two Frances thesis, **147–148**
Soisson, Jean-Pierre, 138
Solzhenitsyn, Aleksandr, 306
Somaliland, 113
Sorbonne, 124
"Soul" tax, 351
Soustelle, Jacques, 80
South Africa, 11
Southern and Antarctic Islands, 113
Soviet, 348, **355–356**
Soviet administration. *See* Administration, Soviet
Soviet agriculture. *See* Agriculture, Soviet
Soviet bloc, 276–277, 285–286. *See also* Eastern Europe
Soviet economy. *See* Economy, Soviet
Soviet foreign policy. *See* Foreign policy, Soviet
Soviet industrialization, 283
Soviet legal theory. *See* Legal theory, Soviet, criminal offenses (USSR)
Soviet legislative process. *See* Legislative process, Soviet
Soviet of the Nationalities, 361
Soviet of the Union, 360
Soviets (councils), 275, 303–304, 308, 346
Soviet succession, 292–293
Soviet Union. *See* Union of Soviet Socialist Republics (USSR)
Soviet (USSR citizen), 356
Sovkhoz, **356–357**
Sovnarkom, 275, 276
Spain. *See* Guide to Countries
Spanish Civil War, 130, 282
Spanish Communist Party (PCE), 250–251
Spartacists (Spartacus League), 193, 234
SPD. *See* Social Democratic party (SPD)
Special Task Formation (*Einsatzgruppen*), 209
Spiegel Affair, 170, **229–230**
Spravka, 304
Spy affairs
  in Britain, **64–65**
  in West Germany, 198
SRP. *See* Socialist Reich party (SRP)
SRs. *See* Social Revolutionaries
SS (*Schutzstaffel*), 209, 213
Stabex, 258
Stadtdirektor, 204

Stadtkreis, 204
Stalemate society thesis, socioeconomic theory, 110, **147**
Stalinism, **357–358**
Stalin, Josef
  achieves total power, 357
  and artistic conformity, 354
  and capitalist encirclement, 278–279
  collectivizes farms, 280
  and Comintern, 281
  and command economy, 283, 319, 320
  control over party apparatus, 298
  and cult of personality, 293, 306
  dominates Eastern Europe, 305
  ends New Economic Policy (NEP), 337
  and Great Purge, 296–297, 322
  industrialization under, 283, 314
  and mass organizations, 334
  named general secretary, 292
  persecutes non-Russians, 348
  at Potsdam Conference, 221
  and principles of war communism, 365
  "socialism in one country," 278, 283
  and terror, 299, 326–327
  and two camps doctrine, 278
  at Yalta Conference, 241
Stare decisis, 10
State and Revolution (1918), 331
State budget, USSR, 319
State capitalism, explanatory theory, **317**, 354
State Committee for Planning (Gosplan), 321–322
State Committee, USSR, 321, 326, **359**
  for Building (*Gosstroi*), 321
  on Labor and Social Questions, 359
  for Prices, 359
  for Radio and Television, 359
  for Science and Technology, 321, 359
  for Security (KGB), 326–327
  for Supply (*Gossnab*), 321
State Council, Russia, 309
State farm. *See Sovkhoz*
State Planning Committee. *See* Gosplan
States, West Germany, 183–184, 191. *See also Land*
  cabinets in 1983, 203–204
  government structure of, 202–203
  list of, 186
  political parties in, 196, 203–204
  in Weimar Republic, 236
Statute of Westminster (1931), 11
Statutory law, 10
Steel, David, 37
Stockholm Conference (Conference on Security and Cooperation in Europe), 264, 265
Stockholm Convention (1959), 259
Stormont, 43
Storm Troopers, 209
Strasbourg, 262
Strauss, Franz Josef, 170, 229–230
Strumabteilung. *See* SA (*Strumabteilung*)
Sudetenland, 205–206
Suez Crisis of 1956, **65–66**
Suez, East of, policy. *See* East of Suez
Suffrage, 20, 57, 58, 96
Sunnydale Agreement, Northern Ireland, 43
Superior orders, doctrine of, 214
Suppléant, 96
Supranationalism, 254
Supreme Allied Commander Atlantic. *See* SACLANT, Supreme Allied Commander Atlantic
Supreme Allied Commander Europe. *See* SACEUR, Supreme Allied Commander Europe
Supreme Court, USSR, 324, 325, **359–360**
Supreme Economic Council, VSNKh (*Vesenkha*), 365
Supreme Headquarters Allied Powers Europe. *See* SHAPE, Supreme Headquarters Allied Powers Europe
Supreme Soviet, 284, 321, 330, 344, **360–362**
Supreme Soviet, Presidium. *See* Presidium of the Supreme Soviet
Surplus value of labor, Marxist theory of, 333
Swastika, 211
Sweden. *See* Guide to Countries
Switzerland. *See* Guide to Countries
Syndicalism, 153

Tadzhikistan, 364
Tamizdat, 350
Tariff union, defined, 249
Tatars, 363
Tax. *See* Value-added tax
Technical-production-financial plan (*Tekpromfinplan*), 340
"The Ten," 254
Territorial divisions, USSR, **362**
  krai, 338
  oblast', 289, 337–338
  preservation of nationalism in, 362
  raion, 338, **346–347**
  union-republic, **364**
Terrorism
  Great Purge and, 297, 322, 357

renounced by Khrushchev, 305
Soviet collectivization and, 281
in West Germany, 224–225
TGWU. *See* Transport and General Workers Union (TGWU)
Thatcherism, **66–67**
Thatcher, Margaret
 and Conservative party, 13
 and elections of 1983, 19–20
 and European Economic Community budget, 27
 and Falklands' War, 25–26
 and hunger strikers, 33
 as prime minister, 54
 and Thatcherism, 66–67
 on welfarism, 76
Thaw, 306
Thiers, Adolphe, 86
Third Estate, 82
Third Force, France, 94, 108, 109
Third Republic, **148–149**
 and Boulanger affair, **149–150**
 and Dreyfus affair, **150–151**
 and MacMahon affair, **151**
 and Panama Scandal, **152**
Thirty Years War (1618–1648), 200
Thorn, Gaston, 244
Thorpe, Jeremy, 37
Tikhonov, N. A., 285
Tiran, Straits of, 65
Tito, Josip Broz, 251
Togliatti, Palmiro, 251, 270–271
Tolkach, 302
Tonkin, 118
Tories, 12, 76–77
Tory democracy, 12, 57
Totalitarianism
 Great Purge and, 322–323
 Soviet secret police, and role of, 327
 Stalinism and, 357–358
 theory of, 210–211
Tous azimuts, 128, **152–153**
Trades Union Congress (TUC), **67–68**
Trade unions
 in Britain, 50, 67–68, **69–70**
 in France, **153–154**
 in USSR, 311, 334–335
 in West Germany, 173, **230–231**
Transformation thesis, political culture, **218–219**
Transit agreements (East and West Germany), 217
"Transmission belts," 334
Transport and General Workers Union (TGWU), 69
Treasury control, **70–71**
Trotskyism, 317
Trotskyites, 282

Trotsky, Leon
 critique of Stalin, 317
 heads Petrograd Soviet, 275
 leads Left Opposition, 357
 revolution, theory of, 331
 Stalin purges supporters of, 282, 322
Truman, Harry S, 221
TUC. *See* Trades Union Congress (TUC)
Turkestan, 363
Turkey, 257, 267
Turkmenistan, 364
Turks, in West Germany, 197–198
Turnover tax, USSR, 277
Tutelage (*tutelle*), 122, 123–124, 133
TVA. *See* Value-Added Tax
"The Twelve," 256
Two-Ballot System. *See* Electoral System: Two-Ballot System
Two camps doctrine, 278, 305, 339
Two Frances thesis, socioeconomic theory, **147–148**
Two-party system, Britain, 2, 52–53

UDA. *See* Ulster Defence Association (UDA)
UDCA. *See* Association for the Defense of Shopkeepers and Artisans (UDCA)
UDF. *See* Union for French Democracy (UDF)
UDI. *See* Unilateral Declaration of Independence (UDI)
UDR. *See* Union of Democrats for the Republic (UDR); Union for the Defense of the Republic (UDR)
UDSR. *See* Socialist and Democratic Union of the Resistance (UDSR)
UDT. *See* Democrat Union for Labor (UDT)
UFF. *See* Union of French Fraternity (UFF)
UGSD. *See* Union of the Democratic and Socialist Left (UGSD)
Ukaz, 309, 330, 344, 360
Ukraine, 319, 348, 349, 363, 364
Ulster, 42, 43, 59, **71**
Ulster Defence Association (UDA), 45, 72
Ulster Popular Unionist party (UPUP), 72
Ulster Unionist party (UUP), 72
Ulster Unionists, 71–73
Ulster Volunteer Force, 45
Ulster Workers' Council (UWC), 72
Ultra vires, 35
Unconstitutional parties, West Germany, **231–232**

UND. *See* Unilateral nuclear disarmament (UND)
Unified Socialist party (PSU), 143
Unilateral Declaration of Independence, Rhodesia, 16
Unilateral nuclear disarmament (UND), 17, 268
Union for French Democracy (UDF), 84, 92, 134, 138
Union for the Defense of the Republic (UDR), 135
Union for the New Majority (UNR), 92
Union for the New Republic (UNR), 135
Union of Democrats for the Republic (UDR), 135
Union of French Fraternity (UFF), 132
Union of Soviet Socialist Republics (USSR), **362–364**. *See also* Guide to Countries
Union of the Democratic and Socialist Left (UGSD), 121
Union-Republic, 289, 318, **364–365**
United Kingdom of Great Britain and Northern Ireland, **73–74**. *See also* Guide to Countries
United Nations
  Belorussia and Ukraine, membership in, 364
  and Yalta Conference, 241
United States, 11
  Berlin blockade and, 160–161
  defends Western Europe, 2–3
  Falklands' War and, 25
  missiles in Europe negotiations, 265–266
  NATO, as member of, 267
  occupier of Germany, 214–215
  at Potsdam Conference, 221
  relations with USSR, 280, 306, 307, 339–340
  Suez crisis of 1956 and, 65–66
  Versailles Treaty and, 232, 233
  at Yalta Conference, 241–242
United Ulster Unionist Coalition (UUUC), 72
United Ulster Unionist party (UUUP), 72
Universities of Marxism-Leninism, 338
University admission, Soviet, 329
University of Paris, 124
UNR. *See* Union for the New Republic (UNR)
"Unwritten law," 10
Upravleniia (administrations), 346
UPUP. *See* Ulster Popular Unionist party (UPUP)
Ural mountains, 362
Urban problems, West Germany, 205

USSR. *See* Union of Soviet Socialist Republics (USSR)
USSR Academy of Sciences, 321
USSR Council of Ministers. *See* Council of Ministers, USSR
"USSR Incorporated," 313
USSR state budget. *See* Budget of the state, USSR
UUP. *See* Ulster Unionist party (UUP)
UUUC. *See* United Ulster Unionist Coalition (UUUC)
UUUP. *See* United Ulster Union party (UUUP)
UWC. *See* Ulster Workers' Council (UWC)
Uzbekistan, 319, 364

Value-added tax (VAT), 258, 262, 271
Values. *See* Political culture, specific countries
Vanguard party, 273, 331–332
Vanguard Unionist party (VUP), 72
Vassal, John, 64
VAT. *See* Value-added tax (VAT)
Veche, 307
Veil, Simone, 262
Verification (*pravo kontroyla*), 295, 296
Versailles Treaty, 211–212, **232–234**
Vesenkha. *See* Supreme Economic Council, VSNKh (*Vesenkha*)
Vichy Regime, 79, 154–155
Victoria, Queen (Britain), 31, 32
Vietcong, 119
Viet Minh, 118
Vietnam, 118, 285, 366
Visitation agreements, 217
Vladimir-Suzdal, Russia, 363
Vogel, Hans-Jochen, 176, 194, 228
Volkskammer. *See* People's Chamber
Volkspartei, 168, 221, 227
Voluntary Association for the Assistance of Army, Air Force, and Navy. *See* DOSAAF
von Bismarck, Otto, 109, 190
  as chancellor, 192–193
von Hindenburg, Paul, 211, 237
von Metternich, Clemens, 190
von Thadden, Adolf, 207
Vote bloque. *See* Package vote
VSNKh. *See* Supreme Economic Council, VSNKh (*Vesenkha*)
VUP. *See* Vanguard Unionist party (VUP)

Waffen-SS (Armed-SS), 209
Wage differentials, USSR, 324
Wales, **74**
  Act of 1978, 17

Index 407

devolution to, 50–51
local government of, 38
politics of, 50–51
population of, 73
Wallas, Graham, 25
Wallis, 113
War communism, 336, **365**
War crimes trials. *See* Nuremberg war crimes trials
War guilt clause, 233
Wars
    Algerian (1954–1962), **80–81**
    Austro-Prussian (1866), 212
    Cold War, 160–161, 214–215, 239
    Crimean (1853–1856), 315
    Falklands (1982), **25–26**
    Franco-Prussian (1870), **109–110**
    French Revolutionary (1792–1802), 139
    Indochina (1946–1954), **118–119**
    Napoleonic (1803–1815), 173, 189, 200
    Prussian, 193
    Russo-Japanese (1904–1905), 315, 347
    Suez crisis (1956), **65–66**
    Thirty Years (1618–1648), 200
    World War I (1914–1918), 193, 206, 232–233, 274–275
    World War II (1939–1945), 213–214, 221–225, 238, 241–242, 282, 363
Warsaw Pact (1955), 366. *See also* Warsaw Treaty Organization (WTO)
Warsaw Treaty (1971), 217
Warsaw Treaty Organization (WTO), 264, 276, **365–367**
Weathermen, 224
Webb, Beatrice, 25
Webb, Sidney, 25
Wehner, Herbert, 227
Weimar Republic, **234–235**
    constitutional system of, **235–236**
    elections of 1933, 237
    lessons of, 159, 235–236
    not like Bonn, **162–163**
    political party system of, **237–238**
Welfare state, **75–76**
Wells, H. G., 25
Welsh Office, 74
West Berlin, **238–239**
    Berlin blockade and, **160–161**
    Berlin wall and, **161–162**
    elections of 1981, 239
    government framework, 202
    Ostpolitik and, 217
    Potsdam Conference and, 222
    representation in West German government, 164, 165, 179
Western Allies, 186, 214–215, 239
Western European Union (WEU), **271–272**
West German bureaucracy, **240–241**
Westminster, 47
Westphalia, Peace of (1648), 200
WEU. *See* Western European Union (WEU)
WFTU. *See* World Federation of Trade Unions (WFTU)
"What Is to Be Done," 296, 331
Whigs. *See* Whigs and Tories
Whigs and Tories, **76–77**
Whitehall, 10
William I
    as emperor of Germany, 192
    as king of Prussia, 109, 192
William II, emperor of Germany, 193
William and Mary, 76
William, Prince (Britain), 31
Williams, Betty, 45
Williams, Phillip M., 146
Williams, Shirley, 20, 63
Wilson, Harold, 23, 70
    foreign policy of, 18
    as Labour party leader, 35
    as prime minister, 54
Wilson, Woodrow, 233
Windsor, House of. *See* House of Windsor
"Wine lake," 246
"Withering away of the state," Marxist theory of, 333
Women in the USSR
    in agriculture, 328
    and equal rights, 280
    and female education, 341
    in party and KGB, 288
    and patriarchal attitudes, 341
    and Supreme Soviet, 361
Worker mobility, USSR, 311
Worker participation in management, 154, 172–173
Workers' benefits, Soviet, 327
Workers' councils, czarist Russia, 355, 356
Workers' Force. *See Force Ouvrière*
Workers, guest. *See* Guest workers
Workers' opposition movement, 291
Working-class Tory, 22, 62
World Federation of Trade Unions (WFTU), 68
Writers' Union, USSR, 354
Writ of Summons (1295), 8
WTO. *See* Warsaw Treaty Organization (WTO)

Yalta Conference, **241–242**

Young Communist League. *See* Komsomol
Young Patriots. *See Jeunesses Patriotes*
Young Socialists (Jusos), 228
Yugoslavia. *See* Guide to Countries
Yugoslavians, in West Germany, 197

Zakon, 284, 329, 344, 360
Zemstvo system, 352
Zero option, 265
Zimbabwe, 16
Zola, Émile, 151
Zollverein, 190, 250